DATE DUE

MAR 1 5 2000			
MAR 3 1 2000			
FEB 1 5 2003			
FEB 2 2 2003			
GAYLORD			PRINTED IN U.S.A.

M

ALSO BY PETER ROBB

Midnight in Sicily

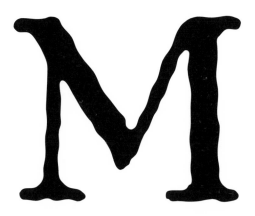

THE MAN WHO BECAME CARAVAGGIO

Peter Robb

A JOHN MACRAE BOOK

Henry Holt and Company | New York

Henry Holt and Company, LLC
Publishers since 1866
115 West 18th Street
New York, New York 10011

Henry Holt® is a registered trademark of
Henry Holt and Company, LLC.

Published in Canada by Fitzhenry & Whiteside Ltd.,
195 Allstate Parkway, Markham, Ontario L3R 4T8.

Originally published in Australia in 1998 by Duffy & Snellgrove.

Library of Congress Cataloging-in-Publication Data
Robb, Peter.
M: the man who became Caravaggio/Peter Robb
p.   cm.
Originally published: Australia: Duffy & Snellgrove, 1998.
"A John Macrae Book."
Includes bibliographical references and index.
ISBN: 0-8050-6356-0 (HB: alk. paper)
1. Caravaggio, Michelangelo Merisi da, 1573-1610.
2. Painters—Italy Biography.   I. Title.
N623.C26 R62   2000
759.5—dc21   99-043576
[B]   CIP

Henry Holt books are available for special promotions and
premiums. For details contact: Director, Special Markets.

First American Edition 2000

Printed in the United States of America

1   3   5   7   9   10   8   6   4   2

I.M.
Murray Grönwall

… marquera chaque soirée de son art personnel, piquant
et concis, un peu acide, excentrique, frôlant légèrement le
clownesque et un charme pittoresque un peu à la Daumier,
comme une poésie exotique de mime et de mezzo, mais
toujours l'interpretation du rôle était rigoureuse …
acteur d'un art si riche et si présent, si habité …

Michel Cournot
Le Monde

Young boys take no care, and never
finish off their things with shadows.
Leonardo

We can only describe and say,
human life is like that.
Wittgenstein

Crime was my oyster.
Weegee

CONTENTS

A NOTE TO READERS

THE FRAGMENTS that tell us what we know about the life and death of the painter I call M float on the surface of a treacherous reality – they're lies to the police, reticence in court, extorted confessions, forced denunciations, revengeful memoirs, self-justifying hindsight, unquestioned hearsay, diplomatic urbanities, theocratic diktat, reported gossip, threat and propaganda, angry outbursts – hardly a word untainted by fear, ignorance, malice or self interest. You have to apply a forensic and skeptical mind to the enigmas of M's life and death. You have to know how to read the evidence. You have to know the evidence is there – you need a feel for the unsaid, for the missing file, the cancelled entry, the tacit conclusion, the gap, the silence, the business done with a nod and a wink. The missing data in M's life and death make up a narrative of their own, running invisible but present through the known facts.

M's career was marked out by crimes. Convention has it they were his. I read the record differently and see him largely as the victim of powerful interests he'd offended. I see his death as murder. I turned from the records of a recent Italian past and found M living in a remote but strange world of parallel powers and crimes of state. I don't pretend to have solved or even fully articulated the problems of M's fate in this book, but I hope that after reading it people may feel that M is a lot more serious than the libel of the criminal genius allows, and that questions about what happened to him need answers. And I hope the book will leave readers dissatisfied with the exquisitely academic orthodoxy that M's life was, like his art, basically orthodox. The *wildnesses* of M's life weren't accidental but were intrinsic to the way he painted. The writer on M who'd known him best, his most disinterested contemporary biographer, remarked of M's art that *maybe that's why the poor guy had so much trouble during his life.*

Roberto Longhi, who did more than anyone to drag M's art back into view, liked to call paintings the *primary documents* in art history. Longhi said that unlike archival documents, the critic's response to the art was the only thing that couldn't be faked. M's paintings are works of his time and for our own, and looking at them long and hard again has been my own primary research, along with retracing the trajectory of his life. The documentary part pieces together the findings of long years of research by many people, whose names are found in the list of sources at the end. *M* is implicitly a report on a great and unfinished collective work of rediscovery. Not that the people who found the documents and identified and dated the canvases would likely share its conclusions. Not that the researchers agree now among themselves, or ever did. Mine is a working hypothesis, a preliminary outline. Though the text is littered with weasel qualifiers, the scrupulous may still find here that likelihood hardens too quickly into certainty – if it weren't so, the narrative would sink under the weight of discussions of the evidence. Conclusions I think are dry enough. There's no romancing.

I owe particular thanks to the recent discoverers who kindly talked with me about what they'd found – John Azzopardi, Fiora Bellini, Maurizio Calvesi, Sandro Corradini, Maurizio Marini, Vincenzo Pacelli. Thanks for their kindness to Pino Bianco, Marco Ciatti, Mario Croce and Princess Odescalchi. For help with books to Enzo Bisso, Lady Drysdale, Rosario Würzburger. Helen Langdon has kindly pointed out two errors of detail that came from quoting corrupt transcriptions. These have been corrected from the original Australian edition of this book, whose publishers, Michael Duffy and Alex Snellgrove, and their staff Gail MacCallum, I deeply thank. I love working with people who know a wing and a prayer is the way to fly. Thanks to Rosemary Davidson and Jack Macrae for joining the wild ride in London and New York and for not falling off. And thanks to Michael Cilia, aged ten, who got the ladder and took me down into the guva and did not fear.

M

M

M? M WAS A PAINTER. This is a book about him. His usual name was Michelangelo Merisi. The first published account of his life, though – and it was by a contemporary who'd known him – called him Amerigi. The second called him Merigi. And when he was one year old and five years old his father's name was recorded as Merici and then Morisi. The painter himself was named as Merisio in Roman court documents and Morigi in another written the year before he died. The further vagaries of the written tongue transmuted him variously into Morisius, Amarigi, Marigi, Marisi, Narigi, Moriggia, Marresi and Amerighi. M himself signed his name Marisi.

Friends uncertain of the surname just called him Michelangelo, or Michele or Michelagnolo, and people who felt uncertain about that as well or who simply knew him less intimately called him generically after the small town of Caravaggio in the province of Bergamo, just east of Milan – where he almost certainly wasn't born but where he spent part of his childhood and where his parents' families came from. M was most likely born in Milan and that was where he learnt to paint. He was born in 1571, although his friends thought he was born in 1573 and indeed so did everyone until recently, on account of M's adjusting his age to make himself a couple of years younger when he went to Rome. Genius was more appreciated in youth and M in Rome was almost a late starter, still unknown when other painters his own age were at the top of the heap and employing him in assembly line work. He died in 1610 in an unidentified location, probably on July 18. M didn't so much die as go missing. He disappeared and his body was never found. No one witnessed his death. Or those who did weren't talking.

His fifteen surnames and the dates and places of his birth and death weren't the only uncertainties about M's life. A lot of what happened between those extremities was no less uncertain. What's known today derives largely from the memories of two contemporaries writing a couple of decades after the events they recalled, ten years or so after M had died. Artists' lives, in those days, were brief. Often in the living, always in the writing. A painter's life was about as long as a who's who entry or a note in a tourist guidebook. This was what artists' recorded lives mostly were, chronological lists of works with a note on technique or the odd illustrative anecdote thrown in. The most intelligent and ambitious of these assemblages — Vasari's in the mid sixteenth century and Bellori's a hundred years later — elaborated an idea of painting that each artist's career was used to illustrate. Neither the individual artist's inner life nor the minutiae of his social existence — the staples of modern biography — was felt worth retailing to anyone interested in the work.

The idea of the inner life spread its dire wings a couple of hundred years after these painters' lives were lived and written, and so did that related idea of unearned greatness now called celebrity. In the nineteenth century they called it genius. The matter of the artist's daily round was ignored because everyone knew that a painter's life was mostly hard and dirty yakka. Time later cast a patina on the old ways, but hard work never acquired real glamour. The early artists' lives were remote, primitive and immensely sane. The people who wrote them were tolerably well informed, close to what they described, and in M's case they're still the main source of knowledge. Nevertheless the first published accounts of M were deeply self serving narratives, each cut and shaped to fit the author's thesis. Each one's version of M was wholly sus. The first was written by a painter he'd humiliated who was out to settle the score for history. The second was by an intellectual whose subtle art historical intent required him to do a personal demolition job on M.

There are more reasons for knowing little about M than a seventeenth century lack of interest in other people's private lives. M lived in a time of ideological cold war that'd split late sixteenth century Europe as deeply as any political divide has riven the old continent in the twentieth. The rise of protestant power in northern Europe had set off a defensive and totalitarian involution of power in catholic Italy. The counter reformation put Italian culture on a war footing — asserted the catholic church's claim to total control of Italians' minds and bodies. It was launched seven years before M was born and it conditioned his whole life. Coercion and persuasion were its twin prongs. The inquisition was the stick, a vast repressive machinery that worked through informants and secret courts to meet ideological deviance with humiliation, prison, torture and burning alive. Art was the carrot, and was enlisted to serve the purposes of the church militant by channelling the imagination's energies into the runnels of catholic doctrine.

Italy wasn't a society that adapted easily to totalitarian control and the church's repressive ambitions were only intermittently and imperfectly realized. The terror network was patchy, and there were usually mitigating elements even in the very worst regime art. The terror and the art were pretty dire nevertheless. Fear and suspicion pervaded the culture. The imminence of terror lurked in what you read, what you did for sex, how you dressed, what you thought about religion, what you knew about science, where your political allegiances lay. It drove private life underground. M lived in a time of bureaucratic power, thought police and fearful conformism, in which arselickers and time-servers flourished and original minds were ferociously punished or condemned to silence.

In everyday life, this meant that – in a way people once hadn't in Italy – you kept to yourself, made sure you didn't talk loosely, and were even more careful about what you put down on paper. It wasn't an age that encouraged gossip, speculation, table talk, wit, paradox or any of the freer and more playful activities of the mind – even among friends. Careless talk cost lives, usually your own. That kind of easy social trafficking was ended that'd once run between the powerful and the artists they patronized, between clergy and lay intellectuals, aristocrats and businesspeople, men and women, old and young. Venice kept up its dazzling promiscuity and Florence a vigorous cultural resistance, but they were now the exceptions and deeply suspect to Rome. The easy brilliance of Italian city culture was gone. Social life was wary, veiled, edged with mistrust. It wasn't a time to leave traces of your private life. Particularly if your ideas and attitudes or your behaviour were likely to draw unwelcome attention. Things, it was understood everywhere, remained among friends. Even the higher clergy, who were anything but nonconformist, kept up their private correspondence in a kind of archly allusive doublespeak and when they were dealing in matters of state it was understood that letters would be destroyed, or the real information saved for word of mouth.

It wasn't coincidental that though M had a cultivated and fluent hand, the only written traces he left of his life were a couple of scribbled receipts. Or that beyond the business accounts of a few commissions, the only records of his daily life should've come from police reports and court transcripts. It was in the nature of a police society that people – some people – ran to the authorities with complaints and denunciations on the slightest excuse, and their long, excited, voluble, angry or evasive verbatim statements are the only place where the very form and pressure of ordinary daily life in these years still lives. The record of ordinary life during the counter reformation in Italy was essentially the criminal record. And since M had his share of run ins with the authorities – more than his share, to be frank – the traces of these that have been found among the vast and worm-eaten record of people's trouble with the law are all we know about how M lived from day to day.

The critics didn't leave much. All the old accounts of M's life and work, in their original Italian, German and Dutch, with introductions and parallel English translations, fit into forty or so pages, most of them on the paintings. Fifty years ago Roberto Longhi printed all the critical discussions of M's work up to the early twentieth century, by Italian, French, English and German writers, in fiftyodd small pages. A good part of those pages were filled by his own commentary. Three hundred years of discussion of M's art and life fit easily into fifty pages. M the man survives as a name in the archives, but the archival facts don't add up to a fully upholstered life. They offer dots to connect, numbers to colour, grounds for hypotheses, data for a mind generated identikit, and what follows here is no more than such an outline. An hypothesis. The outline offered here will fade when more becomes known, but no imaginable archival finding is likely to make the painter M a reader friendly figure – people always found him prickly, his enemies found him violent. His intimates never talked. If you want to know M now, you can poke round a few palaces, alleys and prison cells, quite a few gloomy churches, some ports, a deserted beach or two. Which won't tell you much. And you can look long and hard at the paintings.

The paintings. The art historians have hammered out a workable canon and a chronology of M's work. It's a great collective achievement and years and years of patient drudgery lie behind it. A hundred years ago M's paintings were mostly still rotting in attics and cellars and decaying churches, hidden under crusts of filth, while M's name labelled scores of clumsy copies and crass derivations by later painters who aped his work. Bringing M back to life and sight has been a long, complex and fraught undertaking. The soot of candle smoke, layers of yellowing varnish and crude overpainting have been removed from painting after painting. Rotting canvas, cracked paint, ripped fabric have been nursed back to stable material existence. Images that seemed beyond repair have come back to life, imperfect but real. There are still paintings to be found, doubts to be settled, works to be reordered. But now you can move through a fairly sure sequence of work and try to match the paintings to the known events of M's life. It's been like this for less than a decade.

The paintings are M's great secret. They still have, for a lot of people, the peculiar inaccessibility of the wide open. They delight and disconcert by seeming, like certain works of Tolstoy and Chekhov, to have nothing to do with art at all. They seem to go straight to shocking and delightful life itself, unmediated by any shaping intelligence. The appearance, of course, misleads. In a time when art was prisoner first of ideas and then of ideology, M undertook a singlehanded and singleminded exploration of what it was to see the reality of things and people. He did it with a rigour that, like the work of Leonardo a hundred years before him, meant as much to the origins of modern science as it did to modern art – more so in a way, since what Leonardo wrote about in art only became real in M's hands. M rendered the optics of the way we see so truly that four hundred years later his newly cleaned paintings startle like brilliant photos of another age. These images came out of an attention to the real that ignored the careful geometries of renaissance art as scrupulously as it excluded the dogmas of religion. No other painter ever caught a living bodily presence as M did.

And yet M was able to make art so breathtakingly objective only because he was peculiarly true to his own subjective way of seeing. His visual explorations laid bare his own psyche and his own susceptibilities with a touching frankness and courage – he knew quite well that what and how he painted showed as much of himself as it did of the people on the canvas. M's peculiar personal honesty has more to do with Cézanne than with the painters who preceded him, and in the end it's the reason he fascinates people today. M was the first modern painter. The enigma of M the man is that so little of the few known facts of his amazing life seem to match the subtle and penetrating mind his paintings mirror. Right from the outset of his fame, M the man was known around Rome in the first years of the seventeenth century as a difficult and violent and antisocial person – *wild* was the word most people used – and the later events of his life seemed to confirm the early judgement with devastating finality. The worst and most lasting effect of M's personal history was that it fed back into his art – *was* fed back into his art by hostile intellectuals – to distort the nature of what he'd done. Yet M needed it, that hard shell, to defend his art and his person in a violent and intolerant time. There'd been years before the fame, when he was happy and secure and productive, when he drew no unwanted attention at all.

M's early work stunned his contemporaries because it seemed so real. He dazzled them with a drop of water on a leaf. The quality of his bare skin sent people into delirium. The effects he achieved made people take startled notice, after he took Rome by storm in 1600, of the polemical simplicity of the way he saw art. You painted, M said, from life. You painted what you saw and *a good man* in painting knew how to do *natural things*. The very best – and though it was his own practice M never quite said this – knew, like himself, how to put the natural things they saw straight on to canvas. Forget the interference of preliminary drawing. Drawing was convention, drawing was received ideas, drawing falsified life, was the implication. M didn't draw.

Attitude like this was bound to disturb a profession that saw an arduous training in drawing as the very basis of all art. Not to mention a church that – like the Hollywood studios of a later age – had a stranglehold on the major employment opportunities and saw painting not as a way of showing real life but as the medium for transmitting a set of tightly controlled messages. The counter reformation church demanded and got endless images of the early Christian martyrs and their various grisly deaths. It was the church's way of going back to its roots. People were utterly familiar with and quite unfazed by pictures of torture and death. Pain was the mental wallpaper of the age. Then M did a severed head and you saw for the first time what sawing through a neck was like. M showed you how an old man felt when his hands were nailed down. The irruption of reality into religious art was bound to cause trouble and it did. Almost as soon as he burst on the scene M found himself under attack. The established painters hated him because he subverted the professional structure through which they'd risen – and made the exhausted contortions of *la maniera* at the end of its line look silly. What they most hated was the way M – quite despite himself, because he was a loner – became the universal idol of the younger painters in Rome as the seventeenth century began. They aped his personal style in life and made his work the paradigm of modern art. Even the middleaged painters started awkwardly trying to change stylistic horses in mid career.

M could handle professional jealousy – more or less, in his own violent way – but the institutional hostility was another and more sinister matter. The church's ideologues had laboriously set up and were rigorously policing a system of *decorum* in painting, which dictated what was and what wasn't acceptable in art. It was all set out by cardinal Paleotti in 1584, when M was a boy apprentice painter. Nudity and eroticism were out. So was anything from the pagan classical past – *false gods*. Pain and death were idealized. Anything faintly tainted with heretical incorrectness was anathema. Nothing from real life was to intrude that might diminish or distract from the improving and uplifting image. Dignity was essential. Humour was banished. So was fantasy. Anything *new* of any kind was banned. The trouble, as with the chin jutting totalitarianism of a later age, was that *decorum* didn't occur in nature. A painter who worked only from life was pretty soon going to run into serious difficulties. M duly did.

He was born in 1571, seven years after Michelangelo died, who was the last and greatest artist of the Italian renaissance, and twenty one years before Montaigne, the first modern European writer and a man who thought entirely for himself. M was born seven years after Marlowe, who invented modern drama, and Shakespeare, who *was* the modern European literary imagination – and seven years after Galileo, who made the solar system undeniable and the church's world view irrelevant. Shakespeare and Galileo both outlived M. So did Monteverdi, who was four years older than M and invented opera, and Cervantes, who was twenty four years older and invented the modern novel. Bruno, who was twenty three years older and a tough little nut from Naples, might've outlived him too, if Bruno hadn't been burnt alive in Rome's campo de' Fiori in 1600 for rethinking the universe. M himself was endlessly resilient and had plenty of fight in him to the end, but by 1610 he'd used up at least nine lives and after that there were no more. These names all belonged to the brief amazing moment in Europe's history when the sixteenth century passed into the seventeenth and the modern mind was born. In Italy, if you looked at M's fate and Galileo's, the modern mind might seem to have been smothered at birth. But what M and Galileo did soon spread abroad – was known elsewhere long before they died.

What was M like? His fame was blinding among artists. Real fame always has its special moment. At a certain point in the life trajectory the image becomes fixed, iconic, timeless. M's image was formed in Rome in those very first years of the seventeenth century, when he'd just turned thirty. It was a critical time. The news even then was quickly carried north to the Netherlands by painters working in Rome.

> There's a man called M who's doing wonderful things in
> Rome … he's already famous … he's got no respect for
> the work of any master, not that he openly praises his own
> … says everything's triviality and child's play, whatever it's
> of and whoever painted it, if it hasn't been done from
> life …

The north sent its eager young followers down to Rome. But M had
no assistants, no school, worked alone and angrily repudiated painters
who took up his art as a style. M's views on art were radically dismis-
sive of the usual skills and precepts. He rejected ideas and ideals. He
seemed to eliminate art – all he cared about was life, getting life right.
The fame was always edged with a notoriety that – people felt – had
to do with his art. People related the thrilling newness of the dismissal
to M's unpainterly behaviour. That news too sped quickly north.

> – when he's worked for a fortnight he goes out for a couple
> of months with his rapier at his side and a servant behind
> him, moving from one tennis court to another and always
> looking for fights or arguments, so he's impossible to get
> on with.

Right from the start – and this in 1601 was the earliest news – M's
fame was shading into notoriety. An enemy remembered that

> M was overly passionate and a bit wild. He sometimes
> looked to get his own neck broken or put someone else's
> life at risk. Quarrelsome men hung out with him …

And years and years later people remembered how

> he and his young crowd had the run of the streets, tough
> and high spirited people – painters and fighters – who used
> the motto *nec spe nec metu* – without hope or fear.

Almost from the start things went badly wrong for M, as wrong as
they went right. The rich commissioned his canvases for modish city
churches – and the priests knocked them back. Then the private
buyers pounced. The richest and most discriminating collectors never
doubted M, but institutional endorsement seemed to elude his work.
Each rebuff was a very public affront. His overshadowed rivals were
delighted. Opportunists in the art world went on aping his style, not

understanding a thing. Around this time M's name started appearing in the police records of Rome. Appearing often. There was a string of violent incidents and a major libel trial. He fled the city after an assault, but the matter was settled and M returned. Things only got worse. The moment the fame and the notoriety coincided and became the same thing, the moment when M's image was fixed forever, came in 1606. There was a street fight near the tennis courts, when M was badly wounded and one of his opponents bled to death. It was the moment he fled Rome a second time. And the second time he never got back. He was still trying, and almost in striking distance, at the time of his sudden death four years later. The year was 1610 and M wasn't yet forty.

After that, it was easy for a hostile critic to lock the painting into the life. If M the painter had been famous in his mature work for his powerful contrasts of light and dark, painting his models in a darkened room to bring out their form more vividly, that could be moralized to fashion an image of a painter who

> from his sweet pure early manner ... was driven by his own temperament into the other dark one that was like his own murky and combative behaviour.

Looked at like that, M's whole life was shown as one long desperate flight from himself.

> First he had to leave his home town and Milan and later he was forced to flee from Rome and Malta, to hide around Sicily, run risks in Naples and then die wretchedly on a beach.

It was a seductive story, a great myth if you wanted to bury an awkward presence. Like all great myths it was made from elements of reality and ungainsayable. It served its purpose as the shock of recognition faded and people got tired of the real. Artists like Bernini took what they could use from M and lifted off from real life into the bravura rhetoric of the baroque. And like all great myths, the M story took on a life of its own. After two hundred years of oblivion it was the myth of M that resurfaced first.

A wicked man, said Stendhal. The fable of M the ill starred genius was bound to please in the age of the *poète maudit* and even more in the later age of the sexual outlaw. The strangest index of its potency was the way the myth of darkness got built into the foundation of an academic growth industry. The standard text on M in English spoke in 1983 of *the obvious and indisputable streak of cruelty in M's art* and ventured confidently that

> his criminality seems to be rooted in deep seated psychological problems that transcend purely social explanation.

From a painter like that, how could pictures be other than *flawed and peculiar?* Maybe it isn't surprizing. This late twentieth century stirring of the man's imputed psychosis with the supposed *flaws* of his paintings is an academic updating of the academic job that was done on M three hundred years earlier. It still drips down. At the end of 1996 readers of the *Sunday Times* colour magazine in London were reminded that M *was probably an evil man* and that *inner darkness infected everything that M painted.*

In the summer of 1610, people in Rome were stunned to hear that M was dead. The ever resourceful, ever resilient, ever active, self renewing M? One admirer who'd known him thought his early death was simply irresponsible.

> He lost a good ten years of his life and some of his fame through his own wildness … if he'd lived longer he would've grown …

Another – an enemy at that – wrote that

> If M hadn't died so soon he would've done art a lot of good with his fine style of painting from life …

The modern experts could've told M's contemporaries a thing or two. The modern view is that his paintings show M at the end of the line. M, for his critics looking back, had been heading for death on that *deserted beach* for years, and he arrived there right on time. They'd seen it coming a mile off. The paintings had foretold it all. Modern critics are so convinced by their myth of the way it all panned out that they've persuaded themselves that M's great and tragic painting of his boy lover Francesco Boneri as David – sadly holding out a severed head impressed with M's own ravaged features – was done in the last months of his life, an intimation of the coming end, a *summum* of an ill spent life, a tragic awareness of nothingness and an ironical last minute peace offering to the man who held M's life in his power. It's indeed a deeply, complexly, plangently seductive idea. But the story's wrong, disproven by M's style. That *David* was painted four years earlier.

The wrong dating of this bleak and powerful painting matters a lot to anyone trying to make sense of M's life. The error's doubly false. It shifts the emotional gravity from M's tragic year of 1606, when he painted this *David* – in the time of lucid desperation that followed the killing in Rome. And the painting's own iconic power lends a falsely self aware and tragic finality to his last months, or even years – as if M by 1610 were resigned and knowingly going to meet his death. It's a misreading that spills over into his other last paintings and throws everything awry. The four year switch is false about his art and false about his life at once. It feeds back into the old story. The old myth.

The known facts of M's life were few, and still are. The facts came from the archives. The parish archives of births, deaths, marriages, censuses, payments recorded to builders and craftsmen. The civil archives of last wills and testaments, painting commissions, bank trans-actions, contracts, sales and receipts. The diplomatic archives of let-ters, reports, requests and orders that were flying around the Vatican and the courts and ministates of Italy. The *avvisi* – the sharp and know-ing little unofficial daily news reports from Rome that were the fore-runners of journalism – were always a good source. The serendipitous archives of a few private letters, unpublished poems, whole books in manuscript for private circulation among a certain élite – which included two of the most valuable sources of information on M's art. And the criminal records. These, when the archivist Bertolotti first got into them in Rome a century and a bit ago, turned up the amaz-ing record of M's unknown libel trial in 1603, and the whole series of M's run ins with the law in his Roman years. More's lately been found, and yet more will be. But the findings from the archives need a framework, a context, a meaning. The meaning, the core narratives of M's life, came from two men who'd known M in Rome. The myth came fifty years on, from a third man who'd never known M, but who'd once loved his work.

GIULIO MANCINI WAS a good man to write about M. He combined, as no one else ever would, three remarkable qualities. He knew M and his milieu in Rome at first hand. He was informed and intelligent about art. He had no axe to grind about M as a man. Mancini was a physician from Siena. Like M – who was thirteen years younger – he moved to Rome in the autumn of 1592, apparently

11

after trouble at home and time in jail. He made a brilliant medical career in Rome. It peaked in 1623 when he was appointed personal physician to his old friend the newly elected pope Urban VIII Barberini – even though Mancini moved in libertine intellectual and artistic circles and was known as an atheist with an irregular private life. Maffeo Barberini had himself once been an ambitious young intellectual with advanced views, and had commissioned a couple of paintings from M, one his own portrait. People said that as a doctor Mancini was a rapid and brilliant diagnostician, and some of these visual skills seemed to flow on into a critical interest in painting. He was also known for a certain deftness in extorting paintings he liked from wealthy, ill and psychologically vulnerable patients.

Mancini wrote several self help guides for people on the make, all for private use – one was called *How to get ahead in Rome* and another *Courtierspeak*. He also wrote a book on dancing, a tourist's guide to art in Rome and a text called *What is drawing?* His *Considerations on painting* were another arriviste's handbook – a diagnostic guide for novice art collectors which circulated in manuscript among Mancini's friends. It included – along with tips on how to tell a fake – accounts of the leading contemporary painters and their work, and M was one of these. Mancini wrote it nine years after M died, and his three or four pages were the first and shortest word on M outside a smidgin of Dutch gossip from the turn of the century. Mancini was mostly right on M's early life.

M's memory and his influence on art were already fading in Rome when Mancini wrote in 1619. The doctor dilettante's eye was already cocked at the newer painters. Mancini wrote warmly of M, as he wrote warmly of all artists, but not nearly as warmly as he wrote about Annibale Carracci and his brothers. Their art was innovative too but not so tough and not so violent. The Carraccis were the ones he'd really liked at the turn of the century. Neither could Mancini, who wasn't exactly a craven conformist in his own life, forbear remarking that M's *great understanding of art went with weird behaviour*. Mancini had known M when he was a struggling nobody. He was never overwhelmed by M, and it didn't hurt his value as a witness.

Giovanni Baglione, who wrote next on M, had been, for one brief shining moment, all too overwhelmed. It soon ended in tears – and in a rancour that never left Baglione through forty years of professional success. Baglione was a painter too. He was several years older than M and had started in the null late mannerist style that was the going thing in nineties Rome. *Then*, as Mancini remembered, *he seemed to take up M's*. The year he aped M's heightened drama was

Baglione's finest hour as a painter. But M didn't like plagiarism and he didn't like opportunism and M and his mates made public mock of Baglione, who sued for libel in 1603. The trial gave M a platform for a cruel public putdown of Baglione – who dropped M's manner like a hot brick. The resentment stewed for twenty years, and was still seething around 1625, when Baglione got around to writing a three page bio of M for a book of two hundred *Lives* of contemporary artists that he brought out in the sixteen forties, part art guide, partly a complacent memoir of *famous artists I've known*. Baglione was a part of the Rome art scene, he knew the artists, he knew the paintings, he knew the collectors, he knew the talk. Baglione claimed M's work was overrated, overpriced, undiscriminating and unoriginal, but he'd known M's life in Rome. He knew very little about the prefamous M, and only a little unreliable hearsay about the wild and desperate loops of M's later flight south. But Baglione liked what he heard about how M died. *He died badly, just as he'd badly lived.*

M's image flared once again, briefly and dangerously, fifty years after Mancini and Baglione wrote, before it darkened almost forever. In 1672 the formidable Giovan Pietro Bellori included a life of M in a book of *Lives of modern painters, sculptors and architects*. Bellori was an elegant theoretician, an intellectual who had a thesis about art to expound and no personal concern at all with the merely human side of a painter who was three years dead before Bellori was even born. Bellori was a founding theoretician of the new age of neoclassicism in art and his rigorously selective *Lives* proposed a criterion of ideal beauty and measured modern painters against it. It was anything but a shapeless encyclopedic compendium. There was no place for colourful stories in *his* lives.

Except that in one case, oddly, there was. Bellori wrote his vastly influential work toward the end of a close twenty year friendship with the great French classical painter Poussin. The dreamy, remote, hieratic and exquisite mythological canvases of Poussin – and the strong, extensively expounded and very French neoclassical opinions held by their maker – underpinned Bellori's book. And Poussin's *bête noire* was M. For Poussin, M was the worst thing that ever happened to painting.

> Monsieur Poussin couldn't bear M at all, and said he'd come into the world to destroy painting.

Bellori himself had once admired M unreservedly. Thirty years younger he'd written a poem *To painting* as a preface to Baglione's book, and *the great M* had a whole verse of it to himself, along with only two other painters of the two hundred – beside Baglione himself. After twenty years of Poussin's conversation all that changed, and in the programmatic opening pages of Bellori's own book M was firmly put down as *too natural*. In the strangely select company of Bellori's other lives – there was no Velázquez, no Rembrandt, no Bernini, though Rubens and Van Dijck were there among some now forgotten figures – M was the negative instance, the necessary and instructive opposite, the embarrassing presence who'd turned his back on Beauty and *was extremely negligent about personal cleanliness* and who *for years used a portrait canvas as a tablecloth and ate off it morning and evening.* He'd paid, Bellori implied, the price.

The case against being *too natural* had to be made with due strength, so the decorous Bellori stooped for a little local colour. He knew well what Baglione and Mancini had written and fed their casual anecdotes into something fuller – a less personal, more coherent, more perceptive, more complete, more respectful, more elegant, more serious, more artful and altogether more devastating portrait of M. He called Baglione's book *good for nothing* – said Baglione *didn't understand painting* and wrote only *out of private passion and spite* but filled his copy and another of Mancini's manuscript with vigorous marginal notes. Bellori used second hand knowledge of M's life to bury M's art. It was subtly done. The life was a moralized fable and the image of the painter an allegorical one. Bellori opened on the young M being urged to study *the most excellent marbles of the ancients and the highly celebrated paintings of Raphael*, and

> the only answer he gave was to point at a crowd of men –
> nature had supplied him with enough masters.

By the time Bellori wrote, M's paintings were already ignored, lost, abandoned, mutilated, destroyed, their identities submerged among the work of imitators. Thus it was for over two centuries. The imitators themselves, when Bellori wrote, had long since disappeared or switched camp. M's own name, when not itself forgotten, came to stand for a low and repellent mimesis of low and repellent forms of life. Behind it lurked the obscure memory of the painter's own ugly existence. For Bellori, the darkness of M's mature work, needless to say, matched his *murky and combative behaviour* and his character showed in the way he looked.

He was dark complexioned and had dark eyes, his brow
and hair were black.

Elsewhere, in a private marginal scribble to Baglione's life of M, Bellori went even further. *He wasn't well built and he had an ugly face.* In
the *Life* he explained that

M used to dress in the cloths and velvets of the nobility,
but once he'd put on an outfit he never took it off until it
was falling off him in rags ...

M's image, now fixed almost forever, disappeared into the pictorial
and moral *darkness* with which Bellori had surrounded his name, lost
like *his life and his bones on a deserted beach.*

The case was all sewn up.

1

MILAN & CARAVAGGIO 1571–1592
ROME 1592–1593

Boy peeling fruit
Sick self portrait

O N 14 JANUARY 1571 Francesco Sforza da Caravaggio, who was maybe not yet twenty, attended the wedding of an employee who was ten or so years older than himself. Out of personal liking and respect, the young marchese of Caravaggio was the formal witness to the marriage of Fermo Merisi, his household administrator, overseer and architect. Merisi's family like his wife's came from the small town of Caravaggio, thirty kilometres east of Milan on the Lombard plain. The marchese's sixteen year old wife Costanza was likely also at the celebration. Fermo Merisi lived, like the marchese of Caravaggio, in Milan. He was a young widower, and already had a daughter called Margherita. He was now marrying the twenty one year old daughter of a rather well off local family with property in the district, Lucia Aratori. In the next few years they had four children. No birth or baptism record was ever found for the eldest, but the birth day of the second Merisi son was recorded in Milan as 21 November 1572, and in later legal records of the family Giovan Battista Merisi was always noted as being a year younger than his brother M. There was a daughter, Caterina, born in 1574 and a third boy Giovan Pietro died still a child in 1588.

None of the Merisi children were listed in the baptismal records in Caravaggio. They were likely all born in Milan, where Fermo Merisi rented rooms from 1563 until his death, not far from the Sforza da Caravaggio palace of his protector in the parish of santa Maria della Passerella. A four year gap in the parish's records ended on 20 October 1571, nine months and a few days after the Merisi–Aratori marriage. So M was born just before this. September 29 was the day of saint Michael, the archangel, and M from Caravaggio was almost certainly born in Milan on 29 September 1571, since M's birth day was most likely his name day, as Rubens was called Peter Paul when he was born on June 29 six years later, the day of Peter and Paul. And there was another reason for thinking of Michael the avenging archangel on the day Fermo Merisi's first son was born.

And there was war in heaven: Michael and his angels fought against the dragon; and the dragon fought, and his angels, and prevailed not; neither was their place found any more in heaven. And the great dragon was cast out, that old serpent, called the Devil, and Satan, which deceiveth the whole world: he was cast out into the earth, and his angels were cast out with him.

On earth it was naval war in the Mediterranean between Christians and infidels. The late summer of 1571 culminated in the battle of Lepanto, Christian victory at sea over Islam. That meant glory for the young marchesa Costanza's father. Marcantonio Colonna was the admiral of the papal fleet and head of the oldest and most powerful family of the Roman aristocracy. His daughter's anxiety was at its height when the first Merisi child was born, and triumphantly resolved at sea a week later, when M most likely got his Christian name. The first Merisi boy was born less than two years after Francesco Sforza's own first son. The Sforzas had been the great dynasty of Milan, the Sforzas of Caravaggio a lesser line – the marriage of Francesco and Costanza had begun badly, when he was sixteen and randy and she was twelve and terrified of sex, but it resolved in unexpected consummation a year or so later. Costanza had six children and was made a widow young, when M was still a child – Francesco Sforza died in 1583 and the marchesa Costanza was left to run the Caravaggio estate and bring up the children on her own, with Fermo and Lucia Merisi's young family growing close nearby. A tough and resourceful young widow who ran the estate on her own while her eldest boy Muzio was growing up at the Spanish court in Madrid and the others were children, the marchesa Costanza likely saw the boy M often. Years later she and her family would be closely involved in his fate.

Caravaggio was a quiet place with a single claim to fame. On a spring day in 1432, a peasant girl saw the virgin Mary in the fields outside the town. A spring of fresh water had welled up from the ground where she appeared. A church was built on the spot, but in the fifteen seventies, the original church seemed too small and plans were drawn up for a vaster and more grandiose sanctuary with a cupola nearly sixty five metres high and an interior nearly a hundred metres long. Work started in 1575 and went on until the eighteenth century. An uncle of M's was one of the first contractors for the building, and M had cousins working on it too. There were lots of Merisis in Caravaggio, and Fermo's family was distinguished from the others by the nickname *Quacchiato*. The sanctuary, and the pilgrim traffic it brought, were the biggest and liveliest things about Caravaggio and they hardly impinged on the sleepy rhythm of the town's life. It'd begun as a fortified outpost of the Romans, and since the middle ages had been – despite the odd violent passage of control from Bergamo to Cremona to Milan to Venice, until it was finally wrenched back to Milan by the Sforzas – a quietly prosperous and devoutly right thinking agricultural centre, mainly given over to the cultivation of mulberry trees for silkworms, introduced by Ludovico il Moro, whose name also meant mulberry and who made silk textiles Milan's first industry. Caravaggio's other specialty was growing melons. The sober, regular decency of it all, with the grid of solid, dourly uniform, unpretentious buildings and flat rich land of the Lombardy plain stretching almost endlessly all around in the heavy air, had little to offer impatience or ambition. You'd've had to have quite a stake in the place to stay.

MILAN WAS DIFFERENT. A few hours' ride away, Milan was drama and violence. Milan was governed by Spain and stood on the overland route from the rest of Europe to the Italian peninsula. Milan was close to dangerously protestant France, Spain's rival as the European power. It was on the way from Spain to the Netherlands – in armed revolt against Spanish rule – and on the way from Spain to Austria and the central European part of the Hapsburg empire. It was on the way to the Spanish dominions of Naples and Sicily. Spain had to control Milan and kept a garrison of seven hundred soldiers and heavy artillery in the castle above the heavily fortified city. The Milanese themselves were always complaining about the violent and unruly presence of the Spanish soldiery stationed among them. And about the economic damage done by the military's demand for food and provisions at below cost prices and the extortion of soldiers' pay from the city authorities. Military expenses kept wealthy, industrious business minded Milan in the red and drained more money from the badly bleeding economy of imperial Spain.

Milan was a frontline city for Rome too. Spain's anxiety over France was the political face of Rome's fear of the protestant menace from the north. The cutting edge of the catholic counter offensive was Milan's austere and fanatical archbishop, the beak nosed, hollow eyed, blue jawed cardinal Carlo Borromeo, who went around with his own squad of armed enforcers. Borromeo called them his *armed family*, and used them to face down the Spanish military, whose power he was challenging. Borromeo's enemies weren't only the Spanish. The Milanese senate claimed he'd turned God against Milan, since the normally fertile region of Lombardy had been stricken by a series of crop failures and famines since the cardinal had come to live among them. In 1569 Borromeo survived an arquebus shot in the back while celebrating vespers, in an assassination attempt by members of a religious order violently opposed to the cardinal's reforms of their *corrupt and licentious life*. In 1573 Borromeo excommunicated the Spanish governor of Milan, during the furious clash over the *armed family*, an excommunication which the pope countermanded when the confrontation erupted into armed conflict. In 1579, when the cardinal excommunicated everyone involved in that year's carnival festivities, the pope had to remind him *how great human fragility was*. The lively people of Milan were caught up in such a tight network of Borromeo's dour imperatives and prohibitions that the senate feared a popular uprising. *There is no moment of time ... he does not occupy*, they wrote to the pope. It stayed like that until Borromeo died in 1584. That was the year the twelve year old boy called M went into a four year apprenticeship in Milan with a leading painter in the city.

When M was five Milan was ravaged by an epidemic of the plague that reached the city from eastern Europe via Venice. There were public health warnings in April about the influx of outsiders without health clearances and about the stench of rubbish rotting in the streets. Borromeo organized prayers, sermons and street processions against *the evident danger of plague* and urged acts of penitence to avert the wrath of God. When the epidemic exploded at the height of summer Borromeo's answer was more processions through the city, which he led barefoot and carrying a big crucifix. The upper classes fled the city with their families. The Spanish governor of Milan denied the danger of disease and decreed heavy penalties for leaving. Then he abandoned the city himself. Between August and the end of the year ten thousand died. Carlo Borromeo stayed in the city and impressed everyone by pushing on with all the scheduled rites and processions. His own secretary died of the plague, among others in his household, but he went on attending the dying in the hospices and giving communion to the infected and insisting that all his priests do likewise. *He goes every day to the hospice and wherever there are sick people, and if there's any hope it rests in him*, wrote one Milanese. The epidemic came and went in waves all through the next year, and ended only in January 1578. By then a fifth of the city's people were dead.

A census of Santa Maria della Passerella in the centre of Milan for 1576 recorded the disappearance of whole families from the parish during the epidemic, their members either dead or dying or evacuated to the country. Fermo Merisi and his wife Lucia were listed at home there, and his daughter Margherita and four year old Giovan Battista and a couple of young male servants. The unmentioned five year old M and his other two siblings were surely in Caravaggio, with his father's family or his mother's, out of reach of the epidemic. The others joined them later. The Merisi family may have been feeling out of harm's way by October 1577, when Fermo's father, the family head Bernardino, suddenly died without even time to make a will. That night Fermo died too, equally suddenly and also intestate. A few weeks earlier Fermo's brother Pietro had also died. Fermo Merisi was thirty eight. The depleted Merisi family never went back to Milan. Lucia and the children moved to her father's large house in Caravaggio. Four months later the twenty seven year old widow Lucia became the legal guardian of her four small children. She fought a yearlong legal battle to secure them the greater part of their father's and grandfather's estates. They missed out on their grandfather's big home property, but the boys did inherit three small pieces of orchard and vineyard around Caravaggio, and part of a fourth. As well, Lucia now had her own family's big house at Caravaggio, since her own father had also died.

These were the two settings of M's childhood. Rural, familiar, pious Caravaggio and a busy Milan full of religious zealotry and businessmen and turbulent Spanish soldiery. Time in the shadow of the household whose workings his father oversaw, the castle at Caravaggio and the palace in Milan. A long epidemic of the plague, interminable for a child, and the overnight disappearance from his life of father, grandfather and uncle when he was barely six years old. Life with a young widowed mother and three smaller siblings. Somewhere along the line he got an education. Maybe the Sforza da Caravaggio family looked after the children of Fermo's widow. M's younger brother Giovan Battista went into the church. And the young boy M showed enough talent and keenness as a painter for the family to organize a four year apprenticeship in Milan when the boy was twelve and a half, when his brother was already in the seminary. Their father's brother Ludovico was a priest.

M's apprenticeship contract was signed in Milan on 6 April 1584. By that time the boy was already at work with the painter Simone Peterzano and living in Peterzano's house in Milan, just near his old Milan home. Two neighbours from Caravaggio working in Milan stood in as signatories and in the name of M's mother Lucia undertook to pay Peterzano a total of twenty four gold scudi, the first advance payment of six scudi to be made within six months. Peterzano undertook in return to keep M in his house uninterruptedly for four years – because M was a minor – and have taught him by the end of that time all the skills he needed to paint on his own.

Simone Peterzano signed himself *titiani alumnus,* pupil of Titian, and he was about as good as painters got in Milan at that time. He'd been born in Bergamo, presumably studied in Titian's Venice and had set up in Milan eleven years before he took on the apprentice M. In that dead interregnum of Italian art, when even mannerism was terminal, the century's great painters going or gone – Michelangelo dead in 1564, Titian dead in 1576, Veronese would die in 1588 and Tintoretto in 1594 – Peterzano mixed some of the terminal *maniera* with Lombard realism and some Venetian, if not quite Titianesque sense of light. The light faded the longer he worked in Milan. While he was teaching the young M, Peterzano's own work became noticeably more subdued and austere. Peterzano was toeing the line and it was a sound career move. The customer was always right. Peterzano's new and timely austerity of form and his newly muted colours won him commissions in a number of churches in Milan and nearby that were closely associated with Carlo Borromeo. He even got to do the altar painting of saint Ambrose, the patron saint of Milan, for the cathedral of Milan itself. Other Milanese painters were also hurriedly subduing their styles. It wasn't spontaneous. It was part of the deal. The 1578 contract signed by Peterzano for the frescos he painted in the charterhouse of Garegnano – frescos that contained a shepherd's naked shoulder that reappeared in M's first self portrait, and a saint Matthew and angel that M also remembered long after – included with the technical specifications the written requirement

> that all human figures and above all the saints must be done
> with maximum decency and seriousness and not display

breasts or other members or parts of the body that are not decent and every act, gesture, movement and drapery of the saints be utterly decent and modest and full of every divine gravity and majesty …

And if they weren't, Peterzano was contractually bound

to correct himself and at his own expense every error of art in the work and, in the opinion of the reverend father prior of said monastery, every error committed with regard to devotion.

The year before, Carlo Borromeo had published a *magnum opus* of *Instructions* on the building and decoration of churches. In Chapter seventeen of Borromeo's obsessively detailed second part on decoration, the chapter prescribing how sacred events were to be represented, he set out punishments for painters who failed to maintain decorum. This was the counter reformation in art. Any painter who wanted church commissions – any painter who wanted to work for the richest and most powerful patron of all – had to bear these instructions in mind from now on. Four years after Peterzano signed this contract, Borromeo's friend Paleotti produced his own even more massively and obsessively prescriptive work *On sacred and profane images*. It spelt out the rules of painting, not only in churches but, as his title continued, *in houses and every place*. As mediators of the counter reformation to the unlettered public, painters had a particular responsibility. Tomaso Garzoni put painters between spice merchants and servants and slaves in his vast and amazing compendium *The universal market-place of all the professions in the world*, which came out in 1585 and was reprinted twenty five times over the next century. Like all bestsellers, Garzoni's book displayed a finely honed sense of what was acceptable and what would sell. Painters were admirable people, he wrote,

except when they paint things that are merely lascivious and improper, as when they sometimes do fauns humping nymphs or satyrs copulating with goddesses, or paint vain foliage and grotesqueries in pious places or depict the deity with unseemly images or represent the male and female saints too lasciviously, or form fanciful figures and utterly indecorous caricatures …

Like all the best moralists, Garzoni had a sharp and loving eye for the things he denounced. There'd be little scope in the coming decades for painting the kind of unseemly sensuality he deplored in art – except in a few very privileged and unexpected corners of counter reformation Rome itself.

M WAS BORN into a peculiarly unstable and violent society, a time of prolonged crisis that

> ... twisted and transformed the societies of the Mediter-
> ranean between 1550 and 1600 ... modified the entire
> social landscape ... into, on the one hand, a rich and vig-
> orous nobility reconstituted into powerful dynasties owning
> vast properties and, on the other, the great and growing
> mass of the poor and disinherited, *caterpillars and grubs*,
> human insects ... a deep fissure split open traditional soci-
> ety, opening up gulfs which nothing would ever bridge ...
> the rich stooped to debauchery, mingling with the crowd
> they despised ... society stood on two banks facing each
> other: on the one side the houses of the nobles, overpop-
> ulated with servants; on the other *picardía*, the world of the
> black market, theft, debauchery, adventure, but above
> all poverty, just as the purest, the most exalted religious
> passion coexisted with the most incredible baseness and
> brutality ... at the heart of that society lay bitter despair.

M was about to live intensely all the violent contradictions of this age and Milan a good place to learn about violence. A proclamation by the governor in 1583 blamed Milan's *intolerable misery* on the presence in the city of *louts and vagabonds*

> whether locals or foreigners, without any trade or employ-
> ment ... without possessions or means of support, not
> salaried or servants and not known as nobles, however
> poor ... [people who] attach themselves to some knight
> or gentleman, official or merchant merely in order to keep
> their company, under pretext of real or feigned friendship,
> and guard or help them or ... in order to entrap others or
> carry out some vendetta of their own in the other's shadow,
> or who converse dishonestly mainly in the houses of

prostitutes and in taverns or in games and gambling sessions or stand around like idle vagabonds in the piazzas and the streets, or gather in public thoroughfares or near the very churches to rob or comment on whoever passes, disturbing pious prayers and causing public scandal, or people who being without fixed abode live in rooms, boarding houses or taverns or come and go from the city and even hide in the monasteries during the day in order to kill, wound, rob and do other evil acts by night.

Any such found in the state of Milan after six days, the governor announced, would be sentenced to five years' forced rowing in the galleys. Rewards were offered later that year for anyone who killed or apprehended a bandit or killer, since

a great many robberies, acts of violence, assassinations, homicides and other serious crimes are still being committed in the city

and the authorities went on issuing similar threats and promises against criminal violence in Milan throughout the years of M's apprenticeship, and long after. The particularly murderous wheel arquebus was eventually outlawed, and personal weaponry allowed in the street restricted to the relatively inoffensive one handed sword and standard dagger, but by then M was gone. The Spanish garrison was often reinforced to deal with crises of violence, and undesirables rounded up and expelled *en masse* from the city. The dangerous street life of Milan in the fifteen eighties didn't belong simply to a subculture, or neighbourhoods to avoid. What seemed to be the peculiarly Milanese phenomenon of the *bravi*, the louts described in such anxious detail in the governor's proclamation, the ones who attached themselves as enforcers to members of the nobility and gentry showed how socially promiscuous the violence was. The proclamations themselves were always, apparently, ignored.

With their gauntlets or arm protectors in their hand and their sword and dagger at their side, arquebus in its bag and its iron balls in their trouser pockets … they make themselves bosses of the piazza. They smack their sword against their leg and keep their hand on its hilt, and thrusting and slashing in front of the whole gang in the piazza …

In a livelier variation on the words of the Milanese authorities, Garzoni described how Italy's street gangs moved through the cities, pushing others aside, demanding respect, mocking women, blocking the path of servants

> ... they enjoy being called *sgherri* or names like neckbreakers ... insulting and stealing from the peasant women with produce, pinching them to make them yell, or blush at the indecent things they say and do, then hanging out with the whores and procuresses, joking ... boasting ... fooling around ... stealing their slippers, ruffling their hair, pinching their bums, biting their tits and making them howl like maddened bitches.

The irrepressible turbulence of life in the city and the spirited resistance the Milanese kept putting up to the grimly penitential edicts of Carlo Borromeo in the eighties showed Milan was not much changed since the painter Giovan Battista Armenini arrived in the city from Rome thirty years earlier. Armenini, who wrote a lively account of the greatness of earlier sixteenth century painting in a book that appeared in 1586 – a book written out of an acute sense of loss and decline in contemporary art – remembered when he arrived in Milan as a young painter around 1556. He'd stayed some months in the city and wanting to work as a painter,

> I set myself to work with some of those young Milanese, but I found they were much more given to ornamenting themselves with various outfits and fine gleaming weapons than to wielding pens or brushes in any form of study.

Armenini anticipated the M who had money, fame and notoriety in the streets of Rome. Bellori wrote that M in his glory days fifteen years later

> appeared around town with his sword at his side like a professional fighter and making a show of having anything but painting on his mind.

Armenini's image was a reminder that if M learnt to paint in Milan, he learnt to use his sword there too. The shadow of personal violence passed over his life before he was out of his teens. Giulio Mancini wrote that M studied with diligence for four to six years in Milan, despite the odd wild act he committed from time to time, caused by his heat and great spirit.

Fifty years later Bellori parlayed that *great spirit* into *murky and combative behaviour*, and said M had to leave Milan at one stage after trouble. Privately, he believed M was already a killer. In a handwritten marginal note in his own copy of Baglione's life of M, Bellori wrote that

> he ground colours in Milan and learnt to paint and after killing a companion he fled the town ...

Bellori's word alone wasn't enough to make M a teenage killer. But Mancini had earlier added an almost illegible marginal scribble to one of the copies of his own life of M – it was concrete, detailed and barely intelligible. He wrote, or seemed to write, of a *whore disfigured* and a *gentleman wounded* and *police killed* and M *imprisoned for a year*. The scribble could also be read to make M not a killer but a witness to a police killing, imprisoned for not informing. Something happened in Milan. On either reading, the usually accurate and reliable Mancini had M involved in a killing, and he would've got the story from M himself in Rome. Bellori seemed to get the story of M's crime from a different source. Neither said quite when the killing happened, though both indicated it was shortly before he left for Rome. The Milan police records later turned to dust in the places that mattered – where the criminals' names were written across the top of the page.

M'S TIME WITH Peterzano ended in 1588, and the next year M was back in Caravaggio. On 25 September 1589, stating that he was already eighteen years old, he sold – with his mother's consent – half of one of the pieces of land he now shared with his brother Giovan Battista. The money from the sale, three hundred and fifty imperial pounds, was enough to live on for two years, but nine months later M and his brother together sold the other half to a family solicitor for another five hundred and fifty pounds, using part of the money to buy back the first half, while M took the remaining cash. They did it to pay their and their mother Lucia's debts. The adult countersigning the sale by minors was their priest uncle Ludovico, who was now a chaplain in Milan. Maybe Lucia Aratori was hopeless with money. M'd been selling off family land for three years, and taking all the cash. Maybe she was sick. Three months later, *sound of mind and body*, Lucia made her will, leaving everything equally to her children, and a month later, at the end of November 1590, she was dead at forty. Then the selling really started. Four months later, the small orchard went for a hundred and nine imperial pounds and ten days later the recovered half of the earlier, bigger property went for five hundred and ninety six imperial pounds. M again took all the cash and in return Giovan Battista got sole rights to another small vineyard. The deals were overseen again by their uncle Ludovico, now installed in the archbishopric at Milan.

A year later, on 11 May 1592, came the final divvying up. On the Merisi side only the little vineyard was left, and that was already Giovan Battista's. The Aratoris had the big house where the family lived and another little tract of cultivated land. Giovan Battista got the family house as well as the vineyard, their sister Caterina got half of the tract and the promise of a dowry of two hundred imperial pounds at the time of her marriage. Profligate M had already gone through most of his share of the family property, and had to make do with a small bit of the tract and getting out of contributing to Caterina's dowry. It was the end of family life in Caravaggio, the end of these Merisis. The records of the final division of the family inheritance in May 1592 were the last evidence of M's presence in Caravaggio. The others went on to live their quiet lives and disappear forever into the vast humus of the unremembered European dead. Even the memory of M, after a few wild years of fame, then faded for centuries, and he was known only for a few notorious stories and some darkening canvases.

Giovan Battista, who'd done well out of the estate in the end, went to Rome to study with the Jesuits. Caterina married the next year and eventually had six children. Her fourth child was a boy born on 15 July 1610. Somebody in the district was very up to date on M's career. In a *Description of the town of Caravaggio* written in Latin in 1608, there was a mention of the town's famous M, his new style and *divine ability*, and even a mention of M's being made a knight of Malta, which happened that very year. The family itself can't've heard about their brother. Caterina surely thought M dead, because in 1610 she gave her fourth child the combined names of M and their younger brother who'd died as a boy. The child's name was registered as *Michel Angelo Gio. Fermo*. Three days later, in a strangeness of timing quite unknown to Caterina, M really was dead.

M left this world in 1592 and never went back. He headed south to Rome. In the four years since the end of his apprenticeship, he'd done nothing recorded or remembered, apart from boosting his cash supply by the piecemeal sale of family property in Caravaggio. Bellori said he spent this time painting portraits, but no trace remained. One thing wasn't recorded in documents but impressed in the visual memory and later bodied forth in M's art. He travelled around Lombardy and took a serious look at whatever he hadn't already seen of the kind of painting he'd grown up among – the modest and unflashy Lombard art of Milan, Bergamo, Brescia, Cremona and all the other places in striking distance of home. It was an art – Moretto's, Savoldo's, Lotto's – closely attentive to the natural world and the realities of daily life. It interpreted the miraculous events of the Christian story in images of that life. It was down to earth and unrhetorical painting and it showed how close Lombardy was to Germany and the northern world beyond the Alps. It was a mental universe away from the formality and grandeur of the Roman style that M had yet to meet. Even the greatest and grandest art M knew as a boy, Leonardo's fresco of the *Last supper* in Milan, was still utterly true to the reality principle. Unshowy though they were, these paintings afforded M images he never forgot. He never returned in person to the world of his childhood and youth but its art stayed with him forever. Again and again in the coming years it'd be a precise memory from this early time that took him forward. Though he seemed now to break forever with his Lombard past, in reality it never left him. In Rome they'd have no idea where M was coming from. Rome was so self absorbed and so unaware of what went on outside that it had no handle on what M did. M was a revolutionary painter, but like everyone else he too came from somewhere. He came from Lombardy and a large part of his radicalism was simply a stubborn visual loyalty to his childhood world, his refusal to be impressed by Roman artifice, his refusal to do what all the others were aiming for.

And M went to Venice some time before he left for Rome. Quite likely he went there more than once. Bellori thought Venice was where M fled after the killing in Milan. It wasn't far. Caravaggio was on the frontier of Venetian territory, and there were more reasons for going to Venice than eluding the Spanish police. Venetian painting was a thing apart – still quite unknown down in Rome – and M had likely been hearing from his master Peterzano about Titian and the Venice style. Peterzano's master Titian was ten years or so dead, and *his* great master, when Titian was a teenager, had been a painter who lived briefly exactly a century before M and who now seemed to strike the young M deeply. Giorgione

loved nature so much that he didn't want to take on anything that he didn't paint from life.

His work was famous for its marvellously real rendering of flesh, and
the subtle sense of relief that came from strong shading and contrast –
something Giorgione had learnt from his older contemporary
Leonardo and made better. But the most remarkable thing about Giorgione was that he had no use for drawing in the process of painting.
To Vasari, drilled in Florentine draughtsmanship, this was sheer ignorance – Giorgione was sublime in colour but he never went to Rome,
never saw what the very greatest painting was, didn't understand that
drawing was intrinsic to real art. Giorgione, said Vasari,

> ... used to set himself before living and natural objects and
> imitate them as well as he could in paint ... without doing
> any drawing, and he was sure that painting with colours
> alone, without making drawings on paper was the true and
> best way of working.

For M, Giorgione – not just the way he worked – might've been a
talisman. The enigmatic poetry of *The tempest* and the *Three philosophers* was utterly foreign to M's painting, but there were other things
that lodged in M's imagination. There were powerfully beautiful
portraits of boys, and some decapitations in which the artist's own
portrait figured. The memory of Giorgione and Venetian art was
something else M took with him to Rome, another thing he never
let go of. He knew what he wanted to do and he was a very conservative revolutionary. In the summer of 1592 there was a new pope in
Rome and M was nearly twenty one and he had nearly four hundred
imperial pounds in cash.

THEY ALL CAME to Rome. If you were an artist – a painter, sculptor, architect, stonemason – and you wanted to make the big time
there wasn't, really, anywhere else to work. The more ambitious you
were, as the wracked sixteenth century went into its final decade, the
more important it was to work in Rome. Painters from all over Italy,
and all over Europe – especially the north – were gathering there
among the city's busy huddles of immigrant artisans. Like all migrants

they got their first work from the ones who'd arrived before from their shared place of origin. Rome was full of hopeful artists. None of the currently famous names had any real distinction. None would be long remembered. A few celebrity painters were immensely fashionable. They got the big papal commissions and they had more work and more money than they knew what to do with. Art was elusive. Success was flaunted. Lower down the pyramid people were scrabbling for a job, because there were even more hungry artisans than work in that sudden boom time. Nearly all of them were late arrivals from somewhere else. In Rome the building and decorating trades were on a roll.

It was amazing. None of it was happening twenty years before. And half a century earlier Rome's very survival as a significant centre was in doubt. *Caput mundi*, forget it. Rome had been looted and mostly destroyed in 1527 by the mutinous imperial mercenaries of Charles V. They imprisoned the pope, raped the women, killed tens of thousands and stabled their horses in the Sistine chapel. After the invaders finally abandoned the capital, Rome was nearly finished off by an epidemic of plague. The Tiber broke its banks and flooded the city. The crops failed and brought death by famine. A third or more of the city's population was gone and the ones who stayed among the wreckage were stunned, demoralized and desperately poor. At mid century, decades after being sacked, Rome was still a small and wretched slum surrounded by abandoned ruins.

> The area of the hills had been abandoned and most of the population … was crowded into the bend in the Tiber, into two square kilometres … the Forum was a cow pasture … wolves prowled under the walls of the Vatican … the Colosseum was used as a quarry … in the populated part, unpaved roads were heaped with rubbish from private houses … a maze of alleys less than a metre wide separated the houses of the popular quarters and garbage and butchers' waste gathered in them.

What saved the city was the crisis of Christianity in Europe. Rome was a physical ruin, but at mid century the catholic world entire was facing a vaster and more final disintegration under the subtler onslaught of protestant ideas. The cardinals at the council of Trent dithered and haggled for years before the programme for catholicism's counter offensive was finally drawn up in 1564. The twin prongs of the church's action plan were repression – a reinvigorated inquisition was soon busily burning and torturing the ideologically incorrect and setting up a fine meshed network of informers – and propaganda. And the central thrust of the propaganda drive was to rebuild and redecorate Rome on a newly monumental scale as the home and symbol of a reformed catholicism. This was where the work came from in the fifteen seventies and even more in the fifteen eighties.

The people, seeing that the eternal city did, after all, have a future, started coming back. In the second half of the century Rome's population doubled to a hundred thousand. It was in these last decades of the sixteenth century that Rome took on its modern form, august, grandiose and strategically viable. Thirty wide new roads were driven through the slums from one great piazza to another, linking the key points of a city that had no single centre, repopulating the hills, creating a public theatre for the massed religious processions. Fiftyodd new churches went up and the vast palazzi were built or enlarged – the Vatican, the Quirinal, the Lateran, the Farnese and sixty more, and twenty aristocratic villas. A hundred kilometres of new and restored aqueducts gave Rome a better water supply than any other city in Europe, and the piazzas were serviced and embellished by thirty five great fountains. Houses went up for the doubled population. The centrepiece of it all was the new Saint Peter's, the biggest church in the world when the last stone of Michelangelo's vast cupola was laid in 1590. The huge gilded cross was hoisted into place three years later. A long recovery was reaching its full momentum.

It started out terribly austere, the rebuilding, bleak and even mean, but as the Roman church continued to hold against the protestant battering from outside, and as the inquisition tightened its grip on turbulent elements within, a certain expansive redundancy started embellishing the city's newer fixtures. The worst, people were beginning to feel, was past. Sixtus V, the canny peasant pope who'd been the greatest builder of them all, allowed himself to relax into remarking in 1590, a few months before he died, that Rome needed

> not only divine protection, force of arms and spiritual strength, but the beauty that comfort and material ornaments afford.

This was Rome's condition as the new pope Clement VIII took power in 1592. The more extreme rigours and religiosity of the counter reformation were being quietly neutralized as the amenities afforded by huge amounts of money and a modicum of social stability happily revealed themselves once more. Art, power and pleasure met again in

Rome, mingled and became each other. It was all veiled, discreet, repressed, still a little tentative in the early nineties and always deeply hypocritical compared with the renaissance vigour of a hundred years earlier. The new popes were bureaucrats and ideologues, not aristocrats and earthly rulers. But there were quite a few among the younger, wealthier and randier aristocratic cardinals – if not, or not without a lot of inner conflict, his beatitude himself – who looked back on the courtly lifestyle their families had enjoyed a few generations earlier as something to be recovered and reclaimed for the present. Religious militancy permitting.

Art, for these new young princes of the church – some of them still in their teens – and for the new high bourgeois of international finance – who were making colossal fortunes out of financing the papacy and keeping the Spanish empire afloat – had recovered its central place in the full enjoyment of their private lives. Paintings, not tapestries, were now what the rich wanted to line the walls of their immense and newly built Roman palazzi. And the church needed public art, rigorously policed and ideologically correct, to project itself afresh into the hearts and minds of the people and promote its own greater glory. Public and private met in a blurred and fuzzy no man's land through which a painter had to pick his way with infinite care. A privately commissioned painting for a chapel in a modish city church, for instance, had to be striking and different enough to draw admiring attention to the person paying for it without disturbing that uniform *decorum* that obsessed the newly militant clergy of the newly totalitarian church. So the rising painters, sculptors and architects met with the prelates and barons and bankers who paid them in the studios and palaces of a city that had something about it of a cold war Manhattan and a lot about it of a preindustrial Hollywood. Rome was the world's great image factory. The church needed images to promote its counter reformation. The city needed images for the public spaces of the religious capital. The rich and powerful needed images for the more intimate spaces of their private picture galleries. There were painters clamouring to fill the needs. The only trouble was, none of them was any good.

GRANDEUR WASN'T ALL M found in Rome. The new city was being erected in the middle of farmlands that were falling into irremediable decay, a rural economy slipping into an acute and irreversible crisis that eventually invested the city itself. M arrived in Rome not long after a terrible famine, and in time for a new food crisis in his first winter there.

All of Italy went into a long agricultural crisis in the fifteen eighties. Around Rome the pope was savagely taxing farmers to finance the city's rebuilding. Landowners gave up growing crops, since meat for nobles, tourists and higher churchmen got good prices in Rome. Bandits were ravaging the country – not single outlaws or small bands but proliferating armies of out of work soldiers, drifters and disaffected peasants. They got covert support from the landowners, who were fighting the growing bureaucratic state of Rome and the dwindling of their own feudal power. Sixtus V, the pigkeeper and career cleric who'd risen through the inquisition, kept a copy of Machiavelli's banned *Prince* in his private library and was ready to do what was needed. He launched a ferocious campaign to suppress banditry around Rome when he took office in 1585, lowered the age of capital punishment to fourteen, sent out the military and brought in outlaws – in September 1586 the *avvisi* reported from Rome that

> this year we've seen more heads displayed on the Sant' Angelo bridge than melons at the market.

The outskirts of Rome were briefly pacified. In 1587 the holy father was complaining that only seven thousand local bandits had been killed. By 1590 Rome was under siege.

Peasants were fleeing the land they couldn't work. They joined the bandits or drifted to Rome as beggars and vagabonds. Ten years earlier Montaigne had already noticed that Rome's surrounds were *largely sterile and uncultivated*. 1590 started with torrential rains after two disastrous harvests in a row and in spring the *avvisi* were reporting that *the countryside is deserted and the legate has authority only in the towns*. This time the professional bandits were leading an army of hunger driven peasants, and their leader called himself *the scourge of God*. Sixtus V was paralyzed in the face of the new mass violence. He died that summer and five years of anarchy followed in the country around Rome. The gradual disappearance of banditry after that was less due to the military search and destroy campaign led by the nephew of the new pope Clement VIII than to the alternative employment afforded by new wars in Hungary in 1595 and Ferrara in 1597. The harvests of 1597 and 1598 were the first decent ones in twenty years.

Crop failures and banditry meant that all through the eighties there were crises and shortages in Rome, and the pope was importing grain from Sicily to feed the city. Within a month of Sixtus V's election in the spring of 1585 the *avvisi* reported *forty thousand in arms* over bread shortages in Rome. Action to improve supplies and keep prices down made Sixtus V popular in Rome until the famine of 1590 – that summer, the trapped and hungry Romans were angrily accusing hoarders, profiteers, aristocrats and the Spanish, and the pope died at the height of the crisis. In November a Roman artisan stabbed to death a baker who refused him bread, and at the start of the new year the bulletins reported from Rome that *some new death from starvation is discovered every day.* The new pope no longer dared leave his palace to face the angry crowds, and even during a papal mass he was bailed up by his own serving acolytes who shouted for bread.

Bread rationing was brought in. Peasants were allowed a little more than city people *because they live only on bread and water.* Beggars were rounded up and driven from the city to ease demand, and *the moaning and shouting* of those who stayed in the streets kept Romans awake at night. The clergy were sent packing to their home towns to lighten the burden further, and business in the capital dwindled by three quarters. Carnival was a grim affair in 1591. *Without Ceres and Bacchus, Venus feels the cold,* said the *avvisi.* Who'd feel like late winter sex in the absence of bread and wine? In March the bread ration was reduced by a third. There were riots, deaths, injuries the month after, and a woman led an angry march on the Vatican.

> If the mob had had any leadership, Rome would have revolted,

were the reports. By May people were eating a bread made from barley, *worse than what dogs are fed.* An epidemic of plague swept through the city. Grain supplies eased the famine in Rome that summer and, after a new crisis in autumn, the worst had passed at the end of 1591. But bread prices had more than doubled and food crisis returned in early 1593. This was why M's first months in Rome were so hard.

People recalled the young M as pretty well destitute. He'd arrived in Rome around the summer of 1592, *aged about twenty,* an unknown painter among the thousands,

> naked and extremely needy … He lived there without fixed address and without provision … short of money.

Mancini said M went to stay with monsignor Pandolfo Pucci. Pucci ran the household of Camilla Peretti, the sister of the late pope

Sixtus V. Since she was related to the Colonnas and the marchesi of Caravaggio, and living since her brother's death two years earlier in a wing of the huge palazzo Colonna, this arrangement looked like M's family protectors at work. His uncle Ludovico was living in Rome by now and might've set it up. Everyone probably thought it was a great favour and an ideal arrangement for the young fellow, but of course it was humiliating and claustrophobic and didn't work out. Pucci treated the hungry M like dirt. He put him to work copying devotional paintings – which Pucci sent home to Recanati and were never traced – and expected M to perform *services that were inappropriate to his birth and station.* He was mean as well as demeaning. Bread was short and expensive so the household accountant fed M entirely on greens. Italians ate a lot of salad and cooked greens, something that repelled foreign tourists, but Pucci overdid it. Dinner was always a salad

> which served as entrée, main course and dessert, and, as
> the corporal says, as side dish and toothpick.

M called him *monsignor Salad* and walked out after a few months. He'd been doing some paintings on his own account on the side, which he sold himself, one of them a boy peeling fruit with a knife. The money he made from these persuaded him he could live on his own, and the paintings bought him a few decent meals as well in an eating place where he painted the host's portrait. The painting of the *Boy peeling fruit* survived in a dozen copies and maybe the original – it was M's first known painting.

Baglione made no mention of Pucci and thought M first went to live with an otherwise unknown Sicilian painter – *called Lorenzo*, Bellori added – *who ran a shop turning out crude works.* It was here that,

> being extremely needy and naked, he did heads for a penny
> each and turned out three a day.

Then he might have done half figures for the painter Antiveduto Gramatica, who was his own age and already doing well as a portrait painter. *The big headman* and M were later friends – Gramatica underwent M's influence and attracted the same influential buyers and some of the same enemies – but this early contact seemed brief. In the end – and everyone agreed on this – M went to work in the studio of Giuseppe Cesari. This was M's first breakthrough. Cesari was barely three years older than M but had a good start on him. He'd been brought to Rome at thirteen by a pushy mother, on account of his talent – Rome as Hollywood again – and got his break in the Vatican workshops at fifteen. He was a *strenuous arriviste* who was already the new pope Clement VIII's favourite artist and *the most important official painter in Rome*. In 1593 he was intensely busy, *overwhelmed with commissions* for the Vatican and major projects elsewhere. M, already in his twenties and no chicken, was a total unknown. Looking at Antiveduto Gramatica and Giuseppe Cesari, who were almost the same age and already famous, he quietly removed a couple of years from his age.

It was hardly surprizing that Cesari was taking on extra help. In June 1593 he'd just finished a commission to paint the vault of the Contarelli chapel in the church of San Luigi dei Francesi in the centre of Rome and was about to start on a series of major commissions for the newly powerful cardinal nephew Pietro Aldobrandini. Cesari had been commissioned in 1591 to decorate the whole of the Contarelli chapel and was supposed to have finished the job by now, although he'd only completed the vault. The entrepreneurial scale of Cesari's activities often meant things got left suspended like this. Clients hated this, and in the end he would lose the Contarelli commission – a matter of some moment for M and for art. Cesari was Rome's most prestigious painter and a personal friend of pope Clement VIII, *loved by princes and celebrities*. He was a celebrity himself. He dressed nattily, had elaborately teased out moustaches and a finely pointed wisp of beard and always got around on a horse. Bellori noted savagely in the margin of his copy that Cesari

> was smart and knew how to talk up and flog his merchandise. He was the ruin of a lot of fine minds who followed him – he corrupted and brought down painting and it never would've revived if God hadn't sent Annibale Carracci into the world.

The merchandise itself was often produced by others, something the pope complained about ineffectually. Cesari was a brilliant entrepreneur. He ran a big and busy art factory that he claimed was modelled on Raphael's workshop. It turned out everything from very private erotic cabinet art to large scale religious frescos in the approved counter reformation style. He knew how not to offend. When he decorated the villa Aldobrandini at Frascati for Pietro Aldobrandini, Cesari made lavish use of fig leaves at sensitive points in his depiction of the nude Adam and Eve, and even took care to stick a fig leaf on Adam's bum, out of respect for his beatitude's particular horror of sodomy. Cesari's was *the* art studio in Rome, and Cesari himself, later recognized as the last and most mannered of all the mannerists, was seen at the time as the great modern painter. To be taken on by Cesari meant for M assembly line drudgery and real recognition.

When M arrived in the latter part of 1593 *forced by necessity* to work for Cesari, he

> was put to work painting flowers and fruit, which he imi-
> tated so well that it was through him that they took on that
> greater beauty that delights so much today.

M – Bellori was saying – invented still life, unknown before now in Italy. Some surviving pictures from Cesari's workshop, more like scientific illustrations than art, were maybe some of M's earliest work. On his own later on, he did only one – maybe two – formal still life paintings, but all the work he did in his twenties – when he was most exquisitely alive to the world's feel – glowed with unexpected detail. It caught the eye in the colour and texture of fruit and flowers, the more gorgeously real for being green or faded, pitted or scarred or deformed or split open with ripeness and spilling their seed, the stunning play of light in water or wine and the glasses and carafes that held it, the glint of cheap jewellery, the heft and feel of musical instruments' polished wood, of steel in weapons, the leather, wood and tin of well used daily utensils, the weight, the caress, the fall and folding of cloth, silk, brocade, linen, velvet, lace, wool, the minute clumsy detail of imperfectly closed buckles, buttons, fastenings, bows, the lightness of feathers or hair, the polished darkness of a shell of armour and the softness of human skin itself. Years later his keenest collector remembered that M had

> said that for him there was as much workmanship in a good
> painting of flowers as in one of human figures.

It sounded like a merely technical remark. Yet – set against the hierarchies of renaissance art, or the religious priorities of the counter reformation – M's undiscriminating feel for the real was revolutionary. And his work was most exquisite in rendering the play of light.

> He painted a carafe of flowers with the transparencies of
> the water and the glass and with the reflection of the
> window of a room, the flowers sprinkled with freshest dew.

THE FACE, LOOKING out at you sideways over a bare shoulder, was M's own. The eyes weren't quite fixing you. They were looking through you into emptiness and at the same time slipping downward into a kind of terminally desperate tiredness. The jaunty cast of the slightly parted lips was hardening into a rictus. The lips themselves had a disturbing bluish tinge that like the livid skin of the face and bare shoulder made you think of sickness. Maybe malaria. The eyes themselves were large and round, the orbs pressing out against the lids of skin that held them in. The left eye seemed reddened and larger than the right, and the lower eyelid dark and heavy, as if it'd once been poked with a stick. It'd always be like that, an old reminder maybe of child's play or a street fight. The body, what you could see of it, was lean but not emaciated. The sickness looked seated in the mind. M was sitting behind – and not quite resting his elbow on – a narrow stone slab, one leg stretched out straight along a bench. The inner knee of the bent bare leg might've shown a swelling and a dark bruise. It was hard to see in the lower corner shadow behind the slab. He was not relaxed.

He seemed to be posing as Bacchus. There wasn't a drop of wine in sight or a hint of indulgence in the look, but the off the shoulder shirt and the brown sash, the ivy leaves in his hair and the bunch of grapes in his hand were sending out some kind of classical message. On the corner of the bare slab were a small bunch of black grapes with a couple of vine leaves attached, and two small pale yellow peaches or even apricots, looking very hard and sour. Looking at them set your teeth on edge. Rather as the picture did. The accoutrements were minimal and seemed kind of shrivelled under the unhappiness radiating from the face, autumnal bounty annihilated by the stone slab, the cold shoulder, the livid face, the blank wall behind and their own meagreness. The message died in the cold light of this reality, and the reality itself was gripping.

The grapes, for instance, held in the hand whose thumbnail looked as cyanotic as the lips, were a greengrocer's late summer throwaway, small, irregularly sized, overripe and heavily bloomed. Several on the bunch were already bad and others had dropped off their exposed dry stalks. One was already almost a raisin, with a vivid pocket of powder blue mould caught in its puckered fold. The colours went from a golden translucence through shining yellow to a heavily bloomed greenish matte and the dull brown of the dead ones. Twenty three small grapes were identifiable on the bunch and each had its own size, age and complexion. The bunch looked like a group portrait of a large poor family. The ivy leaves in his hair, on a length of vine ripped from some local wall – bright green, yellowing, brown and shrivelled – were as various. The black grapes on the table were fatter, but the whole lot, plus the two stunted green peaches, would've gone in a paper cone for a farthing.

Anyone seeing this small painting soon after it was done – seeing it a few years, say, before the start of the seventeenth century – might've been struck – as people ever after went on being – by the unaccommodated bleakness of the stare and the random vividness of the fruit. But they would've swiftly dismissed its artless occupation of the space, the emptiness, lack of detail, *design*, finish, stylishness. Forget the appurtenances. Here was a face looking into yours, through you, and it invited you to respond to a gaze, a stance, a moment. Intersecting gazes in a cheap eating place. This raw appeal wasn't art's. It was some kind of raw exercise. The close of the century in art was the contorted glowing twilight of *la maniera*, and if anything lacked *manner*, it was this *Sick self portrait*. Baglione later wrote of M that among his earliest things

> he did some small paintings using a mirror, and the first was a Bacchus with some bunches of different kinds of grapes that were very skilfully done. But it was a bit dry in manner.

Dry was an understatement. It was a formidably uncharming portrait, behind the ivy leaves and grapes. The bare shoulder and the tensed muscles of the folded arm were just as his master Peterzano had done them before in Milan. The cold mortuary light was his own. Fun times? The faunlike eyes held no Bacchic promise of abandonment. What you saw was what you got, and it was isolation and vulnerability, hints of hunger and sickness cruelly underlined by the darkness behind and the bare grey stone slab like a morgue's and the meagreness of the available fruit. That it was a self portrait in a mirror enhanced the bleakness and entrapment. It was hard times for an unknown young painter coming to Rome in 1592, without recommendations, without connexions, or refusing to use them. Food was short in Rome that year. People were dying of hunger.

> He found a model cost too much and couldn't paint without one.

2

ROME 1593–1597

Boy with fruit
Fortune teller I
Cheats
Musicians
Bacchus
Fortune teller II
Lute player I
Lute player II

M WASN'T HAPPY. Cesari was a human figure man himself, and when he picked up on M's skill at doing exquisite fruit and flowers, he wouldn't let M do anything else. In Cesari's factory

> he was working on these things against his will and feeling great bitterness at seeing himself taken off human figures.

Beyond the sheer monotony of it, M surely hated being exploited in assembly line work while Cesari was overseeing major projects and treating even the pope in a fairly offhand way. M's relations with Cesari were never particularly good, and this gave rise to invented stories of insults. He got on better with the younger brother and assistant Bernardino, who was his own age and whose portrait, now lost, he painted and gave to him. Bernardino Cesari was a journeyman who crudely finished off the frescos his brother had begun. *He would have done work of his own*, explained Baglione, *but he was kept busy with his brother's*. Bernardino *loved conversing with nobles and people of higher rank than himself* but he was much less loved in high places than his elder brother. He'd skipped town in the summer of 1592 just ahead of a life sentence handed down in November for extortion and connivance with bandits. He got a papal reprieve the following June – surely engineered by his brother – and was only just back in Rome when M joined the Cesari workshop.

M's problem with Giuseppe Cesari was more specific than workplace discontent and it had to do with sickness or injury. Mancini reported simply that before moving to the Cesaris', M *was attacked by illness and without money* and in the Consolation hospital. This was the hospital of the poor where

> he did a lot of paintings for the prior during his convalescence, which the prior later took home with him to Seville

– or maybe the place was *Sicily*. The Seville destination was a powerful reminder that Diego Velázquez was born in Seville at the end of the decade. The unforgettably desolate image of M at this time was his *Sick self portrait*. Then Mancini added another of his clotted, cryptic and barely intelligible marginal notes, which mentioned that M, *poorly dressed*, had gone with an unidentified Tarquinio and been thrown out – and was then put up for eight months by Bernardino Cesari in the campo Marzio, sleeping on straw on some kind of raised platform. Then Mancini added, with a stab of urgency in the marginal scribble, some disconnected phrases that seemed to say

> Giuseppe sees and is terrified and to distract him wants him to withdraw and flee so he doesn't appear ... where they didn't want him to be seen. Meanwhile a kick from a horse swells his leg and they didn't take him to a surgeon so he wouldn't be seen. He was taken by a Sicilian shopkeeper friend to the Consolation [hospital] ...

These words implied M was with the Cesaris before he went to hospital. Maybe it was another incident, or two separate incidents, but the incoherent drama of Mancini's jotting sounded like a later and more informed account of why M was hospitalized, and there seemed again to be something unmentionable, maybe a criminal episode of violence behind it, given the socially prominent Giuseppe's horror of getting involved. The Consolation was the Rome hospital that specialized in dressing wounds received in street fights. The Sicilian shopkeeper sounded like *Lorenzo*, M's low class first employer. And once M was in hospital, Mancini's note continued, *Giuseppe and Bernardino never went* – to visit M in hospital – *neither did he go back* to them when he got out. The subtext here was that the Cesari brothers had offended on the two counts that mattered most to M – the indignity of the work and quarters they gave him, and their abandonment in his time of trouble. Respect and loyalty both mattered immensely to M. They ran as *leit motifs* through every known episode and every known relationship, and amazingly – given the obstacles he set up – when it mattered he always got them. Cardinals or street boys, M's friends stuck with him. Forget Cesari.

He left the house of Giuseppe to challenge the glory of his paint brush, said the airbrushing Bellori. *Then he tried staying on his own,* wrote Baglione more bluntly. *He wanted to be with Asdrubale*, wrote Mancini in his own margin. Only Mancini, who always seemed to know more about M's beginnings than anyone else, mentioned Asdrubale Mattei, a Roman aristocrat enrolled as a *gentleman amateur* among the founding members of the Roman artists' organization, the accademia di San Luca, and brother of the Ciriaco Mattei who later bought – at sensationally high prices from the superstar painter – three of M's most famous paintings and commissioned a fourth, the *Christ taken*. Asdrubale owned a later lost painting by M of *Sebastian*. He might've given M temporary shelter at this early stage, or financial support while he did *stay on his own* for the next two or three years. M later lived in the Mattei brothers' huge palace – Mancini was likely remembering out of sequence. And when Mancini noted that M *went with* the otherwise unknown *Tarquinio*, he likely meant the painter called Tarquinio who later decorated ceilings in the Mattei palace. M in 1593 was still terribly poor and, according to Baglione, unable to sell the paintings he'd done,

> and soon ran out of money entirely and was so badly dressed that some gentlemen in the profession used to help him out of kindness …

He was scrabbling through the undergrowth of art, getting known by some people who counted but making no money as the Roman poor were starving again.

One of M's newfound allies – *his spokesman*, Baglione said – was a painter thirteen years older than himself. Prospero Orsi lived alone with his mother and was a specialist in the kind of decorative mannerist grotesquerie, ornamental masks, imagined monsters and chimeras which were less and less in demand now the ecclesiastical ideologues had condemned them – cardinal Paleotti had devoted six entire chapters of his book to the insidious threat they posed – and was known as *Prosperino of the grotesques*. He'd been a great friend and admirer of Cesari, Baglione reported, *but after some time, I don't know for what reason, he came to love him little and was one of M's touts and opposed to the cavaliere*. Prosperino, wrote Mancini,

> is the kind of person who likes to help everybody, particularly young people who arrive at court with some talent and no contacts, and to help them he wastes his own time and annoys his friends …

Prospero certainly did this for M, and maybe convinced M to leave the Cesaris after he got out of hospital. Bellori agreed it was Prospero's encouragement that decided M to go it alone. Prospero and M were certainly associating after M walked out. The Cesaris were furious when M deserted in January 1594 and *angrily called Prospero a troublemaker*.

M LEFT THREE paintings behind when he moved out of Cesari's workshop. One was his own *Sick self portrait*. Another was the *Boy peeling fruit*. The third was another single figure with fruit. Now the shadows were sunk to the lower background and a younger bare shouldered boy with thick dark tousled hair and head tilted languorously gazed at you through lazy eyes with lips parted. He was being painted from life and it was hard to hold the pose. He held a very full basket of ripe autumn fruit – an apple, a pear, black grapes, red grapes and white grapes, a late peach, a couple of split dark figs and a burst pomegranate, with plenty of scarred leaf and stalk and one dying spotted vineleaf drooping upside down into the picture's bottom corner. The boy's shirt looked like an off the shoulder bed sheet.

The softer light that ripened the fruit warmed the boy too. His dark hair was outlined against the glow and his cheeks tinged like the peach and the apple and his body emerged from his shirt and the shadows below like the flesh of the figs and the pomegranate. Ripeness, availability and the briefness of earthly pleasures were all there to be seized on. The painting itself seemed entirely taken with the reality it showed. The exposed part of the boy's body, that nexus of shoulder, neck and collarbone nearest you, was rendered with such loving attention to its detail that it outgrew the framing picture and was anatomically odd, though the painting let you forget it. Peterzano had done collarbones like that. The simplicity and the physical intimacy were as startling as the self portrait's. There was nothing beyond the fruit to mediate or distract M's contemplation of the boy. Like the self portrait it plunged you into the enigmatically private. The puzzle never lessened. All of M's paintings would confront you and disconcert you with the intimate reality of individual life but personal meanings were elusive. The later images rarely matched the flickering data of the life as closely as they did now, in the only work he did entirely for himself, unpressured by a client. The *Sick self portrait* matched all the early notes on M's hard times and sickness when he came to Rome. The *Boy with fruit* was more than an object of desire, sweet but not idealized, entirely right as a Roman greengrocer's boy taking a pause in his rounds – although more than one connoisseur over the centuries would take him for a girl. It was a portrait of Mario Minniti and it was full of sexual longing, though not on Mario's part.

Mario Minniti was a Sicilian from Syracuse. He was born in 1577 on December 8, which was Mary's day. When M was working for the Cesaris, Minniti was a boy of not quite sixteen, a younger version of M himself with a wildly precocious curriculum already behind him. Orphaned the year before, he'd soon got *involved in some trouble* at home and fled to Malta on the galleys, and then come on to Rome as a *safe place* when he was still fifteen. He was another hopeful young painter who'd found casual work *with a Sicilian painter who sold pictures by the dozen*. It turned out to be the same Sicilian for whom the young M was just then doing the same thing – the Lorenzo who took M to hospital when he was hurt by the horse. The two of them poor and unknown and ambitious together, M twenty two and Minniti sixteen. Minniti's arrival meant M most likely worked for the Sicilian after he left Cesari, not – as Baglione and Bellori thought – before. Mario Minniti now stayed up at night working on his drawing, making up for the time lost in drudgery during the day, and M was *the spur in his side*. They both hated working in the shop – a real comedown for M after Cesari's – and *decided to leave the crassness of such a master* and live and work together. Maybe Prospero Orsi helped M find *the use of a room* in the palace of monsignor Petrignani, who lived nearby, and where M *did a lot of paintings* in 1595.

M and Mario Minniti lived together for the next five years at least, and Mario Minniti was M's constant and adored model all through that time. And though Mario left and got married some time soon after 1600, and was never M's model again, he was present in crucial moments of M's Roman life after that – and indeed after Rome, and almost to the end. They seemed to keep up a close and constant friendship for the rest of M's life. M's painterly interest in beautiful young Mario of the fifteen nineties was always overtly erotic, and it was an eroticism so charged with longing – basically the *Boy with fruit* done over and over again in subtle variants, until Mario's farewell appearance in the great drama of 1600 – that you wondered whether it was ever consummated. Or if it was, whether it wasn't just casual sex for friendship's sake on Mario's part. The look Mario would return in his portraits never went far beyond the aimiably available gaze of the fifteen year old with fruit, however intensely he was handled by the painter. There was always a sense of M's not quite getting through, never quite disturbing an equanimity in Mario that attracted and frustrated him equally. The Mario paintings were heavy with an inaction that went beyond the early limitations of M's painterly skills. Mario was a wild boy, but not as wild as M – they broke up later because after years with M he was longing for a quieter life – and he eventually became a steady and respected married man running a highly commercial painting business in his home town. All the signs were that the real energy of this relationship came from M. Things would be very different with the boy M took up with after Mario, and very different paintings came out of the later relationship.

There was a wonderful serenity in Mario's painted gaze, an inner repose that M might've envied or simply been entranced by in life, as he worried at its secret in canvas after canvas. Might Mario, though six years younger and still a boy, have afforded, in hard and uncertain times – times that were harder if you were driven by an ambition for your art that seemed to be getting nowhere – an emotional sheet anchor that M badly needed? If that were so, his steadiness was all the more needed as ballast to the influence of someone else M was also getting to know at the same time. This other acquaintance was a quite different kind of friend, and M's connexion an anxious bonding with someone only two years older than himself, but far more professionally established, married with a family and socially sure of himself in a way half starved unknown M could only dream of being. And redhaired, wild, violent, mad as a snake. Of M's two new infatuations, this was the dangerous one.

I'm a gentleman … and I think about eating and drinking and not about minding my business.

Onorio Longhi, whose statement to this effect appeared in the records of a Roman criminal court for 1595, was born in Milan in 1569 but he'd grown up in Rome. His father had come down the year Onorio was born to work in Rome as a foreman stonemason. He ended up one of the first of those Lombard architects, sculptors and builders who largely rebuilt Rome. Martino Longhi the elder worked on the Vatican, on the Capitoline hill complex, and designed some of the major private palaces like the palazzo Borghese. He designed Rome's new granaries at the baths of Diocletian, which were part of the pope's effort to assure and control Rome's food supply. He was another Lombard success story in the capital and owned a lot of buildings in both Rome and Lombardy, including three houses in the centre of Rome. Onorio was the eldest of Martino Longhi's three sons. He'd graduated in law and done some work as an architect himself before his father died in 1591. Everyone agreed Onorio had talent, but no one ever claimed he had his father's calm professional competence. In 1592 Longhi was already in trouble over street skirmishes with his sword.

> He always had such a bizarre mind that hardly anybody could be with him for long … he made himself greatly hated by others,

remembered Baglione, who'd hated him particularly. M – ominously – never seemed to have any problems with Onorio Longhi.

> *I don't carry arms of any kind, by day or by night. The servant who follows me carries it.*

In April 1594 Longhi was taken to court by a painter who accused Longhi of grabbing him by the collar and punching him repeatedly and pulling a dagger on him. *Sometimes I have and sometimes I haven't,* a lady friend of Longhi's, a courtesan, had told another court about Longhi's sword the year before, *seen him wear it in the street when he goes out with gentlemen.* Three other *youths* had been with Longhi when he beat up the painter, but his accuser recognized only Giuseppe Cesari. Maybe M's was one of the unknown faces. *He's got a little bit of blond beard …* Longhi's lady friend had added helpfully about Onorio, *and he goes around in black corduroy velvet.* As M did. In an account of *the Roman families* written some years later, Longhi was described as *a bit the wicked leader of the youth*, and himself told a criminal court in 1595

I usually go around with a lot of different people, people who meet up with me in the street and come along …

One of those people, from now on, would be M.

CLEMENT VIII ALDOBRANDINI, elected at the start of 1592 as an unusually youthful fifty six year old compromise candidate, barely acceptable to Spain's Felipe II, had turned out to be a fussy hands on pope obsessed with minute detail rather than the big picture. The Venetian ambassador said he *wants to know everything, read everything and give all the orders.* His anxieties erupted from time to time in violent anger. He reactivated the index of forbidden books, met weekly with the inquisition and had thirtyodd people burnt alive during his years in power. In 1592 Clement VIII's first thoughts as pope turned to Roman street life. In his first days in office the new pope banned duelling and the carrying of weapons and cracked down on carnival celebrations and the playing of cards or dice games. Once again vagabonds, beggars, gypsies, thugs and louts were ordered out of the city and groups of young men forbidden to move around the city at night.

Women were his special victims – forbidden now to leave their houses after the sounding of the evening *Ave Maria.* Nor could they enter taverns, rent rooms or go to parties or plays. Two days into power he ordered courtesans out of his own neighbourhood around the Vatican, *on pain of whipping, confiscation of property and banishment from Rome.* Two weeks later he ordered all prostitutes herded into a single quarter, the unsavoury Ortaccio, where they and their clients could be more easily policed. Managing the girls was easier said than done. Pius V Ghisleri and Sixtus V Peretti, two implacable inquisitor popes, had tried the same thing and failed not long before, but reminded of this the pope had a tantrum. Panic swept Rome's sex industry – the city's main economic activity and a bigger employer even than art. The women were given ten days to move to the Ortaccio. Some left Rome for Naples but were robbed and murdered on the way. Whippings, confiscations and banishments followed for the ones left behind. The Spanish courtesans, whose erotic arts were particularly appreciated in Rome, were ordered out. A bawd was whipped around Rome on the back of an ass. A married couple of immoral earners were paraded around in a cart, forced to whip each other, before the man's nose was cut off and his wife's ear. Horns and bells were put on the man's head. Intragender sex, *the unspeakable vice*, was another thing the pope was determined to crush. In Clement VIII's first summer a carter was hanged and burnt for this in Rome, the first of several a year for the rest of the Aldobrandini papacy.

Clothes were policed. Sixtus V had already banned women in shirtsleeves from the streets of Rome, and in clothes made of netting, knitted fabric or anything transparent except over stoutly opaque underwear. Women's hair worn in forelocks and jewelled or richly worked panels in their dresses was likewise banned. Clement VIII now elaborated a dress code that required both priests and courtesans to wear an overgarment with sleeves that reached to the ground, black for priests and yellow for whores. Likewise cardinals had to wear their scarlet dress at all times – it was a futile effort to police the pleasures of the sacred college by making its members' comings and goings easier to see. He ordered police to cut off anything that looked like a wanton forelock seen on the heads of women and boys in the street.

In the early fifteen nineties all these measures were raining down on the milieu M lived in – the floating Roman street life of prostitutes, soldiers, gulls, beggars, gamblers, *bravi*, street boys, artisans, painters, unassimilated intellectuals and younger sons – the street corner world of eating places, barber shops and tennis courts that M, moving beyond his first still lifes and single figure paintings, was now beginning to reflect in his art. For his next painting M took a piece of canvas that'd already been used by his former boss Cesari for a virgin with clasped hands – a preliminary sketch for a painting begun around the end of 1592 but which, ultrabusy as he always was, Cesari took twenty three years to finish. M tipped the canvas lengthwise and found the half length shape he liked most of all – a format he'd use over and over for the rest of his life. He used it to paint an instantly recognizable scene of the kind of thing the pope was trying to stamp out. His first work showing more than one figure showed a gypsy girl charming and duping a naive boy.

The voluptuous anxiety of longing in the *Boy with fruit* grew out of a tension between the painter and his model. In the *Fortune teller* the dynamic was all different. It was something going on between the boy and the girl inside the picture and left you free to enjoy it. What made the picture delightful, made it sharp as well as sweet, was the poise between the ingenuous boy and the sly girl – the sweet but silly boy, with his plumes and his gloves and his pleased sense that she was finding him pretty attractive, and the girl who was slipping the ring from the boy's finger with such delicacy that she seemed to deserve it. The two were distributed evenly on the canvas, a pair of opposites linked in the play of their hands and the switch of sexual roles – the boy being pretty, dressed up, passive and duped, while the girl controlled and orchestrated the exchange. The play of the glances was marvellous, especially the girl's. Her role was the painter's – holding things in balance, not being too obvious, keeping it playful. The painting caught a soundless sensuous stillness as the girl gently stroked the boy's mound of Venus and a shaft of golden afternoon light, cut by the shadow of a window sash, caught her obliquely and the boy full on. The same warm stillness of light would be diffused through other of M's paintings that followed. None of these would convey quite the same erotic suspension, in which even the ring filching gypsy girls shared. M did the *Fortune teller* before he had to reckon with other people's tastes. He painted it to flog on the open market and the choice of subject was his own. What he did was quite new – he very notably didn't choose the popular religious subjects when they weren't dictated by a client – and it was a huge success.

Everyone remembered this painting. Real life and delicate eroticism weren't what people were used to in art and the novelty was startling. This was quite different from the gross scenes of common life being done in northern Europe. Mancini thought the *Fortune teller* was as good as painting from live models could get, when it came to putting real feeling into a picture, and added that as *a poor man in his time of need* M sold it for the absurdly low price of eight scudi. Bellori contrived a scene to make the *Fortune teller* the very emblem of M's fixation on painting only from life. In Bellori's fable, M was advised to learn from the greats, and

> the only answer he gave was to point at a crowd of men – nature had supplied him with enough masters. And to give his words authority, he called a gypsy girl who happened to be passing in the street and took her back to his room and painted her in the act of predicting the future ... he did a youth placing his gloved hand on his sword and offering the other bare to the girl, who holds it and looks at it, and in these two half figures M translated reality so purely that it came to confirm what he'd said.

Painters remembered it too, copied it, imitated it, worked variations on it. The *Fortune teller* would become enormously influential through the seventeenth century and beyond, through the eighteenth and nine-teenth. It started a new way of painting, a new way of looking at the world. Nobody would've guessed it when he practically gave the *Fortune teller* away, but M was beginning to change the course of European art. Between the first and the second version of the *Fortune teller* he did another painting whose vivid and loving rendering of the street world amazed people even more. It was another horizontal half length canvas – of three figures, seen closeup in vivid lowlife detail, yet with the same delicate eye for ingenuous juvenile beauty. Bellori described

> ... another deserving equal praise ... of three half figures playing cards. He did an ingenuous boy holding his cards, his head well painted from life, in dark clothes, and turned facing him in profile a youth cheating, leaning with one hand on the card table and the other behind his back, pulling a fake card from his belt, with the third near the boy looking at the signs on his cards and revealing them with three fingers to his mate, who as he leans on the table turns his shoulder to the light in a yellow jacket with black stripes, and there's no inauthenticity in the colour.

The *Cheats* was another leap in quality. It went from two to three figures and a more complexly built three dimensional play around the card table. And here the ambiguities of innocence duped were strung out in a triangle of glances. The soft skinned boy dressed in glossy blackish plum, with little lace cuffs and collar and his dark plumed hat pushed back off his pale face, was perilously abstracted, absorbed in the game, a milk white innocent who thought people played by the rules. The grimacing weatherbeaten bearded figure looming over his shoulder, with the air of a military person resting between wars and wearing what look like odd gloves with splits in the finger ends, was almost a caricature, a figure out of Ben Jonson. The apex of the inverse triangle was the boy in the right foreground, who had one eye on the dupe and another on his older confederate cheat. This boy was the key figure, daringly presented from the back, leaning into the picture in flashy but untidy clothes, with a marvellous cockade billowing out from his hat. Just enough of his face was visible to show that he too was a kind of innocent, wide eyed and open mouthed, full of anxiety about whether he was going to be able to pull off the trick with the card he was slipping from his belt with a dirty fingernailed hand. He stood poised between the other two in the painting's play of forces, the aggressor, but vulnerable, the one who might blow it, the focus of the picture's sexual drama. If an ingenuous boy was being duped here, another was being corrupted by the older man.

And instead of the dreamy erotic tension between the fortune teller and her boy client, a volatile all male trio was poised here to erupt into violence over the card table at any moment. The cards, the dice, the shaker, the gaming board that was already projecting off the front edge of the table, were about to go flying. How it might have ended was implicit in the dark long bladed dagger nearest the viewer, an unadorned weapon with an ominously serious finger grip lying across the rump of the young cheat leaning on the table, a rump splendidly breeched in diagonal bands of gold and burgundy silk bloomers, a rump the abbot Bellori may have had in mind when he mentioned the boy's slightly less striking shoulder.

This was the painting that turned M's life around. It became so much admired and imitated that over fifty copies and variants made by other painters survived. When the *Cheats* was painted M's older friend Prospero

> went around acclaiming M's new style and heightening the reputation of his work – to his own advantage – among the leading figures of the court.

More to the point, the *Cheats*

> ... was bought by cardinal Del Monte, who – since he delighted in painting – set M up and put him in better circumstances, giving him an honoured place in his house among his gentlemen.

What happened, Baglione said, was that when M was at rock bottom and living on handouts, a dealer in paintings near San Luigi dei Francesi whom he called *maestro Valentino* managed to shift a few for him – *had some given away*. Del Monte lived in the palazzo Madama right next to the French church and so happened to see M's work. Valentino seemed not to exist outside Baglione's memory, but two years later the Rome criminal records of summer 1597 recorded a statement from a *Costantino, who buys and resells paintings and has a shop ... next to San Luigi*. Costantino, whose name was so similar to Valentino as to suggest a slip of the pen, told the court he'd been dealing in paintings for four years – so he was already in business when M left the Cesari workshop at the start of 1594. Costantino described himself as a secondhand dealer, and said he lived above his street level shop in piazza San Luigi dei Francesi with his wife and two teenage daughters and two smaller boys. He said he worked alone in his shop and by 1597 he also knew M for sure, since he knew and identified M by name to his interrogators as *cardinal Del Monte's painter* and as living in the cardinal's palace. It was M's first mention in the Rome criminal records, and here he seemed only marginally involved in an act of violence. But the barber at the centre of the affair involving Costantino and M's friend Prospero said he'd earlier dressed a wound M had received from a groom working in a neighbouring noble household.

EVERY EVENT OF M's Roman life from this moment in 1595 was pivoted on this point – for the next ten or twelve years nothing would happen more than five minutes' walk away. The epicentre was this little piazza with the French church of San Luigi, and the great Medici palazzo Madama separated from it by a narrow alley. Palazzo Madama would be M's home for the next five years, his university and his refuge in times of danger. The church was where – five years on – he'd transform European art with his first public work, and where he'd later meet his first humiliating rejection. If you went down that narrow alley, you soon reached the vast and promiscuous meeting space of piazza Navona – place of M's assignations, ball games, friendly meetings, violent attacks and police arrests. If you turned your back on it, and stood with the church and palazzo Madama behind you, you were looking up at the façade of palazzo Giustiniani, home of the banker Vincenzo Giustiniani – who was the richest man in Rome and about to become the most intelligent and committed buyer of M's work. It was one of his grooms who'd wounded M. Leading off the piazzetta to the left was the via della Scrofa, scene of much violence involving M, and it led a few yards on to the campo Marzio, where he'd later rent a house, where the Cesaris lived, where the tennis courts were – and the scene of the terrible and fatal street fight that ended his Roman life. Further on the street led to the other great public space of the piazza del Popolo. In a close radius around piazza San Luigi were the churches that would hold his great public paintings and the palaces of his other patrons and protectors among the Roman great – the Crescenzis, the Matteis, the Colonnas. The future palazzo Borghese was three minutes away. The events about to unfold were unforeseeable, but from his arrival in palazzo Madama the matrix of M's life in Rome was set.

> Cardinal Del Monte, since he had a passion for painting, took M into his home. Now that he had board and an allowance, M's spirits rose and so did his confidence, and he painted for the cardinal a concert of some boys, done from life and extremely well. And he also did a boy playing the lute and the whole thing seemed so alive and true. It had a carafe of flowers full of water, and you could see marvellously well the reflection of a window on it and the other things in the room in the water. And there was fresh dew on those flowers done with the most exquisite care. And this – he said – *was the most beautiful piece he ever did.*

Remembering the younger M's first modest and private successes as a protégé of Del Monte's, Giovanni Baglione sounded like a true enthusiast and a generous admirer. He showed none of the spite and rancour he'd be releasing a couple of paragraphs later when he came to describe M's first public triumph. As a chamber artist painting private works for his protector patron, M was no threat at all to the Baglione who was out grabbing for the big church commissions in the professional free for all of Roman art. When M stepped outside the cardinal's palazzo Madama and became part of the competition, everything would change, including Baglione's feelings about M's art. There was, though, more to it than that. In remembering the Del Monte years Baglione was remembering a different M from the later painter. The persuasively economical sketch of the young painter, released from nagging hunger and precariousness, serenely delighting in the growing skill of his beautiful paintings of beautiful boys, was of a time – the mid to late fifteen nineties – for which nothing was known about M except the paintings he did. Maybe the things he was learning in this centre of the new culture and the technical skills he was developing as a painter absorbed him utterly. Maybe, for the few years he was living with Mario in palazzo Madama, M was happy. His art was. Naturally Mario moved in too.

Francesco Maria Bourbon Del Monte was in his mid forties and a consummate diplomat. He knew how to cover his tracks. He was the confidant of the grand duke Ferdinando I de' Medici of Tuscany and the Medici representative in Rome and his contemporaries never seemed to get beneath the pleasant surface he presented to the world.

> Del Monte's a gentleman, an excellent musician, enjoys a
> joke, takes the world as it comes, lives and lets live and is
> the friend of a few literary people

went one vague anonymous report of 1603. Another of 1599
described his *affable and gracious manner*, and how he'd managed to win
the favour of pope Clement VIII and the cardinal nephew Pietro
through *his pleasant manner*, despite the the handicap of his Medici
ties. Del Monte lived discreetly at the centre of power in Rome, and
he usually did contrive to win people's favour. Great power flowed
through his hands, though like the money he lived off in great style it
was never quite his own. He represented Medici political and cultural
interests in Rome with great efficiency and intelligence, and all
through these years he cultivated intensively his own private garden
of advanced studies in art, music and science, easing the transitions
among public and private concerns with intensive gossip and party-
ing. All intellectuals had to tread with utmost care in that time of ideological closure and repression. None more than those lodged within
the church itself.

As a connoisseur Del Monte had the fineness of mind to recognize instantly the painterly potential of the highly unusual way young
M had filtered a brutal low life realism through luminous Venetian
delicacy in the *Cheats*. He'd picked up a certain erotic vibration in
M's early work, though what happened next suggested he failed to
register its entire range. It wasn't just the painting. The personal loyalty this exquisite mediator went on showing his taciturn and confrontational protégé a few years later, even when M was becoming a
seriously compromising presence, implied something more in their
relations than Del Monte's recognition of genius – that the cardinal
was fascinated with M's readiness to take his art to the edge. In a way
that must've been deeply refreshing in that closeted milieu, M was an
exciting person to have around. There were, of course, no records.

Del Monte's fine feeling for the intricacies of art, power and the
good life might have come from a laying on of hands. When the in-
fant Del Monte was baptized in Venice in 1549 his father's friend
the painter Titian was among the witnesses, along with the sculptor
Sansovino, the critic, pornographer and blackmailer Aretino and the
cream of the Venetian power élite. He was born into a family of
courtier diplomats and intellectuals – his father was in the service of
the duke of Urbino, and Del Monte himself gravitated in his mid
twenties from the small and refined Della Rovere court to Rome, first
into the service of cardinal Sforza and then to cardinal Ferdinando

de' Medici's. When de' Medici left the church to rule Tuscany in 1587, Del Monte was already so close to him that, as the Venetian ambassador to Florence observed, the grand duke

> always eats alone and allows nobody to join him at his table or even to be present while he is eating, apart from monsignor Del Monte, who shares all his most secret thoughts. He never leaves the prince's side, keeps him company even at table ... He's avid for the grand duke's favour, and vastly enjoys being so intimate and familiar with him ... his highness loves him in return, and is glad that he is praised and respected ...

Del Monte got de' Medici's cardinal's seat the next year, and represented Tuscan interests in Rome while Ferdinando I de' Medici was knitting a political and dynastic alliance with France, to build a catholic counterweight to the vast force of Spain's bureaucratic empire. He often returned to Florence to advise Ferdinando about matters *you can't write in letters*. Del Monte for the rest of his life was identified with the French party in a Rome that was politically riven by the rivalry of Spain and France. Thirtyodd years later the French connexion would cost Del Monte the papacy. Del Monte wasn't a specially wealthy man himself, but he maintained a household of two hundred retainers in palazzo Madama, and built up a formidable art collection – nearly six hundred paintings in the end, and dozens of classical sculptures. Over the next five years in palazzo Madama M acquired the depth, the intellectual vigour, the *seriousness* that underlay the technical daring of the works that changed European painting. Nothing in the relation with his new patron was more impressive than M's capacity to assimilate what he found. In a far deeper way than anyone outside imagined, he now *seized and accepted everything with shrewdness and daring*.

THERE WERE LOSSES. M moved in with Mario practically off the street into an environment where refinement and discretion prevailed over all other values. Which was great for a funloving and intellectually restless counter reformation cardinal but stifling for a young painter with a pressing sense of the real. M was starting to engage with the pulsing realities of Roman life in his painting, a reality seen in fascinating tension with the Venetian delicacy of his style and his own erotic susceptibilities. This engagement ended – temporarily, it'd turn out – when Del Monte took him in. Del Monte saw the dimension of the *Cheats* he liked and overlooked the other. Now came the *quid pro quo* of patronage, and the first painting M did for *his cardinal* betrayed a panicky sense of claustrophobia as M was gently directed into a musical allegory slash pederotic fantasy that belonged to no time or place.

The *Musicians* was a crowded half length canvas of four partly nude boys in loose shirts and off the shoulder drapes held precariously on their bodies by the odd loose bow. It was all clearly allegorical. The lute, the horn and the violin and the music scores, all immensely valuable, all came from Del Monte's own musical instrument collection. The youngest boy had wings – Eros himself with a quiver of arrows, helping himself to some grapes in the left rear corner and looking like the *Boy peeling fruit* recycled nude. It was about love as much as music. The central figure, the lute player with an opulent red drape slung over his shoulder, tuned his instrument and looked out of the canvas with parted lips and Mario's tear filled eyes. A Mario whose hair had lately been receiving some serious attention from an expert styliste. The nearly nude foreground boy holding the music for the madrigal was seen from behind, with the knee of his bare left leg apparently thrust into the bare kneed lute player's silken crotch. There was no imaginable space for the lute player's own left leg. M had posed his models separately and superimposed them on the canvas. In trying to accommodate the cardinal's allegorical prescriptions M got himself into a visual tangle and lost sight of real space. Part of the message was lost anyway, when the music was obliterated during the painting's rough later life.

Though these boys were *painted from life, and very well*, technically as well as socially, the dreamily, weepily erotic *Musicians* retreated drastically from the reality of the *Cheats*. The four separately painted figures remained distinct and unrelated and static. They had none of the dynamic glance and gesture that'd energized the *Cheats'* triangular tension. M worked hard for this unreality – at Del Monte's urging? – and repainted the boys' clothes to make them more generalized and allegorical. The regression from real life showed on another level in the way M at twenty three or four painted himself as the boy at the back, looking nearly eight or so years younger than he was – at least as young as Mario and the other boy models when he was really six years older. M was probably adjusting to a shortage of model material, but it was nevertheless startling to see him identify so wishfully, so blatantly with the objects of desire. Yet though this airless musical scene – surely a very beautiful painting before it was ruined – was an involution from the street world of the canvases that'd caught Del Monte's eye, the recognizable feel of the boys' faces raised the question of what exactly they were up to in a real world sense, and what the viewer too was doing in that confined space – what the invitation was. It gave the painting's eroticism a further voyeuristic kick that the ravages of time never quite obliterated.

At least M's *Musicians* were secular and private. In public, and especially in a church, this kind of confusion of the real and the ideal was dangerous. Using identifiable boy models who were available for other things might lead to scandal. Five years earlier it'd happened to Scipione Pulzone – one of the most fashionable and elegant painters of counter reformation Rome and considered a marvel of realism in his day, he'd painted both the pope and Ferdinando de' Medici, down to the minute reflection of a window in the pupil of the grand duke's eye.

> There was no distinction between the living subjects and his paintings of them

and Pulzone's new realism had interested Del Monte too in the early eighties. The Jesuits commissioned an altarpiece of angels from Pulzone for their church, and he painted some boys as *extremely beautiful* standing angels. Then the Jesuits saw Pulzone's angels.

> … they were painted from life and showed various persons known to everyone – they took them down to efface the scandal.

Baglione reported this with regret because Pulzone's boy angels were *so beautiful they seemed to breathe life and movement.*

M wound that tension between a palpably real model and his allegorical role even further and made it laughable in another picture he did for Del Monte about a year after the *Musicians*. He painted Mario as a young *Bacchus*. He heaped an elaborate confection of grapes and withering vine leaves on Mario's dark hair – which was now so thick and long it looked more like a wig than fancy hairdressing – and put another basket of fruit and leaves, among which were an inedibly bad peach, a green pear, a bruised quince, a wormeaten apple and a disintegrating pomegranate, on a table in front of him with a carafe of blackish wine. Mario was leaning on his elbow on some pillows or a mattress heaped to approximate a couch suitable for reclining at symposia, and his sallow looking bare torso was half draped with a greyish sheet that also covered the couch. Or didn't quite cover it, leaving exposed a large patch of the striped mattress ticking below. He was holding a wide shallow glass of wine – a vaguely classical calyx – in his left hand, which was probably his right hand painted in a mirror. The other hand rather obscenely fingered the black bow holding his sheet in place. The startlingly white nakedness of his chest and arm and his pale exposed nipple made his swollen adolescent hands and slightly flushed face look the redder, and rims of black dirt showed under the fingernails – not the last dirty nails in M's art. The heavy lidded gaze and slightly out of focus eyes showed the model had definitely been drinking the prop wine and was finding it harder and harder to maintain the triclinium pose. The surface bubbles in the carafe were traces of a recent pouring, and the grubby hand's wobbly grasp was sending dangerous ripples to the brim of the calyx held toward you.

And toward M, who wasn't able to stay out of the picture, but included a minuscule image of himself – mop of black hair, dark clothes and white collar – standing in front of his canvas and reflected in the very edge of the lower bulge of the carafe, like a tiny signature in the painting's bottom left hand corner. M was making an allegorical painting – and maybe kicking against Del Monte's pressures – that wittily played on the absurdity of the whole enterprise. He couldn't foresee the exploits of modern printers or the way they'd heighten the colours in reproduction, to make the slightly drunk boy in a silly getup look like a grotesque redlipped geisha. Printers would never let the coolness of M's early paintings alone. The coolness of the colours, that slight cast of green and grey, was there to stop the painter's gaze burning up the canvas.

Del Monte wanted a *Fortune teller* of his own to go with the *Cheats* and M looked happier reworking that. He hadn't realized the full potential of this painting and the second variant showed a leap in skill and subtlety – M moved in closer, brought boy and girl more intimately together in a more finely radiant light. He was mastering space and light on canvas. The flat undifferentiated background of the earlier painting now became a real interior wall, with the shaft of side light from a window softened by the shadow of a partly drawn curtain and broken by the harder shadow of a sash. The boy, who'd become a younger, sweetly vain Mario, now leant into the frame and the light, his doublet billowing into the foreground and his hat's plume waving away from it. The gipsy girl's loose white sleeves likewise took on bulk and texture, and the girl herself, losing some of her animal wariness, became slyer, subtler, closer to the gulled boy. The *Fortune teller* sword was the first of a long series of such lethal weapons in M's art – a rapier hilt in complex detail and reflecting the window on its gleaming pommel.

ANOTHER PAINTING GREW out of the *Musicians*, and M called it at the time *the most beautiful piece he ever did*. The new painting showed neither the fancy allegory of the *Musicians* nor the aggressive playfulness of Mario as *Bacchus*. What remained was the single figure of a stunningly beautiful Mario seated behind a small marble topped table in a loose white shirt, fingering a lute, framed by a musical still life of violin and madrigal music and another of flowers and fruit. The elements were artfully chosen and arranged but real. *Voi sapete ch'io v'amo, anzi v'adoro.* You know I love you – I adore you. Music from four madrigals could be deciphered in the painting, and their words all declared love. The boy's parted lips, and his tongue visible against his teeth, showed him singing, while the bass part for another singer – the male part – lay closed on the table – near you, or near M. A film of tears veiled the boy's eyes. The transient blaze of delicate flowers in the carafe, the very ripe flesh of the figs and pears – and the small marrow thrusting its way into the picture – all returned their echo and stopped the erotic tone from getting too sweetly attenuated. The picture needed no explication, though it worked on you far more subtly than the dumbly yearning *Boy with fruit* did. The *Lute player*'s table and the objects created a space that opened to you, invited you and kept you at a distance, while the boy silently sang across it. *You know I love you – I adore you.*

The man who'd ordered the *Lute player* lived just across the way from the palazzo Madama and was in some ways a surprizing buyer for a work like that. Vincenzo Giustiniani was a banker and maybe the richest man in Rome. His family came from Genoa, and that city's financial tentacles reached all over the Mediterranean – and further west to the Americas. Genoa financed the Spanish empire. It was the world's great financial power. That the ruler of the island of Chios, hard against the Turkish coast in the far eastern Aegean, had been Vincenzo Giustiniani's father conformed to the realities of the time – Chios was controlled by the Genoese bankers of the house of saint George and had been a family colony for centuries. For the last forty years the house of saint George had controlled the Spanish monarchy's finances – all the newfound American gold and silver that reached Italy passed through Genoa. But in 1566 Giuseppe Giustiniani had been forced out of Chios by the Turks – a victim of Islam's westward thrust toward Europe. He took his family of three daughters and two sons to Rome where a cousin was a cardinal. His elder son Benedetto was twelve and Vincenzo was two years old.

Giustiniani arrived in Rome with a modest capital of six thousand scudi and when he died in 1600 he was a merchant banker and grain importer worth half a million and he was financing the papacy. Benedetto went into the church and was a cardinal by 1587 – in time to play a decisive part in the election of Clement VIII. Vincenzo went into banking with his father and was twenty six in 1590 when the Giustinianis bought the new palazzo opposite the Medicis' palazzo Madama as their Roman home. Four years later the pope made Giuseppe Giustiniani head of the *depositeria generale* – the most powerful financial post in Rome – because Giustiniani was the soundest banker in the capital.

> No other banker could disburse immediately as much silver as he could to put at the service of his holiness, or wait longer for repayment.

When Giuseppe died in 1600, Vincenzo gave up hunting dangerous game in the wilder parts of Italy and took over as the papacy's chief financier. Benedetto the cardinal was also a financier, in effect the papal treasurer. Even more than his friend Del Monte himself, Benedetto was a diplomatic activist for France's king Henri IV. The *impetuous* Benedetto was on intimate terms with Henri, who wrote to him in late 1599 as *mon cousin*, thanking Benedetto for his help in getting his first marriage annulled – when M went to live by San Luigi dei Francesi, he moved into the nerve centre of proFrench activism in Rome. Vincenzo was the brother more intensely and intelligently concerned with art, especially M's – Benedetto was more conventional – and he had young painters, mainly foreign, living in the palazzo Giustiniani over the years. Like Del Monte he followed their development closely. When Vincenzo died in 1638 the palazzo Giustiniani had a collection of over three hundred paintings – fifteen canvases by M. Although Del Monte had an even larger collection of around seven hundred paintings, only eight were by M. He never tried to elbow Del Monte aside as M's mentor, but Vincenzo

Giustiniani became the buyer who quietly urged M's work out of the hothouse and back into the real world.

Vincenzo Giustiniani was a good friend of Del Monte's and shared a lot of his interests in art and archaeology and music, but he was a very different type. Del Monte was a courtier, bureaucrat, diplomat and politician born and bred and he understood the need for discretion. With sexual and intellectual leanings as heterodox as his were, he needed to – and the startling way he let it all hang out in his final phase thirty years on, after failing in his last bid to be pope, suggested his universal tact and amenability had come at a steep price. His friend and neighbour Giustiniani was a married man and father, a layman, a banker – not quite self made but not yet ennobled and with relatively hard and precarious times a recent family memory. His discretion was even more impenetrable than Del Monte's but it came from a more deeply personal source. It went with a fairly austere protobourgeois way of life and an interest in substance rather than show. Giustiniani's portrait radiated austerity and reserve – a lean and aquiline face, deep and penetrating eyes.

Giustiniani left nothing like Del Monte's stream of correspondence, deft, elegant, purposeful, laced with gossip and perfidy and utterly reticent about himself. Giustiniani did leave a series of short impersonal seeming essays on things that interested him that were greatly revealing of their writer. A friend said

> he could talk about everything, understood everything, even the most recondite sciences

and he wrote tersely and plainly on modern music and painting, architecture – unsurprizing enthusiasms in view of the *Lute player* – and also on the practical arts of good living like hunting and European travel and organizing a banquet and horse trading. It was hard to imagine Del Monte following the younger Giustiniani through bandit country into heavy scrub after wolves or wild boar – Giustiniani's keenness on the chase went well beyond the norm. He had an alert and curious mind for the varieties of people's behaviour and a practical man's relish for materials, tools and processes.

> He'd brought together in his house a group of knights and professional men that had no like anywhere in Europe.

When he was made a marchese he designed his feudal palazzo and laid out its grounds himself – his essay on architecture was based on that experience. When he wrote about painting he remarked that he knew more about the practice of art than the theory – he was close to the painters whose work he collected and he was the man who'd retrieve the situation for M after the shock of his first rejection. But he was fifteen years younger than Del Monte and it showed the cardinal's influence on the banker's early taste that the very Delmontian *Lute player* was Giustiniani's first buy.

Del Monte wanted a singing boy with a lute of his own, and M painted another for him about a year later. He scraped off an old devotional picture, maybe one of his own, and tipped the canvas on its side to paint the half length *Lute player*, just as he'd done before with the canvas used for his first *Fortune teller*. M began his copy from a tracing of the original and then changed it notably. He eliminated the flowers and fruit and brought in a caged songbird, a spinet and a beautiful wooden recorder to make the sense more fully musical. A new placing of the table and the receding pattern of a red oriental carpet enhanced the depth. The objects found a bright new hard edged specificity, while the boy singer lost some of Mario's individuality and became almost androgynous. Bellori in fact took the singer in this later version for *a woman in a shirt playing a lute with the notes in front of her*. Mario might've been transmuted into Pedro Montoya for the later variant. Pedro Montoya was a young Spaniard and cardinal Del Monte's resident castrato. As another member of the household and recorder of its musical activities, M must've known him well.

The art of singing had become highly refined by the end of the sixteenth century and put a new emphasis on the qualities of the solo performer. Vincenzo Giustiniani was interested in the new music as well as M's new art.

> In the holy year of 1575 or soon after a manner of singing began that was very different from the previous one ... especially in the way of singing for a solo voice accompanied by an instrument.

Castrati were all the rage, both as singers in the Sistine chapel and at the richer and more refined of the private functions. Castrati who knew how to play the lute as well as sing were the most sought after of all. In the eighties Guglielmo Gonzaga, duke of Mantua, had been looking around for *eunuchs* to sing at his court who were good catholics and quiet youths ... reliable singers with good voices ... particularly valuable if they can play the lute while they sing.

Giustiniani said castrati

revived the practice of music, and many nephews of popes and other cardinals and princes then came to love it ... all the chapel masters began training various eunuchs and other boys to sing in a new and loving manner ...

The Sistine chapel choir had been recruiting castrati in Spain for decades by the time Del Monte became protector of the chapel in the early nineties. Pedro Montoya had been one of the chapel singers for several years and in 1596, when M painted his later *Lute player*, Pedro Montoya was often noted as absent from the chapel – he was most likely hanging round the palazzo Madama, entertaining cardinal Del Monte's friends at private concerts and being painted by M.

Concerts figured largely in the evening round of Del Monte and his friends – *you should know I play the guitar and sing in the Spanish manner*, a younger Del Monte had written to a friend some years before his elevation – but the resources of music went a long way beyond the social. The Del Monte who was now so intensely interested in M's natural painting had been much taken fifteen years earlier by a book that'd attacked the contrapuntal virtuoso music then in vogue for being *like nothing found in nature* and argued for a recovery of a *simple and natural* music for solo singer and instrument which *aimed only to move others*. The musician who wrote it was Vincenzo Galilei and he was the father of a scientist – no mean lute player himself – called Galileo. And while M was living in palazzo Madama, Galileo was a frequent visitor and M surely knew him. Del Monte had an elder brother called Guidubaldo who was a mathematician and physicist and the man who Galileo later said was the greatest influence on his own early research – for the way he matched theoretical rigour with experimental proof. Guidubaldo Del Monte had written the first ever systematic treatment of mechanics and was about to bring out a work on the mathematics of visual perspective. Four years earlier the Del Monte brothers had used their clout to get Galileo his first decent teaching job, and years later – when Galileo was in real trouble with the inquisition over *what the senses show us* – Francesco Maria would defend him. Del Monte would be one of the first to get Galileo's new telescope and use it to scrutinize the sky. There was a continuity of interest in music, mathematics and physics in this milieu and it all hinged on nature – the evidence of your own eyes and ears. It was a dangerous line to be following under a regime predicated on quite different values. It was why these friends were so fascinated by M's new art.

3

ROME 1597–1599

Jove, Neptune, Pluto
Boy bitten by lizard I
Boy bitten by lizard II
Medusa
Francis & angel
Penitent Magdalen
Fillide
Rest on the flight into Egypt
Catherine

IN SCIENCE DEL Monte was a serious amateur. Beyond his studies of music, archaeology and painting he built up collections in botany and mineralogy, he studied geography, astronomy and mechanics and he experimented in pharmacology. He also experimented in the protoscience of alchemy, and in November 1596 he bought a garden villa at porta Pinciana where he installed an alchemical distillery. He tried to sell it again a year later, then kept it, and around the end of 1597 as a curiosity or challenge he got M to paint the ceiling with an alchemical allegory. Under pressure from his protector or maybe enjoying a *jeu d'esprit*, M produced a work that was so privately placed, so anomalous in its esoteric theme and so exceptional in being his only work not painted on canvas or wood that it remained largely unknown and ignored. Bellori, though, remembered it in 1672, and added a mention at the very end of his life of M.

People still say the *Jove, Neptune, Pluto* is by his hand, in the Ludovisi garden at porta Pinciana, in the casino that used to be cardinal Del Monte's. Del Monte studied chemical medicine, and so he decorated the study of his distillery, identifying these gods with the elements with the globe of the world in their midst. They say M heard himself criticized for not understanding planes or perspective, and responded to the charge by placing the bodies so they were seen from below looking upward, to make them take on the most difficult foreshortenings. It's true that these gods don't keep their proper forms and are painted in oil on the vault, since M had never painted in fresco. All his followers too turn to the ease of oil painting to render the model ...

It was nature in a very anomalous sense. *Bacchus* had played on the ineffaceable chink of daylight that separated myth from the reality of a boy on a dirty bed, but the three sons of Kronos and their imagined beasts dared you to disbelieve them. M's amazing foreshortening powerfully compacted their adult male vigour. They were three muscular variants of a single figure whose Neptune might've been an older version of Mario or even a self portrait. The tumultuous bravura of the foreshortened figures did look like the rising to a challenge that Bellori imagined or heard about. The ceiling's animal figures made the mythic real – the heavy winged eagle carrying Jove, its talons clutching a crumpled bed sheet, the grey flippered seahorse Neptune rode, and Pluto's three headed snarling hound Cerberus, who became three rapidly linked moments of dog behaviour, frames from a dog movie. They were the symbols of the alchemical triad derived from Paracelsus – Jove stood for sulphur and air, Neptune for mercury and water and Pluto for salt and earth. The celestial sphere being moved by Jove – in which a preGalilean sun revolved around the earth – had a brilliant internal glow that must've been refracted through one of Del Monte's mineral specimens. But the myths all faded behind the turbulence of the real men and the almost real animals who embodied it. There was no blank allegorical stasis in this painting, and none of the airless sweetness of the portraits of boys M had been painting such a short time before. The distillery ceiling was charged with a restless male energy and a kind of anger that portended the thunderclap now two years off.

IN THE SUMMER of 1597 a barber's boy named Pietropaolo was beaten up in the neighbourhood of San Luigi dei Francesi and he later appeared curiously reluctant to help police with their inquiries into the case. The youth was held in custody for refusing to identify the person or persons who'd attacked him on a Tuesday evening in mid July, and the authorities themselves were extremely circumspect in trying to identify the individual who'd apparently found a black cloak with metal hook and eye fastenings, a *ferraiolo*, at the scene of the attack and handed it in to the barber's shop where Pietropaolo worked. The barber's shop was five minutes' walk away by the church of Sant' Agostino. Although the finder of the cloak might've been more deeply involved in the attack than his subsequent helpfulness in returning the black cloak implied, there were hints that he might also have been a person of some influence, and so official caution was in order.

The barber claimed not to remember the name of the person who'd brought the cloak to Pietropaolo at the salon while the barber and his family were having their evening meal upstairs. He'd been told the name before, though, and he knew that the man was a painter. The painter had once been to his salon for a trim, and another time to have a wound dressed, a wound Pietropaolo told the barber the painter had received in a fight with a groom working for the Giustinianis. He also said Pietropaolo had told him that Costantino the art dealer from San Luigi dei Francesi nearby had been with the painter when he'd brought the cloak. Pressed to describe the unidentified painter, the barber replied that

> this painter is a young bloke about twenty or twenty five years old, with a little black beard. He's stocky with heavy eyebrows and dark eyes. He goes around dressed in black, a bit untidily, and wears black stockings that are a bit torn.

With professional punctiliousness, the barber added that the painter *wears his thick hair long in front*. Pietropaolo had disowned the cloak and taken it to another barber's shop, because he claimed he thought he'd recognized one of their voices during the brawl. When the art dealer Costantino was then called and questioned, he said he'd been in business for four years selling paintings second hand at San Luigi dei Francesi. On the Tuesday evening in question, he'd shut up shop and gone out for an after dinner walk when two painters he knew passed by.

... one was M from Caravaggio, who's cardinal Del
Monte's painter and the other was a painter too, called
Prospero ... [M's] short with a bit of black beard and about
twenty five or twenty eight years old. They asked me if I'd
already eaten and I told them I had, but they said they
hadn't eaten and wanted to have dinner at the osteria della
Lupa, where we all went together and I kept them company while they ate.

After dinner they'd been sauntering back, the dealer said, when someone came running toward them from piazza San Luigi yelling in fear.
All drew back, and he'd been unable, without his glasses, to see who
the fugitive had been, what he looked like or how he'd been dressed,
or whether anyone had been chasing him. Costantino had gone home
and denied having seen any cloak or having met the two painters sub-
sequently, or ever having been to the barber's shop in question.

When Prospero Orsi was called in, he confirmed that he'd been
that Tuesday evening with *M cardinal Del Monte's painter and Costantino the picture dealer at San Luigi* and that they'd gone to the osteria
della Lupa. M had called on him at home *half an hour before nightfall*
to suggest eating together and they'd picked up Costantino *on the way
there*. Afterward they'd heard *shouting near piazza San Luigi* and been
passed by someone fleeing, someone he hadn't recognized because *it
was dark* and the man had *passed like a shadow*. He added that M had
then found a black cloak and picked it up, saying *it'd be a good idea to
give this cloak to a neighbour*.

The authorities must've been convinced by then that the three
were innocent of involvement in the attack, or that it would be im-
prudent to pursue the matter, because M was never even called for
questioning and the matter lapsed. Questions remained, such as how
M recognized the barber's boy he thought owned the cloak, or
whether he was just trying to do the boy a favour, and why the boy
and his barber boss were so reluctant to identify M, if M had been
unconnected with the attack. The last question put to Prospero was
whether any of the three friends had been armed that Tuesday evening.
Neither Costantino nor he had been carrying any kind of weapon,
Prospero had replied, *although the said M carried a sword*. Was M in the
habit of carrying a sword?

The said M is in the habit of carrying a sword because he's
a member of cardinal Del Monte's household, and I've seen
him carrying one a great many times ... he used to wear

one in daytime, but now he doesn't, only sometimes when he goes out at night.

ONE SPRING NIGHT in the next year of 1598, M was arrested by a night patrol in the few yards between teeming piazza Navona and palazzo Madama. He'd done nothing – he was imprisoned for

> wearing a sword without a licence and carrying a pair of compasses.

Del Monte was out of town at the time, having escorted the pope to Ferrara with a group of cardinals in the pomp of repossession after the papal forces had seized the city back into papal control. In his statement M told the examining magistrate

> I was taken yesterday evening at around [ten or eleven in the evening] between piazza Madama and piazza Navona because I was wearing a sword which I wear as painter of the cardinal Del Monte and I receive an allowance from the cardinal for myself and my servant and I live in his house and am on his payroll.

The infraction was minor – the ban on offensive weapons was commonly ignored. Beyond the glimpse of M out alone in the streets at night, and M's assertion of his dignity as a member of Del Monte's household – which was enough to get the charge dismissed – the fascination of the document lay in the compasses. To a police eye a folded pair of compasses would have looked suspiciously like another offensive weapon, not much different from the long dagger worn and used together with the sword by duellers. As a piece of advanced technology, the instrument for technical drawing and measurement would've been unfamiliar to the police, though it was currently fascinating the literary minds of Europe. The English poet John Donne had lately closed an erotic poem by likening his own and his lover's souls to a pair of *stiff twin compasses*. The erotic allure of the metal compasses and their avant garde promise of precision and control were widely felt. In Italy that same year the poet Guarini had published a madrigal that turned on the same image of compasses for lovers' constancy. The compasses M was carrying when he was arrested probably came from

71

cardinal Del Monte's collection of scientific equipment and might have been the very same massive and lethal looking instrument that would soon appear trampled under the dirty toenailed naked foot of Eros in M's most sensational private commission.

M was likely showing a more practical interest in this state of the art technology, and concerned with what the compasses could achieve in visual representation rather than with their pictorial suggestiveness. As well as the two legged compasses of these poems there existed double compasses that were known as *reduction compasses* or *four pointed compasses* that were used to measure proportions, and maybe M was carrying those. Guidubaldo Del Monte, who was not only a mathematician but a developer of scientific instruments and had designed a solar clock, had also played a part in perfecting the reduction compasses. The year before, Galileo had finished developing his own *geometric military compasses*. And in these years Galileo was in close contact with Guidubaldo, who was finishing off his *Six books of perspective*. When this work came out two years later, dedicated to Guidubaldo's brother the cardinal, it would underline the connexion between mathematics and art by setting out the maths of the sense of depth in vision – the first scientific theory of the vanishing point that renaissance painters had worked out empirically to give their two dimensional images a sense of depth.

ART AS SCIENCE sounded odd as the sixteenth century edged into the seventeenth, but the link wasn't new, just lost or forgotten. A hundred years earlier Leonardo had opened his *Book of painting* on the question of whether painting was a science. His answer was yes. For Leonardo the art of seeing – and representing truly what you saw – was at the heart of understanding the material world. And art and science were joined in that perception. The eyes had once been the windows of the soul. With Leonardo they became man's window on the universe. The image was greater than the word because it was more exact, and precision and beauty were the same thing – the *Book of painting* was full of exultant little riffs on the visual joy of nature and the painter's joy in catching it,

> transparent waters, through which you see their courses' greenish bed, and the play of the wave over meadows and fine pebbles, with darting fish mingling with the weeds ...

There was something deeply moving – to anyone looking back from a later age – in the irrepressible delight with which Leonardo again and again in his notes on painting identified beauty with knowledge of nature.

> It's through seeing that you understand the beauty of created things, the greatest of the things that induce love …

Something of this earlier purity of intent now returned to painting in M's early work. Vasari – recalling a detail in an early painting by Leonardo – might've been referring to M's early still life when he described

> a carafe full of water with some flowers in it, where beyond the marvel of their lifelikeness he'd imitated the dew on them so well that it seemed even more alive than the lifelike flowers.

Leonardo's *Book of painting* wasn't published until an edited version came out in 1651, nearly half a century after M died. But Guidubaldo Del Monte knew the full text – the *codex urbinas 1270* – and he was working on it at this very time for his own study of perspective. M might well have read Leonardo's work on painting himself in the years of his formation at Del Monte's. If it were so, it confirmed a remarkable and critical link. He'd been able to see Leonardo's art in Milan as a boy – the mural *Last supper* above all – and Del Monte in his collection had four small portrait paintings by Leonardo, or copies of them. The times had now made Leonardo's writings almost a subversive text – the counter reformation had rung down the iron curtain of ideology and dogma was now being preferred to empirical knowledge. Soon Galileo would be warning against

> wanting people to deny the evidence of their own senses and submit it to the arbitrary judgement of others, and allowing people totally ignorant of an art or science to be judges of intellectuals … these are the new powers that can ruin republics and subvert states.

Science and art were in the same boat. In 1597 cardinal Paleotti urged the compiling of an *Index of prohibited images*, along the lines of the vigorously policed and highly effective *Index of prohibited books*. It won a lot of support in the college and failed only because the machinery of church patronage already had painting so well in hand that an index of images was superfluous as well as unworkable. Against dogma, and threading through the first part of his *Book,* was Leonardo's insistence that the only knowledge worth having was that which met the test of the human senses.

> It seems to me that those sciences are useless and full of errors that aren't born of experience, the mother of all certainty, and end in known experience – that is when their origin, or means or end doesn't pass through any of the five senses.

The senses were concerning M at the time he was doing his portraits of Mario. Alongside their resonantly suspended eroticism he was making some visual experiments that took his painting in another direction. He was making small essays in pain, surprise, fear and disgust – trying to catch the intensity of feeling in a momentary grimace. He painted a small portrait of Mario, or a boy much like him, with very bouffant hair, a come on rose tucked behind his ear and a slender naked shoulder much in evidence, starting back in mild pain, disgust and fright as a small lizard hidden in the shadows of some foreground fruit nipped the tip of his middle finger. The other hand fluttered back in dismay tinged with an affectation that made you think of Del Monte's hothouse world. The boy looked too effeminate to be Mario, unless the new milieu was getting at him – though his fingernails were dirt rimmed as ever. By the fruit was a glass carafe holding another rose and reflecting the window. The still life was finely done, but the real interest of the painting was in the instantaneous reality of the sudden movement fixed on canvas, the unheard shriek, an effect as far as possible from the time exposure fixity and the glazed stare of the *Bacchus.*

In the *Boy bitten by lizard* M was knowingly or not taking up one of Leonardo's concerns. Though Leonardo's surviving paintings showed faces of an enigmatic and almost unreal serenity – the *Mona Lisa* the most teasing instance – his notebooks were full of vivid sketches of human faces caught in moments of surprise, anger, pain. One of the two longest and most detailed sections of the *Book of painting* was the third, and it was devoted to *the various accidents and movements of man and proportion of the members.* The other was the fifth part, *On shadow and light,* which would be even more central to M's art. Leonardo said movement had to reflect the nature of a man's inner impulse, his attitude had to show a man's intention and the expression on the face had to reflect exactly the inner mental event, so that anger, for instance, shouldn't be mistaken for any other feeling, *and similarly for happiness, melancholy, laughter, weeping and the like.* It was no simple matter, since

> some weep from anger, some from fear, some from tenderness and happiness, some from suspicion and some from pain and torment and some from pity and distress and the loss of friends or family ... and in weeping some look desperate, some ordinary, some are tearful, some yell, some look up to heaven with their fingers clasped below, others look fearful with their head shrunk into their shoulders ...

Leonardo insisted on authenticity in representing emotion – a painter had to note the real thing, real anger, real laughter and not a mimicry of it. *They have to be noted down or memorized immediately.* Weeping for instance, faked by a model, *will be neither spontaneous nor natural.* Once the real thing had been caught in life, it could always be worked up again later, Leonardo suggested, and this is what M did with the second at least of his two nearly identical versions of the *Boy bitten by lizard*.

Mancini and Baglione both mentioned the *Boy bitten* as one of the very first paintings M did in Rome. The picture's vivacity, the boy's deep presence in the space and the subtlety of its oblique lighting all made this utterly unlikely – Mancini was maybe recalling an earlier essay on the theme when he named it as one of the pictures painted and sold for a song while M was still lodging with *monsignor Salad*. *That head really seemed to be shrieking*, Baglione conceded, placing it only a little later. But this painting was something quite new. Among the graceful erotic allusiveness of the roses and cherries, and the boy's seductive *décolleté*, and all the accoutrements of a long held pose as for *Bacchus* or the *Lute player*, the lizard – the adult penis in Greek and Latin poetry, as Del Monte would've pointed out – darted out and threw the usual *mise en scène* into disarray, a sharp and provocative reminder of the reality of lust. The whole thing was *echt* Del Monte. Collecting and systematically studying the ancient art of Rome was one of Del Monte's particular interests, and M had probably seen the Roman copy of *Apollo the lizardslayer* by Praxiteles that later went to the Louvre – the statue in which the god of order became a young boy wondering whether or not to stab a fatly suggestive lizard on a tree trunk. Not that it really mattered. M was never a purveyor of hidden messages.

Charged with erotic aggression toward its subject, the *Boy bitten* was a deceptively playful harbinger of the coming violence in M's work. The concern in the *Boy bitten* to capture sudden movement and sudden pain and fear wasn't merely technical. It showed a new relation of the painter M to his subject Mario, if this boy were he. The change was a shock and a relief after the heavy stillness of longing that pervaded the earlier paintings of Mario. The stillness and clarity contained in the glass carafe and its window reflection – looking like the one Bellori later wrote about with amazement at its skill – set off the picture's flurry of panic and disgust. A storm had broken.

M pressed on into the horror lurking in that harmless penis lizard's nip in another and much more violent essay in painting a scream he did the same year. The other scream of 1598 was fixed on the face of a severed head very like Mario's and not at all nancy – vividly lifelike and freshly dead, blood still splashing from the severed arteries. Baglione wrote that M did a

> very frightening *Medusa's head* with vipers for hair, that was painted on a round shield that the cardinal sent as a gift to Ferdinando the grand duke of Tuscany.

The Medusa, whose hideous gaze was supposed to turn people to stone, was a common motif on combat shields and was terrifying in M's version by virtue of her own horror – the psychic terror at having her head cut from her body. Or would have been. It was the thought that counted. M's monster was actually a boy and remained something of an exercise, Mario's head put to a dreadfully intended but not entirely convincing use. The most striking thing about it was the illusionistic skill whereby M made the severed head seem to project into real space, its jets of blood gushing free of the shield. The illusion was achieved largely by the shadows the snakes seemed to cast on the shield behind them. Their projection made the convex look concave.

In Florence Ferdinando I had been energetically reorganizing his personal armoury and the *Medusa* shield with its horrid image was an artfully chosen present from his man in Rome. Del Monte sent it north in the spring of 1598, or maybe took it himself to Florence in the summer. Three years later an embassy from the shah of Persia presented Ferdinando I with two sets of Persian armour and M's shield was made part of their display, in the hand of one of two models mounted on wooden horses in tournament stance, *clothed in a Persian coat of mail of glittering gold and grey scales forming peacock eyes, and armed with an arrow and a scimitar*, at the centre of Ferdinando's collection of

Medici arms in a large gallery. When the armoury was inventoried many years later and not long before the Persian display was dismantled and the Medici arms collection dispersed forever, a note on the Medusa shield ascribed the painting to M *or perhaps to Leonardo.*

In 1540 a visitor to the Medici collections in Florence had written of a Medusa there with *rare and wonderful* serpent hair painted by Leonardo. So had Vasari in his *Life of Leonardo da Vinci* in 1568, and called it *the strangest and weirdest invention you could ever imagine* and *unfinished* but still one of the best things in the grand duke's collection. Someone else claimed to have seen Leonardo's Medusa only fifteen years before M painted his own version. Leonardo's painting later vanished, or maybe never existed – imagined out of Vasari's long anecdote in his *Life of Leonardo* about a terrifying Medusa like monster the young Leonardo had painted on another shield, an image compounded of dead animals that had shocked his own father with the realism of its painting. If Leonardo's *Medusa* did really exist in the Medici collection, Del Monte knew it. Could M now impress Ferdinando by painting a no less terrifying image? As seemingly real? In the *Medusa* M was taking on Leonardo's standard of realism and emotion in art.

FRANCIS & ANGEL was M's first night painting, his first of full length figures and it showed his first angel. It was his first ever painting of a religious subject and showed the bearded Francis of Assisi *in ecstasy.* It was maybe the very first painting he did for his new boss Del Monte and done even before the *Musicians* – and aptly enough it showed the cardinal's personal name saint metaphorically dying in the world and being reborn in Christ. It was all – the wounds, the ecstasy, the austerity – unexceptionable counter reformation material. The handling was most unusual. Where was the six winged seraph the saint'd seen in his vision? A six winged seraph didn't lend itself to being painted from life. Even more startling than the absence of the seraph was what was in the picture. He had the blissed out saint lying back with unseeing eyes nearly closed between the thighs of a near nude adolescent angel. The mop haired angel wore a pair of stage prop wings and another loosely knotted off the shoulder blouse slash loincloth. His bare shoulder and knee caught the shaft of heavenly light strongly in the surrounding darkness and his figure loomed much larger than the swooning saint's in his coarse habit. The angel looked a lot like a version of the winged Eros helping himself to grapes in the *Musicians* of a little earlier, and maybe even more the duped boy of the *Cheats*, and there was no iconographical precedent for him at all. Was the angel Del Monte's own idea? The face of the saint himself, sinking back between the angel's adolescent thighs, seemed to be the beak nosed and trim bearded cardinal's own.

Around this time Del Monte took another young artist under his wing – Ottavio Leoni, who was seven years younger than M and still in his teens. Leoni was later a friend and ally of M's and an incisive portraitist – he sketched M and Galileo and most of the painters and writers who were M's friends, rivals and enemies. In 1599 Del Monte was praising him to Ferdinando de' Medici as

> a young pupil of mine who works better and more carefully and gets an incomparably better likeness than poor old Scipione Pulzone

– who'd just died. In 1616 Leoni drew Del Monte in his mid sixties, and he showed a sleek and refined high prelate, well fleshed though not fat or gross, with a strong nose, long ears, trim little grey beard and pale, intelligent and slightly protuberant eyes looking out from under a cardinal's little four pointed hat. This was twenty years after M's *Francis* painting. The other memorable image of Del Monte belonged to twenty years before it – a detail in a 1575 painting by Jacopo Zucchi in the Roman church of Trinità dei Pellegrini, and it showed the nattily ruffed twenty six year old Del Monte as an eager sensualist, beak nosed, pointy faced, sharp eyed and avid lipped. The face of Del Monte in his mid forties, fainting between the angel's thighs, was painted midway through this long transition from his younger to his older self. Del Monte kept it until the end of his life. Others liked it too, and several copies – maybe done by Mario with M's help – went into circulation now and were greatly valued.

M's erotic take on saintly ecstasy was an analogue to the mute sexual longing of his Mario paintings, and his essays in catching a silent scream of fear and pain – another go at making real an intensely inward state. The outdoor night landscape in *Francis* evoked the attentive nature painters of his northern youth – the beautiful delicate daisies and woodland foliage in the foreground edge of the picture, the tiny figures of the shepherds by their fire in the middle distance and the strange light streaking the far night sky. For a painter who'd show so little – next to nothing – in the way of outdoor space, M had a feel for the nature of landscape that came from the days he'd looked long and hard at the work of the Lombard painters. Lombardy had always been *the home of simple art*.

> ... in the sixteenth century, Lotto, Moretto, Savoldo and Moroni had paid their respects to the *grand goût* of the paganizing century of Raphael or Michelangelo or Titian and then taken that other path ... with their more attentive humanity, their more modest religiousness, their truer and more careful colours, more detailed shadowing even in the effects of night or artificial light, they'd kept a concern for real people and things. That meant knowing how to mix unassumingly with ordinary people and also how to walk alone through the country, unafraid of mythological stirrings.

Nature wasn't as fraught with ideology as people were. It was M's ordinary people who startled and excited when they turned up in his work in the hyper refined and attenuated art world of Rome. The really dangerous element, from the point of view of political and theological control, was the human. Give people their heads and they started sending the wrong messages. Or none at all.

When, soon after that, M painted the *Penitent Magdalen,* it seemed not a religious painting at all – simply a study of an ordinary modern girl sitting on a low wooden chair drying her hair. Where was the meaning? Where was the prostitute's repentance, her suffering, the promise of salvation? A single barely visible tear running off her nose seemed insufficient. A few trinkets flung on the floor inadequate to show she'd renounced a whorish, meretricious wantonly female past. It was M's first painting of a woman since the gipsy fortune tellers, and Bellori offered a lovingly minute description of the young girl. He was unyielding, though, about the painting's content.

> He painted a young girl seated on a stool with her hands in her lap in the act of drying her hair. He painted her in a chamber, and adding on the floor a little jar of ointment, with some jewels and gems, did her as the Magdalen.

The word Bellori actually used for *doing her as* was *fingere*, which is like the English *feign*, and both words were much used around the time M painted his *Magdalen. Fingere, feigning*, that was what good art tried to do. Shakespeare's truthtelling clown Touchstone would be telling people three or four years later in England, in one of

Shakespeare's own early plays, that *the truest poetrie is the most feigning.*

Truth and fakery in art had never been a simple question and seventeenth century writers on art like Bellori often used the word in the quite neutral sense of creating a likeness. But here a limiting note was inescapable. Bellori was directing back at this beautiful early painting, without quite saying so, the counter reformation demand that religious art be improving. A painting of an everyday girl in an everyday act couldn't, by its nature, represent one of the iconic moments in Christianity's turn against sexuality. The very touching lifelikeness Bellori responded to –

> her face is posed a bit to one side and her cheek, neck and breast are done in a pure, simple and true colouring that goes with the simplicity of the whole figure

– worked against the painting's having any larger meaning for him. *He painted a young girl ... and called her the Magdalen.* Artistically this wasn't enough. Bellori was so intent on giving it an everyday sense of hair washing that he wouldn't see that part of the fineness in the way the girl's features were coloured lay in their slight puffiness and redness from weeping. Unlike M's single boy models, the girl didn't stare out at the viewer – she sat bowed and solitary, locked in a private misery. Not only the swollen face but the redness of her hands and pierced ear and the tangle of undone hair brought to mind the aftermath of an act of violence. The broken string of pearls and the other ornaments looked as if they'd been ripped off her rather than put aside, and recalled not so much the prostitute saint's regret and renunciation as the punitive treatment courtesans were getting in Rome, the police whippings that might come a girl's way if she plied her trade outside the ever narrower parameters allowed. A whipped and weeping courtesan wasn't a rare thing in Rome. And a painter's model, if it were a good looking young woman, was likely to be a courtesan. M did around this time a straight portrait of a courtesan called Fillide holding some orange blossom, and Fillide's likeness then reappeared as the powerful female lead in a dazzling sequence of paintings on nominally religious themes that M did in the very last years of the century. She might've been a friend of the girl who modelled for *Magdalen.*

Just before or just after his simple image of the Magdalen in tears, M used the same girl model, with her tawny hair now done up and her head in a similar pose, as the virgin mother of Christ. The *Rest on the flight into Egypt* showed the suspended reality of the instant out of time, the moment of stasis and rest for the fleeing couple and their baby – the old man and his young wife, and the donkey who carried them. The stillness of an angel's unheard music on a violin pervaded the painting – it was ultra real and magical at once, a peasant family picnic in paradise. This flight into Egypt went through M's Lombardy again and through the Venetian past of M's training. M set the peasant family down in a woody landscape of oaks and Lombard poplars, an overcast sky and low distant hills in brown, green and grey. To entertain them he sent a nude blond adolescent angel with a violin, standing in the middle foreground with his back to the viewer, a filmy white wraith floating over his bum and winding around his legs – he'd flown into the picture on a pair of dirty grey wings borrowed from a Roman street pigeon, wings now projecting out front of the canvas – the wing tips were practically sticking in your eye, the light on the far horizon just behind them. Exhaustion or the music had sent mother and child into placid symbiotic sleep. M did seven surviving mother and child images, and – in the way M saw a small child's face and body and movements and the way a mother held it – they weren't bettered by any other of the hundreds or thousands of such images in Italian painting. Since the mother was sitting on the ground at a slight forward angle, restfulness here was compromised by a sense that she was about to lurch over in her sleep and wake her child. On the angel's other side an elderly and heavy lidded Joseph in a sacklike brown garment sat on the family's bundle of belongings tied up in a blanket and patiently held the music open at a motet based on the *Song of songs*. The angel evidently couldn't play without a score, and was wholly taken up with getting his fingering right on his violin. The kinky end of a violin string hung down from one of the pegs. One further source of Joseph's weariness might have been the wine in the wicker covered demijohn, now stopped with a twist of paper and lying by his feet, and another the unseemliness of letting his gaze fall from the angel's face to his frontal nudity that the long gauzy cloth did nothing to cover. M always painted his boys and angels nude first and then added their light coverings.

In the shadow of the trees behind them and emerging through the foliage, crowding forward between Joseph's head and the angel's, was part of the donkey's face, and while Mary snoozed and Joseph nodded off the animal's huge dark liquid eye was the only one in the picture to be looking really appreciative of the heavenly performer's music. The donkey's eye was brimming with mute adoration. Making the travel worn holy family – the painting's subject and the object of your attention – themselves a weary and inattentive audience for a visually more prominent celestial third party's self absorbed performance on the violin, M made the picture deeply and unobtrusively funny. The angel himself, intent on his unheard playing, was equally oblivious of the way the sight of his own pale adolescent nudity lit up the country stopover. M would be funny again, but he'd never again sound anything quite like this note of serene and gentle humour.

BELLORI LIKED TALKING about M picking up his models in the street and maybe that was how it sometimes happened. More likely they were people M'd known before he moved to palazzo Madama and kept on seeing after that. A lot of M's crowd, the ones who weren't artists or their facilitators or otherwise unspecified *gentlemen*, were prostitutes and *their* hangers on, the pimps, landlords, protectors, friends and mothers who found employment as the women's satellites. As two of the very few working communities in Rome, artists and prostitutes had a lot in common, not least their common intimacy with men of the cloth.

In the spring of 1597, a few months before the episode of the barber's boy and the cloak and a year before the trouble over the compasses, M had appeared as a marginal provocateur in another police report of a tavern brawl among three women. The central figure in the fight was Anna Bianchini, *Annuccia* to her friends and the cops, daughter of a cowherd and a fence for bandits, who'd arrived from Siena on a winter Saturday of pouring rain four years earlier with her mother, brother and sister. She'd been on the game in Rome ever since. She'd travelled down together with another girl from Siena called Fillide Melandroni, who came with *her* mother and brother to join relatives in Rome. The two family groups lived together in the early days while the mothers put the girls to work. When Anna and Fillide were arrested together by the police just over a year into their careers, in April 1594, for being outside the brothel quarter after dark, the judge respectfully addressed them as *donna Anna* and *donna Fillide* even though at that time the girls were respectively fourteen and thirteen years old.

At seventeen, Anna had already appeared in police records more than once as keeping company with painters. A lively quarrel among Anna and a couple of girlfriends called Doralice and Livia had been settled that April evening of 1597 by the police and the three had then gone to the *osteria del Turchetto*, one of their usual hangouts, to make peace over a glass of wine. A few painters were sitting around when the girls came in. The painters and the girls evidently knew each other pretty well already, because when the three women entered one of the painters had remarked loudly *Here's Anna and what a terrific arse she's got*. Anna shot back with *Maybe you're the one with the terrific arse not that it matters to me*. At which point the unnamed young painter fetched Anna a resounding smack on the face and this, for unrecorded reasons that may have had to do with rivalry among the women, set Anna, Doralice and Livia at each other's throats again and the cops reappeared.

Annuccia was described in a police report as being *on the small side* and having *long red hair* and there was other evidence of a lively nature. The year before the scuffle there'd been another incident in the street near the same osteria, when Anna was hanging round with another group of working girls and Prospero Orsi and another young painter – *scandalous people*, a neighbour said later. Things were quiet in the brothel quarter in 1596 and 1597. France and Spain were at war and a lot of the usual men were off fighting on one side or the other. M's friend Onorio Longhi had left in August 1596 to fight for the French, maybe using his expertise in military architecture, and wouldn't return for a couple of years. On this evening, while they were fooling in the street, an old woman of the neighbourhood had passed with a burning coal she'd got from her brother's to light her fire. Her sober dress provoked the girls. Anna gave her the raspberry, and soon everyone was jostling and insulting her, including *the two men … dressed in black*, telling her to *stick her hot coal up her arse*, while the old woman screeched for help. Just when the neighbours had calmed things down again Anna ran up behind her and grabbed the crone's skirts.

Three years later, in 1600, after a couple of years in which, unusually, she apparently got into no trouble with the law at all, Annuccia Bianchini's old turbulence came back one summer night. She was standing by her door with her friend Livia when her former protector passed with his friends, and Anna couldn't resist giving him the raspberry. Words passed, the girls threw stones at the men, and when they reacted – *they wanted to come inside and tried to touch my arse*, Anna later explained to the magistrate – she pulled a knife on them, which a witness saw in the moonlight. It was just another incident whose interest lay in some of the insults exchanged. One of the men called Anna a *whipped whore* and she called him a liar and hit back that he'd done time in the stocks for prostituting women. Having prostitutes whipped and paraded through the city on a donkey's back was one of the ways of enforcing public morality that Clement VIII was keenest on. Annuccia's sudden two year disappearance from the justice records after 1597 meant there might've been some truth in that later insult that she'd been a *frustrata* who then lay low for a while. M's petite *Penitent Magdalen* with the *long red hair* might've been a representation or a recollection of the real Anna Bianchini he'd swapped profanities with in the pub, Annuccia after a brutal run in with the enforcers of sexual propriety. The little flask of balm seen on the floor might've really been needed to heal the cuts, and Bellori, though he was wrong about the hair drying, might have accurately seized on the unimproved and unimproving everyday reality of M's seventeen year old Magdalen.

ROMAN TROOPS LED by the cardinal nephew, art collector and man about town Pietro Aldobrandini at the start of 1598 used a disputed succession in the Este family to bloodlessly seize Ferrara. It was a striking assertion of the third force Clement VIII was trying to build in Rome. In April the pope left Rome on a major city tour leading to Ferrara, where he arrived in May and stayed for seven months. A court of over three thousand went with him – twenty seven cardinals and a retinue of other clerics, musicians, painters and architects. One of the first invited along was Del Monte, who immediately wrote to Ferdinando de' Medici that *his holiness let me know that he wanted me to bring fifteen servants and twelve horses and he'd cover the costs* ... Del Monte and Benedetto Giustiniani were with the pope when a crowd of fifty thousand met him in Ferrara. Pietro Aldobrandini lifted major works by Titian from the Este collection in Ferrara and brought them to Rome. Giuseppe Cesari copied them and Venetian painting started working its way directly into the pictorial consciousness of Rome.

Neither the pope nor Del Monte was in Rome that September, when one of the city's richest men, Francesco Cenci, apparently fell to his death from a wooden balcony on his castle overlooking a precipitous bramble filled terrain in remote mountainous country east of Rome, on the feudal domain of Marzio Colonna. Cenci lived there with his second wife and his daughter Beatrice – a recent arrangement and not a happy one. The Cenci family's immense fortune of nearly half a million scudi had been made, largely illicitly, by the dead man's father as papal treasurer and largely dissipated by the late Francesco, a man of *vulgar and violent character ... tyrannical, miserly and physically abusive* – in 1594 he'd had to pay a quarter of a million scudi to get a charge of buggery annulled. His own sons received nothing and had appealed to the pope for an allowance – Cenci said his sons were trying to kill him and since 1595 had confined his daughter Beatrice with his second wife in the remote castle, to stop her marrying and save on the dowry. The women were held in a bolted apartment and fed through a serving hatch. In late 1597 Beatrice wrote to her brother Giacomo in Rome for help, but her father intercepted the letter and beat her savagely. He moved in himself, and may have raped Beatrice. He'd already tried to rape his stepson.

The castle was in bandit territory and Beatrice – now a total prisoner – tried to have them kill her father, using as go between the castle's ex guardian Olimpio Calvetti, now her lover. It fell through and in the summer of 1598 she got Giacomo to send poison, but her father started making her taste his food. Beatrice – forcing on the family ditherers – got Calvetti and a local labourer to smash Francesco Cenci's head with a hammer while he slept, and fake a dawn fall from the bedroom balcony. Giacomo and their fifteen year old brother Bernardo arrived and the whole family left for Rome straight after their father's hurried funeral. People talked, four local priests made statements and an inquest was opened. The Cencis were kept under house arrest in Rome while Marzio Colonna and the viceroy of Naples and later the cardinal vicar of Rome all ordered separate investigations, but the pope's absence stalled inquiries until the new year. Giacomo Cenci and Marzio Colonna tried to engineer Calvetti's removal in early January 1599 – he was acting erratically and indiscreetly. Calvetti's master Colonna sent him on a journey north but a murder attempt en route failed and two months later Calvetti was back in Rome.

The four priests secretly testified in Rome and the pope ordered his own investigation. Giacomo Cenci was arrested and some weeks later so were Beatrice and their stepmother. Calvetti's accomplice had confessed to the murder under torture in Rome and before dying implicated the Cencis. They stuck to their story of the accidental fall. Wild and contradictory rumours began sweeping Rome, mainly about Beatrice, who was barely twenty and in the words of one *avviso* – *extremely beautiful and sticking so strongly to her version that she's clearly innocent.* Clement VIII was suspected of prosecuting the case in order *to extract cash ... from that opulent inheritance that has been so profitable ... in the past.* The Venetian ambassador said a death sentence for the Cencis, *their estate reverting to the treasury,* would earn the apostolic chamber *the equivalent of over five hundred thousand scudi.* Ferdinando I de' Medici received an urgent plea from Cesare Cenci, uncle to Beatrice and her brothers, who wrote in March to the grand duke reminding him of the Cenci family's long service to the Medicis and declaring them still *most ready on any occasion to give our lives and all we own in the service of your house* and begging Ferdinando's *rightful protection* for Beatrice and her brothers. The grand duke instructed Del Monte to *act in their favour insofar as needed.*

When Olimpio Calvetti reappeared in Rome – the only danger to the Cencis after his accomplice's death – their uncle paid him to leave town again and the prosecution was blocked. Family feeling about the *tall and handsome* Calvetti was complicated. He was Beatrice's lover, which Calvetti's inferior station made unacceptable to her brother Giacomo – he had his servant ambush and kill Calvetti two months later. As a fugitive from justice Calvetti had a price on his head, which was hacked off by his killer and delivered to the authorities for reward. It was a terrible mistake. The servant killer now became a witness against them and so did Calvetti's brother. Nevertheless, confessions were still needed. In August Clement VIII authorized the use of torture on the three Cencis and their stepmother. This shocked everyone, but Clement VIII wanted to curb the resistance of the unruly baronial families to his bureaucratic papal state and to re-affirm the role of the head of the family. And there was the Cenci money. Beatrice, her two brothers and her stepmother underwent the torture of the cord – their wrists were tied behind the back and attached to a rope that was passed over a high pulley. They were hoisted off the ground, dropped from a height and hoisted again. Giacomo and the stepmother soon confessed, but Beatrice, subjected to a more atrocious punishment, resisted for nine hours. Finally even she broke, and the diplomatic reports from Rome all recorded her physical courage.

> She showed such great heart in her travails that she amazed everyone,

wrote the duke of Modena's ambassador. The pope himself *wept when he heard they had all confessed* – Clement VIII was inclined to tears. *Better watch his hands than his eyes*, noted a reporter dryly. What mattered weren't the pope's tears but a signed act of clemency. Pleas for mercy came in from diplomats, aristocrats and high prelates. The Roman clergy called for clemency and so did at least two cardinals. Public appeals were made in city churches. Pietro Aldobrandini was Beatrice's godfather, and she wrote to him from prison on August 20, begging him to get his uncle the pope to hear her lawyers. The pope angrily said he was *amazed there were lawyers prepared to represent such wicked criminals*, and sent them packing. The death sentence for all the Cencis was pronounced on the evening of September 10 and carried out the next morning. Bernardo, being fifteen, was sentenced to life in the galleys after watching his family die. Cenci family property was confiscated.

A huge crowd followed the Cencis to their place of execution. Beatrice was a popular heroine, a beautiful and strong willed aristocratic girl driven to death by her own class.

> People stood jammed together like sardines and the horses and carriages stretched [for miles] … the sun was so intense that many fainted … people were suffocated and crushed by the carriages.

An overcrowded platform collapsed and four people were killed. A mass was then celebrated as a prelude to the public killings. The stepmother Lucrezia was the first to die and she fainted before her head was placed on the block. She was followed by Beatrice, and all the eyewitness reports insisted on the twenty year old girl's extraordinary beauty and the defiance in her *brave … unyielding … virile* behaviour at the end. *She very bravely placed her own head on the block.* Ferdinando I's agent Vialardi wrote that Beatrice

> died in a most holy manner, but protesting and calling for God's vengeance on Clement for not listening to her or studying her defence entirely.

Giacomo was tortured with red hot irons during the procession through the city and then clubbed down, his throat cut, his body hacked to pieces on the public stage. Young Bernardo kept fainting as he was made to watch his brother and sister and stepmother die. While this was happening Clement VIII celebrated a low mass for their souls a short distance away. The women's headless corpses, and the pieces of Giacomo's, were left on display until eleven that night, lit up by blazing torches. The holy father had made his point, though what the Romans took that point to be was beyond even his control. Talk and writing in Rome of Aldobrandini greed and brutality continued with such intensity that in September 1600, a year after the Cencis' killing, Clement VIII personally issued a public prohibition of any written comment at all, whether in large or small format, on the trial, sentence or death of Beatrice Cenci.

When the Cenci family holdings were auctioned off a month later the prize piece, a big property at Terranova on the outskirts of Rome, was knocked down for a song to the pope's nephew Giovanfrancesco Aldobrandini. In December, the pope had to get the governor of Rome to issue a further civil edict against people who

> used their vile tongues in writing notices in various places, filling sheets with calumny and lies ... defaming and dishonouring other people's reputations.

It was an attempt to stifle political comment on Roman affairs by the reporters of the unnervingly frank and informative *avvisi*. They received their warning notices, along with printers and booksellers, five days later. 1601 began in Rome under the threat of a censorship blitz. The defence lawyer for Beatrice Cenci, the one who was bawled out by the pope when he asked leave to present a last ditch defence before she was beheaded, a defence based on Francesco Cenci's rape of his daughter, was a prominent criminal advocate named Prospero Farinacci. At some point Farinacci had lost an eye, and this disfigurement later earnt him a mention in Giulio Mancini's remarks on painting. When Farinacci had his portrait painted, he insisted on a full frontal portrait that gave a total view of his damaged face. The portrait of Farinacci was later listed in the inventory of Vincenzo Giustiniani's collection. The painter – apparently, because the painting disappeared – was M.

◢

WHEN M PAINTED Anna Bianchini's seventeen year old friend Fillide Melandroni – with a very elaborate hairdo and pressing a sprig of highly perfumed bergamot to her breasts – he probably did it for Vincenzo Giustiniani. *Fillide* certainly got to Giustiniani's collection pretty soon and stayed there. Fillide herself was arrested one summer night in 1601 with her protector just near palazzo Giustiniani. The couple's extreme reluctance to tell the police what they were about raised the question whether she wasn't paying a visit to the banker.

Fillide was then at the very height of her career as a prostitute. She was the most sought after girl in Rome and her image, tough, beaut-iful and humorous – a far stronger presence than poor Anna's – was about to appear in M's work as a series of saints and heroines. Fillide's supple, earthy beauty and her ironic glance made her a marvellous model and M owed her a lot. The electric doubleness of her presence, compelling as a fearless young female icon, seductive and subversive as herself, launched M irreversibly into that dramatic mode that – as much as his far more talked about technique of representation – made his greatness as a painter. After M painted Fillide there was no turn-ing back – neither to the unresponsive blankness of an amiably bored Mario model, nor to the charming but purely pictorial stasis of groups like the *Musicians* or *Francis & angel* or the *Rest on the flight into Egypt*. M had his own powerful dramatic instinct and the *Sick self portrait* and the *Cheats* were his strongest early work, but the encounter with Fil-lide was the clarifying flash of light. After M painted her everything else fell away – even his portraits, even still life turned inexorably into drama.

Fillide was M's model, but maybe life played its part in the way he painted her next. Was M in the crowd that followed Beatrice Cenci to the chopping block? Most of Rome was, and most of Rome pas-sionately identified with the beautiful and unyielding young noble girl being crushed by the regime. In 1599 – as the Cenci tragedy unfolded – M painted Fillide for Del Monte in his largest and most formal canvas so far, a painting of saint Catherine of Alexandria – a beautiful and unyielding young noble girl crushed by an earlier regime. M showed *Catherine* framed by the instruments of an imminent ugly death. Nothing transcendental emanated from the added aureole, the martyr's palm or the brutal bladed wheel. The even more sinister and highly professional sword, a long blade designed for both cutting and thrusting, was probably M's own, the one some years later seized by the authorities and sketched in his report by the confiscating officer. The painting was simply the finest M would ever do of a young woman, the only one in which female youth and beauty were the sole object of attention. He did Fillide as martyr saint without parted lips, bared tits and shafts of heavenly light. The girl's direct gaze was more virile than any seen from M's boys thus far, but it was a ques-tioning look and shadowed by a deeply touching and vulnerable uncertainty. It locked into you – her questioning openness required a response, and that was the painting's drama. Her finger rested on the long and already reddened blade. The dark bravura fall and finish of her rich skirt and shawl and the damask cushion framed and empha-sized the unadorned face at their apex, the pale simplicity of the neck and shoulders in their white blouse. *Catherine* was M's most undervalued painting. Bellori named *Catherine* with the *Lute player* for the new depth of colouring in M's work – he was already starting, Bellori said, *to strengthen his darks.*

In the real world, Fillide was coming to the attention of the local police. On the night of Tuesday 11 February 1599 neighbours complained about a big and noisy *mardi gras* party in her house by via Condotti. Young men were seen bearing arms, and since weapons in a whore's house were illegal, the authorities raced to the scene. The guests had evidently gotten wind of the raid, because when the cops burst in they found only Fillide and

> three men, one of whom was wearing a sword and whose name is Ranuccio.

Fillide and Ranuccio were taken into custody, the one as a whore and the other for being illegally armed. That Ranuccio had waited with Fillide suggested, like other aspects of his life, a more than casual connexion with girls on the game. Not yet twenty, Ranuccio evidently wielded some influence, since he was released now without even being interrogated. He was the youngest of the five Tomassoni brothers. The Tomassonis were a family from Terni, not far north of Rome on the way to Perugia. They'd served the Farnese dynasty of Parma for some generations and the brothers were all named after Farnese rulers. The family's service had been largely military. Two of Ranuccio's elder brothers, Alessandro and Giovan Francesco, had lately returned to Rome after fighting for the faith in Flanders and Hungary under Farnese. Alessandro, the eldest, had come back with a permanent limp from a war wound. They were part of that mob of former soldiers who, with the Franco Spanish peace, were again disturbing the quiet of Rome. The common soldiers, out of work and destitute, were now the *vagabonds* against whom the authorities were again busy legislating. An *avviso* of 14 March 1598 reported tartly that

> this morning they've issued a ban on vagabonds, referring
> in particular to returned soldiers who are no more use ...
> and this is how they repay the military today ...

The Tomassonis had joined the other quarrelsome and violent young gentlemen who were at a loose end and finding it hard to readjust to civilian life. The Tomassonis had plenty of useful connexions high and low, however, among the prostitutes and among the higher clergy and aristocracy, and some influence of their own. They may have created a role for themselves as go betweens and facilitators for those younger and sexually busy cardinals and monsignori. The previous November Ranuccio and his brother had helped avert a duel one afternoon outside a barber's shop – testimony mentioned that earlier in 1598 Ranuccio, who was some years younger than M, had been to Perugia in the retinue of the monsignor Cresenzi who'd shortly be dealing with M. Ranuccio and M would soon be meeting in the retinues of the powerful. They'd be meeting on and off for the rest of M's time in Rome, and their last encounter would be fatal.

This was the louche and racy social milieu of Onorio Longhi – people who liked slumming, loved whores and enjoyed a fight. When trouble came they always pulled rank and this almost invariably worked. When M was arrested at night for carrying a sword and compasses in 1598, the first person he'd mentioned was Del Monte, and this would get to be a habit. M might've known Fillide on his own social round of brothel, tavern, piazza and tennis court, or he might've been first asked to paint her as a special friend of the marchese Giustiniani. It hardly mattered. If M at Del Monte's was feeling the preciousness, Fillide set him free.

4

ROME 1598–1600

Martha & Mary
Judith & Holofernes
Basket of fruit
Narcissus
David I
Isaac & Abraham I
John in the wild I

FILLIDE AS HERSELF and Fillide as Catherine – after these M brought her now into his first dramatic painting since the *Cheats* – the first since he'd been in the palazzo Madama. He brought all he'd learnt in that time to bear on an image that formally was much like his picture of card players, now four years and a world away. Del Monte owned a work – which later vanished – inventoried as

> a painting of a *Martha and Magdalen* on wood by Leonardo da Vinci in ebony frame, three and a half palms long by three palms high.

It was a great and strangely rare subject for M to emulate, and M saw what it held for Fillide. He'd already painted Anna looking deeply chastened as a *Penitent Magdalen*, the same figure later on, and the theme had fitted Anna's subdued and mousier look. *Martha & Mary* now caught the beautiful sinner who became Christ's favourite in the very moment of her turning. The sensual woman hadn't renounced beauty and pleasure. She was still in the flower of her beauty and the gorgeousness of her sexual power dressing – and once again thoughtfully twirling a Leonardesque orange blossom against her cleavage – but she was given pause, looking away from her mirror and into the eyes of her drably dressed and passionately proselytizing sister Martha – who was ticking off points on her fingers and pressing her case – in that tiny instant when her life changed utterly.

The whole problem with Anna as Mary in her later moment of repentance had been – as Bellori implied – that in making her real M lost the didactic force of the lesson the painting was meant to impart. It made for a finer painting and a discontented customer. There was no drama in repentance, only moralizing. Anna could've been any unhappy girl, any whipped tart. Now M used the two girls in the same painting. Anna played Martha. Fillide as Mary, in her utter stillness now, was charged with the drama of choice. Mousy but powerful Martha leaned toward her and into the picture across the dressing table, face entirely in shadow and turned away from the viewer, all blurred and shadowy peripheral urgency. The drama centred on Fillide as Mary, caught in full in the still point of her turning life. There was no movement in Mary, but her bright clothes, the life in her *jolie laide* face with its asymmetrical eyes, her creamy breasts and elaborate hair – all seemed to drain into the shadowy conviction of Martha at the picture's edge. The background was dark, the table was dark, the picture was all dark, apart from the dazzling little square of window reflected in the mirror and the highlights of Mary's face and breasts, and Martha's hands. Martha was the future. Darkness was coming into its own. Darkness was defining light. And action was defined by stillness.

DARKNESS WAS NOVEL but hardly new. Leonardo – who'd almost invariably shown his own figures outdoors against a landscape, like the *Mona Lisa* – had also noted down in his *Book of painting* that an

> immense grace of light and shadow enhances the faces of people who sit in the doorways of darkened houses. The observer's eyes see the part of the face in shadow obscured by the darkness of the house, and the part of the same face that's lit gains clarity from the light shining in the air. The

accentuation of light and shadow gives great relief to the face, the shadows being almost unnoticeable in the lit part and the light almost unnoticeable in the dark part. Represented thus, with enhanced light and shade, the face gains greatly in beauty.

M now did in art what Leonardo had admired in life. He put his models in a dark room lit only by daylight from a single high window – almost always out of the picture to the left. He'd been feeling his way toward this from his very first work but he'd never before used such strong contrasts. Light was now modelling the forms. What M saw was what you got. What you saw was what you knew. Things only existed insofar as they were visible. He painted like this in the dark for the rest of his life.

Darkness hid background, panorama, distance, distractions, clouds and sunlight. It eliminated the long view, the big picture. Darkness obscured earthly crowds, mighty armies, mythological masses, heavenly hosts. It removed distant lands and celestial life from view. It fixed the gaze on the drama of the human body and held it there. Darkness therefore had its limitations as a way of pictorially transmitting heavenly glory and earthly hierarchy. At most it could squeeze in the odd individual angel, blown in as it were off course, or Christ as a man among men. If an institutional client insisted, the faintest glimmer of a nimbus might pick out a saint among the ordinary models. Intimacy left little room for exalted station. What darkness and intimacy could do was register the intensity of individual feeling. Like pain. M had already started with a nipped finger and moved to the look on the face of a severed head. Now he turned to the experience of decapitation itself. Not the professional executioner's swift dispatch, the expert assembly line swing that'd produced the massed bandits' heads on spikes displayed on Rome's bridges like *melons at the market*, or sliced through the necks of Beatrice Cenci and her stepmother the year M was painting Fillide. He showed a beheading rather as it might be slowly and clumsily done by a determined but inexpert young woman, and felt by the adult male who'd been ready, a moment earlier, to enjoy her body on the bed where he now lay shocked and dying.

In 1584, while M was an apprentice in Milan, his master Peterzano's friend the painter Giovan Paolo Lomazzo had published a *Treatise on the art of painting* that looked back to Leonardo's example in painting from life. Lomazzo claimed that Leonardo himself particularly loved watching the gestures of the condemned as they were led to execution, observing the way they contracted their brow, the way they moved their eyes, and their whole body. I think it's a good idea for a painter to imitate him and … see the furtive look in a murderer's eye … and the come on glance in a courtesan's …

M's next and last painting of Fillide – they were all done in the space of a year or so, after which his infatuation or her availability seemed to end – was another that seemed to be reverberating with the horror of the Cenci episode. Judith was a popular figure in art and one of the few young female action subjects – Donatello, Botticelli and Giorgione had all done her beheading the tyrant Holofernes. Mostly after the event – like David, the calm young liberator with or without the trophy head. M now showed the intimate and wholly private horror of the murder itself. He returned to multiple figure paintings with a leap into a kind of convulsed and hideous movement he'd barely hinted at before. He now caught the rapt stare of a crabbed servant woman – M's first old working person – waiting at the picture's right edge with a cloth to wrap the head in when it was finally hacked free of the body. He caught the cramped but violent tensing of Holofernes' nude body on the bed, crazily angled from his partly detached head, a repelled and frowning Judith's determined sawing, her grip on the hair of the nearly severed head, and the ropes of blood that jetted on to the pillow and the fold of sheet Holofernes was clutching in his agony.

The dark bedroom setting, the sheets and pillows and blankets and the knotted up heavy blood red canopy overhanging the act, enhanced the stifling, muffled intimacy of the killing and the identity of sex with violence. The drapes that muffled the moans of sex would soak up the dead man's cry. This was very different from the *Fortune teller's* benign look at relations between the sexes. This was sex as war, old testament religion as modern domestic violence. It was sex as spasm, less violent movement than a series of linked tensions – in the gripping hands, Judith's on the sword and head, Holofernes' clutching the bed sheet and the old woman's gripping the cloth – in the contracted muscles of Holofernes' body, arched in death as in orgasm, in Judith's powerful forearms and the clenched muscles of the old woman's face – a face much like those in Leonardo's drawings of old men. Nothing took the image beyond that reality – no history, no structure, no transcendence, no symbolism, just violent death.

FILLIDE MELANDRONI HERSELF was no stranger to a little real life violence. A year and a bit later, in late 1600, she was reported to the police by another courtesan called Prudenza Zacchia who claimed that Fillide and a younger colleague, a girl called Prudenza Brunori and known as Tella, had just that evening forced their way into her house

> and the said Fillide came at me with a knife to disfigure me and she went for my face ... I fended her off with this left hand and she got me above the wrist and wounded me ... they both went for me and beat me up and she got me in the mouth with the point of the blade ... and when they saw I was bleeding they left.

A witness said he later saw Fillide yelling from a window at the complainant, who was standing bleeding in her doorway –

> I got you in the hand you lazy whore. I wanted to get you in the smacker and next time I will.

The nature of this settling of accounts in the brothel quarter was explained by another male witness who described how in the morning of that same day he'd been at Ranuccio Tomassoni's house, warming himself downstairs by the fire while Fillide's friend Ranuccio had been in bed upstairs with the complainant. Fillide herself had then arrived and raced upstairs where she found the two together. *So here you are, you lazy whore*, she'd said. On this earlier occasion too she'd gone for her rival with a knife, but the male witness had disarmed her, whereupon Fillide had thrown herself at the complainant *and torn a lot of hair from her head*.

That it was one of those cases where personal jealousy and professional rivalry were inextricable was indicated by another police investigation of a fortnight earlier. A male client of Tella Brunori's had brought a case against the complainant Prudenza in the later case, and her sister Caterina, who was also a whore. The two lived next door to Tella and six weeks earlier had apparently begun threatening their rival's male client and saying they'd have him killed by their friends. Then one of them had thrown half a brick at him from the upstairs window. The brick, aimed at his head, had hit him in the right leg while he was speaking in the alley with a group of male friends that included *signor Ranuccio from Terni*, causing serious bruising. One of the men present, an aide to the governor of Rome, said he'd seen an arm at the window in the moonlight, throwing the brick, but hadn't been able to tell which sister it'd belonged to. Tella herself confirmed the incident, and she also alluded to the presence of *a certain signor Ranuccio from Terni*. The following Tuesday evening they'd hurled another piece of brick at her client that'd just missed his face, and the aide to the governor of Rome stated the intended victim escaped only *because he'd ducked.* This witness too had mentioned *a certain Ranuccio from Terni.*

When Ranuccio Tomassoni himself made a statement, the version changed. He'd been speaking to Prudenza in her doorway, he said, when the complainant Gaspare had come along and said

> I'm amazed at you, signor Ranuccio, that someone like you should be standing here talking to this whore who's filled me with diseases, a bugger, fucked up the arse.

To which Prudenza had replied coolly

> That's all I can expect from someone like you and if I'd known what you were like before I'd never have gone with you.

At which, in this account, she'd excused herself and gone upstairs, only to be loudly insulted from the street and further accused, in the supporting statement of another of those present, of transmitting the French disease and warts. *Look at the fine fruits I've borne from you!* So Prudenza had momentarily opened the upper window and in Ranuccio Tomassoni's account

> thrown a small piece of tile at him which didn't hit him and was only small anyway.

Ranuccio Tomassoni, in the earlier case, was clearly in damage control mode. He would've wanted to cover for the girl whose bed he was found sharing two weeks later and keep the cops away from the house where she and her sister received their clients. Cops were bad for business, and so was loud talk of sexually transmitted diseases. So why did Prudenza then move on to the offensive against Fillide and Tella Brunori? In both cases the women's resort to violence seemed to express weakness, if not desperation, and the appeal to the police a confidence of victory through law.

In that sense Prudenza's position improved sharply between mid November and early December, while Fillide and Tella Brunori went from being rivals enjoying the benefits of redirected business to angry aggressors. Prudenza in her own complaint was notably reticent about why the others might have attacked her. The only clue was her incidentally mentioned presence in Ranuccio Tomassoni's bed, like the incidentally mentioned presence of Ranuccio Tomassoni as a casual bystander and witness in the earlier incident – the police were treating charge and countercharge as a single matter – the same Ranuccio Tomassoni who'd been arrested with Fillide in *her* house the year before and who seemed to have a working relationship of one kind or another with several of the busiest courtesans in Rome around this time. He appeared in the reports to be well known to both police and other witnesses and to be treated by all with a certain deference. He appeared as a local power in the brothel district, remarkable in one who only turned twenty late in the year of these charges. He was only a year older than Fillide, who in 1600 was nineteen.

Another incidental sign that Ranuccio Tomassoni enjoyed a certain local notoriety came from a report the police made on a quite different matter. This other mention concerned another locally notorious figure and was recorded only three days before the writing up of the charge that Prudenza had thrown half a brick at a former client. M's friend Onorio Longhi the architect was answering charges of trying to force his way at night into a house. The case had dragged on for a couple of years, and on November 14 Longhi was challenging a witness who'd said he'd recognized Longhi's voice in the darkened alley. *If you only know me by sight, how can you recognize me by my voice at night?* Longhi had demanded.

> I recognized your voice because I've heard you speaking with signor Ranuccio at the Rotonda and seen you playing ball there in the Pantani alley,

the witness had replied. Nobody asked him to say who the *signor Ranuccio* was. Called a liar by Longhi, he insisted *I've heard you speak a thousand times.* What Longhi had been heard saying to Ranuccio Tomassoni at the ball game in November 1600 was never specified. Onorio Longhi was going through a particularly turbulent phase at that moment and was in conflict on several fronts. Three days later a sculptor friend stood security for him to the court and also guaranteed what amounted to an apprehended violence order against Longhi in respect of six separate individuals. Two of them were his opponents in the forced entry matter, one was a sergeant at arms named Flavio Canonico, two were an otherwise unidentified father and son from Bergamo and the sixth was Longhi's ball game acquaintance *Ranuccio Tomassoni from Terni*.

The sporting interests and the local street presence of both Onorio Longhi and Ranuccio Tomassoni were amply recorded from now on. Onorio Longhi was already over thirty in 1600 and a familiar presence in the alleys and taverns and brothels over most of the last decade, when he wasn't away at the wars. Ranuccio Tomassoni was just twenty and too young to have fought like his brothers, yet locally on the rise and already a figure of some clout. His name too would appear with suggestive frequency in the Roman police records over the next five years or so. So would M's.

GIULIO MANCINI was a clever arriviste who'd cut a few corners in his time. Nevertheless he was deeply shocked by one early episode in M's life as a painter in Rome. As Mancini told it, M

> had a single brother, a priest, a cultivated and respectable man who when he heard about his brother's fame was taken by a desire to see him. Stirred by brotherly love he came to Rome, and knowing that M was living in the house of the very distinguished cardinal Del Monte, and knowing his brother's strange ways, thought it would be advisable to have a word beforehand with the very distinguished cardinal and explain everything to him. He did this and the cardinal very kindly told him to come back in three days. Meanwhile the cardinal called M and asked him if he had any relatives, and M said he didn't. Unable to believe the priest had lied in a matter that could be checked and was of no use to him, the cardinal sent out to inquire among the people from M's home town whether M had any brothers and who they might be. He found it was M who'd told the beastly lie. Three days later the priest came back, and the cardinal kept him there while he had M called. Shown his brother, M denied knowing him or that the man was his brother. At which the poor priest was overcome with tenderness and said in the cardinal's presence,
>
> *Brother I've come such a long way just to see you, and now*

that I've seen you I've had what I wanted. By God's grace, as you know, I'm in a condition whereby I've no need of you either for myself or my children. Rather it might have been for yours, if God had granted me the favour of marrying you and seeing issue. May God grant that you do well, as I'll pray to his divine majesty in my services, and I know your sister will do the same in her modest and virginal prayers.

M was unmoved by these words of hot and dazzling love, and the good priest left without even being wished Godspeed by his brother. After this it can't be denied that he was a very wild and strange person ...

Giovan Battista had come to Rome around the same time as his painter brother in 1592. He was still in Rome in April 1599 but went back north later in the year – he was ordained by the bishop of Bergamo near Caravaggio that December. Caterina married in 1594 and had her first child the next year, so 1594 was the *terminus ante quem* for *her modest and virginal prayers*. M was fast making a name among collectors but his real fame arrived when he left Del Monte's household, and by then Giovan Battista was gone. The brothers met in Rome before M was really famous, soon after he was taken up by Del Monte. Mancini seemed not to know M's brother was already in Rome and not yet ordained, a seminarian mightily surprised and impressed when he heard that a powerful cardinal had given his *wild and strange* brother *an honoured place among his gentlemen*. After the obscure trouble in Milan, maybe a killing and time in jail, and the seemingly wasted years and wasted money, the early failures in Rome, the poverty and sickness – maybe he thought his brother had changed. It was a time and place where anyone's new success, from the pope's down, would be expected to flow on straight away to the whole family, but M's repudiation wasn't about money. M's savage kicking away of the family props, his refusal to even acknowledge Giovan Battista's existence, however absurd such a denial seemed to his patron watching the encounter, was absolute and final. He'd severed the links. In that moment of angry denial, Giovan Battista's unfortunate reference to M's failure to marry and carry on the family line sounded like a parting jab in family code, a hint at the extreme unlikeliness of M's ever raising a family. Giovan Battista was a student of the Jesuits.

In a life of radical breaks and sudden unexplained departures, it was the only record of M's willing the break with the past – a reminder that behind force of circumstance in M's life lay the will of a man who largely created those circumstances. The train of successes, contingencies and disasters, the powerful friendships and poisonous enmities would all be precipitated by M's powerful sense of self, his steely will to be his own man, create his own life and project his own vision of the world. Mancini, who thought *our age owes a lot to M*, was too conventional and too opportunistic a man to see that the *glory* he applauded and the *wildness* he deplored necessarily went together.

THE GIUSTINIANIS HAD a house guest during 1599 – Federico Borromeo, the late Carlo's younger cousin and very much his creation. When Federico was fourteen his iron cousin Carlo had sent the *tender, impressionable and good natured young boy* to study in Bologna under cardinal Paleotti, who was then gestating his interminable work *On sacred and profane images*. Borromeo was a cardinal in Rome at twenty three in 1587 and sent home in 1595 as archbishop of Milan, where he was trying to follow his cousin's example. So far it was a disaster. Federico liked Rome and art and he'd been forced to take the job. Trouble with the Spanish began in a fight over the seating arrangements for the Spanish governor in the cathedral and soon deteriorated into armed clashes. Del Monte sympathized by mail from Rome – *people here understand the endless battles you're involved in* – and looked after his commissions to clockmakers and painters. Borromeo sent presents of fine crystal in return. A year among his flock and in April 1597 he was back in Rome. Clement VIII was intensely displeased to see him but Borromeo hung on in Rome for five years. In Milan someone leaked a complaining letter he'd sent to Madrid, describing Milan *in the darkest hues of corruption and vice*.

Borromeo was terribly interested in art. He collected paintings. He'd write a book, much later, *On sacred art*. In 1602 he ordered a cycle of fortyodd large paintings featuring the life and miracles of his uncle Carlo for Milan cathedral – most of his commissions promoted the image of the Borromeo dynasty. More privately, Federico liked the novelties of northern European painters. He especially liked the way they did landscapes and flowers in paintings on their own, a minor area of the avant garde that Flemish painters were introducing to Rome. His favourites were the landscapes of Paul Brill and Jan Brueghel's bunches of lusciously decorative flowers in expensive vases. He always visited Brill's studio when in Rome and took Brueghel into his own household for a couple of years. When Brueghel returned home Borromeo wrote him a reference that praised *the purity of his spirit and morals* as highly as his art. Del Monte liked Brueghel's work too, and had eleven paintings by him. Amid the anxieties of ideological correctness, it was easier to unwind in private with flowers and landscapes. Even cardinal Paleotti thought plants and landscapes were acceptable *as long as they were done with proper decorum,* and Borromeo himself later wrote that instead of putting nature into religious painting, where it might get in the way, *it was better to show that variety of scenes in another picture.* As his Flemish favourites did.

Borromeo's five years in Rome were the five years of M's emergence as a great painter − it happened under Borromeo's nose. Dutiful Federico Borromeo wouldn't've responded to the sensuality, the violence or the technical daring emerging in M's art. The exquisite precision and economy of the painter's touch clearly did please him. Borromeo would've loved M's fruit and flowers when he saw them in supporting roles in Giustiniani's *Lute player,* or in Del Monte's *Bacchus* or his *Boy bitten.* He would've wanted them for his own collection − minus the staring boys. And at some time during his years in Rome Borromeo found and bought or was given the painting by M of a *Basket of fruit* which was one of the first real still lifes in Italian art.

M painted over a canvas that'd already been used to sketch a frieze of grotesques like his friend Prospero Orsi's. He painted a small basket of everyday fruit that was so dazzlingly beautiful as a whole and so subtly rendered in colour and texture that you overlooked at first that the pear was past its prime, the apple had a worm hole, some of the grapes were shrivelled, the purple figs were splitting out of their skin, the perfect peach's leaves were eaten by insects, and indeed that all of the various beautiful leaves framing the fruit were in some degree spotted, discoloured, shrivelled. M's still life was anything but still. The cheap basket's leaves were wilting at its outer limits even as the perfectly intact green figs, the peach and the quince and the black grapes with their heavy bloom bulged out of it. Your ranging eye moved in time, covered the haphazard and asymmetrical drama of ripeness. The tiniest marks on the skin seemed to darken under the gaze, as they would've under M's as he worked, and the leaves dried and curled. M enhanced the beauty of the real by showing its life in time − his painterly form and attention revealed the austere splendour of the ordinary, the drama quivering in seeming stasis. His fruit said a lot about M's coming human drama. *Looking at the overlooked,* the *Basket of fruit* was a manifesto.

In case any viewer still imagined that this fruit in this basket − it might've been banged on the table after a tavern meal with Onorio

Longhi or Prospero Orsi – belonged to a lesser order of life and a merely decorative order of art, M obliterated any other element around the basket and leaves. He painted behind and around them a heavy flat pale goldish backing that looked like a wall behind the basket, so that the only other thing seen in the picture was the base band frontally representing the shelf the basket rested on – and from which it projected out of the picture plane into the viewer's face. There was nothing in the picture to distract from the basket of fruit itself, nothing to qualify or explain its in your face presence. What you saw was what you got.

Bellori traced the rise of still life in Italy to M's early work. Other still life painters followed Jan Brueghel's model and aimed for a touch of class in their work by featuring fine crystal and exquisite foods and making their fruits huge and absurdly faultless. And none of these tried anything as optically unorthodox as M's fruit. Vincenzo Giustiniani listed twelve degrees of skill in painting, and put *knowing how to paint flowers and other tiny things* only at the fifth level, though he put M's work at the top. The disparity made him recall something M'd said to him long ago –

> M said once that it used to take as much workmanship for him to do a good picture of flowers as it did to do one of human figures.

The remark was more radical than it seemed, and this was why Giustiniani remembered it – the usual values in art put the human figure above *inferior nature* and human figures in *history* painting at the top. It matched something one of Galileo's pupils reported much later about Galileo's own early observations of nature in the fifteen eighties. Galileo said

> ... the effects of nature, however minimal and hard to observe, should never be looked down on by scientists, but all given equal importance ... nature did a lot with very little, and everything she did was equally marvellous.

Galileo so liked art and drawing in his youth that later he

> used to tell his friends that if he'd been able to choose his own profession at that age he would absolutely have chosen painting.

Galileo never lost his interest in art. Like Borromeo he was in and out of the palazzo Madama all through the years M lived there. In his interested and practical way, he likely looked in on M at work in his studio. If he talked about Guidubaldo's almost finished work on perspective and his own physicist's views on optics he mightn't have got the response he expected from M. Galileo was a scientist and his ideas on art were conventional. The *Basket of fruit* showed that M saw quite differently from those non artists around the palazzo who were articulating mathematical rules for the use of painters. It wasn't only the art lavished on low material that made the *Basket* a manifesto. M's painting over and flattening out of everything behind his fruit made the picture wall behind the fruit continuous with the real wall the painting was hanging on – or tacked to, without a frame, as it once was in the studio. The fruit on its ledge seemed to stick out of the wall and intrude into your own real space. This reversed your usual experience of looking at a canvas – that sense of looking through the picture plane as you looked through a window on to a scene of life that receded away from you. Guidubaldo and Galileo were codifying the renaissance sense of pictorial space while M's painting was leaping toward Cézanne. M's harmless everyday fruit wasn't dynamic in its ripening and dying alone – it was threatening to tip off its ledge and fall on you. Borromeo, however entranced he might've been by the illusion, naturally wanted a conventional frame, which lessened the shock – but holes running along the edges of the painting under the frame remained as hidden traces of the unframed canvas illusion nailed directly to the studio wall that first startled M's visitors.

The *Basket* reworked the illusion M had tried on the *Medusa* shield, and like the *Medusa* it used visual shock to laugh at the rule makers. Their rules of receding perspective were meaningless for an illusory image that had no depth and existed in your visual space and not its own. M was working out very different ways of representing vision in paint – ways that were truer to sense perceptions than reason and logic. The patina of time later coated M's spotty fruit in its cheaply woven tavern basket with an odd beauty that masked its original raw provocation, and the *Basket of fruit* ended up in the limp young hands of the sadly conventional Federico Borromeo, with his timid taste for the gracefully unthreatening new flower paintings. He took the painting back to Milan with him when he returned to face the Spanish governor. He praised it highly in a perfunctory way when he wrote a descriptive catalogue of his collection twenty-odd years later. He evidently hadn't looked at it closely for a while, or maybe ever, because what he wrote was *glorious is the basket ... of vibrant flowers, done by M who became famous in Rome ...*

PAINTING FILLIDE STIRRED M's sense of drama to a new pitch and she painted him into a crisis. Fillide coincided with a new buyer – Ottavio Costa, another banker from Genoa who financed the Vatican and did business with Vincenzo Giustiniani. Costa bought both M's half length action paintings of Fillide – *Judith & Holofernes* and *Martha & Mary* and he later bought three or four other paintings by M. Like Del Monte and Giustiniani, Costa left few traces of his link with M, yet he later played a part in getting M out of his worst crisis. He was the third of that triad of M's early and interventionist patrons who seemed to care for him as much as they did for his paintings. Costa was ten years older than Giustiniani and knew what he liked in M's work – and by commissioning *Judith & Holofernes*, he set M on the way to his great work. After that there was no turning back.

Which precipitated the crisis. Painting for Del Monte in the latter fifteen nineties, M'd put his sense of drama on hold while he prolonged the painting of static single figures and still life. Made them *more* static. Even paintings like the *Francis & angel*, the *Musicians* and the *Rest on the flight into Egypt* were static, built up out of their single components. Now, after he'd played around with his inconclusive and clinical studies of isolated emotion in art, the impulse behind the *Cheats* and the *Fortune teller* was felt again, asserting itself even in his still life. A question of market came into this – the only way a painter could win big public commissions and make a major reputation was doing big *history* paintings of complex action, and M's ambition was being fed by his growing scope and the recognition he was getting now from the connoisseur vanguard. The heart of it though was M's own feeling for the drama of the human presence.

How could you paint *action* directly from life? M painted from life directly on to canvas, like his idol Giorgione. There was no preliminary drawing, no *design* of the image. On M's canvases not even modern infrared reflectography would find any trace of drawing under the paint. The very source of the subtlety and immediacy of his art, above all the living presence of his human figures, was the directness of his working method. It ran against everything Italian renaissance painting stood for – and even more its feeble and denatured present day mannerist derivative. Painting a single figure or a still life straight on to the canvas was abnormal but could be done, but you couldn't do a complex scene of violent action from life. The problem was figures in movement. Giulio Mancini saw the problem clearly, though not the way M handled it. M's working method, Mancini thought,

> is closely observant of real life and always keeps the subject in front of him during the painting. It works very well for a single figure. But composing a *history* and representing feeling come from the imagination and not from observing something real in front of your eyes. It doesn't seem to me that in that case the method works. You can't put the whole crowd of people enacting a history into a room lit from a single window. You can't have someone laughing or crying or walking and get them to freeze while you copy them. So figures done like this are strong but they lack movement and feeling and grace ...

Handling complexity was the function of drawing. Sketching out the preliminaries of a painting, grouping the elements and relating volumes in a meaningful space, weighing light and shade. Doing this you foresaw the problems, knitted the parts into a coherent visual structure, caught the vivid details of life and movement you'd then work into that whole. Drawing was one thing on whose importance those polar opposites and rivals of renaissance art, the abstracting idealist Michelangelo Buonarotti and the empirical realist Leonardo da Vinci, had agreed. Drawing was the intellectual basis of painting, the *idea* of what would be done in paint. The painting, Vasari had written confidently in 1550, *is born from the drawing*. A generation later Armenini, looking back to values that were being lost, wrote in 1586 that the preliminary drawing

> is the work itself, except for the colouring, which is why you can see it was always done so thoroughly and carefully by Michelangelo, Leonardo, Raphael ...

Colour, in this tradition, came after drawing, and was the lesser part of painting. And when painting was done on walls and ceilings, *in fresco* on to damp plaster, as most was, the preliminary drawing was essential. It was done on big sheets of paper that were placed on the wall and traced over with a metal stylus to make light incisions in the damp *fresh* plaster on the wall before painting started. Faint signs of these grooves might remain in the surface of the finished work. Or a lot of holes might be made along the lines of the drawing, and these holes traced over with charcoal. Oil painting on wood panels or canvas was also done from a carbon tracing of the drawing that was transferred to the painting surface by backing the drawing paper with charcoal and running over it with a stylus. Sometimes painters traced incisions when they painted on wood, and even – very rarely – on to primed canvas, adapting the fresco technique to define perspective. Only incisions left faint traces in the finished work. Drawings transferred to wood or canvas disappeared forever under the oil paint.

Painting on canvas was still a fairly recent thing in sixteenth century Italy. Vasari remarked that it had started in Venice, in whose damp sea air wood soon became rotten or wormeaten. Canvas had taken on fast as a more resistant art material that was easily cut to any size, weighed little and was easy to transport. On properly prepared canvas oil paintings were flexible and could even be rolled up. The use of canvas for painting was soon so common that at some point in the sixteenth century people had started speaking about a canvas – *una tela* – to mean the painting done on it. And apart from the mythological oddity of his painting on Del Monte's distillery ceiling and a couple of paintings on wood, M would always paint in oil on canvas. Baglione remembered that *he didn't work in any other way*. Notwithstanding his early training with Peterzano, M would never, ever work in fresco.

Giuseppe Cesari did a lot of work in fresco – when M worked in his studio in 1593 he'd just finished painting in fresco the vault of the Contarelli chapel in San Luigi dei Francesi – but he was probably making more money with his workshop team turning out small quickie canvases on an industrial scale than he was from his prestige commissions for church and nobility. *He seemed to prefer working for people of lower social standing*, said Baglione, remembering Cesari's insultingly offhand manner with the pope and his aristocratic clients. The requirements of scale and speed in his art operations pushed Cesari and his workers to develop new techniques. When they did frescos, along with the incisions they made in copying drawings they also cut lines directly into the damp plaster to guide their painting. A like process – outlines marked in the prepared canvas with the other end of the paintbrush or something similar – was sometimes carried over into the small mass production canvases. M might've learnt the trick at the time he was turning out fruit and flowers for Cesari. The Cesari factory's industrial methods apart, nobody else began a painting like this. It was a technique M now developed as his own rapid way of fixing the critical contours of an image. It was nothing like drawing – he was neither shaping the image nor expressing value, simply fixing a few purely optical relations by scoring lines in the wet priming with the pointy end of his paintbrush. It became a working method unique to M – it let him extend his range to large and complex paintings without betraying that truth to life his art uniquely stood for.

He'd made incisions in some of his earliest paintings – the first *Fortune teller*, the *Cheats*, the *Musicians*, the Mario *Bacchus* and the second *Lute player*. He'd made them on the skirt of Anna Bianchini as the *Penitent Magdalen*, and around the face of Fillide as Catherine, along the folds in her skirt and the edge of the vicious spike on the wheel. They weren't lines made by tracing a drawing, but freehand marks that caught the outline of a head, aligned the angle of the eyes and fixed the contour of a shoulder or the position of a hand. Sometimes they might have served a mechanical purpose, as on the Anna *Magdalen*, where they marked out the pattern of her brocade, the *Bacchus*, where they aligned the tabletop and defined the blue band on his pillow, or on the second *Lute player*, where they marked the details of his instruments and where the outline of his head, hands and shoulders coincided so exactly that M must have used a tracing of the painting he'd done for Vincenzo Giustiniani when he started his second version for Del Monte. An odd foreshortening in the lower part of Anna's seated figure in the *Magdalen* and Mario's left handedness in the *Bacchus* suggested M was starting to use mirrors to fix his image on a plane surface – painting the reflection rather than the model – and using mirrors and making incisions might've developed together.

The value of the incisions M made in his paintings showed up when he did Judith sawing through the neck of Holofernes – his first real foray into doing *history* and action painting, doing it his way without preliminary drawing. Leonardo had written a lot on the problems of history pictures in his *Book of painting*, and his own cartoon of *The battle of Anghiari* and Michelangelo's rival study for *The battle of Cascina* were two lost classics of renaissance drawing, *the turning point of the renaissance*. You drew from life, Leonardo said, and worked it up later.

> When you go around, look and consider where men gather and how they act when they speak, and when they argue or laugh or fight together. Notice the things they do among themselves, and the spectators and bystanders, and sketch them briefly … in a little notebook that you ought to have with you all the time … and don't ever rub anything out

but keep it all and replace your old notebook with a new one when necessary. These aren't things to rub out but to keep carefully, because the forms and actions of things are infinite and the mind can't remember them all …

You had to forget detail, be unlike painters who *wanted every smallest mark of the charcoal to count*, and

> think about the movements that are appropriate to the mental events in the creatures that make up the story, before you attend to the beauty and quality of their parts.

Painting from life, M had to set up a tableau of the event and compose in real life, with models, what Leonardo had urged – not a mere sum of individual figure studies but a *movement* that related the figures, locked them together – and paint that directly. Nude cavalry battles were out of the question, massacres of the innocents and anything requiring heavenly hosts, but events of three or four figures could be managed in a studio, and later on even a ring in angel or two, a borrowed horse or a rented sheep when needed. It took longer than a single study and was harder on the models, holding their frozen action. Particularly hard on Fillide in this case, arms forever tensed in mid decapitation, but also on the male in spasm. After blocking out his composition in real figures, like a photographer lining up a shot, M couldn't simply activate a shutter. He had to paint, and his actors freeze, for longer than any single sitting could last. A few key incisions lightly cut into the wet priming at the start, enough for the needs of M's own visual memory, and just deep enough to show him the contours through the brush strokes of a preliminary *abbozzo* and the earlier stages of the actual painting, would let M recompose the group precisely after his models' lunch break, or when they showed up again for work the next morning – working over time with no fixed image like a drawing to guide him, M needed the marks. The work of painting might bring changes of mind – *pentimenti* and repainting of details, but slight repositionings of the models too – such that the faint incised grooves, where they were visible in the finished painting, didn't always match the figures' definitive outlines. Judith, in this case, lowered her arm in the final version. He linked the central elements of the image on the canvas by marking out Judith's left shoulder and arm, the one grasping Holofernes' head, and outlining the twisted head itself – without the beard – and indicating his radically foreshortened chest. On the right he outlined the old woman's skull – without her scarf – and her throat. These were the deepest cuts and the structurally crucial ones. Other markers were likely filled in by the paint.

Realism like that could be a trap. There was always a tiny gap between the physical reality of the model and the imaginative reality of the event being shown. Fillide Melandroni would always be M's friend Fillide the courtesan, filling in time between professional engagements, maybe her empty afternoons, and for all her wild moments never quite a Jewish freedom fighter out of the old testament. The murdered tyrant was maybe someone M knew from the ball games or the tavern, maybe a professional model, maybe someone found on the street in the way Bellori described for the fortune teller. He didn't lose his head over M's work, and at some point M became aware of a difference between what he saw, what he was painting in his studio in the palazzo Madama, and what he would've been seeing in, as it were, real life. He'd already sketched in the model's convulsed male body and the hideous semi dead face, a horror far more shocking than the earlier essay on the Medusa shield, when M realized that a really half severed head, under tension from Judith's hand grasping it by the hair, would be pulling away from the body as she hacked through the spinal column, would be looking out from the picture plane at a crazier angle than a live model with a fully attached head could accommodate. So he relocated the nose and the left eye, raising them and moving them slightly to the right and adjusting the silently screaming mouth to show the head was coming away from the body.

The fine scorings M left in almost all his work – until he was driven to work from memory at the end – went unremarked by his contemporaries and weren't even noticed for several hundred years. They were the tangible sign of his uniqueness. M never drew. It was why, even when he was offered a fortune to do it, he never painted in fresco. M painted from life.

Not drawing was polemical as well as practical. The year after M arrived in Rome the artists' academy of San Luca was started – or restarted – with the ostensible purpose of giving artists a higher education and the real one of asserting the church's control over art. Federico Zuccari was a notably over the hill late mannerist who had a religious theory of drawing as *a sign of God in ourselves* ... and as president he cloudily expounded on the metaphysics of drawing at the academy's first meeting in January 1594 and appalled the working artists. Young unknowns like M had to submit a drawing if they wanted to join and when Zuccari *called the young painters up to him to show him the drawings they'd done* M didn't respond, if he was even there. He didn't join for years – if he ever did.

M WAS DOING *a lot of private paintings that can be seen in private studies*, paintings that never became well known because they remained concealed in the homes of the wealthy avant garde collectors,

> various paintings for other people ... they aren't accessible
> in public places.

He did a painting of *Narcissus* that was almost his last painting not to have one of the religious themes the market would increasingly impose, apart from a few portraits, and it was already moving beyond the dreamy suspended eroticism of his Del Monte adolescents. Already it was only partly of that early world. M was leaving that refined milieu behind him, creatively if not yet domestically, by the time he painted *Narcissus* around the end of the century, and *Narcissus* had a lot more in common with all the adolescent *Johns in the wild* that were still to come. The painting contained its drama as an inner tension – between a boy and his reflection. The Narcissus myth, of the boy who fell in love with his own image reflected on the water, was the last subject to imagine eyeballing the viewer in the manner of the earlier models. Even so the austere intensity of introspection here was startling.

It was an unusual subject in art. Del Monte had in his garden a copy of the classical bronze of the nude boy pulling a thorn from his foot and M seemed in part to be using it as a model here. Giambattista Marino, a wild and calculating poet on the make who arrived in Rome from Naples in the autumn of 1600, had written about Narcissus four years earlier in his interminable erotic epic *Adonis* – although the poem wouldn't be published until 1622 – and by 1601 M was starting to see a lot of Marino. He later painted Marino's portrait and got a few short poems in return. Marino was mannerist and mannered – he particularly liked things like the *Medusa* and had nothing to offer M – and his Narcissus was the *ungrateful youth* who rejected the nymph Echo and then felt *a new torment of strange love*. M's Narcissus was no object of desire, even to himself. Instead of love or desire or rejection, or even any of that anxiety that his own early *Sick self portrait* might've seemed to foreshadow, M showed a bleakly adolescent scrutiny of a self closed in the circle made by the arc of the

Cheats, 1594, oil on canvas
91.5 × 128.2 cm, Kimbell Art Museum,
Fort Worth, Texas

Isaac & Abraham I, 1598, oil on canvas
116 × 173 cm, Barbara Piasecka Johnson Collection,
Princeton, New Jersey

Matthew called, 1599–1600,
oil on canvas, 322 × 340 cm,
Contarelli chapel,
S. Luigi dei Francesi, Rome

Judith & Holofernes, 1599, oil on canvas
145 × 195 cm, Galleria Nazionale d'Arte Antica, Rome

Peter killed, 1601, oil on canvas
230 × 175 cm, Cerasi chapel, S. Maria del Popolo, Rome

Love the winner, 1602, oil on canvas
156 × 113 cm, Gemäldgalerie,
Staatliche Museen, Berlin

John in the wild IV, 1604, oil on canvas
173 × 133 cm, Nelson Gallery,
Atkins Museum, Kansas City

David II, 1606, oil on canvas
125 × 101 cm, Galleria Borghese, Rome

kneeling boy locked to his own dark reflection in the pond. *Narcissus* was action and contemplation, *history* as well as a portrait. The boy's kneeling was an act and not a pose. His tensed figure, resting on his hands and largely lost in the dark behind the folds of his pushed up shimmering silk sleeves, was pivoted around the pale skin over bone of his boulder like bare knee, jutting out of the dark into the centre of the canvas. The knee took on a luminous life of its own. The boy leant toward the water over this folded knee, framed and isolated by the darkness around him, eye sockets full of shadow, searching out his own image in the black water. Suspended between the search and the gaze, the boy was the adolescent enigma. There was no way M was going to even hint at what he found.

And he did another single figure *history* around the same time – still 1599 or 1600 – a *David* with Goliath's head, another full length study of a kneeling boy, this time more in thoughtful action than active thought. Even more like Del Monte's bronze *Thorn puller* than Narcissus had been, the very young and almost childlike David, swaddled in a kind of sheet, leant into the picture out of its dark depth like Narcissus and bent over to fill the canvas like a teenage quadruped, his right knee and right shoulder catching light and looming out of the picture plane. This David was neither enacting the killing nor displaying the trophy head, but tenderly caught, his face in deep shadow, in a quiet and oddly intimate moment of concentration on simply getting a purchase on Goliath's hair with the cord of his sling shot, the better to carry the head. The dead head itself in the bottom corner was already a mere object and its severing hardly seemed to have mattered – it wasn't now the issue, as it had been in *Judith*. M did the giant's corpse perfunctorily, almost crudely, without interest. It'd become just another landscape feature for the boy to rest his knee on as he bent to the task. At first M had done Goliath's head fixed in the wild eyed open mouthed horror of the moment of death, baring the front teeth and rolling the tongue, eyeballs swivelled to the very edge of the sockets. Then he'd painted out the violence, lowering the eyes and half closing the mouth in the fixity of death. The *pentimento* might've been dictated by a client's revulsion, more likely by his own sense that it presented a glaring distraction from the tender intimacy of the David, whose own features were daringly muted by the shadow. M knew about diminishing returns. Horror wasn't something you evoked at will.

Violence done by a boy or girl on an adult oppressor – Judith's, David's – became a father's on his own young son in Abraham's readiness to sacrifice his son Isaac to the old testament god – a killing interrupted at the last moment by the interceding angel. In a few years M'd be playing on its psychic menace. Doing it for the first time now, he once again shied away from horror. The boy victim was literally overshadowed, resting almost nude on his elbow with his wrists still tied, his face reddened by the fire and swollen with weeping, his father's knife still held against him but the worst moment had passed. M was again deploying that gift that'd dramatized the fading of the fruit in the *Basket* – marking out across the canvas little displacements of time that told you the story. The old woman's eager tension and the ready cloth had braced you for the imminent separation of Holofernes' head from his body. Mary's face and her hand toying with the sprig of flowers had registered her change of mind as Martha talked.

The boy's terror here was still present in his puffy sob racked face. Abraham's knife was still in place and his left hand holding Isaac's head, ready to cut the boy's throat, but the grip had slackened. The angel had caught Abraham's attention and taken Isaac out of his self absorbed misery – he was the focus of the triangle of figures isolated in the dark, the same age as Isaac, maybe fifteen, apparently dressed in a wasp waisted jerkin and pantaloons and badly in need of a pair of glasses for his astigmatism, since M hadn't made an incision to align the eyes. Light fell on the angel's face and the skull and neck of Abraham interrogating him. This Abraham was the first of a long line of formidable strong featured, bald pated, grey bearded patriarchs that'd run through M's work, obsessed with the play of light on skin over bone and the ineradicable dignity of age. It seemed right that the angel stood below the father, not flying above him, and pleading rather than commanding, as Abraham looked down at him – sure enough of his case, shyly confident and arguing as Martha had done, his right hand reaching for the neck of the placid ram who'd come along as the ring in sacrifice.

The play of the lit hands in the dark enlivened and concentrated the drama – Isaac's were limp and tied, Abraham's in a brutal double grip, the young angel's calmly strong. Their arms all reached toward the viewer, drawing the eyes into the picture and lending it depth. The counter play of shadow was even more daring than in *David*. Isaac's face and Abraham's were both turned away from the light, which caught only the angel's directly, and most of Isaac's nude body was in shadow too. Within the half light, the red glow of the unseen sacrificial fire reflecting on the skin matched the bravura rendering of the ram's head and the single piece of firewood charred and glowing at one end. The painting abounded in loving, vigorous detail of a kind

M would never lavish on another picture – partly at least because he'd never again have the time – not skirting the implied violence but buoyed by its own delight in life. Leonardo would've loved it.

The *Narcissus* stayed in Italy, but by various routes never fully traced, the *David* and the *Isaac* both arrived in Spain not many years after they were painted. They were well known and much copied there from early in the seventeenth century. So did a third study of a brooding adolescent – another boy with his face in shadow who looked like the boy M used as the model for Isaac. *Narcissus* had been a kind of pagan forerunner for this study and all the versions that would follow of this figure – he was M's first version of *John in the wild*, the adolescent saint in the wilderness. M painted John almost obsessively, again and again, twice in his very last weeks of life. Painted in this deceptively early looking manner, full of the *Isaac*'s loving natural detail, *John*'s arrival marked the end of M's early years. He was already in the thick of it. These studies of boys, all works that looked back to his art's recent past even as M was thrust forward like the *angelus novus* to the tumult and violence about to engulf the rest of his life, were all painted in the last couple of years of the century. As the fifteen hundreds turned into the sixteen hundreds, M was making it all new.

5

ROME 1600

Matthew called
Matthew killed

BUSINESS BOOMED FOR Giuseppe Cesari all through the fifteen nineties. The more work he did for Clement VIII, the more Clement liked him and the more work Cesari got. The prestige reinforced the more purely commercial business of supplying the commercial market direct with cheapie canvases off his workshop assembly line. Big religious frescos took forever and were a drag. But too much was a long way better than too little, as Cesari remembered very well. He'd been through a relatively rocky patch after Gregory XIII died in 1585 and Sixtus V Peretti took over. Cesari had been Gregory's artistic boy wonder, doing frescos in the Vatican and drawing a papal salary when he was still fifteen. When Gregory died, Cesari went to Naples in 1589. He was back in Rome by the end of the year, and bouncing back into favour with the new pope did some of his best work ever between 1593 and 1595 on the walls of the papal treasurer's family chapel – a dazzlingly illusionistic *mélange* of things he'd picked up from Raphael, Titian, Correggio and Michelangelo, so *épatant* that in their turn they became a model for the vast and gorgeous mythological frescos Annibale Carracci started two years later in the palazzo Farnese. Clement VIII was soon so impressed by what he saw that for the next thirteen years Cesari's only problem would be having more major fresco commissions than he and his team could handle – it meant earlier and less significant commissions now got pushed to the back burner. Work like the Contarelli chapel job.

The Contarelli chapel was in the church of San Luigi dei Francesi.

Mathieu Cointrel, the Frenchman who became cardinal Contarelli, had bought a chapel in this church in 1565 and left his executor Virgilio Crescenzi with the money and instructions for its decoration when he died twenty years later. He'd already paid for part of the San Luigi façade and put ten thousand scudi toward the high altar – there was some question after he died about how Cointrel had made quite so much money in the church's service. Not that anyone was surprized. He wanted scenes from the life and death of his name saint Matthew. Crescenzi contracted with a Flemish sculptor Cobaert for a marble statue of Matthew and the angel for the altar. In May 1591 he contracted with Cesari to fresco the vault and the two side walls of the chapel – Cesari said he'd do the job in a year and a half for six hundred and fifty scudi. It was all spelt out minutely in an attached document – Contarelli wanted an altarpiece of Matthew sitting *in a chair with a book or volume*, about to write his gospel, *with an angel standing beside him larger than life, appearing to reason or in other suitable pose.* On the wall to the right of the altar a fresco of

> ... Matthew inside a store or large room as used for tax collecting with the various things that belong in such an office, a counter such as tax collectors use with account books and money ... Matthew, suitably dressed for the profession, rising from the counter to go to Our Lord, who passing by with his disciples in the street calls him to the apostolate ...

Opposite, a painting of

> ... a long wide place in the form of a temple, with a raised altar at the top of three, four or five steps ... Matthew dressed for celebrating mass ... killed by a group of soldiers ... more artistic to do it at the moment of *Matthew killed* ... wounded and fallen or falling but not yet dead ... a crowd of men and women, young, old and children ... terrified by the event, some looking appalled and others pitying ...

Cesari did drawings for the frescos and actually painted the chapel vault with Matthew reviving the king of Ethiopia's daughter, and the king's and queen's conversion. He was paid for this in 1593. Virgilio Crescenzi had died by now and Contarelli's executor was now his son Giacomo Crescenzi. By now Cesari was getting more interesting commissions from the new pope and his nephew than the minor but demanding Contarelli job. He was seriously overextended – one of the reasons he'd taken on the talented but unknown new arrival M in 1593. In 1595 Cesari was commissioned by Pietro Aldobrandini to do a vast series of fresco *histories of ancient Rome* on the Capitol that kept him busy until the end of his life forty five years later. Giuseppe Cesari no longer needed the Contarelli chapel.

The congregation of San Luigi dei Francesi weren't happy. Contarelli was nine years dead. Now his executor Crescenzi was dead too and after seven years there was still no marble statue. The new painter Cesari had abandoned the fresco job. The chapel was not operative. It was pulling in no income. The congregation became convinced that the Crescenzis were using the Contarelli money themselves – earning interest on the money not being spent. They petitioned the pope in December 1594 – demanded the executor finish work on the chapel and pay the money due for celebrating masses, including nine years of arrears. Nothing happened. The congregation of San Luigi was newly energized when Francesco Contarelli, the late cardinal's nephew, joined the church's administrators in March 1596 – the cardinal had left money to his relatives in his will, slyly ordering that it be paid out when the chapel was finished. The congregation sent a second and extremely testy petition to *the most holy father* Clement VIII at the end of 1596, pointing out that the chapel was *still boarded up* after twenty five years. They zeroed in on Crescenzi again,

> who's never finished it, making excuses now about the
> sculptor, now about the painter, now about one thing and
> now another, and so the soul of the deceased is cheated of
> its prayers and the church of San Luigi is cheated of its
> income ...

They said it was *a national shame* that *foreigners* – French visitors and residents – should see the chapel boarded up for longer than it'd taken others in Rome to build entire churches from scratch. They demanded an apostolic inspection and that Crescenzi *and his brothers who've got rich on that inheritance* be forced to hand over all the money Contarelli had left for his chapel. In July an *avviso* reported that the pope had forced the Crescenzis to hand over all the Contarelli money – *more than a hundred thousand scudi* – to the fabbrica di San Pietro, which administered the church's building work. The Crescenzis blamed the painter. They said he'd already been paid almost in full for the work he'd never done. They were too diplomatic to mention the actual name of Giuseppe Cesari, his beatitude's painter of choice. In September they asked for a payment order to finish the work on the chapel, and in November a payment order was screwed out of the Crescenzis – four hundred scudi payable to Cesari on completion of the two side wall frescos. The order was valid for one year. It wasn't enough to move things along. Late the following March the congregation wrote that the diplomatically unnamed painter still hadn't started. By the end of March 1598 it was clear to everyone Cesari wasn't going to do it – two weeks later Cesari left Rome for Ferrara among the pope's retinue and he stayed away for the rest of the year.

Del Monte knew the Crescenzi family well, and the Contarelli chapel project. Del Monte and the Crescenzis were political allies and social friends. In the summer of 1597 Del Monte mentioned to Ferdinando I that he'd been to dinner with young cardinal Odoardo Farnese and the cardinal nephew Pietro Aldobrandini. After dinner they'd gambled for a while –

> it was a great battle and Aldobrandini and I both lost, and
> I lost more than he did

– and then the three cardinals went out *for an after dinner jaunt* and made music *to the Crescenzi and Macarani girls*. Twenty four year old Odoardo Farnese had been interested in Laura Macarani for some years. Pietro Aldobrandini preferred married women, apart from his one hugely expensive Spanish courtesan. Del Monte remained a sexual enigma. The Crescenzis were worth knowing – prominent in Rome for around seven hundred years, they cared about art. M did a lost portrait of Virgilio Crescenzi, and one of his brother Melchiorre Crescenzi, who was a member of Clement VIII's entourage. Onorio Longhi designed Virgilio Crescenzi's funeral monument. The Contarelli impasse was the kind of diplomatic puzzle Del Monte was bred to solve – a challenge to his skills at making people happy. The blank walls of the Contarelli chapel were M's chance.

The taking of Ferrara in 1598 was a great moment for Roman art. After looking over Venice for himself at the beginning of the year, and being deeply impressed, Pietro Aldobrandini sent Cesari over from Ferrara in July to buy him some Venetian art to supplement the master works by Titian, Bellini and others he was lifting from Ferrara. In Rome these became the Venetian core of a collection that soon included early work by M. Not everyone could be a cardinal nephew, and Pietro Aldobrandini was seizing his moment with both hands. Del Monte also managed to acquire some Venetian paintings of his own including a Giorgione and maybe some Titians – his collection eventually came to include six or seven Titians. Most of the pope's personal attendants would come back from the Ferrara tour with a little something by a recent old master or two.

The high point of the Ferrara expedition, politically and socially speaking, was the elaborate double wedding of the twenty year old new emperor Felipe III of Spain with a Hapsburg archduchess, and the infanta Isabella's with a Hapsburg prince of the low countries. The Spanish empire needed a morale raising show. In Madrid Felipe II had died during the pope's Ferrara visit – eighteen months after Spain's latest bankruptcy, a year after the defeat of its *invincible armada* off England and weeks after Spain ground to a halt in its war with France and began to disengage from the low countries. After the weddings Clement hurried back to Rome to prepare for the holy year celebrations. The holy year of 1600 was being elaborately choreographed as a propaganda triumph of the counter reformation and a massive reassertion of Rome's old role as *caput mundi*. It was no time to allow challenges to established authority, as a radical philosopher called Giordano Bruno was also about to learn. It was no time to cut a *brutta figura*.

San Luigi dei Francesi now had less than a year to fix the Contarelli case before the holy year started. It was thirty five years since Contarelli had bought the chapel and signed the original contract for painting it. What would the French visitors think if they saw the Contarelli chapel still boarded up? Spain's military war with France had ended in May 1598, but Rome was more and more the theatre of a bitter and explosive political struggle for influence between the French and the Spanish. The first sign that things were moving came when the Contarelli chapel finally opened for business on the first of May, its side walls bare. An alert worshipper, glancing around, would've realized that this meant there would now be no frescos of Matthew on those walls – no scaffolding, no tarpaulins, and the chapel never would've opened if such a mess were imminent. A month later the administrators were delegating a group to negotiate again with the Crescenzis. In July one of the Crescenzi brothers signed an agreement with the rectors of San Luigi to pay four hundred scudi for two side paintings in the Contarelli chapel – the painter, nominated by the fabbrica di San Pietro, would be M. Del Monte had been busy. The same day the rectors signed up M himself – all their urgency and all M's eagerness to get the job were in his written undertaking to get it done by the end of the year, or get the paintings finished by others at his own expense. M promised to follow the directions for the paintings earlier given to Cesari. He'd receive as much blue and ultramarine paint for the job as the Crescenzis' own painter Roncalli might decide was needed. Fifty scudi would be advanced immediately. Nine days later a further contract was countersigned by M and all the priests of San Luigi.

> He got the Contarelli chapel job in San Luigi dei Francesi through the efforts of his cardinal,

wrote Baglione. M now had less than five months to produce two huge *history* canvases of a size and kind he'd never tried before. The paintings would fill the upper part of each side wall. He had to combine interior and exterior scenes and deploy large numbers of figures in complex actions. Nothing he'd done so far had come anywhere near the difficulty of this. The time was very short. Not even M could do it in five months. He was late finishing – might've started late, since the canvas supplier wasn't paid until the end of 1599 – but only six months late. After decades of delay, San Luigi got art that made San Luigi dei Francesi and M famous forever.

A BUNCH OF men were sitting at a table. There were five of them and their ages spread over forty years or so. Three were flash young types, a couple of them with feathers in their hats and one of them wearing a sword too. A third stared hatless at a puddle of coins on the table. A rather older man with a beard and a floppy hat was counting the coins and a more elderly clerkly man on his feet peered over the shoulders of the two nearest the money, adjusting the glasses on his nose. There was a bag of coins, an inkwell and pen and an open ledger on the table. The activity was routine, mundane, vaguely lowlife, the young *bravi* looked faintly bored. Was the money the takings of a shop or winnings from cards, a payment to be divvied up or the fruit of a theft?

Two strangers walked in, one of them a robust greyhaired barefoot man with a beard, holding a stick and with a coarse blanket wrapped around him, looking like one of the country pilgrims already flooding into Rome that year – and very unlike the young city blood sitting nearest the door, in billowing silk sleeves with velvet stripes, plume, silk tights and soft shoes. The newcomer was leaning toward the nearest young guy, the one straddling the bench, wearing a sword and looking edgy, saying something in a low voice and raising his hand in reassurance. Behind the greyhaired arrival and largely obscured by him was a taller and younger and strikingly good looking man with a light beard. He too seemed to be barefoot, but all you could really see of him were his neck and face behind his companion's shoulder, and his outstretched arm and hand. He was looking over the heads of the younger ones, gesturing effortlessly to the bearded man in the middle of the group, the one counting the money. The bearded man had seen the newcomers but didn't seem to know them, unsure whether he was the one they were looking for and why they'd want him. He pointed at himself in a way that said *You speaking to me?* The ripple of disturbance hadn't yet reached the end of the table. The others just went on counting the money.

It was unclear where they all were. The space was strikingly bare, quite empty apart from the table, the chair and the bench, and above them a window with open shutters that identified a wall, its panes oilskin or paper. The bare place, the weak diffused yellowish light coming through the panes and the corner on the wall opening on to a larger darker space behind on the left made it hard to be sure if this space was inside or outside. It shared something of each, as if the table were set up in the courtyard of a city palazzo. The light that caught everyone wasn't the muffled glow from the window but a single shaft of intense sunlight that came not from a doorway either but down through an opening high off to the right, above the heads of the standing newcomers but catching the men grouped round the table full in the face. In that odd light in the strange space, everyone, in all his ordinariness, looked caught for an instant out of time and place.

Or forever. Everyone was quite still. The light preserved each figure in its amber. The money counting had been suspended, or almost, and the visitors had barely begun to make themselves clear. This was a moment between two events, drained of busyness and outward drama, full of enigmatic readiness. The stillness lasted as long as you could keep your eyes on it. Which felt like forever.

And yet the very stillness was full of movement and change. A ripple of response to the arrivals was moving from the right across the space of the table, moving with the shaft of light. The plumed youths were caught in the glare and had already reacted. The younger one had leant away from the visitors on to the shoulder of his bearded companion: the other was twisting toward the arrivals and his hand already moving toward the hilt of his sword. The bearded man in the middle had just realized he was the object of the search. The two furthest from the light weren't yet aware of anything. The tall visitor, the one calling the man at the table, was turning to leave even as he beckoned. His feet were already turned toward the exit. The time it took your eyes to follow the tall figure's beckoning hand and move around the table was how long it'd taken him to turn on his heel.

This was how M painted *Matthew called*. The huge canvas, nearly three and a half metres long and nearly three and a quarter high, was almost double the size of the largest painting he'd done before now, and it doubled the number of figures, all done life size. A canvas this size on the wall of a chapel, instead of a fresco, was something quite new in a Roman church. Scale and novelty might've aroused expectations of the grandiose, but M's painting startled people for utterly different reasons. It was a scene from ordinary life, so ordinary and so purged of visual rhetoric and transcendental messages that it demanded attention. It showed Christ calling Levi the tax collector to follow him and be Matthew the apostle, just as Contarelli's old directions had specified thirty five years earlier. But Christ here was almost entirely hidden. Only a head and a beckoning arm appeared from behind another figure's broad blanketed back – most likely Peter's. The glint of the faintest aureole barely helped a viewer to pick him out. And the scene around the table was so everyday, not to say sleazy, that people, even expert professionals, mistook what was going on there. The German painter Joachim von Sandrart, who had plenty of time to study the famous painting thirty years later when he was living at Vincenzo Giustiniani's over the way, described Matthew as shown

> seated with a bunch of rogues playing cards and throwing dice and drinking. Matthew, as if afraid, hides his cards with one hand and lays the other on his chest, and his face reveals the shock and shame that he feels because he is unworthy ...

His mistake was understandable. Sandrart got the setting right, if not the details. Painters often showed Matthew with undesirable associates in his preChristian tax collecting mode – it was part of the story – but M had now taken him so far down into low life that he was breaking cardinal Paleotti's rule against showing things about saints' lives that weren't spiritually *productive ... even if it couldn't be denied they were true*. Even more, M was infringing Paleotti's injunction not to introduce *new* and *unusual* things into religious art's familiar stories, making additions and changes *which trouble our sight more than a little*, but Paleotti had died two years before M began this painting, along with his plan for an *Index of prohibited images*. This was very different from other treatments of Matthew. The German Sandrart saw the use M had made of a 1545 woodcut by Holbein that showed card players in his *Dance of death* series, and pointed it out. With the recollections of M's own earlier genre paintings maybe hovering in his mind as well, Sandrart's confusion was unsurprizing. For M had gathered strength for *Matthew* by charging up on the street and tavern life of the last work he'd done before he turned to dreamy androgynes for Del Monte.

He recovered the vigour and precision of his cheats and fortune tellers, not to mention the very models. The boy leaning on Matthew's shoulder was unmistakeably oval cheeked Mario, back again dressed up and plumed almost as he'd been in the second *Fortune teller*, and the youth facing him showed the same *profil perdu* and pretty much the same features, five years on, as the crooked young card player in the *Cheats*. Now M poured back into his new image of real life all he'd learnt about art at Del Monte's. The new group was vastly more various, subtle and complex in the interplay of its five different individuals than his early essays had managed to be. It was more subtle because now there was no point being made in this look at people doing their thing. They were living their daily life *without hope or fear*. M imbued what might've been a tense, raucous or quarrelsome scene over money – a slice of low life out of a northern European genre painting, or worse, a crassly moralizing setup such as Sandrart thought he'd seen – with the trancelike sensuous stillness of the work he'd done at the cardinal's. These money tellers were in a state of dreamy receptivity like the various earlier musicians. Sitting around in the tranquil boring monotony of their ordinary work – counting money – they were in effect doing nothing, and it was the aimlessness of his daily round that left Matthew open to the word that would change his life. There was no intent on the viewer. This was what Sandrart got more radically wrong about *Matthew called*, and what was really new in it. This was what made it so unlike other religious art and what, if he'd been able to get his mind around the notion, would've disturbed the late Paleotti most of all. The painting's power came from its receptive stillness, a sense of imminence if not immanence.

It seemed amazing. *Matthew's* charged ordinariness was so immediate that it went on being contemporary forever. The receptiveness of mild boredom was amplified in the two boys peripheral to the money counting, hangers on gaudily dressed in what might have been the pages' livery of a cardinal's household or a noble's, in any case Venetian and retro in cut and not designed for office work. The boys were eager to be distracted in their different ways, the edgy blood with his sword and the softer Mario figure – a boyfriend maybe –

leaning on Matthew's shoulder the angle of his head and gaze doubling the older man's.

Suspended between *before* and *after* in the picture, the figures were also lost in space. M conflated the *inside* and *outside* of his instructions, the tax office and the street, into an ambiguous place that was at once interior – the light through the oilskin pane – exterior – the corner opening on the left – and neither. If Christ and Peter had come in off the street, the darkness behind them at ground level made it look like they'd stepped through a wall. M heightened and undermined the in your face reality of the people by an underlying dreamlike weirdness in the sense of place, a weirdness that was partly architectonic and partly a matter of light. Visually it was like a giant version of the *Basket of fruit*. The vast space of flat wall behind and above the figures – the upper part of the canvas empty except for the window with its jutting shutters – made them seem to project into the space of the chapel rather than recede away from it. The immediacy was stunning. People *just like yourself* were looming at you out of the gloom, alive in the light of the chapel's flickering candles as the incense went to your head.

The most daring stroke of all was an afterthought. The apostle Peter, an older man fussing, explaining, reassuring, turning into the action and blocking the major player from view with his dun coloured blanket, linking the low life and the divinity, was a later addition and a brilliant one. In M's original version, exposed by x rays three hundred and fifty years after he changed his mind, Christ made a solitary vertical counterweight on the right to the low horizontal of the group at the table on the left. And he was merely beckoning Matthew in the first version, with a familiar and less than compelling palm downward flap of the hand. Visually, this first Christ was no match for the sprawling life at the table. This was hardly a surprise. It was a sad and ineluctable fact of Christian art that the saviour was nearly always a pictorial dead weight. The more dynamic the art, the limper and weedier the son of God looked as an adult, always the visual centre and hardly ever a source of energy. There were exceptions, but the counter reformation, whose popes and ideologues defaced and more than once tried to destroy Michelangelo Buonarotti's tremendous *Last judgement* because they thought it obscene, didn't produce them. M's own coming work wouldn't always elude this universal truth that Christ in art was a liability.

On his first go, however, by hiding Christ almost entirely behind the anxious Peter, M made a demand on his viewers that was no less peremptory than Christ's on Levi. He forced your eye to follow the gaze of the eyes around the table, to search out and identify Christ in the shadow and movement, to take part in the drama M was representing. The painting's place in the tiny chapel meant that you were looking at the big canvas from close to the life size figures but very obliquely, closest to the young money counter on the left. In a triangular relation with Christ and Levi or Matthew, you were opposite Matthew at the narrow base and Christ was at the high apex. It was very confronting. That Christ, when you glimpsed him in the darkness over Peter's shoulder and behind Peter's head, looked austerely compelling was a plus, and so was his languid new hand movement. Redone, it now looked like Michelangelo's Adam's in the *Creation* on the Sistine ceiling – Christ was the new Adam – and less like a hustler's come on. The group around the table owed something too to the apostles in Leonardo's fresco of the *Last supper* in Milan. From now on M was measuring himself with the best. And putting Christ behind Peter as a modern pilgrim also eliminated the problem of dress. Now M didn't have to choose between the usual costume fakery of biblical sheets and the distracting provocation that would have been involved in carrying over the other figures' contemporary dress and attitude into the Christ figure's. A wholly contemporary Christ would've been a dangerous figure for M, socially and politically. What would've been his class and politics? How you dressed, as the pope's obsessive rulings showed, was a hugely charged and heavily policed issue, and for males of rank choosing the French or Spanish style declared your allegiance. The absence of a table leg, which might've lent some plausible support to the money counting but would've cut across the play of muscular legs in tights, was provocative enough. So, if it came to that, were Christ's bare feet, heading for the exit even as his upper body leant into the picture.

The only natural light in the chapel came from a semicircular window high above the altar. Even in 1599 it didn't let much light in, since on the other side of the narrow alley outside the massive palazzo Madama already lowered over it. *Matthew called*'s imaginary source of its strong oblique internal light was in a corresponding place to the window. It enhanced the illusion, but M, who lived in palazzo Madama, knew quite well how weak the real light was. Hardly more than fifty years later Francesco Scannelli praised *Matthew called* in his 1657 book on Italian painting as *truly one of the most finely coloured, sculptural and natural works*, but added bitterly that

> it is in a place almost entirely lacking in light, so that to the great misfortune of other painters and the artist himself it can only imperfectly be seen.

Sandrart was misled by darkness as much as his own preconceptions. And a few years later Bellori added his voice, remarking of the side paintings that *the darkness of the chapel and their colour remove these two paintings from one's sight*. But M painted for these conditions and not for the glare of electric spotlights worked by coin eating machines four hundred years later. Most of what those later lights would reveal, and colour photography in books, was always invisible to a real observer seeing by daylight or candles. The hidden splendours of M's colour were matched by the revealed intensities of his modelling by light. In the gloom you seemed to see real figures emerging from the darkness, and the inconstant flickering of candlelight enhanced the vivid uncertainty of what you saw. M's art, however richly it'd be made to glow centuries later, and whatever abundance of once hidden detail technology would reveal, was made for darkness. His drawing in paint, his modelling with light, his fanatical fidelity to the contingencies of sight, made up his theatre of the partly seen.

And almost for the rest of his life, M would spend an immensity of care in painting things he never imagined people would see, as if he felt he owed it to the imperfectness of human vision and the hope of improving it. Like the dark part of Galileo's moon, they were there whether you saw them or not. In *Matthew called* he built his first great public painting around the meaning of light, of seeing and not seeing, and it was a statement of intent. The new darkness of his painting – what would most strike people about his pictorial style from now on – was conceived from the start to be indistinguishable from the real darkness of the churches his big public commissions would be painted for, places where it was hard to see. The light and darkness of the world, he was reminding people, was also the light and darkness of the mind. For M and his own life it was all strangely apposite. *Matthew called*, even more than the rest of his work in the Contarelli chapel, changed everything for him, and it was a confluence of his past and his future in painting, a summation of his early things and an announcement of what was coming. From now on, in art and life, things would move faster and faster for M, first wild and then desperate. In a moment Levi would rise as Matthew and walk out the door toward his fate. M would soon be walking out of Del Monte's to his own. For a fraught suspended instant now, the world stood still.

WHILE M WRESTLED with *Matthew*, a long horror culminated a few yards away in the market square of the campo de' Fiori. Giordano Bruno was the most original thinker of his age in Europe, a protean and contradictory writer who mixed religious polemic, the new astronomical science, moral philosophy, knockabout farce and satire with the occult arts of a dying intellectual tradition. A loquacious and excitable former priest from the outskirts of Naples, Bruno had far too robustly independent a mind to be safe in the most repressive phase of the counter reformation. He'd fled Italy just ahead of the inquisition and spent fifteen years crisscrossing the lines of Europe's religious divide, passing like a salamander through the fires of controversy in France, Switzerland, England, Germany and Bohemia. In 1592, under the illusion of a more liberal new pope Clement VIII, he'd ventured back to Venice, *a small lean man with a little black beard, about forty years old.* He was denounced and arrested within weeks. In Rome, he'd spent the seven years of M's early struggles in the inquisition's prison, playing cat and mouse games with the inquisitors – interrogations, investigations, confrontations, bargainings, denials, retractions, explanations, negotiations, compromises and finally stubborn intransigence. In 1599 Bellarmino the Jesuit ideologue gave him a final list of eight things to abjure. Bruno said no. It was a bad moment to say no.

Bruno told his interrogators about

> infinite individual worlds similar to this earth ... they constitute the infinite universe in an infinite space ... I call nature the shadow and vestige of divinity ...

None of it, he insisted, touched on religious faith. It was just philosophy. It was an idea of an infinite universe that seized on the same Copernican astronomy that Galileo was developing as science. Bruno was no scientist – he'd rather sharply remarked that Copernicus's fixed and finite sun centred universe wasn't so new, whereas

> we who look not at fantastical shadows but at things themselves, we who see an airy, ethereal, spiritual, liquid mass, a space containing movement and stillness ... we know it to be infinitely infinite.

He imagined the universe as infinitely many bodies in infinite space – it was tactile and visual, like his notion of the mind. In *The shadows of ideas* he'd written that nature doesn't move from one extreme to another except through the mediation of shadows … shadow makes the sight ready for light. Shadow tempers light … shadows … don't dissolve but keep and protect the light in us, and lead us toward knowledge and memory.

Things themselves, shadow tempering light – M was doing this in paint.

Five days after the Cenci family were killed in September 1599, a fellow prisoner of Bruno's was taken to the campo de' Fiori *tied naked to a stake and burnt alive* – at night, because the French ambassador, whose splendid palazzo overlooked the campo de' Fiori, didn't want *to hear or see that horror*. A couple more followed. In January the pope ordered Bruno's death. In February they took him to piazza Navona. His sentence was read to the crowd and Bruno handed over to the governor of Rome for execution. His books were burnt in piazza San Pietro and put on the *Index*. Making fun of the pope was one of Bruno's crimes – Clement had decided he was Circe's pig in one of the satires, though the inquisitors got the book wrong. Another crime was *maintaining the existence of innumerable and eternal worlds*. Bruno glared at his inquisitors and said

> you may be more afraid pronouncing the sentence against me than I feel receiving it.

He was probably right – taken at dawn to the campo de' Fiori, he was stripped naked and tied to a stake and burnt to death

> with his tongue in a clamp, on account of the very ugly words he used to speak.

Somebody waved a crucifix at him as he burnt, but Bruno averted his gaze. M rethought *Matthew killed*. Did Bruno's burning distract him from his work?

MATTHEW'S FATE WAS outlined in the *Golden legend* by his mediaeval hagiographer and in M's working instructions. He was slain after celebrating mass by a swordsman acting on the enraged king of Ethiopia's orders. The king was lusting after his predecessor's virgin daughter, who was his own niece, and Matthew had publicly rebuked him in a sermon for wanting to violate the sanctity of marriage, because the daughter was a nun and a bride of Christ. Featuring a churchman of rigid principles taking a firm stand against the rampant sexual appetites of the worldly and paying the ultimate price, it was a great vehicle for the counter reformation message. Martyrdoms were in vogue. Its early martyrs were the *heroic guerrillas* of a cleaner simpler past that the church badly needed to remind people of. Carlo Borromeo would've understood the situation perfectly. The sources, it had to be said, disagreed on whether Matthew had been run through with a sword, beheaded or stoned to death. Some even spoke of natural causes. Contarelli was going with the sword, and this was what M had to show on the canvas facing the *Matthew called*, the scene in the church, as Contarelli had minutely specified, Matthew lying wounded but not yet dead at the killer's hands, dismay and confusion in the church.

M had actually begun work on this picture before he put it aside to paint *Matthew called*. It'd presented great difficulties and in the end he had to rework it entirely twice. He'd never taken on a major action canvas before, and if *Matthew called* had grown naturally out of his earlier art, *Matthew killed* emerged from an extraordinarily laboured passage, for so quick and sure a painter, into the *history* mode he was looking for. For M it was a hugely ambitious painting and it must have scared him at the outset. *Matthew called* had doubled his previous number of figures in a canvas to seven: *Matthew killed* doubled that again to thirteen complexly orchestrated figures in violent movement and it called on wholly new resources. The serene achievement of *Matthew called* finally enabled him to do it in the third version.

That there'd been trouble over this painting and a lot of reworking was known at the time – Bellori would report it seventy years later – but only the x ray studies made in the nineteen fifties and sixties would show quite how radically M had thought and rethought on this canvas his whole approach to narrative painting. The history of *Matthew killed*'s three versions was the story of a hop, skip and jump from mannerism to the baroque. In that sense for M the bravura piece he now produced, a brilliant resolution of his difficulties, was no answer at all in the long run. Not for him. The baroque, before it'd been thought of, was an odd place for M to end up, but not as odd as where he'd started from.

When he first started work on the Contarelli contract, the amazingly assured and original M underwent – on the evidence of the x ray photos – for the first and last time in his painting life a major failure of nerve. Anyone would've. He had absurdly little time to do work such as he'd never taken on before. It was his first chance to establish a major public presence and position himself in striking distance of the outstandingly successful Cesari. The risk was great. If he failed to impress he'd greatly embarrass Del Monte, whose painterly creature he was and who'd put his own very considerable authority on the line over the job. He would condemn himself to sink back, probably forever, into the crowd of second raters scrabbling for work in Rome. At best he'd place himself as a chamber artist for refined private clients only. Cesari, as the brilliant man of the moment on the art scene and a dazzling social presence about to be knighted by the pope, as M's contemporary – only three years older – and the original contractor for this job, not to mention the entrepreneur who'd employed M a few years earlier in frustrating and vaguely humiliating work, was the painter to beat.

Cesari – who wasn't doing this job only because he was working on more prestigious commissions elsewhere – was the model for everything M professionally wanted to achieve. So M in his first essay at *Matthew killed* took an approach that had nothing to do with his own instincts and skills and everything to do with the fluent and graceful and very mannered fresco style with which Cesari was just then covering walls all over Rome. It was a mistake, and made worse because M let himself be intimidated by the detailed instructions Contarelli had left for the painting's setting. These had demanded a large temple space, a raised altar and several steps leading up to it, and a various crowd of worshippers moving inside the space. M had never tried composing anything like that before. It implied a deployment of all those geometric arts of perspective and proportion that Guidubaldo Del Monte and Galileo Galilei were so concerned with in painting – Del Monte's book on perspective was due out in weeks or months – and that M had pointedly ignored – defied – in working out his own optical sense of bodies in space, modelled by light. Now he gave in to what he thought the late client had wanted and placed a huge piece of renaissance classical church interior – pillars, cornice, volutes, niche – unless it was a classical ruin seen frontally in the centre of the canvas. In front of that he began several quite small and oddly distributed figures that looked even more diminished against the huge stage backdrop, in the architectonic space he'd mapped out.

He might've been to look at a treatment of this story in another Roman church, done ten or so years earlier by Muziano, the painter originally contracted to do this job back in the sixties. He might have seen preparatory drawings by Cesari, whose sketch for the fresco never did survive. He almost certainly took hints from Raphael's Vatican frescos. To close the deal he might've had to present a proposal of his own along these conventional lines. They were all the wrong models for him. At first there was Matthew standing small and bearded on the right, swathed in a chasuble and showing the palm of his hand against a bulky headless nude standing upright, shorter than Matthew, with a weapon raised above its missing head. Blocking any clear view of the killer was a soldier in a helmet and gym slip showing his back right in the middle at the front, resting his hand on a jutting hip in a very mannered stance. To Matthew's right was a frontal nude adolescent angel, legs apart, book in left hand and a finger of his right raised toward heaven against the killer.

M replaced these – maybe figure by figure, in a gradual process of cancellation and superimposition, as he *drew* in paint on canvas the way he'd found, and not at all in the two distinct phases Bellori would mention – with a stiffly striding upright little killer with a drawn sword out horizontal marching in from the left, even shorter than his forerunner, and a new lower glimpse of Matthew's head, meaning he'd fallen on his knees. A woman, perhaps the nun niece, was now holding her hand to her cheek in horror on the left and a frightened boy acolyte had appeared between the legs of the soldier in the gym slip, and a couple of other faces and hands were identifiable among the confusion. One tiny face floating over the new killer's shoulder looked like M's own. The scene was a lot less static now, but still a mess. The way he was trying to fix it was like moving manikins around in a box. None of the changes touched the real trouble. Neither did trying to make them bigger inside the same compositional frame. The trouble was the box. M had painted himself into a corner.

Driven by lack of time and his own urgency, M abandoned work on *Matthew killed* when he was already well on in this lighter coloured composition to do the painting of *Matthew called*. Charged up after its untroubled realization, he swept back to *Matthew killed* scene knowing what to do. He kept nothing of what he'd left before. He got rid of the confining pictorial box: nothing of the inert and distancing monumental frame was kept. Ideas for single figures were moved, transmuted, energized. The obstructing fence post of the watching soldier was cleared from the centre of the canvas. The cast were pushed around, assigned new roles.

M now moved in close, where he liked to be. Matthew was rotated backward through ninety degrees so that, still with the palm of his hand raised toward his killer, he now lay thrown supine as the killer grasped this wrist and forced the old man toward the bottom of the picture. This assassin was a fleshy nude youth in a pagan loincloth and headband, who bestrode Matthew and readied his sword for the final blow with a theatrical Roman grimace, as in a football replay freeze frame of a slightly out of condition player. Life size, powerfully lit from the left and statuesquely filling the very centre of the canvas, the nude killer and not the wounded saint was now the picture's visual heart. The mixed crowd of horrified believers, all the ages and sexes and social classes Contarelli had wanted shown, were gone. There were no women in the final version. By a quite extraordinary invention of his own that had no precedent in artistic tradition or architectural reality, M seemed to have installed a plunge pool in the darkness below the altar, for the baptism by immersion of Matthew's Ethiopian converts. Matthew was now lying on the edge of that pool, his left arm almost trailing in the unseen water. The scene's pictorial ground dropped away into the darkness of the pool above the bottom edge of the canvas. Projecting forward into that darkness and partly filling it, out of the picture proper, whose plane coincided with the life size Matthew and his killer, and quite apart from the turbine of fear and violence above, sitting and sprawling at the poolside left and right, in the very foreground corners of the picture, were three nude male converts. They were gazing thoughtfully and somewhat langorously, as in the stupor of a bath house, at the elderly apostle about to die a few inches from them. The nearest convert on the right, a fleshy rear view counterpart to the killer and with a three day beard, sat with a naked buttock hoisted on to the poolside at the bottom edge, its cheek almost lapping out of the frame. His companion leant forward, resting his face in his hand and staring intently at the murder being enacted in front of him. The converts' presence was menacing enough for them to look like backup killers, ready to lend a hand if the other needed it, or sextons ready to bury Matthew, if the supposed pool were now a grave. What M's thuggish nudes here could never be was the faithful at prayer, as Contarelli had demanded. This was no ordinary martyrdom.

The steam bath atmosphere was enhanced by a real looking column of thick smoke or steam rising from somewhere between Matthew and the altar. This was actually a heavenly cloud supporting a nude adolescent angel, inadequately winged, who leant forward gingerly to lower a martyr's palm frond, a sort of life line, toward Matthew's raised right hand. The cloud was M's first and last concession to that kind of religious unreality. The nude angel on his feet from the earlier essay had metamorphosed into a clothed pubescent acolyte in the same place, merging in his role with the one seen earlier between the soldier's legs and now fleeing the murder in open mouthed terror, but looking back over his shoulder too, transfixed by the coming death and yet showing more boyish curiosity than real fear.

Who the sinister foreground nudes might've been was unclear because they'd arrived from other paintings and not from life. They looked real enough, and served M's end of projecting his image into the real space in front of it, but in the end they were decorative, not functional – bodybuilder types that'd come from Michelangelo Buonarotti via Zuccari and Cesari. Annibale Carracci, who'd soon be sending all purpose nudes like this prancing and sprawling magnificently over the Farnese gallery ceiling as pagan gods, called them *rent a figures*. They came with the mannerist ethos, which was the only currently available pictorial language for making big visual statements in public. M had started out here trying to accommodate that prevailing public manner and it had been a mistake. The compromise survived in *a few hateful mannerist memories*. M's own way of seeing and his own way of painting couldn't be reconciled with *la maniera*. The anguished working and reworking showed it. Now the whole painting turned into a wildly eclectic sampler of borrowed or remembered figures and poses thrown together as M thrashed around in search of a pictorial language of his own that would make the thing cohere. Figures and groups from Raphael and Titian and Tintoretto were in there with Michelangelo's, mediated often by the work of their recent imitators.

The whole thing in the end was held together by the light. Light blazed in horizontally from the left, from that implied side doorway the witnesses to *Matthew killed* were coming and going through. It caught everyone equally, the saint, his killer, the angel, the acolyte, the mannerist thugs and the street toughs, broke them into reflecting fragments and related the fragments to each other. The architecture was all gone and with it rationally apprehensible space. Only dense brown darkness hid the transitions and bound the bodies into relationship. It was no real space. The altar with a Maltese cross on its cloth was mostly hidden behind the smoke, a couple of steps could be seen below it, and the edge of the pool, if it was a pool, on the left the hint of a pillar – nothing Contarelli would've recognized or the geometers approved, little sense of solid earth at all and no flat surfaces or intelligible cast shadows to give a sense of distance. For M it was fake, but it was baroque and it was a release. Enhanced by the chapel's real darkness and flickering candles, it worked marvellously. Anyone coming down the nave of San Luigi would've seen the pale killer nudes looming out of the dark from a distance, in a space that seemed to open out of the wall into the church's real transept.

Entering the chapel, you found the figures of *Matthew called* close against the wall, as if you'd walked by mistake into a small room where people were doing some shady business.

Matthew killed was an outrageous contrivance and it said a lot for the bravura of its execution that nobody really remarked on it. The critics who would later complain about everything being lost in the obscurity of the chapel might've entertained a few dark suspicions of their own about what was going on, but they'd be unable to verify them by the light of a taper. Sandrart would peer through the gloom at the *marvellous* canvas and think he saw

> Christ, our redeemer, driving the Jews, merchants and customs men from the temple, their stalls and counters all overturned.

The histrionic nude hit man with the headband and sword must've been Christ in this reading. Bellori would see something was wrong, that *the structure and movements aren't up to the story*, which was a way of saying that underneath the brilliance the setting was unreal and the action staged. He was dead on, though by adding in the same breath *although he reworked it twice over* he'd seem to be judging from what he knew about the painting's troubled origin. Mancini felt there was no way M's painting only from life could be turned to *composing a history and representing feeling*, and his remarks about *imagination* were very pertinent to M's difficulties here.

> You can't put the whole crowd of people enacting a *history* into a room lit from a single window. You can't have someone laughing or crying or walking and get them to freeze while you copy them. Figures done like this are strong but they lack movement and feeling and grace ...

Which was precisely the problem with the frozen horrified onlookers and the fleeing acolyte and the overall oddness of the image of a series of violent movements petrified, and why M would never try anything quite like this again. But all these criticisms came decades later. In 1600 the city whose favourite painter was Giuseppe Cesari found *Matthew killed* brilliantly real, though not as brilliant or real as *Matthew called*. M was so new a painter there was no way people could see what an anomaly *Matthew killed* was for him. Fakery was not a problem for the Roman art public.

At the heart of the painting, though, was a moment of stillness and human truth. Matthew, an old man struck down, already wounded and bleeding, weakly fending off his grimacing killer, looked up and caught his attacker's eye for an instant before he died. In that triangle of killer and victim locked together by their hands and their gaze, and in the infinitesimal pause of mutual recognition before the murder, was a powerful immobility like the quiet pervading *Matthew called*, and the murderer was drained for a moment of his strength. None of the surrounding visual flurry quite obscured this truth, though it came close. The angel and the nudes weren't enough to swing a message of transcendence. *Matthew killed* still looked like *a contemporary episode of violent crime in a Roman church.*

The only other truth in the painting – since the nudes, converts or killers, the fleeing acolyte, the horrified bystanders and the tentative angel were merely brilliant and largely borrowed rhetoric – and its only link to social reality, were the sharply diminished fleeing *bravi* at the back, melting away from the scene of the crime with the practised ease of street fighters who knew when trouble was coming. They were the only link with the ordinary workaday world of *Matthew called* and the only figures in which Contarelli might've recognized something of the socially mixed crowd he'd wanted shown. One of these *bravi*, who were hardly Contarelli's counter reformation role models, was recognizable as Mario Minniti, now glimpsed with his sword and lavishly plumed hat as he hurried out of M's painting for the last time, though not from M's life. The furthest figure from the picture plane, making off with a dark cloak pulled around his shoulders and showing a finely shod heel even as he looked back into the picture with intense ambivalence at the event, or maybe at the painting, was M himself.

Only the sharpest eyed worshipper would've noticed in the chapel's gloom and the painting's dark confusion, not just that it was M but that M was more or less nude, weirdly and inappropriately half dressed, turning a naked bum and thigh to the scene and the viewer as he fled like someone caught in a moment of sexual shame. A couple of wrinkles suggested that what looked like skin was maybe flesh coloured tights, which might've covered M with the priests but didn't exactly resolve the matter, not in that darkness and confusion. It recalled the garbled story that'd followed M down from Milan, where if he hadn't killed someone himself he'd at least been a complicit witness who was jailed for refusing to talk. He was linking himself to the thuggish nude converts by the pool in the foreground, as if he'd been with them waiting for baptism moments earlier and was now fleeing naked into the night, after pulling on his shoes and throwing his black cloak – a *ferraiolo* with an iron clasp like the garments that featured as evidence in several episodes of violence involving M – around his shoulders. What was most remarkable of all though was the face he turned back into the scene, flinging an appalled glance back at *Matthew killed*, hypnotized by the stillness of impending violence like Minniti and the young acolyte, waiting for the sword to fall.

It was the third time he'd put his own face in a painting, the first since the early days at Del Monte's five years before, when he'd made himself as young as Mario Minniti really was in the same picture, instead of five years older. Now he went to the opposite extreme and the five years passed seemed like a lifetime. It was a shock. M was a mature adult now, nearly thirty, and had grown the little beard and moustache he'd keep for the rest of his life. He'd have the beard in another portrait included in another painting two years hence and there he'd look a normally lean and active smoothfaced thirty. A couple of years later he'd've recovered his psychic poise. But now after *Matthew called* and *killed* he looked more like forty, overweight, puffy and creased, middleaged already. Even more, he looked deeply disturbed. The face that was supposed to be registering an instant's shock at a murder bore the marks of permanent distress. It was the look of a man living a nervous breakdown.

DAZZLING FAME FOLLOWED, but it got written about later, when everyone who recorded it had a reason – passing fashion, personal resentment, ideological hostility – to diminish, qualify, explain away. Right from the start, in any case, the fame was mixed with notoriety. People rushed to see the extraordinary new work, and nobody writing about M later could avoid mention of the moment he first amazed the public. Some would've preferred to stay silent. Baglione would sourly remember how *he got the Contarelli chapel in San Luigi dei Francesi through his cardinal's efforts* in the tone of one who might've put in his own unsuccessful tender for the job. His obligatory mention was as brief as possible.

> On the right hand, when the apostle is called by the redeemer and on the left hand when he's wounded on the altar with the killer and other figures. The chapel's vault, however, is extremely well painted by the cavalier Giuseppe Cesari of Arpino.

With M's work on the walls, only Baglione would have thought of telling you to look up at the utterly undistinguished ceiling. Yet in the close, competitive, fashion driven, high stake and bitchy world of Roman art, any brilliant newcomer would expect to get worked over. And M was. The Roman jurist Marzio Milesi, the reserved and cultivated member of the city's emerging bourgeoisie who was one of the first and most passionate admirers of M's art, wrote an enthusiastic fifty line poem of *Thoughts on the histories of saint Matthew painted by M* soon after they went on view – one of more than a dozen fervent and unpublished poems and sonnets he'd compose about M and his paintings over the next ten years. Milesi's *Thoughts* concluded with a darkly nonspecific mention of the *hatred* and *envy* already circulating with the fame. The spin Baglione would put on the fame later was that M was praised only because people were jealous of Cesari. Baglione claimed that M's *Matthew* paintings

> helped make M famous because they included work done from life and because they were in company of [Cesari's] – whose skill had aroused some jealousy in his colleagues – and were highly praised by the spiteful.

Baglione's own spite and the deviousness of its expression here were too much for Bellori, who knew the difference between a great painter and a mediocrity. Many years later Bellori underlined that last bit and scrawled alongside it in the margin of his copy *Baglione/Beast*. Not that Baglione was finished yet. Among those who came to see the sensational new paintings in San Luigi, he wrote, *while I was present*, was Federico Zuccari, the jealous and passé establishment mannerist, refounder of the artists' accademia di San Luca and proponent of the metaphysical concept of drawing.

> He said, *What's all the noise about?* And looking carefully at everything, he added,
>   *I can't see anything other than Giorgione's ideas here, in the one where Christ called him to the apostolate.*
>   And sneering and expressing amazement at all the clamour, he turned his back and stalked out.

Everything Baglione later remembered about this time was poisoned by his own impending encounters with M and his art. What the Dutch painter and critic Karel Van Mander reported in his *Book of painters* in 1603 was worked up from reports he'd received from his compatriot the painter Floris Van Dijck, and Van Dijck was a close friend of Cesari's who was in Rome until 1600 or the year after. Van Mander's was the first account in print of M's impact on the Roman art world and the only report to come right out of that first amazing moment. It gave a real time glimpse of M's hard driving ambition, obsessive work and a rivalry to Cesari's preeminence that was already causing unease in that quarter.

> There's a man called M who's doing wonderful things in Rome. Like the Giuseppe [Cesari] already mentioned, he's risen from poverty through hard work and by taking on everything with foresight and courage, as some people do who won't be held back by faintheartedness or lack of courage, but thrust themselves forward frankly and fearlessly, and boldly seek their own advancement everywhere. There's nothing wrong with this behaviour when it's done honestly, properly and discreetly. Luck rarely offers herself spontaneously to people who don't help themselves and usually needs looking out, prodding and urging.

Van Mander's report showed that right from the start M's fame was linked to his revolutionary idea of what painting was about.

> This M's already famous for his work ... he's got no respect for the work of any master, not that he openly praises his own ... says everything's triviality and child's play, whatever it's of and whoever painted it, if it hasn't been done from life, and we can do no better than follow Nature. So he won't make a single brushstroke without close study of life, which he copies and paints.

Zuccari's vicious academic putdown was revealing — it showed he knew how M worked and he knew Vasari's story about Giorgione's painting only from life. It said nothing about M's painting or Giorgione's either. Zuccari knew that didn't matter because he was also aware that nobody in Rome knew Giorgione's art. Among the few exceptions were M himself — had M been talking about Giorgione in the tavern talk Van Mander was reporting? — and Venetian born Del Monte, who'd just got his first Giorgione on the Ferrara expedition. As northerners, Karel Van Mander and his informant Floris Van Dijck were impressed by M's attitude.

This surely isn't a bad way to achieve a good end. To paint after drawing, however close it may be to life, isn't as good as following Nature with all her various colours.

Though a little residual unease at M's fierce radicalism made Van Mander add immediately that

> of course you should've reached a degree of insight that let you identify and choose the most beautiful of life's beauties.

Which was the cue to segue directly into M's unbeautiful and already notorious private habits, since

> ... he doesn't study his art constantly, so that when he's worked for a fortnight he goes out for a couple of months at a time with his rapier at his side and a servant behind him, moving from one tennis court to another and always looking for fights or arguments, so he's impossible to get on with. Which is all quite incompatible with our art ...

Northerners might appreciate radical realism in art, unlike the Roman establishment, but not a painter's failure to be an assiduously professional protobourgeois. *Yet as for his painting*, Van Mander concluded bravely,

> it's very pleasing and an exceptionally handsome style and one for our young painters to follow.

As indeed they would.

6

ROME 1600–1601

Saul I
Saul II
Peter killed

M WAS FAMOUS. He was paid off finally and in full on
July the fourth 1600 for the two Matthew side paintings.
He wrote in the margin of the contract he'd signed nearly
a year earlier a receipt for the final fifty scudi of the four hundred owed
him for the job. Onorio Longhi signed the contract too as a witness
of the receipt, which noted that the two paintings had already been
installed on the side walls of the chapel. They'd been finished some
time earlier – a dispute over a nonpayment to M had led the month
before to one of the San Luigi administrators being expelled, and
this must've delayed the final quittance. Three months earlier, before
he'd even finished, he'd been commissioned to paint another large
painting to be done by June for an otherwise unknown Fabio de Sartis,
who was paying what was now M's going rate of two hundred scudi.
M's undertaking to deliver was underwritten by Onorio Longhi, who
seemed to be seeing a lot of M just then, showing him how to handle
success. Promising in early April to do another major work within
three months implied the Matthew paintings were nearly done –
M did deliver, though not on time, and was paid the balance at
Del Monte's in late November but the painting M did for de Sartis
was later lost and nobody recorded even what it was meant to be of.

And in September, again taking on a big new commission as he
neared the end of the current work – a pattern had formed under
pressure from buyers – M signed another contract, for a second and

slightly smaller pair of chapel side paintings. He didn't sound like the man who was already notorious for doing a few weeks' painting and then hanging around the streets and ball courts for months. Unless M worked incredibly fast on a picture and then held off putting the final touches until he was forced to deliver, or unless he put off starting as long as he could, until driven by a deadline, getting increasingly tense and quarrelsome as the time for work drew near. M's rate of production after the *Matthew called* and *Matthew killed* left little time to waste.

Tiberio Cerasi was yet another hugely rich financier. He was Clement's treasurer, a job he'd bought, and the apostolic chamber's as well. He was also a great friend Vincenzo Giustiniani and moved in the milieu of M's early promoters. He'd just bought a family chapel in the church of Santa Maria del Popolo, on the edge of the huge piazza at the end of the Corso and just beyond the campo Marzio. In late September 1600 he signed a contract with M for two paintings to be delivered in eight months for a fee of four hundred scudi. Suddenly M was earning big money. These three contracts would bring him a thousand scudi in less than two years, along with whatever he got for the paintings for private buyers he did in that time. Cerasi was a canny customer. As papal treasurer he was a colleague of Del Monte's on the fabbrica di San Pietro – so he'd been involved in giving M the Contarelli commission and seen the results. He thought the new man M was the one to go for, but he wasn't so convinced that he didn't first stipulate in their written agreement that M had to show him preliminary drawings and models of what he planned to paint. Cerasi wanted a painting of Saul blinded on the road to Damascus and another of the apostle Peter being killed. Unlike Contarelli he left the details up to M, but he still wanted to know what he was getting. He also wanted the paintings done on panels of cypress wood. M, with his own way of working directly from life on to canvas, and having just entirely rethought a painting three times over in the course of doing it, must've been inwardly appalled at the demand for a preliminary drawing, but accepted the conditions. If things got difficult he was now in a position of strength – the new contract's Latin called him *dominus*, and *egregius in urbe pictor*. To be recognized as *outstanding painter in the city* wasn't bad after a single major commission. And after his masterly resolution of the *Matthew* difficulties M'd've felt able to do anything.

He needed to. Cerasi had commissioned another *egregius pictor* to do his chapel's altarpiece at the same time. Annibale Carracci was the one other strong and original painter in the city – he was eleven years older than M and had arrived in Rome from Bologna three years after him in 1595. He was brought in to work on the frescos in the gallery of the palazzo Farnese and was so busy with his vast private commission that he was still little seen or known in Rome. Cerasi's double commission was a challenge and a provocation to both painters. He was playing them off against each other. Cerasi was evidently very much his own man when it came to art, and a slightly malicious client, if the idea was his own. A strong hint of outside manipulation appeared in the contract – the payment order for M's advance of fifty scudi was made out to Vincenzo Giustiniani. His name turning up there was surely no accident, even though Cerasi was the pope's treasurer and Giustiniani his banker, making Cerasi a client of Giustiniani's. Vincenzo Giustiniani collected Carracci's work as well as M's, and hung their paintings with his works by Raphael, Giorgione and Titian, at the heart of his collection. Ten years later, M and Annibale Carracci were the only two painters active in Rome at the turn of the century that Giustiniani put in the *twelfth and most perfect* class of painters, the ones who had both life and style. Giustiniani would've been eager to see the result of a paint off between the two new painters he most admired. So would his brother Benedetto and his neighbour Del Monte and the Crescenzis and the Matteis and the rest of the avant garde collectors' circle. Tiberio Cerasi wasn't alone in his astute choice.

THE POPE HIMSELF showed no interest in Rome's emerging new art, though he was busy with painting projects. Art for Clement VIII had been less of a priority before the holy year. He'd paved over the piazza Navona and continued Sixtus V's urban works around Rome in a low key way but his interest in art had centred mainly on censoring nudity in churches. A Magdalen's bare breasts had been covered in Saint Peter's on the pope's orders and some provocatively decorated candlesticks modified. Four female allegorical statues on the tomb of Paul III he ordered removed or covered. The rumour that the four allegorical figures were done in the likenesses of the dead pope's concubines made them particularly provocative to Clement. Odoardo Farnese, the pope's descendant, was equally displeased when the allegory of Justice was covered by a bronze dress. *The cardinal didn't find*, reported an *avviso* of December 1595, that marble statues of that kind had ever aroused lust, even though this one displayed a thigh uncovered as far as the crotch.

In other Roman churches veils had been draped over private parts on Clement's orders, wooden statues clothed, paintings covered over. A 1593 edict ordered preventive censorship for all painting in churches and this edict was renewed in 1603 by the cardinal vicar Camillo Borghese, who'd later be more famous as pope Paul V. To move the faithful, Clement preferred the kind of penitential theatre that his gouty walks from shrine to shrine exemplified, and real martyrs to painted ones. Cecilia had been one of the church's very early martyrs. Her remains were accidentally dug up during work on her church in Trastevere in 1599 – in a gold embroidered dress and bloodstained winding sheet, the axe wounds in her neck apparently still visible – and he'd had her reburied with maximum pomp, before cardinals, ambassadors and rapt crowds. Cecilia's new silver casket cost over four thousand scudi. Two years earlier he'd done the same for the remains of the Roman emperor Domitian's niece and her two loyal eunuchs, who'd all died together for their faith.

A million or so pilgrims came to Rome in 1600. They processed through Rome in their impressive masses and Clement washed their feet, or some of them, to great public effect. The pope intensified his own already busy schedule of pilgrimages to the major basilicas. He'd make the visit of the seven churches a hundred and sixty times before he died, and in the course of 1600 did the round of the four main basilicas over sixty times. People were amazed and moved to see the holy father following the processions barefoot and carrying a heavy cross, or climbing the holy stairs on his knees, amazed and moved as they always were too by his public outbursts of penitential tears. Clement's public mortifications of his own flesh were made particularly painful by the dreadful attacks of gout that often drove him to bed. The gout would have been mitigated slightly by his rigorous Friday fasts, which were also famous, but aggravated by the food and drink he consumed abundantly in private on the other days. Despite the penitential show, Clement always struck close observers as *robust and strongly complexioned*, or *fleshy and fat*. One wrote to Florence in December 1599 that right in the middle of a bout of gout, the pope voraciously ate a fish and drank so many of those glasses of that strong wine that's made his attacks more acute that he was falling asleep.

Del Monte told Ferdinando I that Clement loved gourmet foods and *hearty wines or French clarets*. He could drink Chianti too, but only in summer. The pope and his nephew Pietro Aldobrandini were equally fond of the French clarets and equally anxious to secure a supply, so Pietro's trouble shooting mission to France in late 1600 as papal legate was very timely. He took Giuseppe Cesari with him and came back preceded by a shipload of claret and presented twelve barrels of it to his uncle. Clement protested faintly that it was too much, but in the end was prevailed on to accept all twelve barrels. In May of 1600 Clement's twelve year old great niece became duchess of Parma, which was famous even then as a gastronome's delight, and she sent a mule train down to Rome, loaded with Parma hams, cheeses and salami for her relatives. The holy father intercepted most of them. Twenty four men were needed to unload and carry the food into the pope's palace. Against all this the weekly fasts and long walks from one holy place to another had little effect, especially as one of his personal physicians was urging him – as a remedy for the depressions brought on by the fasting – *to fill the intestines with good foods and excellent wines*. When he had to skip a major banquet for protocol reasons, he made Pietro Aldobrandini recount to him afterward exactly what had been eaten and drunk. Clement's household expenses were four times those of his predecessor the canny peasant Sixtus V.

The holy year of 1600 demanded some effort of artistic propaganda and Clement redecorated the Clementine chapel in Saint Peter's. The church's major art project for 1600 however was to redecorate the transept of San Giovanni in Laterano, Rome's cathedral. Costly new silver reliquaries were made to hold what was left of the heads of Peter and Paul, and for the painting of the transept Clement had a team of painters assembled under the direction of his own favourite Giuseppe Cesari. The others were a very mixed bunch. There was the solidly eclectic Cristoforo Roncalli, who was already working with Cesari on the Saint Peter's job, and along with a fading group of late mannerist survivors were some younger painters only a few years older than the youthful entrepreneur Cesari himself, like the Roman Giovanni Baglione and the Tuscan Orazio Gentileschi, as well as Cesari's younger brother Bernardino. His fashionable representativeness and his managerial skills made Cesari the ideal artist, from the pope's point of view, to bring it all together and create the harmonious group of images a revivified faith needed. Cesari's own contribution was the big fresco of the *Ascension*, an utterly uninspired, not to say crude and banal, reworking of Raphael that was considered a great success because its boring sublimity avoided all the frighteningly unorthodox elements that'd drawn such bitter attacks on Michelangelo's *Last judgement* fifty years earlier. That was what the church now wanted to avoid above all, and bad art was a negligible price to pay. Clement was delighted and knighted Cesari, who walked away from the project as the *cavaliere d'Arpino*, in time to join Pietro Aldobrandini on his diplomatic and wine buying trip to France that autumn. The time had come to add the king of France, the king of Spain and the *half crazy* emperor Rudolf II to the pope on his list of clients even as his style *degenerated into vacancy*.

Just as Cesari reached these social heights, two of the contemporaries who'd been working with him on the project, Gentileschi and Baglione, both fell utterly for the radical call of M's new art. The consequences were very different for the art of each, and for their lives. Both Gentileschi and Baglione were about to get entangled with M in ways that would mark all three of them forever.

A WILD SUMMER for Onorio Longhi that holy year turned into a rough autumn. In July 1600, he remembered three months later,

> I was at the French tennis courts … watching a fencing match … and afterward … I went through piazza Navona where they were playing football. Moving up closer to see the game I met [four men I knew who'd been at the fencing] and with them was another they said was from Terni but I don't know his name or anything else about him. They called me over and asked what I'd thought of the fencing match and who'd scored more hits. I told them what I thought … and then the fellow from Terni said I either hadn't seen properly or else I didn't know what I was talking about. I said I'd've bet him ten scudi on the first bout. [One of the others] overreacted and swung a punch and then put his hand on his sword. For my honour's sake and in self defense I went for my sword too and I don't know how many times I hit out or whether I wounded him, because a lot of people separated us. I was alone but

I understand from the duke of Acquasparta, who made peace between me and the other fellow, that he was slightly wounded on one hand.

The judge who was interrogating Longhi on October 25 – and who'd already asked him about a whole series of earlier violent incidents Longhi had been involved in – wasn't interested in the sports fans' brawl and might've realized Longhi was trying to lead him off the track. Or even make him look a fool. He'd just asked Longhi if he knew a Flavio Canonico and Longhi, who was an old hand at these interrogations, had replied that

> unless I'm given further identifying details I neither know him personally nor do I know who he may be.

Had he been involved in

> any episode involving verbal and physical violence with any person in the month of July?

the judge had persisted, eliciting the story of the fight at the football match. *Not that episode,* said the judge, refusing to be distracted, but *another one near the Scrofa?* meaning the street leading to San Luigi dei Francesi, palazzo Madama and palazzo Giustiniani. *Toward the statue of Pasquino?* – near piazza Navona, where people pasted up their anonymous satires on matters like the pope's getting his hands on the Cenci money. Had Longhi said to any person *A penny each to the dickheads,* and if so what response had he received? *Sir,* Longhi replied, presumably drawing himself up to his full height,

> I was walking in the street with certain friends of mine and in the course of conversation I remarked to them that dickheads were worth a penny each. And a passer by, who was accompanied by a certain painter, took this as referring to himself and said to me – and I wasn't speaking to him, neither had I ever met him before – that he ate dickheads like me for breakfast. We came to blows and we parted and I went about my business, because after the exchange of blows the other person picked up some stones to throw, but didn't do so because we'd left … nothing else occurred between him and me.

Had anyone else, the judge asked, come to blows with the said person? *I saw nobody apart from the two who then left*, said Longhi. Asked for names, Longhi said

> With him – that is, with the fellow who got in the fist fight with me – was a painter called Marco Tullio, and with me there was the painter M, who left.

Was M carrying a weapon at the time?

> At that time the said M was convalescent, however he had his boy carry his sword and the boy was with him with the sword when the said fight took place, but the said mr M never drew it from its sheath ... as the said mr M was leaving my adversary drew his sword from its sheath and I don't know what he did with it then, whether he raised it against me ... the said mr M was so sick he could hardly stand on his feet ... when he saw [the other's] sword unsheathed M went about his business ... I don't know whether [the other] was wounded because with me he only traded punches ...

Architect Longhi was a violent man currently out on bail. The law was catching up with him around this time over a long series of assaults and brawls that often seemed to involve the same people in recurrent faceoffs. The criminal records implied but never explained, mainly because Longhi was so consistently unhelpful and misleading in his answers, a set of factional allegiances and more or less stable antagonisms. Onorio Longhi only ever gave anything away when he knew his interrogator already knew the answers, and then his own responses turned minimal, cautious and legalistic, as they did when he was asked about the incident involving M. Some of the incidents might have been merely casual, though you never knew. Two days earlier he'd admitted under questioning that

> about a month ago I bawled out a boy and kicked him in the arse, a greengrocer's boy at Macel de' Corvi, because he'd knocked down a young page of mine ... it's not true I hit him on the head.

Fruiterers' boys in Rome were a lot more likely to be beaten up than painted. When the judge asked him about the night of the dickheads, Longhi, who revealed himself rather less subtle an operator than he might've liked to believe, took some pains first to conceal M's presence and then to minimize M's part in what he described as a fight between himself and the unknown person met by chance. That Longhi was covering for M, who couldn't have been quite so unsteady on his legs that night as Longhi was suggesting, became clear when he let fall that it was cardinal Del Monte's chief of staff who'd settled things between the opponents and got a promise from all parties to suspend the violence. *I believe*, Longhi added with a casualness that would've fooled no one and certainly not this interrogator.

Flavio Canonico, the unknown person, turned out to be a former sergeant of the prison guard at the castel Sant' Angelo, and M had wounded him slightly on the hand with his sword. Onorio Longhi was named as M's accomplice. Three and a half months later, on 7 February 1601, criminal proceedings under way against M for assaulting Canonico were suspended, peace having been made between the parties. In playing down M's role in the incident, Longhi had also concealed whatever part was played by the painter Marco Tullio. This painter would later die young and receive a brief but emotional tribute from Giovanni Baglione that made great play on the never achieved *honours* implied by his surname Onori, and saluted him as a youth of great promise whose death before his time *has left the bitterness of desire*. He'd been mentioned in police records as having been with the courtesan Anna Bianchini, M's model and a girl who hung out with painters, when she was arrested once four years earlier. He was identified by Baglione as a young painter who worked with Federico Zuccari and whose career was promoted by Zuccari. Any young painter known that July as Zuccari's boy would've given M and his friends grounds for intense hostility. July was the month Zuccari had publicly sneered at M's first major work as a ripoff from Giorgione. July was the month Longhi witnessed its payment. Longhi's street talk insult about *dickheads* had surely been directed at the painter and not the unfortunate former guard who got in the way. M drew his sword because M knew his was the honour to defend.

Although in the Canonico case the real object of interest was M, and M's trial was later aborted, the judge on October 25 wasn't quite finished with Longhi, even after he'd wrung from him the key admissions about M and his sword and the role of Del Monte's administrator in brokering peace. Just before he let Longhi go on this day, the interrogating judge swung back abruptly to Longhi's account of the violent tussle in piazza Navona, the story Longhi had used as a smokescreen to cover M, the story the judge had tersely said earlier he wasn't interested in. Now the judge asked him if he knew the name of *the person from Terni* he'd fought with, and the names of his own associates that day in July when swords were drawn at the football game. He was fishing for the name of Ranuccio Tomassoni from Terni but Longhi wasn't biting. Longhi replied that *according to what he'd understood* the person from Terni's name was *Luca Ciancarotta* and that as for himself, there was nobody with him. *I went alone to that place.* The judge, who perhaps found the name of the otherwise unrecorded *Luke Broken-shank* ever so faintly implausible, then asked Longhi if he'd ever had

> any disagreement and argument with a certain Ranuccio Tomassoni from Terni, and if so when and for what reason.

Longhi replied promptly

> No sir. I've never had any argument with Ranuccio Tomassoni from Terni … he's a friend of mine and in the past there's never been any disagreement whatever.

Promptly but not entirely convincingly.

> Had he ever tried to attack the said Ranuccio, either alone or with associates and if so with what person or persons?

Again, Longhi protested too much.

> My dear sir, there's no such thing because as I said Ranuccio is a friend of mine. Only a few days ago he had dinner with me, and I neither argued with him nor assaulted him.

Longhi must have been questioned over three days, because the end of the court record is dated October 27. He was now dismissed and given three days to prepare a defence. Why did the judge want to know about Longhi and Tomassoni? No records were found to answer that question. None of it seemed to matter – these were ordinary pointless clashes between Rome's sexually active and socially insecure males. Artists who wanted to be taken seriously as fighting men – people like Longhi and M – were peculiarly liable to friction with military people like the Tomassoni brothers who lacked outlets for their skills. Unspoken matters of sex, politics and art – things nobody would mention to the cops – made the clashes explosive. None of it'd matter, except that six years later the interminable chain of intermittent street clashes and growing mutual loathing would erupt in a prolonged and savage group duel that left Ranuccio Tomassoni dead, M and another badly wounded – M, Longhi and a Tomassoni brother would be fugitives, M with a price on his head.

WHAT WAS WRONG with M now? He'd painted himself looking puffy, aged, sick and distraught in the middle of 1600. Answering questions about an episode of street violence that'd taken place later the same month, Onorio Longhi was now making much of the fact that M was *recovering from an illness* and *hardly able to stand on his feet on account of his illness*. He'd only have made such play on this defence if it were generally known and verifiable. The boy carrying his sword was a detail people would remember. And Longhi's story of the fight had a certain inner coherence that suggested Longhi had indeed provoked it and that M had only intervened at the end, grabbing his sword and lashing out in a rage, catching one of the others *on the hand*.

M really had been sick. Giulio Mancini the art collector was Del Monte's physician and had treated him. Mancini wouldn't mention the illness in his notes on M's life and Mancini was a good doctor – he evidently found nothing remarkable in whatever made M sick in 1600. Whether M's new illness had anything to do with his stay in the Consolation hospital six years before, or the slightly malarial lividness of the *Sick self portrait* of that earlier time, or whether it was a psychophysical collapse brought on by the stress of the revolutionary effort involved in the *Matthew* paintings, M wasn't in good shape to deal with the sudden clamour of notoriety, neither the art world jealousies nor the inane adulation and imitation.

In 1600 M could afford the expensive and *noble* clothes Bellori described, and to keep a boy servant. He could start looking and acting like Onorio Longhi's social equal. M cared deeply about rank, or at least about being properly respected, but not about bourgeois style or comfort. It was typical of someone suddenly flush with money to spend it on things he was meant to want but didn't really care about – *once he'd put on a suit he never took it off until it fell off him in tatters*. Three years earlier he'd been described to the police as dressed *not too tidily in black* and wearing *slightly ripped black stockings*. Nothing much was changed outwardly. And now in the year of his vast success Longhi was always there too, present when the contracts were signed in the offices and when the swords were drawn in the street. Longhi had a powerful sense of his own worth and an explosive temper from way back, and as M's elder and more professionally established friend he'd've been the leader in the early days. In the summer of 1600 M's sudden wealth and fame might've urged Longhi on to even more extreme acts of self assertion than usual. And M in a weakened state was suddenly finding himself the object of unwanted new attentions of several kinds. Who egged on whom hardly mattered. M and Longhi were a volatile combination.

The clash with Marco Tullio Onori and Flavio Canonico marked M's entry, at Longhi's side, into the Roman criminal records. Before that there'd been only the routine arrest two years earlier for being abroad armed at night and his vivid nonappearance in the 1597 incident of street fighting in the via della Scrofa near San Luigi. The violence began in perfect synchrony with his public emergence as a painter, and more soon followed. On November 19 that year, while the charges against M were going ahead over this July incident, a complaint was laid against M by Girolamo Spampa, who – in the uncertain nineteenth century transcription of the record – reported that he'd been attacked by M the previous Friday evening on his way home from studying at the academy. He'd stopped at the candle seller's in via della Scrofa to get some candles when

> the defendant came up with a stick and started hitting me with it and hit me quite a few times. I tried to defend myself ... some butchers came with lanterns and then M pulled out his sword and hit me with it. I fended it off with my cloak, which it slashed as you can see, and then he ran off ...

Spampa was insulted as well as attacked. Being whacked from behind with a stick and the flat of a sword humiliated him, made him morally and socially unworthy of the gentleman's proper frontal use of fists, or the point or the cutting edge of a sword. There was no other testimony. It looked like more factional violence in the art world, and the timing linked this episode too to the acclaim and jealousy released by the *Matthew* paintings, still M's only public work. M was defending his art against people he saw as its vile deniers or maybe worse. Once again the object of his violence was a younger painter linked to the academy – assuming Canonico had just got in the way of Marco Tullio. And both injured parties withdrew their cases against M within two weeks of each other in early 1601 in exchange for M's promise not to attack them again. It looked a little as though someone had leant on the victims. Someone was cleaning up after M.

The end of the holy year and the start of 1601 were something of a legal watershed for others as well as M. Two days before Spampa laid his charge of violence by M, Onorio Longhi found a Milanese sculptor to underwrite his promise not to molest any of the half a dozen miscellaneous people he was apparently then in conflict with. There was Flavio Canonico of the *dickhead* incident. Another was the former manservant he'd been fighting with for years over the alleged theft of his possessions while Longhi was away at the wars – *You fucking thief I'll kill you with my own hands*, he'd said to his former employee. Another his former landlady.

> Open up you stupid whore … and if you don't shut up, if you say another word I'll break this sword over your head,

he'd said to her. Two were the unknown father and son from Bergamo. And the last named in the court records was Ranuccio Tomassoni. And two days before this a witness in the stolen property case had identified Longhi as the person he'd seen playing tennis in the Panatani alley and heard speaking – in a raised voice, presumably – *with signor Ranuccio at the rotunda*. What Longhi was discussing with the younger man he'd strongly protested three weeks earlier was *a friend of his* and whom the court now deemed in danger of attack by Longhi, was never explained.

Ranuccio Tomassoni, the youngest son of the chief of the guards at the castel Sant' Angelo – where Canonico had served as a sergeant – was also floundering, at the time the court considered him under threat from his good friend Onorio Longhi, in the fast shifting legal and sentimental sands of Fillide Melandroni's bashing of Tella Brunori – tearing her hair out and trying to slash her with a knife while Prudenza was in bed with Ranuccio. Fillide was M's friend and model, but whether M came into this wasn't clear. It was all very complicated, lustful and foulmouthed. It was very violent in a seemingly random way and almost unimaginable as a milieu or a moment conducive to the reinvention of European art.

SOMEONE ASKED ANNIBALE Carracci what he thought of M's painting of Fillide as *Judith* hacking off Holofernes' head – soon after it was painted most likely – and he said *I don't know what to say except that it's too natural*. The remark – one verbally challenged painter on another – was coming from the painter who fifteen years earlier, when

M had yet to even start as an apprentice in Milan, had in Bologna been charging into the effete unrealities of *the manner* with a series of works – a *Butcher's shop*, a *Bean eater*, a *Boy drinking* and a *Dead Christ* as a shocking bloodied open mouthed corpse, all from the early eighties – that were far more *natural* in their abrasively everyday subjects and vigorous, relaxed immediacy of treatment than anything M had done by 1600, or would ever do. When in 1583 Carracci made the move from this real life work to religious commissions at the age of twenty three – the same inevitable move M was now making – he did a *Crucifixion with saints* altarpiece that drew howls of protest, much as M's work later would in Rome. The archbishop of Bologna was Paleotti and Paleotti had just the year before laid down the counter reformation law in his *Discourse on sacred and profane images*. Carracci's Christ was a stocky dying peasant hoisted against a leaden sky, and the faces around his knees were faces from the streets of Bologna. There wasn't a glimmer of the transcendental in the scene. The painting lacked smoothness and finish. It was done in the same strong strokes that Carracci used to catch real life on canvas. The whole thing was utterly lacking in *decorum*. When it came to being *natural*, Annibale Carracci had a few credentials of his own.

He was eleven years older than M. As a restlessly innovatory assimilator and combiner of influences – Venetian light, Lombard reality, the central Italian art of drawing – he'd come a long way already when he turned up in Rome in 1595 to work for the Farnese family – specifically for young cardinal Odoardo. In Rome Carracci discovered and assimilated the great art of the surviving marble sculptures from ancient Rome. Carracci also found the monumental nudes of Michelangelo Buonarotti's Vatican frescos. For Annibale Carracci these new discoveries were timely, even necessary, because his main job in Rome was to fresco the ceiling and walls of the great gallery of the palazzo Farnese with a joyously various celebration of *the power of love*. The love was, for once, profane. Bellori later tried to read Carracci's masterpiece as an allegory of the struggle between sacred love and profane, but the supporting evidence he marshalled was extremely thin. Carracci's exuberant scenes of the loves of the pagan gods, taken for the side panels from Ovid's *Metamorphoses*, under a vast and tipsy wedding procession fresco on the ceiling of the *Marriage of Bacchus and Ariadne*, had no sacred component. By May 1601, the huge ceiling fresco was finished after several years of more or less singlehanded work by Annibale. Nominally it celebrated the marriage of Odoardo's elder brother Ranuccio Farnese, the duke of Parma, with Clement's great niece Margherita Aldobrandini.

It was a marriage that needed a boost from art. Ranuccio was already thirty when it was contracted, and had nearly died of an illness in 1598. The Farnese dynasty needed an heir. They'd failed in a lengthy bid for the hand of Maria de' Medici, whose uncle the grand duke Ferdinando I was saving her for Henri IV of France, and other moves toward the duke of Bavaria's daughter or perhaps an Austrian Hapsburg girl had stalled when the dying Felipe II of Spain failed to come through with the massive dowry required. The Farnese family needed a good dowry after the financial drain of the old duke's ruinous military campaign against the protestants in the Low Countries. The Aldobrandini family, former functionaries of the Farnese dynasty, were a social comedown but while Clement was pope their money supply was practically inexhaustible. The Aldobrandinis, for their part, were making the most of the papacy and they too had originally been aiming higher. Clement had wanted to marry Margherita to Henri IV himself, who wasn't interested, ditto Ferdinando I de' Medici's eldest son and the duke of Savoy. The Aldobrandinis were *parvenus*, the Farnese line strapped for cash and the marriage a last resort for both sides.

The Aldobrandinis made the mistake of making the first move and in reply the Farnese family demanded an immense dowry. Negotiations were tense, and when they were settled in September 1599 the bride's father complained to his future son in law about the *avidity* displayed. Del Monte immediately wrote to Ferdinando I that the dowry was *secretly far more than it appeared*, and the Tuscan resident in Rome estimated that the Aldobrandinis were paying the almost unbelievable sum of three hundred and fifty thousand scudi for their marriage into a ruling family – the Venetian ambassadors thought even more – and *everyone knows that in the end it'll all come from the Holy See*. The pope had to use the Jesuit theologian Roberto Bellarmino, mediator in the Bruno heresy case earlier that year, as a negotiator. Del Monte gleefully reported to Florence that Ranuccio announced his engagement *to his holiness's niece* in December 1599 without once naming his fiancée's family. The bride's father was the pope's nephew Giovanfrancesco, who got the Cenci estate for a song a couple of months earlier. He'd worked for Ranuccio as an estate manager and ten years earlier he'd been caught thieving from the Farnese accounts and jailed. The matter was hushed up, but was one of the reasons Ranuccio was determined to screw all he could get out of the Aldobrandinis now. The bride was twelve and still prepubescent when the marriage was celebrated in May 1600. Her only sibling Silvestro nearly matched this precociousness the next year when his great uncle

Clement made him a cardinal at fourteen. Margherita's wedding to Ranuccio Farnese was a low key affair on the pope's orders. She cried all through the ceremony, Del Monte reported, and wished she could've been a nun. The wedding procession moved through Rome under pouring rain. As a dynastic breeder the bride was damaged goods, much operated on as a child in the genital area and unlikely to bear children, a fact kept hidden during the prenuptial bargaining. The first ten years of marriage were a series of abortions and miscarriages, and when she finally gave birth to a live son in 1610, he was an epileptic deaf mute. Only in 1612 was a viable heir to the duke of Parma born, and by then Ranuccio had been cursing the Aldobrandinis for years for cheating him in marriage as well as business.

None of this brokered wretchedness emerged in the joyous pagan erotic energy of Annibale Carracci's frescos. They decorated the gallery that held the Farnese collection of ancient sculpture and played among the appearances of real, sculpted and painted nude figures in a vertiginously witty *trompe l'oeil* that made the most of the carnal opulence Carracci had found in Phidias and Michelangelo. They were an amazing anomaly in the art of Clement's Rome, and one the man who commissioned them, Ranuccio's younger brother the cardinal Odoardo, was anxious Clement should never see. Odoardo had already clashed with the pope over the female nude on the tomb of his forebear pope Paul III, and put up with a whole series of other small humiliations inflicted on him by the vindictive pope Aldobrandini, who resented Farnese wealth and power. Nobody doubted where Clement would've stood on *The marriage of Bacchus and Ariadne*. Immoral carnal pagan deities were the kind of thing cardinal Paleotti had denounced in art even more fervently than the indecorous naturalism of Carracci's youthful work in Bologna.

> Christ our lord shed his blood in order to extinguish their memory totally, and now it seems that many Christians instead of painting that Christ who demolished the Joves and the Junos with the holy cross, are trying to revive their memory with chisel and paintbrush.

The cardinal nephew Pietro Aldobrandini was another matter. As a heavy consumer of sex and art he appreciated such things and was invited to the unveiling of the ceiling at the end of May 1601. He was so impressed he immediately presented Carracci with a gold chain worth two hundred scudi and commissioned a painting from him.

The *avviso* that reported this spoke of a new flowering of art in Rome, *no less than in the past*, and added that

> Now we await the completion of the hall on the capitol by the cavalier Giuseppe, the two paintings that M is doing for the chapel of the late monsignor Cerasi the treasurer and the main painting in the same chapel by the above mentioned Carracci, all three paintings in short being quite excellent and beautiful.

M had been the sensation of Roman art for less than a year. Already he had a rival. The *Matthew* paintings were last year's sensation. The Farnese gallery ceiling was this year's, bigger and newer and easier to see. The report caught a general eagerness among the connoisseurs to see the work of Rome's two most exciting new painters facing off in the same space, just as Cerasi and Vincenzo Giustiniani had anticipated the year before. The report's loose phrasing managed simultaneously to imply that Carracci's altarpiece wasn't yet finished and that M's side paintings were. This was doubly inaccurate, though the state of work in progress was hardly clear. The *avviso* also guilelessly conveyed the intense awareness of each other that M and Carracci must've had by now, an awareness that flowed into the way each handled his commission. They'd known about each other long before the public knew either. The *avviso* also referred glancingly to something that'd happened at the beginning of that same month, before the wretched wedding and the unveiling of the pagan marriage carnival. The treasurer Cerasi had died on May 3 at the age of fifty seven, and the art for the chapel where he was now entombed was in the hands of his heirs, the governors of the Consolation hospital. An earlier *avviso* reported this on May 5, mentioning that Cerasi was buried in the

> very beautiful chapel that he was having done ... by the hand of the very famous painter M ...

and not mentioning Carracci because Carracci's big moment was still a few weeks off.

Annibale Carracci's painting was ready early in 1601 to be seen by Cerasi before he died. It was full of an energy that portended the Farnese ceiling. The colouring was bright and light – Annibale's work was getting lighter as M's darkened – the clean *hard shelled* surface enhanced by painting on wood, the figures and the composition idealized, sculptural, muscular. Carracci was assimilating Raphael as well as Michelangelo and classical sculpture, but there was also a glance at M here in the clean finish, the drapery, something real in the onlookers' faces. Carracci's was a frank and untroubled performance. M got into difficulties. Somebody – and since the client was dead it wasn't clear who – didn't like his two paintings. Baglione, always quick to serve up the bad news on M, claimed that

> he did these pictures first in another style, but the owner didn't like them and cardinal Sannesio took them, and M did the ones that can be seen there now – in oil because he didn't work in any other way. Fame and fortune, as they say, carried him through.

A Sannesio family inventory did later list

> two large paintings on wooden panels, one showing a saint Peter crucified and the other the conversion of saint Paul in gold frames.

The rare use of wood identified these as M's originals, done like Carracci's altarpiece on panels because the chapel was damp and the very resinous cypress wood was resistant. The *Peter* on wood later disappeared. Why weren't they liked? The contract M signed in late September 1600 gave him eight months to deliver, until late May. Cerasi died that month and probably never saw them. Giacomo Sannesio was a good friend and *familiar* of life loving and art loving Pietro Aldobrandini and three years later a cardinal himself. It looked as though the problem never was a big one, and that Sannesio simply wanted to get his own hands on these paintings, maybe taking advantage of the confusion when Cerasi died. M's first painting of *Saul* on the road to Damascus went straight into Sannesio's private collection and M replaced it with a canvas that was far more disconcerting than the first – and went up without a murmur of protest from anyone and stayed there. M took a cut in his fee – he got three hundred scudi instead of the stipulated four – maybe for being six months late, maybe for not supplying the stipulated sketch in advance, maybe for having worked on canvas, and maybe because the *owner* needed a little financial inducement not to like the first versions. Giacomo Sannesio would've been quick to make the necessary adjustment.

A year earlier M had rethought *Matthew killed* on a single canvas, and the evidence of his travail was buried under the surface of his finished painting. When he did *Saul* now, M did a fully realized first work before doing an utterly different second version. The second *Saul* on canvas showed how conservative and unresolved the first version on wood was – the change in the two paintings done weeks apart revealed the volcanic discontinuities underlying M's work. The first *Saul* was M looking back at his past. It wasn't even dark, and under its bright surface and the frantic energy of its composition it glowed with the colours of Lombard nostalgia – outdoors always meant home. Like the flight into Egypt, the road to Damascus went through M's childhood country. The foreground was all arching twisting bodies – Saul improbably half supine – how was he holding himself up, now that his hands were shielding his eyes? – his muscular grey horse out of mannerist central casting arching and foaming at the mouth, the old soldier's contorted trunk and a faint cowering figure behind him, an all too bodily and fairly uncouth looking Christ in a nosedive to the ground, barely restrained by a plump young angel. The streaked dawn light in the distance appeared above flat Lombard plains, and the splintered tree Christ and his angel had just crashed through was a lovingly rendered Lombardy poplar. The painting was all agitated detail. It was marvellously done but busy – the hugely plumed helmets, the flapping leather ribbons of Saul's Roman skirt and the glimpse of his scarlet cloak, the rearing horse's mane and tail, the shaking poplar leaves and the torn branch, the old soldier's beard and sleeve – none of it showed what M'd lately discovered about the concentrating strengths of darkness around lit bodies. M was no nearer to solving the problem of action than in *Matthew killed* – the same embarrassment of frozen turmoil was now set in a strangely elegiac early morning aspic. M couldn't allow himself a lesser painter's solutions. His own sense of the real allowed him none of the fakery others got away with.

That was the first time. What made M see Saul so differently now? A look at Annibale Carracci's altarpiece. This was the painting his own had to cohabit with, and like M's first *Saul*, Carracci's painting was bright, packed, solid, energetic. Its strong sculptural design made it all the harder not to see the whole thing was deeply, truly inane – the virgin breaststroking her way upward through the air with a slight smirk on her face, eyeballs rolling heavenward, half a dozen bodiless winged heads of bellcheeked cherubs peeping out from beneath her armpits and her feet, her gravity defying drapery fluttering upward as if she were falling not rising, the onlookers looking like they'd seen it all before, one of them apparently signalling to a concealed crane driver winching the virgin to the heights. And who was that more voluptuous figure cleaving to the virgin like a Siamese twin? It was all quite free of indecorousness, lasciviousness, superfluousness, humorousness, seductiveness, ideological incorrectness. It was a wholly professional job. Annibale Carracci had come a long way from his Bolognese *Butcher's shop*. This was utterly unreal and very Roman – the extreme logical consequence in art of the kind of compromise M had just made in *Saul*. Carracci was as good as it got. To get away with this kind of scenic unreality you had to generalize, surrender or sublimate your feeling for the textures of the perceptible world. And there was the problem of movement. Carracci had simply generalized it out of existence – a woman floating up into the sky surrounded by a lot of winged babies' heads wasn't susceptible to a quick reality check – while M's first *Saul* looked real enough to be merely hectic. So now he threw it all out. If M couldn't – in the same mimetic act – paint from life and paint action, then action had to go.

The horse said it all. The horse wasn't in the original story. The Jewish functionary Saul, on the road during a search and destroy mission for the Roman empire against Christians in Damascus, was simply surrounded by light. He *fell to the earth*, heard the voice of Jesus, remained blind for three days and had to be led the rest of the way to Damascus where he became Paul the Christian convert and ideologue – although the unseen Jesus's remark to the sprawling Saul that *it is hard for thee to kick against the pricks* implied the presence of a mount that'd done just that. A rearing horse had long been standard in treatments of Saul. Michelangelo's Vatican fresco had one, Raphael had one and there was a splendid one in Milan M knew by the Lombard painter Moretto. The visible presence of Jesus was normal too, with or without heavenly host. A rearing horse didn't lend itself to painting from life and although M scored lines to fix all the human models on the cypress panel, he made none for the horse because the rearing horse was never there. It was invented, or worse, copied from someone else. It was a fantasy horse.

If M was going to have a horse it had to be a real one. A real horse meant not a rearing Arab charger but some workhorse that could be hired from a local carter for the necessary time and led clattering up Del Monte's stone stairs into the studio where the lighting was controlled and the painting materials kept. Which is what M got. A somewhat restive carthorse, skinny, skewbald, swaybacked and large headed, feeling the heat – M was working on *Saul* over the summer of 1601 – and the confinement, drooling over its bit, weary with standing still and concerned, in a horselike way, with finding a solid uncluttered space to plant its right foreleg, disturbed by the waving limbs of the sprawling model playing Saul under its feet. A horse looked an awful lot bigger close up in a dark confined space and M played on that. Only a perfunctory boulder or two now remained of *the road to Damascus*. Forget high noon. The new work played on confinement and darkness by going in even closer and working from somewhere down near the floored Saul. M might've seen it only after the horse was led in. He left traces of a quite different work under the surface. An incision in the priming around the horse's raised hoof fixed its position because this time the horse was real. The blinding heavenly light had dwindled to a rather feeble lantern glow. The powerful external force was gone, everything was interiorized and quite still. The new painting emanated silence.

It was very indecorous.

> The rear parts of horses and other animals are never seen frontally but placed behind, as a part unworthy to be seen.

Saul's blind eyes made his cropped head look even more military, like a Roman bust, as he looked up sightlessly into an undifferentiated forest of bare legs, the barefoot groom's with their ropey veins and horny toenails and the horse's. How he'd got down there wasn't clear – it looked like *an accident in the stables*. The weary beast standing over Paul had thrown nobody. Paul's red cloak, plumed helmet and the absurd ribboned skirt were props recycled from the first version, but now the brilliant red had faded to dun, the leather ribbons were less noticeable than the horse's dangling reins, and the helmet almost lost in the darkest bottom corner. Paul might've been opening his arms to Jesus or groping for a helping hand up, from the intent and placid groom, who hadn't even noticed him lying there flat on his back. You saw it all at a raked angle as you looked at Annibale Carracci's *Virgin* in the narrow chapel. Paul's prostrate body was directly aligned with your own line of sight, and the suffering carthorse sideways on. In the play of light and darkness, Paul, horse and picture plane made a three dimensional vision swung out forty five degrees toward you. This wasn't the kind of setup the theoreticians of perspective had foreseen. It sucked your eyes away from the tasteful Carracci altarpiece into an hallucinatory *mise en scène* that had the pony's bony workaday rump projecting massively and indecorously toward Annibale's glossy, demure and untouchable heaven heading virgin. From the altar what you mostly saw was horse's arse. *The history is quite without action* was all Bellori was able to say about it – he had no words for this life size view of a tired carthorse's hind quarters. Bellori wasn't the only one to have a problem with the immortal skewbald. Neither did Mancini or Baglione mention it. Almost nobody bothered to copy it. Annibale Carracci was probably the only person in Rome with an eye to see what M had done to him.

In *Peter* opposite, M worked around the same life changing insight. He painted stillness, not action. He saw art lay not in the history you *told* but in the human truth you *showed*. It was the artist's old truth, a lesson that had to be relearnt for every time and every art. In *Peter* M dramatized a reality that matched the business of horse care, which was the sheer hard labour of torture and execution. *Peter* was worked out as intimately as *Saul* – no transcendental presence, no onlooker, no witness to the killing of the old man beyond yourself, and you were taken in as close as anyone could get. It was another strictly private event. The executioners weren't grimacing nude thugs like Matthew's assassins. The three faceless labourers hoisting Peter upside down on the cross he was already nailed to – two faces turned down and away, one caught in deep shadow – were concentrating on the job in hand, absorbed in the effort of getting him in place to die. The immobility in this painting wasn't the stillness in *Saul* but the momentary stasis of mechanics – Peter's weight on the massive cross meeting the muscular effort being made to raise him. Peter himself was a well known painter's model from the via Margutta nearby instantly recognizable to the first people who saw the painting in Santa Maria del Popolo. The others were likely neighbours too.

Darkness was closing in here, nothing visible beyond the four figures, the cross, the rope, the shovel, an abandoned greenish cloak and a small boulder like a loaf of bread that might've been the same one seen in *Saul*. The figures themselves, compact, busy, practised and impersonal as nurses, worked in brisk physical intimacy with the old man they were putting to death. One wrapped his arms around Peter's legs to steady the cross, the other pulling on the rope was using his own thigh to steady the victim, the face of the kneeling shoveller with his shirt rucked up under the cross was inches from Peter's. The image of this effort was skewed obliquely and as daringly as *Saul's*, bringing the cross's upright nearly into line with a viewer's sight, so that Peter was seen feet first and the figures emerged from the darkness with a rounded solidity. No part of which was more rounded or more solid than the kneeling labourer's arse projecting hugely into the viewer's face, just above – in the near bottom corner at eye level – the filthiest sole of a bare foot M ever painted. The still point around which the visible effort pivoted was Peter's face – M's first rendering of a really old man, the beginning of a long imagining of age. Peter's fading eye brought back to sharpness for a moment, not by pain or fear but by the sudden bodily disorientation, was something of the order of *Pray you, undo this button*. Like Lear's this was a modern death – unmediated, unadorned, unexplained, a death without promise of transcendence, without vindication, death as nothing other than itself. It was another amazing discontinuity. Years seemed to have passed between the first *Saul* and the second, done weeks apart. Now *Peter* looked like nothing so much as M's paintings of age and death that were years away – it was a look into the future of M's art.

In June while he was starting the second versions on canvas of the Cerasi *Peter* and *Saul* paintings, M signed a contract for a new work and it referred to him as *resident in the palace of … cardinal Mattei* – where the new contract was signed. It wasn't clear whether the move was definitive – in October he had another brush with the law for carrying an unlicensed weapon at night, and told the police he was *on cardinal Del Monte's payroll*. The arresting officer wasn't convinced and jailed him anyway. It did look as though M left the palazzo Madama in the first part of 1601 and that he spent the next couple of years with the Mattei brothers. No contrary evidence emerged, and he did a lot of work for Ciriaco Mattei in this time. Mario had lately left to marry *so he could live more quietly* – it looked the moment for a change of life and a flexing of his suddenly won independence of Del Monte. Other things were changing too. On the personal front M's immediate future was being signalled, just as he signed the new contract at the Matteis', by the puffy faced angel with reddish brown hair and a broad nose in the first *Saul*. He came floating into the painting's top right hand corner and stopped the fatal nosedive of the dark and shaggy plummeting Christ. It might've been an image of the boy's role in the life of dark and shaggy plummeting M. The tawny haired angel's name was Francesco Boneri, Cecco for short, and he was about twelve when he entered M's life the year Mario got married. Whether Cecco also moved into the cardinal's household with M wasn't recorded. If he wasn't living there on a permanent basis, Cecco certainly spent a fair amount of time in M's studio there over the next year, because he spent a lot of time being painted nude by M. The Matteis soon got to know him pretty well in any case, since M's second full frontal nude of the boy went straight into Ciriaco's collection. Cecco's arrival was about to tie M's art and his life into an inextricable knot.

7

ROME 1601–1602

Maffeo Barberini
Matthew & angel I
Matthew & angel II

S UMMER TIME WAS fun time and nobody was more aware
of this than the younger members of the college of cardinals.
The wealthier and social minded set. In 1601 M was being
found more and more often in their retinues – street fighting at night
wasn't the only relief from the mental drama of the Cerasi canvases.
The social set included young Odoardo Farnese, whose gallery in
the finest palace in Rome Annibale Carracci had just covered with a
riot of neopagan nudes. He was three years younger than Alessandro
Peretti da Montalto, whose great uncle pope Sixtus V Peretti had made
him cardinal when he was fifteen years old and who was now fabulously rich. One of Montalto's young courtiers had described him in
spring as

> a soft youth, and so given over to pleasures that he neglects
> almost everything else

and in summer he was more so. Odoardo was two years younger than
Pietro Aldobrandini, who'd been made a cardinal by his uncle the
present pope and was rapidly becoming fabulously rich and whose
niece had just married Odoardo's brother and who was nearing thirty
like the painter M. The eldest of these friends was cardinal Alessandro d' Este who was thirty two. No more than five years separated
the eldest from the youngest of these pleasure lovers.

Francesco Maria Bourbon Del Monte was a good deal older and nothing like as rich as the younger ones, but great company and he liked the younger cardinals and he was very well connected. They were a close little group and enjoyed sharing the good times with each other. On the first Sunday of July that summer, Odoardo Farnese had had them all to lunch in his garden, where an *avviso* reported that they ate *splendidly*. The next day, the *avviso* went on, *they all did the same at signor Marzio Colonna's palace at Santi Apostoli*. The next Sunday they were all at a big wrestling tournament put on in the evening by the Colonnas outside their palace. One of Odoardo Farnese's grooms was the winner, but the cardinal himself had left for Parma the day before and missed the triumph. He was still away on August 9 when cardinal Montalto's brother the marchese Peretti invited them all to another garden banquet, for which the host

> had ordered in at great expense from many places many different kinds of really excellent fish.

Not everyone was a cardinal at the seafood barbecue but nobody brought his wife. Nobody ever did. These were male occasions and the only women ever present were *honest courtesans*, who were strictly professional girls, ones who had enough class and cultivation to grace high society as well as satisfy the guests. One of the most sought after girls in the Rome of 1601 was at the lunch that day. Her name turned up in the police report of an incident that took place when some of the guests decided later that afternoon to go for a jaunt outside the city. The officer in command of the checkpoint at the porta Pinciana reported that three coaches and some men on horseback were approaching toward evening *opposite the gateway to cardinal Del Monte's vineyard* when the first coach galloped through the road block as its passengers screamed to the driver to stop. As the officer's men overtook it, three girls jumped from the thundering coach – shrieking with laughter presumably – and were apprehended. One of them, who was very flirtatious and insolent to the commander – *if you want to beat me up, go ahead officer* – was Domenica Calvi, known as Menica from Siena, even more familiarly Menicuccia, around sixteen years of age, nearly two of these spent on the game in Rome. The other two were her sister and another colleague.

> When I saw you outside I was screaming to the coachman to stop but he didn't want to because he was scared of the cops.

She'd provoked the whole incident to impress the cops, whom she knew, with her influential connexions. Now she was mocking them. The commanding officer's report doggedly reported her words.

> *Lieutenant I kept telling the coachman to stop but he refused to listen to me.*

And when [he] told her *You've got to go to jail* she said *I want to go by coach and not on foot.* A lot of gentlemen had reached us by now from the two coaches she'd left behind and they lent her a coach and so she was driven to jail ... when she got inside the said Menica told one of the gentlemen

> *Oh, Sir, I left my silver cup with the prawns in the coach, see that it doesn't get lost.*

When Menica was interrogated by the magistrate the next day, she naturally kept her mouth shut about the cardinals she and her sisters in arms had been in the coach with, and apart from remembering a *signor Ottavio Doni* she kept her mouth shut too about most of the gentlemen who'd made up their escort. Whether M ever entered into Del Monte's social milieu as part of his retinue on jaunts like this – not particularly likely in the light of his own known social habits – he did at some point get to know Menica Calvi, as he already knew Anna and Fillide, because three years later, under interrogation about his role in a street fight, he insisted to the police that while the rocks were being hurled in the street he'd been chatting with Menicuccia, *who lives in that street,* he added helpfully. Where they'd been heading this summer day was Del Monte's country lodge, the one whose laboratory ceiling M had painted with *Jove, Neptune, Pluto.* It was one of Del Monte's favourite retreats, *a very lovely and delightful place* where he used to invite friends for musical entertainments. It was so delightful that Pietro Aldobrandini four years earlier had decided he wanted it and Del Monte, because his friend was the pope's nephew, had to give it up. Pietro Aldobrandini was like that. Everything he liked he wanted. Everything he wanted he expected to get. It was the whole point of being the cardinal nephew. Del Monte had told Ferdinando I at that time that Aldobrandini had looked out at the villa Medici estate from the verandah of Del Monte's lodge and said loudly *That's the pope's vineyard over there* and then turning toward Frascati had added *And that's the Capranica vineyard and that's the one I want.* A couple of years later in 1599 he'd got another country house and graciously given Del Monte back his own. It was good to have Del Monte on side.

Menica Calvi went on to have a long and brilliant career in Rome, at least as brilliant as the other Siena girl Fillide's, and a lot more soundly managed. And this from starting seven years behind. Menica's adolescent high spirits never frightened off the cardinals or seriously alienated the police. On her way down from Siena in 1599, when she was around fourteen – she was coy about her exact age and always managed to keep it out of the court records – she'd stopped off in Orvieto where a girlfriend from Siena helped her get started professionally. Menica was a fast learner. She knew the value of a good address and when she arrived in Rome in early 1600 she set up in a smart central neighbourhood, in the via del Babuino, renting a big house of several floors with parking for a coach and stables for the horses. She had silver cutlery and crystal wineglasses for her visitors, and she received them in a big fourposter bed topped by a

> domed canopy in turquoise damask silk from Bologna with matching bedcover and surrounds,

with expensive gilt embossed leather on the bedroom walls. Barely a month after Menica's arrival in Rome cardinal d' Este was so struck by her that he sent two of his men around one evening to bring her back to his palace. This was good news and bad news. Menica had only been a year with the cardinal before an *avviso* reported he'd had to return to Modena, *to recuperate from the heavy expenses sustained at court*. Meanwhile Menica was *taking the airs* dressed in *cloth of silver with gold roses*. She was also taken sick at this time, in the spring of 1601, and frightened enough to make her will, but bounced back quickly enough to be surprized a couple of weeks later by the police in the company of two of her regulars, barons who moved in the young cardinals' set. She took up music lessons that spring. *I can't play, only strum*, she explained to a magistrate who wanted to know about the sounds of music coming from her house. Around this time Montalto took up with her as well.

Menica Calvi sustained her brilliant career over many years. She understood about investing her earnings and she died at fifty a very wealthy woman. Over the five years that followed their summer jaunt in 1601 she and M would both come into glancing contact with third parties that implied a common milieu, but the summer outing to Del Monte's place in the country would be the only documented link ever made between them. M had painted Menica's colleague Fillide several times, and another of her neighbours and coworkers would shortly become M's most seen female model. Fillide was identified as Judith, Catherine and Mary Magdalen through the named portrait he also did of her that Vincenzo Giustiniani owned, the one destroyed in Berlin. Nobody ever identified Menica as a model in M's work, though he knew her and she impressed people no less than Fillide did with her looks and intelligence. Maybe he did paint her. In the same *big room* of Vincenzo Giustiniani's gallery, where he hung all his paintings by M, the inventory made when he died listed next to *a portrait of a Courtesan called Fillide ... by the hand of M* another

> half figure portrait of a famous courtesan on canvas still unfinished ... by the hand of M.

This time the girl was unnamed and the painting then lost, but she might've been Menica Calvi and why her portrait should've been the only picture M ever left unfinished was a total mystery. He might've been working on it at a time he suddenly had to leave town.

IN AUTUMN 1600 a poet arrived in Rome – on the run from Naples – who quickly turned his attention to the art sensation of the moment. Giambattista Marino was two years older than M and in the same urgent need of patrons and protectors M had known earlier. Marino's bright career in Naples had run into trouble when he got a wealthy businessman's daughter with child and was jailed in 1598 after her death in a botched abortion. Marino was now under death sentence for falsifying papers to help a friend facing execution – connexions let him escape to Rome. He was a far more accomplished operator than M and soon found a place in the household of monsignor Melchiorre Crescenzi, and M painted portraits of both Marino and Crescenzi before Marino's next career move to the household of Pietro Aldobrandini in 1602. Nearly all M's portraits were later lost, as these two were, and he did quite a few of his friends around this time, as well as the commissioned ones of patrons like Benedetto Giustiniani. He painted Bernardino Cesari, the cavalier d'Arpino's rougher younger brother, Onorio Longhi and his wife Caterina Campani, the courtesan Fillide Melandroni and the other *famous courtesan* who might've been Menica Calvi, maybe his friend the miniaturist Sigismondo Lair.

Nothing in their respective arts joined M and Marino in a common feeling, and no line of Marino's ever implied that M's painting meant more to him than the occasion of a conceit. Marino had a cold and facile mind and a verbal style that had more to do with the cerebral contortions of mannerist painting than anything M was doing in art. He was also monumentally on the make, and after a very bumpy twenty year ride he did eventually make it big, as court poet to Louis XIII of France. Like anyone with an eye for painting, Marino was struck now by the newness and force of M's art and by his success and on some level seemed to really admire him. Marino the poet found in art the pretext for a series of conceits to wrap poems around. Art versus nature was an infinitely variable old standby, and Marino worked and reworked the old ties of poetry and painting with tireless enjoyment of his own ingenuity.

Many years later Marino thought of making a collection of poems called *The gallery* – each poem written on a painting – and he used it to solicit the gift of paintings for possible inclusion in the forthcoming major collection. The promotional plan was coolly received but *The gallery* finally came out in 1620 and included poems on M's *Medusa* shield, on M's portrait of Marino and a third on the portrait of Melchiorre Crescenzi – the poems were probably written when Marino and M were friends in Rome and when M did these paintings. They were merely conceits, like the brief and frigid poem Marino wrote on M's death. M later got a mention – along with Cesari, Baglione and everyone else whose name still came to mind – in the interminable erotic epic *Adonis* he published in Paris in 1623 – a poem unthinkable in turn of the century Rome. The great artistic enthusiasm of Marino's later life was Nicholas Poussin – Marino brought Poussin to Rome and got him to illustrate the *Adonis*, and Poussin abhorred everything M stood for in painting. M surfaced in a few flickering memories of a shared real life in Rome in some of Marino's later sonnets – a game of cards that seemed to be built around the image of M's *Cheats*, dice games, ball games and tennis matches in the campo Marzio, where Marino likely spent time with M and Longhi and their push.

Marino wasn't the only writer excited by M's painting as the seventeenth century began. The poet Aurelio Orsi, who'd got himself a post as the secretary to Odoardo Farnese and was the brother of Prospero Orsi, had earlier written a poem in Latin on the penitent Magdalen. It mentioned the marks of a whipping and was probably done with M's painting of Anna Bianchini in mind. Orsi, whom Mancini thought *a very fine poet in both Latin and the vulgar tongue*, belonged to a group of poets and intellectuals called the accademia degli Insensati. Its most powerful member was Maffeo Barberini, a fast rising young prelate who also fancied himself as a poet and published his first slim volume in 1606. Many years later, when he was the pope Urban VIII who condemned the old blind Galileo, Barberini would be called the *divinus poeta* and encouraged to believe he was a very great poet indeed as the editions of his work multiplied through catholic Europe. Barberini had studied poetry with Aurelio Orsi and maybe the Orsi brothers guided this artistically susceptible young power broker – papal legate to the court of Henri IV in 1601, back to Paris in 1604 as papal nuncio, cardinal by1606 – to sit in 1598 for his portrait by M. These were the days when Prospero

> was acclaiming M's new style and boosting M's work – and getting credit for it – among the leading figures of the court.

M painted Maffeo Barberini at thirty, newly appointed clerk of the chamber by Clement VIII, fleshy, eager, happily crushing his letter of appointment in one sausage fingered hand and pointing dynamically out of the frame with the other, like any good pol in his photo opportunity. Marino faked amazement at M's portrait likenesses – *I saw another self, or rather myself … divided in two* – but Mancini the diagnostician more subtly thought M caught a person's inner life in a way that excluded the kind of superficial likeness that came easily to lesser painters. He was maybe thinking of the Maffeo Barberini portrait in particular, since he was Barberini's doctor – it was quivering with an ambitious thirty year old's eager self confidence. Barberini himself was convinced enough by M's art to commission another painting from M five years later. By 1603 M was famous, his personal life rocky and the second work he did for Barberini was one of the most intimately disturbing things he ever did, a sadistic handling of Cecco Boneri. But in 1598 to commission your portrait by M was an act of cutting edge patronage.

A third member of the Insensati group was a poet from Genoa called Gaspare Murtola – as heavily into the poetry of the brilliant conceit as Marino, he wrote some short poems on paintings by M that unlike Marino's showed some real feeling and appeared very soon after the paintings themselves. In 1603 Murtola published madrigals on *The fortune teller* and the *Medusa* shield, and two or three more devoted to a painting M had done only a year or so earlier. The paintings that most seized Murtola's imagination were the ones of boys that were about to send a quiver of excitement through Rome. Like Marino's, Murtola's poems played tediously on art and nature, and the naturalness of M's art and nature's own artifice – and so on and on – and each poem tried to match its painting's effect. M's early paintings were being pounced on by these avant garde poets as emblemata of emotional states – another *insensato* did a poem on a boy bitten by a scorpion that recalled M's *Boy bitten*. M's small experimental paintings were visual equivalents of a poem turned on a single conceit and M was likely encouraged to try them by the poets he was getting to know. Poems and paintings generated each other reciprocally. The *Medusa* head, M's most cerebral early experiment, was the poets' favourite, and as soon as he moved on to larger, complex *history* canvases and religious themes the libertine poets' interest waned. And M, leaving Del Monte, was moving beyond the little avant garde circles and into contact with intellectuals who left fewer traces.

Marino and Murtola later got tangled in a murderous public rivalry – poets had an even tougher struggle for patronage than painters – and in 1608 Murtola tried to shoot Marino in the streets of Turin. But in 1601 they were sharing the Roman umbrella of Melchiorre Crescenzi. In this milieu Murtola was friendly with a connoisseur of independent means, a *good, but prolix* antiquarian, art collector, critic and poet called Marzio Milesi. The very private Milesi admired the painter M with extraordinarily personal intensity. By 1601 he'd already written several poems on M's painting, and there'd be more than a dozen poems in Italian and a set of epitaphs in Latin on M over the next ten years. Milesi never published any of them, though he surely circulated them among his circle – they were made to be seen, designed to convince. Under their decorous veneer, they were polemics. The poets Orsi, Marino and Murtola used M's work as a pretext for their own, especially Marino. Milesi's poems were directed straight at M himself, and they were the first written response to his art.

Three short poems were addressed to the painter *still young* – from a poet one year older – and the first grabbed his name and plunged into an assertion that M was Michelangelo Buonarotti's equal and *like* him,

> If you look like this in your green years
> What will you do when you're ripe?

The M phenomenon would defeat Art *and* Nature, the poem decided, breaking out of the dichotomy other poets were still playing with.

The second one began just as ringingly on the modernity and newness of M.

> Let the ancients and the finest make way for you
> Angel M, painter of our century ...
>
> Let someone else imitate things ...
> You make them live and true ...

The third upped the stakes even further. It borrowed Homer's salute to Virgil from Dante's *Inferno* and adapted it for the peremptory opening *Admire the highest painter* and then went on to imply M needed a Dante to do him justice. *He stupefies the world ...* By the end M had become a kind of messiah of art.

> O happy century of ours in which we see
> What since ancient times we've [only] thought and believed.

These were strong words from a withdrawn and scrupulous intellectual, and only their ringing conviction saved them from sounding excessive and absurd. The poems were only eight or nine lines long, but Milesi then took the second one praising M's newness and worked it up into a fifty line effusion describing *the histories of saint Matthew*. It ended in defiant modesty, after repeating that *my great M* had *astonished the world in our century*.

> O you my notes, and I know you aren't a song,
> Or anything to arouse people's admiration,
> But don't hesitate to make yourselves heard,
> And if hatred or envy coming from anyone
> Says there's another equal to this praise
> Say that time alone will make him so.

Milesi clearly felt close to M, and close to M's own way of seeing his art, but maybe the closeness was more imagined than real. The enmity and jealousy Milesi was noticing over the *Matthew* achievement, and M's need of a spokesman, weren't necessarily felt like that by M himself. Milesi's world of erudite amateurism wasn't M's round of intense work interrupted by desperate pleasures – Milesi showed it when he exclaimed at the rapid and copious way M produced *marvels*. Yet his words assumed that a reader would recognize that hostility to M as real, even in that early moment of M's success, so there must've been something in it beyond Milesi's partisan anxiety. The insistence on the really phenomenal nature of M's art – *stun* and *stupefy* recurred in his praise – seemed at times to be implying a certain unworldliness in the artist himself. Maybe Milesi saw M as unable to handle the hostility to his work that was already forming among intellectuals. At least there were others like Milesi who were on M's side.

The painters were the ones who were really divided over M. Unlike the writers they were interested in how he did it – in the painting from life and more and more in the lighting M used in *strengthening his darks*. From the start he'd used a strong oblique source of light to shape his models' features, painting by the strong light of a small window in a dark room, such as his studio at Del Monte's must've afforded, and exploiting the contrasts. In the night scene of *Judith & Holofernes* he'd tried overhead lamplight to get even darker surrounding shadows and an even more localized source of light. The increasingly radical experiments with light led to the *Matthew* paintings – *Matthew called* used sunlight through a window, though not in a simply natural way, and *Matthew killed* an artificial source, and both matched the real light in the place where the paintings hung. When the flood of private and public commissions followed, as it now did, this was the look people wanted. And it was the look young painters wanted too, for their own canvases. The promise of powerful effects directly achieved and the seemingly liberating ease of the antiacademic lesson of life combined to make M an irresistible example to the younger artists, even as the academy itself hastened to take him in. Bellori described with elegant succinctness and a pleasing neoclassical irony the phases of M's deepening style, its appeal to young emulators and the feelings it aroused in the academy.

> Caravaggio, as he was already being called by everybody after the name of his home town, was getting himself noticed more and more every day for the tonality he was introducing. It was no longer soft and lightly coloured as it had been earlier, but wholly marked by strong shadows and using a great deal of black to give relief to the forms. He took this working method of his so far that he never let any of his models out into the open sun, but found a way of making them stand out against the dark brown air of a closed room. He raised a lamp up high so that light fell straight down on to the main part of the body and left the rest in shadow, to gain strength through the contrast of light and dark.

176

So that the painters then in Rome were taken by the newness of it, and the young ones in particular all descended on him and hailed him alone as the only imitator of life. Looking on his works as miracles, they vied with each other in following him, stripping models bare and raising lights. They now ignored their studies and teachers, and everyone easily found in the streets and piazzas his own master and models to copy from life. The ease of it attracted others, and only the old painters broken in to the old practices remained stunned by this new study of life. They never stopped attacking M and his style and spread it around that he didn't know how to come up out of the cellar. They said he was so weak in invention and drawing, and lacking in decorum and art, that he used to paint all his figures by a single source of light and on one plane without any depth of perspective.

But none of these charges slowed the flight of his fame.

THE PEOPLE WHO came to stare in 1600 at M's *Matthew* paintings on the side walls of the Contarelli chapel might've been too amazed or too deeply envious to notice that the chapel's prime position behind the altar was surprizingly still vacant. It remained an empty space all through the following year. The gap was no oversight. As in all the Contarelli affair, a delicate, complicated and long drawn out situation had developed. The lack of an altarpiece had nothing to do with the delays in getting the side wall paintings done, but since M had so stunningly retrieved the situation there, and redeemed years of embarrassment by producing Rome's most brilliant new art, it was almost inevitable that all the people with an interest in finishing things off should've thought of trying to repeat their earlier coup. They turned to M again.

When Mathieu Cointrel's original plan fell through for his earthly memorial in the French church – the paintings that were never done by Muziano – he gave the prime bit to an artisan who'd become a personal protégé. He still wanted the chapel's ceiling and side walls painted in fresco with scenes of Matthew's life, but the altarpiece would now be a pair of marble sculptures representing Matthew writing his gospel with the help of the angel, and Contarelli wanted these done by the Flemish sculptor Jacob Cobaert who lived in Rome. Cobaert started roughing them out in a garden Contarelli rented for him to work in, and when Contarelli died at the end of 1585, the first thing his executor Crescenzi did about the chapel art was formalize Cobaert's commission for the statues. A long contract was drawn up at the end of 1587 and its conditions betrayed a certain unease about progress made to date – or at least Crescenzi's brisk determination to wrap up this part of the job as soon as he could. Cobaert's fee was huge – a thousand gold scudi plus seventy per annum expenses for his assistant and *pleasures of the table*. The down side for Cobaert was that if he didn't finish the job in four years he got nothing.

Unease was confirmed. Nothing was ready when the time was up in late 1591, but the conditions had been a bluff and the contract ran on through the time Giuseppe Cesari was supposed to be painting the frescos. It was formally renewed yet again after another four years had passed in January 1596, but still Cobaert failed to deliver the goods. He wasn't up to the job. It was all very sad. Cobaert was an elderly craftsman *excellent in doing small things* in ivory, gold and silver. With a life size marble saint and angel he was way out of his depth.

> He spent the rest of his life making this statue, never let-ting anyone see it, unable to leave it alone, like someone with no experience of marble, and he didn't want to take advice or help from anyone. He went on until he was about eighty years old and turned gaga and couldn't finish it …

And, Baglione added, laying it on,

> he had no dealings with anyone and lived like an animal and wouldn't let man or woman into his house … he was solitary, suspicious and melancholic and trusted nobody …

In early 1602 the news was that Cobaert had finished the Matthew part of his sculpture group. The necessary angel, after more than fifteen years' work, was still to come. Francesco Contarelli was now a rector of San Luigi and more eager than anyone to see the sculpture in place and his uncle the cardinal's chapel finally completed. He was also a good personal friend of the Crescenzis and wanted to close an episode that'd now dragged on for nearly forty years. On January 8 a removalist was engaged to collect the statue from Cobaert's studio and install it in the chapel. The long wait was almost over. Such a long expense of effort promised something special, and M's dazzling paintings raised hopes of a repeat performance with the statue.

Anticipation surged. The statue was lifted into place. What happened next – for Baglione – was a hoot.

> The Contarellis were expecting a divine work, or a miraculous one. When they saw it they discovered it was a dreary failure and didn't want it in their chapel …

Three weeks of intense covert dealing later, gaga old Cobaert, doing extraordinarily well out of family loyalty, gave up all claim to the last three hundred of his thousand gold scudi and was formally released from his undertaking to turn out a further marble angel

> because said statue installed in said chapel does not satisfy the illustrious master Francesco Contarelli …

who along with the whole congregation now wanted

> to place above said altar in place of said statue a painted image of the same saint Matthew …

Maybe somebody had foreseen all this, because within days a new contract was prepared and on February 7 M signed to do a painting of the angel dictating his gospel to Matthew, *the one and the other with body entire*, payment a hundred and fifty scudi and delivery by pentecost, within three and a half months. The Contarelli chapel was saving a hundred and fifty scudi, and Francesco Contarelli took the old man's statue home and kept it there *at the foot of the stairs* for the rest of his life. A painting above the altar had been his uncle's original idea. Not, probably, the kind of painting M did. *Matthew & angel* was the world's funniest work of Christian art, so wildly funny it was clear even M hadn't foreseen the devastating effect of painting the Christian icon from life. He did an angel who was

> an insolent kid draped in a trailing sheet like something in a parish hall pageant,

and the angel was nothing beside M's new Matthew. Unlike the astute businessman of *Matthew called,* or the elderly priest he became for *Matthew killed*, the Matthew who went up over the altar was a puzzled barefoot peasant taking an adult literacy lesson from God's smirking pubescent messenger.

This wasn't funny the way a lot of current religious art was. M's art wasn't kitsch – the joke belonged to his own way of seeing the transmission of holy writ and this was why it had consequences. Kitsch was altogether different. The counter reformation was art's first great age of kitsch – never before had such terrible intensity of feeling found expression in such insanely constricted imagery, but it took a certain kind of observing intelligence to enjoy it, and without your own contribution the art stayed simply dire. Kitsch was Cesari's *Santa Barbara*. When Cesari was commissioned by Pietro Aldobrandini to paint the patron saint of the bombardiers of the castel Sant' Angelo, about five years before M's Matthew commission, he produced a santa Barbara that garrisoned soldiers would appreciate, a santa Barbara with a touch of Betty Grable, on the tacit understanding that the cardinal's uncle Clement VIII wouldn't be invited to the unveiling ceremony in the church of the castel Sant' Angelo in 1597, or ever hear about the painting. The pope wasn't, and didn't. He would've been deeply shocked. Santa Barbara, a tad plump and with a face like the one on Annibale Carracci's virgin, only with her hair unbraided and falling wantonly, was rolling her eyes up toward an angel who was wrapping her in a bolt of ultralight fabric. Except that one plump breast had flopped free of the drapery. It was the breast, and his own nephew's complicity with his favourite painter in its exposure, that his beatitude wasn't to know about, though it was a very small concession in an otherwise highly decorous painting. The breast survived, suspended between what was acceptable and what not, until catholic zealotry draped it in the nineteenth century and restorers bared it again in the twentieth.

M was now a rival of Cesari's. That he might've found his old employer's santa Barbara funny was suggested by the way he worked her into his own new painting. In the insolent and androgynously pubescent boy angel he now mimicked Barbara's drapes and plumply sinuous posture, known in the mannerist trade as the *serpentina*, particularly the way the flimsy fabric sat on the soft belly and slightly raised thigh, and the tumbling hair. Barbara's serpentine stance was merely formal, an antecedent of the cocked thigh bathing beauty pose, but M's angel took advantage of his own sinuousness to wrap himself around the seated saint, breathing out the words and guiding Matthew's horny hand across the open book with soft fingers, as Matthew wrinkled his brow and stared in amazement at the elegant Hebrew he found himself writing.

M had promised in his contract to have the painting ready by pentecost, which came on May 23 that year. The contract had been very insistent on that point.

M must have finished it with all perfection and with the
utmost possible excellence of workmanship and deliver and
install it thus finished and perfected in the above named
place, which was in place of the white marble statue.

That gave him three and a half months and he delivered on time. The
delivery date mattered because pentecost was a major fixture on the
French calendar in Rome. Every year the community held a special
service in San Luigi attended by the ambassador of France and all the
cardinals professing loyalty to the French crown. The celebrations of
1602 were particularly significant as the first attended by France's new
ambassador. Philippe de Béthune had arrived in Rome the previous
October to lead Henri IV's new diplomatic counter offensive against
the Spanish dominance in Rome. After his absolution by the pope
and his remarriage to Maria de' Medici, Henri IV was determined to
seize the initiative from Spain and rebuild the French party inside the
college of cardinals. What wasn't yet part of Béthune's brief was his
imminent intervention in M's turbulent personal life. The presence
of Béthune and his retinue from the embassy of France and of the
fourteen proFrench cardinals who'd accepted the invitation to the service and of the French and proFrench community in Rome were
meanwhile why the priests of San Luigi were anxious to have M's
altarpiece ready that day.

It was the priests, Bellori emphasized, who rejected *Matthew
& angel*. Whether it was the august occasion itself that made them
lose their nerve, and whether they knocked it back before or after the
pentecost service – whether the painting was seen in place by the
ambassador and the cardinals – the drama and publicity surrounding
the rejection made the experience a burning humiliation for M, and
left him, in Bellori's account *despairing … desperate*. It was the peasant
Matthew who really upset people. He was sitting in the Savonarola
chair previously used by the young money counter in *Matthew called*,
dressed in a shortie tunic like asylum inmates' issue, bare armed, bare
legged, barefoot, his cloak or blanket slung across the chair, toenails
blackened and remaining hair ruffled, being patronized by this cheeky
kid with a pair of swan's wings on his back. The gospel he was writing was supposed to be arriving as dictation directly from God in the
original Hebrew, the angel serving as intermediary. This was the story
but it supposed some sort of active participation, not this polite puz-
zlement as of a labourer grandparent being taught to surf the net. The
saint's uncouthness projected itself forcefully into the chapel. The job
of replacing a third rate sculpture invited M to enhance the relief like

illusionism of his image, so that the dirty foot at the end of Matthew's crossed leg was jutting out over the altar, its black nailed big toe poking into the face of any celebrant priest.

M's aggression was frontal and inescapable, but it was mild after the big horse's rump obliquely facing the heavenward soaring virgin Mary in the Cerasi job he'd just finished, or the labourer's arse thrust in your own face when you looked at *Peter.* Yet this time people were really upset. *Nobody liked it,* said Baglione bluntly and Bellori later elaborated the reasons.

> When he finished the middle painting of Matthew and it was placed over the altar, it was removed by the priests who said that that figure had no decorum, nor did he look like a saint, sitting there with his legs crossed and his feet rudely exposed to the people.

People seemed not to mind the rather sexy adolescent angel, pressing up against the middle aged saint in a quite earthly way, or else they overlooked him in outrage at the barefoot illiterate Matthew. M had drastically misjudged prevailing orthodoxy and the strength of institutional feeling. He'd shown none of Cesari's skill at matching product with client, or Carracci's brilliance at generalizing problems out of existence. M's extraordinary public successes, and what he'd lately got away with in the Cerasi paintings, had encouraged a certain obliviousness of other people's values, or a feeling that the power of his art made him immune from them. M was shattered by the reaction to *Matthew & angel.* Bellori wrote that the rejection – evidently very different from what'd happened over the first versions of *Peter* and *Saul* –

> greatly upset M and left him almost despairing for his reputation … [he] was desperate over this affront …

His distress was ingenuous though hardly surprizing. His *Matthew & angel* wittily and beautifully played over the space that separated the church's mannerist artifice, in the joke of the preteen angel, from the reality of an illiterate working man's effort to grasp the message of the Book, in this case his own. The drama of Matthew's calloused foot invading the space between canvas and viewer, more daring than any optical bravura he'd ever shown before, also made sculptural fun of the *dreary* rejected *statue in white marble* lately carted off. It was a deeply benign canvas, filled with the serene and sanguine enjoyment in human incongruities he'd last shown in the *Rest on the flight into*

Egypt, but now more inward, more deeply real in its empathy with Matthew's human bafflement. Humour, however, was the enemy of *decorum* and nothing mattered more than decorum. *Matthew & angel* had to go. *The affront* to his new reputation was a shocking rebuff on his home turf at the French church, a few yards from Del Monte's and Giustiniani's and a worrying turn in his new life as a public painter. It was much worse now than with the first transitional versions of *Peter* and *Paul*. *Matthew & angel* was a mature and wholly realized painting. If *the priests* didn't like his work in San Luigi, between the acclaimed *Matthew* paintings of less than two years earlier, where could he hope to succeed? In the face of M's and the art academy's cardinal *protector*, the rejection was a sobering display of ecclesiastical clout. Vincenzo Giustiniani saved the day.

> Intervening with those priests, he took the picture for him-
> self and got him to do another different one,

whisking it over the road into his gallery to hang with the *Lute player* and more recent work. Bellori said he hung it in a place of honour. Baglione claimed Giustiniani was so infatuated with M's work that he took it simply because it was a painting by M. M did another *Matthew & angel* for San Luigi that was deemed decorous and stayed in place over the Contarelli altar. He received his final payment from Francesco Contarelli, acting for Crescenzi, on September 22. This was four months after the original delivery date, but in just seven and a half months he'd painted not one but two full paintings.

M's resilience was his strength as a painter. He was able to rethink his art in the process of creating it – resolving the imaginative dilemmas with a wholly new conception of the subject. On life painting he was intransigent. On his imagining he was best when goaded into seeing that compromise was useless. Pressures on his imagination from outside had produced his most original work. When *Matthew & angel* was rejected things were different. He'd already given the subject his best shot and now he demonstrated a more prosaic inner resource, a different kind of impressiveness that in the long run he needed no less. He showed now that he was able to control his own exuberance and respond to other demands in a way that didn't compromise his art. M now drew on resources Annibale Carracci would've envied and that maybe Carracci's own painting had made M aware of. The discipline even seemed to strengthen his painterly technique. The second *Matthew & angel* was a strong, simple, austere, even fine paint-ing, and terribly controlled. The playfulness of the first version had evaporated and left a stony residue of form and brilliant mineral colour. It was impeccably decorous. Or seemed to be. A longer look revealed some discreetly subversive reminders of his own autonomy.

The second painting showed in its absences what'd offended in the first. The new Matthew was no longer a vigorous amiable peasant but a gaunt old greybearded man, the model from *Matthew killed* recalled to duty, bare feet no longer in your face but away from it, covered from neck to ankle in a dun coloured tunic and an orange cloak, holding the pen unaided and even quite expertly in his hand. The angel was older and tougher looking – even loutish – and no longer standing pressed against him but hovering overhead in a totally non-physical manner that allowed room for no misinterpretations. Any potentially disturbing former sense that the two might've been enjoying their proximity was replaced now by a distinct vertical gap of black space between them, and a startled or anxious look on Matthew's face. The new angel was held up or weighed down by a sinister pair of dark wings – almost invisible in the dead black space that surrounded and separated the two figures and took up half the canvas – and a turbine of freshly washed bed linen. The smallness and apartness of the two figures, brightly suspended in a lot of darkness, was unlike M and looked like a willed breaking up of the powerful and unsettling synergy of his earlier locked double composition. In a very Roman and slightly thuggish manner the angel ticked off items on red adolescent hands with black rimmed fingernails – not Del Monte's type of dreamy beauty at all, though the lively earlier angel might've passed. M was answering his priestly critics by throwing Matthew's relation with the angel into reverse. The subversiveness of his new treatment lay now in the unlikeliness that this particular angel would have much enlightenment for the intellectual old saint, who indeed looked a bit startled, frightened even, at the flying street kid who'd disturbed him at work. But the incongruity was now muted, generalized and controlled, put beyond the reach of hostile critics.

M made every effort to succeed in this second picture, wrote Bellori – no doubt truly. What gave strict decorum the lie was the old saint's uneasy stance and M's newly playful use of forward three dimensionality in his pictorial space. The angle of Matthew's vision propelled the angel out in front of the picture plane. That Matthew was standing right on the plane was shown by the bench. He was resting his knee on the same wooden bench the *bravo* had sat on in *Matthew called*, whose front corner had now lost its solid footing in the painting, and he was about to topple out arse over tip into the space above the real altar. Bringing Matthew crashing down with it, if not the angel who'd put the disconcerted Matthew into this precarious stance. In soothing the guardians of orthodoxy, M had supplied them with a visual booby trap. They wanted decorum and he gave them counter reformation slapstick.

NOBODY LIKED IT, claimed Baglione, but Vincenzo Giustiniani snapped up *Matthew & angel,* straight away *simply because it was a work by M.* The marchese, wrote Baglione, was the dupe of a public relations job,

> persuaded by the great fuss about M that Prosperino of the grotesques was making everywhere.

Prospero Orsi was playing *promoter* of M's art, he claimed, because *he had it in for Giuseppe Cesari.* Mancini remembered it the other way round, that Cesari resented Prospero Orsi as a troublemaker for leaving the Cesari art factory and taking the young M with him seven years earlier. Prospero apparently did a good job on M's behalf, because Giustiniani wasn't the only wealthy private collector to fall for his pitch.

> In fact he got signor Ciriaco Mattei to fall for his noise too, and M ... got many hundreds of scudi out of that gentleman.

Bellori, who never knew him and gave no reason, later said Prospero was acting out of self interest in making M known. Mancini, who did know him, said Prospero was the kind of person who always went out of his way to help younger artists get started. M himself remained close to Prospero Orsi for over ten years of daily life, from the time they met until M left Rome. Prospero went bail to get M out of jail in 1605, and showed himself a friend when M was a wanted man and there was nothing to gain except recognition of M's art and maybe M's freedom. In 1602 M's art no longer needed advertizing. Del Monte commissioned no new paintings after M left the palazzo Madama but Vincenzo Giustiniani, Ciriaco Mattei and Ottavio Costa were now pressing to buy M's work. Del Monte was likely pleased that his protégé had made it into the wider world and felt his work was done. There was no sign of a break between them. Whatever his personal living arrangements, M continued for years to invoke Del Monte's magic name when he was in trouble with the authorities, and Del Monte was always ready to intervene discreetly when needed. He understood M was difficult and he knew M was the greatest painter of his time.

The large public drama of M's *history* paintings for Contarelli and Cerasi was matched by the intensity if not the scale of the private excitements aroused by the work he was now doing for the wealthy. Outsiders had to imagine what privileged access to the galleries of the powerful might let them see, and the art world's eager talk soon amplified its new sensations. The unseen and the merely heard about afforded a special kind of *frisson* and the complicated play of double standards made art a minefield for the client. Daringness of treatment was even more likely to get mixed up in second hand reports with scandalousness of theme. If the trouble in the churches was mostly the doctrinal correctness and decorum of the images, the problem rearing its head in private collections was mainly erotic, and there the problems of decorum took on a whole other sense.

Clement VIII probably heard about Carracci's erotica on the Farnese ceiling from his nephew Pietro. What mattered was that he shouldn't clap eyes on it personally. The palazzo Farnese on the campo de' Fiori with its gallery of pagan nudes was safe from a papal visit, protected by Aldobrandini jealousy of Farnese wealth and power. Even so, young cardinal Odoardo, who'd conceived the whole project largely as an assertion of autonomy and a smack in the eye to the canting pope, lost his nerve as work proceeded – especially now the two dynasties were linked by the marriage of Ranuccio Farnese of Parma with Margherita Aldobrandini. Both sides were hoping to gain from this union and nobody wanted trouble. Annibale Carracci's later paintings on the walls were a lot more demure than the erotic riot on the ceiling and some of them verged on the moralistic. None of the many female nudes in the Farnese collection of classical sculpture was installed as planned in the gallery niches. Delicate white veils, as the frescos were applied to the wet plaster, were hastily inserted between grasping male hands and plump female pudenda. There was talk, years later, of Agostino Carracci's having left town in a hurry just ahead of Clement VIII's punitive wrath. Agostino was also a painter and the rumour may have been connected with the hand he was giving his brother Annibale on the frescos. Agostino's two contributions had been the most erotically daring of all and had to be censored. When cardinal Bellarmino called at palazzo Farnese, he urbanely suggested cardinal Odoardo clothe some of the naked wretches he'd seen on entering, *as winter was coming on and they'd feel the cold*. Odoardo Farnese quickly said he would, but anxiously explained he couldn't actually *remove* them because they were *done in fresco in the wall*. The constraint bound everyone. Twenty years later Mancini could venture that erotic art was fine if it remained concealed in marital bedrooms where it could stimulate the making of vigorous babies, but nobody was saying even that in 1600.

The most violent sexual anathemata of the counter reformation were cast against the sexuality of women, and it was displays of female sensuousness that the church most abhorred in art as in life. Only the female nudes were banned from the Farnese sculpture gallery when the ideological screws were tightened. The male nudes were allowed to stay. And when M's first altar painting of *Matthew & angel* was found unacceptable at San Luigi dei Francesi, the priests' objections were all about the unseemly representation of Matthew as uncouth and illiterate and unmindful of his big dirty feet. Not a word at the time of anyone's worries about the very earthly prepubescent seminude angel voluptuously invading Matthew's personal space. The church's real sexual war in the counter reformation was with female sexuality. Even the *unspeakable sin* of intragender sex was a lesser problem, and it had to be flaunted before the torturers and executioners went to work. If sexual interest was displaced toward boys in a time like this, as it naturally was, since boys were neither women nor men, then that sorted well enough with the benign lack of interest in the polymorphic perversity of younger males that had always prevailed around the Mediterranean. Neither the old testament nor the new testament nor the fathers of the church had had a great deal to say on the specific matter of sex with boys. None of it was new. Pederasty was old as the hills. Only the furious sexual policing was new in life and art, and its counterpart in the way women's bodies were put to sexual work in Rome's biggest and practically its only industry. The issue in both cases was control. When suddenly everything was fraught with ideology, boys had the unusual freedom of being ignored. It suited M, though it was unlikely he ever worked things through as a matter of strategic choice. It meant he could treat his own erotic feelings in art with a freedom he'd never have been allowed if those feelings had been for women. Boys were a window of opportunity.

THIRTY YEARS ON, gouty and nearly seventy, the marchese Vincenzo Giustiniani in 1632 invited a young German painter in Rome to prepare the catalogue and engravings for an illustrated book on his large collection of classical and modern sculpture. The painter Joachim von Sandrart, in his mid twenties, spent several years in the palazzo Giustiniani working at his art, cataloguing the sculpture and looking after the Giustiniani collection of more than three hundred paintings. The *Galleria Giustiniana* came out in 1635. Sandrart got on well with the aging marchese – his brother the cardinal was ten years dead and Vincenzo himself had only a year or two left – sketched with Claude Lorrain in the garden and called on the elderly Galileo Galilei while he was undergoing his second trial by the inquisition. Forty years later, Sandrart published in Germany in 1675 a vast compendious book of his own on art through the ages that included information about painters whose work Giustiniani had collected. One of them was M.

Though the whole art scene had changed out of recognition by the sixteen thirties, and entirely different tastes prevailed in the new age of baroque, Giustiniani was still passionate about the painter whose art he'd collected thirty years earlier. He had fifteen canvases by M in his gallery, but one in particular had fascinated the young German. Sandrart remembered that

> This piece was hung on open display in a room with a hundred and twenty others by the most outstanding artists. On my advice, though, it was covered with a dark green silk curtain. Only when all the other paintings had been properly seen was it fully revealed. It made all the other rarities pale …

The anxious young German was probably less worried about the way M's painting eclipsed the others in the room than concerned that this was the kind of painting that belonged behind green curtains. Visitors might be shocked. The hardworking and punctilious outsider was more concerned about other people's opinion than the unbuttoned and fabulously rich old marchese. He'd never shown any personal susceptibility to the painting's specific content and liked it because it was a masterpiece, a masterpiece he'd commissioned thirty years earlier that still astounded people. None of Giustiniani's visitors seemed to mind the painting either. Sandrart recalled that

> a prominent *cavaliere* liked it so much that he offered a thousand *pistole* for it in front of us all. When I reported the

offer to our patron and asked him for a response – he was sick with gout at the time – he laughed and said

Tell the noble cavaliere that if he can get me another picture of the same quality, I'll pay him double that, two thousand pistole.

The *pistola* got its name because it was small, new and powerful. It was a gold coin worth two scudi. Giustiniani was being offered two thousand scudi, ten or maybe fifteen times what he'd paid, and he was saying in reply that M's painting was worth twice that. Baglione had implied that Giustiniani at the turn of the century was buying up M's work irrespective of quality, because he had a thing about M. The unnamed *cavaliere* who thought he was making a big gesture in Sandrart's presence knew only the painting. Thirty years on M the painter was already half forgotten. His painting of *Love the winner* was still astounding people.

8

ROME 1601–1603

Love the winner
John in the wild II
John in the wild III
Meal at Emmaus
Doubting Thomas
Christ taken

*L*OVE THE WINNER still brings a rush of colour to the unwary viewer's cheek. Four centuries after it was painted it stays irrepressibly fresh and lively and sexy. It was utterly clean and simple, floating amazingly free of interference, above the dead weight of a church ridden culture. It seduced everyone. It offered a boy as object of desire – the boy, more precisely, offered himself – yet it was utterly free of pederastic repression or pervy idealizing fantasy. The boy was real, happy, confident, himself. The change of tone from the muted longing of the *Boy with fruit* and the *Lute player*, or even the tipsily level stare of *Bacchus* could hardly be greater. Startlingly, this was sex without guilt. The open self assurance meant that people tended not to have a lot to say about *Love the winner*. Its high spirits needed no elucidation. Which left little room for the historians and critics, who mostly fell back on the very things the painting and its subject were laughing at, to elucidate the serious matters of government and war, art and learning that were being trampled underfoot. M's still life – the violin, the lute, the music, the armour, the coronet, the set square and compasses, the pen, the manuscript and the bay leaves, the great globe itself, glinting with goldleaf stars under the boy's soft bum – was exquisite, as good as any he'd done, but not enough to draw eyes from the grinning boy. His eagle's wings were formidable, but the dark predator's feathers only set off the bare skin and the pliable body. The frontal nude with his legs spread made you look at him alone. The painting afforded no other resting places for the eyes. Prepubescent *Love* filled most of the canvas with his compact torso, and his immature dick was the painting's inescapable visual focus.

The boy himself was so intently observed that the allegorical trappings seemed invisible, weightless, blown out of sight by the boy's lively here and now, and none of their interpreters' efforts over the centuries would ever quite manage to claw them back into the picture. To counter reformation connoisseurs with an inveterate and hideously overdeveloped habit of reading every image for its message, and then appreciating its *style*, a painting that annihilated message and style with its physical presence was deeply shocking. Or would've been if it weren't so disarming. M's Eros was not an intimidating presence. When such an utterly exhausted and meaningless emblematic presence in art as the boy Eros – the profane counterpart of the vastly more common and even more inane Christian angel – suddenly made you look at him *as* him – *a person not an object*, somebody might've said – the effect was stunningly, bracingly new.

For M it wasn't new at all. He was returning to the days before he took on *history* painting, hitting the central nerve of his whole undertaking in art, rendering the visual truth of what was in front of his eye, filthy toenails, discoloured teeth and all. If you were used to benignly gazing at the young boy in art – the kind of neopagan art lately renewed by Annibale Carracci on the Farnese ceiling – of the plump, cheeky, pretty well sexless *putto* as witness and ornament to the gods' adult sexual pleasures, with or without cherubic wings, indeed with or without body – Carracci again, adjusting to the realities of counter reformation Christianity with his winged heads in the Cerasi altarpiece – peeing into helmets, peering under skirts, riding dolphins or crabs as they had at Pompeii, wrestling, simpering, tumbling through the clouds and adoring virgins in the *trompe l'oeil* air – the grinning boy M chose as *Love*, posed naked on a crumpled bed sheet with a bunch of props scattered at his feet and offering himself as a player in the game and not just an instigator, seemed like a reality you'd never seen before, or ever imagined.

Lacking decorum as well as his clothes, *Love the winner* wouldn't please the church's critical theorists. Forget the wanton forelock. He was a reality the more urbane ecclesiastical art lover might prefer not to be seen paying any attention to at all. The year earnest Federico

Borromeo stayed in the palazzo Giustiniani – just before he was forced back to his job in Milan in the autumn of 1601 – might've overlapped with the time M was painting *Love* for Vincenzo Giustiniani, just before 1602, and if it did Borromeo was certainly shown the new painting Vincenzo Giustiniani was *going overboard over*. A carefully vague anecdote Borromeo told many years later suggested he remembered it. Laying down the law in his 1624 treatise *On sacred painting*, he still seemed to be feeling that particular shock of the new, reverberating down through the years. Borromeo was objecting to realistic nudity in art, and wrote primly that

> we ourselves know a man of noble family who, wanting to impress his visitors with a painting he had in his house, invited everyone present to observe how the hairs on a naked leg could be counted one by one. Thus he displayed his own ignorance and the painter's. And the mass of the people likes things like this, and unfortunately enjoys the very worst things …

The man of noble family who wanted to impress his visitors sounded very like Vincenzo Giustiniani, with his attention to workmanship and his feeling for detail – and delighted with his new painting. Only there were no hairs on Love's legs and it was hard to think of any real painting of a hairy legged nude Borromeo might've had in mind. Love's legs were notably smooth and soft. But one thing people always remarked on was *Love the winner*'s meticulously feathered wings. Giustiniani would've been talking up the individual feathers on the wings, not the hairs on the leg, and cardinal Borromeo now displacing the detail to avoid any shaming mention of the notorious work, any giveaway sign it'd stuck in his mind for twenty years and more, and maybe at the same time remembering despite himself and all too vividly across those years the seductive detail of the dark eagle's feather curling over and caressing the boy's hairless thigh.

Nobody recorded who it really was, the living and breathing original of *Love the winner*. Models didn't count. The others in M's artists' push would've known him, but being a boy he didn't matter. Even the identity of Fillide took some tracing, and Fillide was a famous courtesan whose named portrait by M could be matched against her roles in other *histories*. People talked about this boy, though, gossiped about him – when a painting was as famous as *Love the winner* and got the whole force of its impact as a portrait of a real boy, talk was inevitable. Even subliminally, the painting's directness determined how people referred to it. *A sitting Cupid painted from life*, Baglione called it.

> A life size Cupid after a boy of about twelve ... [who] has large brown eagle's wings, drawn so correctly and with such strong colouring, clarity and relief that it all comes to life,

remembered Sandrart. Yet the boy's identity did matter. His identity mattered because he was M's new lover and it mattered that he was M's lover because he figured in some of M's most remarkable and deeply felt and radically intimate paintings. *Love the winner*, after the angelic glimpse in the first *Saul*, was the first. And it mattered in the longer run too, because this twelve year old grew up to be a painter himself, and one of M's first followers, though distinctively his own painter. And it was as a painter he later left an extraordinary visual reflection on the nature of his early life with M. Little might be known about him – it was enough to see he mattered more than anyone else in M's life. M's art showed that.

So who was he? They were still talking about the boy fifty years later, around the middle of the century. There was an Englishman in Rome from 1649 to 1651, an art lover called Richard Symonds, who kept a kind of art diary with notes on the paintings he saw in various collections. Symonds visited the palazzo Giustiniani thirteen years after the marchese's death to see the paintings. He scribbled down at one point, in a confused mixture of his own English and his informant's Italian, a few lines on M's *Love the winner*. His concern, like Sandrart's fifteen years earlier, was to fix the image in a few words and record the huge sums certain people were still offering for the painting. Sandrart heard nothing from the impeccably reserved Vincenzo Giustiniani – who would've known everything – about the genesis of the painting of the boy *Love*, only that the model was a twelve year old boy. Symonds, though, heard as well some old gossip about who M's model had been. Its source was a Giustiniani family member and Symonds wrote it down with the rest. His diary entry on *Love the winner* read in a scribbled jumble of Italian and English

> Cupido di Caravaggio
> Card. di Savoia proferd 2 milia duboli p il Cupido di Caravaggio
> Costò 3 centa scudi:
> Checco di Caravaggio he calld many he painted was his

194

boy – haire darke, 2 wings rare, compasses liute violin &
armes & laurel
Monsr Crechy vuolle dare 2 milia dubole
it was ye body & face of his owne boy or servant thait laid
with him.

The name Symonds transcribed phonetically was Cecco, which was
affectionately short for Francesco. In his jumbled and elliptical scrawl –
Checco di Caravaggio he calld many he painted was his boy – Symonds
noted of the model *he [was] calld* Cecco and that *many [times] he* –
meaning M – *painted* him and that Cecco *was his boy*. The same boy
had made his first cameo appearance the year before *Love* as the angel
staying Christ's nosedive in his first version of *Saul*. Soon after *Love*
M painted him as a full length nude John the baptist in a painting
nearly as startling and sexy as *Love the winner* and a lot more ideologically unsound. For M, 1602 was the year of the nude boy Ceccos,
and they were the only full nudes he ever did – his only two paintings of joyous and untrammelled sexual energy.

Symonds elaborated what he meant by saying that Cecco *was his
boy* in the note's last line, *his owne boy or servant thait laid with him*. The
story Symonds heard wasn't contradicted, if not quite fully confirmed
either, by a parish census document surviving from 1605, three years
after M painted these nudes. It listed as living with M in his rented
rooms in Rome a certain *Francesco* described in the census as M's *garzone*, being his assistant or servant, age unspecified, *his boy*. The work
of a painter's boy included grinding his colours, stretching and priming his canvas – It was prentice work for a youngster learning the
basic skills of the craft. It was what M himself had been sent to learn
from Simone Peterzano in Milan at the age of twelve and a half, and
that Peterzano had contractually promised to teach him. The relationship of master and apprentice wasn't necessarily formalized and financially binding, as it'd been in the training sought by M's careful family,
and the boy, as a servant, wasn't quite a pupil. Serving as the painter's
model was a normal part of duties and sleeping with his master – they
were alone in the household – not unknown for servants and artists'
models to do. Painter and boy, according to church records, were regular communicants at mass. The boy was learning how to paint. The
name meant nothing to Symonds, though he might've reflected on
the oddity of the boy's name being remembered at all fifty years later.
Being remembered wasn't the normal fate of servants and artists'
models. But Cecco as a man achieved his own distinction, and thirty
odd years before his name was mentioned to the English tourist,

Mancini named *Francesco, known as M's Cecco* as one of the most talented painters working in the late M's style. His name was Francesco Boneri and a family of artists called Boneri had been working in the province of Bergamo, where the town of Caravaggio was, all through the sixteenth century. Cecco's parents probably lived in that dense community of Lombard artisans working in Rome – there was a notable community from Caravaggio itself in the campo Marzio – and it were unsurprizing if they'd put their boy Francesco to learn painting from M.

Marzio Milesi, M's unlikely friend, wrote a short poem *To a young boy painter, student of M* whose praise of the boy's brilliant beginning sounded quite sincere, urging him to continue as he'd begun. He followed it up with another *To a young boy, excellent painter* that was even more enthusiastic. Since Cecco did later become a remarkable painter, it was surely Cecco Milesi was writing about here. Mario Minniti was too old, and he was never a really good painter, despite the odd flash of later brilliance. Another candidate was also too old. The *servant* Bartolomeo who was mentioned in 1603 might've been Bartolomeo Manfredi, another early follower of M's mentioned by Mancini along with Cecco. A very few years after M's *Love the winner* Manfredi did a strikingly violent and explicitly sexual painting of a young man beating a nude adolescent boy, but Manfredi was already twenty when Milesi wrote and hardly *a young boy painter*. Symonds got Cecco's name slightly wrong. Mancini had him not as the Cecco *di* Caravaggio of Symonds's broken Italian, as if he were of some established family, nor as Cecco *da* Caravaggio, as if he came from the same town as M, but Cecco *del* Caravaggio – the Cecco who belonged to the painter from Caravaggio. M's Cecco. Mancini knew the adult painter's name was Francesco. He likely remembered him personally from the time he'd modelled nude for M at the age of twelve, so he called him by the affectionate nickname the boy had had in those days. Giustiniani later bought a painting by Cecco. Did he know it was done by the model of his favourite painting? Its painter was unidentified in the inventory. It was a big horizontal canvas of *Christ driving the money changers from the temple*. It showed Christ on the right and the thuggish money changers grouped on the left in a raked light – it was reminiscent enough of *Matthew called* to suggest why Sandrart, when he came to write it up years after seeing it, misremembered M's subject as the one of the painting by the unknown Cecco that he'd seen in the palazzo Giustiniani.

Like its owner Giustiniani, all the poets went mad for M's painting of *Love the winner*. It was an immediate sensation in the advanced circles of 1602. Gaspare Murtola promptly wrote three ecstatic madrigals on it – or him – that were published the following year – *Don't look, don't look on Love ... he'll set your heart on fire* – and Marzio Milesi, who maybe wasn't yet aware the model was a promising painter himself, wrote a Latin epigram earnestly quoting Virgil – *omnia vincit amor*. Murtola also did a fourth and no less intensely felt madrigal urging M to paint another young boy too.

> If, wise painter,
> You want to paint Love
> Paint the young boy
> The pretty Giulietto
> Each lovely as the other
> Each amorous as the other
> And if you want to paint him blind
> Look on his lovely form
> When all languidly he sleeps.

The *pretty Giulietto* was never otherwise mentioned or identified. Maybe he was a young friend of Murtola's own, who he thought made an even better Love than Cecco did. Maybe Giulietto was the other young boy M painted that year as the first angel, the one teaching Matthew how to write Hebrew. This boy was never named and a lot of people later mixed him up with Cecco among M's boy models of the first years after 1600. He wasn't the same boy, though, and something of that angel's androgynous voluptuousness came out in Murtola's poem. M had painted Giulietto as Narcissus a couple of years earlier – or a boy very like him – and he'd do him again, but not as Love, a year or so later, when he was already adolescent and no longer pretty, as a very young and beardless Christ. The feeling running through Murtola's poem was that however striking and seductive M's painting of *Love* might've been, the boy Cecco himself, with his bad teeth and streetwise grin, wasn't a really suitable embodiment of Love. He was less *lovely*, less *amorous*, less *languid* than playful Eros with his wings and arrows ought to be. The minor poet Murtola was voicing the very values of the slack and exhausted convention that M's painting had boldly thrown out, aesthetic and erotic values that M himself – as in the first *Matthew*'s angel – had been highly susceptible to until now.

It was the way incipient sexuality came across as toughness in *Love* that gave it the sexy edge, made people catch their breath. Cecco as *Love* joined, as it were, the divided values of Matthew and the angel.

He was the hard peasant man and the voluptuous child in one. His wings weren't a stately white swan's like the angel's, but a dark carrion seeking bird of prey's. Cecco was well on the way from being the golden haired fullfaced child in the first *Saul* to being the yelling young lout about to be knifed in the next year's Isaac. M's painting was getting harder, more energetic and assertive, and so were his boy models. The new angel, when M redid the *Matthew* altarpiece within months of the first, was so thuggish and menacing as he spelt out the gospel on his dirty fingers that the second Matthew turned into a scared pensioner fearing a subway mugging from the air. Cecco survived the early putative ravages of child sex abuse and grew up to become a vigorous and assured painter with a strong feeling of his own for the energy of lowlife types. As an artist he was very much his own man, one of the most distinctive and subversively original and one of the most brutally realistic painters in early seventeenth century Italy. He was still in Rome in 1620, and soon after that he registered the oddest long delayed aftershock of his first encounter with the long gone M, and those early days when he modelled nude as M's *Love*. The memory returned in an immensely strange painting of himself twenty years after *Love the winner*, a painting that was hyperrealist, illusionistic and at the same time – insistently – merely an image.

All that came a long time later. In 1602 Cecco was on the cusp of adolescence, and if *Love the winner* played on his immaturity for the sake of the theme and – yes – sexual decorum, the other painting M did of him that year, the other full length nude, showed his body more male, his limbs longer and muscles harder. M did this new painting in a way that upped the ante of his visual provocation to an almost insane level. 1602 was the year M thought he could get away with anything. Either that or he simply didn't care. Amazingly, he came through unharmed. Eros had given M and his client Giustiniani a certain limited room for manoeuvre. The boy Love was traditionally playful. He'd lost his really dangerous charge of sexual anarchy long, long ago, before the end of preChristian times. Greek Eros had been tamed to Roman Cupid, made a child, and now lived on as a plump and sexless *putto*. A pagan symbol of sexual love was by definition unreal and valueless in the Christian era, a coin in a currency passed out of use. The church was naturally still far from happy about anything pagan because sexual pleasure came with the territory. The pagans had never entirely been neutralized, and Odoardo Farnese was realizing that his new ceiling was a more radical provocation than he'd foreseen. It'd already provoked M to show what radical really meant, what a charge a tired old pagan topos like *Love* could still be made to pack. Taking on the meanings and the imagery of the church in power was different again. This was what M now did.

Cardinal Paleotti had been very firm and very clear about *the paintings of false gods*, but he never got around to writing the third book of his treatise, which was going to concentrate on *lascivious painting*. He died before he could put paid, among other things, to

> arguments used by painters to justify showing nude and lascivious figures or indecent acts

or make clear why

> bodies must never be stripped naked to paint nudes from life.

It was a tall order, and hardly surprizing that he kept putting it off until it was too late. More than sex on its own, the cardinal's major worry was sex worming its way into religion. He knew it always did, given half a chance. He'd been planning to set out clearly *which saints may be shown partly nude and in what way* and why *youths' lascivious faces must on no account be used for saints'*. Paleotti did well to die when he did. Offending on every imaginable front, M's new painting of Cecco came on as a counter reformation ideologue's ultimate bad dream. Whatever Ciriaco Mattei was expecting when he commissioned M to do a painting of his eldest son's name saint, John the baptist, it sure wasn't what he got. Mattei got M's *owne boy* filling the canvas in a state of total frontal nudity – at least in the sense of exposed genitals, though he was twisting round from sideways on – grinning out over his shoulder in a maturer and more insolently sexy way than he'd grinned as Love, his limbs arranged in an adolescently awkward and wildly improbable anticipation of a nineteen fifties art studio *beauties of the male physique* pose with an oily art studio sheen to his skin, leaning so far back that his legs were almost waving in the air and being nuzzled by a *horny old ram*. A raucous teenage laugh was ready to break out like a thunderclap. The sittings with the rented ram had clearly been a lot of laughs. What this had to do with Christ's visionary forerunner in the wilderness, who

> had his raiment of camel's hair, and a leathern girdle about his loins; and his meat was locusts and wild honey

and calling the priestly caste *O generation of vipers* was unclear. The leathern girdle was happily cast off and John looked far too laid back to be denouncing anyone.

What did Ciriaco Mattei think when he saw it? Was he secretly delighted that M had come up with an image of his own carefully concealed subversiveness? Maybe certain *tendencies* the painter had played on? Did he like it as a doting father for expressing his own eldest son's real or imputed exuberance? Was he blind to art and simply thrilled to have scored another canvas by the most talked about painter of the moment? Utterly uninterested except in the prestige? Or was he deeply shocked, but too decent and well bred a man to do other than pay up and shut up? Was he so dazzled by the exquisitenesses of the ram's head and the foliage that he missed the big picture? Was he provoked or lulled into accepting the painting by his livelier younger brother Asdrubale, who liked M's art a lot? Was M's name so dazzling in Rome at that moment that with private clients he really could do what he wanted? The questions came hard and fast in the wake of the big unanswered question. How did M get away with it? The Mattei family were continuous, socially, politically, culturally with those other patrons and clients now congregating around M, and in one way they were so worldly and so serious that most of these scenarios were unthinkable. They were long established, and experienced art patrons – deeply informed and energetic students of archaeology and collectors of sculpture, ambitious builders who employed leading painters on complex decorative schemes. They had enough awareness to know what they liked and enough money and enough clout and enough discretion to be exempt from priestly anathemata. And yet, and yet –

While he was living with the Matteis M did the two *Saul* paintings and the two *Peter* paintings for Cerasi, the two *Matthew & angel* paintings for Contarelli, the two nudes of *Love the winner* and *John in the wild*. And he did three incomparable paintings for Vincenzo Giustiniani and Ciriaco Mattei – *Doubting Thomas*, the *Meal at Emmaus* and *Christ taken*. He did a *Sebastian* for Asdrubale Mattei that was later lost and a new version of *Isaac & Abraham* for Maffeo Barberini – a painting which ominously showed *his owne boy* yelling in fear as he was brutally put to the knife. The two Mattei years were marked out by Cecco's first childlike appearance as the angel in 1601 and this squalling frightened adolescent Isaac in 1603. It was a relationship that lasted much longer, but these looked like the limits of its serene early phase. These two years were the time of M's most prolific and inventive painting, the time when he was most himself, working freely and rapidly in the close and immediate half length format he now made vividly his own. How he actually lived in those two years remained almost completely unrecorded. An enigma. That he was living with the Matteis at all during that time was only inferred from an incidental annotation in the contract of June 1601. The amount of work he did for the Mattei family in that time seemed to confirm it – and that Cecco was with him and that they gave M the support and the freedom he needed, two years of good sex, plenty of money and untrammelled imagination, an outwardly domestic time maybe, a stable and happy time with Cecco and not a single run in with the police. The only time like it had been the tranquil and productive years with Mario at Del Monte's. The years with Cecco at the Matteis' were more adventurous and more assertive and they ended in trouble. But for now M was exulting in hard won painterly powers. Nothing like this time would come again.

The strangest part of it was who he seemed to be living with. Cardinal Mattei was the last person, you might think, to take over as protector of the most provocative and nonconformist painter in Rome. Ciriaco yes. Asdrubale yes. Cardinal Gerolamo no. He seemed to have no interest in art whatever. He left sixteen paintings when he died at the end of 1603. For a man of his wealth and standing this was like nothing. Del Monte, with none of Mattei's personal resources, owned six hundred paintings and fifty or so marble sculptures. There were acres of bare walls in Mattei's vast palazzo. It was called personal austerity. Mattei was neither a diplomat and power broker like Del Monte nor one of the good time set among the wealthy younger cardinals. He'd been made a cardinal by the fanatical Sixtus V Peretti and was famous as a zealot of the counter reformation and for his closeness to the strictest Franciscan order. He was not the kind of person you could imagine amiably wandering in to peer over M's shoulder as Cecco posed naked with the ram. When M left the cardinal's palace, or close to that time, he was under arrest. He'd become a liability and an embarrassment for quite other reasons, and three months later his distinguished host was dead. Mattei's will specified *no images* in his memorial. It was unlikely he and M had ever had a lot to say to each other.

And yet his was the branch of the catholic establishment that first cocked an eye at M's new art. The Mattei family was personally close to the late Filippo Neri, the counter reformation's militantly simple campaigner for a one on one relationship with God. Though Neri used to warn his penitents not to stare too hard at images, a religious movement like Neri's that theatrically embraced poverty and simplicity and a one on one relationship with God found it could relate to an art of painting like M's that spat out the hieratic and the transcendental and took its models off the streets – that was so radical it seemed like an anti art. The movement thought maybe it could use an art like that. Neri by the time he died in 1595 was a charismatically saintlike figure adored by Rome's vast floating population of the poor and homeless – the barefoot pilgrimages and ostentatious fasts of Clement VIII were based on Neri's. Pietro Aldobrandini had been a personal student of Neri's too, maybe not the best bearer the movement ever had of its message of cheerful renunciation, or not as far as food, drink, women, real estate and art were concerned. Neri's Oratorian movement had clout and had its eye on M. In 1602 the interest crystallized into a commission to do a major altarpiece for the Oratorian church in Rome, the *new church* of Santa Maria in Vallicella.

JOHN IN THE WILD frolicking with the ram seemed to be no problem for the people who mattered. The painting was not only acceptable, it was hugely popular – Ciriaco Mattei wasn't shy about letting people see it. Eleven copies were made of it – eleven surviving copies – one by M himself for a client who wanted a less insolent grin and some heavy shadow in the groin area. It was the first time he'd copied his own work since the *Boy bitten* and implied a pressing demand. Nothing known about M made you think he'd've been a patient and willing duplicator of things already done. The Mattei brothers' greatest obsession in art was collecting and arranging the marble statues that piece by piece were still being prised out of the Roman earth. Like the Giustiniani brothers, Ciriaco and Asdrubale both had a huge collection, Ciriaco's arranged in an elaborately landscaped garden. They'd've liked the sculptural feel of *John in the wild*, created by the play of light on the contours of the body. The springing youthful energy coiled in *John* and *Love* was form as well as finish. When the early enthusiast Scannelli in 1657 thought the

> nude *John* ... couldn't have shown truer flesh if he were alive, just like ... *Love*, which is maybe the best of M's paintings for private clients

he wasn't talking just about skin, but the muscular potential beneath it, the sense of imminent movement that M would do so well in children. The Matteis might've realized too that the sculptural feel of Ciriaco's *John* and *Love* derived from more than the way M had lit and modelled the play of flesh under smooth skin. The boy's slight body was arranged as *Love* in a way that was startlingly like the statue of *Victory* by Michelangelo Buonarotti, and like the painted Bartholomew in the *Last judgement*. As *John* he sat like one of the monumental, slab muscle packed and steroid pumped blankfaced nudes on the Sistine ceiling, their massive rolling slowness exactly mimicked in the laughing quickness of a barely adolescent boy. Once you caught the visual reference – and it was one M's contemporaries in Rome could hardly miss – it looked like a joke, a very cheeky takedown of the magnificently idealized gym queens in which M's namesake *sublimated* sexual into religious longings in the neoPlatonic as well as the Freudian sense. Michelangelo Buonarotti had brought it on himself. He'd been Rome's last great artist, and for a new painter of major ambitions he was the necessary point of reference. Annibale Carracci was showing that in his Farnese frescos. M had found Michelangelo's frescos of *Saul* and *Peter* on the Pauline chapel walls merely useful. Sex was another story, and if M's own handling of male nudity made Michelangelo's look sexless, that was more an assertion of his own sense of the real than a comment on Michelangelo's. The *Last judgement* looked carnal enough in its day – Aretino called it *bathhouse art* when it was unveiled. M's two boy nudes said a lot more about his own art and his own sexuality than they did about his feeling for Michelangelo Buonarotti's. Their sexual exultancy was his business.

Giustiniani was quite aware of Michelangelo's shadowy hand in M's studies of Cecco. It was what he meant when he later included M in the tiny group of superlative painters, the ones whose work combined truth to nature with the compositional strengths of *la maniera*. His own *Love* and his friend Mattei's *John* were the most emphatic of a lot of direct and indirect compositional reworkings from other artists in M's work. Most of the images M drew on came from Lombard and Venetian paintings he'd seen as a boy, or on his journey south to Rome. They were a repertory of forms retrieved from deep in his young imagination's memory, and acted out in life by the models in front of him, though hardly ever, as here, conscious and explicit and laughing citations from the work of his namesake. The haunting of M's painting by forms drawn from the work of great and lesser forerunners was a reminder that memory always played its part in the act of seeing and imitating. It'd do so in a different but matching way in M's later work too, when hunted and on the run he painted into the faces of the real or imaginary casual models he picked up to work from in his stopping places the remembered features of the models he'd known and loved in Rome.

John in the wild was the unlikeliest religious painting ever done and went on confusing people forever over what it was *of*. The lamb of God being a randy old ram and John's usual cross nowhere to be seen didn't help. Around 1620 Gaspare Celio, who'd worked for Mattei and seen the painting a few years after it was done, recalled it as a Phrygian shepherd – *pastor friso*. Giovan Battista Mattei when he died in 1624 left it to *my only lord and master* Del Monte under its proper name and his own. The ancient cardinal was surely delighted to have it, but three years later he too was dead and before long the painting was being inventoried among his others as a *Corydon*, reclaiming it for classical pederasty as a shepherd out of Theocritus's or Virgil's pastoral erotics. *John* was a kind of swansong, though it sounded like a yell of triumph at the time. M was invincible that year – money being thrown at him, the rich and powerful jostling for his work, out of Del Monte's gilded cage – though it was all illusory. It was a one in a million coincidence of the moment of sexual exultancy and the peak of *avant garde* notoriety. The taunting irreligious fuck me *John* for the doting Matteis was a one off hit. So was Giustiniani's pagan boy sex triumph *Love*. He never did anything remotely like them again. Neither were they like the other work he was doing even then. Two other paintings M did for Mattei, just before and just after *John*, and another for Giustiniani in the same months, were crowded human dramas, vivid, intense and utterly serious, miles from the lightheartedness M showed in his treatments of Cecco. But they still didn't look religious.

CIRIACO MATTEI MARKED two payments in his own meticulously kept account books for July and December of 1602, and they roughly marked when M began and finished *John in the wild*. The amount paid came to a fairly modest total of eighty five scudi, because John was a single figure. The larger payments to M that were recorded before and after these in Mattei's accounts were for much more complex paintings. In January 1602 M received a hundred and fifty scudi for a painting of the *Meal at Emmaus* and in January the following year he got a hundred and twenty five scudi for a *Christ taken*. M did a third painting too at this time, a *Doubting Thomas* for Vincenzo Giustiniani. Baglione thought he did the *Thomas* for Mattei too, because he painted it in the Mattei palazzo, but there was no record of payment by Mattei and five years later *Thomas* was securely in the Giustiniani collection.

Small format, private client, intimacy and trust – now M explored the resources he'd created with his great and arduous achievements in public *history* painting. These smaller canvases were histories too, but now M moved nearer, composed more tightly, caught the inwardnesses and closenesses of people's relations with each other. In the heartbreaking felicity of old Peter's dying look – at those few crumbling stones you knew would be the last thing those cloudy eyes would ever see – he'd discovered that old people might be more than specialty figures with striking facial landscapes, more than a mere addition to the variety of human types a *history* required, more than the contrasting servants of youth and beauty like clumsy Matthew to his angel or the old servant woman to Judith. In his maturity M discovered the beauty of age in people, as he'd already enjoyed the living variety of fruit and leaves, and all the related beauties of the used and abused, the worn, the lived, faces, hands, clothes, tools, and that this happened at the very time he was exulting in Cecco's unmarked adolescent vigour was no less amazing than the simultaneity of all his different and dazzling technical gains. And sentiment didn't come into it. Bellori couldn't forgive him for making painters want to paint *common bodies without beauty* and the real and imperfect world.

> People started imitating vile things, seeking out dirt and deformity … if they have to paint armour, they choose the rustiest, a vase is never a whole one but broken with its spout missing … clothes are coarse stockings, britches and big hats and when they do bodies they put all their effort into doing the wrinkles and marks on the skin … the fingers knotty and the limbs deformed by disease.

Much would be made ever after of M's intent in choosing his models off the street. It was seen as polemical realism, kicking sand in the faces of weedy late mannerists, or seen as a polemical exaltation of the disinherited that might've expressed a special sympathy with the followers of Filippo Neri *the Christian Socrates* – the sharper minded of whose acolytes certainly felt that what M was doing afforded interesting but dangerous possibilities. It was an intellectual's delusion that M might've had a programme. The simplicity of the trained mind was always to imagine all others as itself. M's greater simplicity was to like his models because they were what he saw. He told Giustiniani that there was as much *workmanship – manifattura –* in painting a still life as in doing one of people. Compared with the radicalism of putting flowers on a par with people, M's dismissal of the human distinctions of rank and beauty made these look like hair splitting.

Pushed into *history* by the demands of the market, he now made it peculiarly his own in these chamber histories for private buyers. His concern was still with two things, the form and finish of the image itself. The finish was being refined and intensified by his experiments with light, the bodies powerfully present, lit by a single source, isolated by surrounding darkness. Form was now the multiple play of bodies in a small space, looming out of the dark to fill the horizontal half length canvases with two, three, four human figures locked in existential crisis. The *histories* were biblical, the scenes were what he could assemble in his studio. Beyond their very availability, what M probably liked most about his models was being able to make them do what he wanted – keep a sword up or swing a severed head for hours, stand in despair until their head spun and the blood drained from their raised arms, stand hieratically all day with a powerful child struggling to break loose. The models evidently didn't mind M's treatment of them. They kept coming back, turning up in painting after painting.

M was never more vigorously himself than when he painted these horizontal three quarter easel paintings for his private clients in Rome. They afforded him a format that was intimate but not restrictive and which matched what he could manageably stage in the studio and paint from life. None of them took so long to do that energy and invention died on the job and the dead hand of official requirement never descended. The destination of a private gallery relieved him of the doctrinal anxieties and dangers that surrounded anything public and promised a warm response. The rapid production blended continuity and variety of treatment in a way that encouraged experiment. These paintings were the mature and natural outcome of the work he'd been doing at Del Monte's in the latter nineties, transmuted and energized by the dramatic exigencies of biblical *histories*. The year around 1602 and 1603 was a year of horizontal marvels.

The first thing M did for Ciriaco Mattei was the *Meal at Emmaus* at the end of 1601 – of the moment where his two followers recognized the executed Christ in their dinner companion when he broke and blessed the bread. It invited, and got, a treatment that looked back at M's earlier figures at a table and the interplay of human figures and still life. The basket of fruit was again projecting off the front edge of the table, the fruit itself rich and spotted as in life, the light on the water carafe exquisite. *Giulietto* as the startlingly young and beardless Christ contrasted with the older, rougher disciples as he'd done with

Matthew when he played the angel, and the abrupt amazement of their recognition was like the peasant Matthew's. The figure on the left – his out at the elbow sleeve catching the light as he pushed back his chair – was marvellously done, but none of the four figures seemed to be quite in synch. It was the problem of action again. M's disturbingly level gaze made the overripe fruit in its cheap basket and the plain glass carafe and the broken bread and the scrawny chook with its claws in the air no less a part of the picture than the Christian protagonists – the food and drink were framed and protected in the deep space made by the gesturing arms, the fruit poised to be sent flying out of the front of the picture when Cleopas sprang up from the Savanorola chair. And it made the host – who was there for the very purpose of demonstrating his profane unseeing exclusion from the mystery – no less compelling a figure than the apostles, his shadow splattered on the wall as in a flash photo, the patient provider of food who'd also spent a lifetime courteously attending to other people's conversations, partially heard and imperfectly understood.

Scannelli in 1657 found the *Meal at Emmaus* a painting of *terrifying naturalness* and he was a doctor. Quite how disturbing M's loving attention to the palpably and visibly real might be to catholic orthodoxy registered in Bellori's reaction a little later. Bellori – who could delight in a painting by M of men around a table when the men were card players representing nothing beyond themselves – praised the *natural colouring* but hated the rest.

> In the *Meal at Emmaus*, apart from the uncouthly country forms of the two apostles and the Lord shown as a beardless youth, the host's standing by with his cook's cap on and on the table there's a plate of grapes, figs and pomegranates quite out of season.

Fruit out of season mattered, in an image of the Easter mystery, but the painting was done in the autumn of 1601. It may not have been ideologically correct but among painters and clients the *Emmaus* was a great hit. Twenty odd copies were made that survived.

Even more were made of *Doubting Thomas,* which M now did for Giustiniani and was even more brutally real in its handling of Christ's reappearance. People still wince when they see Thomas's finger stretching the skin over Christ's ribcage and probing the bloodless slit. *Thomas* was an austere study in browns of four figures, bare of objects and setting, a man showing his operation scar to his workmates. The four figures were locked into a powerful composition of heads, hands and shoulders, the lines of folds in cloth, wrinkles in brows, strands of hair. Thomas and the other apostles were burly, bent, tanned and creased with outdoor work, and the browns were their glowing life. The Christ was young, slim and ringleted, but dead – or formerly dead – and the painting took its power from the subtlety with which it played on his likeness and unlikeness to them, his closeness to them and separateness from them. His face in half shadow showed the kind of abstracted intentness with which anyone might study an old spear wound between their ribs, raised to another level of regret.

IF YOU WERE a painter and wanted work in Rome you did religious art, and religious art meant – emphatically – paintings that were not like *John in the wild*, and also not like the all too human encounters of *Emmaus* and *Thomas*. M could get away with paintings like these for his eager individual clients, but even as these private buyers were paying big money for it, his work was starting to disturb the guardians of established culture. Wealthy individuals like Contarelli or Cerasi – churchmen who'd made personal fortunes in very questionable ways out of their work inside the church – could commission whatever art they wanted for their chapels, but the results had to be approved by the priests of the church where the art'd be seen. And however rich and influential the benefactor and however famous or fashionable the artist of his choice, that approval wasn't necessarily forthcoming. Three years after M's dazzling public debut in San Luigi dei Francesi, neither the catholic church itself, the biggest and richest art patron of all, nor any of its constituent religious orders, had yet commissioned any work from the painter M.

M knew this and he kept trying to come to terms with prevailing values in art and religion. He needed to sell his work. He wanted people to see it – more people than tiny groups of the ultra rich. In the working and reworking of the Contarelli and Cerasi side paintings he'd started with ideas that conceded a lot to late mannerist ways of visualizing religious scenes – to decorous ways of presenting the Christian story – and he only abandoned or redid them because, in the end, they were incompatible with his way of seeing. It was recognizing that incompatibility that urged him to his great new imaginings. The problem he then faced when the first *Matthew & angel* was knocked back was simply a shock. It was something he hadn't foreseen – he'd had no doubts here, the painting was clearly a masterwork – which was why he struck people as *despairing* until Giustiniani interceded to let him try again. On 7 January 1602 Ciriaco Mattei had noted a payment to M of a hundred and fifty scudi for the *Meal at Emmaus*. A year later, on 2 January 1603 Mattei paid M a hundred and twenty five scudi for *a Christ taken in the garden*. A year had ended in which M had been humiliated over *Matthew & angel* and bounced back triumphantly, even as he was pushing his most liberal collectors to the limit with *Love the winner*, *John in the wild*, *Meal at Emmaus* and *Doubting Thomas*. He now tried very hard to get seriously in line with the *Christ taken* and the effort resulted in a powerful painting riven by its own inner tension. It turned out, for quite contingent reasons, to be the last painting he'd do for the Matteis, the last fruit of a serene relationship with deeply congenial patrons, and probably the end of serenity with Cecco too. In that sense the anxious violence of *Christ taken*, a painting more like *Matthew killed* than anything else he'd done in the last three years, announced the deep disturbances of the year just starting. In 1603 M hardly painted a thing. Other things were on his mind, and one of the few paintings from this time implied trouble with Cecco as well.

When his own follower Judas betrayed Christ with a kiss for cash, and Christ was seized at night by the Roman soldiery, it was the great black moment in the Christian *history*, fraught for the faithful with the intensities of the coming passion. In a time of inquisition, censorship, spying and torture in the Christian world, of torn loyalty, secret betrayal, anonymous denunciation, nocturnal arrest, and of exemplary public whippings, humiliations, beheadings and burnings alive for crimes of opinion and morality, the arrest of Christ was also a peculiarly charged, a peculiarly political and *modern* moment in the Christian drama. M's treatment showed all this. The hugger mugger drama in the night, scuffles, whispers, shouts, the kiss, the torches and the drawn swords, panic, resistance, resignation – it was made for M and he seized the chance. Again he moved in close and exploited to the utmost the panoramic intimacy of a three quarter length horizontal canvas, filling the space with seven crowded figures cut off at the knee. It was a wonderfully fluent articulation of distinct individuals into the best *action* picture he ever did. Everybody was sweeping from right to left across the canvas, soldiers, onlookers, a panicking disciple, Judas himself lunging into Christ's face with lips still puckered from the kiss – everyone except Christ himself, the one slight figure on the left who stemmed the surge. The painting was like a dynamic reworking of the group in *Doubting Thomas*, only this more complex cluster divided the canvas down the middle, into a right side of jostling armoured soldiery and darkness and a left side of three interlocked faces of Christ and disciples framed in strongly coloured drapery.

What held it together was the reaching figure of the helmeted and armoured soldier at the front, the great black shell of his shoulder catching a brilliant gleam of light in the very centre of the canvas, the iron cased arm reaching over Judas's and the heavy mailed hand joining Judas's grasping fingers to pull Christ into the centre of the picture. The soldiers were brutal and menacing but never inhuman. The elderly soldier with the straggly moustache and a badly rusted helmet, uselessly tugging at the fleeing disciple's red cloak, might've been imagined by Cervantes, and his superficial likeness to the old soldier in the first *Saul* showed how much more deeply human M's gaze had become in a year and a half, how his human register had widened.

It was among the soldiers that M now placed himself, at the back of the crowd, peering over heads for a glimpse of the action, so that the upper part of his face was white in the light and the rest in shadow. He was no longer puffy and distraught, as he'd seen himself in *Matthew killed*, no longer fleeing the violence, but newly young, eager, deep eyed, tensed toward the human confusion, and holding a lantern above the faces in the dark. It was how he lit his models in the studio, hoisting a lantern overhead in the darkened room, and a way now of saying that this was how dark deeds at night were lit in real life. The lantern also illuminated M's own artfulness, since the real light source, the source in the studio, was out of the picture. The *real* light was coming from elsewhere. Twenty seven years later the young Spanish painter Velázquez spent a year in Rome at the age M was when he did *Christ taken*, and his own later paintings showed he looked long and hard at M's work. If Velázquez ever got to see *Christ taken*, he might've liked its painter's wink at the irreducible artificiality of the real in art, winked back and stored the idea away for future use.

The soldiers were so powerfully done that they overwhelmed the icon at the heart of the picture. They got a lot of help from the icon himself. Christ here was a long way from the smooth cheeked full-faced boy breaking bread at Emmaus, and had nothing of the austere intense disinterestedness of the figure in ringlets showing Thomas his wound. The pasty figure being seized had regulation hair and beard, sanctimoniously lowered eyes and fingers knitted like a bashful virgin in a silent movie. Like the apostle behind him – frozen in a stylized cry that owed everything to artistic precedent and a lot less to real feeling than, say, the boy acolyte's in *Matthew killed*, let alone M's own open mouthed anxiety in the same painting – Christ was not real. He was unreal in a way that was perfectly in line with the counter reformation idea of how Christ would look. Maybe M did it for the fading cardinal Gerolamo, who now had less than a year to live. Maybe, unnerved by his own unremitting provocations over the previous year, he just blinked. If compromise was his intent, he achieved it for a fatally weakened painting. Bellori was reassured enough by the propriety of the central figure to turn his enthusiastic attention to the rusty helmet, the visored face, the raised lantern – the things that really interested him. The lower foreground was almost painful, where Christ and the arresting officer were side by side. A marvellous overlap of strapped and buckled armour on a powerful male haunch dressed in red with gold – an intricacy of iron, leather and satin, of plates, nails, buckles and ribbons – was juxtaposed with Christ's mincing laced white fingers and the idly symmetrical folds of his turquoise wrap. *Christ taken* was full of life and danger pressing in from its edges, and empty at its heart. If he meant it to, M's little move toward accommodation didn't help with new commissions – probably it went unnoticed. Suspicion was being registered.

In August 1603, six months or so after M did *Christ taken*, cardinal Ottaviano Paravicino wrote a letter to a friend and colleague Paolo Gualdo in Vicenza inquiring about the new painter M. It was a letter whose elaborate indirection suggested how uneasy the church's opinion makers were becoming about M's take on reality. Paravicino was one of the most influential cardinals and belonged to the very nexus of clerics, Filippo Neri's Oratorians, who were most interested in what M was doing. As a boy Paravicino had been tutored by the ultra devout Cesare Baronio, now cardinal and confessor to Clement VIII and currently thinking mainly about death. The tutor Baronio was so shocked by the lustful images he found in the palazzo of the boy's father the marchese Paravicino that he took to them with a paintbrush and obliterated the scandal of nudity himself. Young Paravicino, having learnt early to tread carefully around art, went on to twenty years of *spiritual formation* as the pupil of Filippo Neri, *employed in the humblest tasks.* Paravicino, *a little hunchback with an alert face,* was made a cardinal for his success as papal nuncio in turning back the protestant tide in Switzerland during the eighties. Later in Rome he collected his mentor the dying saint's last phlegm in a cuspidor. Paravicino had been one of the cardinals who'd supported the proposal for an *Index of prohibited images* seven years earlier.

Paravicino was writing to a good friend in Vicenza – a churchman without great ambitions, linked to the Jesuits of Padua but more interested in the arts and good times than a career, who knew Tasso and Palladio and would later be a friend and defender of Galileo –

for information about the painter M. The letter itself was a prime piece of ecclesiastical high camp, though its tone was steelier and more menacing than Del Monte's benign malignancies. Fishing for confirmation or denial of a rumour he didn't want to spell out but sounded pretty sure of, the cardinal, in an archly tortuous series of pseudo jocular hypotheses – Filippo Neri had promoted *Christian cheerfulness* among his followers – was trying to discover whether his friend – who'd been in Rome a short time before – had been in contact with M and maybe even commissioned a religious painting from him. The cardinal clearly thought his friend had. The cardinal called M an *excellent painter* to show his awareness of M's current prestige and implied that he knew money had already changed hands. But the letter, in its joky fictive mode, imagined M himself saying that if he'd done one of those paintings of his, paintings that were *midway between sacred and profane*, the cardinal's ecclesiastical friend *wouldn't've even wanted to look at it*. Or so the cardinal made clear he preferred to believe. He'd clearly had a look at *John in the wild*, or one of the others at the Matteis'. He surely remembered the trouble over *Matthew & angel*. Religious art that was *halfway profane*, from the church's point of view, was halfway wildly unacceptable.

Paravicino was also fishing for information about M's possibly dangerous opinions and the answer he got was lost. It was all the more unfortunate in that the cardinal's own next letter to Vicenza made it clear that the answer to his insinuations was *copious*. His friend was clearly rattled, and felt there was a deal of explaining to do. Which was hardly surprizing. The cardinal was uttering a friendly and lightly coded threat to a potential client of M's, or an informer on him, and this cardinal's was one of the Roman church's most powerful voices. In case his good friend got the wrong idea, cardinal Paravicino then amiably hoped his friend the monsignor's summer holidays *in villeggiatura* out of town were going well, and closed with an arch allusion to the friend's close attentiveness to a young widowed duchess.

Cardinal Paravicino was revealing a tizzy of anticipatory nerves over what M was going to perpetrate in the big altarpiece a private admirer had lately ordered for a chapel in the Oratorians' *new church*. Piero Vittrice, *butler* and later *wardrobeperson* to pope Gregory XIII had died in early 1600. Vittrice had a chapel in the new church and his heir and nephew Girolamo Vittrice, some time in late 1601 or early 1602, commissioned an altarpiece from M. The chapel was closed in early 1602 for reconstruction work and some time after this, when the size of the new painting was fixed, M began work on *Christ's burial*. No records survived of the contract or payment, but by the beginning of September 1604 the painting was well in place. M himself, who'd been so conspicuously shattered when *Matthew & angel* was knocked back, probably began his second big work for a public altar with a certain inner dread. After that first brutal intimation of limits he took greater care. Some unidentifiable time in the nearly three intensely busy and increasingly fraught and violent years between early 1602 and late 1604 – and most likely in the earlier part of 1603 – M painted his most lavishly praised and most frequently copied painting in a Roman church. He'd made very sure there were no problems with his second altarpiece. Everybody thought it magnificent, the best thing M ever did – *they say* added Baglione darkly. Bellori too thought *Christ's burial* M's best work and described it in detail –

> the whole nude is painted with the strength of the most exact imitation.

By the summer of 1603, however, M was facing much more urgent trouble than a discreet thumbs down from an influential prelate. He was about to be arrested for criminal libel of one of the church's favourite younger painters. Things were starting to come apart.

9

ROME 1603

Christ's burial

*C*HRIST'S BURIAL WAS a deeply moving picture for all the wrong reasons. Not that any of its admirers seemed to notice, then or ever after. It briskly eliminated mourning, swooning or keening and got down to the practical question of manhandling a naked corpse and lowering it into the ground. The physical awkwardness was clear when the process was seen from below. Christ did for once look like a real corpse and a dead weight, a well made man killed in his prime, his lips already turning blue. It was a strictly private burial, two close male associates, John and Nicodemus, dealing with the body and three women formerly close to the deceased pressing up close behind. The dead man's mother showed considerable self control in her set face, while one of the younger women, a very pretty girl whose fancy hairdo was coming undone in wisps, was bent forward crying quietly to herself. Only the third woman, a young relative at the back, made a slight show of public emotion with her upraised hands.

The moment of stasis in the action had come when this group had arrived at the edge of the stone slab and finished moving forward. The two men were about to lower the body. Everyone was bunched up close into a single sculptural group. A curving declension of bowed heads led the eye ineluctably to the horizontal reality of the dead body. They were all on top of each other, the corpse's legs encircled in Nicodemus's arms, John taking the weight of the torso with his fingers in the wound, the women backing up behind – the five living figures were quite distinct, none looking at another, locked in their own thoughts but locked together by the intimacy of the task in hand, a collective unity packed into the canvas. They were felt as a looming solid presence. M's fascination with three dimensionality in painting – not in Leonardo's old renaissance sense of perspective and a depth that receded from the plane of the picture's surface, but as an invasive bodying forth out of that surface – went back to his experiments with the curved surface of the *Medusa* shield, the *Basket of fruit* on its ledge, sticking out from the wall the painting was hanging on. Now it was solid figures looming out of the dark. He was always having quiet slapstick fun with this illusion of physical imminence, with the fruit basket about to topple off the table in front of Christ in *Emmaus*, Matthew's stool about to crash out on to the altar and send the saint flying, or turning the space of a chapel where the viewer stood into a palaeochristian plunge pool. This was a painter who enjoyed training his black poodle Crow to walk on its hind legs.

Now he was realizing this effect of physical imminence as an answer to the old question of *action* in narrative painting. If *feeling* could be rendered in its moment of stillness as inwardness, *action* could be done as the stillness in which movement impended into your space – it was the acrobat's trapeze at its furthest point from you, about to swing toward you and be grabbed. The friends burying Christ were neither facing nor in profile to a person looking at M's painting. As the corner of the stone slab they stood on made clear, jutting massively out of the bottom at the viewer, their impending movement was diagonal to the picture plane. Nicodemus caught the viewer's eye with a sharp and wary *sideways* glance out of the front of the picture. This pulled you into a peculiar and almost furtive intimacy with the event – like an actor glancing at an observer in the wings – as the visual aggression of his elbow, jutting like the slab sharply into the observing eye, made the viewer even more of an intruder into this private and sorrowful task.

Most powerfully, though, it made the whole group look as if it were going to follow Nicodemus's gaze and swivel round toward the viewer and dump the body – since anyone in the chapel was looking up at these figures from somewhere down in the tomb, which was more of M's subdued visual fun – if not in your lap at least on the altar below the painting. M had set up a powerfully monumental group in his studio – a group whose sculptural classicism the critics all admired in the finished painting, as they were intended to – and then moved his easel over to paint from the corner. It was a move that his Nicodemus model, lately seen as Thomas probing Christ's wound, clearly found disconcerting. He was unaware that the oblique glances he kept shooting over at the painter from his long bony face, and his pointy elbow and the curve of his hunched back and his big feet with the raised veins over the ankle bones, sturdily planted at eye level, would be at the heart of a great pathos.

Christ's burial was a triumph of fine tuning. M now knew how to seize the telling instant of utter stillness that always occurred in any collective event, between one movement and another, like the stillness of a pendulum at the furthest point of its arc. Busy tumult vanished from his work. The technical solution to the problem of painting *action* from life was a matter of perceiving the stillness and inwardness that was present even at the height of violence and confusion. M understood people's infinitesimal reflective detachment from their own acts, and in painting the surface of events he seemed to see through their momentariness to a permanence of inner meaning. M would go on painting *histories* of violent group action to the very end of his life, and more and more they were images of austere and monumental stillness.

EVERYONE THOUGHT GIOVANNI Baglione was the same age as M, and they believed M to be two years younger than he really was. Two years was no great fib, but Baglione took a whopping eight off his own age. When Baglione later included a fairly extensive account of his own achievements – carefully airbrushing over certain key connexions – among his *Lives of the painters*, he feigned modesty and disguised the self promotion by pretending it'd been added by the publisher. He wrote about his own first work back in the days when Sixtus V was making Rome over. Baglione did his first known work in fresco on the walls of the Vatican library in 1589, and remembered that he'd painted

> two big *histories* with figures from life, and he brought them
> off so beautifully and frankly that pope Sixtus, seeing this
> work done by a young boy of fifteen, was utterly delighted
> by it.

But the parish record of Baglione's death on the second last day of 1643 – the year after his *Lives* were published – noted that his age was seventy seven. In 1589 the artist whose boyish precocity had so thrilled the pope was actually twenty three and not fifteen. And so Baglione was five years older than M. Being a Roman, he was active early on the scene and did a lot of frescos in churches around Rome in a mannerist style that drew on the work of his junior Cesari. Cesari duly appreciated the older painter's assimilation of his own kind of mannerism and made a point of gathering Baglione into the team assembled to work in 1600 under Cesari's direction on Clement VIII's holy year project of redecorating San Giovanni in Laterano.

Another painter employed on the same project in 1600 was in his late thirties, a Florentine goldsmith's son born in Pisa in 1563, three years older than Baglione and eight years older than M. He'd arrived in Rome in his mid teens to live at first with his uncle, who was a captain in the garrison at the castel Sant' Angelo. Orazio Gentileschi had begun painting only in his twenties, after early work in his father's craft. He was a self taught late starter who lacked a painter's formal training. He too, like the *soi disant* boy prodigy Baglione, was one of the crowd that had worked on the frescos in the Vatican library at the end of the fifteen eighties. In the following decade he'd begun the slow crawl toward creating a painterly identity for himself in his first public commissions. Gentileschi was another good friend of Cesari's and another natural for the team redoing San Giovanni in Laterano. In 1595 Gentileschi worked on designing a dead cardinal's catafalque with Onorio Longhi and maybe it was through Longhi that at some time toward 1600 Gentileschi got to know M.

While they were working under Cesari that year, producing dreary official art for the holy year – Baglione working very much in Cesari's own manner and Gentileschi still without an easily identifiable style of any kind – M was doing the *Matthew* side pictures that inflamed the teeming world of Roman painters that summer. Each responded to what M was doing in symptomatically different ways. Gentileschi was already part of M's and Longhi's social push and likely knew well from watching him how M worked from life straight on to canvas. He began a long slow sedimentary accumulation of M's early experience in painting on canvas. He'd been working for all his first painting years under church supervision as one of a large team, subdued to an official ethos and group discipline that allowed him none of the personal scope the young M was enjoying in his private easel work for Del Monte and friends. Knocking forty, Gentileschi now reversed M's step from private and small to big and public. He borrowed M's pair of swan's wings, the ones lately used for the rejected *Matthew & angel*, and did some paintings of his own of *Francis & angel* that were oddly like M's earliest religious paintings.

Orazio Gentileschi was making M's experience his own. He was one of the few who learnt a nearly unlearnable lesson and he learnt it because he had resources of his own. A few years later he'd pass on what he knew to his only daughter. Artemisia Gentileschi was one of the seventeenth century's most formidable painters, Italy's greatest woman painter ever. Her own work was full of her father's spirit and fuller, in its urgency and violence, of her father's wilder younger friend's – of the art of the difficult man she'd known as a child, of the painter who left town suddenly as she was reaching puberty and never came back and was already dead the year she did her first important picture as a precocious girl of seventeen.

Giovanni Baglione at the same time was ending the early phase of his long and appallingly prolific career and getting ready in 1600 to jump ship. He'd seen the future and decided it worked. He liked the look of the new century's new art and decided to make it his own, maybe after eyeing what Orazio Gentileschi was already doing in this direction, since Baglione's *earliest works in this style are more reminiscent of Gentileschi than M.* Like Gentileschi, Baglione too did a version in 1601 of M's innovative early painting of Francis in the arms of an angel. Baglione's had an extra angel standing by. Gentileschi and Baglione were now shadowing each other's moves, rivals as emulators of the younger M. Whoever was first to do a *Francis & angel*, it was Gentileschi who first did a painting – later lost – of *Michael archangel* for the church of San Giovanni dei Fiorentini. Baglione hit back with a *Divine love* encased in massive armour like the archangel. This was the painting that turned things ugly. *Divine love* wasn't only, as Gentileschi later claimed, done as a challenge to his archangel. It took on M and his most *piquant* and celebrated work, *Love the winner.*

Giulio Mancini had as much trouble as modern historians locating Baglione on the art scene and sounded puzzled when he wrote that Baglione

> went off following the style of the cavalier Giuseppe [Cesari] for a bit ... then he seemed to attach himself to M's, and lately he's taken up a style of his own ...

This was later, when Baglione had been trimming his sails to the winds of fashion for nearly twenty years, and was a successful and socially prominent painter and a *cavalier* like Giuseppe Cesari. Someone a very prominent member of the medical establishment like Mancini could even meet socially. *He behaves quite decently,* noted Mancini appreciatively, *extremely easy to get on with.* Unlike the late M, whom Mancini remembered with something like horror when he looked back and who was *impossible to get on with.* At the start of the century, however,

Baglione was heading into middle age without having perfected the bland adaptability of either his later painting or his later manners, and his rivalry with Gentileschi and his emulation of M were about to get him entangled in the worst and most humiliating thing that ever happened to him. An episode that knotted his gut and filled his mouth with bile whenever he thought about it, even when he was forty years older and famous and the others were dead or forgotten. Giovanni Baglione was about to take up the new realism. At the time it looked like a great career move.

Baglione painted a *Divine love conquering earthly love* for Vincenzo Giustiniani's elder brother, the cardinal Benedetto. He took the two boys who'd modelled as the angels for his *Francis* and rejigged them as sacred and profane love. Sacred love, a youth with strange slanting heavy lidded eyes and a mane of tawny hair like a Tina Turner wig, was dressed in full body armour that left only his head, arms and feet bare. He was equipped with a fantasy of splayed feathers as wings and stood over a nude and supine, suggestively but tastefully posed Profane love, theatrically making as to impale him with an allegorical thunderbolt. In the bottom left hand corner a murky devil looked away in defeat. It was certainly one of the best things Baglione ever did, but when the play of light on real surfaces – the technical tricks Baglione was lifting from M – was brought to bear on such a rhetorical allegory the effect was subtly ridiculous. The prominent cocked leg encased in its plates of armour looked like a mutant grasshopper's.

Baglione's painterly challenge to the preeminence of the marchese's sensational nude boy *Love the winner* was also a sanctimonious courtier's appeal to the counter reformation proprieties, and on this level at least it worked brilliantly, as Gentileschi remembered.

> It was a *Divine love* that he'd done to compete with an *Earthly love* by M and he'd dedicated it to cardinal Giustiniani.

The cardinal brother, relieved to have an acceptably orthodox counterweight to M's provocative masterpiece in the collections of palazzo Giustiniani, rewarded Baglione ostentatiously with a gold chain, just as Pietro Aldobrandini had given Annibale Carracci a gold chain worth two hundred scudi in admiration for his Farnese gallery frescos the year before. The display of approval got up M's nose – an extravagant reward for a painting that was at once cheaply derivative and smugly critical of his own most daring work. By flaunting it in San Giovanni dei Fiorentini as well, opposite Gentileschi's probably likewise armoured and striding *Archangel Michael*, Baglione made a second enemy with the same painting. *People didn't like it as much as M's*, Gentileschi said some months later of Baglione's effort, using carefully neutral tones and pretending not to know too much about the episode, *even though it was understood the cardinal gave him a neck chain*. Gentileschi clearly didn't think much of Benedetto Giustiniani as a judge of art. He told Baglione what he thought too, probably in more vivid terms than he later used to recall it.

> The painting had a lot of faults and I told him he'd done
> a grown man and armed when it should've been a naked
> boy and so he did another who was all nude.

But the second painting Baglione did wasn't quite *all nude*. It was a replica of the first, only Divine love had shed his armour and donned a hideously fancy and fussy girdle. A brocade skirt was hitched up on the thigh of the cocked leg, now smoothly nude. There was one other small difference in the new version. The dark skinned pointy eared devil, whose face had earlier been turned away in shame, was now looking back in dismay over his shoulder, resting on his hand and staring wide eyed at the viewer – or indeed the painter – showing a light scurf of facial hair and a mouthful of bad teeth. The devil's grimacing face was unmistakeably M's. This was wanton provocation. If Baglione thought that *Divine love* with an exposed thigh would silence all critics and even let him mock, in the hypocritical name of counter reformation moralism, the painter whose art he was trying to hijack – and maybe he really did believe that with his facile brush and winning establishment ways he could make short work of a rebarbative and vulnerable genius like M – he had another think coming. It came pretty soon, though at the time Baglione was gloating pictorially because he thought he had it made. There was more than the gold chain.

BAGLIONE WON A major commission for the Jesuit church in Rome, from the father general of the society of Jesus himself, Claudio Acquaviva. The commission was to do a huge altarpiece for one of the chapels – an immense *Resurrection of Christ*, almost eight metres high by four and a half wide, one of the biggest paintings in seventeenth century Rome – and M had wanted that commission very badly for himself. The Jesuits were the counter reformation's ideologues, and Baglione's image of *Divine love* trampling and impaling a naked and defenceless Earthly love promised that the exciting, glamorous and prestigious new *chiaroscuro* realism could be combined with a tasteful assertion of high catholic values. In Baglione. Baglione was offering ideological reassurance a few months before cardinal Paravicino felt the need to put out his uneasily facetious feeler about M's religious art. Baglione got the job. He already had sound institutional credentials as a Cesari man, and if Acquaviva and the Jesuits could've foreseen M's radically disturbing handling of the resurrection theme that came a few years later, they'd've felt their caution well repaid.

Only it was a dud. Baglione flopped. The big screen spectacle opened on Easter Sunday 1603, but the huge canvas, *done with love and care*, Baglione insisted defensively decades later, was an evident failure. It was so much a failure that late in the century the Jesuits silently removed it and replaced it with another canvas. And after it was taken down, Baglione's *Resurrection* as silently vanished out of art history. Only a small preliminary version afforded a glimmer of what it was – as a matter of art and not just personal resentment – M and his friends now so savagely attacked. Baglione's great stylistic compromise split the canvas in two. Top and bottom came from opposing poles of Baglione's eclectic mind. Above, a perfectly conventional late mannerist risen Christ in loincloth adopted a stock pose with banner among a perfectly acceptable heavenly orchestra of swooning angels and cherubs playing their instruments on small clouds. Most of the strongly *chiaroscuro* bottom half was stolen from M's *Matthew killed* – unrelated bodybuilder semi nudes, *sleeping soldiery* who looked as if they'd wandered in from another scene – as indeed they had. Some looked dead, but a left handed nude on his feet wielding a knife irresistibly recalled Matthew's assassin, and another sprawled along the bottom foreground was aping in a vacuum the role of the nude at the pool's edge in M's painting. There was plenty to feed M's fury here.

That spring, M and his push – specifically Onorio Longhi and Orazio Gentileschi – moved in for the critical kill. Frequent visits to the church – the Gesù one of the symbolic centres of the counter reformation – and loudly voiced and savage criticism of Baglione's art inevitably got mixed with merely personal rancour and commercial rivalry – since big commissions were a cutthroat business – and mutated, as the sweltering malarial summer came on in the close little world of the painters' Rome, into the viciously intimate and physical. There was no way, in any case, to draw a line between art and money in the matter of intellectual property rights. Anger at the theft was mixed with contempt for the uses the stolen goods were put to. None of it was new. M had been reacting violently to imitators ever since the *Matthew* paintings went on view. In the autumn of 1601, when he'd just finished the Cerasi *Saul* and *Peter* paintings, a younger painter had gone to the police accusing M of a nighttime attack in the via della Scrofa.

> ... the said M came up and hit me from behind with the sword he was carrying and caught me on the arm. As I turned to defend myself the said M inflicted many other blows on me, such that if the neighbours hadn't heard the noise and come running, I might well have been wounded or even killed by the aforesaid who moreover insulted me and called me a fucking prick and other insulting words.

The complainant, who claimed M was *continually committing similar offences and attacking people*, was a painter several years younger than M who was eagerly taking up M's way of doing still life, despite M's vigorous attempts to discourage him from riding in his slipstream. His name was Tommaso Salini and everyone called him *Mao* and he was a friend and follower – apparently the one and only friend and follower – of Giovanni Baglione. M sardonically called him Baglione's *guardian angel*. Mao was an equivocal hanger on. He'd earlier been in trouble with other fellow painters as a slanderer and thief, and even his mentor and great defender Baglione later remembered him as having *an excessively free and mostly biting tongue*. Many years later he'd be involved in a bitter public feud with M's friend – his early employer and later his follower – the painter Antiveduto Gramatica, who loathed him.

In 1603 Mao was sticking with Baglione. Mao was, M said, the only painter who praised Baglione's disastrous *Resurrection* when it was unveiled that Easter Sunday. And when the attacks on Baglione and the jokes and insults from M's friends got vicious that summer, it was Mao who got hold of copies of some of the scurrilous poems about Baglione that were circulating among the painters. In his own account, he went to work on Filippo Trisegni, who was one of the eager young painters burning to work in M's way, a beginner to whom he'd lent art materials in the past, and a couple of days later Trisegni came up with a poem addressed to *Gian Coglione*, or *Johnny Prick*.

Johnny Prick can surely be called
he who goes attacking those
a hundred years his better.

In painting I mean since he wants to call
himself a painter like the man in mind
whose colours he doesn't deserve to grind.
No painter's better than he, no matter how
many he shamelessly names
and that proverb's right too when it says
he'll curse himself who wants praise.

I'm not in the habit of washing my mouth
or praising someone who doesn't deserve it
like his idol does for sure.

If I wanted to go on about
the shitty things this guy's done
a month, two months, wouldn't be enough.

Come over here a bit, you who want to attack
other people's paintings when you know
your own are still nailed up at home
because you're ashamed to show them out of doors.

Actually I feel like giving up
there's too much stuff here to go on about
especially if I start on the gold chain
he doesn't deserve around his neck
if I'm not wrong he'd better wear
an iron one around his feet.

Everything he said with feeling
I'm sure it was because he was drunk
as indeed he should've been
otherwise he'd've been a fucking prick.

Salini claimed Trisegni told him this poem, or pair of sonnets – slightly
confused over its pronouns, which mixed up the attacker and his
victim, but deeply felt nevertheless, attacking Baglione for attacking
M – was the work of Orazio Gentileschi and Ottavio Leoni, the young
portrait painter and protégé of Del Monte's. Trisegni denied saying

any such thing. Spurred on by this discovery – Salini said – he invited Trisegni around to his home a few evenings later *to look at a picture* and Trisegni sat down and copied out from memory a shorter and saltier poem against Baglione – one he'd apparently given Salini earlier and that Salini had lost – that incidentally happened to be even more wickedly obscene about Mao Salini's own wife. The second poem, which might've lost some of its finer effects in the phases of memorizing, recollecting, copying and recopying in the area of piazza Navona and the campo Marzio, apostrophized Baglione as *Gioan Bagaglia*, or *Johnny Baggage*. It went

> Johnny Baggage you don't know a fuck
> your pictures are picturettes
> we'll see with work like that
> you'll never make a cent
> to buy yourself some cloth
> to make yourself some little pants
> to show the world the part
> of you that shits
> So take what you've done
> your drawings and sketches
> to Andy the grocer
> or wipe your arse with them
> or stuff them up Mao's wife's cunt
> since you're no longer fucking her with your big donkey's
>   dick
> O painter pardon me if I don't worship you
> but you're unworthy of the gold chain you wear
> and an insult to art.

Johnny Baggage – Salini said Trisegni told him – was the work of M himself and Onorio Longhi. Salini raced back with this to Baglione. Whether or not he'd sought the doggerel out on Baglione's instructions, Mao Salini now strongly felt it was his duty as a concerned friend to make sure Baglione was fully aware of the obscenities circulating on his account. When he read them, Baglione sued M, and Onorio Longhi, Orazio Gentileschi and Filippo Trisegni for criminal libel.

When Baglione laid his suit before the governor of Rome on August 28, its terms made clear that the issue was professional rivalry over the big commission for the Jesuits. M had wanted the job, Baglione said. Neither M nor any of his friends would ever deny

225

that the *Resurrection* contract had been the trigger. Impervious to further ridicule, Baglione attached the two handwritten poems to his deposition – *whose* handwriting it was mattered – identifying them punctiliously as

> that which begins *Johnny baggage* and ends *an insult to painting* and the other ... that begins *Johnny prick* and ends *otherwise he'd've been a fucking prick* ...
>
> You should know that I am a painter by profession and have practised this profession here in Rome for many years and now it happens that I have painted a picture of the resurrection of Our Lord for the father general of the society of Jesus ... the said M tendered to do it himself, for which reason the said M out of envy as stated, and the said Onorio Longhi and Orazio his friends and followers have gone around ... attacking myself and my works ... the above named defendants have always persecuted me, they have emulated and envied me, seeing that my works are more highly rated than theirs ...

That same day the court took a deposition from Mao Salini, who was generous with names and innuendo. Salini said he'd had the poems two or three months earlier, so it'd taken Baglione a while to act. He said Triseghi had identified M and Onorio Longhi and Orazio Gentileschi as the main authors, with help from Ottavio Leoni, and insisted that M and Gentileschi had wanted the Jesuit commission themselves, that Longhi had given them a hand as their intimate friend who'd already fought with Baglione in the past. A painter called Lodovico from Brescia had distributed them to various other artists,

> in particular to a certain Mario, a painter too, who lives on the Corso.

This was Mario Minniti. He also claimed, one thought leading to another, that Triseghi had got the sonnets

> from a fuck boy of M's and Onorio's called Giovanni Battista, who lives behind the Banchi.

This carefully nonchalant piece of extra helpfulness would stall when M flatly denied knowing anyone *young* of that name living in that area. A certain Wildean or Clintonian casuistry in the precision of M's denial nevertheless left a sense that the *fuck boy* was real, was maybe even Cecco, whom M had painted as a nude boy John the baptist some months earlier – Salini would hardly have mentioned him if he wasn't at least plausible, and the name and address indicated that he was even hopeful of dragging him in to testify, like the painter Mario. Too detailed a knowledge of people like that might've reflected, of course, on Salini himself. As it was, this added detail suggested too that the imputed past whereabouts of his friend the complainant's *donkey's dick* were weighing on Salini's mind along with the memory of being beaten up by M.

It took the authorities a couple of weeks to pull in M, Gentileschi and Trisegni. Longhi was out of town and out of reach of the law. On September 11 M was arrested in the piazza Navona. Trisegni was taken at home over lunch. Gentileschi was brought in the day after. When Trisegni was interrogated the next day he cast himself as Mao Salini's concerned friend. Trisegni had felt his helper ought to see the obscene and defamatory doggerel about him and Baglione that was circulating among the painters. So when he heard someone reciting the verses in question, Trisegni said he

> pretended I liked them and asked ... for a copy ... and when I'd copied them out I went and found the said Tommaso and I said to him that he ought to be aware that while he was going around attacking other people's paintings people were attacking him too and I told him I wanted to show him something that'd been done against him ...

Mao Salini, naturally enough, was greatly stirred up by what Trisegni brought along and eager to know who'd written them. But Trisegni had no desire to be a troublemaker. He did a little more stirring.

> [Mao] badly wanted to know who'd given them to me and who'd written them but I never wanted to tell him because I didn't want to make trouble. Yet he kept on very insistently demanding to know and he named a lot of people, particularly M and the said M's servant Bartolomeo, and Orazio Gentileschi and [a couple of unidentified others] and asked me if it was any of them. And I said it could be one of these – maybe it *is* one of these, but I don't want to tell you his name.

Trisegni had his own agenda here. He wanted to make it in the art world and he knew that Mao Salini like Giovanni Baglione had been at work on M's techniques for a couple of years already. He now said he'd reveal the names if Salini would show him how to paint *a human figure with strong cast shadows* in M's way. Salini was unpersuaded by this offer. He never did teach Trisegni how to paint with shadows *and so I never told him.* But Salini badly wanted to see any further material about himself that Trisegni might come across, so Trisegni went back to his source and copied out the second poem for Mao in a grocer's shop. Trisegni made it very clear to the court that he personally knew nothing about poetry and copied it out badly, running on the lines. So who were the authors? Trisegni told the court his source had told him it was

> a young guy who was a student of logic – or was it physics? – who was really good, a master of the art and available to write sonnets to order for a woman if I wanted. He told me he was a university graduate and wrote exquisite verse.

A faint air of pisstaking that hung over this part – if not indeed all – of young Trisegni's evidence was reinforced by his immediately following statement that when he took the poem he'd copied at the grocer's round to Mao and Mao told him he'd lost the first – the one advising Baglione to *stuff his drawings up Mao's wife's cunt* – Trisegni was able to help out by copying the whole thing straight out again from memory. Trisegni's volubility might also have been the logorrhoea of a defendant having an acute panic attack. The next day Trisegni and Salini were brought face to face and each accused the other of lying. Trisegni denied he'd

> mentioned, told or specified the name of anyone who might have composed or distributed the said sonnets and poems.

Salini insisted he'd been given the names – which he avoided repeating in Trisegni's presence –

> and in particular that he'd got them from someone who lives behind the Banchi whose name he specified to me and also the fact that he was the fuck boy of the persons I specified in my examination ...

Meanwhile the police had searched Gentileschi's and Longhi's homes and found some unrelated handwritten poems in both. These showed their competence as versifiers, though Gentileschi insisted *I know how to write but not too correctly.*

It looked bad. Whatever the picky and unforgiving professionals of the Roman art world were saying of his mammoth *Resurrection,* and however much father Acquaviva might've been quietly regretting the installation of this ill conceived giant turkey in the Gesù church, Giovanni Baglione had the seal of approval of the society of Jesus and the Jesuits stuck by their choices. The Jesuits were the one leading order of the counter reformation whose churches never accommodated any painting of M's – unlike the Oratorians, the Augustinians and the Dominicans – and Acquaviva's choice of Baglione to do the *Resurrection* had been – according to Baglione himself in his lawsuit, a rejection of M. Baglione had said

> I painted a picture of the resurrection of our Lord for the father general of the society of Jesus, needed for a chapel in the church of the Gesù … the said M tendered to do it himself.

M never denied this. The probing Paravicino letter of a few weeks earlier seemed to show an awareness that the Jesuits had decided they didn't approve of M – part of its edge lay in its recipient Gualdo's close links to the Padua Jesuits. Acquaviva was another of those who like cardinal Paravicino had favoured the project of an *Index of prohibited images* when Paleotti floated it seven years earlier and the Jesuits were unlikely to recognize their notion of the Christian *mystery* in M's fixation on rendering the form and feel of the here and now. The Jesuits' painter of choice for the *Resurrection* had also worked as a painter for the pope, another thing M, for all his fame, had never done. M and his friends had attacked a rising member of the art establishment and their obscene defamation of Baglione, if proven, might be seen, much more dangerously, as an assault on Baglione's institutional patrons. For several years, M had eluded – with the help of Del Monte's discreet interventions – the consequences of a series of acts of violence. Now, over some doggerel verse, he and his friends were already in jail. M himself was all too clearly the real object of Baglione's suit. How he handled his own deposition was a matter of some moment.

FOR A MAN of few words, M did well when they brought him out of jail to testify. The words were still few, but they were telling. For a man who habitually and most effectively expressed himself with a paintbrush or a sword, he now showed a fine sense of theatre and a powerful way of lying in his teeth. The lies in no way vitiated the force or the interest of what he had to say. M would die leaving no letters, no table talk, no notebook or treatise. On 13 September 1603 for the first and last time in his life he spoke on the record about his art.

M spoke tersely. After the preliminaries –

> I was taken the other day in piazza Navona, for what reason
> I don't know ... I'm a painter by trade

– he was asked what other painters he knew in Rome.

> I think I know nearly all the painters in Rome. Starting
> with the good men I know Giuseppe Cesari, Annibale
> Carracci, Federico Zuccari, Pomarancio [Cristoforo Ron-
> calli], Orazio Gentileschi, Prospero Orsi, Giovanni Andrea
> Donducci, Giovanni Baglione, Gismondo Laer, Giorgio
> Todesco, Antonio Tempesta and others.

He placed himself astutely in the landscape of art politics. Giuseppe Cesari, Annibale Carracci, Federico Zuccari and Cristoforo Roncalli were the establishment pantheon in 1603 – to start with their names was a profession of orthodoxy. Then came his own friends Orazio Gentileschi and Prospero Orsi, and Giovanni Andrea Donducci. Baglione was squeezed in neutrally ahead of the eminent northern Europeans then working in Rome – Sigmund Laer and Georg Hofnagel and their Italian follower Antonio Tempesta. M added pointedly that *nearly all* of them were friends of his, though they weren't all *good men*, and he was asked to say what he meant by *good men*.

> To me the term *good man* means someone who knows how
> to do things well – that is knows how to do his art well –
> so in painting a good man knows how to paint well and
> imitate natural things well.

And this was the only direct recorded statement M ever made on art. Its minimalism would've shocked the *good men* whose names he was invoking. It was about as untheoretical as you could get – polemically untheoretical – but it was a bit abstract for M's interrogator, who swiftly moved back to personalities and unsubtly asked M which painters were his friends and which were enemies.

> Of the ones I've mentioned above, Giuseppe Cesari, Giovanni Baglione, Orazio Gentileschi and Giorgio Todesco aren't friends of mine because they don't speak to me. The others all speak and converse with me.

This elegantly combined *faux* humility with a nice bit of equally *faux* water muddying that linked the man suing him with one of his co-defendants. Unfortunately Gentileschi would later inadvertently blow this pretty fiction in his own deposition. And who, M was asked, were *good men*?

> Of the painters I've named above I consider good painters Cesari, Zuccari, Roncalli and Carracci. I don't hold the others to be good men ...
> Good men are ones that understand painting and they'll judge to be good painters the same ones I have, and the bad ones. But the bad and ignorant painters will think good painters who are as ignorant as they are ...

After a bit more shillyshallying on both sides M was finally asked what people thought of Giovanni Baglione. His answers now were no more eloquent but they were more deeply felt.

> I don't think there's any painter at all who thinks Giovanni Baglione is a good painter ... I've seen almost all Giovanni Baglione's work ... most recently the *Resurrection of Christ* at the Gesù ... I don't like that painting of the *Resurrection* there at the Gesù because it's clumsy. I find it the worst he's done and I've heard no painter speak well of it. Of all the painters I've spoken to nobody liked it.

M then added, as if to himself,

> – Unless it was praised by a guy who always goes around with him, the one they call his guardian angel. He was there to praise it when it was unveiled. They call him Mao.

He told them he'd been to see Baglione's painting with Prospero Orsi and Donducci, and been back to look at it again other times when he couldn't remember if there'd been other painters with him or not – adding testily *I don't know how long this story's going to keep doing the rounds*. Asked whether Mao was a painter and whether he'd seen any work by Mao, M replied acidly that

> maybe he does dabble and daub but I've never seen any work by that Mao.

Asked about the others, he told the interrogator that Onorio Longhi was a great friend and that he knew Ottavio Leoni, though he'd never spoken to him, and claimed Orazio Gentileschi hadn't spoken to him for three years. He said Mario used to live with him once but that he'd left three years earlier and he hadn't spoken to him since. Mario had indeed broken up with M nearly three years earlier, but the lack of contact here was as believable as the alleged three year silence from Gentileschi. Mario was still around. M said he knew a Lodovico but had never spoken to him. His servant Bartolomeo had left two months earlier. And he definitely knew no youth called Giovanni Battista, in particular none who lived behind the Banchi *and was young*. He was not in the habit of writing verse in either Latin or the vulgar tongue. The conclusion was emphatic and categorical.

> I have never heard either in verse or prose, in Latin or the vulgar tongue or anything of any kind whatsoever that made any mention of Giovanni Baglione … I have never been informed that in any verses in the vulgar tongue any mention has been made of the said Giovanni Baglione or of the said Mao.

It was a finely judged exit line. M had managed to keep the whole discussion on the exalted level of professional practice and himself above the squalid milieu of boy fucks, donkeys' dicks, wives' cunts and shitting arses that the poems Baglione had presented reeked of. M was after all the *egregius in urbe pictor* and habitually described as *famosissimo*, and the authorities were evidently intimidated by his bearing as a major artist. They hadn't pressed him on any of his answers. M had set the tone throughout and Baglione had been largely ignored, an undistinguished marginal figure whose faults and low standing M only elaborated on when specifically requested. When M was marched off again to the governor's prison in the Tor di Nona his interrogators must've been almost convinced.

GIOVANNI BAGLIONE WORRIED that they were. M had been a tough and effective defendant who'd yielded nothing and made a discreetly damaging attack on the complainant. Filippo Trisegni had held his ground against Mao Salini. Onorio Longhi had become an extremely adroit performer in his frequent criminal examinations and if he were taken would make Baglione's going very hard. The case against them needed beefing up, and the same day M was cross examined Baglione came up with material to boost the original charges he'd made two and a half weeks earlier. Baglione had evidently decided that his former colleague Gentileschi was the weak link in the defence and the best hope of getting at M. He now produced an angry and abusive letter he said Gentileschi had written him not long before.

Baglione had made a visit to the sanctuary at Loreto, and Gentileschi had asked his old colleague for a silver medallion or effigy of the madonna he'd brought back from the shrine, a little talisman from a catholic holy place. Gentileschi had offered to pay for it, and as a *well mannered gentleman* was deeply insulted when Baglione sent his servant around with two souvenirs of lead and a message that he was out of silver ones and that anyway it was the *devotion and not the value* that mattered. He sent the servant back with a furious note – the document Baglione now eagerly produced for the court – that said among other things that Baglione ought to *hang a little heart on that chain you wear around your neck, as an ornament to match your worth.* The chain in question was the gold neck chain Baglione had lately and notoriously had from Benedetto Giustiniani for doing the *Divine love* to rival his brother Vincenzo's earthly *Love the winner* by M. *And since,* Baglione argued in his new deposition,

> in the sonnets made against me he mentions a neck chain saying I ought to wear an iron chain instead and in this note he also talks about the chain saying I should wear a little heart instead of a chain, I say more strongly that it must have been him together with the above mentioned who did those sonnets and defamatory rhymes …

Gentileschi was interrogated again the following day, and when he too was asked about relations among Rome's leading painters, he explained that he was a friend of all of them *but there's also a certain rivalry among us.* Out came the story of the painting Baglione did to rival M's *Love* and win ecclesiastical approval, and how he hung it opposite Gentileschi's *Archangel Michael*, and what Gentileschi said and how Baglione did a second semi nude version.

> And I haven't spoken to Giovanni Baglione since that affair of the *Michael*, mainly because going around Rome he expects me to raise my hat to him and I expect him to raise his hat to me. Even M, who's a friend of mine, expects me to salute him … it must be six or eight months since I've spoken to M, although he sent round to my place for a capuchin monk's habit and a pair of wings that I lent him and it must be about ten days ago that he returned the monk's habit.

So much for M's three years. The wings and the monk's habit must've been the ones Gentileschi had used to paint his own versions of *Francis & angel*. Gentileschi was more loquacious than M and even than young Trisegni, talking too much, giving away too much rich detail for his own good or M's, on a painter's daily round in Rome and M's prickly insistence on being first among equals. Unwisely and gratuitously he mentioned the episode of Baglione's gold neck chain even before his interrogators produced the note. Confronted with the note he talked even more, and the court transcript noted tartly in Latin that he got tangled up in his own words. He was saying basically that *it does and it doesn't look like my handwriting*, that he recognized the handwriting as being *like* his own but not necessarily *as* his own, *because I write in different kinds of hand*. Beyond the specific need to deny the charge, there was a peculiar honesty in Gentileschi's answers, an attempt at frankness within the absurd parameters of the charge, an absence of real malice toward Baglione that was very unlike M's barely controlled contempt, and an admiration for M that didn't exclude recognizing that he made great demands on his friends. Baglione had intuited correctly that Gentileschi was the weak link in the defence. With his back to the wall, Gentileschi like M denied everything, but after the prolonged waffle over the handwriting, his denial came too late.

No record was found of the verdict or the sentence, but it turned out badly for M. He'd taken his distance very clearly from Gentileschi, but it wasn't enough. Two weeks after his interrogation he was still in the governor's prison of the Tor di Nona when the French ambassador Philippe de Béthune intervened to secure his release, *moderating the other decree already made*. The ambassador was likely responding to a request of the proFrench diplomat Del Monte, and the cardinal's failure this time round to settle M's problems with the law, on his own very considerable authority as a senior cardinal and representative of Ferdinando I de' Medici, showed how seriously things had now turned out for M. Even more so did the fact that even the representative of *the most Christian king* of France lacked clout to secure his full release – on September 25 M was put under house arrest, and if he left home without written permission he would be sentenced to row in the galleys. Even if these provisions were more formal than real, they were a further humiliation for the *pictor praestantissimus* after weeks in jail. There was no reason to believe the new sentence wasn't for real, or that Béthune's intervention at the highest diplomatic level had been undertaken lightly. The *other decree* might've been extremely grave – less than three years earlier the same governor of Rome whose tribunal was now sentencing M had announced the inclusion of criminal libel among those crimes punishable by death.

There might too have been M's former sitter and present client Maffeo Barberini behind the French diplomatic intervention. Two months earlier Barberini had paid M the third of four instalments for a painting M was doing for him of *Isaac & Abraham* – the canvas showing Cecco Boneri as a yelling boy Isaac about to get his throat cut. Barberini had become friends with Henri IV when he'd been papal legate in France two years earlier, standing in for the pope at the Christening of the newborn French *dauphin* and he was about to return to France as papal nuncio in late 1604. M received Barberini's final payment for the *Isaac* on 8 January 1604, three and a half months after the French ambassador got him out of jail. Philippe de Béthune, maybe not coincidentally to his rescuing M from jail, had been locked in a prolonged diplomatic struggle with Acquaviva and the society of Jesus ever since he'd taken up his posting in Rome. Henri IV in his protestant days had banned the Jesuits from France, and their readmission had been one of Clement VIII's conditions for Henri IV's embrace by the catholic church. The king of France was still deeply suspicious of the Jesuit operation and was stalling on letting them back in. Negotiations had reached deadlock in 1602 when the conditions presented by Béthune had been rejected by Acquaviva. The Jesuits were a thing Maffeo Barberini would have to take up with Henri IV when he was posted to Paris at the end of the following year. On the first of September 1603 Henri had announced some concessions in the edict of Rouen and Béthune's highly unusual intervention on M's side three weeks later looked like part of a new round of diplomatic manoeuvres – a show of support for the artist the Jesuits had rejected and might've had some oblique part in sending to jail. The Jesuits' painting in their Roman church was after all the issue in the trial.

On a personal level, Béthune might've wanted to do something for M's art. He knew it well from San Luigi dei Francesi. Seven years later there was a strange sequel to Béthune's intervention, and it pointed to Maffeo Barberini's being indeed involved with Béthune in getting M out of jail. Probably he just wanted his painting finished. It also implied the incident was deeply felt and keenly remembered by Béthune himself. In the summer of 1610, a fortnight after the news of M's mysterious death reached Rome, Barberini, now a cardinal and thirteen years off being elected pope Urban VIII, mentioned casually in a letter of August 3 to his brother that the French ambassador had asked to borrow and have a copy made of *my Abraham done by M*. It was the painting M'd been working on for Barberini that earlier summer, the painting Béthune's rescue operation let him finish, the *Isaac & Abraham*.

ANOTHER ITEM MISSING from the records was the fate of the others. They probably came out of jail with M in a package deal on the defendants. A few months later Orazio Gentileschi was recorded as living back home as usual in via Paolina near Santa Maria del Popolo. Filippo Trisegni never learnt to paint figures with cast shadows – at least he never made a name for himself and disappeared from art history. Two months after the trial Onorio Longhi was again in Rome. He was the only one of those charged with libel who showed any sort of a way with words, and he'd been writing verse since his days as a law student, before he took up his father's profession of architecture – fairly proFrench and antiSpanish verse as it happened. As long ago as 1590 he'd written a poem to celebrate the birth of Ferdinando I de' Medici's first son and much more recently a very partisan song for Henri IV's marriage to Maria de' Medici. He now burst back into the Roman scene with a violence that showed that nothing was settled, nothing forgotten. Mao Salini gave his version of what happened to police one Sunday that November.

> I was in the church of the Minerva with my friend mr Giovanni Baglione to hear mass and while we were standing there waiting I saw Onorio Longhi who was standing in front of us staring at me. He was saying something I

couldn't hear very quietly with his mouth. He beckoned me with his head and I approached and asked him what he wanted and he started saying

I'd like to make you swing from a wooden scaffold you fucking snitch.

To which I replied that he was insulting me in church and that he wouldn't've used those words outside. So the said Onorio told me more loudly to step outside and said I was a prick and a snitch if I didn't and said he was going outside to wait for me. He went straight out the Minerva's back door and grabbed a stone and said

Come outside you sneaky snitch.

I told him he was lying in his throat and to throw away the brick so we'd be on equal terms. Then mr Giovanni Baglione came out and held me back ... a friend of Onorio's said *Drop the knife* ... Onorio yelled *Get the knife off him* and at the same moment threw the brick at mr Giovanni. It hit his hat but didn't hurt him and then Onorio started to come at me. I had a stone in my hand and told him to stop or I'd lay him out right there, but he kept on coming at me saying *You fucking snitch.* I denied this and went back into the church and he went away ...

We came here straight away to report him, Salini went on importantly. But first he went back to the church to get names of witnesses, and walked into trouble again.

I found him again in the church ... and he came at me again with his sword under his arm and and started saying *Come on out, come on out you filthy spy.* I told him to mind his own business and that unlike him I had no weapons and Onorio replied

Come out, come on out, you sneaking insulting smart alec spy ... so you don't want to come outside – then I'll be waiting outside your house for you ...

and ... Giovanni Baglione and I were going home down the Corso at the intersection of the via della Croce ... and ... we saw Onorio outside the door of my house and he came straight up to us and said

Right, go and grab your sword – I don't want to give you any trouble until you've got a sword,

but I didn't trust him and went inside the tailor's shop

by the butcher's on the via del Corso and mr Giovanni went into the baker's shop that sells bread and wine and charcoal … he started saying

You filthy prick of a spy, come on out and bring your sword – I've got a bone to pick with you, snitch.

While he was speaking there were a lot of people around who saw and heard what was going on – the barber next door to the tailor, the owners of the baker's shop … Tommaso Della Porta the sculptor and an old man called mr Annibale …

Longhi was arrested that day. Giovanni Baglione made a statement confirming everything and going into some detail about the damage done to his hat by Longhi's brick, and two days later so did witnesses. Longhi's fury however had been entirely directed at the sidekick and not at the man who'd brought the criminal charges against him – maybe he'd heard about the *snitch*'s repeated mentions of *M's and Onorio's fuck boy*. Maybe his wife had heard too. The sculptor Della Porta said he was a friend of both Longhi and Baglione and had led Longhi away because he *didn't want to see them hurt each other*. The barber had seen *a redbearded man armed with a sword* shouting at a painter who'd retreated into the tailor's shop and another *who said he was a painter too* hiding in the wine seller's shop. Another shopkeeper had been disturbed at Sunday lunch, and gone out to see a crowd of people and a man with a sword *red in the face* threatening two others he didn't recognize, but since they fled into the tailor's and the wine seller's and nothing more seemed to be happening, the shopkeeper returned to his lunch.

There'd been a nasty undertone to the trial – nastier than the ostensible cause – and both sides tried not to acknowledge it directly in their testimony. On the face of it Baglione and his *pupil* Salini had been grossly slandered out of professional jealousy. But the gross verses were themselves a response to unspecified attacks, as the poem *Johnny Prick* made clear. This was the one the *snitch* Salini claimed had been written by Orazio Gentileschi and Ottavio Leoni, and in its angry choked up way it was all about Coglione Baglione's contemptible attacks on an artist the writer, or writers, greatly admired. There was no reason to disbelieve Salini on who the authors were – Gentileschi's intense admiration for M came out when he was cross examined. The poem's very lack of specificity was its point. The attacks on M had been in some way unmentionable – the handwriting was hard enough to decipher let alone interpret – and the mention of *washing out my mouth* reinforced a sense of the unspeakable. Washing out the mouth was what you did to get rid of something really foul, like lies of a particularly hateful kind, and evoked a different order of language from – say – the contemptuous remarks Zuccari had made about what he claimed was the unoriginality of M's *Matthew called*. The obscenity didn't feel gratuitous. It voiced a moral squalor.

10

ROME 1603

Isaac & Abraham II

THEY NEVER STOPPED attacking M and his style and spread it around that he didn't know how to come up out of the cellar.

It wasn't true – not until late in 1603 at any rate – what the resentful old mannerists said about M. The landscape M did now – a background glimpse, but integral to the picture, placing its moment of violence and drama and fear in a deeply reassuring setting of quiet continuity – was the last such glimpse, though, of the outdoor world in M's work. It did mark a change of tone, a final break with the painted northern world of his first twenty years. After more than a decade in Rome of formation and triumph, a great urgency now came into his work. After this painting, M's big public commissions and half figure *histories* would be interspersed with a series of intensely solitary and introspective single figures, brooding in their isolation. The social world of his youth disappeared from his work along with the pagan subjects and the still life. From now on, M's experience was rendered entirely through his imagining of the figures and images and events of the Christian drama. And the visual correlative was enclosure and isolation in the middle of darkness, out of sight of the larger social world. After this he really was more and more a prisoner in his cellar studio, trapped like his models *in the dark air of a closed room.*

M started painting *Isaac & Abraham* in the spring of 1603 – soon after Baglione's unfortunate *Resurrection* was unveiled and before the crisis it led to – using the same horizontal three quarter format he'd lately used for the *Meal at Emmaus, Doubting Thomas* and *Christ taken*. He had to suspend work on it when Baglione went to the police with the poems and didn't finish it until he came out of jail in autumn. He wasn't finally paid off until January 1604. *Isaac* was a new commission from Maffeo Barberini – a response to what Barberini had seen or heard of M's reimaginings of biblical events in entirely human terms – and it was close up, urgent, unadorned and intimate. Barberini was evidently still pleased with the dynamic gesturing portrait M had done of him in 1598, and freshly impressed too, if he hadn't seen the new work himself, by what Del Monte told him when they met in Florence in 1602. He'd done *Isaac* before – the patriarch Abraham with his knife out and ready to slit his own son's throat as an offering to the old testament god, the angel interceding at the last moment, the ram making itself available as a substitute sacrifice – and the earlier version had been a much more rigorously controlled study of figures in darkness, a close sculptural group in the glow of a fire and a little heavenly highlighting. It'd been a very gentle study – within the terms of an event set up to diminish merely human love – thoughtful father, weeping son and sweetly reasonable young angel. The new version took the old man last seen looking on in *Doubting Thomas* and before that as the second *Matthew* writing with the angel, and before that as Peter, looking less disturbed than his forerunner at the orders he was being asked to carry out, sceptical at the last minute stay of execution. He still had his son under his thumb, which was pressing cruelly into the boy's cheek as the hand held his neck to the stone. Isaac was Cecco – stripped naked, hands tied out of sight behind his back, face pressed down sideways and bum arching upward in struggle, white and distorted, yelling his head off. It looked like a sexual assault in the grey morning light – peasant violence on a child labourer somewhere on the outskirts of town. The upward jutting knife blade stood for rape and murder. Beside the boy's writhing and his terrified yell of resistance, both the serenely intervening angel and the ram, looking in sideways from opposite edges of the canvas, were a lot more formulaic than M's earlier rams and angels. They carried no freight of meaning here. The violence was on its own – so nakedly that M, pressured by circumstances or Barberini or a late loss of nerve of his own after the trial, muted and muffled its force with some last minute changes.

The oddly crude and unconvincing angel was actually a makeover – Cecco was doubling roles. M had painted him as the angel too, and – as infra red reflectography would show – then disguised and idealized him into something *Leonardesque*. Cecco's small chin and delicate lips are evident in the infra red reflectogram inside the blocked in profile. These highly individual features were then masked over by extending the profile outwards to give the figure a suitable idealized countenance

– and above all to make Cecco as angel look different from Cecco as Isaac. It was Isaac who was really the whole centre of interest in M's second imagining of this *history*, and in the earlier stages his nude body was much more visible before it was obscured by Abraham. M made a lot of incisions in the priming of this canvas to fix the models' contours, and

> The most fascinating lines occur in the figure of Isaac; the whole of his head as well as the features of his face are indicated. An arc … defines the alignment of the eyes and a little *hook* gives a preliminary indication for the nose. The open mouth was of crucial importance for the picture's impact, and M carefully marked the position of the lips with incised lines … two diagonal lines define his right thigh, clearly visible in the reflectogram, while the U shape line must, by extension, record the placement of Isaac's genitals. So important had the leg seemed to M that he initially blocked in the dark area around it.

The trouble was the boy's projecting body interfered with the flat serial arrangement of the figures across the canvas – *frieze like* as in *Judith & Holofernes* – and his leg ended up concealed behind Abraham's sleeve, wrist and cloak, his genitals behind the knife handle. So that

> the tightly compressed pose of Isaac – his right leg bent back over his left, his right arm tied behind his back – is almost impossible to read without the aid of the information provided by the incisions and infra red reflectography.

This meant that the original violence being done to the boy's trussed and folded naked body was partly painted over and obscured as the painting was completed. Even as it was, the part of Cecco left in view under the descending knife – his twisted neck, the white deactivated shoulder, his open bawling mouth and the faint curve of his squirming bum – was the picture's vital centre, drawing the eye irresistibly, leaping out from the deadness of the rest with ugly energy. The

Abraham who took up so much of the canvas was a finefeatured face on an inert and bulky bundle of heavy cloth that fell in unconvincing folds – he'd nothing of the tense and edgy way he'd knelt on his stool before, looking over his shoulder in an almost identical pose as Matthew with the angel. The angel here, and the ram, were verging on the perfunctory and looking too much like each other for comfort.

The strongest bit of human figuring here was Isaac, now unrelentingly drained of any attribute of charm or desirability, showing only the physiology of fear and pain. You had the feeling that some real pain was used, maybe in the pressure of that thumb, to achieve the desired effect. Cecco himself had visibly changed in a couple of years from the chubby goldenhaired child angel of the first *Saul*, through the pubescent tough of *Love* and the longer limbed adolescent *John in the wild* to a pasty unsettled teenager with bags under his eyes and clammy hair – a streetwise Roman who knew making a lot of noise was the best defence. Cecco Boneri's was a much more remarkable metamorphosis than any in the earlier and longer series of Mario Minniti portraits. It had to do not only with Mario's being older when M first knew him, and already formed, but with M's being younger then too, adoring in the early pictures and in thrall. He was older now, a lot older than Cecco Boneri, knowing and lustful. Whatever the pictorial *mise en scène* required, there was never any idealization of Cecco.

Isaac & Abraham was interrupted in the painting. Maffeo Barberini's account books for 1603 recorded part payments to M of twenty five scudi on May 20, ten scudi on June 6 and fifteen on July 12. In August, when M might've been expected to be getting round to completing the painting, the feud with Baglione reached the height of its virulence and on August 28 Baglione went to the police demanding that M and the others be charged. M spent only a couple of weeks in jail, though things had clearly turned out badly when the ambassador Béthune intervened and got him out on September 25. The feud, the trial, imprisonment, uncertainty and its aftermath of unabated anger would've reduced his will and energy to paint for some time after that. Then there was the housing question. M's trial and apparent conviction for obscene libel of an establishment painter made him a very embarrassing member of a cardinal's household. Whether he was still living in the palace of cardinal Mattei at the start of summer 1603 or whether he'd returned to Del Monte's – and he'd been picked up in piazza Navona, a few steps from the palazzo Madama – it was clear he couldn't go back when he came out of jail. Since he remained under house arrest and wasn't allowed to leave home without written permission – facing the horrible penalty of rowing in the galleys if he did – having his own independent home was quite likely a condition of being allowed house arrest, maybe part of the deal engineered by Béthune and M's ecclesiastical backers. M contracted with a widow named Prudenzia Bruni to rent a two storey house with attic, cellar and a courtyard garden with a well in the lane of san Biagio in the campo Marzio. He moved there on his formal release from the Tor di Nona prison, and the rental arrangement was evidently part of the deal. The house was near the studio where he'd once drudged for Cesari, and closer still to the Tuscan ambassador's palace. After years of precarious or subordinate lodgings in other people's houses and palaces, his house, nothing fancy but big enough, was now M's first independent home and studio in Rome. It was also, for the time being, his prison. Here he finished off the *Isaac* for Barberini.

M had placed sexuality and violence at the painting's centre in the assaulted nude body of Isaac – quite unlike the gentler weepier handling of the boy in the other *Isaac* several years before. But now M subdued all that blatant pain he'd created. He partly obscured Isaac's bare body with Abraham's bulky drapery and filled out the canvas rapidly with the perfunctory angel and ram. The cruelty in the closeness of the knife, humiliation in the pose, brutality in the thumb grinding into his cheek – these were part of the painting's origin, but after the trial M seemed to lose his nerve and go to some lengths to muffle the violence. He handed the finished painting over to Barberini around the end of the year. The final instalment of fifty scudi was noted in Barberini's account book on 8 January 1604. It brought M's total payment to a hundred scudi.

DID THE JESUITS put Baglione up to his libel suit? Baglione was behaving in the months before the trial like a man who felt he had institutional power behind him. His frontal assault on M as a painter with his own *Divine love* was a remarkable provocation in itself. He followed it up with a very pointed and poisonous allusion to M the second time round, when he gave the devil a face and made it M's. The pictorial insinuation wasn't a light one – could hardly have been a more emphatic nod and wink in the direction of the inquisition. That the naked devil was grovelling with a naked and sprawling adolescent *earthly love* doubled the dose of allusive poison. Mao Salini's elaborately casual mention of the *fuck boy* in his later deposition was dropped on well prepared terrain.

Even if he'd wanted to, there was no way M could respond to this kind of insinuation. His reaction – and his friends' – was the spluttering angry obscenity of the verses circulated and some loud and savage mockery of Baglione's dud *magnum opus* for the Jesuits, whose very public failure must've been vastly more satisfying. Baglione's prompt and confident response in pressing criminal charges – a wholly justified confidence, it turned out – reinforced the sense of a hidden sanction to the whole exercise. The whiff of heresy that clung to Baglione's image of the devil wasn't merely wanton. Baglione never could've got away with suggesting something that didn't evoke a *suspicion* already lurking in ecclesiastical minds. Onorio Longhi's rage at Salini for being a *snitch* and a *spy* also implied that Salini had been tattling behind the scenes about dangerous matters – religious, political or sexual – that never came out in the trial.

Some things were unmentionable in a civil court. There was the *vitium nefandum*, which was the sin literally *not to be mentioned*, and there was heresy. They were matters for another court, matters of belief or morality of interest to the inquisition, and you only raised such things if you were going for broke. People burned for such things. The *holy office* was the controlling institution of the papal dictatorship and if its time of really savage repression was past, the crisis of authority over and public burnings getting rarer, the machinery of repression kept ticking over. The burning of Bruno and the others in the holy year had been the last direct assertion of control – and that'd been more a piece of admonitory theatre than a really necessary act of repression. Crimes of belief in the strictly doctrinal sense were now making way – since the revived inquisition, up and running beautifully in all its complex articulation, still needed human material to work on – for thought crimes of a more nebulous kind, antisocial thinking or behaviour that threatened or questioned the new order of church power.

> By now terror reigned supreme. But the terror was courtly, intangible, ceremonious, made up of anonymous denunciations masked with a smile, of betrayals hidden behind scruples of conscience, of a meticulous legality always observed with care. It was the moment of the uncommitted, the mediocre, the legalistic, the churchgoers, the *academics* and their acolytes ...

It was the moment of people like Baglione. Control was still needed, but it was now more subtly exercised through the mechanism of the confessional, the dense network of constant lowlevel monitoring of people's thoughts and deeds that the Jesuits had perfected, the base structure on which the society of Jesus was erecting the front line educational and ideological defence of catholic orthodoxy. It was inevitable that the confessional, with a little discreet urging from the father confessor, became a vehicle for retailing what other people were up to as well as your own sins.

> As soon as confession became an obligatory and minutely controlled practice, the desire grew stronger to use it as a place for informing on people and gathering information.

It wasn't that the inquisition stopped playing a major role. But in the first years of the seventeenth century it was playing a new role, reaching into other areas of private life and behaviour.

> In the late sixteenth century, the courts of the Roman inquisition ... started concerning themselves with other questions. By the end of the century, superstition, magic, cursing and other things had taken the place once occupied by heresy ... the court moved more cautiously on the ground of sexual crimes ... but it clearly evolved from being a heresy court into being a court of collective morality ... it intellectualized social practices and applied the rule of suspicion, interpreting the various kinds of deviant behaviour as heretical.

As the inquisition lowered its profile and extended its activities at the turn of the century, Italian society was modernized, imperfectly, along ideological and totalitarian lines. In the new regime of papal dictatorship,

> Truth is elaborated and transmitted by a network of power that reaches every individual ... removes him from the warm embrace of tradition ... and imposes new rules ... family and social tradition, the behaviour of shop, workshop and market, the rules that govern relations with others – all others, including God and the saints – enter a shadow zone: the authorities start from attitudes of suspicion and criticism ... values oscillate – in a society

dominated by an ecclesiastical power system – between faith and morality and a growing emphasis on police control: a police of the faith ... that is continually turning into *the vice squad.*

Heresy was far more dangerous ground than sexual morality, and neither party dared venture on it in the trial. But something was going on in the summer of 1603. The layered insinuations contained in cardinal Paravicino's tentacular letter of inquiry about M were one sign, in the evocation of

> a priest who seemed impeccably orthodox until he opened his mouth.

Paravicino was likely aware when he wrote to his friend in Vicenza of some disturbing unspecified discoveries that were being made just then about the late cardinal Contarelli, the French Mathieu Cointrel whose chapel in San Luigi M's *Matthew* paintings so famously adorned. A week or so after cardinal Paravicino wrote his urbanely exploratory letter, Francesco Maria Vialardi, the Roman agent and informant of Ferdinando I of Tuscany – who'd been imprisoned himself with Bruno years earlier – reported to Ferdinando that

> It's said that some really nasty things have been discovered about cardinal Contarelli, so much so that his holiness has said he really was a heretic, more specifically a Calvinist, and that his dealings were altogether quite wicked.

Contarelli had been dead nearly twenty years, and whatever this news meant, it looked like the product of antiFrench stirring at a time when Philippe de Béthune was engaged on a vigorous diplomatic offensive on France's behalf in Rome. Béthune's immediate mission was to convince Rome of Henri IV's goodwill and the total sincerity of his reconversion to catholicism. His longer term aim was to build a counterweight to Spain's massive influence in the college of cardinals. This was something Henri IV's footdragging over readmitting the Jesuits to France can't've helped him do, and the timing of Henri's September 1 announcement at Rouen of concessions on the Jesuits, three weeks after the report on Contarelli, looked, well, interesting. Béthune himself personally embodied the uncertainty of Henri IV's newly refound catholicism. He too was a political convert and a religious liberal, and before being posted to Rome had been France's ambassador to Scotland, where he'd facilitated James VI's succession to Elizabeth I in England.

So if there were reasons to believe there was more than painters' professional rivalry behind the libel trial of M and his friends – though it was clearly exacerbated by the vicious scrabble for commissions, violent factionalism and personal jealousy – it looked as though other forces also lay behind the French ambassador's very unusual intervention to free the painters. Something much more serious was being held against M than the writing of scurrilous verse, and since that thing wasn't dealt with in the trial or its aftermath, it remained, whatever it was, in the air. In a culture of suspicion, whatever dark posthumous secrets might've been uncovered about cardinal Mathieu Cointrel, they flowed on to contaminate the painter who memorialized him. That the painter was engaged nearly fifteen years after the suspected heretic's death wasn't, doctrinally speaking, the point. Hadn't the offending *Matthew & angel* adhered meticulously to the dead cardinal's own detailed prescription of how the saint and the angelic transmitter were to be represented?

The *culture of suspicion* was grounded in canon law since the twelfth century. *Suspicio* translated into *praesumptio culpae*, the presumption of guilt, and was the basis of the inquisition's whole procedure. But whether the suspicion attaching to M was doctrinal or sexual or both, nobody really wanted to drag out anything that would involve the inquisition. Once the inquisition interested itself in someone, the investigation went on forever and usually ended badly – eight years passed between Bruno's arrest and his burning. M was close to some of the most influential ecclesiastics and laymen in Rome – Del Monte, Barberini, the Giustinianis, the Matteis, the Crescenzis for a start – and a lot more were eager to own his paintings. Recourse to the inquisition wasn't desirable. M had to be kept painting. The available sanctions against libel and slander afforded quite severe penalties, like death, or the threat of it, in a much more easily controlled lay ambit.

The punishments for defamation were aimed at anyone who challenged the church's monopoly of information. The *Index of prohibited books* covered the upper reaches of the information range, but the papal state had also been irked over the last few decades by the proliferation of well informed and often pungent *avvisi*. Pius V had suppressed them briefly thirty years earlier and Gregory XIII a few years later had sentenced their writers to slavery on the galleys and Sixtus V a decade after that had a police proclamation issued against *slanderers and defamers of others by means of avvisi or otherwise*. Clement VIII had been particularly distressed by the way the *avvisi* described his handling of the Cenci affair four years earlier, and brought in the death penalty for defamation. A more local form of comment that the defamation laws were also intended to suppress – a form much more like what M and his friends had been doing with their verses against Baglione – was the satirical verses people pasted up at night on the statue of Pasquino, near M's nocturnal stamping ground the piazza Navona.

The ugly personal clashes of 1603 in the courts and in the streets did no harm at all to Baglione's career. Legally and professionally he came off best, though the *Lives* showed that the experience rankled for the rest of his long and busy life. After his run in with M, he dropped his version of M's style – which was mannerism with shadows basically – with a clatter. He was scared stiff by now but superficial enough not to be put off his stride. He was back at work on a new commission later that same year and did three paintings for the crypt of Santa Cecilia in the Trastevere, where Clement VIII had reburied the saint's relics with great pomp in 1599. The pope was particularly pleased that cardinal Sfondrati was spending twenty five thousand scudi of his own money on a major restoration, including the plumbing of the bathroom where Cecilia had survived an attempt to suffocate her with hot steam before being finished off with an axe. The axe murder itself was represented over the altar in white marble. Baglione's new contributions were all *banally devotional in tone* but Baglione, who had a way of pleasing whichever pope was currently in power, remembered that *Clement ... liked them a lot* and *honourably rewarded* him. He scaled the heights of official art four years later in 1607, with a commission to paint *Tabitha's resurrection* for Saint Peter's itself. The job got him made a *knight of Christ* by Clement's successor Paul V and by then he was a quasi official painter to the papacy like Giuseppe Cesari. Qualitywise it was downhill all the way. From time to time, like a reflexive twitch, a small visual recollection of his brush with M would surface in one or other of Baglione's later paintings but when he could he tried to bury the memory. In his disguised autobiography, he couldn't resist boasting about his *Divine loves*.

> For Giustiniani he did two paintings of *Divine loves*, trampling earthly love, the world, the flesh and the devil under their feet, carefully done from life, and they can be seen facing each other in the hall of his palace.

But he mentioned them way out of chronological order, to cover his tracks and airbrush the unnamed M out of the picture. Just possibly, he'd even done a third to compete more directly with M's, one which really was *all nude* and *a child* as Orazio Gentileschi said at the trial, identifiable as a hideous deformed looking child with a misshapen head, a hump back and stumplike wings. This *Love*, if it really was Baglione's, was born of a monstrous hubris and was surely one of the paintings Gentileschi's verse claimed Baglione kept

> still nailed up at home
> because you're ashamed to show them out of doors.

It certainly got no mention in his autobiography and would've dismayed his institutional backers on more than one ground. All the same, the unpleasantness of 1603 was a career breakthrough for Baglione – professionally he never looked back. Neither indeed did his sole follower, *snitch* and *guardian angel* Mao Salini. For M, 1603 was the summer things began to go obscurely wrong.

WEIGHING HIS WORDS, M named in court *the good men* among the painters of the day. There was the contorted old academic idealist Federico Zuccari – a nod to the institutional past – and there was the very eclectic and successful Cristoforo Roncalli, twenty years M's senior. There were near contemporaries like Annibale Carracci – out of the commercial loop as he plunged, on the Farnese ceiling, into an overhead neverland of guilt free pagan sex that was now a serious worry for Farnese – and the pope's favourite Giuseppe Cesari, who'd industrialized late mannerism. These painters were Roman art at the pre M moment – theirs were the names anyone might've chosen. They were the darlings of the Roman establishment and there was no alternative to the establishment in Rome. M's interrogators would've been nodding in pleased recognition and sage agreement with M's opinions. When Giulio Mancini outlined his amateur's sense of what mattered in Roman art in the first years of the seventeenth century, he grouped the artistic currents under the names of Carracci, Cesari and Roncalli. But ahead of them he put a fourth, who was M.

M's terse and immensely intelligent replies to his interrogators had linked himself implicitly with the recognized masters of the day and so with the upholders of the prevailing order in art. The last thing he could afford to do was identify himself as a rebel or innovator in his thinking. The crime of the heretic was to rebel against Rome's order, and M's French connexion, if it were more than accidental and contingent, brought him among a party that was even more obsessed with the affirmation of order than France's rival Spain, as obsessed as papal Rome itself.

> It wasn't Spanish culture that promoted the new demonization of the rebel. The epicentre was France at the end of the sixteenth century ... thirty years of revolts and civil wars had struck the nation's heart and pushed it to the brink of ruin and disintegration ...

M saw that the dangerous hidden currents in the trial were pulling him toward generic rebellion. His minimalist account of his art – *imitating natural things* – was finely judged as clear and reassuring to the police mind as well as quite sincere. It kept well clear of the ideological rocks. He did what he could. The trouble was that among the artists M *was* seen as a rebel and an innovator. The younger ones were deserting the styles and institutions of officially acceptable art – everything the accademia di San Luca stood for, when it could be pulled into line – to flock unwanted after M. And whether he wanted to or not, M was starting to fit the identikit that was then being assembled of the rebel the seventeenth century would love to hate. From a right thinking point of view, M had all the right attributes of the social rebel.

> Pride, murky ambition, contempt for society, untrustworthiness and denial of the rules of honour even in personal relations ... sometimes immorality and sexual excess, as they were then understood – libertinism and homosexuality – and religious indifference completed the picture ...

This was an image of the *political* rebel, as it was propagated in the tracts of the time. It was intended to

> overpower or make disappear the political motivations of opposition and resistance, and assimilate the image of the rebel to those of the common bandit, the individual outsider, deviants from universally recognized and accepted norms of behaviour.

For M it meant that whether he liked it or not his art was political. He was being typecast. The extreme distaste that vied with Bellori's admiration for M toward the end of the century had everything to do with M's repudiation of *universally recognized and accepted norms* in art, and this *deviance* was inseparable in Bellori's account from the role of ringleader he assigned to M, the dangerous head of a bunch of young subversives. M's *art* was subversive, as

> ... the painters then in Rome were taken by the newness of it, and the young ones in particular all descended on him and hailed him alone as the only imitator of life. Looking on his works as miracles, they vied with each other in following him ... ignored their studies and teachers, and everyone easily found in the streets and piazzas his own master and models to copy from life. The ease of it attracted others, and only the old painters broken in to the old practices remained stunned by this new study of life.

That M loathed being imitated – what lay behind the Baglione libel trial – and was so intensely jealous of the art that cost him so much – working fast had nothing to do with untroubled facility – that copying his techniques could be *physically dangerous*, in the eyes of his critics had nothing to do with it. Bellori was evoking an art world phenomenon he was born too late to have known directly, but Baglione knew it all too well, lived through it and remembered it resentfully to the end of his *Lives*. Scattered through his tiny biographies were the distant traces of M's first and passionate following. When Baglione wrote about Carlo Saraceni, for instance, he presented him as a promising youngster who'd come down from Venice – Saraceni arrived in Rome in M's marvellous *Matthew* year of 1600 and was seven or eight years younger than M – full of eager intentions and a quick learner. But then

> he got it into his head that he wanted to imitate the style of M and abandon the studies that would've made an excellent artist of him – the same thing happened to others too. His style was a bit slack, as his work shows ... [it]'s recognizable by its weakness of style ...

The enthusiasm, and the irritation it caused, were intensely personal. Saraceni so wanted to be like M that he copied the manner, the dress, the allegiances, the lifestyle.

> He was a joker, and always wanted to go round dressed in the French style, though he'd never been in France

and didn't know how to speak a word of the language. And since he made a show of imitating M – who always went around with a black poodle called Crow that did wonderful tricks – Carlo Saraceni used to take a black dog around with him too, and called him Crow just like M's dog – laughable behaviour, really, thinking that appearances matched the reality of achievement.

Sad, really. Especially if your own only follower had been a Mao Salini, who made no impression at all on anyone else. Carlo Saraceni kept up in middle age what he'd learnt young from emulating M. He was knocking forty when Mancini remarked that

> when necessary, he gives a good account of himself with weapons in hand.

Saraceni wasn't the only one to throw away his youthful promise by following a false master, a master it was all too easy to emulate because all you had to do was copy from life. There was Bartolomeo Manfredi too, who might've been a student of M's and the *servant Bartolomeo* whom Salini mentioned in the trial as having distributed copies of the slanderous poems. The known name and the active part in the painters' feud seemed to show that *Bartolomeo* was more than mere domestic help. Manfredi was younger than Saraceni. If Mancini were right, and Mancini knew him, he was as young as sixteen or seventeen in 1603. He arrived in Rome from his home town Mantua as a young boy and at first studied painting with the very establishment Roncalli.

> But then he grew up and gave himself over to imitating M's style, and he got to the point where a lot of his works were taken for M's own, and even painters were taken in ...

Even Baglione had to admit Manfredi was good – Mancini and Bellori both thought he did work that was finer than M's – but he was firm that in the end the bad example showed through.

> He painted no big public picture, either because he didn't have the heart for it, or because his drawing wasn't up to it, or the occasion didn't present itself ... if [he]'d had good drawing to go with his good paintings, he might've done wonderful things ...

Fifteen years later, Giulio Mancini liked Manfredi's *distinguished appearance and fine behaviour* – very good company on the rare occasions Manfredi was feeling sociable.

> At such times expense is no consideration, but they don't happen often.

Manfredi was successful early – had his own servant by 1610 – and seemed to feel no need to prove himself with big public commissions, happily reworking M's themes in easel paintings for private clients like Vincenzo Giustiniani and earning big money doing it. The painting Mancini thought *maybe the best thing he's done* was maybe also Manfredi's first, and it happened to be strongly linked with both Baglione's *Divine loves* and with the *Isaac & Abraham* M was working on at the time of his trial and imprisonment in 1603. Manfredi's *Mars whipping Love* showed a nude and smoothskinned adolescent Love sprawling on the ground – very much like the same figure's position in Baglione's two paintings – being thrashed with a knotted rope by a vigorous young working class Mars, as a barefoot, crouching and equally proletarian Venus tried to restrain him, and a breast popped out of her dress. Unlike Baglione's inertly posed Love, this boy was writhing vigorously, blindfolded and yelling, his wrist clamped in Mars's powerful grip, his unmarked white bum twisting toward the viewer as the knotted cord flailed above Mars's head began to descend. The painting was quite unlike any Manfredi did later, and both the boy's pose and the painting's charge of sexual sadism came directly from M.

Baglione felt friendlier when he remembered Orazio Borgianni, or seemed to, although Borgianni was another of M's fiercest and earliest young followers in art and life. Borgianni was a year younger than Mario Minniti and a couple of years older than Carlo Saraceni and may not even have been in Rome when M and his friends were on trial. He'd been around – worked in Sicily as a boy in the nineties and gone on from there to Spain for several years. He was back in Rome the year before the trial, and off to Spain again the year after, and it wasn't until he returned to Rome for good in 1605 that his work showed what he'd learnt from M. Baglione relished immensely the story of how Borgianni was later plunged into a fatal depression after being cheated out of a major commission by a colleague's evil machinations, and presented him as even in his early days an ingenuous Othello like man, quick to anger and fearsome with a sword but easily manipulated by others – *weak minded*, even.

Orazio Borgianni was a free man, and so he sometimes liked to get into fights with other people. He was formidable and generous not so much in his intelligence as in his physical strength ... he quarrelled with quite a few people. M used to speak very ill of him, and if he hadn't been equally good at handling weapons himself would've had a very nasty experience at his hands. A doctor who tried to outsmart him over a painting got a very ugly beating with a stick.

The too clever doctor Borgianni beat up sounded very like the smart and unscrupulous Giulio Mancini, who later strangely overlooked Borgianni in his account of contemporary painters, although he mentioned practically everyone else imaginable. If Baglione wasn't simply lying about enmity between M and Borgianni, and he probably wasn't, he was thinking maybe of some irritation in the early days, when Borgianni might've been too keen and too unskilled a follower for M's taste – too much for a spiky genius already plagued with other young painters like Saraceni aping his dress, his manner and his black dog, so soon after the ill intentioned opportunist Baglione had first plagiarized his work. Rome wasn't a big town and the artists' quarter of the campo Marzio was even smaller. The hostility didn't last in any case, as Baglione knew all too well. Three years after the first trial Baglione would be back in court pressing further and graver criminal charges, this time against M together with Saraceni and Borgianni, whom he identified as M's *adherents*.

Baglione was as clipped as he could be about his old colleague Orazio Gentileschi, but at the end judiciousness failed him.

> If Orazio Gentileschi had shown a more flexible disposition, he would've turned out really well. But he was more like an animal than a human being ... he had his own opinions and offended everybody with his satirical tongue and we've got to hope that God in his kindness will pardon all his faults ...

He was even terser about Onorio Longhi, who

> always had such a bizarre brain that it was hard to stick with him for long ... he made himself greatly hated by the others.

The *unreliable* Prospero Orsi got the briefest of notes.

> This man was a great friend of the cavalier Giuseppe Cesari
> d' Arpino and made great efforts to copy his style in his
> own paintings ... but after a while for some reason he
> stopped being his friend and became one of M's touts ...

There was no mention at all of M in the life of Antiveduto Gramatica. Neither M's early work in the nineties nor his later influence on
Gramatica's style were recalled – only Antiveduto's later *great hatred* of
Mao Salini. Evidently Baglione didn't associate Gramatica with the
stress and humiliation M caused him. Saraceni, Manfredi and Borgianni were the first of M's militant young followers among the
Roman painters. Prospero Orsi was too old to learn new tricks and
made do with energetic praise, but M's exact contemporary and early
employer Antiveduto Gramatica soon started assimilating things he'd
found in M's work. They were the scouts or the vanguard of an army.
A story about this time in M's life – a pure invention but very telling
in its own way – was retailed by Carlo Cesare Malvasia in his book
on Bolognese painters that came out six years after Bellori's work.
The count Malvasia had a weakness for any good story and especially
for anything that raised the profile of a painter from Bologna. Lionello
Spada was a painter from Bologna five years younger than M, and
another eager follower – people called him *M's ape*. Malvasia couldn't
resist sending him off to Rome a few years earlier than the records
showed, where

> he was given a warm and loving welcome by M, who
> remarked that he'd finally found a man after his own heart.
> I don't know why, but Lionello threw himself at M's feet
> and all he tried to do was please him in everything. He
> even stripped naked and acted as his model. Maybe because
> he wasn't unlike M in his habits, and his weirdnesses
> matched M's own wild temperament. But I do know that
> M didn't turn out as Lionello had imagined him. Too rash,
> as he used to say later, and just as much in his painting as
> in the way he lived. Unattractive in appearance and quite
> vile in his inventions. The only thing he was really good
> at was realistically doing the real life in front of him ...
> ... so [Spada] tried unsuccessfully to get away from
> him a number of times ... M took him to Naples and kept
> him prisoner there for four full days, modelling for a saint

John the baptist. He locked him in the room and fed him through a little window, so he wouldn't escape. He'd done exactly the same thing in Rome, in his *Matthew called*, when he painted Spada as the one with his back turned ...

The interlude ended with Spada's following M to Malta and falling for a beautiful black slave girl there – this was the kind of thing being said and implied about M in less austere milieux than Bellori's after M's death. And doubtless earlier. Malvasia caught the weird and dangerous glamour that surrounded M's name and offered an exuberant lowlife analogue of Bellori's more urbane and pointed invention of stories to match the art. Lionello Spada really was infatuated with M the painter – though he surely never met the man – and found in M along with the new technique a feeling for the male erotic violence that Malvasia's anecdote was trying to talk around and that Spada showed in paintings like his *Cain killing Abel*, which looked like a teenage homosexual rape. Although Spada didn't arrive in Rome until 1608, the notion that the youth seen in *profil perdu*, the one looking like the younger Robert De Niro, was really Spada went on being aired forever. His sword in the painting – *spada* – was the clinching visual pun.

WHEN M WAS let out of jail on September 25, an undertaking was signed on his behalf that he wouldn't

> attack or cause to be attacked either the life or honour of the painter Giovanni Baglione and the painter Tommaso alias Mao.

The promise implied a fairly reasonable fear that M would now move from words to deeds against Baglione and his sidekick and indicated that trial and imprisonment had exacerbated and not stifled the original quarrel. Onorio Longhi showed that as soon as he was back in town. Neither were Longhi's hurled brick and threatened duel the only bodily price Baglione would pay for running to the cops, nor the squashed hat the only damage Baglione's wardrobe would suffer, but the sequel was a while off and M himself would never be personally involved. M himself had neither the time nor the disposition for any lingering rancour. His weeks in the Roman governor's jail and the business of setting up house on his own – and being confined there – were interrupting a series of commitments that continued to accumulate irrespective of his problems with the law. Nobody cared about a painter's private life and M's judicial track record wasn't yet unusual for his milieu. It wasn't discouraging the private clients who kept wanting to put big pictures by M into their chapels in the major Roman churches. His brilliant job on the *Burial*, at once daringly new and soundly orthodox, had reassured people and kept them excited by his work.

One of the commissions he still had to do went back to 1601. When M was working on the *Saul* and *Peter* paintings for Cerasi and had lately gone to live in the palazzo Mattei, a neighbour and friend of Del Monte's and the Giustiniani brothers had commissioned a painting of his own. Laerzio Cherubini was a self made man in his fifties who'd arrived young in Rome as a *poor foot soldier*, studied law and had a brilliant career as a criminal and civil advocate. He was now a figure of considerable power in the church's legal administration and – surely egged on by his neighbours – he too now wanted a major work by the great new painter. Cherubini was also one of the three official custodians of the newly built church of Santa Maria della Scala in the Trastevere and got for himself the first and biggest private chapel that was decorated in the church – some said the design was Onorio Longhi's, though it probably wasn't. The new church was given to the Carmelites and Cherubini's chapel was dedicated rather unusually to the virgin Mary's *transit* to heaven and intended for the saying of masses for the dead. From M on 14 June 1601 Cherubini commissioned a painting for the altar showing *the death or transit of the blessed virgin Mary*. It was supposed to be finished and delivered by the end of the following year.

The price wasn't specified. Maybe Cherubini had doubts about the art he was being urged to commission. Maybe he and M simply couldn't agree on a price. M got an advance of fifty scudi and Vincenzo Giustiniani was named in the contract as the arbiter of the final price to be paid. Giustiniani had played some discreet part in M's Cerasi contract nine months earlier, but his role in the new contract implied that both M and his new client had utter trust in Giustiniani's critical acuteness and integrity. Giustiniani was offering himself as a guarantor of M's art to a client who might've been getting uneasy, losing his nerve at the last moment about buying into anything too, well, *unusual* – using his authority as a connoisseur and collector to promote M's work and further his career. Giustiniani was putting his mouth where his own money was. In the end Giustiniani would see that M got paid more for this commission than he got for any other single painting he did in Rome. It was indeed the biggest canvas he ever did. But it was a long time coming, long after the term agreed in the contract. M's deluge of public and private commissions were the likely cause, though the chapel may not have been quite ready for the installation either, a reason or an excuse to put the painting of *Mary dead* on the back burner. No documentary evidence survived to show when M did finish and deliver *Mary dead*, but the evidence of his work itself made it seem that he got round to it in the later part of 1604, some time after the other major public work he took on that year.

SOMETHING ODD HAPPENED in Loreto. Nobody knew quite what it was. Maybe someone was withholding facts. Enough contradictory statements converged on Loreto and M at the end of 1603 to show it did happen and it seemed to involve work, rivalries and acts of violence. Loreto, everybody knew, was the place northeast of Rome near the Adriatic coast where the house was in which Christ was born. Angels had flown it over from Palestine. Now it was a holy shrine and a place of pilgrimage and one of the most visited places in catholic Europe. Montaigne had made the four day pilgrimage there from Rome twenty three years earlier, and found the holy house

> a very old and mean little brick maisonette, longer than it was wide.

Baglione had been there and brought back the cheap little lead souvenirs of the Madonna that so angered Orazio Gentileschi. Images of the Madonna of Loreto were seen around the churches of Italy.

> The Madonna of Loreto was often, but not always, shown in flight with the house in which Jesus had been born, miraculously transported by angels from Palestine ...

Toward the end of 1603 – after October 25, when his month of house arrest expired – M left Rome on a short mysterious trip. It was his first time out of town since he arrived in Rome over ten years earlier. A letter was written on the second of the following January by an aristocrat from Tolentino in the Marches who was living in Rome.

Lancellotto Mauruzi had heard M was in Tolentino to do an altarpiece there and wrote to tell the local priors that M was a

> most excellent painter of great merit, in fact the best there is today in Rome.

He urged them to treat M well. M never did the painting, or if he did it was lost – maybe the letter got it wrong. Tolentino was near Loreto and M had lately signed up to paint the local cult Madonna. That summer, a week before M's arrest on the libel charge, the family of a man called Ermete Cavaletti, dead the year before, had bought a chapel to bury him in. It was the first on the left in the church of Sant' Agostino – a few steps from the piazza Navona. The will specified a painting of the Loreto Madonna over the altar, and at some unknown time after September 4 and before he left town, M contracted to do it – an iconic and devotional painting very different from the religious *histories* he'd been doing up to now. It was a reason to go to Loreto – get the feel of the place, see the art, check out the iconography of the flying house. The angelic airlift wasn't a thing you could do from life in the studio. Loreto was a busy place then. Clement VIII had ordered enlargements to boost pilgrimages. It made business sense. Twenty years earlier Montaigne said the place was pulling in ten thousand scudi in cash offerings and remarked that the money was clearly not at that time being ploughed back into decorating the church – gifts and money came in daily and the priests were *quite nonchalant* about accepting them. Baglione's trip had clearly been to suss out the chance of a painting engagement in Loreto, maybe after a tipoff from somewhere in the upper reaches of the hierarchy. Baglione got nothing, but in early 1604 Cristoforo Roncalli did. Baglione claimed M tendered unsuccessfully too.

> [Roncalli] ... got the holy house job at Loreto ... but M was among the others competing with Roncalli and M was so furious at being cut out that he got revenge by having a Sicilian traitor wound Roncalli, though only with a light cut.

The *Sicilian* sounded like Mario Minniti, if there were anything in the story. Baglione clearly believed there was and Baglione wasn't a liar – though frescos weren't M's thing and he was there long before Roncalli got the job. And if M was a harsh critic of his contemporaries, he wasn't professionally jealous or vindictive. If he were, Roncalli might've stuck in his gullet. Adaptable, amenable, eclectic, Roncalli – also called *the Pomarancio* after his home town – was a painter who made himself agreeable to everyone. *The experts like him more than ordinary people do*, remarked Mancini of Roncalli. He was nearly twenty years older than M and moved in the same circuits – everywhere M arrived he found Roncalli had been there before him. When M was working on his *Matthew* paintings, it was Roncalli who decided how much expensive blue and ultramarine paints he'd be allowed, because Roncalli was the Crescenzi family's painter of choice. M, who was militantly averse to the kind of *beauty* Roncalli's work embodied,

> didn't use blues in his figures … and if he did employ them sometimes, he muted them, saying they were poisonous colours.

Socially, Roncalli was everything M wasn't. *He always had this glamour from working for the nobility* remembered Mancini, and was at home with the church establishment and its preferred painters – Roncalli too, like Cesari, like Baglione, became a *knight of the cloak of Christ.* Cardinal Crescenzi had fixed it with the pope for Roncalli to have his cavalier's cloak,

> given to him by cardinal Ottavio Paravicino in his private chapel, and the godfathers who girded on his sword – as is the way – were the cavalier Domenico Passignani and the cavalier Giovanni Baglione.

Paravicino was the cardinal who'd been inquiring into M and his art with such urbane menace. Glimpsed here with Baglione and Roncalli he seemed like someone photographed at a mafia private function. By the time this ceremony took place, M had a death warrant on his head. Did M maybe sense how things were stacking up, see that however good he was he'd never be allowed the recognition granted a Roncalli or even a Baglione, and did he lash out again? Did he have Roncalli cut?

Baglione got things wrong – M would never have put in for a fresco job – but he wasn't the only one who believed it. A little later Passeri thought M actually got the job at Loreto but angrily refused to take the young painter Guercino along as his assistant and so lost it to Roncalli. The story appeared in Passeri's life of Guercino, a leading painter of the next generation. The administrators, Passeri wrote, were *perplexed* by M's *bestiality* and wanted young Guercino to go along as a *moderate companion* to keep him *reined in*. The myth of the violent M was well implanted by the time Passeri wrote, and he had M slamming a hot poker into the floor by the fire as the terrified Guercino spoke. Passeri's story seemed independent of Baglione's, and though it too failed to hang together – M's friendship with Guercino was chronologically impossible – it pointed to a lost *urstory* about M and Loreto that was really true. The idea of M slashing out now against exclusion made sense.

He was lashing out in other ways. In late April – around the time he was working on his Loreto Madonna for the Cavallettis – he was in the osteria del Moro – a usual working artists' hangout *at the Maddalena* in the campo Marzio – with a couple of friends one day at lunch when he attacked the serving hand in a rage. The serving hand had lacked *respect*. The indignant and frightened waiter rushed over to the cops and told them breathlessly that

> I brought them eight cooked artichokes – that is four done in butter and four in oil, and the defendant asked me which were the ones done in butter and which ones in oil. I told him to smell them and he could easily tell which were cooked in butter and which were done in oil. Then he got in a rage and without saying another word to me he took a china plate and threw it in my face. It hit me on the left cheek here where I've got a bit of an injury. Then he stood up and put his hand on one of his friend's sword that was on the table and looked as if he was going to go for me with it but I got out of his way and came here ...

A painter – a maker of copies, in this workaday eating place – who'd been sitting with another group said that when M asked how to tell the artichokes in butter from the ones in oil, the serving hand had said *I don't know* and picked one up and stuck his nose in it.

> M took it badly and got up in a rage and said
> *It seems to me, you fucking prick, that you think you're serving some two bit crook.*
> And he grabbed the plate with the artichokes in it and threw it in the bloke's face. I didn't see M put his hand to his sword against him.

M's hairtrigger touchiness over respect, or the lack of it – not long out of jail and feeling he was being treated like a *cheap crook* by a merely uncouth serving youth – came from knowing how exposed he now was, in no longer belonging to a powerful cardinal's household. There was a real reason for this violent expression of personal insecurity. Yet though he may not have known it, interested and influential parties were still concerning themselves with his well being. When the case came to judgement in June, M was convicted of assault but in the register of convictions for such offences the space for his sentence to be indicated was – in the only such case in the register – left blank. Somebody with clout had intervened and, going by the sentences listed in the same register as meted out for other assault cases, the move had maybe kept M from doing some forced rowing in the galleys.

11

ROME 1604

Pilgrims' Madonna
John in the wild IV
John in the wild V

A FLYING HOUSE with clouds, sunlight and angels around it and the Madonna on board – no way M was doing that. The Cavallettis knew this quite well from the work M already had showing in three other nearby churches. The Cavallettis never complained and were surely mightily pleased – even, or especially, by the attention grabbing fuss – when M rethought her image entirely, and brought the *Pilgrims' Madonna*, for the first time, entirely down to earth and the present day. He did her as a sexy young housewife coming to the front door of what looked like a very ordinary Roman home – a handsome doorway, the frame a bit chipped and a patch of stucco missing from the wall, exposing the bricks beneath – still babying the overgrown naked boy child in her arms and gazing unseeingly – unlike her child, whose eyes were on the human – with a kind of stoical modesty at a patch of ground in front of the shabby couple kneeling devotedly below the doorstep. The shabby couple – they must've just knocked – were a bearded barefoot man in his thirties with patched britches and a considerably older and worn looking woman, old enough to be the man's mother, who'd already lost her teeth and had her hair scarfed against roadside dust. They both had walking staves, resting on their shoulders for the moment as they touched their fingertips in devotion, and the staves showed who the couple were. They were the pilgrims.

No need for M to go to Loreto to do a field study on people like this. Every year a good thirty thousand of them arrived in Rome – a third of the permanent population – and maybe half a million, a million, a million and a quarter had poured in for the holy jubilee four years earlier. For M the pilgrims were a memory from childhood, of the peasant worshippers who used to visit Mary's shrine in Caravaggio. In small places like Loreto and Caravaggio the pilgrimage was an exercise of belief through the great effort of the barefoot journey. What M caught now in his models' bodies – the man's crouching, tensed and forward leaning, the woman's almost rocking back in ecstatic repose, her eyes fixed on the Christ child – was that physical intensity of felt devotion. In Rome the pilgrim was a rather more complicated figure. There were a lot of reasons other than piety for coming to Rome. In Rome the wealthy pilgrims like Montaigne were indistinguishable from tourists, and the poor were assimilated to the masses of poor, unemployed and destitute people who drifted into the capital seeking refuge from rural poverty and banditry, along with the criminals and sexual adventurers. These were the hordes of all too visible poor the Roman authorities didn't know how to handle, with policies that swung wildly between mass expulsion and mass lockup, between simple persecution and a charity that felt like imprisonment to its beneficiaries. Poor pilgrims were indistinguishable from homeless beggars, at once models of active counter reformation piety, an urban blight in the new showpiece Rome and a growing social menace. Giordano Bruno, who'd been around and knew the life of European cities, had made a pungent summary of the urban drifters and homeless in his *Ash Wednesday dinner*, and grouped religious pilgrims in his fourth and lowest class of all

> a mixture of the desperate, servants whose masters have turned against them, survivors of great storms, pilgrims, the useless and inert, who've lost resources to steal, who've just escaped from jail, con men …

Bruno had seen them in London, he'd seen them in Paris and in Italy he'd seen them

> on the steps of San Paolo in Naples, on the Rialto in Venice, at the campo de' Fiori in Rome.

Montaigne had thought – wrongly, but tellingly – that there was nobody in Rome who lived by his own labour. The conditions of life were changing all around the Mediterranean, and the privileged figure of the pilgrim in Christian Europe was starting to be lost among the frightening masses of rootless poor. In Rome the problem grew and grew. By 1693 a reformer was writing that

> Since Rome is the capital and in the end the centre of the Christian world, the poor of all nations stream in here, looking for some consolation for their own misfortunes. A lot of them come for business and when their resources run out they're forced to beg and end up liking it … infinite crowds of vagabonds and parasites … wander among the houses and churches all over the whole city, approaching people and extorting, almost violently, the money they then spend in the most shameful and scandalous ways …

It was just what Sixtus V had been saying, in much more violent terms, over a hundred years before. Since poor, grubby, needy and appallingly *numerous* pilgrims of the lower order were looked on with suspicion and hostility, not to say loathing, by respectable Romans, their prominence in a Roman altarpiece could only aggravate the unease that M's completely new handling of the Loreto Madonna was already causing. Baglione, when he retailed what right thinking people felt about M's new work, likely remembered that soon after the *Pilgrims' Madonna* went on view in Sant' Agostino there was a new crackdown on the kind of people it showed. An *avviso* reported from Rome in September 1604 that

> an edict was issued last Sunday against the vagrants present in great numbers in the city. Within ten days they have to find employment or move out. The penalty for failing to do so will be time on the galleys.

After five months of systematic search and arrest by the police the warning was repeated. Meanwhile, Baglione wrote of M,

> … he did a Loreto Madonna painted from life with two pilgrims, the man with muddy feet and the woman in a dirty torn bonnet. Because he trivialized the attributes that a major painting ought to have, the lower classes made a huge fuss over it.

Baglione mentioned the new wave of excitement at M's art only because the *huge fuss* came from all the wrong people for all the wrong reasons – reminding you it wasn't the first time dirty feet had been a problem in M's art. And since the greatest offence of these destitute pilgrims or vagrants in showplace Rome was being seen at all, putting two of them, life size and closely observed, over a major altar with *their filthy feet on display* was a provocation. It was a shock of recognition for the people themselves, who weren't used to seeing themselves reflected in others' eyes at all, let alone as art. No wonder they *made a huge fuss* when they flocked amazed to see it. Paleotti had known that *the mass of people are idiots* and suckers for realism. Borromeo later sighed that

> these things are crowd pleasers, and unfortunately the crowd likes the very worst things … ignorant ordinary people admire only the errors in painters like this and don't know how to appreciate art and see whether there's anything really beautiful in it …

Roncalli's graceful work, for instance, was never a popular hit – *experts like him more than ordinary people do.* It wasn't just the grubby poor. The young mother herself in M's new painting fed the sensation, and there were reasons for thinking that she was part of the problem for the right thinking. The pilgrims' Madonna was now a young Roman housewife, stunningly beautiful in early motherhood, her legs languidly crossed as she leant against the doorway in a fulfilled maternal daze, getting the rather shabby *holy house* to take some of the weight of the big child in her arms. She looked as if she'd come out for a gossip, or to catch the late sun and a bit of alley life. She was barefoot, but dressed in silk and velvet, a loose sleeved pomegranate top with a hint of *décolletage* and a grey silk skirt pulled tight over her thigh by her cross-legged stance. It was the first time M had used this gorgeous Venetian red since the musical boys in his first work for Del Monte and he never would again. It seemed to mark an erotic surge, a peculiar voluptuousness of perception. Her clothes, in the Roman alley, and her athletic tiptoe levitating stance that faintly recalled the story of the flying house, marked her subtly as different, along with her looks. Her superb Greek profile – dark thick hair, dark jutting brow, heavy-lidded eyes, big straight nose and small mouth – was caught against the darkness in M's oblique afternoon light. This was a carnal and sensual Madonna. She was an icon remade.

The council of Trent had been categorical in banning any kind of innovation in religious art, and when he spelt out what this meant, along with a sharp reminder that matters of ideological correctness were very much the inquisition's concern, Paleotti had particularly dwelt on the kind of newness that offended against *decorum* by showing the holy family, the saints and apostles doing everyday things and living ordinary lives. Paleotti's imagination or his indignation had run away with him here, and he mentioned the Madonna fetching creek water for her baby, en route to Egypt, or Joseph picking fruit, the baby Jesus playing with a bird. The more domestic things got, the more reprehensible they were. Paleotti had let his mind play aghast over ideas of

> saint Philip asleep in bed, saint Andrew eating at table, saint Petronius getting dressed or saint Agnes taking off her shoes … the Madonna doing needlework … saint Peter with his mother in law … saint Paul tanning hides …

M's very domestic image of the mother and child catching some late sun on their front doorstep in the company of a couple of vagrants was getting dangerously close to offending here. Neither the expensive clothes nor the statuesque pose that'd maybe been taken from a classical sculpture nor even the last minute haloes added to mother and child did much to relieve the deeply physical dailiness of the pilgrims' Madonna.

The *huge fuss*, as far as the locals were concerned, wasn't just over the pilgrims or vagrants who loomed so large in the canvas. It was over the Madonna herself. She afforded another shock of recognition. She was far too strikingly individual not to be identified as the courtesan Maddalena Antognetti. Lena lived in the neighbourhood with her mother and sister, both of whom were also on the game, as it was played in the upper reaches of the Roman church. She'd been the lover, in her teenage heyday a few years earlier, first of the *soft youth* cardinal Montalto and then of monsignor Melchiorre Crescenzi and she belonged to the upmarket group of girls that included Fillide Melandroni, Menica Calvi and Tella Brunori. She was now intensely involved with M himself. Whether the involvement was a consequence of her modelling work, or whether her role in that painting came about because their lives were already entangled, a tumultuous and violent episode in her life was beginning that was part of a more general comedown from the gilded days and nights she'd spent a few years earlier. Life was closing in on Lena.

Making Lena the pilgrims' Madonna was a risky move for M. Lena's wasn't exactly an unfamiliar face around town. This was a very different move from painting Anna Bianchini or Fillide Melandroni as the Magdalen for a private collection. The council of Trent had specifically banned *all sexually attractive beauty from images of holy figures.* Recognizable faces in public religious art were always a danger in any case, and never more so than when you had rivals and enemies to point this out. Federico Borromeo was very firm on this point, and might've had the *Pilgrims' Madonna* in mind when he wrote that

> we cannot but reprove those artists who chose persons who
> have lost all good name and graft their faces and figures on
> to images of the saints – and do it so exquisitely that they
> are immediately recognizable.

Even Mancini agreed this was a shocking practice – *living persons shouldn't be painted in the role of saints,* and he singled M out as particularly offending in this. Yet the *Pilgrims' Madonna* had a trouble free life. M nicely played off for a second time the startling newness of his painterly treatment against an image that was orthodox enough to pass. His clients the Cavallettis and the church must've been so gratified by the popular acclaim and the crowds M's work was bringing to Sant' Agostino that they put aside any worries they might've had about the filthy barefoot pilgrims and the all too recognizable strong faced courtesan Lena with the grey silk taut over her thigh.

Why then was the *Pilgrims' Madonna* so undistinguished a painting? Beyond the bold, voluptuous and disconcerting presence of Lena the courtesan as the model for the virgin Mary, beyond the in your face dirty realism of the life size street people, and behind the sensuousness of M's painterly surface, lay a kind of votive stasis. It was odd. It'd been too easy. M had been working obsessively for four years now at a single task. He'd had to apply his early mastery – his way of seeing and rendering the play of light on bodies in darkness – to the newer requirement that he show complex human movement, action, relationship. The effort was being rewarded because the demands of the big *history* commissions were taking his acquired skills into new areas, enriching and deepening them, socializing his art. He was learning deep things about the stillness that was a part of movement, about the contemplative repose that belonged to all action. He was understanding the moments of awareness that precede and follow action – ugly, practical Nicodemus glancing out of the picture, as the others stayed locked in their varieties of private grief, to see where they were going to lower the body. In extending and refining his technique he'd learnt things about human nature and the way people were together, the dynamic way they related in space. The marvellously visual tension of the effort made the interest of his paintings. But here he relapsed.

In the *Pilgrims' Madonna* there was no real implied before and no imminent after, just this emblematic stasis. Mute adoration implied no connexion. The virgin mother looked blank, withdrawn and almost bored. She was being treated as an object – a statue – or worse, an idea, and Lena the model showed the strain of it. She was psychically absent. This was painting as illustration of an idea, and the tableau's giveaway sentimentality was picked out in the chubby forefinger of the Christ child blessing the humble poor. The awful priestly finger-wagging from a child was M's worst – his only – lapse into counter reformation kitsch. The slight angling of the massive doorstep away from the picture plane was a pictorial convenience that had none of the displacing force of the painter's diagonal take on the *Burial*. That'd thrust you into a radically private and intimate view of death and loss, as the obliquity of *Peter killed* had brought you face to face, as he strained up toward life, with the old man's last moments. Here it all seemed flattened out and drained of spatial drama. In his newest public work M had come up against the fact that there was no way he could animate a doctrinal given. The more intensely you felt the peasants' pathetic devotion, the more its object the Madonna became remote, inert, hieratic. She was no longer one of *the natural things* he'd invoked at his trial, and nothing could bring the two realities together. After a long look the picture's gorgeous detail cloyed. As none of M's adoring early paintings of boys had done, the new work tasted of sugar. In a way that the bleakest and cruellest of his later paintings would never be, the *Pilgrims' Madonna* was slightly repellent.

RUNNING A HOUSEHOLD turned out not to be one of M's personal strengths, although he kept the house in vico San Biagio for nearly two years. It all ended unpleasantly. In the summer of 1605 M had to leave Rome for a while in a hurry and his landlady Prudenzia Bruni – who lived with her son and daughter in a house adjoining the one she let M – took advantage of his temporary absence to get some compensation for the eighty scudi owing her for six months' unpaid back rent and major damage to a ceiling. He never went back. The court order taken out by Prudenzia Bruni marked the end of M's tenancy in the only home of his own he ever had. She evidently locked him out and the house was soon relet to a new tenant. The inventory made in his absence of the things he'd left behind shed a sharp light on to the way he'd been living since the autumn of 1603. Along with the damage to the ceiling, it also raised some questions about the way he worked.

He'd rented a house to come out of jail to that was nothing like the luxury homes nearby maintained by establishment painters to whom image mattered, people like Zuccari and Cesari. Zuccari lived up the hill at Trinità dei Monti, and Cesari's place – where M had stayed with the two brothers a decade earlier – was just nearby. Lena lived a minute's walk away on the Corso, which was useful for her modelling sessions. The place M took as house, studio and temporary prison was decent enough, a two storey place, new or newly fixed up, with a large room and two smaller ones both upstairs and downstairs, with a cellar below and a verandah upstairs looking out at the back on to a courtyard garden with its own well. This was unpretentious but adequate and the rent was forty scudi a year, which was nearly double the average for the neighbourhood. It'd been let more or less unfurnished, and M was no homemaker. There was almost nothing in it.

After laconically listing enough personal belongings to suggest M had been basically camping out in his nice rented house, with a few sticks of furniture, the very short inventory, evidently following the lawyer inventorist's passage upstairs and his final arrival in the room M used as his studio, listed at the end the working materials M had abandoned when he left town in a hurry ...

> *Item* two large unpainted canvases.
> *Item* one old chest with various rags inside.
> *Item* three stools. *Item* a big mirror. *Item* a mirror shield.
> *Item* three other smaller pictures.
> *Item* one three legged bench.
> *Item* three large unpainted canvases. *Item* one large painting
>   on wood.
> *Item* one ebony case with a knife inside.
> *Item* three bed bolsters.
> *Item* one high wooden easel.
> *Item* one small trolley with various packets of coloured paint
>   pigments.
> *Item* one halbard. *Item* two other unpainted canvases.

M must've taken all his paintbrushes with him. The presence of the two mirrors not among the personal effects but among the painting things showed that M was still – in some way – using mirror reflections in setting up his work. Right at the outset of his painting career in Rome, M had used mirrors, as Baglione remembered and the early *Sick self portrait* showed. When Baglione mentioned *some little paintings done in the mirror* as M's first independent efforts he was underscoring M's poverty and isolation in those early days – his failure to make any sales, his poverty, his terrible clothes. But if mirrors were still among the few essential working items ten years later, they were now more than an economy measure, and likely always had been.

The younger M had been fascinated by the play of light on glass and through glass. The meticulousness with which he rendered what happened to sunlight on a carafe of water or a glass of wine, the way that light was trapped in the heart of shadow the carafe then cast on a white tablecloth, the way the light caressed the bulging surface and gave the glass form even as the rays were refracted through glass and water and left their own stamp on the glass's surface, in the shape of the rectangular window through which they'd arrived – this loving attention to the ways of the energy at the source of his art was still being given play a couple of years later, in the flask of water and the glass of white wine on the table of the *Meal at Emmaus* he'd done for Mattei at the end of 1601.

From then on, as the pressures of making complex human figure compositions mounted, M's concern with reflected and refracted light retreated to the implicit and the practical. From being the end of his painting it more and more became the means. How could it help him paint? He no longer needed mirrors to provide him with a model, though he would've continued to use them when he occasionally included a self portrait in a *history*, like the one in *Christ taken*. Yet what the lawyer found in M's abandoned studio seemed to indicate that mirrors were still integral to M's work in the studio. What wasn't clear was how he used them. Some of his early paintings did have the look of reflected images. Anna Bianchini was painted as the *Penitent Magdalen* somewhat from above, with an oddly foreshortened effect about her skirt and the stool she was sitting on, as if M had been standing quite near her and painting not Anna but her reflection in a downward looking mirror on the wall overhead. And unless Mario Minniti was left handed, when he stood in as *Bacchus* M painted his reflection in a mirror.

Mirrors weren't new in painting. They fascinated the mannerists in the previous century as a means of modifying images. Parmigianino's *Self portrait in a convex mirror* was an overt and extreme case of playful experimentation among many less obvious ones like his own *Long necked Madonna*. Images elongated in a mirror's distorting reflection lent a more aristocratic beauty and elegance than anything mere nature had to offer. When Garzoni wrote about mirrors and mirror makers some time before 1585, in his huge compendium of trades, his imagination was entirely caught up with their manifold power of weird illusion. Practical uses in art or science went unmentioned. Garzoni didn't mention painting, but he was writing at the height of mannerist preciousness and his outlook showed it. As a popular moralist he was firm about mirror making that

> in the end this art is quite vain and useless to the world and used more often for worldly amusement than anything else. It shows itself more trifling and bizarre than good and useful.

M's use for mirrors reached back beyond the mannerists to Leonardo. Before the mannerists began playing with mirrors as a way of modifying and improving on nature, Leonardo had been emphatic that the mirror – the *flat mirror*, true undistorting – was *the painters' master*.

> When you want to see if your painting corresponds over-all to the thing painted from life, get a mirror and reflect the living thing in it, and compare the reflection with your painting ... [and if you've done it right] your painting too will look like a natural thing seen in a big mirror.

Leonardo's vocabulary here – *la cosa ritratta dal naturale ... una cosa naturale vista in un grande specchio* – sounded much like M's when he said at his trial that skill in painting meant knowing how to *dipingere bene et imitar bene le cose naturali*, paint well and imitate natural things. Leonardo's advice to match painting with a mirror image as a simple reality check was compatible with his insistence on the importance of mathematical perspective in creating a true image. But sometimes Leonardo implied that the mind itself was like a mirror. Earlier in the *Book of painting* he noted that

> the painter's mind should be like a mirror and always take on the colour of whatever's its object and fill up with as many likenesses as there are things in front of it.

At times, when he wrote about painting, Leonardo's urge to understand and control nature – and linear perspective was a means of doing this in art – gave way to this notion of a receptive intelligence that extended to all the functions of the mind and made the painter's mind a unique microcosm. The painter was not as other men, but a being apart. Developing the idea of a mirror mind, he added

> The painter should be solitary and consider what he sees and speak with himself, choosing the most excellent parts in the appearance of everything he sees. He should be like a mirror and change himself into as many colours as there are in the things that appear in front of him. Doing so, he'll seem to himself to be a second nature.

When Leonardo wrote about linear perspective for painters in the *Book of painting* – he dropped the idea of writing on the maths of it when he heard Piero della Francesca already had – he was drawing on what'd gone before in the way of theorizing about space in art – Alberti's chapter on perspective in his book *De pictura* in the fourteen thirties and Piero's more rigorously mathematical treatise *De prospectiva pingendi* fifty years later. And the notion behind all the theories of perspective and behind the painting practice the theories tried to codify was that a painting was like a window. Looking at a painting you were looking out at more or less distant objects that lay beyond the picture plane. Leonardo himself advised the use of a pane of glass to fix a scene for painting. In M's time Guidubaldo and Galileo were still thinking on this model. When Leonardo wrote more subjectively about the way the world impressed itself on the mind through the eye, as a kind of feeling mirror, and the way the mind's response matched what it saw, he was looking as it were inward rather than outward, from the picture plane toward the perceiving self. He was also looking forward rather than backward in time, anticipating concerns with the way people perceived the world – the very nature of seeing – that were becoming a matter of very intense study in several quarters a hundred years later, at the time M was painting in Rome. The uses of the mirror, in the first years of the seventeenth century, were of more than metaphorical interest.

When M was working in Rome, the mirror was part of the instrument called a *camera obscura* – lately developed and refined in Naples by the scientist and playwright Giambattista Della Porta.

> In a small circle of paper, you shall see as it were the Epitomy of the whole world.

In its simplest form the *camera obscura* had been known since ancient times and used as a kind of pinhole camera for viewing eclipses without having to stare at the sun. Della Porta had shown for the first time in 1589 how a *camera obscura* with a lens and a mirror could be used to cast an image on a screen – his *Natural magic* was a major work on optics that also contained the first theoretical account of the telescope. Galileo's later actual telescope was also, as it happened, anticipated by Johannes Kepler in a book published in Frankfurt in 1604, the same year M was working with mirrors in the studio of his newly rented house in vico San Biagio. Kepler too failed to develop his telescope discovery – at least partly because the main object of the research described in his book wasn't the telescope itself but the *camera obscura*. Kepler was interested in understanding and refining the workings of the *camera obscura* for astronomical use in observing the sun. Doing so involved understanding the optical working of the human eye itself, and in his 1604 book Kepler gave the first accurate account of the way the eye's lens formed an image on the retina. Suggestively, he called that image a *picture*, implying that the image was to some extent at least a creation of the seeing eye and not an objectively transmitted datum. Kepler wrote that *vision is brought about by a picture of the thing seen being formed on the concave surface of the retina*. His own interest in sight stopped with the formation of that upside down image, and he left to philosophers and neurologists the question of how it related to human perception of the world. What he'd found, going back to the problems with the distorted solar images rendered by the *camera obscura*, was that the human eye itself played a part in the distortion and that

> the origin of errors in vision must be sought in the conformation and functions of the eye itself.

Seeing this meant making a distinction between things in the world and their image, or *picture*, or representation on the retina. *Ut pictura, ita visio*, sight was like a picture.

SEEING THE WORLD as an image on a screen, or a mirror, or the retina of the eye, and seeing a picture as a projected, refracted, reflected image was a rather different way of thinking about visual art from the idea of looking out on things through a window. The mirror was an emblem and maybe an enabler of the newly accessible inwardness in painting. M's great struggle with *Matthew killed* in 1600, when he'd wrestled with prospectival painting and finally thrown it over for images of an hallucinatory vividness – hallucinatory because they were looming at you out of the picture plane instead of receding behind it, not caught in a grid of perspectival lines but swimming at you in all the unnerving clarity of their strong relief out of the murky dark, and because you weren't sure where you stood in relation to them, so that everything was unsettled, mobile – had been the point of no return.

There'd been signs before that, like the *Basket of fruit* projecting on its ledge, the *Medusa's* severed head seeming to float in a concave space. And one painting M had done just before the *Matthew* side paintings had the force of a proclamation. In 1599 *one large mirror* had let him paint *Narcissus*, and the mirror had entered the painting itself as the sheet of dark water spread out in front of the kneeling boy. The mirror was asserting its part in the creation with polemical force. The painting included the boy and his image, what he was and what he saw. Just as M was starting to *strengthen his darks*, he'd done a painting that was half reflection, life seen in a glass darkly so that everything was even more subdued than the real boy looking down, almost engulfed in lightlessness, and all you saw were shadows and some brilliant points of light. The boy's billowing hitched up sleeves, a mass of dazzling creamy silk above, were reduced in their reflection below to the merest highlights. It was what M was doing in his art, stripping it down so that you had to work down from these minimalist highlights, and when he started painting for the churches you'd be picking out these points of light in the gloom of a badly lit chapel, in the mean daylight arriving through a small dirty window high overhead or the flickering yellow flames of candles, to recreate the image in your own mind. *Narcissus* was a manifesto for M's new art.

So was the other painting he'd shown a mirror in, the *Martha & Mary* he'd done just before *Narcissus*. The mirror in that painting was the other one, the convex *mirror shield* that M had taken to his new lodging and the lawyer later found there. In *Martha & Mary* the mirror's part was more pictorial. Yet the mirror did also make the painting's dazzling focus a tiny and brilliant white rectangle on its upper curve. That point of brilliant light was the reflection of the high small window or skylight that lit the scene M was painting, as a high and focused light source out of sight to the left lit most of M's scenes. Mary draped her arm over the mirror with her fingers pointing at the diamond of white light in case you missed its significance, and Fillide's deformed ring finger on her left hand, which'd last been draped on the hilt of *Catherine's* long and murderous sword, showed – like the teeth missing from the ivory comb lying by the makeup dish with its scrap of brown sponge – that natural light lit up real life.

The mirror was convex, like the one Parmigianino used for his playful *Self portrait* and like the mirror on the back wall that reflected Van Eyck's *Arnolfini marriage portrait*. A convex reflection enhanced the immediacy of what was near and central and minimized the peripheral, and the one shown in *Martha & Mary* was also a *dark* convex mirror that obscured neutral tones and left only the highlights – useful in heightening images like the ones M was now painting. Looking with horror at your own reflection in a mirror like this, you'd see something like the severed head of the *Medusa* painted on its round shield – to look at M's painted shield with its floating head and writhing snakes would elicit that horror. M's painting imitated and provoked a horrified reflection in a *mirror shield* like the one in his studio. Was it his own mirror, or Leonardo's earlier realization of the same effect that'd given M the *Medusa* idea?

The square of light the mirror reflected in its darkness in *Martha & Mary* was the illumination from high up that all the early critics said M used to light his *mises en scène* in a dark walled space. It wasn't at all, as Giulio Mancini pointed out, *natural*. M and his followers were distinctive in lighting their work, Mancini wrote,

> with a single light coming down from high up, without reflections, as it would from a window into a room with the walls painted black. So with the lights being very light and the shadows very dark, these come to give relief to the painting, but in a way that's not natural. It wasn't used or imagined in other centuries by older painters like Raphael, Titian, Correggio and the others. Working like this, this school's very attentive to reality and always paints with the living model right in front of it. It works well for single figures, but ...

Sandrart said the same thing.

> ... to bring out those effects of relief and natural roundedness better, he used dark vaults or other shadowed rooms with one small light above, so that the light falling on the model made strong shadows in the darkness ...

And so, with his own moralistic forcing, did Bellori.

> He took this working method so far that he never let any of his figures come out into the sunlight. He found a way

of setting them off against the dark air of a closed room and taking a high light that came straight down on to the main part of the body and left the rest in shadow. That way he achieved strength through the contrast of light and dark.

The particular setting – the dark closed space and the single light source above – were so intrinsic to M's whole way of *imitating natural things* that the nature of studio space available was of crucial importance to him. In the vast high ceilinged palaces of Del Monte and the Mattei brothers he'd presumably found it easy to get the kind of working space he needed. The studio in the palazzo Madama likely had its own role in M's discovery of the painting environment that suited him, and pushed his art in the direction it took. But the modest two storey house he was renting from Prudenzia Bruni didn't offer the same convenience. When she later went to court against M in his absence, her claim was upheld for eighty scudi. Part of this was for six months' unpaid back rent and the rest for repairs to a damaged ceiling. Six months' rent was twenty scudi – the cost of fixing the *broken ceiling* was put at a year and a half's rent. It was unlikely to have been an accident, and hard not to think that M found it necessary to knock a hole in the ceiling of his studio to get exactly the right kind of overhead lighting he was looking for. Why the obsession with setting the scene and getting the lighting just right? It was, as the formidably empirical physician Mancini remarked, *not natural*. But imitating natural things was only ever part of the story. M also believed a *good man* ought to *know how to do his job well*, and for a painter that meant *knowing how to paint well*. *Natural* had nothing to do with the painter's theme – quite different from young Annibale Carracci's early *Bean eater* or *Boy drinking* or *Man and monkey*, or *Butcher's shop*, which all showed a feel for ordinary people in their vigorous unglamorous everyday lives that was never M's.

Was M ever aware of that more subdued and private disaster that was working itself out in parallel to his own in another part of town? It was the awful pull of the eleven years older Carracci's – a marvellously vital and more variously resourceful painter than M – alienation from the humanity of his art, as he generalized, classicized, giganticized, idealized, mythologized it out of existence to oblige Odoardo Farnese and his other Roman patrons. Bellori chose to see it as a kind of divine intervention in art – Annibale Carracci's being sent to save painting from the opposed and equally hideous fates of mannerism and naturalism. M's own course ran parallel to Annibale's, but M was moving in the reverse direction. Inwardly and outwardly, the precious dreamy solipsism of ten years earlier was being transmuted now, under the pressure of M's unmovable constancy in his own ways of seeing, into a terrible sense of the limits of life.

Natural in M was only the utter fidelity to his own optical sensations, the minute fixation on his own visual contact with the world, a contact that became more intense – more ecstatic – as M inexorably reduced it to the picking out of ever feebler highlights, exacerbating the contrast between light and dark, visible and invisible, and recreating a world of forms and textures out of the glinting reflections in the dark. He made you do it too, follow the strenuous play of his eye and mind, creating the forms in the darkened theatre of his studio. This was *natural*. All the rest, in the most literal sense imaginable, was window dressing. Whether M's use of mirrors went beyond using them to frame the figures he was painting and fix them in two dimensions – whether it extended to practical experiments with Della Porta's *camera obscura* of the kind Vermeer and other painters would later be making in the low countries – wasn't clear. The *camera obscura* had been well popularized in Giambattista Della Porta's bestselling new edition of his book, which had been around for some years, and it had to enthral a painter obsessed with optical images. But M and Vermeer were painters fascinated by the way reality impinged on their own direct vision of things. An interest in its working as an analogy of their own sight, and a feeding back of its images into the way they rendered their own on canvas, didn't necessarily translate into its use as some kind of mechanical aid. What mattered for M was what his own eyes saw.

There was plenty of empty space in the rented house – an empty room, more or less, both upstairs and downstairs – for arranging his models the way he needed them. M painted his *histories* in parts – into the studio at vico San Biagio he brought the local people as models, wearing their ordinary clothes, and set them up with cheap everyday objects like the ones found in his house. The whole thing existed only in the unifying imagination – real components assembled into an oniric whole. The hyperrealistic detail that he painted *with the living model before him* became part of something that couldn't be found in the workaday world, but it was the everyday reality of the details that made the dream seem real. The missing leg of the money counters' table, Mary's body levitating in its red dress, the uncast shadow on the table of the meal at Emmaus, Saul's disappearing leg – none of them made sense, but you saw and believed. M's paintings had always turned faults into new strengths. The boy musicians jammed into their unreal space were a young painter's awkwardness – the hallucinatory space of Matthew's killing was a dreamlike and fluid and haunting theatre of the mind.

A friendly darkness now bound and united the things the mind bodied forth. Darkness was the dream medium in which the images swam. Darkness smoothed and obscured the illogic that linked things in the mind. The conniving gloom of a Roman chapel suggested and enhanced the darkness of the mind and the darkness of the world. Only the mind could relate the world's shreds of life into a whole. M's darkness wasn't a black emptiness – it was full of hidden life and movement, like the night. Things people never saw he worked as fully and lovingly as he did the brilliant highlights. M was making his art harder, asking more and more of you, forcing you to peer into the gathering darkness to make out the objects of your visual pleasure. More and more, you were having to create those objects for yourself.

ADOLESCENT JOHN WAS the ascetic and solitary precursor of Christ. He was the boy who spoke with *the voice of one crying in the wilderness*. The figure of John as a lonely brooding boy caught M's imagination early and held it to the end of his life. He painted more versions of *John in the wild* than of any other figure – at least eight. The series was like an intimate running commentary on his life. M's first *John* was one of the very last of his early idyllic paintings of boys. Around 1598, when he did his first version of *Isaac & Abraham*, he painted the same boy as a young *John*. It was also the time of the *Basket of fruit*, and this first John was surrounded by foliage, sunlight falling on different angled leaves and playing over their dimples, their veins, their ragged edges – John was awkwardly holding up his cane cross, and the sheep sitting at his feet had the pompous and hieratic look of an animal conscious of posing as a religious icon. The boy himself though, nearly nude – and here and as Isaac he was M's first full length boy nude – was rendered in a complex and subtle play of intense light and deepening shadow that was already mapping out the contours of bodies to come. The boy's downward looking face was in shadow, as in Isaac, and his intense, moody, lowered eyes and inwardly directed gaze caught, like the shifting intensities of light on his soft body, the changeability and uncertainty of adolescence. Fragile, withdrawn, vulnerable, he wasn't much of an image of Christianity's militant and uncompromising forerunner for a newly militant church.

Then again, neither was Cecco, laid back, grinning and totally nude. It was Cecco's cheerful grin that gave that painting its peculiarly disconcerting look of a holiday snapshot. M gave his own intensely lighthearted sexual intimacy to the way he painted Cecco as John, but he certainly wasn't the first painter to do John as an appealing boy more or less stripped of any ideological dress. Leonardo and Raphael had both done it before him. Though only M's Cecco John frankly displayed his genitals, the most radical thing about this *John* was the way the painting registered its subject's own amusement, the delightful charge of pleasure M set up for you to share.

By the middle of 1604 a lot had changed in M's life. The nude Cecco had last been painted at the start of the year, twisted and yelling with a knife at his throat. M now went back to the figure of John, but using other models – the sexual electricity of the Cecco paintings was out of the series. It was in the two intensely inward paintings of John he did now in a time of trouble that M made this figure peculiarly his own. As the difficult year of 1604 went on, after he'd done Lena as the *Madonna*, maybe around the time of the April artichoke violence at Moro's, M went back in mind to his fairly untroubled first assay at John with the green leaves and sunlit wall – and took it up again in a painting he did for Ottavio Costa. He reworked it with another model seen in a similar way in a similar pose, or a mirror image of it. The new boy was older, more deeply frowning, the foliage was now dead and brown, the background dark, the sheep was gone. The delicacy of the first painting, where the red cloak spread around him enhanced the warm tan of the boy's skin, was screwed up in the new version into a harsh light that broke up the image of the boy's body into areas of livid white skin and irregular patches of deep shadow. The cloak was so vast and heavy it seemed to be swallowing the boy's body, and its red now showed up his pallor. Under his tousled hair, the deep shadows of his eye sockets, and the shadow under his cheekbones, nose and mouth, all turned the boy's sensitive white face into something like a death's head. The younger and earlier model's softly slumped body and almost childish splayed legs were now tensed and hollowed, bent with an early adult exhaustion, a thin shoulder, a forearm, a knee catching the full intensity of light, ribs and joints delineated and the rest of the body eaten up by darkness. Age seemed determinant in M's treatment of his John models – he moved from the tender handling of the first and youngest through frankly expressed desire of Cecco's active body to a kind of identification now with the more nearly adult figure of his deeply introspective third. The complicated breaking up of the body's image into extremes of light and shadow implied a fragmented, disturbed, unrested mind, and it was a disturbing and disorienting figure to look at. The raking light from overhead was no longer shaping the figure out of darkness. It was blasting the body to brilliant pieces.

M did another and more sanguine *John* not long after this lunar hallucinated boy. There was even less here to identify the model with its ostensible subject. The new version was in the horizontal format M liked and the tougher looking model was painted in a similar stance but seated much lower, the image cut off at the knees, and he might've been sitting naked on the edge of a bed – the wilderness setting was almost totally obscured and the red cloak looked like a bed cover. The lower centre of gravity had something to do with a regained sense of stability – the previous John looked as though he were slipping off a high stool. The brilliant coldness of the earlier light on flesh was gone now, and so was the sense of fragility – the new model had a labourer's robustness, and his suntanned face and neck, and his tanned forearms identified him as an outdoor boy. The big work roughened hands – Roman police were just then telling legit labourers in the city from illegal beggars by checking their hands – the food bowl, the everyday white undergarment instead of the animal skin, had come with him from the real workaday world. The densely textured creaminess in the simplified painting of the torso, the economically splendid folds of the dark red drape and the barely suggested background marked a new, confident urgency in M's art. The warmly rendered body and John's lowered gaze – eyes unseen and features almost hidden by darkness and the mop of hair, except for the very carnal mouth – gave some sense now of anonymous sex rewarded, release from anxiety, the comfort of strangers, carnal peace. Darkness and light were less ferociously opposed. By the time M did this *John* it might've been 1605.

THE HAIRTRIGGER TOUCHINESS M'd shown over the artichokes at lunch in spring found nothing in the street life or the political climate of Rome that summer to calm it down. A new ambassador had arrived from Madrid at the end of 1603 whose crass arrogance rapidly alienated the Aldobrandinis – the pope appointed in June 1604 an overwhelmingly proFrench set of new cardinals that swung power away from Spain for the first time. The French ambassador Béthune was delighted to see the Spanish shooting themselves in the foot but it stirred the animosity of the old money old power proSpanish Farnese, and a small incident in the August dog days flamed into a military standoff between the Aldobrandinis and Odoardo Farnese that brought Italy close to civil war. So much for the Roman third force. When Odoardo Farnese was barricaded with an army in his great palazzo, it was inevitable that two of the Tomassoni brothers were on hand – the Tomassonis had been military servants of the Farnese for generations.

Young Ranuccio missed the chance to take up arms with his brothers because he was in jail at the time. Two days earlier he'd been *playing the lute at the window of my house*, which was only a few metres from M's, when a neighbour's daughter called for help during a scuffle with police trying to collect an unpaid debt – *so I put down the lute and grabbed my sword*. Ranuccio had blocked the police with his sword on the stairs. *What insolence is this?* he'd said to the cops. *Get back. Don't you know who I am?* In fact he was only a young wannabe, and being arrested meant that once again young Ranuccio missed out on the action and the chance to establish a presence among the people with clout. By the time he was out it was all over – Odoardo Farnese had humiliated the pope. Life on the streets was more polarized than ever between the French and Spanish parties.

And M was in fresh trouble. On October 17, a month after Odoardo's standoff with the pope was settled, M was arrested and jailed again. It happened on a Sunday evening. He'd eaten at the osteria della Torretta – steering clear of Moro's after the artichoke incident six months earlier – halfway between his rented place and Ranuccio Tomassoni's. He'd eaten in the company of Ottaviano Gabrielli and Pietro Paolo Martinelli. Gabrielli was a bookseller in piazza Navona and ran a significant business – he'd bought up an aristocrat's entire library four years earlier for a thousand scudi, and a good part of another just the year before. Two years earlier he too had been tried and jailed for libel, in an unconvincing case that really seemed to be about the sale of prohibited literature. He admitted this and minimized it when he was interrogated now. Gabrielli wasn't much intimidated by his run in with the law – he went on selling the works of Giordano Bruno after they'd been put on the new *Index* in 1603. M was quite likely a customer of Gabrielli's. He had a case of books in his house around the corner – twelve books, likely to have been essential ones, much read and referred to in the rudimentary and utilitarian household or campsite M was running in vico San Biagio. Nobody bothered to list their titles when M's landlady brought in the lawyers and noted among his things

Item another case with twelve books inside.

Martinelli was a courier. It was a very Roman profession. News was a vital item of consumption, and the information business was another of the city's essential service industries, like sex, food, tailoring and art. Rome couldn't work without political, financial and military information, speedily transmitted. The Rome Madrid linkup was the first regular postal service anywhere and by now Rome was connected directly to all the main European cities. Spain, France, Genoa and Venice had services in and out of Rome despite the pope's determination to get a monopoly on communications – ambassadors, bankers and the pope all ran their own couriers, and a good man could halve the normal four days that separate Rome from Milan or Venice, and get to Florence or Naples in a single day instead of the usual two. Martinelli was evidently a good man, one of the pope's own couriers. That he also worked for Pietro Aldobrandini made him seem more than a routine messenger, evidently a trusted man. The others didn't refer to him as Martinelli. They called him *Fright*. A perfumier was arrested with them later, an anxious little man who denied any connexion with the others and whose name nobody else could remember.

Each of the three gave a quite different stonewalling account of what happened after dinner at the Torretta. Only Martinelli actually mentioned the dinner at all, and he said that after eating they'd set off on foot toward piazza del Popolo. They were about halfway there when they were arrested for throwing stones. Everyone denied doing anything, and everyone was too far away from everyone else to see anything anyone else might've been doing. Martinelli said he'd gone on a long way ahead, talking with another friend. Gabrielli told his interrogators he'd had dinner in a different eating house with *a youth called messer Aurelio* and that they were on their way to visit a *girlfriend* of Aurelio's called Giovanna when he got involved in M's arrest.

Was Aurelio Prospero Orsi's brother, the poet Aurelio? Gabrielli had lagged a long way behind, talking with his friend, had been aware of no stones thrown and *would've turned back if I had*. M didn't mention dinner, and said he'd been with Martinelli and Onorio Longhi in the street and had met up with Gabrielli and friend just before his arrest. He claimed he'd been chatting with Menicuccia *who lives in that street* when he heard stones flying – thrown, he thought, at his friends. Menicuccia was Menica Calvi, the famously beautiful and clever courtesan who'd been on the summer outing to cardinal Del Monte's country place three years earlier, when she was arrested for insolence to the authorities. *Insolence* was complicating M's own arrest now – he was accused of using offensive language to the arresting officer. M said the corporal in question provoked him with his insolence every time they met, but made a point of denying explicitly that he'd ever said the corporal *sucked cocks or anything at all*.

There was a sense in all this testimony that a lot of shadowy unnamed figures were moving around in the dark of the episode – one or two getting mentioned in passing by mistake – as the various accused responded in the best southern Italian manner by saying nothing of substance and throwing in a few irrelevant details as a smokescreen. It sounded as though the police had interrupted a fairly large scale rock throwing street fight in the dark, one that'd pitched M, an Aldobrandini courier, a fairly radical bookseller and Onorio Longhi and maybe others as well against a bunch of unknowns. M now asked Gabrielli to run to Del Monte's palace with a message to the cardinal of M's arrest, which the bookseller did. M also asked Gabrielli to go and speak to *a gentleman* in the household of Olimpia Aldobrandini. Olimpia Aldobrandini was Pietro Aldobrandini's sister and niece of the pope. This was the first trace of a continuing Del Monte connexion – there'd been no other recorded link between M and Del Monte since M had moved out nearly four years earlier. It meant M still felt Del Monte would cover for him when there was trouble with the law – and that the cardinal had likely had a hand in cancelling M's earlier criminal sentences. But if now M simply needed help in another brush with the police, why did he send a message to Olimpia Aldobrandini's as well? M's show of arrogant assurance – when the cops were blocking M in the street the scared perfumier heard him say *In any case I'll be out tomorrow* – implied a quid pro quo. As if, in the street fight a few minutes earlier, he'd been taking the Aldobrandinis' side. Which was unequivocally the French side.

Was M being picked on by the police? Or was he trying to provoke them? Was it just a tense and turbulent time on the streets – merely personal or a matter of perceived allegiances? That there was a real and persistent hostility between M and the police by now – that the arrest and insults of October 17 weren't a momentary thing – seemed confirmed when a month later M, alone this time, was stopped again at one in the morning of November 18 and asked whether he had a proper licence to carry his sword and dagger. M did, and when, having checked it, the officers in question handed it back and – in their leader's own account – wished M a courteous *Good night*, M replied with an obscene insult. The patrol officer sent *my men* back after him. M was arrested and tied up, repeated his insult more extensively and was put in the Tor di Nona jail.

A couple of months later a kind of reconciliation was engineered between Odoardo Farnese and Pietro Aldobrandini, who'd gone on being furiously hostile ever since the summer faceoff. It was too late for Clement VIII, who'd been missing a few beats under the stress and had a massive stroke at the beginning of February. When he died a month later, everyone agreed it was the Farnese uprising that had finished him off.

12

ROME 1605

Mary dead
Crown of thorns I
Ecce homo

THE GIRL MIGHT or might not've been Lena. She looked like Lena. Lena in a completely plain red dress with long sleeves and a full skirt that came down to her ankles. Lena lying on her back with her right hand resting on her stomach and her left arm straight out sideways. Her bare feet straight out in front of her, the bare toes of each foot tipping out slightly. Lena with her head tipped back, lolling over toward you, the muscles of her face and mouth relaxed and her eyes closed as if she were asleep.

Or dead. This was Lena Antognetti – though not everyone thought the supine girl looked like her – last seen earlier in the year leaning in a doorway with an overgrown baby in her arms. Now she was Mary again, not aged at all, but this time dead. M was finally getting round to painting the work he'd contracted to do in mid 1601, three years earlier. The contract was for M to paint *the death or transition of the blessed virgin Mary* and M had chosen the death. A *transition* would've brought to mind and eye bodies flying through the air and squads of angels once again, the peril he'd just avoided in his last painting of Lena. He'd avoided the flying house but made a tiny compromise with the theme, by having Lena stand on tiptoe on her front doorstep. This was the nearest Mary got to flight. M's interest here was death. Not death as resurrection, transcendence, rebirth, vindication – death given meaning, death that gave life meaning as it did in all the religions and in none more than in the one which promised its faithful the *resurrection of the flesh* – of which there was little hope offered here. This was death as the loss of physical life, death as coldness, weight, silence, immobility. Death as human emptiness. Death as pure absence. Death as the end of the road. It was death as a very fresh experience, death as that moment when everybody around suddenly realized there was nothing more to do, that the physical care and the comforting were no more use and a person was now a corpse.

Someone had loosened the tight lacing of the bodice that constricted Mary's breasts. Maybe she'd pulled it undone herself. Her body was flung out in an abandoned way that made death look like the end of a violent inner struggle. Nobody around seemed much use, and you felt the need for action there. On the floor below her feet, in the very bottom foreground, was a big and glinting copper basin with a wet rag hanging over its side – water and a cloth from soothing the girl's last moments, or vinegar ready for washing the corpse? It was all you could see around her, apart from the back of a kitchen chair, a back wall blotched with damp and some raftered wooden ceiling. All the rest was bent heads and hands and feet and yards and yards of heavy drapes. The young girl slumped on the low chair in front of the body, head bowed, face hidden, body doubled over, was the same young girl with the braided hair pinned up from her slender neck and wearing a tunic who'd been folded into her misery in the *Burial*. She was the only living female there, and the only one who might've done some good. Her sleeve was folded back from her wrist – but she'd been unable to start, or go on with, her work of washing the dead girl. It looked like

> the death of a local woman … in a rented room … a scene
> … from a night refuge.

The five men standing or kneeling beside her, another half dozen behind who didn't yet seem aware of what'd happened – one of them the lawyer who was paying for the painting, Laerzio Cherubini – were the disciples, clumsy, encumbered, slowed and muffled into immobility and silence by their long and heavy blanket cloaks, made into something poor but obscurely monumental, as if they'd been wrapped by Christo. Some of these others were familiar too. Standing in tan cloaks at the left and in the centre were M's two old models for his first and second *Matthew & angel*. The young man standing by her head in a bottle green cloak, resting his cheek on his fist, was the same John who'd lowered Christ's body in the *Burial*. Hanging over them all was this massive red curtain – a large bed's or a sleeping alcove's, maybe the one from M's own curtained two poster bed in vico San Biagio – hitched up by a cord and looming heavily over everyone, taking up a good third of the space, its darker shadowed red picking up the brighter surface of the dead girl's dress and *spreading itself everywhere like a disease of the retina.* The overpowering drapery, the bent figures and closed mouths were the visual analogue of a muffled sob. Under the heavy red curtain, a group of M's old studio crowd was filling the stage in a theatre of loss.

There was only one person who really mattered here and that was the dead girl in the red dress herself. She didn't take up much space in the huge canvas and her incomparably beautiful flung back head took up hardly more than a point on its surface. But the light, welling in yet again from the upper left, fell right on her, made the red dress glow in a way that seemed to charge the body with more pulsing vitality than any of the living showed, and coming in almost from below, brought her features for a moment back to life. In front of the body, the light also caught the seated girl's – Mary Magdalen's – bare nape, her hand, her white sleeve and something of her orange tunic, and it was over the little foreground hill formed by the light falling on the crying girl's rounded shoulders and not far away that your eyes were drawn to the dead girl's face, lying like a more distant hill in a landscape of female outlines, or a rising sun beyond the rolling intermediate terrain of her own arm and breasts. The dead girl's face was inescapably lit up in the crowd as the point toward which your eye travelled along the converging bright red axes of her body and her outflung arm.

M was drawing your eye into his picture through an oblique take on the main figure – making you follow a diagonal into the picture, forcing you into a third dimension. There was a faint recall here of the diagonally canted cross old Peter had been trying to lift himself from, in the way the dead girl's bare feet jutted forward toward the left and her hand stuck forward to the right. To orient yourself in the space of the picture you had to find your way in to the deep centre the limbs came out from, above the weeping girl on the chair, and the centre was a point by the radiant dead face. The painting was ready for the drama of your encounter when you reached the chapel – as you approached from the left, swung into the chapel and stared up at the canvas, whose bottom was high above eye level. Once again M had painted a drama to be seen in a real place, to be seen in movement as you approached it, to catch your eye and pull you in.

The lines of the bystanders' shadowy bare feet and their shining bald heads converged on the same dead face, and the hang of the curtain followed the movement overhead. A lot of the visual movement was now across the surface of the painting, and there was none of that powerfully plastic three dimensional shaping of the figures by the light, or of that aggressive projection into the space in front that M had built into the *Burial*. The paint itself was now so thinly and lightly applied that the very weave of the canvas showed through and left the work looking almost unfinished in parts. Instead there was a lot of diffused light, atmospheric and deeply coloured semi shadow, which the direct light merely complicated by bringing out a lot of random seeming details from the gloom – the side of a neck, part of a hand or a skull, an ear, a nose, a fingertip, a cheekbone – and these seemed merely to break things up and recompose them, like the pitiless white light that broke up the body of the intensely brooding young *John* M did around this time. The apostles lost their personal individuality and became parts of a larger shared and choral grief, from which only the young girl was kept out. And she, and her sorrow, were assimilated to the dead girl in the red dress herself.

The canvas was so big, the biggest M ever did in Rome, that someone thought the damage he did to the ceiling might've been done by trying to move it out of the studio. And when it got to the church in Trastevere *Mary dead* was knocked back immediately. It was taken down and shut away. Hardly anybody got a chance to see it. It was quite unacceptable. It was far too bleak, not to say tragic, for a chapel where masses for the dead were celebrated, and the lack of any glimmer of a heavenly afterlife was rubbed in by the austere realism – the stained wall, the basin and the damp cloth – that tied Mary's last moments all too explicitly to life and death in the poor and crowded quarter of the Trastevere around the church. Nobody directly involved ever set out the barefoot Carmelites' reaction to M's painting, but when his follower Carlo Saraceni had a go at the commission a few years later, Saraceni's substitute canvas – which showed people kneeling and marvelling around a Mary who wasn't dead at all but sitting up in a chair in a much more upmarket setting of vaults and pillars, gazing heavenward with hands clasped in prayer – got knocked back too. Saraceni had to do another, and his second version was basically the same but with a celebratory orchestra of tumbling cloud borne *putti* – not naked of course – painted in overhead, brandishing harps and violins and roses to make the coming ascent fully explicit. Only then were the barefoot Carmelites happy. In the Saraceni painting they decided to keep, Mary wasn't yet dead but sitting up in a thronelike bed and already on her way. It was something a bit upbeat.

Something to make people feel good about death. Something utterly unlike M's dead girl in a red dress.

The art scene people, when they looked back on the affair, remembered a quite different aspect of M's painting, though one that might've weighed with the barefoot Carmelites as well. There were different versions of this. Mancini, who wrote first, said nothing of bleakness or ideological incorrectness and recalled that the barefoot fathers had the painting removed from their church because

> in the figure of our lady he'd painted a courtesan he loved, a meticulous likeness done without any religious qualities at all.

Mancini mentioned the case more violently and more extensively, in the course of a rather uncertain earlier run through the requirements of *beauty, decorum, grace* and so on in painting. He'd written that

> Some moderns … when they represent our lady go and paint some dirty whore from the brothel quarter – which is what M did in the *Transit of our lady* at the Scala, and why those good fathers didn't want it and maybe [that's why] the poor bloke suffered so many troubles in his life …

Did Mancini, around at the time, know who M's *dirty whore* was? He sounded completely confident of her identity and of M's feelings about her, and if he didn't go into further detail it was presumably because he felt the personal detail wasn't all that important – M wasn't the only painter who did this, just the notorious example who came to mind because there'd been a major rejection. Mancini's feeling that M's troubles began with the rejection of *Mary dead* seemed to be linked with her identity, and that made sense if he knew she was Lena. M's relation with Lena was about to plunge him into new violence and real trouble. Baglione had a different take on the painting's rejection. He wrote that

> It was taken away because he'd indecorously done the Madonna swollen and with her legs bare.

Bellori took this further and made her a real corpse – he said the painting was removed because M *had too realistically copied a swollen dead woman.*

At some point long afterward, the word *swollen,* used by Baglione and taken up by Bellori, who never saw the painting, to mean *swollen in death* gave rise to the story that M had painted not just a whore's body but a whore suicide's — doubly sinful — fished from the Tiber and swollen from its immersion. The trouble with the legend was that it obscured the real implication of Baglione's phrase, which was that the model might've been pregnant. Once somebody had murmered that to *those good fathers* — and there was just enough of a hint of a rise in the girl's belly for the suggestion to stick — there was no way M's painting was staying in place. The idea, though, was less the point than the image itself. The idea of a whore was negotiable. Everybody did it — where else could painters get their models? Lena had passed as the pilgrims' Madonna. The trouble here was the way M had shown a woman — carnal, human, abandoned and flat on her back, a real being heavy with a sense of sleep, sex, birth and death. Talk about lack of decorum.

LENA ANTOGNETTI DIDN'T seem to be pregnant enough in late 1604 to be impeded in her professional activities. On the second of November a police patrol reported picking her up late at night while doing the rounds. She was

> wearing a cape and it had struck three in the morning and
> since the said woman is a courtesan I sent her to prison.

Wearing a cape meant she was wearing a man's outer garment to avoid notice. It was two weeks after that that M was picked up not far away at one in the morning. Lena Antognetti's personal life was going through a rocky patch in late 1604 and it was going to get rockier. One of the things that was complicating it seemed to be a connexion with M. In December 1602 she'd had a baby boy and the birth of her child seemed to close her career as the lover of prominent clerics. The Christ child she'd held in the doorway for the pilgrims was likely her own son — the boy would've been the right age, about two years old, and he'd shortly reappear a year older in 1605, in M's third and last painting of Lena. At the start of 1603 Lena had put the child out to wet nurse and in March she went to live with Gaspare Albertini, who was a lawyer and a literary intellectual, a member of the Insensati group.

M's connexion with Lena was about to plunge him into his most dangerous act of violence so far and precipitate a crisis in his life. What that connexion was, and how it led to the violence, was recounted in a story heard and transcribed seventy years after the event by the biographer Giambattista Passeri, *painter and poet* and friend of the Roman baroque artists. It was a story Passeri later excluded from his life of Guercino, the younger painter Passeri mistakenly thought had known M in his early days in Rome. Passeri's story about Lena and M also had its shortcomings, but it began to make sense of the connexion between them, and between M's life and his paintings at that time. It trimmed down, censored, shaped events into a little fable. The trimming might've been Passeri's own moralizing and literary touch, or it might've been all he knew, the way the story had been passed on for half a century. It was right in its basic facts and stewed in the baroque legend of M the excommunicated outcast.

When M painted the picture that's in Sant' Agostino in Rome ... the virgin Mary with her child in arms and two pilgrims adoring her, he lived ... in those alleys behind the mausoleum of Augustus. Nearby lived a woman with her unmarried and not unattractive young daughter. They were poor but honest people, and M tried to get this young girl to model as the mother of God for the painting he had to do. And he did manage to get her, after offering a fee that they were too poor to refuse. So he had his way and did what he wanted. The girl was being courted by a young lawyer, who'd already asked her mother a number of times if he could marry her and always gotten no for an answer. The mother was a simple woman, an innocent, and shuddered at the idea of giving her daughter to lawyers, who all went straight to hell.

The young man was annoyed at being rejected, and tracked the girl's movements everywhere. He noticed that she often went to M's house and stayed there for some time – since he was painting her. Angry and jealous, he ran into the mother one day and said to her,

My good woman, since you're so careful and watchful, you can keep that nice young daughter of yours. You won't let me marry her, and then you go and take her to that painter scum and let him do what he wants with her. You made a great choice and it shows the type you are. You refuse her to someone like me for a wife and give her to that ill fated outcast as a concubine. Well you can keep her now and a lot of good I hope it does you.

He turned his back on the mother and stalked off,

leaving her in total confusion and bitterness. The woman decided that in all innocence she'd made a terrible mistake in taking her daughter round to M's. The lawyer was right to abuse her. She went straight round to M's herself and burst into tears over what'd happened. M smiled bitterly at her charges and asked her who'd upset her so badly. She indicated who it was, and the lawyer was instantly recognizable as the person who was always going up and down the street outside. M consoled her and sent her home.

Furious at what'd happened – and he was a very violent tempered man – the next morning M put an axe under his arm and went out to look for the young man. It was a Wednesday and Wednesday was market day in piazza Navona, and by chance M found him there in front of San Giacomo degli Spagnoli, the Spanish church by the Triton fountain. He went up and said *It's time you learnt how to behave yourself* and gave him a massive blow to the head with the axe. The young man collapsed on the ground, covered in his own blood.

By good luck the lawyer didn't die after the attack, though he was very sick and he was weak for a long time after it. After he recovered he lived for a long time near San Luigi dei Francesi, and it was several years before the matter was finally settled.

Passeri took no position on what might've gone on between M and Lena in the artist's studio, though he implied there'd been no sex. That quite reasonably left entirely open the question of M's sexual orientation. The whole thing was a folk memory rooted in fact. The facts, as even the criminal records showed, were rather more complicated, and sex was the enigma hovering over Lena's relation with M. Did they or didn't they? In any case, the real young lawyer was merely unlucky. The reality of the criminal records seventy years earlier was this. On a summer night in 1605, at eleven o'clock on the evening of Friday 29 July, a junior lawyer called Mariano Pasqualone presented himself to the criminal court and showed them a fresh wound in the left side of his head *with much bleeding*, the court record noted in Latin. Pasqualone had come to make a statement to the effect that M had just then assaulted him with a sword in piazza Navona. Pasqualone had been strolling with a companion in front of the Spanish ambassador's palace, he said, when

I was murderously attacked by the painter M … I felt a blow to the head from behind. I fell to the ground immediately with a wound in my head that I believe was caused by a blow from a sword.

He hadn't seen his attacker,

but I haven't had dealings with anyone except the said M, and just in these last few evenings in the Corso he and I had exchanged words over a woman called Lena who lives at the bottom of piazza Navona … and is M's woman. Now please dismiss me so I can get some medical treatment.

When the wounded man went to find a doctor, his companion, who was a Vatican scribe, testified that when he'd seen Pasqualone suddenly fall to the ground,

I turned around behind and saw someone with an unsheathed weapon in his hand. It looked to me like a sword or a dagger. He immediately sprang away and turned toward the palace of the very illustrious cardinal Del Monte – I mean up that alleyway. He was wearing a short black cloak off one shoulder …

The wounded lawyer wasn't a jealous suitor – just an unlucky functionary. He was used to trouble, but this time he'd been the bearer of unwanted communications in a matter that was already complicated, tense and violent. Lena's common law relationship with Gaspare Albertini wasn't working out. Motherhood wasn't her thing and monogamy with a fairly low level professional, for a girl used to hanging out with rich and hedonistic cardinals and other friends, must've been drab and quite a letdown. Two weeks after Lena was picked up hurrying home shrouded in a man's cloak came M's six am arrest that November for insulting the police. He was stopped not far from Lena's place. When he was next arrested six months later, it was after five o'clock in the morning and in the via del Corso, opposite the church of Sant' Ambrosio, where Lena lived.

Someone – his best friend – was telling Gaspare Albertini about Lena's other life with M and the lawyer had recourse to a little domestic violence. He had troubles of his own, with a new lover called Silvia whose husband was taking matters to court. On June 28 things suddenly got worse and Albertini cut Lena up in the face. She packed up and went back to her old place on the Corso and three weeks after the attack she went to court with a friend and reported her ex de facto's violence against her. This was on July 19. Moving back to the Corso turned out not to be an ideal solution either. Lena's place there was above a greengrocer's shop run by a woman called Laura Della Vecchia and her daughter Isabella, and the day Lena was reporting her old lover, M was in jail at the Tor di Nona for defacing the women's shop front. The women had been talking about the people upstairs's behaviour or maybe complaining directly to Lena about the scandal and this had angered M and now mother and daughter were determined to drag him through the courts. They sounded much more like the originals of Passeri's *poor but honest* mother and daughter than anyone in Lena's family, where all the women were on the game. Prospero Orsi and Cherubino Alberti the painters and Ottaviano Gabrielli the bookseller and a tailor called Girolamo Crocicchia went over and paid bail of a hundred scudi to get M out of jail and on forfeit of another hundred scudi they underwrote an apprehended violence order against M – guaranteed he wouldn't insult or assault the greengrocer women or cause them to be assaulted.

Into this overwrought mess stepped Mariano Pasqualone, who worked in one of the legal offices of the cardinal vicar of Rome. One of Pasqualone's jobs was delivering court orders prohibiting couples involved in scandalous relationships from seeing each other. Maybe he was told – or had taken it on himself if he were a canting right thinker – to warn people off who were living irregular private lives, since Pasqualone said *I haven't had dealings with anyone except the said M*, and that *he and I had exchanged words over a woman called Lena*. M reacted savagely. After the malignant greengrocer women Pasqualone was a moralist too many. But it was one thing to beat up other painters in the street and another to wound a legal functionary of the ecclesiastical state. M had got it badly wrong this time. He'd attacked a middle level representative of the prevailing order – Pasqualone was the lawyer who'd first questioned Beatrice Cenci about her father's death seven years earlier. The best thing to do was skip town. Let the dust settle, let Del Monte see what could be worked in the way of damage control.

Which was what M now did.

CAPTAIN PINO AND his squad of the Capitoline division had arrested M near Lena's place on the Corso between five and six in the morning on May 28. It was two months before M's attack on Pasqualone and he was wearing a sword and dagger without a licence. M tried a little bluff when they asked to see his permit. He admitted that

> I haven't got a written licence to carry a sword and dagger. Only the governor of Rome ordered the police chief and his corporals orally to let me be ...

This cut no ice and captain Pino pulled him in, but just in case M really did have influential cover, Pino carefully sketched M's confiscated weapons in the margin of his written report. Just in case his action was ever queried. It shouldn't've been. Sometime in the six months since his last arrest in the early hours of the morning M's licence to bear arms had been withdrawn. Either someone had it in for him or he was getting a record as a dangerous person. It wasn't exactly surprizing. His art seemed dangerous to many but it entailed a vulnerable openness on M's part, an exquisiteness of feeling that'd've had some need of social armour for going about the ordinary business of life. On canvas M was showing an ever more intense and nuanced awareness of physical presence, an absorbing empathy with other people's ways of being in the world. His awareness of others increased its range with almost every new painting. Ten years earlier he'd started – subjectively – with himself, and young boy objects of desire. He'd broadened his range into young, physically interesting, various and vigorous models of both sexes. Now he was more and more often including deeply felt and loving renderings of the old, the work worn, the poor, and a few children and animals springing with life. And on the streets he was widening the range of his enemies.

The street fighting had to be a release from the ever less bearable tensions involved in the painting – the higher pitch of violence coincided roughly with his work's new depth. His earliest violence had been directed at hostile or opportunistic painters – M's public behaviour first became a matter of comment when M was doing the *Matthew* canvases. It was renewed now – in the seemingly random and pointless flareups like the violence in the eating house, the obscene provocations of police – as he toiled with the largest, barest, greatest work, the most tragically reduced and essential canvas he would leave in Rome. *Mary dead* was strong because M dared to be weak, giving up even the bravura resources of his own painterly powers to show a true thing. Hurled rocks and artichokes, arrests and imprisonment, were the price M paid for doing it. So it looked.

Now there was Lena too. M was most involved in Lena's life, or so the accumulating fragments of evidence implied, in the summer of 1605. Maybe it'd been going through most of 1604 as well – during the painting of the *Pilgrims' Madonna* and *Mary dead* – flaring up in 1605 when Lena's own domestic situation got more difficult and more violent. The clamorous notoriety of Lena as the *Pilgrims' Madonna* in a local church can't've helped, nor the shock of rejection and removal around the end of the year of *Mary dead*. And the street life was hardly calm.

The streets of Rome in 1605, during the interregnum after Clement VIII's death in March, were even more volatile than they'd been in the summer of 1604, and just as polarized between the partisans of France and Spain. When Alessandro de' Medici was elected pope Leon XI on the first of April it was a French triumph – then he picked up something nasty and twenty seven days later he was dead and things were more tense and unstable still. They were verging on anarchy. A couple of days after the new pope's death, a wild street fight between the factions in via Condotti with drawn swords left several wounded and maybe some dead. The Roman police chief and his men were taking in some of the arrested when they were confronted by an armed band in campo Marzio, led by three of the Tomassoni brothers, one of them Ranuccio. They made the police hand over the prisoners – *otherwise we'll cut you all to pieces you fucking pricks* – and drove the patrol out of the neighbourhood, where Giovan Francesco Tomassoni was district head. In mid May a new conclave elected the proSpanish bureaucrat Camillo Borghese and the day he was crowned pope Paul V was the day M was picked up for carrying unlicensed weapons. The new pope's first thought was for his family, and two months later he made his sister's son a cardinal. Scipione Borghese was still in his twenties, five years younger than the painter M in whose work he was about to take the keenest interest. The day after Scipione Borghese became a cardinal, M fled Rome after cutting Pasqualone's head open.

IN THE TWO years between the libel trial and his bashing of Pasqualone – when he was arrested and jailed on five separate occasions – along with his two altarpiece paintings with Lena and his two new versions of *John in the wild*, M did two paintings of Christ humiliated and maltreated by his captors. They were both done for private clients and continued a line of pictorial thinking he'd begun with *Christ taken* for Mattei just before the trial. For Massimo Massimi he did a vertical painting of a middleaged barechested Christ, seated and stupefied, passive and wooden, being crowned with thorns by three snubnosed, faunlike crophaired soldiers looming over him. One of them gripped Christ at the waist as in a vice, another yanked the cord tight that bound his wrists, the third jerked his head back by the hair, and as Christ looked up in pain and apprehension at the lookalike killers standing over him, his hands convulsed in the spasm of the tightening cord, there was a sense of worse to come. The fear and pain were no more than physical – the painting was a study in human rights abuse, the military's maltreatment of a frightened civilian caught at the ugly moment when things were turning worse. The sharp pain of the cord on the wrists brought the edge of sudden fear into the eyes, the rush of apprehension of all the worse to come. The powerlessness and humiliation would've been less acute if the Christ figure had been meeting the violation with some resource of his own. What made this model so unlike Christ and so much like anyone else was the lack of understanding in the eyes. No larger purpose was working itself out here. The sadism shocked you because this was everyday work. Nothing was put on. The understatement was appalling. *Where are you taking me?* Into the painting's darkness was where they were leading the prisoner.

Massimo Massimi loved it and commissioned M to do another just like it. Massimi belonged to another old and powerful Roman family and owned the palazzo Massimi alle Colonne, which was a couple of minutes' walk from piazza Navona and San Luigi. He was himself a close younger relative of the Giustinianis and the Matteis and had been a *district chief* for longer than Giovan Francesco Tommasoni. He was also an extremely busy and wealthy young financial entrepreneur of a kind that was only just coming into existence and deeply into collecting art and decorating the family palace as an affirmation of his place in Roman society. A decade or so later the business empire would begin to collapse, and by the middle of the century it had become so complete that Massimo Massimi was forgotten and his art collection sold off and dispersed. In 1605, however, he was rich and getting richer, about M's age and looking around for art to buy.

On 25 June 1605, a month into the Borghese papacy, four weeks after his last arrest and four weeks before his run from Rome, at the height of his involvement with Lena, M wrote – in a cultivated hand and spelling his family name differently, in the one surviving document in which he wrote it out in full, from the way everyone would write it thereafter – that

> Io Michel Ang.lo Marisi da Caravaggio
> undertake to paint for the most illustrious Massimo
> Massimi, having been paid in advance
> a picture of the same size and value
> as the one I have already done for him
> of ChriXt's crowning for the
> first of August 1605. In faith
> I have written and signed in my own hand
> this day 25 June 1605
> Io Michel Ang.lo Marisi

He was giving himself five weeks, a short time even for him. Having pocketed the money he was under some pressure to deliver. What M did deliver – and exactly when was never recorded, though it surely wasn't before he fled Rome after the July 29 attack – wasn't one of his great paintings. Maybe it was a mistake on Massimo Massimi's part to pay for art in advance. Maybe it was the distracting conjuncture in M's private life. It was an *Ecce homo* – Pilate showing the stripped and beaten Christ to the mob – the next phase of the passion, the next frame in the iconic comic strip after the crowning with thorns and utterly consonant in tone, though the stress was shifted now from private pain to public humiliation. Did M propose the subject or did Massimi? At the very least Massimi must've liked the idea of another work that developed the sadomasochistic dynamic of *Thorns*. Maybe he demanded more of the same.

The painting M now did for him showed a quite different Christ from the blocky, white and frightened middleaged figure Massimi got before. The new Christ was young, slender, smoothskinned, tanned, almost beardless, apart from some downy facial hair. He stood almost frontally to the canvas, naked except for a strip of steambath issue cotton slipping over his hips. His wrists were tied in front of him and the twined thorn branches jammed over his forehead. His face was lowered, largely in shadow, big heavy eyelids covering his eyes, a long overlip above a resolutely closed mouth. It was an expression of great delicacy, hemmed in by shadow. Its strength, though, came from its relation to the two figures on the right. In the foreground was a lean greybearded pointy eared Pilate with a floppy wide black beret like hat pulled rakishly over one eye. His eyebrows were raised in theatrical query, the high forehead a mass of furrowed skin. M'd always had a weakness for the wrinkled brow and here he indulged in folds of turtle neck. Pilate's face wasn't unlike Christ's, a generation on – fine, narrow, long nose, large eyes, high forehead and pointy faunlike ear – but it was done as caricature, in crudely heavy strokes, such that people would be trying ever after to identify the original. Andrea Doria? Surely Galileo Galilei? The painting's buyer? – but he was too old for Massimo Massimi, though he sure was a hardbitten business-man.

Pilate's query to the crowd had been whether – exercising his governor's prerogative of mercy for one man – he should release Christ or the condemned prisoner Barabbas. This merchantlike Pilate might've been offering Christ for sale. The demure and girlish nudity on display was powerfully enhanced by the gesture of the tall, slim and swarthy figure standing behind Christ – between Christ and Pilate – in an open necked shirt and a piratical turban or sweatband on his head. He was holding open over the bound and helpless Christ's shoulders a brown cloak or blanket. He'd just removed it, to reveal the nudity, or was just replacing it, and his framing gesture gave an unequivocally sexual sense to the way the bound body was laid bare. The man's gaze, while Pilate stared out of the canvas and fixed you in the eye with his question, was fixed on Christ with a delicate and deeply private blend of gentleness, brutality and lust. Shoved to the back, this illdressed and unshaven proletarian loomed over the son of God and the sleek exponent of worldly power. The whole thing looked like a scene at the slave market. Christ was on offer.

The analogy wasn't a remote one for anyone living in the Mediter-ranean. The endless war with the Turks had reached a kind of stasis, and after the ruinously expensive failure of Clement VIII's land cam-paign in the east, neither the Christian nor the Islamic forces had the means or the will to make a decisive move. Life in the Mediterranean now went on in a permanent state of low key warfare between the power blocs. Its normal form was the piracy or privateering in which both sides combined war and normal business. Mediterranean piracy included a busy slave traffic in the soldiers and sailors taken as prison-ers of war and the women and children seized in shore raiding parties and it was practised on both sides. In Algiers at this time there were twenty five thousand Christian slaves. All the big Italian seaport cities – Genoa, Naples, Venice and the others – were implicated in the slave traffic. It was big business.

> For over a century, hunting the infidel would remain some-
> thing between a high risk sport and a normal economic

activity for the warlike aristocracies of the western Mediterranean.

The Tuscany of Del Monte's boss Ferdinando I de' Medici was a major player in this and Livorno was one of the main Mediterranean cities to run one of the

specialized markets created by privateering ... the market in human beings.

The Christian powers were like Islam, and

... they too had their bagnios, their slave markets and their sordid transactions ... it was not merely in Algiers that men hunted each other, threw their enemies into prison, sold or tortured them and became familiar with the miseries, horrors and gleams of sainthood of the *concentration camp world*. It was all over the Mediterranean.

A lot of the privateers and slave dealers on the Islamic side were renegade Christians from Italy, prisoners who'd turned, or people, especially from the south, driven by poverty and the chance of fortune into the flow of *Christianity's silent haemorrhage*. In 1605, the year of this painting, a Spaniard who'd spent five years as a prisoner in Algiers at the time of M's childhood published a memoir in which he remembered of his captor Uchalì that

He'd been born in Calabria, and was a highly moral man who treated his slaves most humanely. There were over three thousand of them, and when he died his will provided that they be divided between the grand Turk – who always shares equally with the deceased man's children – and the renegades who'd been in Uchalì's service. I was given to a Venetian renegade who'd been captured as a ship's cabin boy, and of whom Uchalì was so fond that he became one of the man's pampered favourites, and indeed turned into one of the cruellest renegades I ever saw ...

This was Cervantes remembering as *the captive* his own five years' imprisonment in the freshly published first part of *Don Quixote*. So a slave market scene made a natural modern setting for Christ's betrayal and killing. The analogy mightn't've appealed much to one of the

M by Ottavio Leoni.

M hunted. From *David II, 1606.*

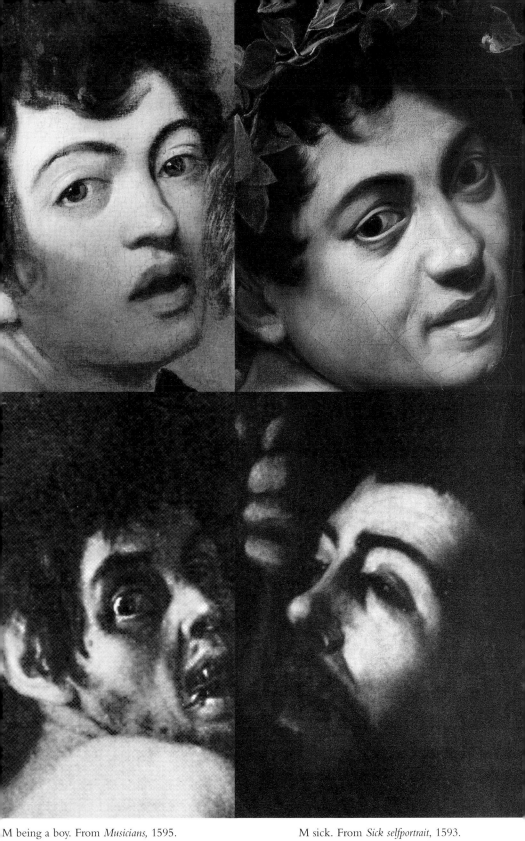

M being a boy. From *Musicians,* 1595.   M sick. From *Sick selfportrait,* 1593.

il. From Baglione's second *Divine love,* 1603.   M at the end. From *Ursula transfixed,* 1610.

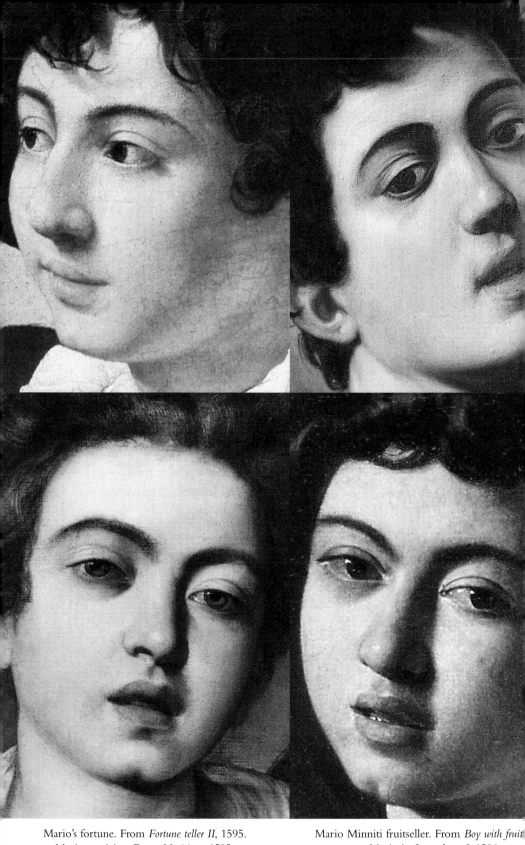

Mario's fortune. From *Fortune teller II*, 1595.
Mario musician. From *Musicians,* 1595.

Mario Minniti fruitseller. From *Boy with fruit*
Mario in *Lute player I*, 1596.

Cecco Boneri flies in. From *Saul I*, 1601.
adolescent. From *John in the wild II*, 1602.

Cecco love. *Love the winner*, 1602.
From *John in the wild III*, 1602.

Fillide Melandroni. From M's lost portrait, 1597.
Fillide thinking. From *Martha & Mary*, 1598.

Fillide unbroken. From *Catherine*, 1
Fillide killer. From *Judith & Holofernes*.

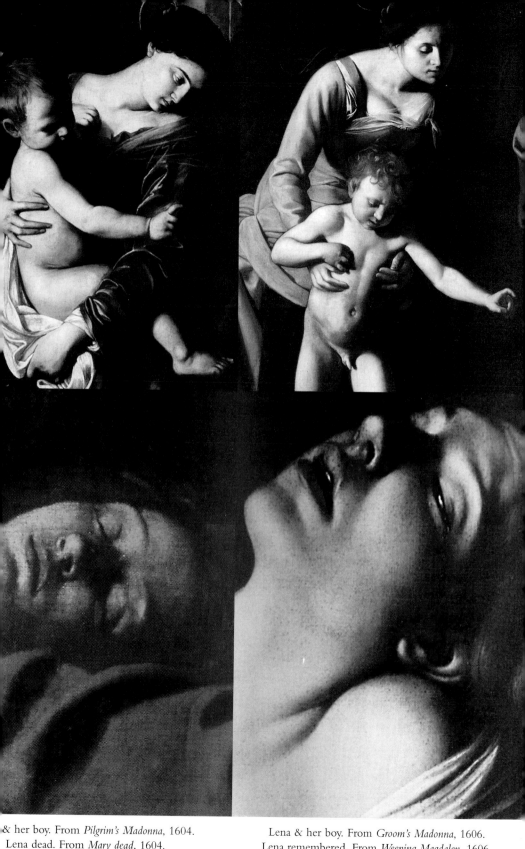

& her boy. From *Pilgrim's Madonna*, 1604.
Lena dead. From *Mary dead*, 1604.

Lena & her boy. From *Groom's Madonna*, 1606.
Lena remembered. From *Weeping Magdalen*, 1606.

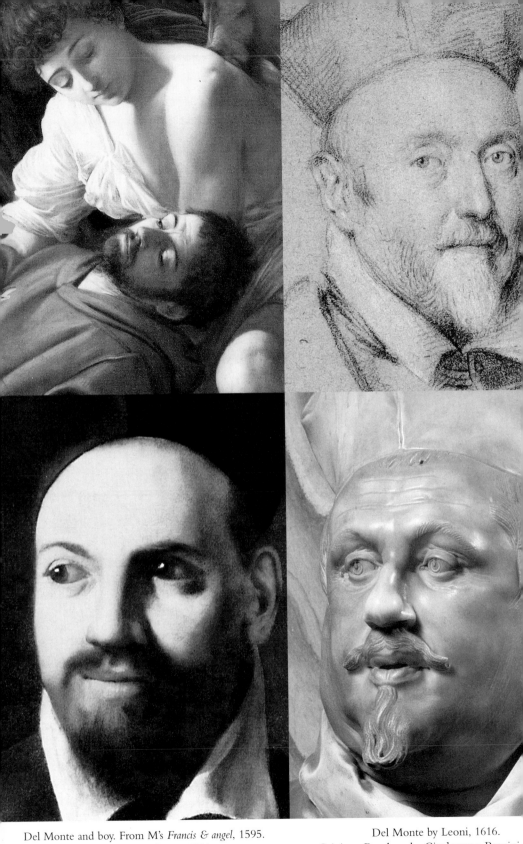

Del Monte and boy. From M's *Francis & angel*, 1595.
Maffeo Barberini by M, 1598.

Del Monte by Leoni, 1616.
Scipione Borghese by Gianlorenzo Bernini.

new breed of wealthy financial entrepreneurs who also had his close ties to the Oratorians and their cult of Christian poverty and simplicity. In any case M's brutally erotic treatment would've disconcerted an owner of the *Thorns* who – M's contractual note implied – wanted and expected more of the same. The pain of a cord being pulled savagely tight around wrists was one thing, the violation of the cane sceptre thrust into the helpless tied hands was another. Maybe Massimo Massimi gave the painting to a relative called Innocenzo Massimi who was later a papal nuncio in Madrid and a bishop in Catania, because Bellori claimed the painting *was taken to Spain* and a copy turned up in Messina.

Each time M treated the inertly suffering figure of Christ in his passion – the dead weight that Christian art had to carry – he invested the figure with intensely human interest. But it was interest of a wholly impersonal and almost cruel kind. The asexual fear and brutality of the Massimo version, and the clearly hinted erotic sadism of the *Ecce homo* – they were both quite cool and clinically curious looks at physical violence. They were done from the outside. They entirely lacked the deep subjective inwardness or the tragic simplicity of the way he'd handled the dead *Mary* or the bleak loneliness of moonlit *John*. At a time when he had some grounds for feeling scourged and mocked himself, while his own life creaked and splintered under the stresses being put on it and the tensions inside, M in his work made no identification at all with the passively maltreated figure of Christ. If M had played a part in choosing to paint this series of humiliations, his own stance toward the matter was closer to the delicately animal jailer's, lifting the blanket from the graceful nude body, than it ever was to the stripped and mocked and suffering Christ's. It was as if that thought'd never occurred to him.

M WENT NORTH. He went to Genoa. This was soon known around Rome, where he was supposed to be working on a painting for Cesare d' Este, the duke of Modena – the ruler forced out of Ferrara seven years earlier by the pope – a painting that was due at the end of the summer. The duke had commissioned works by the two best painters in Rome, M and Annibale Carracci, and was eager to see the results. He'd timed his commissions badly, for the year when both were in deep personal crisis. Annibale Carracci after finishing the Farnese gallery was irretrievably gone in a far worse state than M, who was nothing if not resilient. It was all very difficult for Fabio Masetti, the duke's ambassador in Rome. On August 6, a week after M was seen running toward Del Monte's palace, he reported that

> It'll be impossible to get the paintings for the Madonna chapel by September, because M's wanted by the authorities for wounding a deputy of the vicar's lawyer Spada. I understand he's in Genoa ...

The duke insisted, and eleven days later, just after the midsummer holiday, the ambassador wrote that

> I've been around to the painter's home this morning, and I found neither him nor anything new to report. His young men excuse him on the grounds of the recent holidays. All I can say ... is that every day I'll go round there or send someone around, but as I wrote before he has to be humoured. M is wanted by the court, and is in Genoa.

Three days later he was obliged to follow up with further bad news.

> The more his highness shows he desires the paintings, the greater is my regret at understanding that it will be impossible to realize this desire. There's no use even thinking about M's one. As for the other by Carracci, although I put my hand on it every day, and although a lot of heads and so on are already finished, I've been told it won't be ready by Christmas. I've also been told that anyone wanting a properly finished job from types like these can't afford to upset them. I beg your highness's understanding and assure him that I won't fail to do everything I can. They're now negotiating the terms of M's return. As soon as a settlement is reached he'll be back, and I'll be breathing down his neck.

Why did M take refuge in Genoa? It clearly wasn't a blind choice, and the person who advised him to go there was likely the same influential *they* who was currently negotiating on M's behalf for him to return to Rome without being jailed – almost certainly, that is, the tirelessly discreet and loyal Del Monte. Maybe not only Del Monte in this case. The Giustinianis were Genoese and so was Ottavio Costa. Maybe Giustiniani and Del Monte together worked out who would accommodate him and protect him when he arrived in Genoa. But something else was coming into play now too, something that reached a long way further back into M's life than his connexions with Del Monte or Giustiniani.

In 1600, the year M leapt into fame, Costanza Colonna the marchesa of Caravaggio had come to Rome. She'd presided over M's first years of life when she was a fifteen year old mother in Milan and Caravaggio and by 1600 at forty five she was the widowed *old* marchesa of Caravaggio after her son's marriage to the new one. In the summer of 1600, Costanza Colonna first went to Genoa to see off her brother, cardinal Ascanio Colonna, who was leaving by sea for Spain, and to drop off one of her sons with relatives there. The relatives were people with clout, even by Colonna standards. Her brother Fabrizio's daughter Giovanna had married Giovanni Andrea Doria, head of Genoa's ruling family, and was now *princess of Genoa*. Then the *old marchesa* came south. In Rome Costanza Colonna went to live in the palazzo Colonna and look after the affairs of her brother Ascanio during his five year absence in Spain. She stayed on the scene through the five years of M's growing fame and notoriety. In May of 1605 Ascanio came back to Rome, and that summer her mission was completed. If she hadn't already left, Costanza Colonna was getting ready to head back to Milan at the time when M slashed open the head of the vicar of Rome's lawyer's deputy.

Ascanio Colonna and his sister Costanza Colonna organized M's flight to Genoa. There was no one else it could've been – they sent him straight to their niece's husband, the prince of Genoa. On August 24 – nearly a month after his flight and when M was already back in town – the ambassador Masetti was reporting back to his employer on M's dealings with *prince Doria*. Going to the Dorias in Genoa meant going to the heart of power. Needless to say, the ambassador's source of information was Del Monte, and Del Monte probably got it straight from M. The Genoa visit was a remarkably swift, highly coordinated and entirely successful intervention that got M out of deep trouble. It was first new sign of the Colonna dynasty's presence in M's life in ten years or so. Within months the Colonna family network would be called back into play for M again, more urgently and extensively still, and after that they were never out of his life. M's escape to Genoa in the summer of 1605 was the moment the Colonnas became the hidden orchestrators of the rest of his life. Whether they ever intended it, whether M was glad of what they did, whether they did as well as they might've for him and whether they were acting in M's real interests at all, would run as unanswerable questions through the events of the coming five years.

With the ambassador of Modena after him for his painting, and Massimo Massimi wanting his, M might've rolled up the *Ecce homo* canvas and taken it with him to finish off while he waited in Genoa for the dust to settle and Del Monte to strike a deal with the criminal court. It wasn't just that the crudity of the Pilate figure made him look painted in singularly difficult circumstances. It was that Pilate himself looked strangely like Andrea Doria, not the present prince but an ancestor painted in 1526 by Sebastiano Del Piombo in a canvas then in Genoa. Either that or M used the memory of it when he finished off the work in Rome. It was a bit of a backhander as a compliment to his hosts.

THE HARRIED AMBASSADOR Fabio Masetti reported to his employers on August 24 that

> I'm doing whatever's humanly possible for his highness's pictures and looking all over for help and favours. I asked … Farnese's secretary if he'd very discreetly use the cardinal's authority to hurry Carracci up, and I've often visited Carracci myself, without much good coming of it.
>
> Hearing M had turned up in Rome in the hope of a peaceful settlement, I appealed to Del Monte to order him to send his highness's picture and he readily promised me to do this. But Del Monte can't rely on him and says he's got *a very wild mind*. Del Monte told me that prince Doria had been after him to paint a loggia and was prepared to pay him six thousand scudi for it, but M still wouldn't accept the commission, even though he'd practically promised to do it.
>
> The idea had come to my mind to feel M out as to whether, since he's still wanted by the law, he might've been happy to move here [to Modena], where he could've given his highness every satisfaction. But when I discovered how unstable he was I did no more about it.

Two days after the ambassador sent off his latest report for the impatient art lover in Modena, M appeared in Rome before the vicar of Rome's solicitor on August 26. The groundwork had been laid and M – who'd've got back earlier and been primed by Del Monte on what he had to do – made a formal statement that was written into the record. He said he was *really sorry* about his attack on the attorney and that if the situation repeated itself he *wouldn't do it again*. M justified his deeply insulting and furtive form of assault, the same he'd used years earlier on his *unworthy* enemies in the art world Marco Tullio Onori and Mao Salini, by remarking that the lawyer Mariano Pasqualone had refused to wear a sword during the day. Following the formula of honour, M added rather ominously that

> I hold that with a sword in his hand mr Mariano can speak for himself against me or any other person.

He solemnly undertook

> not to attack [Pasqualone] or cause him to be attacked either directly or indirectly, publicly or secretly.

Peace was then formally sealed *with a handshake, embrace and a kiss of peace.* The *quid pro quo* was that Pasqualone and the vicar's legal office dropped all pending charges and inquiries against M. And indeed no further trouble was ever recorded between M and the legal functionary. But any inference drawn from this solemn embrace that M had come back to Rome calm and chastened and purged of anger was soon belied. Del Monte was lowering expectations for diplomatic purposes when he told Masetti about M's *very wild mind* and his unreliability, but he was probably quite sincere and even edgy and alarmed. For ten years he'd been deeply and publicly committed to fostering M's genius, and now the whole thing looked like blowing up in his face. And at the most delicate political conjuncture, when Del Monte's own position in the newly modified Roman power structure was freshly insecure and undefined.

The fresco was an excuse. Anyone who knew M and his utter and unshakeable refusal to have truck with fresco painting, and the approach to art that fresco entailed, knew that no fee – and six thousand scudi was a breathtaking amount, maybe a joke on young Marcantonio Doria's part, to see how far M's refusal went – would change his mind. Marcantonio Doria was only twenty and mightily impressed with M's art. He and M had become personally close as well, and his wild offer was made to keep M in Genoa. M told Del Monte about it as soon as he got back to Rome and Del Monte passed the information on to Masetti as a way of exalting his painter and putting the lesser urgencies and the lower offer of Cesare d' Este and his ambassador in their place. There was still an undercurrent of concern in the way Del

Monte spoke about M – maybe he said more. He convinced Masetti of M's instability and maybe believed that back in Rome M was still in a dangerously disturbed state.

M had nowhere to live – he went back home to vico San Biagio and found himself locked out. On July 30, the day after he'd skipped town, Prudenzia Bruni went straight to court about the six months' rent M had left unpaid, and the cost of repairing the damaged ceiling. On the very day M was making up in court with his victim, the other court sent a functionary around to vico San Biagio to make an inventory of the property the court was seizing. There wasn't much left to seize in the house M had abandoned a month before. He was living there, according to the parish records of June 6, with *Francesco, assistant*, and both were – wisely – keeping up their church attendance. This *Francesco* was likely Francesco Boneri. M hadn't painted Cecco since he'd done him as a squalling Isaac with a knife at his throat nearly two years earlier. By 1605 Cecco was a youth of sixteen or so.

The two storey house they shared until M's flight, with three rooms on both floors plus verandah and cellar, had almost nothing in it. Downstairs there was a cheap wooden sideboard with two brass candlesticks on it. The sideboard held glasses, carafes and straw covered wine flasks. There were a couple of plates and a couple of knives, two salt cellars, a chopping board, three earthenware pots and a ladle and a water jug. There were a couple of stools and a small table with two drawers. No cooking pots were listed – it sounded as though M and Cecco lived on takeaways when they weren't eating at one of the nearby painters' and artisans' hangouts. When he was absorbed in a painting it was likely he hardly bothered with meals. M's indifference to gracious living was still a matter of comment for Bellori over fifty years later, who reminded his readers with a shudder that M

> was extremely negligent about personal cleanliness and for
> years he ate off a portrait canvas, using it as his tablecloth
> for breakfast lunch and dinner.

In the sitting room the inventorist noted a couple of little bedside tables, a picture and *a small safe covered with black leather* containing only a pair of torn trousers and a ripped jacket, a guitar, a violin, a dagger, a pair of earrings, an old belt and a door knocker. There were two swords in the room, two *hand daggers* and a pair of old green pants, along with a smallish table, two old straw bottomed chairs and a small broom. Some of these things sounded like props from the paintings. The earrings might've been the ones flung on the floor beside the

Penitent Magdalen, the same smart pearl drops on black velvet ribbons that *Judith* had later worn as she sawed through Holofernes' neck. One of the straw bottomed chairs was last seen in *Mary dead*. The violin had been on the floor under Cecco's naked leg in *Love the winner*. The holy family had a straw covered wine flask on their *flight into Egypt*. The door knocker sounded like a prop got and then not used for the front doorstep encounter with the *Pilgrims' Madonna*. The torn trousers and jacket and the old green pants might've been for models to put on – for someone like the male pilgrim kneeling by the doorstep – but they also sounded like formerly glamorous appurtenances of M's own town wardrobe. Although it sounded as if he leant more to Spanish elegance than French practicality, Bellori later claimed M's character showed in his very dress and behaviour,

> using as he did the noblest cloths and velvets to adorn him-
> self – but then once he'd put on an outfit, he never left it
> off again until it'd fallen off him in tatters.

Even then, it seemed, he didn't throw them away. Any of the jugs, glasses, plates, carafes on the sideboard could've found their way into a still life or the simple dinner table of the *Meal at Emmaus*. The point wasn't so much whether any of these particular *items* was or wasn't *as seen in* a major devotional picture now showing in a church near you as that any of them might have been. What you saw in M's pictures were the objects of everyday life in its most basic domestic register, and there was no way an inventory of the things in M's household could distinguish between utensils and props, between what he needed for life and what he needed for art. Were the two swords and *hand daggers* for real or for posing? They surely weren't, in any case, his main sword and hand dagger. They would've gone with him to Genoa.

And in the bedroom upstairs, the

> *Item* one mattress. *Item* one bolster. *Item* one blanket …
> *Item* one bedstead with two posts

– were these the actual sleeping arrangements? Or the curtained bed where Holofernes had his head sawn off, John the baptist sat looking round for his clothes and the dead Mary lay back under the hoisted red curtain? They were the same, probably. M ate and slept with the images his mind called up. Invented or not, Bellori's image of him eating off one of his old canvases told an essential truth. The *Item one folding bed for servants' use* sounded more severely practical, something for Cecco's use. The chest with the twelve books inside seemed to be in the bedroom, by the majolica pitcher for ablutions.

Through in the studio proper, with its easels, mirrors, its finished paintings and big unpainted canvases, and its little bedside tables and trolleys and chests with paints and rags, the only seating was afforded by three stools. Whether he ever got his *stuff* back again nobody recorded. He never went back to the house and Prudenzia Bruni let it again to a new tenant a few weeks later. What those finished and unfinished canvases might've been that the inventorist found, and who got their hands on them, nobody ever revealed.

13

ROME 1605–1606

Jerome I
Jerome II
Paul V Borghese
Fruit & veg
Grooms' Madonna

M WAS ANGRY and humiliated, locked out of his house, his *stuff* confiscated and having to make his peace with the lawyer who'd stuck his nose into his affair with Lena – furious with his landlady. Five days later he went back to the alley where Prudenzia Bruni lived in the adjoining house and threw rocks at her window shutters at one o'clock in the morning. She went straight back to the police the next day to lay a complaint against *the painter M of no fixed abode* – as the record crushingly described him – and showed them the smashed shutter and stones still inside the window.

> He came back again later with some others, playing a guitar, and they stopped on the corner of the alley and he was talking with his mates and I couldn't hear exactly what they were saying.

Out spilt the whole story of the unpaid rent and the broken ceiling, M's seized possessions. *He smashed my shutter to get back at me and there were three others with him ...* The neighbour she named as a witness, who was *the wife of Pietro the courier* – maybe the one involved in M's earlier stone throwing incident a year before – prudently insisted she'd gone to bed hours earlier and hadn't heard a thing. *They can ask Maddalena about it*, Prudenzia Bruni had added, but whether she was talking about *M's woman* Lena Antognetti was never clear, because the investigation never got round to her.

M now had to make his own accommodation with the new order and remake his life. M signed the peace deal with Pasqualone in the Quirinale palace antechamber of the newly elected *most illustrious and most reverend lord cardinal Borghese* and witnessed by his associates. The new pope himself was in residence in the Quirinale. It was the power centre. It seemed likely the cardinal nephew himself had a part in the deal, and though he was already far too august to be present officially in settling a squalid case of grievous bodily harm, Scipione Borghese might've used the occasion nevertheless to look over the exciting and difficult painter whose work he was finding he liked so much. Scipione Borghese wasn't yet thirty and he'd only been in Rome three months. He'd grown up poor and was eager to put the lean times behind him. He'd been a cardinal five weeks when M entered his antechamber that August and in the government only a few days. Next month he'd be secretary of state. Pietro Aldobrandini was still clinging on to power as chamberlain, but soon to be eased out of Rome and dispatched to distant Ravenna. Scipione Borghese had a feel for the uses of money and power. He was less of a politician than Pietro Aldobrandini, and given less room for initiatives of his own. Paul V wasn't the type to delegate and Scipione was distinctly subordinate as diplomat, courtier, interpreter of the holy father's will. Scipione anyhow wasn't overly keen on administration, but found he liked art a lot and he liked a lot of it.

Paul V understood that a bureaucrat pope of undistinguished family had to show straight away that he personally was in control. Paul V began with an exemplary execution. A right thinking domestic servant had drawn the authorities' attention to an unpublished life of Clement VIII written by her employer. It described the Aldobrandini regime as a tyranny and compared Clement VIII to the emperor Tiberius. Paul V had the author publicly beheaded for *lèse-majesté*. The Venetian ambassadors reported that the wildly excessive punishment *scared all of Rome* and that the new pope seemed *immensely rigorous, severe and inexorable*. Which was just how Paul V wanted to be seen.

Scipione's task was to establish the Borghese family and elbow aside the Colonnas and the Orsinis and he set about it with a will. Four years into the Borghese papacy Scipione's annual income was knocking a hundred thousand scudi. Three years later he was pulling in a hundred and fifty thousand and by the end of the papacy fifteen years later nearly two hundred thousand a year. These colossal sums let him buy up whole principalities and feudal states and eighty farming properties around Rome. In the fifteen years of the Borghese papacy the public deficit went from twelve million to eighteen million scudi, and over a million scudi went directly to the pope's two nephews. Not to mention the privileges that flowed to the papal family through side doors. And Scipione Borghese was, if anything, greedier for art than he was for cash and real estate. He became a great builder, a great decorator, a great collector of antiquities and a lover of modern art. He was eager for the coming thing and the good life, whose final effects were marvellously rendered in marble by Bernini the year before he died thirty years later – the genially glazed little eyes, the lips parted by the weight of the plump cheeks and abundantly flowing jowels, the whole mass of liquefying flesh sliding down beneath the cardinal's biretta that sat on the back of the head like something out of a party cracker, toward a body held in below by an imperfectly fastened button. But in 1605 Scipione Borghese was still the poor provincial relative whose uncle had just won the papal lottery and he was seizing the day. In Ottavio Leoni's portrait of that time he had beady, avid eyes, cheeks already filling out and small wet looking lips. He was five years younger than M, poised and ready now for a lifetime of personal gratification on an heroic scale. His quickness of mind and his eye for the main chance and his feel for the up and coming must've made M's present difficulties seem like a gift. No wonder the case was resolved under the new cardinal's wing.

Maybe it was now that Scipione Borghese commissioned or extorted the painting M did for him of Jerome writing. Maybe it was a little sweetener thrown in by Del Monte when he was setting up the deal, or offered by M himself when the papers were signed. The matter was private enough for no record to be left of exactly when or for whom or for how much M did this painting, but it came out of this time and seemed to belong to Borghese from the start and it wouldn't be the last sweetener M'd find himself needing to offer Scipione Borghese. Bellori was unequivocal that the painting was done for Borghese.

> For the same cardinal he painted saint Jerome absorbed in writing and reaching out his hand with the pen to the inkwell.

Jerome, the elderly hermit translating the Bible from Hebrew to Latin in his cave, surrounded by his skull and his books, was the source of the Vulgate's authority and the council of Trent had decided the Vulgate was the one legitimate source of knowledge. Jerome was a staple of counter reformation art and one of its dreariest subjects. Dashing off this emergency work, M threw sclerotic scholastic piety out of the window and galvanized the subject in his favourite threequarter horizontal format. Limbs, books' paper and vellum, drapery, the wooden table itself, skull and pen were combined into an extended and almost abstract still life in tones of brown, white, red, a painting whose slashing bold economy of strokes and rawness of presence would convince some people he'd left it unfinished.

But it was more than a still life — *Jerome* like the *Basket of fruit* was charged with a subtle drama. The old man, who had a powerful generic likeness to the old models from *Peter killed, Matthew & angel II, Isaac & Abraham, Mary dead*, now older and scrawnier, sat wrapped in a cardinal's mantle that looked like an urgent homage to the newly appointed Scipione, at the far right of the canvas, his own skull gleaming as he bent over his book and reached out distractedly toward the inkwell. The form and movement of the old man's endless seeming prehensile extension, in all the folds of its loosening skin, the covered ridges of its aging muscles and veins, the creaking articulation of its joints, down to the dirt rimmed thumbnail on his tanned manual worker's hand and the plucked looking quill the hand was grasping, the uncertainty of the pen tip's unguided approach to a not quite seen inkwell perched on an uncertain heap of massive old books and a wobbly death's head, halfway across the canvas from the other skull housing the old brain that'd absently sent it on its mission, filled the painting with tension, uncertainty and — in a way that recalled the tipping stool of that other elderly and distracted recorder of the religion's most sacred texts, the Matthew who looked so like this Jerome — imminent slapstick. If the *Ecce homo* had been a merely hurried work, *Jerome*'s headlong violence of execution was a unifying and electrifying *tour de force*. Who would have thought the old man had so much blood in him? Scipione Borghese — his later behaviour showed — loved it.

M'd done another painting of *Jerome* not long before, maybe for Vincenzo Giustiniani or his brother the cardinal. It was another unrecorded work that might've been the *half figure of Jerome* listed in the Giustiniani archive. It was actually a vertical canvas, but it was posed like a half figure that'd been extended above and below, the kind of mistake a distracted inventorist might've made. The painting used the same old model and painted him in a pose that eerily reproduced his most recent *John*, sitting with a bare torso and the red mantle around his knees – it was like the boy imagined sixty years on. It was a quieter preparation for the Borghese version, without the subdued drama of the inkpot and books but a lot of attention to the folds in the skin on the old man's belly, and on his brow and wrists, smaller versions of the larger folds in his clothes. The leisurely and contemplative work on this figure clearly enabled the whirlwind assurance and economy of the job M rushed for Borghese, which he must've done very soon after the first.

The tenderness and amusement that M's art always showed for old people, the loving unselfconsciousness with which he reproduced the much lived in carapaces of the working old, and the unsentimental distinction – sensuous appeal even – he could find in a bald skull, a wrinkled forehead, a horny foot, uncertain movement and not very clearly seeing eyes – suggested that when he was a child he'd spent a lot of time in the company of old people. Observing them. Maybe he invested his elderly models with memories of the grandfather he lost in the plague when he was hardly six years old. The loving attention was directed at the old of both sexes, and it was the exigencies of *history* that made him more often paint old men than old women. Every new art defined its newness in part through its choice of material, and although the people who attacked M's realism were never explicitly ageist, the ugliness and deformity they found unpleasant in his paintings came from the models' age as much as their poverty. It was quite new for a painter to show as much feeling for the realities of age as for youth and beauty. Even Leonardo had turned age into caricature. M showed a deep feeling for its frailty.

The young maternal woman was just as deeply felt a figure in his art – M more than met the requirements of catholic iconography when it came to doing a mother and child, as he was about to show with Lena again – but there was a curious absence from his work of anyone like a virile father figure. Beyond adolescence, M's male imagery leapt from unattached *bravi*, workers and thugs to patriarchal age, skipping man as achiever, nurturer, teacher. In a range of studies from life that took in marvellous small children and animals, the figure of a man you might admire or trust, a sense of male respect, was quite absent. It made you think about M's early years in Caravaggio and Milan, useless and impertinent thoughts about the father who also died when M was a child of barely six. And about how slim the chances were, in the weird and unreal society of Rome's theocratic dictatorship, for a man born without privilege, to create some happiness and self respect in his own life. You were reminded again of Montaigne's impression of the universal idleness in Rome, the envied idleness of the higher clerics and the frightening idleness of the destitute. The idleness of a city almost without trades or professions, in which the churchmen were playboys or bureaucrats, the lay men were condemned to be courtiers, all the pretty girls and boys seemed to be prostitutes and all wealth was inherited old money or extorted new. There'd be a small and remarkable group of exceptions to this rule of absence in M's work. It'd come almost at the end, and he had to leave Rome and Italy to do them.

M couldn't afford to get negative now. Things might be looking up. He'd lived in Rome through the entire thirteen years of the Aldobrandini papacy without getting any encouragement or patronage at all from the establishment and with plenty of small signs of suspicion and hostility. He'd been given all his chances by a small circle of enthusiasts, whose network had also brought in his few private commissions in churches. Paul V, as far as art went, seemed to be no improvement on his predecessor – a renewed taste for big public works like Sixtus V's went with an inertly conventional preference in painting – but when his nephew Scipione hovered into sight over the pickings M must've sensed the difference. Pietro Aldobrandini's main interests had been politics and sex. Scipione Borghese liked art, as well as other consumer goods. He was committed to bringing back the good old days. The renaissance had shut up shop long ago but the poor boy from the provinces was busy reinventing himself as a renaissance prince, like Ronald Reagan playing the cowboy. He had the money to do it. He liked parties. He liked food, and

> ... some descriptions of his banquets and their menus have survived. The lists of hot and cold courses of meat and fish, fruit and vegetables, pastries and sweets, wines and liqueurs go on forever. It's unimaginable how a human stomach could take in even a tiny part of all the courses ...

Between meals he was clearly interested in M. It wasn't that he had any particular insight into what M was doing or felt any personal affinity with it. He knew nothing, really, about painting at all. Neither would he learn much. He'd been developing his taste and growing into his role as collector and connoisseur for fifteen years or more when the Venetian ambassador described him as notable for

> the mediocrity of his learning and a life devoted largely to cultivating pleasures and pastimes.

Scipione Borghese liked art and for the moment at least he liked all of it. He was setting out on a career of collecting everything and M was as interesting as anyone else in 1605. M was keen to play along. The mirage of official patronage was floating into sight.

The cardinal was pleased with these and other works M did for him, wrote Bellori, including paintings that Scipione Borghese wouldn't get his hands on until later,

> and presented him to pope Paul V, whom he did a portrait of sitting down and was very well paid for it.

It looked like things were starting to pan out, and an invitation to paint the pope was too good to refuse, although portraits were never M's thing – Mancini would always insist M couldn't get a good physical likeness, making the point that likeness and art in a portrait weren't the same thing – and especially not portraits of people like Paul V. Even the young Bernini, later a master of vivid and flattering portrait busts of people in power, was defeated when he did Paul V a dozen years later. He produced a smoothly inert eggshaped marble head with sightless slits for eyes and a stubborn little pursed mouth fringed by an obscenely anal wisp of moustache and beard. He made Paul V look like a central committee member on the dais in Red Square. M did no better now in 1605, though his was surely an excellent likeness, identifiably a younger and hairier and slightly slimmer version of Bernini's egg. He caught the pope stiffened in a posture of blank hostility and disapproval. The holy father's stumpy, bulky body was wedged into a high armed throne, narrow eyes staring out suspiciously, lower lip jutting and mouth fixed in a descending curve, fat hands hanging off the arms of his throne with the papal ring well on show and the kissing slipper peeping from his ample skirt. This was no touchy feely pontiff like Clement VIII. No maudlin theatre here. Neither did the new pope show that formidable *gravitas* that diplomats and court reporters were retailing to the world. This was the image of an insecure bureaucrat, a functionary not yet comfortable with absolute power. M's hurried handling of the fabrics was very fine. His acute treatment of their wearer was insolently disinterested, almost entymological. His beatitude could've been anyone. The pope's reaction wasn't recorded. No papal commissions followed.

CUTTING HIS BEATITUDE down to size on canvas and throwing rocks through his landlady's window weren't all M was doing on his return to Rome to show that he was in no way downcast by his enforced flight and the arranged peace. He took up with Lena again. At the end of October he signed a contract for another altarpiece – his first commission for a church since *Mary dead* had been knocked back. He took the job at a giveaway price that showed the weakness of his current standing. It'd put him back in the public eye, he must've thought, and lead to other things – and again it'd show Lena as Mary, the third such altarpiece in a row. He was certainly pushing it. Their relations were already notorious. This was what'd led to the violence against the lawyer Pasqualone. It was why the fruit and veg lady and her daughter, Lena's neighbours, had got him jailed. The two episodes had likely been linked. If the women reported the *scandalous* goings on, the court was bound to intervene. M had assaulted Pasqualone a week after his friends had bailed him out of jail, with the promise not to *offend* the two women.

Pasqualone was settled, but there was a painting that looked like a working out of his feelings on canvas, another work in the satirical, polemical vein that was running through M's work that summer and autumn – M having the last word to Laura Della Vecchia and her daughter Isabella in a still life of early autumn fruit and veg. On a massive chipped marble slab tabletop, whose corner jutted out at you like the tombstone in the *Burial* or the *Pilgrims' Madonna* doorstep, was a cheap wicker basket of fruit and vine leaves, a heaped replay of the Borromeo *Basket of fruit,* and of the fruit basket on the table's edge at the *Meal at Emmaus.* A strongly defined and almost vertical shaft of light fell on the table from slightly left of centre, as though through a hole in the ceiling. The muted palette recalled the colours of the *Pilgrims' Madonna.* Only this time the fruit basket, with its plums, grapes, peaches, a pear and an apple – the apple with the dark scar of a worm's boring, the peaches, and indeed the apple too, with a more striking than usual resemblance to pale human buttocks – wasn't in the centre foreground. It was shoved to the left rear, behind a couple of ripe pomegranates, one of the husks slashed open to show the glowing moist red seeds, and on a bed of their own leaves laid down on the slab's projecting near corner, six or eight very ripe figs, soft skin abraded and one of them too, split open in its ripeness to display its mass of reddish purple flesh and tinier seeds. Even these small and delicate fruit were jostled aside by the rotundities of a mass of big melons, marrows and pumpkins that took up the bulk of the room on the slab. One of the pumpkins at the front was slashed open like the pomegranate to show a crescent shaped gash of its voluptuous moist interior. So was the watermelon, revealing its pink flesh and slippery black seeds. The marrows were long, uncut and remarkable. The subtle and delicate youthful drama that played over M's only other surviving and identified still life, the early *Basket of fruit* Borromeo had taken to Milan six years earlier, was supplanted here by tumultuously physical free for all of *vegetable love*, as one long curved marrow thrust itself diagonally across the slab toward the moist gash of a pumpkin. Behind it, another smoothly elongated marrow was rearing even more suggestively into the viewer's face, its end caught in a brilliant play of *chiaroscuro* contrast, looming into the picture in the centre of the falling shaft of light, coming right at you through the fruit as unmistakeably the head of an engorged penis.

Whether M painted this big and wildly erotic fruit and veg for himself – to let off steam – or as a shared joke with a sympathetic client who was in on his personal difficulties, or as a picture he expected to palm off as just another still life on an ingenuous client – but it was far too in your face for even the sourest counter reformation prude to miss its thrust – was unknown. The painting was ignored in all the surviving records until an inventory of cardinal Antonio Barberini's collection made in 1671 listed

> a picture ... representing various fruits placed on A Stone Table in A Basket hand of M

and valued it at fifty scudi. Barberini wasn't born when M did the painting, but he was a nephew of M's client Maffeo Barberini – made a cardinal when his uncle Maffeo became pope Urban VIII – and more importantly he bought up part of Del Monte's huge collection when Del Monte died in 1627. He was an eager accumulator of art, an emulator of Scipione Borghese, and Bellori saw M's *Cheats* in his collection. Bellori didn't mention seeing any thrusting marrows or slashed pumpkins on the cardinal's walls and when he allowed himself a little rush of genteel enthusiasm for M's still lifes of fruit and flowers and praised him as the originator of *that greater beauty we so enjoy today*, he sure wasn't thinking of *Fruit & veg*'s turgid cocks and moist cunts. It was a joke Del Monte might've enjoyed – and maybe M's way of giving thanks in kind for Del Monte's recent good offices.

PAUL V WAS in a hurry to finish the new Saint Peter's, to God's greater glory and his own. The latter would be made permanent by placing his name in huge letters on a grandiose redesigned façade as *first of the apostles,* which provoked a few sour jokes when the job was completed over a decade later, from people who thought the first of the apostles was Peter. Paul V wanted a bigger church, to house the crowds and control the flow, and he got Carlo Maderno to design an elongation of the nave in Bramante's and Michelangelo's original Greek cross design into a Latin cross. He got moving on this front in his first months in power. The radical rebuilding entailed tearing down what remained of the ancient Constantine basilica. This ran against impassioned opposition from some of the older cardinals, Baronio and the Oratorians in particular, attached to the church's more austere beginnings, but with a strange timeliness in September 1605 a block of marble crashed down from the old building's wall and almost smashed an altar. Clearly the faith required something newer, bigger, more impressive. Demolition entailed moving out some long standing tenants, temporarily at least, and reviewing the whole system of accommodation priorities in the grand new mother church of catholic Christendom.

The papal grooms'd had their own chapel in Saint Peter's almost forever. As the renaissance church had grown up over the old one the chapel had been shifted around several times already, so it was nothing new for them when their chapel in the old nave was deconsecrated in October 1605 and moved to a new place in the already built part of Michelangelo's new church, ready for the nave's rebuilding. The move was temporary, but the grooms hoped to make it permanent and they wanted a striking new altarpiece. The old one *didn't fit* the new location. On the last day of October, the grooms decided to commission a new painting and several members were delegated *to deal with the Painter.* At some point they decided this would be M. *The Painter* was just then lying in the house of his lawyer friend Andrea Ruffetti recovering from some nasty injuries. A week before the grooms decided on a new painting, investigators from the criminal court had called at Ruffetti's house, just by the palazzo Colonna, to interrogate M and found him lying in bed wounded in the throat and the left ear. Who'd wounded him, and why, was what the investigator and his assistant wanted to know. M wasn't talking.

> I hurt myself with my own sword. I fell down the stairs here. I can't remember where exactly. There was nobody around at the time ... there's nothing more I can say.

He was placed under house arrest. There was no indication what this was about, though the investigating lawyer clearly knew what he was after. Why didn't M talk? His *omertà* seemed to mean he was deeply compromised, or that whoever wounded him enjoyed powerful and dangerous protection. It was an unsettled time for M and he was short of cash, hardly surprizing if he'd lost his house and possessions and the only work he'd done since coming back to Rome was a couple of paintings *gratis* for Scipione Borghese and Del Monte. The trip to Genoa would've cost him and he'd likely spent the *Ecce homo* payment well before he did the painting. Maybe there were other reasons too. Two weeks before the lawyer called, he'd been round to see Masetti, the duke of Modena's ambassador, who was still waiting for the promised painting, Masetti promptly reported back on October 12 that

> M came around looking for me this evening. He wanted an advance of twelve scudi on the painting he's doing for his highness. He promises he'll have it finished soon. I had him paid immediately … and said I'd like to know how much he wanted for the job, so I could inform them back there and he said to get them to send fifty or sixty scudi …

Three weeks later he was on his feet again and back for more. On November 5 Masetti wrote

> M's been round to see me and says the picture's nearly finished but he needed money. I told him to see he does something worthy of his highness, and that he won't be short of money if he does …

Ten days later M was back again. On November 16 Masetti wrote again.

> M came round to see me yesterday evening. He asked me for another twenty scudi and said the painting would be finished this very week and that he'd bring it round to me. To keep him on side as effectively as I could I gave it to him, but I insisted that he had to bring me the painting. As soon as he sends it, I'll inform his highness what qualified judges think of it.

But M didn't bring the painting. He'd reached a low point. After years of living with powerful protection, working with amazing productive intensity and earning far more than he ever needed – there was a limit to what he could spend on paints and canvas, food, drink, clothes and weaponry – he was now being put up at a friend's and cadging advances on a painting he never got round to doing. The hardheaded papal grooms must've seen *the Painter's* physical and financial weakness when they came round to negotiate their commission, because they apparently swung the deal for the absurdly low price of seventy five scudi. The going rate for a big altarpiece was around two hundred. For his last, the rejected *Mary dead*, M'd got two hundred and eighty. Why was he getting a quarter that fee for a comparable job a year later? An altarpiece in Saint Peter's was an extraordinarily prestigious commission. It would've been great publicity and a way of relaunching the Roman career that was all he cared about as a painter. Forget Genoa. Forget Modena. However much they were prepared to pay. The grooms of course knew this and would've played on the prestige factor in their bargaining. M might've had to undercut another candidate. It may also have been he was promised more. Seventy five was what, five months later, he got.

At any rate the deal was done. On the first of December the grooms paid him an advance of twenty five scudi. M stayed on at Ruffetti's place and did the painting there. Ruffetti the attorney belonged to that circle of youngish intellectuals and professional people M'd been moving in over the last few years. M had friends outside the art world, more outside maybe than in it, and they made up a milieu it was hard to define and harder to reconstruct because they all seemed marginal to the world of power and money. Quite a lot – on one level – could be known about M's clients, almost nothing of his friends. Ruffetti was a friend of Onorio Longhi's as well as M's, had studied law with Longhi and had been with him the day he came back to Rome after the libel trial two years earlier and challenged Giovanni Baglione to a duel outside the church. Another of the group was Marzio Milesi, the very private lawyer and amateur of archeology who wrote the passionately inelegant poems in praise of M's painting, and who was in turn a friend and correspondent of that Paolo Gualdo in Vicenza about whose contacts with M cardinal Paravicino had been so intensely curious. It was a milieu in which M's sitter and client Maffeo Barberini moved, in the days before the rise and rise began that'd take him to the papacy and pull him away from an embarrassingly freethinking past. Maffeo Barberini was keen on poetry, like most of the circle, and would be extremely put out, years and years and years in the future when his old friend and M's the libertine erotic poet Giambattista Marino turned up in Rome after years of living at the French court in Paris expecting some kind of official sinecure from his old mate the pope. A friend of Barberini's was a wit and libertine called Gian Vittorio Rossi, also known as Nicio Eritreo, who was also a friend of the libertine doctor and art collector Giulio Mancini. Long afterward, when most of the group were either dead or rich and powerful, Rossi wrote *a very lively portrait* that

> outlined Mancini's atheism, his extraordinary diagnostic skills ... and his unscrupulousness in extorting from his clients the paintings about which he was *intelligentissimus*.

How deep were M's friendships in this circle? Realizing your potential didn't come easy for intellectuals in a repressive age, and the only people here who really succeeded in their careers, Barberini, Mancini, Marino, were all consummate operators in their different ways. Were the others men who preferred to cultivate their own garden in these grim times, or were they simply second raters? Bruno was burnt alive for ingenuously rethinking the universe. Tommaso Campanella, the other great intellectual rebel from the *mezzogiorno*, escaped the inquisition's death sentence by faking insanity and in 1605 was entering the seventh year of his imprisonment in a dank and lightless underground cell and rethinking society as *The city of the sun*. He had twenty three more years underground to go. Galileo Galilei – who knew how to play the power establishments – also moved in this milieu of academies of friends, these semi facetious, semi formal and intensely serious networks of free minds and critical intellects, pedants and phonies that formed, shifted and reformed themselves in the interstices of theocratic power and included powerful churchmen like Del Monte and Barberini, intellectuals deeply interested in the science that was about to become wholly the prerogative of the protestant north. And in the radicalism coming from the south – when Bruno was brought to Rome by the inquisition and a few years before Campanella was jailed, Del Monte was in contact with Campanella and writing to Ferdinando I about his ideas in a critically sympathetic tone. These cardinals kept open their lines of communication without ever renouncing power. Barberini became pope and Del Monte came close. Maffeo Barberini's contradictions were exquisite – as Urban VIII he got Tommaso Campanella out of jail and presided over the inquisition's condemnation of Galileo Galilei.

BASHING AND SLASHING the legal functionary Pasqualone – even though M formally conceded he'd broken the code of honour in the way he'd done it – was another case of M's defending himself, *his woman*, his private life against the interference of neighbourhood snitches and the church's policing of personal morality. Personal violence was often the only way of resolving things. The law was even less likely to render human justice in sexual matters than in – say – questions of property. The law's concern was order, and the sexual order was a repressive system of militant hypocrisy. Rome's sexual weirdness – the huge floating population, the armies of single men, the armies of young girls caught up in the vast articulation of the prostitution industry, and swarms of available and ideologically non-existent boys, all of their lives entangled with the pervasive and invasive powers of an inquisition that was increasingly shifting its interest from religion to sex, the luxury and indulgence and idleness periodically dashed by the moralistic frenzies of dictator popes, the church's obsession with appearance and decorum over realities and the morbid sadomasochistic ideology loaded on to sexual imagery and behaviour, the fascination and loathing invested in female sexuality, the wild excitements and cruel repressions of a society where sexual pleasure was everywhere on sale and always wholly illicit – none of this made for a stable or satisfying sex life, whatever your preference and whatever your status. What – in that Rome – could ever be *normal*?

The perverse embrace of sex and religion was everywhere in the painting of the counter reformation. The repression, the titillation, the sadomasochistic fascination with pain, the unnaturalness of it all. It'd been worse in Lombardy earlier on, when Carlo Borromeo's counter reformation was biting more fiercely, and the ravages of the plague supplied the physical horror.

> Swordplay in the sacristy … languors and resentments … flowers, muscles and pestilence … beauty dimples and hideous wounds … underage delicacies …

In Rome it was more formal, more stifling, duller. Nailed hands, rolling eyes, exposed breasts, floating veils, bleeding wounds and cherubs' heads on wings – the dire panoply that'd become the standard – well, strike those *breasts* – catholic iconography for the next four centuries. Secular reading offered a related mixture of sex, death, frustration, incest, pain, voyeurism, nymphomania, pedophilia, sadism, repentance. In this chamber of horrors, the freshness and frankness of M's figures were stunning. People talked about them as matters of style – and still do – but before style, before technique, came a way of seeing, a frankness, and unimpeded directness of vision that saw the person, or indeed the thing, in and as and for itself. And this was only in part a property of art. It was the same whether M was painting young boys, strong girls, or fruit or flowers. It was the quality of gaze. Annibale Carracci matched that frankness – and then sold out, went bland. When M turned – he couldn't refuse – to the Christian classics of torture and suffering people wanted to commission, he did them with the same ingenuous freshness he'd put into his early fruitsellers and luteplayers. Physical violence had never seemed more immediately and intimately and shockingly *painful*. After the swooning and the fakery and the self laceration and the secret lusts, M showed the real horror of violent death. As he'd earlier shown the real taste of an apple. The life in a direct gaze. There was no way M's attachment to the real, what he could see and feel in front of him, could limit itself to matters of style.

It seemed almost beside the point that M was erotically drawn to boys – no big deal for his contemporaries, who only found the matter worth mentioning if they wanted to score a point in a vicious libel trial or explain the dazzling vividness of his most famous painting with an anecdote about the model. Donne got excited around this time at the idea of his girlfriend's going to Italy, travelling incognito in boy's clothes and being leapt on lustfully by *th'indifferent Italian*, and an actual traveller, the Scotch protestant William Lithgow, returned home from his nineteen years of *painefull peregrinations* reporting that the Italians were even worse than the infidels in their liking for boys – Italians found it

> a pleasant pastime, making songs, and singing Sonets of the beauty and pleasure of their *Bardassi*, or buggerd boyes.

It was always like this. Nothing in people's sex lives now had changed from the past, only people no longer talked about sex of any kind. Sex was dangerous. Neighbours were watching and the Roman inquisition was always eager to hear what they might have to say. M's unfortunate fate of being known as the painter assassin, the killer genius and the gay icon had nothing to do with his private life and everything to do with the startling freshness of his art. Pain was everywhere in painting, and so were male nudes and you hardly noticed – until M did a naked boy or an old man being murdered and it was like seeing them for the first time. M never made that furtive concealed sadomasochistic identification of sex and pain that ran like a central nerve through the religious art of the time – even the mimed rape in his second *Isaac & Abraham* was frankly violent and openly sexual. Being frank about sex in repressive times was what made M first a shocking and later an iconic figure. A hundred years earlier nobody would've noticed or cared, but anything was fair game in the ideological wars of the counter reformation. Now art and private life could each be used to condemn the other. The early warning shot'd been Aretino's vicious and insinuating letter to Michelangelo about the *Last judgement* in 1545, which linked art and personal life by mixing an attack on the great fresco's *bathhouse art* with innuendo about Michelangelo's young male friends.

Seventy years before that, Leonardo as a young man of twenty four had been charged in Florence with fucking a seventeen year old boy – the inconclusive trial followed an anonymous denunciation and ended in dismissal and was likely a political attack on the Medici family, since one of the other youths charged was a Medici relative. The seventeen year old apparently put out on a regular basis. Nobody found it odd when at forty Leonardo took a ten year old boy into his household as a pupil, a boy Vasari described as

> stunningly beautiful and graceful with lovely thick curly hair that Leonardo adored – and he taught him a lot about art.

Leonardo's drawings and notes – *thief, liar, stubborn, greedy* – and other sources indicated that the boy Salai was an untalented delinquent of remarkable beauty. He stayed with Leonardo for twenty six stormy years and later died of a gunshot wound. Some obscene cartoons labelled *Salai* and drawn by his other apprentices in Leonardo's notebooks – under Leonardo's design for a bicycle – implied art wasn't all Leonardo was teaching young Salai. A drawing of *the angel in the flesh* done some time after 1510 showed an androgynous Salailike figure lifting up a flimsy shirt –

> We see a foreshortened view of an erect male member. The angelic smile is transformed into a faunlike grin further reinforced by the animal structure of the head ...

– which in a painted up and pelt clad version became the *John in the wild* that was Leonardo's last painting. Nobody was surprised or outraged by Leonardo's behaviour around the start of the sixteenth century. His admirer Lomazzo was inventing a dialogue forty years after Leonardo's death – and just as the counter reformation was about to bite in the fifteen sixties – in which Leonardo alluded to Salai and praised pederasty as an art friendly activity. There was nothing unusual about M's sexuality or the way it was reflected in his art. What was new, a hundred years after Leonardo, was the way repression made the art and the life sexually daring and subversive as Leonardo's never was.

ANNIBALE CARRACCI IN March that year finally finished his work on the Farnese gallery for Odoardo Farnese. He'd been working on the job for a few months shy of ten years. He'd produced, against the odds of history and culture, a vast, light, airy, joyous and sensuous life affirming masterpiece, full of a coiled erotic energy that sang out against the fear and repression and prurience of the time. The gallery itself still wasn't quite completed, but Carracci had signed off. He'd had some kind of a stroke. It seemed to have been caused partly by physical exhaustion but not entirely, and after a while he got over the physical attack, but not the rest. Mancini noted the symptoms with medical brevity, and hinted but wouldn't commit himself on the cause.

> Once the gallery was finished, either because he didn't feel he'd been paid what he deserved or because of some other misfortune or blow he'd received, or for some other reason, he was overcome by a deep depression accompanied by loss of mental faculties and memory. He could neither speak nor remember anything and was in danger of sudden death. Then after treatment he became able to do a few things ...

Baglione also remembered Carracci as being in a near fatal depression that year, and offered a much more precise account of the cause.

> From the prince's [Odoardo Farnese's] magnanimity he expected an honourable recompense for his labours, but he was disappointed. A certain don Juan, a Spanish courtier and favourite of the cardinal's, thinking he'd show how much care he took of the prince's interests, had Annibale presented with a saucer containing – for ten years'

continuous labour carried out with exquisite care – a tip of five hundred gold scudi.

There was no reason to doubt Baglione's word. He was around at the time and these were the kind of details another painter remembered. Mancini fairly clearly knew too, but had his own reasons for not going into it. Maybe there was more to the story, as he implied. It was a devastating blow to Annibale Carracci's self esteem. It was worse than an insult. It was like nothing. He'd thrown his life away on the Farnese gallery. On March 12 Odoardo Farnese wrote to the duke of Modena, apropos the d' Este commission, simply that Carracci had had a stroke. The ambassador Masetti, chasing it up four months later, reported on August 6 – while M was hiding out in Genoa – that Carracci had left the palazzo Farnese and moved into rented accommodation. *He wants two hundred scudi, would you believe, and seems more temperamental than ever*, wrote Masetti to Modena on October 8 after calling on him yet again about the duke's painting. It made M's demands look very modest. But he had some ground to make up. From time to time Carracci would get it together and do some small painting, but for the last five years of his life, until his death at forty nine in 1609, Carracci painted almost nothing. It was a weird parallel to the fate that was overtaking M – utterly different in every detail yet strangely, underneath all the accidents of contingency, the same. It was the prerogative of the powerful to betray their servants. You played their game or you played your own. The end was the same.

The idea that a painter could suffer a devastating breakdown simply because he felt his work was held of no value wasn't one seventeenth century Rome had much time for. Particularly when that painter's masterpiece was a work of lighthearted pagan eroticism. It was Annibale Carracci and not M who fixed the long term course of Italian painting, but there was a lack of sympathy – disapproval even – for the founder of neoclassicism that soon found its way into accounts of his premature end. Even though everyone liked Annibale. Bellori, who strenuously reinterpreted the eroticism of the Farnese frescos as an allegory of divine love, after pages of fulsomeness hinted at syphilis, which he called *amorous disorders* and Sandrart spoke primly of his *wicked life*, which was something none of Carracci's contemporaries ever noticed. It wasn't – suggested the fate of an infinitely likeable, hardworking, modest, adaptable and eager to please painter of genius – that M was queering his own pitch.

Carracci managed, like M, to string Cesare d' Este's ambassador along nevertheless. Both of them, the ambassador reported in mid

January of 1606, were holding out the hope of delivering the duke's finished works *today or tomorrow*. Ambassador Masetti was hardened by now to this kind of sweet talking and added grimly that

> if the past's any guide to the present I fear we'll have to go on being patient for a few more days.

He suggested getting Farnese and Del Monte to put pressure on their respective protégés – overestimating the influence each still had. M was clearly getting embarrassed over the advances he'd extorted for the nonexistent painting and *he blushes whenever he sees me*. There was no chance of getting it now. M was working on the *Grooms' Madonna*.

M PAINTED the grooms' picture at Ruffetti's place in piazza Colonna. It had to include Anne, who was the grooms' patron saint and Mary's mother. M combined her with another painting of Lena *looking a bit older* as Mary and her boy, who was growing fast, as the Christ child. Leonardo had painted the virgin and child with Anne as a family group – M, acting on instructions, combined Anne with a rather touchily doctrinal picture of stamping on the serpent of original sin. Different readings of a pronoun in *Genesis* led to fights over who'd crushed the snake, Mary or Jesus. Pius V announced in 1569 that they both had, so M showed the child's foot on the mother's, as in a painting he'd likely seen in Milan as a boy. If he hadn't seen the original, he'd seen a print, which reversed the pose of mother and child, as he now did. It made a vigorous life painting of mother and son, but left old Anne as a marginal onlooker, looming over the action but not a part of it. M's non painterly friends were struck by this painting – probably the first time they'd been present at the act of creation, and Lena's visits with her boy for the sittings at Ruffetti's would've caused a stir. The arrival of the wrinkled and toothless model for Anne less of a one. Marzio Milesi wrote an enthusiastic poem on it, and Ruffetti got another of their circle, Giovanni Castellini, to write an epigram marking the painting's completion. The epigram later disappeared, but Rossi was impressed enough to remember it fifteen years on and try to retrieve it. Castellini was an expert archeologist, and the figure of Anne seemed posed after a lately unearthed Greek sculpture – he was also expert on visual symbols and had helped in the compilation of Cesare Ripa's 1593 *Iconology*, the ready reference book of symbols that was every painter's handbook for over a century.

M got around his symbolic instructions by making it all utterly domestic. Lena, her large breasts thrust into a conspicuously tight and low cut dress, was all maternal pride and encouragement as she leant forward over her well muscled nude boy, growing and vigorous and frowning with concentration and effort, and showed him how to put his foot on the head of a viciously whipping snake. The snake, under everyone's indulgent gaze, looked like some kind of intriguing domestic pet. It was a family snap, but strangely bleak for all the maternal domesticity – the setting was very dark and quite bare. There was only the rectangle of overhead light on the dark wall. There was a lot *of* the wall, of a cold greenish black that looked like the wall of a waiting room or a prison – the high, weak overhead illumination enhanced the dungeonlike feel of the setting, which was hardly warmed by Lena's red dress or her child's skin, a grim darkness into which wrinkled old Anne, in her voluminous dark dress, had largely receded – a deathlike darkness.

Pressed for time, needing the money, distracted maybe by a press of onlookers in his friend's house, M knew quite well that most of the painted surface in his big works for churches went unseen and now he was acting on it. Before he'd lavished as much care on what he knew would be invisible in a dim chapel. This time he left it out. *Mary dead* – its *feathery* technique in the way he'd applied the paint, the rudimentary blocking in of some of the furthest receded figures, merging outlines of heads, shadows, swags of drapery that'd left the painting looking almost unfinished – had signalled a new recognition that not everything you saw was equally important. The girl's sprawling, raked body was what mattered, the rest was reverberation of that presence, ripples in the visual pond. In the *Grooms' Madonna*, the utter absence of context also looked back to his very first altarpiece, the rejected *Matthew & angel*. Housewife Mary and boy child were locked together physically and rendered as powerfully rounded real presence like the peasant saint and boy angel in the early painting, and the absence of background gave these figures too, leaning forward out of the picture plane, the look of sidelit statues. Jesus here looked like an old statue of the child Hercules. Or real people, next door neighbours. But Matthew and his angel had filled the whole canvas, jammed into it, bulging out of it. Context was the Savonarola chair and the heavy book with its Hebrew letters. Background hadn't been an issue because there wasn't any space for it. In the new painting, Mary and boy took up less than a lower third of the canvas, small lit figures surrounded by a great darkness. Anne was something else again, a monumental figure who seemed out of scale with the others, sketched in almost monochrome brown, done with stark, essential slashes. Light on Anne was shades of bronze darkness. Anne, staring out of the shadow with the haunted vacancy of age, was the future of M's art.

So what went wrong now? On 13 March 1606 the grooms got fifteen chestnut wood boards for mounting the painting in their new chapel and had them trimmed by a carpenter. On April 8 M wrote a note declaring the canvas finished and himself *happy and satisfied* with the painting he'd delivered to the grooms. Though Rossi remembered him as having finished it by the end of 1605, the canvas seemed to be delivered and installed in Saint Peter's some time in these three and a half weeks, when the wood was bought for mounting it. On April 14 the grooms' account books noted a payment for carpentry to install the painting – and two days later they laconically recorded a payment to two workmen for the removal of M's painting from Saint Peter's to their own church. They'd had to take it down at once. M's painting of the *Grooms' Madonna* had been on view for some time between a day and a month. A month after his painting had been carted off, on May 19, the grooms recorded that two payments totalling a miserable fifty scudi had been paid to M. It was the third time he'd had an altar painting rejected, and this time it was from Saint Peter's itself. Three weeks later the grooms also lost their altar in Saint Peter's, and immediately started negotiating for a new one. Why? Mancini was silent about what happened. Baglione wrote only that M's canvas *was removed by order of the cardinals of Saint Peter's workshop*. Bellori said the painting was taken down because

> the virgin with Jesus as a naked boy were indecently painted, as you can see in the villa Borghese.

He was probably right, particularly if the cardinals picked up on Lena's identity. As old Anne faded into the dank gloom of the background wall, and in the absence of anything else to catch the eye except the snake, Lena's prominent pale breasts, and the warmly sexual portrayal of the Christ child with his little jutting dick prominently shadowed on his innerthigh would've been all, when the painting was installed, you would've noticed.

The grooms later got another altar in Saint Peter's, then lost that too. Reasons were never recorded. They knew M's painting was a liability, because they got rid of it as soon as they could. Less than a month after recording the final payment to M, they voted to sell it to a private buyer for a hundred scudi. Everyone was happy. The grooms had disposed of a painting that'd brought them trouble – being, probably, the reason they lost their new altar in Saint Peter's – and making a profit on the resale, as they pointed out with satisfaction in the records. An informed private buyer got a major canvas by the leading contemporary painter for half the going price. The private buyer in the case happened to be the cardinal nephew Scipione Borghese. Baglione thought the grooms *gave* him the painting, and they practically did – he was now well on his way to building up a collection of M's work at throwaway prices. Everyone was happy except M, probably, when got his derisory fee a month later.

The strange thing was that the eight cardinals directing the fabbrica di San Pietro included Del Monte, Benedetto Giustiniani, a Crescenzi, Ascanio Colonna – M's admirers and patrons, who'd likely proposed him to the grooms in the first place. Ascanio Colonna's grooms belonged to the commissioning organization. There was another figure involved here who spelt trouble for M – the old cardinal Gallio, a friend of the late Carlo Borromeo's, fanatic of the counter reformation and intransigently proSpanish. He'd built the church that rejected *Mary dead* a year earlier and for some reason the grooms now turned to him when they were looking for a new altar. He had clout in Saint Peter's and would've been ready to pounce on new offences. Maybe he recognized Lena. The overriding figures in Saint Peter's, though, were his beatitude himself, and his adviser and executive Scipione Borghese – now poised to snap up M's painting the moment it was taken down. It was something to think about. The more so in the light of coming events. By the time Scipione Borghese got his hands on the *Grooms' Madonna* M was gone, and the painting's fate determined by quite other factors. By the end of May for M everything had changed.

THAT SPRING VINCENZO Giustiniani left Rome for a six month tour of northern Europe. If Giustiniani was finding the first year of the Borghese regime unusually heavy going, he gave no particular indication – he may even have been on a discreet mission for the pope. He was building up his network of financial relations through Europe. The lives of the two painters he believed the greatest then at work seemed to be cracking up that March – Annibale Carracci had just had his nervous breakdown, M was hurtling between rejections and street fights – but there was no way of knowing how far this impinged on the marchese, whose collection of five hundred paintings was the thing he perhaps most cared about, but not the only thing. He now owned fifteen paintings by M. Maybe Vincenzo Giustiniani was bored. The few writings he left showed a restless intelligence hungry for concrete facts and pleasurable details, an enjoyment of practice and process and technique. His piece on travel showed how much he relished it. People learnt *prudence*, he wrote, by reading and experience –

> experience of holding public office at different levels in your homeland, concerned with politics and economics in war and peace

– but this wasn't enough.

> Without leaving home, nobody can understand the different customs, forms of government and ways of making war, of cultivating the land and building, ways of dressing, the properties of food and wine, the different kinds of horses, the many ways of travelling and the variety of cities and provinces …

Every place had some good quality of its own that others didn't attain, and what mattered was *being able to know at first hand what you read about*. Tipping generously mattered too, and not getting into arguments while on the road in foreign countries. People got offended, he noted, if you haggled over prices in Germany. Giustiniani was an architect who worked on the design of his own family palazzo out of Rome – and laid out its gardens – and the church nearby. No wonder he seized on the crystalline sense of the real in M's art more intelligently and consistently than anyone except maybe his friend and neighbour Del Monte. No wonder he was drawn now to the new practical and scientific entrepreneurial cultures of the protestant north. He must've intuited that this was where the future lay, in Germany, France, England, the low countries. The arrival of the Borghese team of pope and nephew, with their double whammy of political reaction and gross consumption, maybe weighed on his spirits. As the man who financed the papal deficit he knew more than most about the economics of decline and what lay behind or under Rome's gorgeous façade.

Giustiniani's long tour in the summer of 1606 included business and pleasure. He invited Cristoforo Roncalli along in his party and did rather better than the professional at identifying the painters of the pictures they saw *en route*. In Paris he stayed with Maffeo Barberini, who was made a cardinal that September, and the former French ambassador in Rome who'd got M out of jail after the libel case, Philippe de Béthune. He also took along a secretary, Bernardo Bizoni, to keep a record of the journey, and when the party got to Nuremberg on May 8 there was a dinner party in the house of some expatriate Italians, *very lavish*, the secretary Bizoni noted, *twenty two at a round table*.

> There were toasts to the health of the senate of Nuremberg, to the republic of Genoa, to cardinal Giustiniani, to signor Vincenzo ... to monsignor the treasurer of Rome ... to the grand duke [Ferdinando I of Tuscany] and the grand duchess and to cardinal Del Monte ... after the toasts had been proposed and made, with so much wine and big glasses, everyone fell asleep and vomited, from the signore marchese [Vincenzo Giustiniani] on ... in Germany all important deals are concluded with a toast.

Passing out at a formal dinner wasn't Giustiniani's style. He must've felt terrible next day, and later remarked in his travel advice that in Germany you either avoided social occasions altogether or went *prepared to drown in drink or even die from it*. Bizoni went on to list the senate members and other businesspeople present. It was a business dinner, and the interest of the record was the high place given in Giustiniani's home thoughts from abroad to Del Monte. It was to be the only piece of documentary evidence that survived to demonstrate the closeness between M's great patrons, the two souls of discretion who lived over the way from each other by piazza Navona in Rome. Or even that Giustiniani and Del Monte knew each other at all.

14

ROME & PALIANO 1606

Weeping Magdalen
Francis I
Francis II
Meal at Emmaus II
David II

T WO DAYS AFTER M's painting was removed from Saint Peter's, Rome was on the brink of war with the Venetian republic. Paul V provoked a crisis that'd been gathering for years. Rich, cosmopolitan and ideologically unsound, the powerful republic of Venice was a problem for the pope and for Spain – by 1606 the only part of Italy that'd stayed free of Spanish control. Spain mobilized its forces along the Lombard border – which ran by Caravaggio – while Bellarmino and the Jesuits worked on the theology of intervention. Venice had France and the protestants on side and a European war suddenly looked likely. Neither France nor Spain could afford a war, however – Venice yielded nothing and Spain eventually forced Paul V to pull back. Rome depended on Spain more than ever. The illusion of ten years earlier, that Rome could create a papal third force, independent of Spain and France and conditioning both, had evaporated utterly.

What the *interdiction* caused in Rome in the spring of 1606 was a new flareup of the factional violence in the streets. Cardinal Bellarmino was abused in the street and his retinue beaten up. Scipione Borghese's staff were attacked. Sunday 28 May 1606 was the first anniversary of the Borghese regime. The solemn processions to the French and Spanish churches, the firework displays over the castel Sant' Angelo and the boats on the river, Paul V's cavalcade, all took place in a volatile city full of disturbances, brawls, insults in the streets. One episode that day was of particular violence. In the confusion, excitement and the gang brawls that were sputtering all over the city that Sunday afternoon, it seemed like another projection of the slightly panicky excitement that shows of power always elicited in a people highly practised in reading the signals. So the event was reported the next day, and over the following days, in a series of letters and *avvisi* that were dispatched to various smaller capitals around Italy. The event got a certain coverage, caused a certain flurry in various circles, because of the intensity of the violence and the relative notoriety of those involved. Like every death, though, this one happened at the intersection of lines that were drawn from way back, and had been converging inexorably for years. Not much was known about exactly what happened or the identities of everyone involved, and the reports fell into a series of contradictions and uncertainties that were never, later, fully resolved. There was enough to see that more'd been at stake than a small bet, and more'd driven the main opponents together than a fault at tennis.

The tennis fields were in the campo Marzio. The via della Pallacorda ran outside the Tuscan ambassador's residence, villa Firenze. Along the other side of the palazzo di Firenze was vico San Biagio, where M's old house was. *Pallacorda* was the forerunner of Wimbledon lawn tennis, and the street went on being called after the playing field long after it'd been built over. It was a couple of minutes' walk from the Tomassoni house in San Lorenzo in Lucina. It was an habitual hangout. You played and you bet on other people's games – this was where, five or six years earlier, the witness in one of Onorio Longhi's court appearances remembered seeing him play tennis, and remembered seeing him talking with Ranuccio Tomassoni at the Pantheon nearby. In those days, prosecutors had been convinced Longhi had assaulted Tomassoni, but Longhi denied it, claimed him as a friend, said they'd lately dined together. In 1600 Ranuccio Tomassoni was barely twenty. In 1606 he was a married man who still hadn't found a stable profession but he knew his way around the households of several cardinals and had extensive experience as a protector of prostitutes and had lately been flexing his muscle on the streets as a political gangster with his military brothers.

One of the very first reports caught the moment.

> 28 May 1606. The celebration of the pope's coronation
> began, which was on May 29 of last year 1605, and the
> same day on the grand bank [of the Tiber], celebrating the

occasion and fighting and competing with each other in the boats, somebody took a swing at someone else and the other hit back and inflicted a wound that killed him. That same evening in campo Marzio the painter M wounded and killed Ranuccio from Terni with a blow to the inside of his thigh – he was hardly confessed before he died and was buried next morning at the Rotunda – and then his brother captain Giovan Francesco pulled his sword and killed another soldier – former captain – from castel Sant' Angelo, and in the same fight Giovan Francesco wounded M and another.

Late that Sunday night the surgeon barber on duty at the Tor di Nona prison noted that he'd operated on a Petronio Troppa from Bologna – the soldier who'd taken M's part – for sword wounds in the left arm, thigh, shin and heel, removing seven pieces of bone. The patient, he noted tersely in Latin, was *likely to die or remain crippled*. With equal brevity the church recorded Ranuccio Tomassoni's death and burial next morning as the *avvisi* had it. A private letter sent to Modena a couple of days later, on May 31, offered what became the current account of what happened, slightly exaggerating the deaths and injuries.

Two evenings ago the celebrated painter M, accompanied by a captain Petronio from Bologna, clashed with Ranuccio from Terni and after a brief fight the painter was fatally wounded in the head and the other two were dead. The fight was over a fault call while they were playing tennis, by the grand duke's ambassador's place.

In fact only Ranuccio Tomassoni was dead, as other reports soon made clear. M was badly wounded in the head, but he disappeared from the scene. Petronio, near death, was imprisoned and treated and would eventually pull through. Three days later the always well informed informer and agent Francesco Maria Vialardi sent an *avviso* to Maffeo Barberini in Paris that filled out the details more accurately.

The same day [May 28] there was an argument over a bet near the grand duke's palace between a son of the late colonel Luca Antonio Tomassoni from Terni and M the famous painter. Tomassoni died from a wound inflicted when he fell down while he was retreating. Then captain Giovan Francesco his brother and M's friend captain Petronio from Bologna joined the fight and Giovan Francesco fatally wounded capt. Petronio and hit M in the head. He and M got away and Petronio was jailed, where he still is.

A more detailed report sent to Ferdinando I in Florence the same day, maybe by Vialardi himself as Tuscan informer, added the detail about M's hit to the thigh and said that Ranuccio's brother had held Petronio prisoner – and the very pertinent further fact ignored by others that M and Ranuccio *had quarrelled two days earlier*.

If this were so, the story that went down in history – of the dangerously impulsive and murderously quarrelsome painter lashing out at some near unknown, or even *a young friend*, over the utter triviality of a point in a tennis match – needed some radical revision. The idea that M's killing of Tomassoni might've had antecedents recalled the letter the duke's ever hopeful ambassador Masetti had sent to Modena three days earlier, in an exasperated mood of relief and cynicism.

> The painter M has left Rome badly wounded, having on Sunday evening killed another who provoked him to a fight. I'm told he's heading for Florence and maybe he'll come to Modena as well, so he can make them happy doing as many paintings as they want.

He was wrong about where M was headed, but the story of the provocation further queried the version of a spontaneous flareup over the score in the tennis match. Del Monte's old childhood playmate, namesake and patron Francesco Maria II Della Rovere the duke of Urbino also got an *avviso* sent by his own informant – who was maybe Del Monte himself – on May 31 about the killing and M's flight. This presented the fight as bigger, fiercer and more protracted than the other reports suggested, in fact

> ... a very notable conflict with four on each side, the leader of one band being a Ranuccio from Terni who died soon after a long fight ... they say the cause of it was a question of a gambling debt, of ten scudi that the dead man had won from the painter.

Who were the others? They all fled, but they were identified in the warrants issued by the investigating magistrate exactly a month later. Ranuccio Tomassoni was dead and Petronio Troppa was near death in jail. Warrants went out for Giovan Francesco Tomassoni and two brothers of Ranuccio's wife of three years, Ignazio and Giovan Federico Giugoli. On the other side, for M and Onorio Longhi. That left one unaccounted for. There were reasons for thinking the fourth on M's side was Mario Minniti.

What happened? And why? Another *avviso* of May 31, little known, longer than the others and kept in the Vatican's secret archive, tried *to recount the event and its cause differently* but only raised more questions. It evoked a major street fight, remarked that nothing like it had happened in Rome for a long time and estimated that *maybe twelve* men had been involved on each side. It confirmed the story that M already owed Tomassoni ten scudi, said he'd delayed paying the debt out of contempt, and in an opaque phrase added that

> to avenge some offence, M had put together six hundred scudi ... in preparation for flight.

That M was planning to run made no sense. Rome was the only place M wanted to be. It sounded like an explanation after the event. The phrase used might've meant *to guard against contingencies*. In any case, the report added, M had been passing the Tomassoni house with friends – actually a couple of blocks from where the fight was reported – when Ranuccio Tomassoni came out armed and confronted him. The two had fought alone and M had been wounded, at which point captain Petronio had come to M's aid and Giovan Francesco had intervened on his brother's side. The brawl then became general.

M seemed to have been bailed up and fought his way out. The report confirmed the earlier bad blood between M and Tomassoni. Its mention of an earlier *offence* against M recalled his obscure wounding seven months earlier, about which he'd obstinately refused to say a word when investigators found him convalescing in Ruffetti's house. The Tomassoni gang would've been a formidable enemy – the whole episode made sense in the light of their intimidation of the police and their political violence in the street a year earlier and the lesser episode the year before that. And the evidence of hostility between M's close friend Onorio Longhi and Ranuccio Tomassoni went back for years. The idea that M was being menaced and stalked by the Tomassonis was strongly confirmed by Mancini's couple of lines on the incident. Mancini, telegraphic as ever, said of M – not mentioning Tomassoni by name at all – that finally, as a result of some events that meant he was running the risk of being murdered, in self defence he killed his enemy. He was helped by Onorio Longhi to defend himself against the massive aggression.

A picture was beginning to form. M had made the mistake of owing Tomassoni money at a time – the time of Lena, legal problems, flight to Genoa, loss of his house and property, the need to offer sweeteners to the new papal family – when his finances were in a bad way. The little painting he did was free offerings or work already paid for long before. M's repeated and humiliating requests for small advances from Masetti confirmed the need. That wasn't his style and *he reddens whenever he sees me.* The debt was an occasion for the Tomassoni brothers to hassle and intimidate M, who was also on the other side, now the losing side, of the political divide. Ranuccio Tomassoni may have nursed an old resentment of M's friendships with the prostitutes, from the days when Tomassoni had been trying to turn an honest penny as a courtier pimp, before he married a friend's sister and found a new outlet in his brother's control of local government in the campo Marzio. On May 28 M was attacked or goaded into fighting.

> First they fought with racquets and then he took up arms
> and killed the youth,

wrote Bellori gracefully and inventively of M and *a young friend of his,* long after the event. Giovanni Baglione, who like Mancini was in a position to know, gave an incidental hint about what happened afterward. Baglione's line – twisted as usual by old rancour – was that M went looking for trouble. A reluctant respect for M's courage nevertheless seeped through what the epigone of *prudence* had to say.

> In his overly passionate nature, M was a bit wild and sometimes he used to look for a chance to break his neck or put someone else's life in danger. He spent a lot of time with men who had quarrelsome characters themselves. Finally he clashed with Ranuccio Tomassoni, a young fellow with a very good style, in a difference over a tennis match. They challenged each other, took up arms, and when Ranuccio fell M wounded him in the prick with the point of his sword and killed him. They all fled Rome ...

There was clearly more to the story, when *they all fled* at the end of it. The phrase that mattered in Baglione's account was his description of Tomassoni as having *a very good style*. The style – as the theatrically self important language and gestures Ranuccio used in his 1604 clash with the police showed – was the formal and obsessively dignified Spanish manner the young Tomassoni was clearly cultivating, in line with his family's proSpanish allegiances. That Baglione was impressed enough to mention it meant more than point scoring. M had killed a *comme il faut* young man. It meant Tomassoni had a social standing that impressed the socially anxious and insecure Baglione and compared very impressively with the social nonentity M's total lack of status. Ranuccio Tomassoni, as various *avvisi* recalled, was the son of the late colonel Luca Antonio who was very well remembered by the proSpanish aristocracy for his miltary services to the house of Farnese. The death of a Tomassoni would be particularly displeasing for the new Spanish aligned pope. The Tomassonis now had political clout. Maybe the still recent memory of a subtly pisstaking portrait stung his beatitude afresh when he heard of the killing.

Baglione seemed to know too how the fight ended. Several *avvisi* referred to a wound in the *thigh*, which was to say *groin*, but Baglione's specificity made clear that the final blow was a gesture that went disastrously wrong – not a thrust in the fight, but a humiliating little parting flick with the tip of his sword at the fallen Tomassoni's dick, an insulting denial of Tomassoni's ever so valued manhood. Unfortunately for both Ranuccio Tomassoni – whose *bravo* style, lately mutating into *hidalgo* pomposity, had seemed an overcompensation on the part of the youngest son in a family of soldiers and thugs, the boy too young to have proven himself in the field against infidels and heretics like his father and his elder brothers – M's flick severed an artery and Tomassoni soon bled to death. Did the boy pimp, the street bully, the child father, the political gangster, the unproven youngest son, the would be *sgherro* and hounder of the greatest painter of his age, feel, as consciousness faded and his blood drained out through his penis, that this was a man's death he was dying? It didn't look like that to family and friends. Death administered with contempt was another reason for a moralizing pope to harden against M, and for Tomassoni's family to remain implacable in wanting M's skin.

ONE DEAD, BLOOD spilt into the ground, one near death. The fighters scattering as word spread and police asserted their presence. The women of the Tomassoni clan – the dead man's mother Olimpia, his wife – appearing to reclaim Ranuccio's body and prepare it that Sunday night for a hasty burial next morning. His widow arriving as her two brothers fled into the late spring evening. Her small daughter crying. Giovan Francesco Tomassoni reverting from street fighter to his role as district head of the campo Marzio, taking charge of Petronio's barely living body, *a sack of bones, broken within* – and then realizing that he too had to take flight. Badly wounded in the head – some at the scene thought fatally – M making his way or being helped to where he took refuge in someone's house. The news passing along the nerves of Roman power. In some way, in some sequence, these events followed the death of Ranuccio Tomassoni by M's hand.

M holed up somewhere for a couple of days while his wounds were dressed and he recovered some strength and the network of his friends and protectors was activated again. It was less than a year since he'd run to Genoa, but he was in a far more desperate need now, wanted for the infinitely graver crime of homicide, and a compromising presence in even the most powerful person's household. There was a gap between the first news of the killing on Sunday and the *avvisi* of the following Wednesday, which implied he'd only just left Rome that day. Many years later, Sandrart wrote that M first took refuge in the palazzo Giustiniani – a less likely hiding place than others nearby and the marchese himself was away from Rome on his European journey at the time. Past history made Del Monte's over the way a tested and more likely refuge. It was most likely of all that while Ranuccio Tomassoni lay bleeding to death M staggered or was dragged into the grounds of the palazzo di Firenze. The Tuscan ambassador Giovanni Niccolini's residence was part of Del Monte's domain, and the fight'd happened right outside it.

They all fled from Rome, wrote Baglione succinctly, *and M went to Palestrina …* Bellori said that

> He fled from Rome under pursuit and without money and found refuge at Zagarolo in the kindness of the duke, don Marzio Colonna,

and Bellori was confirming what Mancini had noted earlier, that

> he was forced to flee from Rome and his first stop was in

> Zagarolo, where he was given secret refuge by that prince,
> who knew him very well,

and it fitted what Baglione remembered and ambassador Masetti's report four months later, that M was at Paliano. Zagarolo, Palestrina and Paliano were all neighbouring feudal territories belonging to the Colonnas. They were all within striking distance of Rome, about fifty kilometres west of the city and slightly to the south.

Once again, it looked as though Del Monte saved M's skin. Del Monte was tied to the Colonnas by more than his cousin's son in the Colonna household in Rome, more than his Sforza descent. The marchesa of Caravaggio, Costanza Colonna Sforza and her brother cardinal Ascanio Colonna had another sister, Giovanna, who'd been married to Carlo Del Monte. Carlo, killed in battle a very few years earlier, commanding an infantry company at the siege of Ostend in the low countries, had been the son of the mathematician Guidubaldo Del Monte. Del Monte's nephew, that is, when family ties counted for everything, had been a war hero married to the prince of Paliano's daughter, son in law of the victor of Lepanto. And Del Monte was close too to Marzio Colonna, the duke of Zagarolo – some years later he mentioned Marzio's son the new duke in a letter to the duke of Urbino as *my relative and very special friend*. He must've arranged for Colonna – who apparently already knew M well – to take M into initial hiding on his Zagorolo territory. Don Marzio's wife's family were the lords of nearby Palestrina, where M moved on later in the summer, still under the protection of the Colonna family network. Ascanio Colonna, as it happened, was appointed bishop of Palestrina a week after M killed Tomassoni. Later still that summer M moved on to Paliano, a little beyond Palestrina to the west.

Costanza Colonna's late father Marcantonio – and she was M's marchesa of Caravaggio – had been made prince of Paliano by the pope in 1569. When M arrived there in 1606 its ruler was Marcantonio's grandson, Filippo Colonna, and as Marcantonio's children, both the marchesa Costanza and cardinal Ascanio Colonna had an interest in the principality as well. Costanza Colonna by then had gone back north and Filippo Colonna may have been in Spain that year – Ascanio Colonna was probably the man in charge at Paliano. These were the places where the Colonnas gave M refuge, and if they did it *secretly*, and if they kept him on the move around their various feudal territories over the next four months, it was because M could hardly have been more at risk. The Colonnas, in sheltering M, were now – in principle at least – running grave risks themselves, protected only by their own clout.

Del Monte was M's hope in Rome. Getting the injured party to swear off and make peace was the absolutely necessary first step toward getting the authorities off your back, as M well knew. He needed to repeat the settlement he'd got from Pasqualone the year before. At first he seemed optimistic about pulling it off – loyalties apart, he knew how badly private clients in Rome still wanted his work – and six weeks after the killing the ambassador Masetti reported to Modena that he understood M was trying to arrange his return to Rome. In September Masetti repeated that M *expects to be allowed back soon.*

The hopes were dashed. Some time after killing Ranuccio Tomassoni M learnt that he'd been sentenced to death. He may have known before he even left Rome, while he was recovering in hiding in one of the palazzi of his Roman protectors, that he was under *bando capitale.* This time the usual moves brought no result. It may have been they were never tried. Clout had its limits, even Del Monte's, where Paul V was concerned. Del Monte around this time acted effectively to get an amnesty for another killer, but on M the pope was unyielding. Maybe in M's case Del Monte didn't even try. M failed to get back to Rome. The pope was implacable and M's sentence remarkably cruel. The *bando* was a criminal equivalent of the old English marriage banns, the announcement of a criminal sentence, *the public intimation of a sentence to be carried out.* A person who'd been sentenced by the proclamation of a bann was a *bandit,* and when people were sentenced to death in absentia like this, explained a legal manual called *On criminal judgements and their practice in the Roman curia* written by a cardinal De Luca later in the century, *in Rome we call them life bandits.* It was an even uglier and more terrible sentence than it sounded. If you were under a capital bann, anybody within the territory of the court's jurisdiction was allowed to kill you, with the further option, added the cardinal,

> of severing the head in order to present it to the judge …
> to claim the reward offered.

Although a *bandit* could only be killed within the territory of the court's jurisdiction, the cardinal further noted that

> some zealous magistrates and officials customarily … have bandits killed in foreign territory, or taken live and brought back for punishment, or get their heads in order to put

them on display, rewarding rather than penalizing those who bring them in.

If you were brought in alive, you had no right to a trial, other than a summary identification process, before proceeding directly to your execution *by axe, garrotte, club or fire*, according to your crime, social rank and the custom of the country. This was now M's likely fate, and it'd hang over him for the rest of his life.

What happened to the others? The authorities were after them too, but they never had a death sentence hanging over them. They were all *banditi* and driven from the territory of Rome, but theirs was the *bando d'esilio*. Only M was under a *bando capitale*. Onorio Longhi fled to his home ground Milan and joined the Spanish army there as an engineer. He never saw M again. Mario Minniti went home with his Roman wife to Syracuse on the eastern coast of Sicily. Giovan Francesco Tomassoni and Ranuccio's widow's two brothers fled to the safety of Ranuccio Farnese's Parma, whence they too eventually began petitioning the pope for a return to Rome. Rome was where the action was.

Onorio Longhi's role in the fight was confirmed by more than his name in the warrant. There were his own later words in his appeal to the pope five years after the event, when he was negotiating to be allowed back to Rome. He'd fled to Milan, his native ground, and by 1611 M was dead and it made no difference any more what Longhi said to achieve his aim of a pardon. He'd been banished from Rome because he was *present*, Longhi said in the appeal he addressed directly to Paul V, at the homicide committed by M on Ranuccio Tomassoni, for which he held no blame – in fact that day

> he was keeping M company as a loving friend to prevent
> any disorder happening and urging him to keep the peace,
> as God was his good witness, and his own conscience.

If Paul V handled the appeal personally and knew Longhi, he might've allowed himself a small pursed smile when he read these words. Longhi however was able to bolster his petition by informing the pope that

> he has obtained peace from the party which has always
> been well aware of his innocence

– *peace* being that formal expression of your willingness to let bygones be bygones and not press further charges that Pasqualone had made with M in 1605 – the Tomassoni family came round to accepting Longhi's version, at least to the extent of dropping the matter five years later. So they did in the end with Mario, though it took time for him too.

Mario's presence as the unnamed fourth man on M's side was an inference, but a plausible one. A long time later Mario's Sicilian biographer described how *after ten years' residence in Rome*, he returned to Sicily with his Roman wife. Once he got back to Syracuse Mario

> wasn't able to move around freely on account of a homicide he'd accidentally committed, so he took refuge in the Carmelite convent there.

The ten year span about matched the time M had known Mario, from their first days together, drudging in Cesari's workshop, to the fatal showdown with Tomassoni. Sicily was Spanish territory and Minniti should've been out of reach of Roman justice, but unlike M he had no known powerful friends and was a painter at risk. He was a born survivor, which implied a cunning to match his rashness, and on his home ground in Sicily. A spell in a safe house made sense, while he sussed out things back home, assessed the risk of arrest and extradition. The *accidental homicide* was likely Tomassoni's killing and at first the family was unrelenting.

> He tried a number of times to obtain a pardon from the dead man's relatives but it was always denied him. Finally his good qualities became so evident that the authorities intervened with those nobles and ... he was freed.

M recovered that summer on the Colonna estate at Paliano and by September was ready to move on. It was the dogged ambassador Masetti, still hoping against hope to get a painting out of M, or at least recover the duke's money he'd unwisely advanced him, who reported in a letter of September 23 that M was at Paliano and near recovery – Masetti's news was maybe a little old, because less than two weeks later M was already in Naples and collecting payment in advance for a painting he promised to deliver by December.

Over the summer of 1606 M was trapped in the torpid middle of nowhere, through three months or more of stifling inland heat, sick and weakened from his head wounds, as the thought insinuated itself that however much optimism and resolve he mustered about fixing things up, getting an amnesty, going back and starting again, things would never be quite restored. Life was irrevocably changed. However odious Ranuccio Tomassoni might've been, he was a young man now dead and M had killed him. M had to think of himself as a killer, and nothing in his life and art from now on would give grounds for believing he was ever less than appalled. Or that the awareness ever left him. And beyond homicide was the penalty for homicide. What would become of him? Killer and victim were caught together in the terrible intimacy of violent death.

WHAT M DID in this grim moment of his life was what he always did. He went straight back to work. It was reflexive, a part of his life. Though he surely needed to make some money in readiness for his next moves, painting defined his being and was a necessary part of recovery. M spent nearly four months on the Colonna estates at Paliano and did three paintings there, maybe more. This work marked, in ways that were all inseparably a part of each other, a moment when M's art changed radically. The change had to do, materially and practically, with his never again belonging to a settled community of friends and models and clients. From the summer of 1606 until the summer of 1610 he would be without sustaining continuities, without the Roman life he'd clearly loved – always on the move, sometimes with a heartstopping urgency, working at great speed in more or less makeshift circumstances and dogged by new and terrible realities in his mind and daily life. Always fixed on return to the centre. More intimately, it had to do with what he now knew about losing life violently and forever.

It wasn't simple, the way it showed in his paintings. There were still the discontinuities of treatment, that endless backward and forward movement of anticipation and recall around the point where his painting was at any moment – the restlessness that later made his work so hard to date and put in order. It wasn't even entirely new. The early signs of the direction he was now taking had all been there in the increasing urgency of his last year in Rome. That urgency itself had been growing ever since the violent impact of M's coming out into the larger world in 1600, through the drama of the trial in 1603 and the preliminary flight of 1605. The ugly and futile incident that changed M's life irrevocably into tragedy had been a black dot on the horizon from the start. It arrived as something arbitrary, casual, pointless and yet it was M's logical and ineluctable act of resistance against the dreadful pressures that'd been converging on him in Rome. The bleakness that now came into his way of seeing had already been there in his great Roman painting of *Mary dead*. So had the first signs of violent speed, a savage economy of technique quite other than the rapid sure delicacy of the way he'd laid on paint before. He turned necessity into art. Its first sign was a painting unlike any other he'd done before or would ever do again.

> They all fled from Rome and M went to Palestrina, where
> he painted a Mary Magdalen,

said Baglione. It was Lena, imagined with her head thrown back, hair loose and shirt falling off her shoulder, fingers tightly clasped, leaning on her elbow, tearfilled eyes closed and lips parted in an ecstasy of abandonment and loss. There was nothing else in the picture. She was resting on a bundle of sticks that were mainly hidden by her red cloak, and she was sinking out of the picture in despair. If a diagonal line were imagined from the top right to the bottom left corner of the canvas, her three quarter figure filled only the bottom half. The rest was almost impenetrable darkness. Formally, the picture drew on M's recent paintings of young John or old Jerome, it was a female ana- logue to those and it was done in the same powerfully limited range of tones of brown, white, red. Formally Lena was Mary Magdalen, but context, symbols, all pointers to extrinsic meaning were entirely gone. She might've been a woman deserted by her lover, a woman whose child had died, a woman betrayed. It was a female image of exhaustion and despair whose energy was all turned inward. The sight- less eyes were closed against darkness, the hands held only each other and the lines of the folds of her clothes – the white shirt and the red cloak were the only things visible beyond Lena herself – did nothing but enclose, follow and enhance the distraught lines of the woman's body.

The power lay in these lines, the physical energy of the suffering in the flung back body, the unprecedented intimacy and vulnerability M showed in painting the face thrown back and lit by a raking beam from below. The soft neck, throat and shoulder took the force of the light, the upper part of the head was lost in the darkness at the edge of the painting. Mouth, nostrils, eyes were penetrated by the cruel oblique light – it was a violation of identity. Her face, cast so far back and lit so rakingly from below, lost its conventional connotations and recomposed itself in an almost cubist manner into an unfamiliar land- scape whose markers were all awry, eyes below the nose, mouth and left eye two similar forms balancing each other, ear tucked in behind the shoulder, so that her identity seemed to disintegrate into an assemblage of recognizable but alien features as you gazed at the painting, and it took a great effort to see her whole. What you usually saw was hidden in shadow, what was hidden now *swollen in light – a tragic negative*. In a polemical vindication of Lena's part in his rejected tragic masterpiece of a year and a half before, M had taken Mary's reversed face from his painting of *Mary dead*, applied a more radical light, distorted its still beauty into the living but incipiently deathlike distress of the open mouth seen from below with a glint of upper teeth, added the silent movement of the tear gathering under the eyelid and sliding almost imperceptibly out of the corner of her eye.

Had he used a model? There was something faintly unreal about the way the figure's echoing and concentrating lines in the joining of her arms, the flowing of her hair and the folds and creases of her clothes were abstracted into a thing in itself, Edvard Munch like, that implied M was painting a feeling this time rather than a living model in front of him, a memory of Lena in a moment of abandon. The likeness and unlikeness of this figure to Lena's as he'd painted her before reinforced the feeling. He'd never before done a painting that seemed so simply and deeply personal, a painting that seemed to relate so directly to the exhaustion and despair you might've presumed M himself was feeling now. The strangeness lay in its ambiguity, the way the image hovered at some point between an objective rendering of a distraught young woman and an internal and subjective rendering of his own inner state. The fascination came from his rendering his own feeling in female form, as if only a female capacity for pain were adequate to what he himself was now undergoing. In the woozy, flowing female lines of Lena remembered, M lost for the only time in his painting life his crisp cool take on reality. To represent his own state he identified with Lena.

It was an extraordinary image, *one of M's finest*. Soon it was recognized as one by other artists. M took the canvas with him when he moved on to Naples and there it aroused intense interest among other painters. Immediately they imitated it. A huge number of copies and variants were done, more copies than were made of any of M's other paintings. M's memory of Lena abandoned – his image of physical abandonment – entered the vocabulary of Italian painting as an unconscious citation, used by painters who eventually would've had no idea where the image came from. The early copies showed how remarkable M's rendering of Lena's tilted face was, at that angle in that raking light, how difficult it was to catch. None of the others got the mouth right, the eyes, the planes of her cheeks – sophisticated painters like Louis Finson, working not from life but from a portrait that'd already resolved the projection on to a flat surface, produced crude and clumsy distortions of M's subtle work, mouth and eyes ugly and askew. Finson copied it several times and never got it quite right. These painters had studied drawing, but only conceptual variations on the standard poses – Lena's face by M lit from below was like a whole new animal, a form of life never seen before, and they couldn't render it.

Years later, Lena in despair was assimilated into another artist's far better known work, one of the most famous works of art of the Italian seicento. Leonardo might've remarked that Gianlorenzo Bernini's great sculpture of *Teresa in ecstasy* of 1652 was a lesser work than M's modest *Magdalen* because Bernini, working in marble, didn't have to render the contours of an ecstatic and flung back female face in two dimensions and he didn't have to light it. Transmuted into baroque erotic marble, in *Teresa* being impaled and again in Bernini's later sculpture of *Ludovica Albertone* writhing in ecstasy, M's conception lost its radical cast and its disfiguring human anguish – the lips and eyes swollen with weeping – and became at once more mystical, more sexual, more theatrical and more demure. Worldly, brilliant, entrepreneurial, a man as much in tune with the powers of his later age as M was alienated from his, Bernini owed a twofold debt to M in his great *Teresa*. The cheerful pubescent angel transfixing the saint in ecstasy was a correspondingly polite baroque descendant of grinning Cecco clutching his arrows as *Love the winner*. Half a century after M's death, it was unlikely anyone noticed.

The peculiar power of M's female image of suffering showed by contrast with a male counterpart, of *Francis* deep in thought. This other painting from the time of M's refuge after the killing showed a bearded Francis kneeling in a frayed habit, bent over a book propped open on the ground by a wooden crucifix and a skull, his fingers intertwined like the Magdalen's supporting his chin. It was a lot more conventional as a saintly icon – halo, book, crucifix, skull – and instead of female abandonment and vulnerability, this Francis presented male focus, concentration, a quite different kind of inwardness, leaning forward and down, the whole painting brought to a tight focus on the high lit point of the sharply angled nose and the many emphatic wrinkles in his brow. The eyes below were lost in pits of shadow. It was a powerful work in near monochrome of greys and browns, done with that rapid, essential *savagery* of brushstroke, picking out the lines of light that defined dark masses, that he'd shown in the final Roman urgency of the old woman who was Anne and that'd be the defining mark of his work from now on. The setting was another impenetrable wild darkness – as in the *Magdalen* a few perfunctory strokes of dark brown on darker brown in the background suggested a tree trunk, a few dead leaves. The mute and lonely intensity of this Francis was bleak, heartbreaking, but its register was narrow, pinched and dry beside Lena's imagined agony as the *Magdalen*. If Lena – you might venture loosely – had been painted by the man who'd been hounded from his own life, *Francis*, with its hint of self portraiture, was the work of the man who'd killed. It was his second *Francis* – his third counting that very early painting of Del Monte fainting in the arms of a boy angel. He'd done another of a robuster Francis in a ripped habit holding a skull and meditating on mortality like Hamlet in the graveyard, another unrecorded painting and harder to date – maybe he did it now, or perhaps it belonged to early 1603, the year Orazio Gentileschi recalled at the libel trial in September having lent M a monk's habit and a pair of wings six or eight months earlier. Francis joined John and Jerome to make up that trio of alienated males, young, mature and old, brooding and remote from human society, that M painted again and again. They were the images of thought, of an integrity maintained through isolation, solitude and poverty and he made them his own.

There was no record of this *Francis*, nor did any of the early writers mention it, but it belonged inescapably to M's months of refuge at Paliano – marked by its twinship with the *Magdalen* painting and its handling's closeness to the work in the other painting M now did in hiding. His new Paliano painting was a reworking of his earlier half length *Meal at Emmaus* and it showed the change come over him. The new painting was made on the template of his first version. It kept so closely to the forms and gestures used before as to be a consciously darkened restatement of it. The illusionistic exuberance was all gone, like the outflung arms and the vivid teetering fruit. There was no vivid colour, no beardless boy Christ, no bread roll body and blood obstructed by the upturned claws of a roast chook, no play of light refracted through glass and water and wine. The joyous engagement with the simple things of the everyday world that enlivened M's early mature work was gone. Darkness had come down over the table – the same table, covered by a similar patterned carpet with a white cloth on top, all now in deep shadow. All that was on it now were two bread rolls, one broken, a pottery jug and a plate with a couple of lettuce leaves. In arrival was a piece of roast meat on the bone, brought by an ancient, downcast, deeply furrowed and introspective crone, a new figure on the scene – or so she looked for a bewildered instant, before you recognized her as a reappearance of the ancient Anne M'd done six months or so earlier. Subliminally but ineluctably she was also an older beardless replay of the brooding Francis he'd just done. She and the cook – he an older, shrunken, faded and furrowed replay of the capped host from before – now towered over a small, subdued Christ. The Christ himself looked like a worn and older reappearance of smooth cheeked Giulietto, no longer dressed in scarlet and white but in drab dark greenish grey, tired head bent forward, minimal gesture of wearily raised hand. The apostle on the left was younger, sketched in briefly as the back of a head of curly hair, a dark green shoulder and a slash of umber blanket, he too keeping his spread finger gesture of amazement and revelation to the absolute minimum. The one on the right was a sun baked, sun stupefied peasant with huge ears, a neck like a riverbed in drought and big, dark, knotted hands. There were no big shadows cast on walls. Everything outside the five side lit heads and shoulders and the narrow strip of tabletop was in deepest darkness, and the darkness pulled the figures together, made them, isolated as each seemed, a little human group in which Christ was no more than human and even the ancient serving woman hovering on the fringe belonged.

M WAS STANDING at the crossroads again. Every five years or so in his life as a painter, he'd made a choice that changed everything. The choices were always obvious enough – what'd mattered was the way he took them up. Somewhere back in the early unrecorded time of Milan and Caravaggio there'd been a moment – around the time his mother died in 1590 and the family goods were divvied up – the time he'd spent feeding his visual hunger and some of it maybe in jail and on the run, which had been the time of his original resolve to paint, in the face of the things he'd failed or refused to learn as a boy from Peterzano, the universal skills of drawing and fresco painting he'd rejected. Then there'd been his first real break, after his arrival in Rome, the chance offered in 1595 by Del Monte's interest and hospitality – the material security, the intellectual stimulus, the discreet pressure or encouragement to paint a certain kind of work. That ended in the technical challenge of translating five years of perfected chamber art into big complex public pictures, the moment that'd come when the *Matthew* commissions were fed his way in 1600. He'd seized each of these moments and exploited it in unforeseeable ways, turned a difficulty into a strength, and each time he'd taken the art of painting down a new road.

What came now didn't even look like the shadow of a chance. And what he made of necessity had none of the dazzling innovation of his first things for Del Monte's gallery or the walls of the Contarelli and Cerasi chapels. It was a kind of involution. From now on, always on the move, M would be forced more and more often to abandon what he'd made the very principle of art before, painting with *l'esempio avanti del naturale*. And there'd be no one around to really notice the change, no more of his Roman clients' loving intensity of gaze, prolonged over the changes of the years. His work was so much a matter now of fleeting needs and makeshift circumstances that you wondered whether he was aware himself of the difference it made, not having models, having to work faster and faster before he moved on. Did he realize how much it threw him back on his past, how much of the work he did now was painted from memory, memories of light striking a head, a hand, memories of faces themselves? M after Rome was more and more often forced to paint at speed, and once again the technical exigencies became a principle of art. He'd stored so much in his mind, in those years of fanatically catching at the traces of the real in a darkened room, and now it was all he had. He'd be living off it until the end, hacking away at it, reducing it to essentials, a Beckettian minimum, glimpses in the dark. It was what he wanted to do. It'd be, after the arduous years of fidelity to *natural things*, strangely liberating, despite the horror of what sometimes floated into sight out of the mind's darkness.

Now he did the most intimate and desolating work he'd ever do. Sparely, rapidly, meagerly applied paint, so overwhelmingly personal in its tragic intensity that people would always want to see it as among his last things, though it was only an intimation, a laying down of the parameters for the new work coming. It was a painting of David holding Goliath's severed head. The boy and the head were almost lost in darkness, under a few streaks of tentlike roof – there was a crescent moon of Goliath's suspended face, a little more of David's, gazing down, half of the boy's bared chest and the single radically foreshortened arm that grasped the head, a few brief folds of his loosened shirt and his baggy peasant pants, a length of glinting sword blade. Nothing more. The image might've been defined by negatives, by absences. It was meant to be the triumph of righteousness over power and arrogance, and it came out of the dark as an occasion of deep sorrow. Goliath's head was appallingly human in death, the blood darkening on the forehead wounded by David's slingshot, his left eye still flickering with some life, mouth open for one last exhausted breath, discoloured teeth glinting dimly – and the boy David wasn't holding it out as a victory offering but staring down with a tragic regret that was unbearably touching because he was so young. There was a sense in which David seemed the victim and not the agent of a human horror. How could his skinny arm bear the weight of that still suffering head?

The question had a particular force because the severed head was M's and the boy holding it out in sorrow was Cecco. Bellori remarked on M's presence in his *David* –

> a half figure of David holding up by the hair Goliath's head, which is his own self portrait, and gripping the sword. He painted David from a bareheaded youth with one shoulder coming out of his shirt, and did him with a powerfully dark background and shadows –

and twentyodd years before Bellori someone else in 1650 said that M

> in that head wanted to portray himself and in the David he portrayed his Caravaggino.

The affectionately possessive diminutive was a reminder that this was the same year somebody else told the English traveller Symonds that in *Love the winner* M painted *ye body & face of his owne boy ... thait laid with him.* Did Bellori hear this too, but feel that unlike the self portrait it wasn't the kind of thing one drew attention to?

One of the measures often taken against those wanted for capital crimes, wrote cardinal De Luca in his *Criminal judgements*, at least against those guilty of *more serious or scandalous crimes,* was ignominy.

> The image of the *bandito* is displayed in public places ... for ignominy and the mortification of relatives and as an example and a terror for others and also so that strangers, thus informed of the sentence and the person, may be invited to kill him and claim the reward indicated.

In *David*, M painted his own wanted poster, a reminder that anyone was invited to kill him and bring back his head for cash. *Nec spe nec metu*, as they'd said in his push back in Rome. He'd push on *without hope or fear*. But if the *David* were meant to exorcise terror by imagining the worst it didn't. Murder by beheading was something he'd treated so far only once, in the far from deeply felt *Judith*, and that work was a lot more interested in beautiful Fillide's frown of concentration, and her bare forearm hacking away under the old woman's intent stare, than in the wide eyed horror of the man writhing on the pillow and losing his head. Now M was launching into a theme that would recur again and again after this *David*, and in the next few years he'd show it at least half a dozen times again.

The amazing thing about this *David* was the return it showed of M's poised mastery. Facing the worst had let him recover his fullest powers. The painting in its bleakness had a subtlety of finish in which its surface and its image came together as they had in his most deeply tragic Roman painting – *Mary dead* of a couple of years earlier. *David*, too, was already looking forward to the teeming masterpiece of figures in darkness he'd paint in Naples in the coming year. The folds of David's shirt, the blade of his sword were bravura pieces of simplification, a few thin streaks of white paint that transformed themselves into soft folds and steely edge against the blackness. The cruel light that'd raked across the Magdalen and broken her features up gave way here to something more diffuse, an atmospheric subtlety that was the more elusive here in that only darkness surrounded the figures. M made it a dense and vibrant darkness out of which David's twisting torso and his forward jutting arm didn't break free as they might've, like the elbow of Nicodemus in the *Burial*, or Matthew's bare foot in M's first rejected painting. The boy's extraordinarily sculptural figure didn't stand out with the hard edged solidity of the earlier figures, nor was he made up of brilliantly reflecting highlights in the dark. He was immersed in something larger, subtler, finer.

The painting's fascination came too from the tension it made you feel between the subject and the way it was shown. You didn't need to recognize M's face or Cecco to feel this. It came from the deeply sorrowing figure of the boy. If the picture showed that David was victim as much as agent of the recent violence, it came out in a sense of adolescent uncertainty about what made you act. He had the look of a boy guerrilla in a wire service photo. And the assassin as victim was where M came in. M provided his own portrait for the severed head, but he'd also entered the skin of the reluctant and regretful boy killer.

It was, of course, Cecco, although the suddenly fragile and deeply shadowed face and body had changed from the chubby goldenhaired child angel's of five years earlier, and from the exultant and insolent adolescent's that followed. You could still tell it was Cecco. The features were his and especially the boy had Cecco's ear, the same large red projecting generously curved ear M had put into every portrait, most visibly on Cecco nude as *John*. M was always big on ears, their shape and angle and their individual convolutions, the way they caught the light and glowed. They were less active but almost as expressive as people's hands. The slender fragility he had here was partly illusory, the effect of David's sideways stance and the darkness eating into the outer contours of the body, reducing its visible surface. The chest and shoulders were quite broad. If Cecco Boneri had been twelve around 1601 and 1602, he was now seventeen, as he looked in this painting, thinner, wirier and on the verge of manhood. The question was whether this image was a memory of Cecco, or was it a rendering of Cecco in the flesh? Did the *garzone Francesco* leave Rome with M to keep him company in hiding on the Colonna estates? He probably did. A reason for thinking this *David* was painted from life, beyond the subtlety and individuality of the features, which were done quite unlike Lena's remembered face in the *Magdalen*, was the unusually detailed incisions M left in the surface, defining the outline of David's head, the alignment of his eyes and particularly the outline of the radically foreshortened arm and hand that were holding out the head. He'd used detailed lines like these once before, in the difficult foreshortening of John's leg in the *John in the wild* he did for Ottavio Costa in 1604, and he'd almost never use them again. Another reason for thinking that Cecco stuck with M that summer was that later, in Naples, M painted him again.

THE SUMMER'S HIDING ended and – likely a few days behind the actual state of play – Fabio Masetti reported on September 23 that M was still at Paliano. If M was still there he was packing his bag, because less than two weeks later he'd signed a contract in Naples for a major work. Naples was several days' journey away from the Colonna estates. It was, given the banditry that paid particular attention to the busy traffic along the two hundred kilometre route between Rome and Naples, a risky journey. For M, with a death sentence hanging over him and his head now proclaimed as a nice little income supplement for whoever took the trouble to hack it off, it wasn't a journey to make alone. Going to Naples at all showed how far M was now beholden to his aristocratic protectors, and how fine a line might've been drawn between his being their guest and his being their prisoner. What else could M do? Onorio Longhi had made for his family's home town of Milan. Mario Minniti had gone home to Sicily. With-drawing to your home base made sense in times of trouble. You had a network of family and friends to give you a bed, look out for you, set you up, rebuild your morale. Longhi and Mario, though, weren't on the run from a death rap. M was too well known, and if he had a previous conviction in Milan, not to mention a possible outstanding warrant over a much earlier killing, he had several strong reasons for staying away. Neither did he have any family left to speak of in Cara-vaggio. There was only his sister and his priest brother somewhere in the district. And he'd broken irrevocably with them, denied their exis-tence. Unlike his friends, M had no home to go to.

He'd've been more than welcome in Modena or Genoa and other places besides. Florence, maybe Venice. Mantua. Yet he now went to Naples, which was a city quite outside his circuits of acquaintance so far, and a choice of destination that would take him deep into Span-ish Italy and determine everything that happened to him thereafter. To a painter, Naples offered nothing like the densely cosmopolitan community of peers or rich and the sophisticated market he'd known in Rome, a city in which even the lumpenproletariat rushed to see an important new altarpiece and there were bankers and cardinals with a taste for the avant garde and the money to indulge it. The smaller ducal courts of the north were run by dukes and princes equally eager to build prestige by cultivating the new. Naples was not state of the art. It held, however, its own surprises.

And Naples happened to be where don Marzio Colonna, lord and duke of Zagarolo and the first to give him refuge, mainly lived. Marzio Colonna was a member of the vicerealm's *collateral commission* and five years earlier he'd been the mayor of Naples who presided over the celebrations for the birth of the infanta of Spain. Felipe III had made him a *knight of the golden fleece*. Seven years later Marzio Colonna would die in Naples. The duke of Zagarolo had clout in Naples and he was heading back to the city at the end of the summer on his estates. He could give M safe conduct through bandit territory and put him in touch with the right people on arrival. It may've been that right from the start M was thinking of Naples purely as a staging post, that he'd already formulated – together with the Colonnas – the project that would take him on to Malta early the following summer, as part of his plan to regain lost ground and prepare his return to Rome.

15

NAPLES 1606–1607

Seven works of mercy
Andrew killed
David III
Rosary Madonna

APLES WAS A shock. It was a shock for everyone. After fourteen years in the city that considered itself the *caput mundi* and the centre of everything that mattered, M in the autumn of 1606 found himself in a city that was at least three times the size of Rome – the biggest metropolis in Europe after Paris – on one of the most stunningly beautiful locations on earth. Naples had more than trebled its size in the ninety years of Spanish rule, and grown tenfold in two hundred years. Its three hundred thousand or more inhabitants, though, were still jammed inside the confines of the old city, on a town plan that'd been marked out by the ancient Greeks and was now occupied hodgepodge by magnificent new baronial palaces and the teeming and ageless warrens of the poor. In Rome the buildings commonly reached three storeys, and M had known a city marked out by the wide straight streets, the vast piazzas and splendid fountains of Sixtus V's urban renewal. In Naples houses went to six or seven floors, towering over narrow sunless alleys. This was the capital of the kingdom of the two Sicilies – most of southern Italy plus the islands – and it had the attributes of real wealth and power. Naples was, as Cervantes had reminded readers of *Don Quixote* the year before, *the richest and most depraved city in the whole world*. And Cervantes knew because he'd lived there. When M arrived there, *Naples had no equivalent in Christendom*.

> The whole of southern Italy flocked to the city, both the rich, often very rich, and the hopelessly wretched poor … peasants from throughout the provinces of the vast, mountainous and pastoral kingdom … were attracted by the *arti* of wool and silk … by the city's public works … by domestic employment in the households of nobles … [and by] the countless religious establishments with their throngs of servants and hangers on …

> Naples was excessive in every respect … an overpopulated and disquieting city … order could never be maintained, and at night the only law was that of the strong and cunning … it was the most astonishing, most fantastically picaresque city in the world … a more hard working city than its very bad reputation gives it credit for, but that reputation was not undeserved …

Beside all this the *caput mundi* M had lately fled was in many ways a poor and rather demure thing. Rome was an elegant but unproductive show city. Naples had all the attributes of manifold economic life, production and consumption from hardscrabble desperation to unparalleled idle opulence. And it had the appurtenances of real power. Militarily, for instance. Naples garrisoned the massive forces that maintained Spanish power in the central Mediterranean, a riotous and parasitic soldiery that lived promiscuously off the Neapolitan populace. The city sustained as well the courtiers of the local nobility, the retinues of the Spanish rulers and the imperial bureaucracy of the occupying power.

Which was what Spain was, in Naples, and the people hated it and never forgot it. In 1510 and 1547 armed revolt by the people had forced the Spanish to abandon their plans to introduce the Spanish inquisition in Naples, and these were only two of the periodic uprisings of Neapolitans against Spain that would continue through the next century. One of the reasons for Neapolitan poverty, amid all its natural and geographical resources, was the rapacity of viceroy after viceroy. These were aristocrats from the court of Madrid given monarchical powers and liberty to profit from their appointments in whatever way they could, while the city ran up huge deficits. The poor were hurt most by the viceroys' profiteering, but from time to time they found allies against Spain in Neapolitans further up the social scale. In 1585 the Spanish viceroy provoked a massive armed revolt by increasing the price of bread in Naples while exporting local grain to Spain. The uprising was, in the end, savagely repressed, but it marked the beginning of organized opposition to Spanish rule in Naples, and was the forerunner of the great revolt of sixty years later.

The seaport was the busiest in Italy and the city around it contained a busy community of foreign merchants and financiers. The endless influx of new people from the surrounding country, the closeness to the sea's international traffic and the local fishing fleets made Neapolitan society more heterogeneous and less isolated from the daily realities of life than Rome's febrile society of priests and prostitutes, and even more cosmopolitan. And the physical promiscuity in which everyone lived meant that while life in Naples was no less hierarchical than elsewhere, there was more contact among the different classes – they were living on top of each other. The stories and songs and theatre of popular life fed directly into the high culture – in the stories, for instance of M's contemporary Giambattista Basile or the demotic vigour of Bruno's dialogues.

Naples was also a centre of the counter reformation and no less priest ridden than Rome.

> Even considering Rome's dogmatic and normative rule, Munich's bigotry and missionary fervour, Spain's mystical and repressive impulses, Paris's great population and culture, Naples was the real capital of the counter reformation, and reflected its successes, its ambiguities and its failures.

But it was also a city that kept asserting its religious and intellectual autonomy against Rome's dictates, as Sixtus V found in 1586 and Clement VIII discovered in 1594, when they tried to replace by force the friars of two Neapolitan convents with more acceptable adherents of the counter reformation and were driven back by armed popular resistance on both occasions. One of these was the convent of San Domenico Maggiore, where Giordano Bruno had begun his career and where Tommaso Campanella had studied. They and their acquaintance the Neapolitan scientist and playwright Giambattista Della Porta, inventor of M's *camera obscura* and the telescope, and like the others tried by the inquisition, were, with Galileo Galilei, the most original thinkers in Italy at that time. It may or may not have been coincidental that M was about to undertake two commissions for the church of San Domenico Maggiore in his very first months in Naples.

When M arrived in the autumn of 1606, the viceroy of Naples was don Juan Alfonso Pimentel de Herrera, known for short as the conde de Benavente, *one of the grossest, most incompetent and arrogant rulers the city had known*, and the city was in the middle of *a particularly serious food shortage* that'd been approaching crisis for the previous couple of years. The viceroy was taking advantage of the famine to do a little profiteering for himself and his business partner, and eliminating the functionaries who'd become embarrassing witnesses of his activities by having them publicly executed for real or invented irregularities. The previous year he'd slapped a big new tax on fruit, in case people looked for alternatives to bread and pasta. Salt was already seen to. In January of 1607 the inspector general sent out by Madrid to investigate Benavente's administration put a lot of the viceroy's associates on trial, including several of Marzio Colonna's colleagues on the *collateral commission*, but Benavente sailed on undisturbed. By the following spring, the Naples correspondent of Ferdinando I de' Medici was writing to the grand duke in Florence, in April 1607, that

> the famine is so great throughout the kingdom that whole communities come to Naples and go around the city crying *bread, bread*, and so many poor people have fallen that I pray to God the plague doesn't take hold of this city, because people are dying in the streets and nobody's doing anything about it.

So M found the world's *richest and most vicious city* in a state of crisis, or most of its population. Beyond a few contracts and receipts for work he did in the city, no record of any kind would survive of the time M spent in Naples – where he stayed, who he knew, how he spent his non painting time. It was likely that he behaved for a while with more circumspection than usual. Apart from the Colonnas and their circle, which included the Spanish ruling group – and he'd hardly be mingling freely in their social life – M was on his own in the crowded, difficult and *disquieting* city. It wasn't the moment to be acting up. He was also very busy with commissions. Through Colonna connexions or because his fame had preceded him, M had all the work he could handle in Naples over the winter of late 1606 and early 1607.

> He immediately found work because his style and his name were already well known there,

wrote Bellori. No wonder his social life was low key, in the middle of famine. At least he seemed to have Cecco for company. By the time summer came he was off again, though not for long.

On October 6, within days if not hours of M's arriving, a Naples bank issued a payment order for two hundred ducats in the name of Niccolò Radolovich. It was for an altarpiece showing the

> Madonna and child surrounded by choirs of angels, plus saint Dominic and saint Francis embracing below, with saint Nicholas on the right and saint Vitus on the left.

Radolovich was a very prominent local businessman – a shipowner and trader of Croatian origin, related through his mother to the recent pope Gregory XIII – and it sounded like he had appallingly conventional taste. M had never done *choirs of angels* in his life. He refused to do them, and that'd been the whole trouble over his masterpiece *Mary dead*. And there were four saints to galvanize into life below. There was no record of M's thoughts as he banked the money the same day, or when he withdrew most of it three weeks later. But the promised painting was never traced or convincingly identified, although there were reasons – a later painting in Naples that seemed to be derived from it – for thinking it might've been done. The money was good and he needed it and he could hardly afford to mess around with his first client in Naples the way he had the duke of Modena and the relentless ambassador, when his life was falling to pieces in Rome. It still didn't sound like M, somehow. He'd undertaken to deliver it by December.

Though – beyond the few contractual fragments – there was no documentary record of M's life in Naples or the impact Naples had on him, there was the evidence of his work. That was unequivocal.

> Political paralysis, poverty, famine, epidemics, volcanic eruptions, earthquakes, Saracen raids, banditry, organized crime, bureaucratic corruption, crippling taxation, the arrogance of their Spanish rulers and the exploitation of the local barons – none of it got the better of the people.

The same went for M. His life and career were shattered, he was separated from the people and place he loved, he had to live under the hideous threat of a price on his head, he had the inner knowledge of himself as a killer, he'd lately hit the depth of isolation and loss – and now he rebounded with dazzling energy. Naples brought M back to life, and he showed it in painting one of his very greatest works.

M WAS MISSED in Rome. People were quietly working to gather evidence in his favour, although the chances of a pardon were slim. Ranuccio Tomassoni's wasn't a death that could be treated lightly, given his family's standing, and the Tomassoni family clearly blamed M alone for the death. Paul V was making a point of establishing a reputation as iron willed and inflexible in matters of law.

A document later turned up in the archives in which a surgeon testified on July 24 that he'd lately been treating a mattress maker's son called Francesco, who was now fully recovered from a head wound inflicted on him – and a note somebody else had added on the back of the page indicated that this certified recovery counted *in favour of M*. The two months elapsed between the date of the certified recovery and the fatal brawl made it look as though Francesco might've been a peripheral victim that day in campo Marzio. He was evidently in the Tomassoni camp, maybe a local youth enlisted by Giovan Francesco, and evidence of his recovery would count to minimize the case against M. Someone was clearly hunting for testimony useful to M. The document was dated, by a slip of the surgeon's pen or the scribe's, 1616 instead of 1606. For his friends and protectors, M's hash was far from settled. His shocking flight from Rome convulsed the art world. A rather surprizing consequence of this was the reappearance of the egregious Giovanni Baglione on centre stage. Most surprizingly of all, he was taking M to court again. *In absentia*. This time Baglione's accusation against M was rather more serious than it'd been three years earlier. This time Baglione was accusing M of premeditating a murder. He wasn't referring to the death of Ranuccio Tomassoni, although he clearly felt that recent event would make his own case more plausible. Baglione was now accusing M of trying to engineer his own murder.

In late October, two or three weeks after M had surfaced in Naples, Giovanni Baglione was on his way alone from an autumn Sunday afternoon mass at his local church of Trinità dei Monti – so he claimed to the police in the deposition he made from home some days later – when he was the victim of an assault. He'd been coming down the steps when his assailant, who'd been

> hiding behind a pillar, attacked me with an unsheathed sword and landed me a blow on the back that cut through my cloak and jacket as you can see ... and then aimed an overarm blow at my head, which landed flat on my left arm ... I drew my own sword and in so doing wounded a finger on my right hand [here the court recorder duly noted in

Latin the presence of a *small scar* on Baglione's right index finger] and then we exchanged several blows until my sword broke, because I believe he was wearing armour on his chest … and the people arrived and separated us.

Another painter testified that he'd seen the hooded assailant lying in wait on the steps for Baglione with his sword drawn, and identified him, as Baglione had, as a *beardless* youth named Carlo Bodello, whom the witness knew by sight. At the time Baglione, who got himself identified as *knight* on the court transcript, although Paul V wouldn't get around to making him a *knight of Christ* until the following year, was nearing the zenith of his prestige and was president of the painters' accademia di San Luca. The *outgoing* president – the election of the painters' new president three weeks earlier was in fact what Baglione wanted to tell the court about, even before he got to the assault. The attack, he said, had everything to do with it. Baglione identified the beardless youth who'd attacked him as an aspiring painter, a hatter's son who'd turned up at the academy three weeks earlier for the election of the new president. Baglione had tried to have him thrown out as a minor and not a member of the academy. Young Bodello had stood his ground,

> and he told me he was a painter like the others and wanted to stay … but I made sure he didn't vote.

Baglione said young Bodello had been set up and incited to attack him. Behind Bodello, he claimed, were Carlo Saraceni and Orazio Borgianni. Saraceni and Borgianni were two of M's earliest and most passionate followers among the young painters of Rome. Saraceni was the one who'd got a black poodle of his own to be like M. They'd been planning, Baglione claimed, to stack the meeting three weeks previously with supporters like the beardless hopeful Bodello, to swing the election of *a chief of their own kind* to the presidency. When they failed, they'd put the youngster up to this revenge attack. And if Saraceni and Borgianni were behind Bodello's attempt on his life, Baglione added, behind them stood M himself.

> … they did this because they were and are hostile to me and followers of M, who is my enemy – in fact I understand various people have given [Bodello] things and told him to murder me and take the news to M, who'd pay him well for it …

Baglione's servant testified that he'd been holding his master's horse outside during the election meeting when Bodello had come out at the end with Borgianni and Saraceni and another, and that he'd overheard Borgianni say to Bodello

> You didn't do what I wanted. That fucking prick was there ...

without knowing who the *fucking prick* might've been. The painters then went off together and he couldn't hear the rest of what they said because *I stayed there holding my boss's horse*. What followed Baglione's accusations, and how they weighed on M's standing with the pope – who was the only person now who could decide his fate – was lost in the archives. No records of further proceedings would be found. It was hard not to relate what was going on here in the election jockeying to a recent dispensation of the newly elected Paul V. The previous year the pope had granted the accademia di San Luca the annual right – on saint Luke's day – to free a condemned man. This gracious nod in the direction of the academy's seriousness and the stresses of the artistic temperament was suddenly a concession of some moment. It might've been designed with M in mind. His beatitude must've been kicking himself. Its usefulness, though, would depend on having the right man at the head of the organisation – a man who'd put in the right request. Not Giovanni Baglione or any such successor as Bagli-one might want to hand pick. In late 1606 the right man wasn't in place. The attempt to put him there clearly failed, but it did show that M now had a committed minority following within the official artists' body – which seemed to be riven by murderous internal tension – and that his followers were ready to do almost anything to get him back to Rome. It was that year that even M's old friend Prospero Orsi, who like M himself in his earlier years had never bothered with the academy before, took the trouble to get himself nominated. Anything to make up the numbers.

A HOUNDED MAN, M came to Naples, and Naples took him in.

> I was an hungred, and ye gave me meat: I was thirsty, and ye gave me drink: I was a stranger, and ye took me in:

naked, and ye clothed me: I was sick, and ye visited me: I
was in prison, and ye came unto me.

Kindness to strangers was a duty of Christian charity and it'd lately
taken on a peculiar weight. The counter reformation held out the
hope that you might be saved in the next life through your good works
in this. Carefully dosed social assistance was also a way of keeping a
lid on social unrest among the scary new masses of urban poor, and
nowhere were the poor more numerous or more assertive than in
Naples. In Naples the words from Matthew's gospel had been the
founding text for seven young aristocrats, younger sons of some of
the city's better families, still in their twenties, when in 1601 they'd
set up an organisation to give comfort to the poor, the sick, the dying,
the imprisoned. The growing mass of destitute in Naples afforded
plenty of scope for social work. The young men's original intent had
been to undergo a little personal mortification by dirtying their own
hands every Friday in the most desperate corners of the city, like the
hospital for the *incurables*. Five years on their original intention, probably to their relief, had been overtaken by the very success of their
initiative. They'd attracted a lot of followers and a lot of money. The
project became institutionalized as a charity fund the year after they
started and gathered the approval of Felipe III and pope Paul V. A
large amount of money was at first mostly put into a hospital for the
destitute and then into assisting prisoners, rescuing slaves and other
such work. By 1606 they'd built their own church, and they held their
first meeting in September there, a few weeks before M arrived in the
city.

Some time in October or November of 1606, the young gentlemen commissioned M to do a painting for their main altar. The fee
was four hundred ducats, double what he'd got from Radolovich. The
nobles wanted a major statement from a major painter. The *pio monte
della misericordia* was a cutting edge institution of social assistance and
it had to show. The theme was the *Seven works of mercy* – the six named
by Christ in Matthew's gospel, plus burial of the dead, which was a
real hygiene issue in Naples. Dogs were chewing the corpses of prisoners dumped outside the city jail, and that wasn't the worst of
it. And since Neapolitans and the people of the south were greatly
exposed to Islamic raids on the coast – Capri had been torched by
a Turkish landing party – an eighth item was added to the programme
of good works, the ransoming of Christian slaves from the infidel.
The ten thousand foreign slaves in Naples weren't a concern, and in
any case slaves weren't, it seemed, part of M's brief. He did, though,

have to show all seven other activities in the space of a single canvas. It was an unprecedented demand in Italian art, and sounded like an iconographic nightmare.

By 9 January 1607 M had delivered the finished painting and collected his fee. In an astonishingly short time he'd completed a work that was technically more complex and difficult than any he'd taken on since the *Matthew* side paintings. He'd finished his greatest public painting since *Mary dead* in the same brilliantly improvisational manner of those earlier breakthrough works – x rays would reveal the *Seven works* as the first canvas since *Matthew killed* where he'd radically rethought his composition in the process of painting it. It was as if, coming to Naples, he'd recovered his young man's flair for seizing new solutions on the wing. The *Seven works of mercy* was a long way from the muffled tragedy of *Mary dead*. It was full of the same wild crowded life he'd packed into his début *Matthew* paintings six years earlier. As a solution to the problem of an unusually difficult commission, the *Seven works* was brilliant. As an image of life refound, it was a marvellous intuition of the street genius of Naples. After the monumental, devastated stasis of *Mary dead*, *Seven works* seemed irrepressibly in movement, and like all things in movement, strangely provisional. The works of mercy were fleeting.

Naples was and is a city

> that transforms any collective occasion into a theatrical rite – funerals, executions, public processions or neighbourhood brawls.

Nobody could've responded more keenly to this enhancement of the everyday than the painter who saw Christian *history* embodied in his friends and neighbours, playing out *actions* he painted *from life*. Or been more aware of the extraordinary changes wrought by Neapolitan light and darkness on the city's spaces – the blackness of the narrow alleys, the close unlit interiors, then shot through at a certain moment of the day by a dazzling oblique shaft of blinding Mediterranean sun or brought suddenly alive at night by the flare of a lit torch. As the Neapolitans spilt out of the cupboards and stairwells where they slept like litters of puppies and made the courtyards and alleyways and tiny sloping piazzas their living room, who more than the painter of *Matthew called* would've been alive to the promiscuous interplay of inside and outside, public and private, in which every moment and act of human existence was observed by others, became a *spectacle? Dramatize, dramatize*, urged Henry James. Every Neapolitan did that from birth.

So M did the *Seven works of mercy* as street life and as theatre. Into the closed black ambiguousness of an alley corner at night – say, the corner of via Tribunali and vico dei Zuroli, a few metres from where the painting would hang – he crowded his protagonists. This was mercy as everyday life, a mercy without pity, pathos, gratitude. Mercy as the satisfaction of basic needs. Mercy, indeed, as business. At an unseen doorway on the left, a stocky rednosed host welcomed a traveller with a pilgrim's cloak and stave and scallop shell on his widebrimmed hat, an emaciated redbearded figure who might've been Christ incognito. *I was a stranger, and ye took me in.* The host's rather northern European look made you wonder whether he mightn't've been the German land-lord of the locanda del Cerriglio, where M later stayed in Naples and where he was maybe living now. Behind mine host a bearded local or Samson in the desert drank water greedily from an ass's jawbone that might've been a wineskin, a coarseness that horrified Bellori. *I was thirsty, and ye gave me drink.* Below these, in the bottom left hand corner were two inevitable Neapolitan figures, an almost invisible cripple crouching in the shadows with his crutch, and a shirtless barefoot *lazzarone* sitting on the ground. A young *bravo* in a plumed hat, a bil-lowing sleeved apricot silk shirt with a broad black stripe and frilled cuffs and gloves, and fully armed, was hacking through his long cloak with his sword, dividing it between the two at his feet. Swords could be put to good uses too. *I was naked, and ye clothed me.* He was a more thoughtful reworking – after a six year gap and in a painting where everyone was coming across as rather tense – of the *bravi* in *Matthew called* and he crystallized that early memory running all through the *Seven works,* as the nude *lazzarone* was a thinner and more finely muscled relation of the foreground nudes of *Matthew killed.* The *bravo* stood, in a classless way, for the young men who'd set up the flourish-ing charity enterprise, and his sad face looked like a memory of M's hallucinated and introspective moonlight *John's* of three years earlier, the inward gaze of a young man with the world weighing on his shoul-ders. *I was sick, and ye visited me.* There was another pilgrim behind him, hidden except for an ear catching the light and the tip of his staff. These figures on the left foreground were crowded, seven of them jammed into a quarter of the canvas. Space opened out behind them on the right, where through the barred window of the prison – the real prison was a few yards down via Tribunali – the starving old bearded prisoner sucked milk from his daughter's breast, as she hitched up the rest of her bodice as best she could and looked round over her shoulder, lips shaping themselves into a Neapolitan preventive verbal strike at anybody who might feel like making a comment. *I was an hungred, and ye gave me meat … I was in prison, and ye came unto me.* Milk, actually, a couple of drops of which had splashed on to the old man's beard and were running down the hairs, *just as happens in everyday life.*

The noise the prisoner's daughter had heard behind her was a labourer holding up the bare feet of a corpse. The livid soles of the dead feet were appearing around the corner, followed by a deacon holding up a torch and himself half emerged into sight around the corner. The body beyond the feet and behind the wall was an unseen memory of Lena laid out in *Mary dead* – the angle was the same, even the place on the canvas. *The noncanonical act of burying the dead.* The picture's main light came from the front left, but the deacon's torch now lit the scene from the back, opening up the narrow space between the buildings, creating the depth in a tunnel of legs and feet running from the sprawling *lazzarone*'s, through the *bravo*'s, and the daughter's to the undertaker's at the back. The phosphorescent flare of the torch at the back, the glaring reflection on the priest's chanting face and his white surplice – whose folds were like the folds of David's shirt in the painting from Paliano, as the glint of the *bravo*'s drawn sword by the cripple's face was like David's blade – struck Bellori for the way *it lights up the colour and enlivens the composition.* It was, apart from the lantern he'd held up to *Christ taken,* the only time M put a light source inside one of his paintings, and it might've surprized him to know how many of his followers would later fill their dark interiors with torches, lamps, candles, fires.

Everyone at this street corner was wholly taken up in his or her own business – the endless task in the Spanish south of looking after number one. Most eyes were lowered, no eyes met in this grimly solip-sistic busyness. The daughter was sullenly performing a filial duty as she gave her father milk, the *bravo* was lost in his own thoughts as he offered his cloak, mine host was hustling up business and the cadaver's transporters were long dulled to mortality. Nothing, really, could've been less uplifting. They were all, though, being watched. Unseen above them – taking up most of the space in the canvas's upper half – was a turbine of spread wings, bare shoulders and damp bed linen. Two angels – curlyhaired local *guaglioni,* nude teenagers locked in embrace, one with his arms around the other, the second cleaving the air in flight, were filling the space between the buildings with their wingspans, suspended heavily in the close air above the human anxiety below. The attentively watching boys, who in later times might've screeched up on a Vespa, were themselves being looked down on from a window or balcony lost in the darkness, by a young woman who was gazing down on the street scene in the manner of young housewives and holding a lively boy child, writhing away from her and captivated by the street life below. You'd hardly have guessed, but this was the Madonna. She and the acrobatic angels, it suddenly struck you, weren't so much unseen as ignored by the participants in the mundane struggle for life below. They were a usual part of the scene. Never had huge spread wings on boys' backs looked so, well, *everyday*, as they did here tangled with the drying bed sheets, wingtips peeping through the jail bars and the spans casting a huge shadow on the wall.

The thing about Naples, M had understood, was that reality wasn't necessarily what it was elsewhere. This was the city where, after crushing the last rebellion over bread prices of twenty years earlier, the Spanish viceroy had ordered a monument erected near the church M was painting for – on the site where the demolished house of the revolt's leader had been – a monument that displayed the severed heads and hands of all the rebellion's leaders. A contemporary account reported that after the terrible end of the hunger revolt

> they say a fiery cart rolls through the city, and a man on horseback with black torches who comes out of the prison and passes the place of the monument and the heads cry out.

The angels – another memory of *Matthew*, this time of the angel in the second altarpiece – were clearly local boys, one model's tensed arm and flattened hand resting on solid air as he posed, and the mother and child had a breathcatching beauty of a kind that flourished briefly everywhere in those dank alleys, though the girl giving milk below was finer and more real. This Christ child was the best child M ever did, maybe the finest in his amalgam of beauty and realism, of all the thousands Italian painters had produced. He was a Neapolitan child who by the age of – say – three had seen it all already, whom nothing in human life or death could surprize – innocent and eager nonetheless, lively, energetic and *amused*. When life was theatre, its participants learnt early to appreciate good entertainment, and that went for the holy family too. These onlookers were so seamlessly a part of this earthly and urban scene, Mary and child, that it was surprizing to discover that they might've been added in, and not part of the original conception at all. And in one earlier version, mother and child were placed lower over the angels' arms and the child was to the left of the mother. This was a run of the mill celestial apparition that M had been forced to include by the governors and he must've made them so small and inconspicuous because he hated doing it, being precisely the same instance of sickening devotional unreality he'd earlier refused to put into the *Pilgrims' Madonna* and *Mary dead* – until he revolutionized the holy mother and child by making them into earthly figures at the first floor balcony, peering down precipitously into the street, linked to the drama below by the way the child's enthralled excited gaze reflected what he saw and held the confusion together. It was improvisational genius. It thrilled his clients, made realistic sense of the mother and child and unified the theatre of the scene below.

Down in the street the confusion got so confusing that M had reworked that too. The drinker who disgusted Bellori had originally been at the centre of the canvas, so the man holding the corpse – whose shadowed face looked strongly like M's own – was backing right into him. Shifting him to the far left eliminated the confusion of the two groups and afforded the needed light reflected by the drinker's bare chest. On the right, M made the irruption on to the scene of the deacon and the corpse more dramatic by thickening the prison wall to block out a large part of the figure he'd already painted. The priest's whole face and shoulders had been visible at first – now he was just heaving into view around the corner. The effect was like the drama of Christ's appearance in *Matthew called*, which M had heightened by hiding him behind the added figure of Peter. M shifted the milk girl's pose as well. None of these changes below involved the kind of radical rethinking M had done in *Matthew killed*. They were traces rather of a fine tuning that was likely made necessary by the speed at which he was working, a series of adjustments to the basic structure to enhance clarity and drama of a very big canvas – bigger than *Mary dead* and his biggest so far – and a hugely complex composition with sixteen figures in related but distinct actions.

For once, the clients loved their altarpiece and thought it worth every ducat of the four hundred they'd forked out. The *Seven works of mercy* caused such a sensation in Naples that six years later the governors of the confraternity noted with immense satisfaction they'd several times been offered two thousand ducats for M's canvas, but they formally resolved that *it can never be sold for any price and must always be kept in the church*. A few years later they decided not to let it even be copied. They were getting edgy because the conde de Villamediana, one of the most powerful figures in the viceroy's court, the head of a gay camarilla and a collector of M's work – he was later murdered in a sexual intrigue in Madrid – had his eye on it, and his request to have a *copy* made had been laden with innuendo about the right thing to do. Its impact on art in Naples was immense, although in another strange parallel with the great *Matthew* works in Rome, the painting was so dark and so badly lit in the church it was done for – a church which was replaced later in the century by the octagonal lantern church where the painting's been ever since, as the governors determined – that visitors would always be complaining that they couldn't see what was going on. When they described it, they usually got things wrong, which was understandable. By the time the marquis de Sade, who showed a lively interest in M's work most of the time, looked in on it in 1776, he found the painting *singularly blackened* and *not worth seeing*.

Seven works revolutionized painting south of Rome and it shifted the centre of gravity of Italian painting to Naples. The *Seven works of mercy* was unlike any of M's other paintings. Its animation – the variety of impulses feeding into its harmonious sense of movement – its passionately ranging attentiveness to the conditions of life, its bravura heightening – anticipating the whole of the baroque in a single canvas, yet flowing back into an enhanced sense of the real – shot through with a dry and loving humour – the wholly unsolemn and sometimes subversive way it shared in the generosity it was celebrating – were unique. *The greatest religious painting of the seventeenth century.* Maybe you could strike *religious*. A fleeting, vivid dreamlike night scene, *no more hallucinatory than Naples itself.* It was the painting of a man who'd come back to life. For M, although he'd never do anything like *Seven works* again, it marked the start of a new phase, the freeing up of all the stored experience he'd gained doing his great Roman *history* canvases, the *Matthew* paintings and *Mary dead* above all, so that he could now produce, as he would, a series of large and complex histories very fast and with great improvisational flair, working from memory more often than models, not simply living off the accumulated technical capital of his Roman years, but investing that ease and mastery in daring new visual experiments. Even the smaller paintings that looked like hurried assemblages of figures and poses from the repertory in his mind – and sometimes, as the pressures grew, were – in the very speed and economy of their making were stabbing at essentials and preparing the ground for the racked, stripped, bleak enormousness of his very last *histories*.

THE VICEROY OF Naples, Juan Alfonso Pimentel de Herrera, conde de Benavente, wasn't too distracted by the people dying of hunger in the streets of Naples that winter, or too taken up by his speculations on the grain shortage, or too worried by the corruption trials in January of a lot of senior members of his entourage to notice what was going on in the art world, and the brilliant new work M had done for the *monte di misericordia*. The conde had lately been involved in restoring the tomb of saint Andrew, which was in the crypt of Amalfi cathedral just down the coast from Naples. Andrew was a favourite saint of the Spanish royal family's and this was a high priority project ordered by Felipe III. By 1607 the altar was almost finished. Andrew and his crucifixion were on the conde de Benavente's mind that winter. Particularly the story of how the ancient apostle, tied up and left to die, had gone on preaching to an audience of twenty thousand and stirred them to insurrection. To fend off the riot the proconsul ordered his untying but Andrew wasn't to be cheated of his martyrdom. He'd been saved when the workman taking him down had been paralyzed in the act and Andrew had died anyway. At least the riot was avoided. It must've seemed a vaguely comforting outcome to the viceroy, as new disturbances loomed in Naples that spring, and this was the scene he now commissioned M to paint.

M did a full length canvas with the old man expiring tied on the cross plumb in the middle – though at an angle to the picture plane – a workman mounted on a ladder beside him like an electricity repairman. Their feet were around eye level, and the other figures in the picture – the bearded proconsul in rakish plumed hat and upper body armour, an old crone and two barely seen extra workmen – were all cut off at the waist. It was, basically, a very hurried repertory piece. The woozy old saint was faintly unconvincing, if you had in mind the tremendous dying Peter M'd done five years earlier, though his raddled and cruelly extended old body was finely done, with what seemed an unusual attention to the raised arteries visible above the groin. The workman was a faceless cipher, his clothes a few brief slashes. His colleagues were mainly identifiable as an ear and a gaping mouth respectively. The watching proconsul – glinting armoured shoulder, hand on haunch, evanescent plumes – was attractively alert, like an architect on a job site, watching the labourers struggle with an intractable reality.

M'd changed his mind on the old woman watching. She was one of those hard lean peasant women past the age of childbearing M was noticing more and more. The first had been almost a caricature, the old servant in the Fillide *Judith*, waiting to gather up the severed head in an old cloth, the moment it came free of the neck. That was eight years ago now. People always thought these old women in M's paintings were derived from ancient portrait busts, as though they needed to be dignified by classical precedent and there weren't live originals all around him, exactly as there'd been for Roman sculptors. Old women had come back into his art as the old kneeling pilgrim and old grandmother Anne in two of his Lena paintings, and again as the shadowy old serving woman in the *Meal at Emmaus* he'd lately done in hiding. They were starting to engage M's interest as much as his old men. They lacked, on the whole, the old men's carefully rendered upright frowning ruffle haired dignity – attractiveness almost. The old women verged on the grotesque. To the world they were objects of contempt and ridicule, their usefulness long gone. But for M they had a compact and irreducible vitality, a lean beady eyed alertness and had come through so much that they seemed indestructible or expressions of an endless capacity for hurt. As he moved south, M was going to find more and more of these old women for his paintings. The one in *Andrew killed* at least still had her teeth. When he first painted her, M had her standing with her hands clasped under her chin. Removing them as he did exposed a big goitre on the woman's throat. Goitre was a common disease among the poor in the country around Naples – and around the Caravaggio of M's childhood – and if the devotional sense of the deformity was to remind people of Andrew's protection of people with throat ailments, its visual force brought you up against a human and social reality that wasn't only emblematic. Deciding to show the goitre was more than an iconographic choice.

The viceroy too was hugely pleased with the painting M knocked off for him. He took it back to Spain when he repatriated in 1610, as Bellori knew, and hung it in the Benavente palace in Valladolid. When the family collection was inventoried in 1653, it was identified as an *M original* and valued at fifteen hundred ducats, far higher than the price put on the works by Rubens, El Greco and Bosch in the same collection. The valuation was made by a friend of Diego Velázquez, and it looked as though M's perfunctory work might've been known to his greatest follower. Benavente had another painting identified as M's in the same inventory, but it disappeared. He wasn't the only one to return home to Spain with work by M. The conde de Villamediana, who'd unsuccessfully tried for the *Seven works*, left with – Bellori claimed – two of M's paintings, one a *Boy holding an orange blossom*, another work that disappeared, and *the half figure of David*. Villamediana repatriated in 1617, after spending a lot of his six years in Italy putting together a big collection of work by *good men* to take back to Spain. In 1615 he was reported to have spent twenty thousand scudi on paintings in Naples and Rome. He didn't have long to enjoy his harvest. Five years after he got home Villamediana was murdered in Madrid, and his painting of *David* by M was bought the next year by the prince of Wales, who became Charles I of England and was beheaded.

This *David* was M's last painting of Cecco. He did the half figure in early 1607 on a wooden panel over an old mannerist allegory tipped on its side. A lot had changed since the days of the other devastated and darkness infested image of Cecco as David he'd so recently made in hiding. There was *a moral clearing* in the work M was doing now, after the *murkiness of the senses* in the other David. The clouds had passed. In the new version David was invested by a strong light coming from the left and a weaker light from the right, and they restored to his face and body a clarity of outline and a rounded sense of solidity and a glint to his now wide open eyes. The darkness of the background – a browner, warmer black – was defining, not invasive. M no longer saw his own in Goliath's more generic head – if anything it now looked like an enlarged imagining of Cecco's own as it'd be in maturity. There were parallels in the pose and shape of the head, and the hair was the same, but it was too lightly featured to be fearful in itself or for the likeness to stir more than a small subliminally troubling recognition. The severed head in this painting was a neutral kind of trophy, and there was a kind of weary fulfilment in the youth, as if he were returning from a day's hunting. The dillybag slung across his chest and the heavy sword resting on his shoulders and the air of radiant health – the colour in the mouth, the glinting eye – enhanced the idea of outdoor activity. Sport was in the air here, activity good in itself. No points were being made, or fears expressed. David's clothes were done with the same rapid simplifying economy M was showing in all his paintings now, perfecting the art of the effortless crease. The play of light on the skin – the soft shadows made by tendons, bones, veins, muscles under the surface – was a sensuous marvel. Cecco was painted a little from below, leaning slightly away from you and above the looming out thrust head, and his image was ever so slightly glamorized, like a Herbert List photo of a German boy between the wars. This was a tense, athletic revisiting of the Del Monte chamber art of ten years earlier. It was M's last study of Cecco and like the earlier painting of *Narcissus* it was out of series – really it was out of time, looking neither forward nor back, unique.

M in the spring of 1607 was moving with effortless newfound energy and speed through a series of utterly diverse commissions that could only be related by subtle links of style. Outwardly, in theme and treatment, they all seemed quite unconnected. He was taking on anything, and not everything worked. The remarked on new lucidity of image reflected M's clearsighted urgency about recovering the ground he'd lost, remaking his reputation, gathering his forces for a new assault on Rome. M knew the Ranuccio Tomassoni killing had been the final act of a year or more of disintegration in his life, and he knew it'd shown in his work. Delays, haste, broken promises, failures to deliver – these were the failings that'd counted, and they explained the manic professionalism of these months in Naples. He did one particularly deadly and alien job, with the same clarity he'd put into *David* – it only partly came off as a painting and it certainly failed to please whoever it was pitched at. By the end of the summer it'd ended up on the open market, and since it had the unappealing look of a rejected custom job for someone else, nobody bought it. Fame's appeal had its limits.

This new altarpiece was a mysterious unrecorded commission that seemed to have parallels with the elusive Radolovich job. He'd arrived in Naples and immediately won that commission for a big altarpiece – theme and payment were documented but the painting itself never found. Now for an unknown buyer and an unknown altar at an unknown price he did a huge *Rosary Madonna*. The painting was a brave or cynical attempt to kick life into a formal full dress piece of counter reformation iconography – much like the one Radolovich had wanted and spelt out in his contract, but with different saints and theme – and deciding whether M had succeeded or not depended on what part of the painting you were looking at. Several things about the painting pointed to a link with his rescuers the Colonnas. And a request from them, in the circumstances, would've been something he couldn't refuse.

The picture showed, under a great swag of knotted red curtain that was a formulaic recycling of the one that'd hung so powerfully over *Mary dead*, a virgin and child sitting high up, on some kind of unseen throne, flanked by saints Dominic and Peter the martyr in beards and monks' habits, and below, kneeling and clustering around Dominic, hands grasping for rosaries, were three barefoot Neapolitan *lazzari*. Kneeling by them, looking directly up at Mary and the baby, were a young mother and her small child, and, almost squeezed out of the side of the picture and looking at neither the holy mother and child nor at the saints but glancing over his shoulder at you, was a black clad white ruffed middleaged man looking as though he'd commissioned the painting. The painting was an heroic and nearly successful attempt to make this hieratic counter reformation pyramid of power live. The naked Christ child was clearly bored, for starters. His gaze was swivelling off field and he looked about to squirm out of his distracted mother's grasp and scramble down. The two gaunt ascetic saints – Peter martyr had a helpful identifying axe cleft in his skull and a few splashes of blood on his cowl like a lapel tag – were both in power huddles, Dominic with the Madonna herself, who was making a finger jabbing point as he leant toward her, holding out his rosaries like a distracted street vendor. Peter was indicating the Madonna to someone out of frame and surrounded by two shadowy advisers, one of them a marvellously sexless figure in a hood whose frowning attentive face seemed to be floating free against the darkness like a mask. The distinguished bald figure was squeezing sideways into the frame, shuffling acrosss on his knees and glancing back over his shoulder to make sure he could be seen, in a way that emphasized – if you were so lazy or ingenuous that you hadn't already noticed – that the whole setup was a carefully staged photo opportunity *ante litteram*. He was hanging on to Dominic's cowl in case they got parted in the jostling, when their closeness mattered for the picture. They all stood there making their emphatic gestures, as in the group pic at a conference of foreign ministers – except for Dominic, who clearly felt a dork, standing there with his rosaries.

In the lower foreground, beneath the dark suits – and even the Madonna was power dressing for the occasion in navy blue – were *the people*, or at least five selected representatives, grouped on their knees in careful eager spontaneity, gesturing toward the dangling rosaries. Nobody painted a bare foot's filthy sole like M, got the right gradations of impacted dust. These figures were faking it but at least they were real, and they brought with them some of the dirt and movement from the alley of *Seven works* – like the young *lazzaro* on the right, under his thick black hair and sunburnt face, catching the light on the white skin and muscles of his naked shoulder and arm and the heavy dun folds of the huge blanket he was otherwise wrapped in, down to his dusty feet. On her knees opposite him, in dull green, gold and white, with pinned up hair, looking like the weeping girl in *Mary dead*, her head leaning back into the picture plane for a better view and gaze directed above the staged tableau at the other mother and child in the room, was the young woman with her kneeling toddler, a few months older than the son of man on his mother's knee. These two were the finest thing in the picture, the only kneelers seen in real detail – the mother's protective hand, the intricacies of their apron strings, the child's bulging diaper and heartbreaking little shoes.

The interlocking and overlapping differently angled pyramids of people, with the Christ child right in the centre, the vivid clarity of M's images and the way the glances and gestures bounced your gaze, pinball like, around the structure until you hit the virgin and child and the lights flashed – all this persuaded you at moments that the thing was really alive. The visual game let you forget for a moment the ghastly exaltation of priestly power that determined the structure – the people all grovelling here in the dirt before not even the virgin – only the young mother noticed *her* – but a grim monk, and clamouring for holy beads. The faces were as sharply observed here as the ones in *Seven works* – they were the same faces, some of them, Dominic was maybe the drinker recycled, and the Madonna of the rosary herself was certainly, with a little added bodyweight, the girl with the beestung lower lip who'd last been seen breast feeding her jailed dad through the bars. There was enough life here, trapped in the diabolical intricacy of the visual structure, a crayfish pot for the eye, almost to convince, but not quite, because when you got to the heart of the matter there was nothing human there. All you found was doctrine. The dazzling symmetry and the cleanly plastic modelling of the figures were sinister simplifications after the stubborn randomness of *Seven works*. That painting had been the exhilaratingly provisional outcome of a battle between the painter's organizing mind and the intractable vitality of his material. The only reworking in the *Rosary Madonna* had been an adjustment to make the Madonna bigger and raise her even higher above the crowd. Even the *Pilgrims' Madonna*, which anticipated this sellout three years earlier, was rigorously, messily human by comparison. Bellori never saw the *Rosary Madonna*, which was in Antwerp when he got to Naples in 1661. He would've loved it.

Nobody ever worked out for sure who the man in the ruff was, looking out of the canvas, who M did this painting for or why it was put on the market a few months later. The red curtain was tied to a massive fluted column, a *colonna*, and this brought to mind the mighty family that'd saved M's neck. The Colonnas had a column as their family emblem. They were also particularly attached to the cult of the Madonna of the rosary, who they felt had intervened to enable Marcantonio Colonna's victory over the Turks at Lepanto. A sister of Costanza, the marchesa of Caravaggio, and cardinal Ascanio Colonna, had married the Neapolitan Antonio Carafa, duke of Mondragone, who'd also fought at Lepanto with his father in law Marcantonio, and in 1606 their son Luigi Carafa Colonna became the owner of the *Magdalen* M had painted at Paliano in the image of Lena. The thirty fifth anniversary of the victory at Lepanto was coming up in October, a week after M's own thirty fifth birthday. The Colonna family chapel in the church of San Domenico Maggiore was dedicated to the Madonna of the rosary, which made it almost inevitable that M had done this painting for the Colonnas, quite likely as a present, in thanks for what they'd done for him the summer before. It wasn't one they wanted and the painting was put up for sale straight away. An unsolicited gift might've clashed with the family's own plans for the chapel. They might've simply preferred the cash – Marzio Colonna for one was going through a bad patch financially. They might've been uneasy over a public reminder of the family's link with the painter. They weren't art people, the Colonnas, though they did hang on to the Lena *Magdalen*, which stayed in the family for centuries. Evidently they knew what they liked. So who was the man in the ruff? He was too old to be Marzio Colonna, who died at the age of thirty four, or Luigi Carafa, who was barely forty that year. It looked like Marcantonio Colonna himself, the victor of Lepanto.

On September 15 the Naples agent of that great collector duke Vincenzo I Gonzaga of Mantua – who had what was probably the best collection of paintings in Italy at the time and had people constantly on the lookout for new collectibles – mentioned in a letter to the duke that

> I've also seen a few good things done here by M that'll be up for sale ...

This was followed up ten days later by a letter from the Flemish painter Frans Pourbus, who was also acting for the duke in art acquisitions, telling the duke about

> two stunning paintings by M's hand, one's a rosary done as an altarpiece – it's eighteen palms high and they won't take less than four hundred ducats for it ... I didn't want to make an offer without knowing your highness's intention, but they've promised me not to let go of it until they're advised of your highness's pleasure ...

The duke didn't come at the offer. He may have smelt a rat in the price and the sweet talk, and he wasn't wrong, because the *Rosary Madonna* by then likely belonged to a couple of friends of Pourbus, the painters Finson and Vinck. These were two other Flemish painters then running a studio in Naples who were also friends of M's – someone later recalled Vinck in a letter as a *great friend* of M's and Finson copied M's *Magdalen* and his *Andrew killed* in M's studio. Finson took the *Rosary Madonna* to Amsterdam several years later, along with the other work of M's that Pourbus had tried to flog to the duke, a new version of *Judith & Holofernes* M had done in Naples. That painting later disappeared, but a copy seemed to survive in Naples. As for the *Rosary Madonna*, Peter Paul Rubens and some others bought it after Finson's death for a church in Antwerp.

16

NAPLES & MALTA 1607

Crown of thorns II
Whipping I
Whipping II
Salomè I
Jerome III

I N THE SUMMER of 1607, when he was offered the *Rosary Madonna* for his collection, Vincenzo I Gonzaga maybe felt he'd lashed out enough already on work by M that year. In 1607 the Flemish painter Peter Paul Rubens, six years younger than M and a rising star in European art, was working in Rome. He was painting the high altarpiece for Santa Maria in Vallicella, the church that held M's painting of *Christ's burial*. M's picture was working on his mind, and a couple of years later he did his own version of it. Rubens was also keeping up a sideline in advising Gonzaga on art to buy there, as the painter Pourbus was doing in Naples. This was something Rubens had been doing ever since the duke had engaged him seven years earlier to paint portraits in a series of beautiful women that figured large in the Gonzaga enthusiasm for art. Rubens had been in Rome since 1605 on his current sojourn, and had known that Laerzio Cherubini was stuck with *Mary dead*, since the barefoot Carmelites refused to have M's painting in their church. Rubens had seen the painting himself and thought it M's masterpiece. Early in 1607 he looked at it again *and liked it even better.* He urged Gonzaga's ambassador to buy it for the collection in Mantua. The ambassador got a second opinion, took a look himself, and wrote to the duke's chancellor in Mantua. He personally wasn't entirely convinced, but then he wasn't an expert on art. As a diplomat he did know a thing or two about reputations.

> I've been convinced more by the others' opinions than my own impression of it, but I'm not up to understanding the hidden technical qualities that make the picture so much admired ... but the painter is one of the most famous doing modern work in Rome and this picture's thought one of his best ... and it's true you can see some bits of it are quite exquisite ...

He forgot to mention the price, and wrote again a week later

> It slipped my mind to tell you the price ... has been settled as two hundred and eighty scudi – we did what we could to improve on that but the owner says he won't even think of losing a single penny of the price he paid for it. The painting's quality argues for it – it's lost none of its standing from being out of the painter's hands and rejected by the church it was given to ...

Two eighty plus twenty as a fee for Rubens, *who's gone to a lot of trouble to swing this deal for us*, made three hundred scudi. The deal was done, but the painting wasn't handed over for another month – *I was afraid they were making a copy*, wrote the ambassador, who had to apply a little diplomatic pressure through ecclesiastical channels. It wasn't dispatched to Mantua for another fortnight, because

> All this week I've had to put the painting we've just bought on display, so the painters from the university could see it. A lot of them have come to look, including some of the most famous and they were very curious. This picture's been talked about a lot, but until now almost nobody's been able to see it. It's certainly been a great satisfaction to let them enjoy it to the full, because it's been praised as a remarkable work of art ...

So, in M's forced absence and two years after its rejection, *Mary dead* finally received the acclaim and wonder of his Roman rivals. Their interest was all the more intense in that they knew it'd be a while before Rome saw any new work by the wonder of the age. The ambassador had no reason to play down the art world's acclaim, but it sounded unanimous in Rome now, as it hadn't been in the fourteen years M worked there. It'd taken a great painter to recognize another. M's reputation was soaring. It was as if he'd died already.

For a Roman art collector M might as well have been dead. If there were no more paintings coming on to the market, it hardly mattered what your resources were, what you were prepared to pay. M was now out of reach to all his old Roman clients – none bought anything more from him once he was in Naples, unless Vincenzo Giustiniani got a single painting. Ottavio Costa got the *Meal in Emmaus* painted when M was hiding at Paliano, and that was the end of it. Rubens had special access and that enabled the Mantua coup – even then it hadn't been easy to get the painting. Not for love or money was the story. People were sitting on what they had. So if you were a neophyte collector, unlimited financial resources were no use at all in helping you find work by the most exciting and famous painter of the day. It would've been mortifying to have money and nothing to spend it on – and never more than in the fortnight in April when the entire Roman art world was jostling for a first and last glimpse of M's greatest work. This was now the situation of cardinal Scipione Borghese. He was already thirty and only just getting started. He had a great art collection to build and only the rest of his uncle's life to do it in. And M's work was out of reach. If he could ever have imagined allowing himself to entertain such a thought, there might've been moments when Scipione Borghese really resented his uncle's implacable and unforgiving hostility toward the man who'd done that subtly mocking portrait of him. Then again, having the power of someone's life or death in your hands gave you a certain leverage. If he didn't know it already, Scipione Borghese didn't take long to learn, as he inexorably gathered judicial powers into his own hands over the next three years.

Scipione Borghese had already, of course, brought off his own little coup in the rejected altarpiece department. He'd bought the *Grooms' Madonna* at what amounted to half price after it was rejected from Saint Peter's. It wasn't clear, in that murky episode, whether the definitive refusal of M's painting had come before or after May 28, when M killed Tomassoni. Maybe it was the later thought of hanging a new altarpiece in Saint Peter's by a man now wanted for homicide that was the problem. The likelihood remained, whatever the exact sequence of cause and event was through April, May and June of 1606, that Scipione Borghese manipulated events to get his hands on M's last Roman painting for a song. Borghese had already realized when he got M's *Jerome* in 1605 that it helped a collector to have a hold over an artist. He'd only been a cardinal for a couple of months when he got *Jerome*, and had, so to speak, lost his collector's virginity in that episode. When you were the cardinal nephew and secretary of state there were many ways you might gain and use the power you needed over artists, and over the coming years Scipione Borghese would be exploring all of them with flair and resourcefulness and a steely unyielding determination that in this field at least would match his uncle's. It helped that for art's sake he was prepared to cut corners.

Now, the anguish of seeing *Mary dead* whisked off to Mantua at the end of April – why hadn't he thought of that painting before? – why hadn't people *told* him about it? – urged Scipione Borghese to decisive action. His mind turned to the blithely unsuspecting Giuseppe Cesari, *knight of Christ* and painter to the popes, the kings of France and Spain and the holy Roman emperor in Prague. The cavalier d'Arpino was at the apex of his prestige and wealth. He was currently working on the mosaics decorating the dome of Saint Peter's. He'd been busy on this for the last four years, but not so busy that he hadn't had time to buy a palace on the Corso that he was about to have completely made over, or have another palace built in his home town Arpino. Scipione Borghese knew a few things about Giuseppe Cesari, because he was a favourite painter of the Borghese family as he'd been of the Aldobrandinis. He knew about the *cavaliere*'s art collection of a hundred and six paintings and he almost certainly knew about his hobby collection of arquebuses. The arquebuses were, technically speaking, prohibited weapons, so it was, technically speaking, quite correct of the judicial authorities to arrest Cesari in a whirlwind operation, confiscate his goods and sentence him to death. This'd be a shock to anyone. It certainly demoralized Giuseppe Cesari, who liked to cut a dash on horseback with his sword but wasn't really a man of steel.

Cesari's art never recovered, lost all its *élan* after he was flung into jail. At least the death sentence was suspended when Cesari did what he knew he had to do. On 4 May 1607, a few days after *Mary dead* left Rome for Mantua, Cesari signed his collection of paintings over to the apostolic chamber, along with a *pro forma* fine of five hundred scudi for possession of prohibited weapons. After duly deliberating on the matter, pope Paul V decided three months later that all of Cesari's paintings should be transferred to the care of the cardinal nephew Scipione Borghese,

> even when they were by the hands of the most excellent painters and whatever price and value they reached.

There was a lot for Borghese to enjoy in what the law sent his way, as the cavalier d'Arpino tottered blinking out of jail to pick up the threads of his life. The eyes of the lot were three early works by the painter of the moment. There was M's very first surviving work, the *Boy peeling fruit*, and there were his two exquisitely autobiographical paintings, the *Sick self portrait* and the first picture he did of Mario as the *Boy with fruit*. It was unlikely Borghese recognized either the distraught and haggard greenish faced young painter on hard times or the ravishing sleepy eyed boy Mario when he oversaw the hanging of his new possessions – Scipione Borghese had still been a shabby teenager in the sticks when they were done, and his beatitude's police inventory identified the subjects only as *a youth* and *a boy*. These were paintings the unknown M had given or sold for a song to Cesari, maybe he'd just left them behind when he went off to work on his own and set up house with Mario. Or maybe Cesari's sharp eye had picked them out earlier on, among his employee's assembly line production. Now they were worth far more. Now Scipione Borghese had five paintings by M. In three more years he'd have seven. The exact manner of his coming by the next two would be rather more obscure and complex than the way he'd acquired his first four – tied up with the fearsome events that overtook M in the summer of 1610. Borghese saw now that his future as an owner of M's work would depend on the way he used his powers to pilot M's return to Rome, on the way he made him pay for papal mercy. This will to control M's personal fate determined Borghese's moves on M from now on.

Later, as the years and decades passed, Scipione Borghese would be less obsessed with M's art and more eager to get his hands on work by a new and coming generation, people whose names were now hardly known and whose careers fell beyond the present story's span. His involvement with some of them would show, however, that he never forgot the lessons of his early days as an art collector. Five years later, when his own former protégé Guido Reni, who was the new celebrity painter in Rome, got angry at his insulting and unprofessional treatment by the Borghese papacy and stalked off the job – which happened to be the Borghese family chapel – and went home to Bologna, Borghese moved to have him jailed when he refused to return, and only an intervention to the pope saved Reni from prison or exile. And five years on again, when the painter Domenichino, another of the most appreciated of the new generation of painters, did a canvas of *Diana with nymphs at play* on commission for cardinal Pietro Aldobrandini in 1618 – a sexy lot of nude or barebreasted nymphs bathing, dancing and shooting arrows, since by then the boring old rigours of the counter reformation were fading fast – Scipione Borghese wanted it for himself. The ingenuous and *dreamy* Domenichino preferred to stick with his original client and Borghese had to jail him until he released the canvas. There was too the matter of the Raphael altarpiece that Borghese had ordered stolen at night from a family chapel in Perugia and brought to his collection. Borghese was more into art than politics, but in art he was a ruthless politician.

Now, even as he was gathering Cesari's hundred and six canvases to his bosom, and as *Mary dead* headed north in a cloud of dust with a stash of holy candles and the latest three volumes of cardinal Tosco's *Works*, the signs were that Borghese was already putting out feelers to the friends and protectors who'd been trying to negotiate a deal for M's return over the past year. The signs came in further letters from the dogged ambassador Masetti to the court at Modena. Even Masetti had come to accept that he was never going to see the painting M had been promising to deliver *within days* nearly two years earlier, but he was determined to recover the thirty two scudi M had weaselled out of him. Masetti was probably responding to a flurry of irritation and impatience from the duke of Modena that the rival duke of Mantua had snapped up *Mary dead*, when he reported on May 26 that

> It hasn't been possible to recover the money on account of a homicide committed by [M], for which he was *bandito*, but since the killing was accidental and since he too was seriously wounded, they're negotiating an amnesty for him and there are hopes of a pardon. And when he does get back I won't fail to recover those thirty two scudi …

Masetti reported a week later that he'd even written to M – whose precise whereabouts in Naples were evidently well known in Rome – demanding the money back, and unsurprizingly he hadn't received an answer.

> … I doubt I'll get anything out of him as long as he stays *bandito*, but the moment he appears in Rome I'll be quite unforgiving, and I'm terribly sorry his highness's kindness and humanity has been repaid so ill …

His highness evidently wasn't getting the message that there was no hope of a painting by M, because by midsummer Masetti was forced to write, on August 20, that

The greater the desire shown by his highness for the paintings, the sorrier I feel that it's impossible to realize the said desire – there's no use even thinking about M's, and as for Carracci ... Right now they're negotiating a peace settlement for M. He'll be back the moment it's agreed on, and I'll be breathing down his neck ...

If a settlement of M's case really was imminent in the summer of 1607 – and Masetti had no reason at all to raise new false hopes in Cesare d' Este now, since the duke was already unhappy – what went wrong? A lot of powerful people had very strong reasons for wanting M back in Rome. The homicide was nothing whose resolution by the pope would've raised an eyebrow – Masetti was already indicating how the terrain of an *unfortunate accident* and *suffering on both sides* had been prepared. People were busy working for a solution. Everyone expected allowances to be made in cases like this. But M didn't come back. What now started moving inexorably toward the tragic outcome of three summers later looked like a tangled drama drenched in the blackest irony of misunderstanding and cross purpose. From a Roman point of view the legal and diplomatic problem seemed to be headed for a brisk solution in 1607, one that Borghese was surely intending would be even more in his interests than his last settlement of M's problems with the law. The Roman point of view, however, wasn't the only one that counted.

The trouble was that M himself seemed unaware of whatever deal was being hammered out on his behalf. And in the meantime M was pursuing a plan of his own. Although he looked like a painter singularly incapable of those little accommodations and compromises that made up most people's lives – unable to handle painters who were plagiarizing his work, unable to deal with troublesome lawyers or neighbourhood thugs with good connexions, unable to soften the radical edge of his art and conform to the religious correctness of the day – unable to do anything other than paint – when he was looked at from a different angle he showed quite other qualities of resilience, fight and sheer bloodyminded determination to do whatever he had to do in the service of his art. He was quite ruthless in pursuing his ends and adopted when he needed it the confrontational manner and the expert swordsmanship of the day to settle his problems. He also knew how to secure the loyalty of the buyers and protectors most useful to him. There wasn't much he could do about the church, but his professional relations were otherwise excellent. M was still the man who'd

... risen out of poverty through hard work and taking on everything and looking ahead without fear ... [one of those people] who won't be kept down by faintheartedness ... who thrust themselves forward frankly and fearlessly and seize their chance where they can ...

What he saw and felt with his lucid and penetrating painter's gaze, the delicacy, the disconcerting frankness, the deep empathy with women and the old and the sexual susceptibility to boys that showed up in his work, weren't necessarily on display in the streets or in the *salotti*. M knew how to look after himself, how to protect his gift. M was a man who'd often got into trouble, sometimes big trouble, and who'd always known how to get out of it. Tomassoni's killing and his own near death cleared the air and brought him back to what mattered, his work. He'd done at least three major paintings in the summer of convalescing and hiding, and ever since he'd arrived in Naples he'd worked in a blaze of professional fury. By the end of the year he'd produced an indisputable masterwork, a painting that matched any he'd done in Rome. He'd also come within a whisker of pulling off the impossible, in producing a great work of counter reformation orthodoxy. He'd won a personal commission from the viceroy of Naples, who was the most powerful man in Italy after the pope. He was now producing a formidable series of other works, working harder and faster than ever before.

M was not in 1607 a drifting psychopath. He was working maniacally to recover what he'd lost, and neither his known temperament nor his professional behaviour in those months indicated that he'd be merely hoping for the best on the legal and political fronts. M wasn't a man to hang round waiting on the graciousness of his beatitude. He had plans of his own, plans in which the Colonna family were involved and which had maybe been laid while he was still in refuge on their estates. Naples was M's first step on the comeback trail. The next, for reasons that must've seemed compelling at the time, particularly in the lack of news from Rome of moves toward a pardon, was Malta. What happened from now on, for anyone trying to follow his traces, would be a deeply disturbing sequence of often baffling events. Great patches of uncertainty now followed. M would leave paintings in Naples, Malta and Sicily, and a few sure documentary traces of his increasingly convulsive movements and activities. These traces made you think of movements and activities he was less and less the master of, gave you a sense of hidden forces prompting, directing, leading on. Some terrible new events in his life would be lit by sudden flashes of light and followed by patches of darkness.

ONE PAINTING M did get up in San Domenico Maggiore – forty five years late – was the *Whipping*. On 11 May 1607 he received from a Tommaso De Franchis a part payment for a painting of the whipping of Christ for the De Franchis family chapel there. The commission came from within the same group of clients he'd already been working for – a De Franchis brother and a Carafa were among the governors of the *pio monte della misericordia* who ordered the *Seven works*. The De Franchis family were high bourgeois still five years off from becoming aristocrats. M was quickly building a new network in Naples, though there was no sign that they shared the informed commitment to his art he'd won from his Roman buyers. Efforts like the Carafa *Rosary Madonna* and the viceroy's *Andrew killed* implied the opposite – that he was prepared in Naples, needing money or supporters or both, to do things like taking on rigidly ideological art and dashing off a vigorous but formulaic work for a client who couldn't be refused. The Carafas' lack of interest in the *Rosary Madonna* looked symptomatic – they probably cared for art as little as their relatives the Colonnas, whose intensely protective concern for M's person never seemed to translate into a commission. M in Naples was astonishingly prolific, and his omnivorousness for new commissions made some infelicities inevitable. Not every painting could be a *Seven works*, but the altarpiece he did for De Franchis was the other great painting of 1607.

The *Whipping* seemed another painting that was quite unique, as much *sui generis* as *Seven works*, but it wasn't. It belonged to a whole series of very similar paintings M painted over these months. All of them showed whipping or some other of the forms of torture that were so intimately a part of the Christian religious experience, and never more exquisitely so than during the catholic counter reformation. They were a shock. M's earlier work had never trucked with joy through suffering – when he did a head being hacked off, or an old person nailed up and left to die, the result was sheer physical horror and a kind of painterly innocence that made it all even worse. The subtler workings of the stories of Christian suffering he'd done three or four years earlier had sparely played on the drama of the moment before – of confusion, betrayal, arrest, denunciation, humiliation, hugger mugger panic and darkness, a cord tightened around the wrists and the sickening fear of apprehended violence, psychic pain, not physical. People watching other people being led off – and you were one of the watchers. M skipped the exalting message, gave you only the fear. They were extraordinarily modern apprehensions, lying in wait under their layers of dirt for the twentieth century to see them.

In Naples physical pain became strangely congenial to M's art. After waking with the astonished social vision of *Seven works*, he headed in a quite other direction, cutting into a new and strange vein of private feeling. *Whipping* was the biggest and most monumental of a group of five or six closely related paintings he did toward the end of his first time in Naples. All of them showed a powerfully sculptural male nude being tortured by a couple of workmen. The figure was usually a Christ but there was a Sebastian who was almost the same. One way or another, most of these soon disappeared from view, so the force of M's obsession in this year was dispersed and *Whipping* for a long time seemed to stand alone as an enigmatic and experimental work. But there was another *Whipping*, a canvas from this time in Naples that remained unknown until it was identified as M's in the nineteen fifties. There was another again, known only through copies. There was the closely related *Sebastian* that Bellori called *one of his best works* and said was taken to Paris – it too remained known only through copies.

The painting that led into it was a horizontal, three quarter length painting of the *Crown of thorns*. It recalled the subdued workaday tone of the Cerasi paintings of five years earlier – the two workmen quietly concentrating on jamming the thorn twigs on to Christ's head with canes as the supervising officer, in a vest of glinting black scaled and riveted armour like the soldier's armour in *Christ taken*, his cream shirt protruding at the cuff and waist and collar, and wearing a finely plumed hat of the kind M had earlier enjoyed painting on Mario, languidly rested his hand on a raw wooden trestle and gazed obliquely and unseeingly downward in a pose of deepest boredom, his face in shadow and his right ear catching the strong oblique light descending into the frame. The officer was a bored version of the plumed and alertly interested proconsul watching Andrew die. What this *Crown of thorns* lacked was any sense that what was going on particularly mattered. The four overlapping figures were locked in a powerful circular turbine, and the clean, luminous way M rendered the bare shoulders of Christ and the two workmen were a reminder of what he'd achieved doing Cecco's bare skin in *Love the winner*. The problem, as far as the painting's interest went, was that recurring bugbear of Christian art, the slack and passive figure of

Christ, whose glassy eyed air of someone sitting out a hair shampoo at the barber's was enhanced and not concealed by the rhetorically off the shoulder placing of his red mantle. Just where your eye was most intently focused, interest died.

It was a complex and subtle study of bodies, an interlocking pattern of heads, hands, shoulders, chests and an interplay of bare skin and cloth and armour, abstracted from the *history* and its meaning that they were supposed to be embodying, a painting without any narrative interest at all, beyond a certain languidly clinical feeling, as the golden afternoon light played rather more strongly than usual over the exposed skin, for the sensual possibilities of physical pain inflicted and suffered. The play of forms and surfaces, in the neck, arm, shoulder and ribcage of the workman in the upper right hand was a marvel. The armoured officer was finely done and he looked appropriately dreamy, because he was extraneous to what was going on. This painting's interest was the intimate interlocking of torturers and torturee. The painting was about how it was to give pain and feel pain, and how close pain and pleasure sometimes were, how voluptuous suffering could be on a golden afternoon. You didn't need a man in armour to show you that, though armour showed up the nakedness of skin.

When drama and tension were gone, and torturers and victim were locked inseparably into a much more private exchange of pain and pleasure, the superfluous observer might as well leave the picture. And so he did. In the *Whipping*, M reworked the languid half figures into a huge and complexly disturbing full length canvas. Christ's bent head and shoulders were exactly the same, but this painting no longer pretended to be a drama – with all others excluded, tension gone, thugs and victim were left alone in their intimacy. There was a figure in place of the lounging officer, looking into the picture in the same way, but he was now a third torturer – mainly visible as a white shoulder – kneeling down to knot himself some twigs and eager to join the action. The torturers now had identities and movements of their own. There was the heavy, balding middleaged one on the right, there for stolid control, and on the left a wiry vicious maniacal terrier of a man, mouth open and the white of his eye glinting as he lined up his first blow with a sportsman's care. The curly haired youngster kneeling was looking up distracted, excited by the pain already starting, slower off the mark. The colour was almost monochrome, tones of sepia and gold shading into darkness – no afternoon sun flooding this scene. The light invested only Christ and the other figures were drowning in darkness and a dull highlight running down the stone pillar was all you could see beyond the four, and above them there was only more darkness.

The Christ M painted for De Franchis was quite unlike the slender and vulnerable figures who'd mainly been his previous saviours. This Christ was powerfully built, verging on the overweight, larger than his assailants and the most physically formidable figure in the picture. As a nude he was more like a figure by M's namesake Buonarotti, with the soft fleshy abundance of the *ignudi* on the Sistine ceiling. His strongly lit torso looked as though it were swooning balletically toward the picture plane, though he was in fact being worked by his tormentors. His legs were buckling because one man had a foot behind his knee, and his head wasn't so much lolling sideways as being yanked there by a hand grasping a hank of hair. He was, of course, offering no resistance but that stolid mass would take some subduing. The massive inertia of Christ's pale torso held the incipient violence in check. The whole thing was so perfectly balanced – giving and taking, acting and suffering, pain and pleasure – that the beating seemed voluptuously suspended in the darkness, taken out of time, as your eye moved slowly round its anticlockwise circuit.

It hadn't been so at the start – it happened while he was painting it. At some point M had changed tack. When x rays were made of the canvas in the nineteen eighties, they showed a carefully finished and highly individual portrait face under the shoulder of the tormentor on the right, looking up into Christ's face. It was, maybe, a portrait of Tommaso De Franchis. It had a bourgeois look. As M originally imagined it, the *Whipping* had included at least one further presence, and the exclusive concentration on torturers and victim, and the circular completeness of their relation only came as he worked on it. This was the transitional work, the one that stepped fully into the voluptuousness of pain. Having got to that, M did two more paintings of Christ being whipped and they both maintained or concentrated even further that intensity of focus, still reworking the same central figure – though using different models – of a powerfully built nude Christ with a forward leaning torso, face down, nape of a strong neck running on from the shoulders in a horizontal line.

One was a painting that survived only in copies, a three quarter of Christ tied nude between a torturer looming over him from behind and another seen closeup below him in front. In that intensely intimate image the figures filled the canvas. And there was another, the *Whipping* found in the nineteen fifties, a three quarter length painting where the victim was leaning out of the canvas to the left, and the real interest had shifted to the two strongly individual models as journeyman torturers doing their job without animus. And then there was the *Sebastian* – the surviving copies showed it was a very close variant on the Christ paintings. A rather plump nude youth in a loincloth, looking much like the De Franchis Christ, hands tied behind him to a tree trunk, two men kneeling by him, a single arrow in his side. In these paintings of pain inflicted and undergone, M did a tightly related set of variations on a single, obsessively recurring figure of an adult male nude. The model changed, the pose hardly at all. Both the figure itself – youthful but mature – and the multiple treatments of a single image were unique in M's work. None of the pressures of rapid production could explain the intensity of this voluptuous fixation in a painter so immune the rest of the time to languorousness and so little inclined to repeat himself. Even old Andrew on his cross in his death swoon had been an early version of the image. It was as if something in Naples had got to him – pain as a sensual experience was somehow a very Neapolitan thing. Naples was a pleasure loving city, violated by the Spanish. Everything was a sensual experience in Naples, and you had to take your pleasures where you could.

M never returned to the enjoyment of pain and never again worked and reworked a single theme like this. What he did return to was the image of the southern labourer. The lean and sunbaked features of the poor and the old of the *mezzogiorno* would be a constant presence in his *histories* from now on. At this moment the wiry snub nosed, crop haired satyrlike figure who appeared in two of the paintings of the *Whipping* – demonically snarling in one, almost solicitous in the other – was also unmistakeably the deeply thoughtful servant killer holding John the baptist's head to *Salomè* in a half length painting of this time. Salomè, her face averted from the dish, was the model from *Seven works* and the *Rosary Madonna*, and between her and the killer floated the downcast figure of that other constant presence, an old woman's mask of stony misery.

The big *Whipping* earnt M two hundred and ninety ducats but it wasn't installed in San Domenico Maggiore until 1652, after the De Franchis chapel was enlarged and remodelled. Twenty three years later it was displaced by a much venerated wooden statue of the virgin Mary which was believed to perform miracles and carry out acts of revenge on the incredulous – she destroyed the family of a doctor who thought hygiene more important in time of plague than her miracles. That was counter reformation Naples. The three quarter *Crown of thorns* that preceded the *Whipping* went to Vincenzo Giustiniani's collection in Rome. Was M in touch with Giustiniani? There was no way to tell. The problem in trying to trace M's movements and activities in 1607 was that not even he could produce so many paintings in six months. If after completing the big and complexly innovative *Seven works of mercy* in early January – having maybe done the vanished Radolovich painting before that – he'd gone straight on to do the *Rosary Madonna*, and the *Andrew killed* for the viceroy and the portrait of Cecco as *David* and the new *Judith & Holofernes* his painter friends were trying to flog in September, there remained the De Franchis *Whipping*, another very big canvas he'd had to radically rethink and restructure while he was working on it, then the second version of *Whipping*, the *Crown of thorns* that went to Vincenzo Giustiniani, the lost third *Whipping*, the *Sebastian* and the *Salomè*. All the circumstantial and stylistic evidence meshed to place the origin of these paintings at Naples in 1607. Ten canvases, two of them very large and demanding, couldn't be done in six months. And on the twelfth of July, after a week or so at sea, M was already in Malta. This meant he returned to Naples at the end of the summer to finish his commissions over the winter. Then he went back to Malta.

WHY MALTA? M was a huge success as a painter in Naples. He was though, personally very exposed. Masetti's letter indicated he was being closely tracked from Rome, and although he was outside Roman jurisdiction he wasn't far enough away from it. He was vulnerable to a *coup de main* and uncertain of intentions in Rome. Somebody put it to M that Malta, and the knights of the order of saint John of Jerusalem who'd installed themselves on the island seventy six years earlier, offered powerful contacts, security, work. Malta and the order also promised, if all went well, a reward that M, in his hunted and outcast state, found immensely desirable. That was a knighthood in the order of saint John. That would offer status, a social anchor – there was no way M would've ever been made a papal knight like Cesari, Roncalli and Baglione, even without the homicide – and attach him to a powerful network of solidarity and protection such as M at that time could very much use. The order had both prestige and political clout in Rome. A knight of the order of saint John of Jerusalem was a very different figure from a – well, a social nobody and a killer, however good a painter he might be. A knight got special treatment even after committing major crimes. A knight might hope for a pardon.

The order of saint John was military, aristocratic and exclusive, and only influence could get you in. The knights were hard men, their organisation a strange nexus of austere monasticism, aristocratic militarism and criminal adventurism. They made their own rules. They were a bulwark of Christendom in the strategic centre of the Mediterranean and forty two years earlier they'd made their modern name by resisting a long and bitter siege of Malta by Turkish forces. Malta was

> Italy's maritime front against the Turkish threat [and had to] provide a naval base for the Spanish fleets, to offer resistance to Turkish armadas and to defend its own territory against pirate attacks.

Malta was also a base for Christian privateering and raids on north Africa, and the Christian centre of the Mediterranean slave trade. As members of a religious order that was also a needed territorial and military power, the knights of hospitaller Malta had a certain fearsome independence of Rome and Spain. They'd risen up in revolt, for instance, when Rome tried to introduce the inquisition into Malta. A compromise was later reached, letting in an inquisitor with limited powers and a very strict diplomatic brief. For the inquisitor

> apart from Jews and Muslims passing through and the island's small population, the main problem was the quarrelsome and violent company of the knights, *young men with little practice in discipline and great lovers of licence*, so the inquisitor needed to use *skill ... mistrust of everyone ... pleasantness and affability with all.* Above all he had to consult first with the grand master in every case and act covertly.

In accommodating Europe's more turbulent young nobles, hospitaller Malta worked in some ways as a kind of aristocratic forerunner of the French foreign legion, at once a release mechanism for the home powers and an agency for dirty work abroad. By the start of the seventeenth century it wasn't even so tough any more. The life of the knights of the order was becoming, as the threat of an Islamic invasion of Europe receded, less and less monastic and increasingly *brilliant, privileged and arrogant*. It was already heading toward the condition observed by a visiting French aristocrat a hundred years after M's time there. Life was *far from austere*, the count remarked pointedly, and hospitaller Malta *might've been called Little Gommorah*. You could see the attraction for M. To become a knight, though, was an extremely remote and unlikely ambition for M to cultivate, or even think of. It cost a lot of money, and the order didn't accept homicides. M only went to Malta now because he knew he had contacts there and a real chance of improving his situation, even if a knighthood must've seemed no more than a mirage.

There were several possible contacts. Preeminently, there was Fabrizio Sforza Colonna. The second son of Costanza Colonna Sforza, the marchesa of Caravaggio, was around M's age. Fabrizio Sforza Colonna had more in common with M than shared childhood memories of Caravaggio and Milan in the seventies. Five years earlier he too had committed some serious crimes – crimes in fact maybe including a homicide, maybe something unmentionable because it went unmentioned. Since he was a member of such a powerful dynasty, and a knight in the order of saint John of Jerusalem and the order's prior of Venice – along with his uncle cardinal Ascanio Colonna – the pope wanted to avoid holding the trial Fabrizio Sforza Colonna faced in Rome. Particularly as his mother, Ascanio Colonna's sister, was then living in Rome at her brother the cardinal's palace. This was just what the knights hospitaller of the order of saint John of Jerusalem were for. The pope sent the aristocratic criminal Fabrizio Sforza Colonna to Malta, to be tried there by his own order. The Tuscan ambassador had mentioned the marchesa of Caravaggio's presence in Rome when he reported to Ferdinando I from Rome in July 1602 that

> his holiness's galleys arrived six days ago … bringing the prior of Venice Sforza from prison in Milan, and they'll shortly leave for Sicily and Malta, where they'll hand him over to the grand master …

In Malta Fabrizio Sforza Colonna spent four years in prison – comfortable prison that afforded some freedom of movement. He was confined to the island for three more years after his release in 1606 and even after that he was forbidden to return to Milan without the pope's express permission. The new pope did, however – through Scipione Borghese – allow the order to appoint Sforza Colonna head of the fleet,

> general of the Malta galleys and of Felipe III king of Spain in Lombardy and Piedmont.

It was, given Malta's place in the Mediterranean, its dependence on sea power and its role in the war on Islam, a post of great significance. The fleet had grown a lot since Alof de Wignacourt had become grand master in 1602. Sforza Colonna's contribution mattered because Wignacourt was developing systematic privateering as a government controlled Maltese industry and was himself a licensed operator. Venetian merchant shipping was particularly at risk from the knights. This resolution of Fabrizio Sforza Colonna's problems with the law pleased everyone. He was in reality allowed to leave Malta, and didn't even have to surrender control of the Venice priory. At the end of June 1606, a few weeks after M had gone into hiding on the Colonna estates, the grand master Alof de Wignacourt wrote to the marchesa Costanza Colonna to say how happy he was at the way things had turned out for her son Fabrizio and how much he hoped Fabrizio would stay on in Malta.

Ascanio and Costanza Colonna likely thought of their nephew and son Fabrizio in Malta when they mapped out possible moves for M, maybe while he was still being sheltered on their properties. In any case, Fabrizio Sforza Colonna in January 1607 was in Marseille to collect a new galley from the shipyards there and another being built for the order of saint John in Barcelona. Wignacourt wrote to him there, mentioning among the news from home that the Maltese forces had just intercepted a couple of ships *loaded with good stuff*, and taken a hundred and eighty slaves as well. On the voyage back Sforza Colonna stopped at Genoa and Naples and he reached Malta on July 12. This was the day, other sources showed, that M also arrived in Malta from Naples. The conclusion was hard to avoid – M travelled south on Sforza's galleys.

Other friends and clients of M's had strong links with Malta too, which were activated in the summer of 1607. One was Ottavio Costa, the Genoese financier – who a few months earlier had taken the *Meal in Emmaus* M'd done in hiding. His wife's uncle was the marchese Ippolito Malaspina, knight of saint John, prior of Naples and until he resigned when Paul V was elected in 1605, commander of the papal fleet. Malaspina was also an intimate and adviser of the order's grand master Wignacourt. Wignacourt had written to Malaspina in February 1607, looking forward to Malaspina's imminent return to Malta, and Malaspina may have come on the new galley with Sforza Colonna, and maybe M – Wignacourt had written to Sforza Colonna instructing him to give Malaspina passage back to Malta. Malaspina was the recipient that summer of a painting by M which included his coat of arms on the canvas. He might've known M from Rome, because he'd lived there from 1603 until 1605 when he was admiral of the papal fleet – he'd bought a palazzo on the piazza Navona and certainly would've been mixing socially with his relative and M's patron Ottavio Costa in those years. Ottavio Costa now owned a house on Malta that he'd bought from Malaspina and one of Costa's sons was already a knight in the order of saint John, and another would be later – their names later appeared on their great uncle Malaspina's tombstone. If Malaspina was connected with Genoa and M through the Costas, he was also the cousin of Giovanni Andrea Doria, the prince of Genoa, who'd two years earlier sheltered M on his earlier flight from Rome and whose wife was a Colonna – and whose young relative Marcantonio had vainly offered M a fortune to fresco his *loggia*, and had been trying to get a painting out of him ever since. There was, finally, the coincidence that twelve days after M's arrival in Malta, a cousin of the marchese Vincenzo's, Marc'Aurelio Giustiniani whose brother Orazio was a knight in the order, presented a petition to the grand master offering the order a property at Venosa in southern Italy. Giustiniani arrived around the same time as M, and maybe with him, and if he did their travelling together may not have been fortuitous. The next month Wignacourt wrote to cardinal Benedetto Giustiniani about the successful outcome of the visit. The whole dynastic umbrella of M's powerful protectors was quivering over Malta when he arrived there.

For anyone interested in M, the Giustiniani offer wasn't the most exciting formal deposition being made a fortnight after he arrived. The most intriguing was M's own. Not that he was giving anything away, as usual. Two days after the Giustiniani petition, on July 26, M found himself being interrogated by the inquisition. Not about himself. The court wanted to know about a painter it'd heard about, who'd just arrived in Malta and who apparently had two wives, one in Sicily and another in Malta. The inquisition felt strongly about bigamy. A remark had been reported, a few words let fall in a conversation at the house of a Sicilian knight on July 13 – M had been talking with this knight, with whom he'd arrived in Malta the day before. At a certain point in their conversation the knight had broken off and turned to another person present – or so that person claimed when he went to the inquisitor – and told him that

> a painter's come here on the galleys, and he's got two wives, one in Mussumeli [in Sicily] and one here in Malta.

The informant named M, who was interrogated about it on the twenty sixth, and M said he knew nothing about it. He knew only that there was a Greek painter staying in the knight's house, who'd arrived on the galleys a fortnight earlier, which was to say the same day as M and his Sicilian host. It was nearly two months before the inquisition got around to interrogating the knight, and on September 18 he too said he knew nothing about it – he muddied the waters further with an involved story about a Sicilian peasant bringing a mare across to Malta, and a joke the peasant had made when the knight had facetiously offered him one of his household slaves as a bride. The inquisition at this point gave up.

The episode might've had no more than its considerable interest as a record of when M reached Malta, and of the poisonous atmosphere he'd landed in – if a man's casual joking remark on a social occasion in his own home could be so swiftly retailed to the inquisition by one of his guests – if the mention of a Sicilian painter with two wives hadn't had a curious echo in the known facts of Mario Minniti's marital history, as they were later recorded. Mario had arrived in Rome at fifteen not directly from Sicily but via Malta, where he'd fled on the Maltese galleys after trouble in his native Syracuse. What if he'd got married there? He later married a Roman wife and took her back to Sicily. She died, said the biographer, and he married a noblewoman. There was no hard evidence here, just enough to raise the thought that if Minniti had been involved in the fight in which Tomassoni died – the *accidentally committed homicide* his biographer also vaguely mentioned – he might've fled Rome not separately but together with M, and have followed him to the Colonna territories and down through Naples to Malta. And that M had made some unwise crack about his friend's marital complications to their host. Mario Minniti was in Malta later on, and eighteen years later he left one of his best paintings there, an *Ecce homo* with a wooden, uninteresting Christ framed by a corrupt and wizened Pilate on one side and on the other a stunning sloe eyed, openmouthed slender teenage soldier in a glinting helmet worthy of the master.

Did Ottavio Costa, learning of M's presence in Naples around the time he picked up the *Meal in Emmaus* that M had painted on the Colonna estates, decide to see what he could do for him? If he did, it were natural, thinking of connexions in Naples, to think of his wife's uncle Ippolito Malaspina. Maybe Costa set in motion M's voyage to Malta with Malaspina on Fabrizio Sforza Colonna's galleys, arranged introductions on arrival. Malaspina might've already developed an interest of his own in M's work, after seeing it at Costa's palazzo in Rome or Genoa, or hearing about the painter from his brother in law. Particularly if he wanted to commission something for his order's home church in Malta. Something along the lines of *Who was that interesting painter Ottavio had told him about? The one he'd met in Rome at Ottavio's a couple of years ago? The one whose work Ottavio collected? The one in trouble with his beatitude? He was in Naples? And available?* Or maybe Malaspina just bumped into M in the grand master's palace on the island in the summer of 1607. Or at admiral Fabrizio Sforza Colonna's place, the other admiral's, with whom he had so many naval dealings.

MALASPINA DID ORDER a painting from M in Malta. A *Jerome* for the chapel of the *Italian tongue.* Each nation or *tongue* represented in the order had its chapel in the church of Saint John, and that year Malaspina, prodded by the circumstance of M's presence, decided to do something for his. M did him a three quarter length canvas of *Jerome writing,* and down the right hand side of the canvas ran a brown strip that might've been formed by the edge of an open bedroom door and at the bottom of it, in the corner of the canvas, was the Malaspina coat of arms. This *Jerome* was another three quarter length study of a barechested man writing, with a red blanket around his knees. It couldn't, however, have been more different from the hallucinated and ruffle haired ancients of his earlier two versions. This Jerome was no gaunt and fragile distracted old translator of ancient texts. He was an active, powerful man in his sixties who'd just roused himself from rest to jot down a memorandum. From the man's fit, muscular body, straight back and his weatherbeaten face and hands, it looked more likely to be a disposition for troop movements or a note on shipping schedules. He had a beaky nose that looked made of bronze and a deep vertical cleft scored in his lean cheek, as though from staring into the sun for hours at a time over the years.

The face had a certain generic likeness to the Andrew's of earlier in the year and a couple of portrait faces M would do of knights in Malta the following year, but it was subtly and utterly itself. The eyesight wasn't quite what it'd been, and the marvellous detail at the painting's centre – the detail that made it *action* and not a mere portrait, let alone a generic saint's image – was the barely parted lips of the commanding mouth, the glimpse of lower teeth, as the nearly closed eyes under creased lids – the sun, again – focused on the page. Writing wasn't altogether this saint's thing – there was a subliminal humour in the tension between the reality of the action man model and the pernickety values of the scholar saint, and it went right back to M's barefoot peasant *Matthew* of five years before, gaping at the scripture he was writing with the angel's guidance. M knew now about not going over the top. There was a little extra too, another glance at a less recent past in the little still life cluster of bread roll, upturned skull and crucifix on the table, done with the vividly detailed care M always gave to still life. *There was as much workmanship* in painting a skull as a living head. The old sense of fun was back here too. The crucifix, with its tiny nailed Christ splayed on his back, was about to topple off the bedside table, and the largely toothless skull had rolled over on its side and was painted from below as a weird *objet trouvé* and not as a *memento mori*.

The painting was full of understated energy, the leader unbuttoned in his tent or his cabin, having shed his clothes but not the habit of command, jotting down some orders to give at dawn. The body and its pose recalled the mop haired John's of three years earlier, the one who in the desert seemed to be sitting on the edge of an unmade bed. The angle of the head, the muscle joining the base of the skull to the shoulder, was a visual reminiscence of both Andrew and the beaten Christs of the same year, reworked in a vein of tensed concentration. Everything else in the picture was reduced to an almost abstract formal grouping by M's deft and slashing strokes – the plane of the table, the ample folds of the red blanket, the sacklike brown bed and the darkness above it – done with the same jabbing economy with which the subject was scribbling his notes. The torso was done with a light modelling subtlety that derived straight from painting *Whipping* for De Franchis.

> Ever since he was a youth he'd wanted to realize his natural inclination for the art of soldiery and sail against the Turkish predators. Indifferent to the ambitious power of his father's feudal baronage, he left all control to his brother Andrew and joined the convoys of the knights of Jerusalem ... he was made prior of Naples and given the grand cross of Malta ... advancing in age, valour and experience in his noble art, he had the glory of being called by pope Clement VIII in 1604 to be captain general of all the ships and galleys of the papal power ... decorated with the golden grand cross by the grand master of the order ...

If the sitter for this painting were Ippolito Malaspina himself, who was sixty three in 1607, he must've loved the subtle, humorous, deeply human and quite formidable image of himself as a man of religion who was also a man of action that M created. Malaspina's close friend the grand master Wignacourt must've been deeply impressed as well, maybe even a little envious, because he invited M back to Malta some months later to do a series of portraits of himself that he evidently liked no less. Whatever little local difficulties Mario Minniti might've encountered over his wives, M himself seemed to be a great hit. If Minniti really was the man with two wives, he managed to pass unremarked in Malta on that occasion and left before M to go back to Syracuse. He might, if the bigamist were he and the inquisition was sniffing around, have left on the first available galley. Galleys sailed frequently, as it happened, from Malta up the east coast of Sicily to Syracuse and Messina in the summer months. It was easy for Mario to go home.

M's own movements at this time were a puzzle. It was long well known that he left Malta in October 1608, and the inquisition records establishing his arrival as 12 July 1607 made it seem he'd spent fifteen months Malta. There were problems with this conclusion, and one of them was how he would've passed the time. By the autumn of 1608 he'd've done three paintings for sure on Malta, maybe five altogether. Given his working habits, three or five paintings in fifteen months was a meagre rate. In Naples there was the opposite problem – that not even M's speed and intensity of work seemed able to make ten works in six months a plausible proposition. There was a further problem too – a major commission M did around this time in Naples that he couldn't've begun, for contingent reasons, before the end of 1607. M's July visit to Malta was most likely a short summer visit to test the waters, maybe specifically to carry out the *Jerome* commission for Malaspina and see whether there was more work to be rustled up on the island. And he probably went back to Naples toward the end of the summer – to be there when the *Rosary Madonna* and *Judith & Holofernes* were put up for sale in late September. Naples too, was directly linked by sea to Malta, and over the summer months the galleys were coming and going all the time. For someone who knew both Fabrizio Sforza Colonna the Malta admiral, and Ippolito Malaspina, the admiral of the papal fleet, travel arrangements were hardly a problem. In Naples he'd done his great breakthrough painting for De Franchis in May – *that* date was recorded. It was likely – if undemonstrable – that most of the paintings he did to develop and vary that figuring of the male nude and his assailants were done in the last months of 1607. By the start of 1608 he had a major new commission on his hands, a set of three paintings for a chapel, and by the time that was finished in late spring, he headed back to Malta. The theoretically possible alternative to this, that M painted in Malta canvases that were ordered from Naples and sent back there on the galleys, was more than intrinsically unlikely. M's great care in studying the lighting and the architectonics of the places where his public paintings were installed, his creation of painted dramas around the specifics of place, made it unimaginable that he'd work by mail order.

M clearly liked what he found on his first reconnoitre – requests for work and maybe already some hint of advancement, a promise even. And the people who mattered in Malta clearly liked what they saw of M and his work – when he came back the grand master Wignacourt got him to do two major portraits and another military leader had himself done as well. In no time at all Wignacourt seemed to take a particularly intense liking to M, although he knew all about his past and the killing in Rome. Maybe, in the skewed society of Malta, the killing was seen as a plus. No effete dauber M. He was surely encouraged in his good opinion by Malaspina and Sforza Colonna. Wignacourt was so impressed that the following winter, while M was back in Naples, he set machinery in motion directed at removing the obstacles to M's entry into the order of saint John of Jerusalem as a *cavaliere magistrale*. Whoever first floated the idea, it was hard to imagine Wignacourt would've done this without having heard from M how passionately he desired such a knighthood. It was another reason for M to return to Malta next spring. Which he did, and at first everything was marvellous. M was on the comeback road at last. Fifteen years on, he was still one of those

> who push themselves forward boldly and fearlessly, and everywhere seek their advantage …

17

MALTA & NAPLES 1607–1608

[Resurrection]
Wignacourt & page
Antonio Martelli
John beheaded
Love sleeping
John in the wild VI
Annunciation

ALOF DE WIGNACOURT, while M was working on his pain sequence back in Naples, was putting out feelers from Malta. The feelers reached toward Rome. On 29 December 1607 the grand master wrote to his ambassador to the holy see. The feeler came softly as an elaborately probing instruction. Wignacourt reminded his representative that the order of Saint John, when it particularly wanted to honour someone of great valour, might confer a knighthood on the candidate directly. It could dispense with the normal probationary period – which was a time of real military trial – before admitting him to the order. The order of Saint John was, in 1607, a fighting corps bound by military discipline, operating along a real though ambiguous front line against Islam in the Mediterranean – being a knight hospitaller was not a matter of flummery and flattery in the manner of the papal knighthoods of Cesari and Baglione. The order now had

the opportunity of acquiring to the service of our religion a most virtuous person of the most honoured qualities and manners and whom we hold our particular servant.

In order not to lose the services of this most valued person – mention of whose identity the grand master very elaborately skirted – Wignacourt wished to make a *knight of the grand master* and – here came the crunch – he ordered his ambassador to ask his beatitude to kindly allow the order *once only* to confer the magistral habit *without obligation of trial* and

> that having committed a homicide in a brawl should not be an obstacle to him.

When he were granted the dispensation, the candidate

> would straight away share the other knights' rights of canteen and allowance.

It was a garrison thing. The new knight would be there serving with his peers. The implication that the request involved a military man, the kind of person who got involved in soldiers' brawls, would've kept suspicion even further from the papal mind. A hint of artistic merit and his beatitude might've smelt a rat. And just in case the ambassador, or indeed pope Paul V Borghese himself – who presumably had no reason whatever to link this remote sounding and non specific application now arriving from Malta with the Tomassoni family unpleasantness in Rome of eighteen months earlier – and why would he? – didn't fully weigh the gravity of the request, the grand master underlined in the letter to his ambassador the value he put on a positive outcome, which

> ... as it is most intensely desired by us, so we most warmly urge the matter upon you and await its earliest possible resolution ... we shall pay all costs involved ...

The ambassador put out his antennae and what they picked up was reassuring enough for the grand master Wignacourt to address himself directly, five weeks later, to his beatitude Paul V himself and not feel too worried about losing face in a rejection. By that time there was a second unnamed candidate for a fast tracked knighthood, though only one of the two *who have desire and devotion to dedicate themselves to his service* had committed homicide.

> And notwithstanding that one of them has formerly committed homicide in a brawl ... may he receive this most

singular favour for the great desire he has to honour such virtuous and meritorious persons.

His beatitude's reply to his *beloved son* the grand master was filed in the form of a much corrected draft document submitted for the pope's approval, which granted Wignacourt leave to make his two candidates knights *even though one of them committed homicide in a brawl, as long as there is no other legal impediment.* The ground had been cleared.

M WANTED TO do it himself and it was out of envy that the defendants went around badmouthing me and attacking my work.

When Giovanni Baglione had taken M and his friends to court for libel in 1603, he was responding to a series of attacks on the big painting of *Christ's resurrection* he'd recently done for the Jesuits. There was a lot to laugh at in Baglione's effort, going by the small surviving preparatory painting he did, with its clumsily adapted ideas stolen from M. What nobody knew was how M would've handled the theme, in the utterly unlikely event of a successful tender to the suspicious and ideologically hypertuned Jesuits. The victory over death in Christ's triumphant emergence from the tomb and his rising to heaven was the crucial and exultant moment of the Christian history. It was also, in its very denial of mundane reality, the hardest moment to imagine represented by M. The trouble over *Mary dead* had all started in his refusal to accommodate Mary's corresponding *transition* to heaven in that painting, and in his anchoring his image in the tragically mundane moment of her earthly death in a squalid room. Now, five years later in Naples, M had his chance with Christ.

Along with its foreign financiers, foreign court, fortune seekers, soldiers, prostitutes, beggars, displaced peasants and wheelers and dealers, Naples like Rome had its resident communities of businesspeople and craftsmen from other regions of Italy. As in Rome, there was a big group from M's own Lombardy, and this community had its own Neapolitan church in Sant' Anna dei Lombardi, which was near the rough house *locanda del Cerriglio* where M hung out in Naples – the church was a little further up the hill called Montolivieto. In this church a man called Alfonso Fenaroli from Brescia – about as far to the east of Caravaggio as Milan was to the west – acquired a family chapel on 24 December 1607. He commissioned M to do an altar-piece of the *Resurrection* and two side paintings, of M's favourite subjects *Francis* and *John*. M likely did them in the early months of 1608 – when paintings were done for two other family chapels acquired on the same day. The artists engaged for the others were Carlo Sellito and Battistello Caracciolo – M already had enthusiastic followers among the young painters in Naples and these two were the first. Battistello grew into a major artist. The church was destroyed in the earthquake of 1798 and M's paintings lost. The two Fenaroli side saints sank out of sight. But from comments recorded over its hundred and ninety years of known life it was clear that the Fenaroli altarpiece was a very different matter – *Christ's resurrection* was M's lost masterpiece.

Faint echoes of it in paintings by Neapolitan contemporaries were clumsy and attenuated memories. Neither were the few remarks that were made about it in print particularly admiring, but they did show what startled people in M's version of *the resurrection of the flesh*. The first mention was the shortest, a footnote somebody added to one of the manuscripts of Mancini's *Considerations*, which noted simply that M's Naples painting of the resurrection was *bellissimo*. What made it beautiful? The first description of any length came in 1674 from an exact contemporary of Bellori's. It was published two years after Bellori's *Life* and shared its idealizing prejudice against the merely natural. Luigi Scaramuccia in his guided tour of Italian painting, the *Elegance of Italian brushes*, looked first at the *Seven works of mercy* and found it *totally bizarre* – was disapproving but stimulated – and when his imaginary party under tour leader the *genius of Raphael* moved on to *look more curiously* at the *Resurrection*, its members were even more excited and perturbed.

> They observed Christ not as he's ordinarily done, agile and triumphant in the air, but painted in that terribly fierce manner of M's with one foot in the tomb and the other resting on the ground outside it. They remained somewhat apprehensive at such wildness, and Girupemo asked his master the Genius if he had any idea why M had done it like that. To which the Genius replied,
>
> *Whatever the painter's achievement in this bizarre work, and however much people like it – since everyone enjoys the newness of its inventions – those of us who understand painting have to criticize it for not showing Christ our lord with anything like appropriate decorum. It's a great painting of a man, not an ideal, which means he couldn't do a single thing without a live model in front of him.*

– The tour leader being also a master of the fashionable putdown. Eighteen years later, someone else wrote that in the Fenaroli chapel

> there are three paintings by M and the one in the middle shows the resurrection of the lord who's jumping out of the tomb with a lot of soldiers sleeping. It's greatly admired because the figure in the middle looks as though he's coming out of the picture. Some art experts say it lacks style because there's no glorious majesty.

Style, once again, meaning *decorum*. A century after Paleotti, *decorum* was still riding high, though by the end of the seventeenth century it'd been watered down into something like mere conventional *good taste*. It was M's lack of taste in this painting that fifty years later offended the writer of a survey of art in Naples, in showing Christ

> coming out of his tomb looking almost frightened – a low idea, and indecent when shown.

Almost the last mention of M's painting before it disappeared, and quite the most intelligent, came twenty years after this from a French tourist in Italy, who was breathing the fresher air of the enlightenment as Italy sank into clerical obscurantism, an amateur quite uninterested in antiquarianism, let alone correctness, and full of enthusiasm for his own pleasures and discoveries. By 1763 Charles-Nicolas Cochin found nobody even remembered that the Feneroli *Resurrection* had been painted by M. He knew M as the painter of *Seven works* –

> I couldn't work out the subject. There are angels high up, on the right a woman breast feeding an old man, a torch &c. The picture's very fine, but very black.

– and of *Whipping*, which he thought *very fine ... greatly blackened*, but not of the *Resurrection*, which struck him more than either.

> It's a very singular imagining – the Christ isn't in the air at all & walks among the guards on foot – it gives a very low impression & makes him seem like a convict escaping from his guards. The life model moreover is a thin man & one who's suffered. The pictorial organization is very fine & the style is strong & felt with taste. It's very blackened. The artist's name is unknown. A fine piece.

413

For Cochin the *low* effect of M's painting was the source of its radical drama. In M's consummate style, this was Christ as a man, and not the massive Michelangeloesque figure who was Christ in the *Whipping*, but a thin man who'd had a hard life. This was the resurrection not as an airborne triumph of clouds, shafts of sunlight, cherubs, ecstatic gazes and clean white flowing linens and amazed earthlings below – how could it ever, being M's? – but an emaciated, lately dead man stepping blinking into the daylight like a prisoner just freed from a concentration camp or like a survivor of the plague. It was the only way M would've done it. Visually too, utterly M. The powerful composition. The enveloping darkness. No *glory*. No *majesty*. The risen figure looming out of the canvas, not receding like someone seen through a window, stepping with his feet on the ground, not flying heavenward. Most extraordinarily of all, what nobody imaginable would've dared except M – the wretched build, the fearful, apprehensive look of the unexpectedly released prisoner, blinded by the sudden light, picking his way through the sleeping guards, wondering what was coming next, not yet believing his luck, furtive, suspicious, *frightened* and frightening to the viewer – what an image of the way Christ rose from the dead to heavenly glory. To an unbeliever four hundred years later, it sounded stunning. Seen as a wholly earthly event, the idea of a man who'd died and come back to life was an intensely personal imagining for M in Naples, the subjective analogue of *Seven works*. Acclaimed like the *Pilgrims' Madonna* by the people who recognized themselves in it – *people enjoy it ... acclaimed for its newness ... greatly admired* – dismissed by the trained minds of M's age and the next, by the time it found a – foreign – admirer ready to take it on its own terms, M's name as the painter was already forgotten, and thirtyfive years after that the painting itself had disappeared altogether. It seemed an exemplary fate.

M STARTED THE Fenaroli paintings – there were no records for the paintings themselves – early in 1608. By late spring he was back in Malta. The Fenaroli commission for three large canvases, and maybe others done in that period, meant he couldn't've arrived much before May, when the sea was good again for sailing. A very personal sense of urgency had transpired from the formal language of Alof de Wignacourt's letters to his ambassadors and the pope, and it can only have come from Wignacourt's anxiety to see himself in a canvas by M. The extraordinary intensity of M's Malaspina *Jerome*, the physical way it combined psychological immediacy and mythic impersonality, Wignacourt wanted for himself. He sounded, too, genuinely affectionate toward M, and every mention of M's time on Malta confirmed this in some way. On Malta, M was a hit.

So although there was no hard evidence at all of when exactly M's Maltese work was done or in what order he did his next paintings, the very formal portrait of Wignacourt with his page was probably done first to appease the grand master's eagerness for M's services. More even than M's other portraits, this one creaked and groaned with the tension between the containing formality – a portrait had to be a likeness and it had to flatter the sitter's sense of himself – and M's response to visual phenomena. The formality was embodied here by the great suit of full body armour, which limited individual life to the head. The portrait head was so finely done – with enough of the Malaspina *Jerome* about it to please Wignacourt immensely – that the armour looked a tad out of place. The setup of the painting, the choice of armour, the helmet, the pose were likely prompted by Wignacourt's idea of the image he wanted. The way the great beetlelike casing took over in its own right – less a projection of virility, strength, valour than a complex set of glinting surfaces – was M's response. Again he was turning everything into still life. The grand master was standing in a kind of photographic studio no man's land that drained the armour of the strength it was supposed to convey. It was all very benign, and saved Wignacourt from looking like a mechanized monster, along with the diffused light and brown tones and the touching informality of the right fist made vulnerable as an upturned palm. That was a second thought, opening out the mailed fist, and made the metal casing almost human. It was flattering – the pose hid the wart on the left side of the grand master's nose – and slightly pisstaking, as M always was with authority figures – the stumpy splayed legs – and very finely poised.

Or would've been. The young page boy coming into the picture from the right threw everything awry. The grand master seemed unaware of him, gazing sternly off and upward into the middle distance the way he'd decided to, but the skinny blond kid was upstaging him like mad without even trying. The grand master was sealed inside his own ideal conception of himself, while the boy gazed sharply out from the edge of the picture at you, and by bringing you into the picture his eye contact set a whole new set of questions in motion. His intense interest in the painter left the grand master suddenly in danger of looking foolishly unaware of what was going on around him. And M's intense interest in the boy left you with a sense of the painter's gaze straying compulsively off to the right when it was meant to be picking out the grand master's innumerable rivets. A *Don Quixote* situation was threatening to undermine the whole ennobling thing. The boy's was such a subversive presence that he looked almost added in later, and the odd alignment of the four feet – was his page standing in front of Wignacourt or alongside? – raised the old problem M'd had with the *Musicians* fifteenodd years earlier. The parts didn't fit the pictorial space. Had he painted master and page separately and had trouble relating them? The canvas was nearly ruined by restorers in the eighteenth century, which didn't help you decide.

In 1608 Alof de Wignacourt was evidently delighted. Bellori had it that M did another portrait of the grand master as well.

> He painted him standing in armour and sitting down unarmed, in the grand master's robes ... and for these the grand master rewarded him with the cross.

Baglione too said M was made a knight as a *sign of merit* after doing this portrait. The other portrait disappeared but a couple of pictures of Wignacourt that seemed copied or derived from such a work remained in Malta. The machinery of M's induction into the knighthood, set in motion by Wignacourt's letters to Rome months before, just kept moving forward.

Whether Wignacourt went on being totally happy with his own image after he saw the stunning portrait M also painted of one of his close colleagues on the order's governing council was a question. It was the best portrait he ever did, an inward study of an aging man of action who was also a cunning power player. Fra Antonio Martelli like Ippolito Malaspina had been one of Wignacourt's electors in 1601, and had since moved rapidly through a series of increasingly powerful posts in the order. He'd been prior of Hungary, admiral of the fleet and was now prior of Messina in Sicily, a fighting fit seventy four. In late March of 1608 Martelli was given formal licence to leave Malta to go and run the priory in Messina. He probably left in April and just before that M painted him three quarter length in black, with a huge and shimmering eight pointed Maltese cross in white silk on his chest, hair cropped like a marine's, a couple of grey hairs in the trim beard, a few folds of loose skin at the shirt collar, a glint of rheum in the eye and lips slightly puckered over some unseen gaps in his teeth – but lean, upright, weatherbeaten as the Malaspina *Jerome*, one hand on the pommel of his sword and the other fingering his rosary beads. The figure was the very model of a Christian fighting man. The face was a study of age held off by alertness, a wariness in the eyes and mouth that was amplified in the body's slight tension, the gut sucked in under the buckle on the belly, the slight twisting and reaching for the sword as if in response to a newly sensed danger. Unlike the Malaspina *Jerome*, this knight needed his props, lacked the effortlessly commanding assurance the other mustered even sitting naked on the edge of his bed. The three portraits M did on Malta showed distinct identities but an extraordinary family likeness among the sitters. It had the feel of an M deeply in thrall to the idea of the patriarchal virility these old knights embodied. His fascination with old men, the fragile dignity and Learlike pathos of his exiled and martyred old saints, was briefly charged with a feeling of hope and strength in age. Compared with the physical intensity M caught in his two supporters, Wignacourt looked not so much mythic as an affable accommodating politician.

He was certainly very accommodating to M. A lot of exceptions were made for M over his admission to the knighthood, beyond the overlooking of the homicide of Ranuccio Tomassoni. Wignacourt wanted M admitted immediately to all the usual rights of bed, board, seniority and allowance granted to the young knights in the year they had to spend *in convento* – on the island – before they entered the order definitively, but *without having to pass the tests*, as Wignacourt twice put it in the letter to his ambassador in Rome. The main practical test – apart from the courses of instruction in religion and morality – was *doing the convoys*. After being nominated and making their profession – solemnly promising to obey the vows and rules of the order of Saint John – the candidates had to spend part of their probationary period serving on the Malta galleys in the war against the Turks in the Mediterranean. M was excused this – his name never appeared in the lists of those serving in the time he was in Malta. Joachim von Sandrart, who later went all the way to Malta to see the huge canvas M was about to paint, wrote around the middle of the century that M had *generously outfitted a ship for the fight against the Turks*, something he maybe heard on the island, meaning M bought his way out of service at sea. His productivity in Naples and Malta in 1607 and 1608 showed he also eluded the requirement that all novices spend a year *in convento*.

He was made a knight on 14 July 1608, exactly a year – and two days – from his first arrival, as if he'd never left. But he skipped the service at sea, as Wignacourt's letter had foreshadowed, and probably the endless lectures on the spirit of sacrifice and the knightly ideal – the thought of M sitting on a bench with a bunch of unruly youngsters and being instructed on the glories of being beheaded for the cause and on what to do if a spider fell into the consecrated wine was kind of implausible – and a scrap of evidence much later suggested the residency requirement might've been waived too, that he might indeed have gone back to Naples to handle his outstanding work over the winter. It was the strangest and most unreliable scrap of evidence imaginable, but it pointed, in its erratic way, to other possibilities as well. It was a half page thumbnail sketch of M's time in Malta, the work of an anonymous eighteenth century friar, as transcribed and abridged in the hand of a nineteenth century count. The version got almost everything wrong, but in an interesting way that pointed to other possible facts behind the mistakes. It sounded like an oral memory written down by someone with no sense of history, an islander living in an eternal present, and it said Wignacourt had called M to Malta in 1608

> to decorate the … church and its oratory and with the pope's approval made him a knight. Then M left without having done anything else and returned to Rome where … he was professed in the church of Sant' Anna in Borgo … after being professed he returned to Malta to do the convoys on the galleys, and at that time he did the *John beheaded* for the oratory at the request and expense of the prior of Venice fra Stefano Lomellini … and the portrait of prince Wignacourt … and two half length *Jeromes* …

M had left Malta and come back. The writer seemed to be mistaking a real voyage to Naples for an impossible journey to Rome. The church name looked like a mistake for Sant' Anna dei Lombardi in Naples, where M did his *Resurrection*. It lent weight to the idea that M went back to Naples. The other curious mistake was naming the prior of Venice as the person who commissioned M's Malta *Beheading*. Stefano Lomellini was a later prior and the writer got the wrong pope as well. At M's time the prior of Venice was Fabrizio Sforza Colonna – maybe M's great Malta work was commissioned by a fellow criminal and not the grand master Wignacourt at all. There was an independent hint in a letter written in Venice that might've meant the Colonnas were involved in this commission.

The letter was written on 7 September 1607 and addressed to cardinal Federico Borromeo in Milan. It was sent from Venice by his cultural affairs secretary who was rooting around for old codices and other manuscripts in Greek and Arabic for the cardinal to put in the *Biblioteca ambrosiana*, the library he'd founded in Milan that year. The secretary, who'd been in Naples the previous winter when M was working there, was now organizing a search for manuscripts in some of the Greek islands – islands linked with Malta – and arranging to have money sent on to the places the cardinal's buyers planned to visit. The banker Castellari who'd be forwarding the money was casually identified in the letter as the one who was doing the same for M in Malta. Or so the banker's jargon implied. M was mentioned by name in the letter, though not Malta. It wasn't clear who'd be sending money to M, Borromeo himself or some of his close relatives and contacts in the Colonna family. Cardinal Borromeo – and his staff – seemed to be remarkably well informed of the clandestine M's movements south of Rome.

That money was being sent to M from Venice fitted the thought that Fabrizio Sforza Colonna was ordering a painting as prior of Venice and paying out of priory funds. A big commission by Sforza in late 1607 sounded right. He'd just brought M to Malta, he was newly out of jail himself and appointed to a key post as *general of the Malta galleys* – a major canvas of *John beheaded* for the new oratory by the great painter of the day would've made a fitting act of commitment to the order of Saint John and everything it stood for. A generous fee from Venice for the huge canvas M was about to paint might've been how M could afford to fit out a warship at his own expense. It made for a nice reciprocity – the warrior giving a painting and the artist giving military hardware. Being admitted to the order of the knights hospitaller normally took a lot of money. M didn't belong to an aristocratic dynasty that could buy him his knighthood, and whatever the circuits of commissioning and payment, the huge canvas of *John beheaded* was inevitably seen as M's deeply felt act of adherence as well, maybe, as his payment in kind for admission to the order.

M LOVED SWORDS. He was an expert swordsman – in the campo Marzio two years earlier he'd been cornered and fought his way out – and a painter who figured the hilts and pommels with caressing exactitude in his art, and could render the flash of a blade in a couple of smears of white paint. Malta could bring relief and vindication by the sword, the consolation of action. *We want*, the grand master said of the unnamed M in his preliminary letter to Rome, *to console him by giving him the habit of knight of the grand master*. Was M *consoled* by the social identity and weight a knighthood gave him, or by being identified as a man of action? *In order not to lose him*, the grand master had also written. He wanted M to glorify the order, and himself. The knights had been on Malta less than a century, firmly established there for less than half that. They needed art to project their strength, and until M came into their ambit there was none. What they needed, beyond the power portraits of the leader such as M had already done, was a major image of their patron saint, a defining visual statement of what the order was about. This was what he now gave them. In return they made him a man. *Quid pro quo*.

John the boy in the wilderness was M's favourite saint – the John M found in Malta was the end of the story, not the radical boy but the adult John who was furtively beheaded in jail in a setup by Herod. The setup was Salomè's dance and the request that couldn't be refused, to silence John's attacks on Herod's sexual morality. This had a resonance for M of a quite different kind. It reminded him of the price on his own head, the lurking dangers of a police action or a bounty hunter's knife. He'd done his first ever handling of the John's beheading a few months before, in the half length painting in Naples, of the snubnosed executioner presenting Salomè with John's head on a platter. It'd been a first reaction to the cult of the saint's beheading, a souvenir from Malta. For the knights, beheading as an image of exemplary suffering was real enough. In 1608 the memories of the long and terrible Turkish siege of 1565 were still fresh. The older knights remembered how the Turks had taken the fort of Saint Elmo at the height of the siege and massacred the knights there on John's birth day, June 24. They'd stripped the corpses and decapitated them, and slashed a cross in the bodies with their scimitars to mock them. They'd lashed naked headless corpses to boards, arms out in the form of a cross, and sent a string of them floating over the harbour to the knights still besieged on the other side. The attempt at terror failed. The grand master saw the raft of headless corpses and had his Turkish prisoners beheaded and shot their heads from cannon back across the water at Saint Elmo. These were the examples of discipline and sacrifice from living memory that had to be drummed into the riotous youths from the noble families of Europe during their year *in convento*, before they were admitted to the knighthood.

The place where novice knights were instructed in the values and disciplines of their religion was the oratory of Saint John beheaded which had been finished two years before M first arrived in Malta, added on to the order's church of Saint John. It was built over the remains of the knights who'd died in the siege and since – all dead knights were called martyrs, even the ones who'd died in bed of old age. The oratory as M found it was a high, narrow rectangular room of austere and simple design – eighty years later it was gussied up in high baroque style by the Calabrian painter Mattia Preti, but when M arrived it was bare. Here M painted a huge canvas – more than five metres wide and over three and a half metres high, reaching across the entire width of the oratory above the plain small altar at the east end – showing John's beheading. Something for the novices to gaze at as they learnt how to be knights of Saint John.

It was remarkable how, under the pressures of his own impending fate and the recent history of Malta, M went quiet now. The shrieking horror and pumping blood of his early *Judith* were gone, and so was the busy crowded drama of *Seven works*. The vast scene he painted was alive but quite still, unreally real as a big window cut through the east wall to the outside, as if you were seeing, large as life or even larger, a group of working people carrying out an everyday horror in an inner courtyard. You saw a big arched doorway, framed by great rusticated blocks of stone such as you saw everywhere in the big buildings of Valletta and which might've lain right behind the wall. On its right was a low grated window and through it two prisoners were peering, as you were opposite them, at a semicircular huddle of figures framed by the arch. A heavy rope hung down in front of the window and passed through a massive iron loop set in the wall. A stocky figure with heavy legs and shaven head and big beard and a bunch of big keys at his waist, *in Turkish clothes*, was pointing authoritatively – a foreman, the jailer. He was pointing at a heavy ornate brass bowl being held down by a girl, a servant, or was it Salomè in housework clothes with her sleeves rolled well up? The foreman's lowered eyes weren't following his pointing finger but were directed slightly away from the dish and toward John's head on the ground. John's head was still attached to his body, lying prone with his hands tied behind his back, naked except for his brilliant red cloak – the only real colour in the dark vastness of the canvas, beyond an acid, pepperminty flash of the jailer's jacket – and his little shred of animal skin, his *raiment of camel's hair*, left over from the early days in the wild. M's John wasn't the adult, bearded prophet other painters showed, but a smoothfaced longhaired youth only a little older than the young Johns he'd shown in the wild. His head was about to be severed. Most of the work had been done, and cleanly. John was dead and the blood had drained from his face. The sword blade was lying gleaming on the ground beside him and there was little blood on the ground. Bending over John was a crop haired executioner, naked except for a cloth wound into bloomers around his hips and a leather belt holding the sheath of his butcher's knife. It was August 29 and the slow, minimal movements in the oblique light looked like events at the end of a long hot summer afternoon. The executioner was reaching down and grasping a hank of John's long hair in his fist, to get a purchase on the head and clear the neck for the final cut with the knife he was reaching behind his back to draw from its sheath. It was the weariest and most indifferent movement you ever saw, the last act of a busy day, and everyone wanted to get it over as quickly and quietly as possible. The heavy silence was palpable. It must've been an effect of the dark heavy overhanging space. The only person present with no immediate task was an old woman, beyond maybe just waiting on Salomè, one of those old women M now saw everywhere present at scenes of horror – purged of grotesqueness, pathos or even the specificity of a goitre, just a dried out dark dressed whitehaired old woman with long nervous fingers that she was pressing to the sides of her head, the only participant who was also a witness, the only one who understood. The figures were at once monumental and dwarfed by the dank stone spaces around them.

This was the first painting since *Matthew called* that seemed to be set in a real architectural space. The reason was the same. The place where this was happening was here and now. The courtyards were the courtyards the viewer passed through every day. Coming in to the long narrow chapel, you saw a group of life sized figures standing around in the large real space beyond the altar, glimpsed them in that moment of stillness in movement M knew how to catch. M's vast illusionism was grandiose and banal in austerely stunning combination, the huge unfilled courtyard space around this quartet of, almost, domestic employees. This was bringing Cinemascope and Todd AO and Panavision to painting and using it for street photography. You felt as in the *Calling* a hushed stillness and a weird everydayness, a knot of people engaged in ordinary work. The figures looked even more ordinary. These weren't the highly social individuals M had painted earlier, picked out by dress and manner. The extraneousness of personality was being burnt away, in the ever more essential brushstrokes. People, M's style was concluding, were more alike than otherwise. Eight years earlier M had shown a complex interplay of different physiques, ages, temperaments in the response to Christ's beckoning gesture. Now the four agents of John's death made a perfect choral semicircle as they bent over the body. It was only as you drew near, coming down the oratory, that you were fully aware it *was* a body they were bending over, the longhaired youth with the not quite severed head. It was a muted, accumulating horror that you needed to get close to see. Gesture revealed more than facial individuality and the movements were all the sober economical acts of doing. What counted was the act, and each was a part of a private, shameful business. You weren't invited to look. Like the appalled and fascinated silent prisoners behind the grate, you had to perve.

Bellori was so fascinated by what he heard about this canvas that he too, like Sandrart, made the strenuous sea journey south from Rome to Malta just to see it. M's contemporaries Baglione and Mancini hadn't even tried to say what happened when M moved out of their Roman ambit. They knew he'd been to Naples and Malta, but had no idea what he'd done there – Bellori, decades later, tracked the paintings down. The description he left of *John beheaded* came from someone who'd looked long and hard and close up at

> the beheading of the saint, fallen to the ground, while the butcher, as if he hadn't hit him right the first time round with the sword, draws the knife at his side, seizing him by the hair to separate the head from his body. Herodiade stares intently while an old woman with her recoils from the sight, as the prison warden in Turkish dress points at the hideous mutilation.

The idealist Bellori, when he talked about M's work, always found himself drawn, in spite of himself and his principles, to particulars of the raw human drama he was describing. It was the same when he described *Seven works* – all that energy of delighted observation in describing art he was bound to condemn. He noticed too the emotive part style played in the execution of the great Maltese *John*.

> In this work M employed all the power of his brush, and worked at it with such violence that he let the priming of the canvas show through its half tones.

He was talking about everything of M's that was to come. The huge empty spaces overhead, the slashing rapidity of the brushstrokes, the repertory of known faces and gestures – the old woman would soon be seen again, and figures peering in the gloom like the prisoners, and the jail warden's stocky widelegged stance recalled Wignacourt's in his armour – the unerring economy of the white highlights that defined a body's presence in the dark, now made their definitive appearance. *John beheaded* cleared the stage for the works of M's last flight, and showed how much he could do with almost nothing.

M did other paintings too on Malta. For Francesco dell'Antella – another member of Wignacourt's inner circle, a Florentine like Martelli and the grand master's secretary for Italian affairs who'd been active in the effort to win Paul V's *placet* for M's knighthood – M painted, maybe as thanks for his efforts, a small horizontal painting of *Love sleeping*, which was in some ways the weirdest painting he ever did. The supine child Love, nude and asleep with his wings spread out under him, quiver and arrow in his hand, had none of the glowing elastic flesh of Cecco at twelve years old, and none of the charm of the lost earlier treatment of *Love asleep* that'd shown the *pretty Giulietto* and elicited an ecstatic madrigal from the poet Murtola on the sleeping boy's *sweet languid little form*. This new one looked *like a dead baby* and its body was being eaten by the invasive darkness. The slightly distended belly, the unevenness caused by displacement of the muscles, the small teeth showing between the half parted lips seemed almost repulsive. The oblique light thrown up under the lolling head broke down a child's appealing features into a new and unfamiliar assemblage of projections and orifices – it was like Lena's face as the Magdalen's, but uglier. The child's body was completely objectified, as if the painting were an exercise in draining the subject of all the associations a viewer might bring to bear on an image of a small child. This one wasn't a child you wanted to touch. It might as well have been a dead rabbit. Unless it contained a joke – about, for instance, the erotic interests you renounced when you became a chaste knight of John – it must've spooked dell'Antella. As if to answer deathliness of the *horrid* painting of *Love sleeping* for dell'Antella, at some stage, and maybe now in Malta, M did a small painting of a very young *John in the wild* drinking at a water source, leaning forward on a rock and into the picture, only his head, shoulders and hands visible, with a sketch of wild horizon above him. The clean vigorous visual idea here – the angle of the head and shoulder and the play of light and shade on the boy's face and body, the frank and unselfconscious lack of *decorum* in the kid's mouth distended to catch the cold splash of water – were as full of energy as ever. This painting owed its treatment to the Lena *Magdalen*, and its tone – the almost asexual tenderness toward a younger boy – to M's very first known painting, of the young *Boy peeling fruit*. Movement in M's art was never linear.

The last known Maltese painting went to France and was tied up with the other candidate knight for whom Wignacourt had to get a dispensation from the pope. At the start of 1608 the bastard son of Henri II, duke of Lorraine's eldest son, had turned up in Malta wanting to become a knight in the order. He came with powerful recommendations, but his candidacy provoked violent tension between the knights of the French *tongue* and the Germans, who didn't want him. The problem took some handling by Wignacourt, with appeals to Scipione Borghese and others. The Lorraine candidacy was helped along at the end of July by a visit to Malta from prince François of Lorraine, a knight in the order who arrived with six galleys and stayed for a week.

> He gave gold chains and other rich gifts to almost all the other knights and palace officials.

The duke of Lorraine, who took power in 1608, presented an *Annunciation* by M to the church in Nancy some months later, and it looked as though it'd been commissioned by his novice knight grandson early in the year and taken away by prince François on his galleys that summer. The eighteenth century capuchin monk, in his wildly but suggestively inaccurate summary of M's time in Malta, also mentioned a visit to France by M, and it sounded like a scrambled memory of M's painting's journey to France. The French connexion was through the ongoing aristocratic soap opera of M's powerful backers. The duke Henri II of Lorraine had married the daughter of the duke Vincenzo Gonzaga of Mantua who'd bought *Mary dead* through Rubens – and she was the sister of the cardinal Gonzaga who was about to enter M's life in a big way. And the duke of Lorraine's sister Christine just happened to be the wife of Del Monte's employer Ferdinando I de' Medici. Relations among the Lorraines, the Gonzagas, the Medicis, the Colonnas, the Del Montes and the Borromeos were a tangle of intermarriages, and these were knotted into the canopy through which M was swinging with apparent ease. Wignacourt himself was in contact with Costanza Colonna that year, commiserating over the death in the summer of 1608 of her brother cardinal Ascanio and smoothing the passage of the priory of Venice entirely into the power of her son Fabrizio. And Federico Borromeo was closely in touch with the Lorraine court at Nancy in 1608.

What M himself thought about his relation to this network was quite unknown. The type of power relation between an artist and his patrons would have seemed so inevitably a part of things he probably didn't even think about it. With someone like Del Monte he had long standing relations that involved great mutual respect as well as reciprocal self interest. The question was rather how it seemed right now. How far were these people simply enabling him to achieve the social rehabilitation he wanted and how far were they deciding his fate among themselves and for themselves? Did he feel their interventions as liberating, did he feel grateful or did he feel increasingly hemmed in? Who was prompting his moves? How gladly did he paint for them? And how disinterested were they in their facilitations? He was the most acclaimed painter of the time, his work a must have for the powerful. Did his protectors simply want to keep him in their own circuit of influence and milk him for his art?

Why should the Colonnas, a family whose record showed its members quite singularly indifferent to the visual arts, among the great Italian dynasties of the time, a bunch of military minded philistines most of them, feel any affection or respect for a man whose only claim to attention was being the outstanding painter of the time? The surely pretty tenuous and remote matter of his father's onetime service to the family can't have counted for much. The idea that Costanza Colonna, for instance, might've nursed a maternal feeling for this strange and violent tempered killer with an eye for handsome boys, just because he was born soon after her own first child and in the days of her father's military glory – was this any more than a maudlin latter day art historical fantasy? There was no way of telling. It was true that Costanza's own son Fabrizio might've sensitized her to the travails of the black sheep. M himself was unlikely to harbour sentimental illusions about the powerful. His art ran contrary and so did his earlier prickly guarding of his own autonomy. He was also a man of his time. He'd honed the acute survival instincts of the socially precarious and knew quite well how little the rich and powerful were swayed by feeling when their own political or material interest might be at stake.

The *Annunciation* was damaged terribly over the years, and what mainly survived was the angel, taken brilliantly from behind, chastely swathed in a sheet and a sash, glaringly lit on his sheeted rump and back, whose stiff protobaroque swirls were as fine as the damp sheets' in *Seven works*, holding his wings spread perfunctorily for flight but actually kneeling securely on a rocklike cloud placed on the ground, his bum looming at you out of the canvas, like the elbow in the Rome *Burial*, or the risen Christ who was unnerving people in Naples, stepping out of the tomb and out of the canvas with a jailbreaker's look on his face. This angel's face was largely hidden behind a dazzling white shoulder and arm, naturally tanned on the forearm and hand reaching down to Mary. His head was a bit like his new young drinking *John's* – another take on the same figure. She was a masklike face, a pair of folded hands, the folds of a verdigris cloak, and her bedroom appurtenances of mattresses, curtain, straw bottomed chair and a household basket she'd put down beside her when she fell to her knees.

That summer Fabrizio Sforza Colonna came back to Malta from a raid on Turkish shipping with seventy four slaves. Bellori heard that Wignacourt was so pleased with M's job on *John beheaded* that

> beyond the honour of the cross, the grand master put a
> rich gold necklace on him and made him a present of two
> slaves, along with other displays of respect and satisfaction
> with M's work.

The slaves, maybe, came from among the new arrivals, and the gold necklace Bellori heard about was likely one of those handed out by François of Lorraine on his goodwill visit. By August, M must've been getting to enjoy being a knight and receiving these considerations of his rank. To having an identity, to feeling he belonged. A sign of a quite new personal mood was that he'd finished off *John beheaded* with his own signature. Not only was it the biggest painting he ever did, it was the only canvas he ever put his name to, and his signature was written in the blood that ran rather thinly from the not quite severed head. M wrote *f Michel A* and maybe more that was later lost, a macabre *jeu d'esprit* that linked his name with the still present thought of his own head being severed, maybe exulting in the thought that as *fra' M* he was out of danger or nearly so, linked his name as *fra' M* with his *brother* knights, and linked his name with the iconic saint of his most intimate imaginings. It was a strange touch, at once flippant and fearful. It asserted his new identity and recognized how fragile that new identity was. He finished the canvas around the time he became a knight, or maybe he raced back and added his mark as an exultant afterthought, to immortalize his memory for all the generations of new knights passing through the oratory. When Wignacourt formally made him a *knight of obedience* on July 14, the document of M's admission pointed out that he was being knighted for his merit and not his birth – making clear that a less talented painter never would've made it, forget *burning with zeal* – and that he was expected to turn his talent to the greater glory of our island Malta and our order. The order had chosen M because he was the best and wouldn't be superseded or outperformed. The grand master included a reminder that this had been made possible *by a papal authorization specially granted to us for the purpose*, and you wondered what Paul V Borghese would've thought if he'd known. It wasn't exactly a simple gift.

You could, too, reading the grand master's Latin, almost sense M's quickening dread at hearing he was now expected to stay put in Malta and paint – at thinking that if he was no longer quite a hunted exile he'd just become a kind of prisoner.

MALTA WAS A small island and the garrison society of the knights hospitaller was a tight, closed and physically isolated world – tied to the complex and conflicting rules of an order that was religious and military, charitable and elite, a group of randy, riotous youths from different countries and languages held in check by hardened and cunning old military men and overseen by religious zealots of the counter reformation. However much M might've dreamed of being a man's man, feared and respected as a fighter not a painter, secure in his status, this wasn't really his kind of place. There was an island world outside the knightly order – the teeming port city of Valletta, with its fast growing floating population of privateers, slaves and slave traders, soldiers of fortune and prostitutes, the Malta that was evoked by the nineteen year old Spanish mercenary Alonso de Contreras when he described a north African raid of six years before M's arrival.

> We took all the women and children but only a few of the men because a lot got away. We entered the city and sacked it, but the booty was nothing because they're dirt poor around there. We loaded seven hundred people and the miserable booty on the ships. But then more than three thousand Moors arrived on foot and on horseback to rescue them, so we set fire to the city at four different points and got away in the boats. Three knights and five soldiers were lost through their own greed. So we got back to Malta pretty happy and I spent my own wretched earnings on the girls of the town, who are so pretty and so cunning that they soon get hold of whatever the knights and soldiers own. A few days later, the grand master Wignacourt, who knew about my experience in the east and knew I spoke the language, ordered me to leave for the levant with a frigate, to get news of the Turkish fleet's movements ...

Contreras was back in Malta when M was there, after more military intelligence work for Wignacourt and profitable raiding on the side. His girl had been fixing up the house.

> They were all glad to see me back – they'd already sold the soap and the slaves I'd sent them.

Along with his major booty, he'd picked up a *bey*'s mistress, *the most beautiful woman I ever saw*, two small boys, a renegade and two Christian slaves in his last neat side operation. The furious *bey* had pursued him across the Mediterranean.

> He was convinced I'd had his woman, and if he'd caught me he would've had me fucked up the arse by six blacks and then impaled.

In Malta Contreras was putting his private life in order.

> My girlfriend had gone through nearly everything I'd earned with such effort and then I found her in bed with one of my mates, a guy I'd even done favours for. I practically finished him off with a couple of blows and when he recovered he got out of Malta in case I killed him. The girl ran off too. Later she sent an endless series of people around begging me to take her back, but I didn't and I soon filled her place. I only had to choose, since the girls in Malta thought I was one of the best things going.

For Contreras at twenty five the life was all getting a bit stressful and he was about to go into religious retreat back in Spain. For the leaders of the order of Saint John of Jerusalem, the contamination of this real world of sex, death, commerce and servitude aggravated the problem of controlling the young knights. They were already a handful – they were rich – their steep and increasing entry fees a main source of revenue for the order – highly aristocratic – they had to produce evidence that all four grandparents were noble to get in – and young – the entry age was eighteen, but *there was a growing tendency to admit younger boys as pages*. And they were away from home, in most cases to their noble families' great relief.

> Young men on their first tours of duty in Malta [were] no longer in touch with the senior members of the convent

who kept their retinues in the city. This led to much duelling and lawlessness ...

The influx of younger boys really got going under Wignacourt, who since he'd become grand master in 1601 had made an effort to cultivate the amenities on Malta – M's very presence being a manifestation of his *mission civilisatrice* – and had introduced live music at meal times and *surrounded himself with a large crowd of adolescent pages*. The attractive young page of the official portrait was rare in art but one of a whole mob of aristocratic boys in real life. The tavern life of the port would've suited M greatly in his leisure hours, but he may have had some trouble, when he wasn't painting, escaping the maybe invasive and stifling hospitality of his host and patron the grand master and his coterie of leading knights, and this was a situation that his own admission to the order would've aggravated. From now on M had to behave like a knight. Then again, there were compensating presences around Wignacourt. Nothing was known about M's daily life in Malta. Did he join the grand master at table, with the musicians and the page boys? Or did he eat in the refectory of the Italian *langue* with the teenage aristocrats? Did he ever get away to the waterfront taverns and their slavers and their sly and pretty girls? Given M's temperament and inclinations, and given the unstable and intermittently explosive nature of an aristocratic community that was moving rapidly and unevenly from the sacrificial heroism of forty years earlier to the *Little Gomorrah* of ninety years later, and given the underlying ambiguity of M's relation to his aristocratic peers – he could never *really* be one of them, and indeed was only a *knight of grace*, since to be a *knight of justice* you had to be nobly born – along with a possible sudden realization, even as he grasped the prize, that he was now caught in a gilded cage, you could see in retrospect that the long hot summer of 1608 held the makings of more trouble.

It came seemingly without warning – and when it did come there was no indication of what the trouble was. But it was big trouble. It was even worse than the killing in Rome. On July 14 M was solemnly inducted, by virtue of special interventions of the grand master and the pope himself, as a knight of the oldest and most exclusive aristocratic warrior caste in Europe. By the first days of October he was imprisoned in the *guva*, a bell shaped hole eleven feet deep dug into the sandstone inside the huge complex of fort Sant' Angelo that rose directly above the grand harbour of Valletta. The *guva* was a prison for errant knights of Saint John, a prison you could leave only if someone brought you a ladder or a rope, and prisoners normally left the *guva* only for their place of execution. By October 6 M had got out of the *guva*, escaped from the fort and fled Malta. The criminal commission of the order that day recorded the information of M's detention and his secret escape, ordered his arrest and a report on how he'd managed to escape – which was an amazing feat. Not to say, for a man alone and unaided, impossible. But the *list of crimes committed by knights* of the order contained no record of any crime by M, or indeed any entry between 1605 and 1609. Whatever M had done, it wasn't something the order of Saint John could bring itself to utter in its copious and carefully kept records. The inexorable process was now set in motion that led to M's being formally and publicly stripped of his so eagerly sought knight's habit before the end of the year and *removed and thrown out of our order and our community as a foul and rotten limb.* None of the documents that recorded the investigation of his escape and his expulsion from the order, or any subsequent document of the order, mentioned the crime for which M was now so swiftly and irrevocably removed. The reticence of the institutional procedure – and even the strange violence of the language of expulsion was strictly *pro forma* – masked something personal and unspeakable. The kind of offence only death could settle. The formal closure that followed in Malta opened the way for private vendetta. Every move M made from now on showed he was wholly awake to this. M now really was a hunted man.

18

MALTA, SYRACUSE & MESSINA
1608–1609

Lucy's burial
Lazarus raised
Nativity I

ORT SANT' ANGELO rose like a giant sandstone ocean liner out of the rocks of a promontory guarding Valletta's grand harbour. The fort had been built up over an old mediaeval castle and it was from here the grand master and his six hundred knights had held off the three month Turkish siege of 1565. A series of sheer walls descended in steps to the sea on all sides, each step high enough for a fall to be fatal. The *guva* was dug into the ground at the very heart of the complex, a simple underground hole carved into the rock below a small opening, too deep for unaided escape, into whose walls below were gouged the desperate marks and messages of transgressor knights spending their last days and nights alive. One of them in terror of impending death had scratched an image of his own funeral hearse into the soft damp stone. It was a frightening place to drop into, even with a ladder and a friend. Somehow M got out of that hole, out of the fort and out of Malta. There wasn't yet the Torre Orsi, the control tower built soon after at the harbour entrance to intercept escaping prisoners and slaves. When he next surfaced M was in Sicily.

Not a whisper, not a squeak. There was nothing at all in the record to even suggest what might've happened in Malta between the middle of July and the end of September. Neither did the committee of inquiry that Wignacourt set up with a bureaucratic flourish establish anything worth knowing about how M got out of the *guva* and off the island. On October 6 the *criminal commission* was formed to trace and summon M and *gather information about his flight*. This was the first indication that something was wrong, the first documentation of M since his knighthood. On November 27 it was announced that the information had been obtained about

> how fra' M, being detained in prison in the castel Sant' Angelo, did escape

and calling an assembly of the knights *to strip him of his habit*. And five days later, the knights were summoned by the tolling bell to the oratory, where *the said fra' M* was called by name four times to stand before his peers. When he failed to materialize, a symbolic stool was duly stripped of a knightly habit and M was expelled from among his brother knights as a *foul and rotten member*. The ritual formula of the *membrum putridum et foetidum* carried a faint but unmistakeable reminder of the *membrum virilis*, and you wondered how many of the knights now gathered to hear it uttered knew or wondered of a sexual crime as the root of M's new and terrible trouble.

The knights of Saint John heard only, on this public occasion, that M *did escape by means of ropes from the said prison*. This was apparently all the criminal commission had learnt in its month and a half inquiry into how M had got out of his escape proof hole in the ground death cell. Or all it was saying on the record. You wondered what the assembled knights were saying to each other. Maybe they knew nothing. Everything about the way events unfolded suggested the matter was being covered up at the very highest level. The talk, though, in that closed community, would've been worth hearing. The anathema was cast on M underneath his own masterpiece. The spartan and windowless oratory of Saint John was where the order held its criminal trials – M knew this when he painted what was then its huge and only and transfixing image. The knights were crowded on to pews along the side walls to watch the trial, and the accused, when he was available, stood in a dock directly under the severed head of M's John. An engraving of such a trial made not long after showed that the knights on such occasions had a great deal to say among themselves about the proceedings, and even a few things to laugh at. If M'd been caught he would've been in the dock there, in front of his own painting, to be ceremonially stripped of his cavalier's cloak when the sentence was read out. *In absentia*, the order made do with the surrogate habit ripped from a stool.

M knew the rules, and had likely been familiar with them for a long time. The order's statute book had been printed in Rome in 1588 with illustrations by Giuseppe Cesari, five years before M went to work for him, and maybe there was a copy in his studio. M knew these pictures, because in *John beheaded* he'd taken the image of the Maltese arched stone gateway and the barred window from the illustration of the death penalty for murder. The engraving showed two condemned knights peering from their cell, much like M's prisoners, at two free and virtuous knights standing by Saint John's church. Behind them was the sea, and a condemned knight sewn live into a sack being thrown into the water from a dinghy. The knights watching trials would've got M's pictorial allusion to statute XVIII, *prohibitions and penalties*. If M himself had killed again in Malta, this would've been his fate. But precisely because the crime and its punishment were so standard you'd've expected it to be named in the sentence. Even duelling would've been enough to get M expelled from the order. Given the novice knights' propensities, duelling was made a serious crime, and one knight was just then finishing a two year prison term for fighting a duel. This was an even more banal offence, not something to suppress from the record.

It was soon known in the larger world that M had got into trouble in Malta, but none of the accounts picked up and recorded by the biographers afforded anything of substance on what the trouble was. It was all vague and secondhand and uncomprehending. Mancini knew about Malta and the knighthood, but seemed unaware of any trouble at all. Baglione wrote that

> After I don't know what kind of disagreement with a knight of justice, M caused him I don't know what kind of offence and got imprisoned for it, but he scaled the prison wall at night and fled.

Sandrart, who'd even been to Malta, knew nothing. Bellori, who likely had too, was the most forthcoming, and he was struck by the sheer drama of M's reversal of fortune.

> M felt immensely happy with the honour of the cross and the praise for his painting, living in Malta with personal dignity and great material well being. Then his disturbed mind suddenly made him fall from his prosperous state and from the grand master's favour. He came into ill advised conflict with a very noble knight, was enclosed in prison and reduced to a state of physical collapse and great fear.

> To free himself he risked great danger and scaled the prison
> by night and fled unrecognized to Sicily.

Bellori, or his informant, seemed to know more than the others, more maybe than he was saying here. Whatever M did, it specifically and suddenly alienated Wignacourt – the main if not the sole architect of M's success in Malta and a man who'd seemed, in his letters to Rome, to have a particularly strong personal feeling for M. And whatever the *conflict* was, there was no mention of violence this time. Bellori would've seized on any hint of violence, to add weight to the Rome incident and reinforce the pattern of his subtly moralizing version of M. Instead he had to fall back on other character defects, about which he was equally insistent – this wasn't his first mention of M's *disturbed mind* – but which as a high toned churchman and idealist intellectual he wasn't going to specify in print.

So there was no real ground here for the standard inference that M had got involved in another street fight with an influential person. Baglione's *knight of justice*, Bellori's *very noble knight*, was probably just the De Varayz who was the senior knight who *ex officio* filed the complaint on M's escape, and who'd presumably imprisoned him in the first place. The long current alternative reading, that M was expelled from the order because the Rome killing unexpectedly came to light in Malta, was made invalid by Wignacourt's preventive request and Paul V's special allowance before M was knighted. That M was a killer had been no problem at all for Wignacourt. Neither had it been a problem for his beatitude, at least in principle, because Wignacourt had got the answer he wanted within days. Paul V and his nephew Scipione Borghese might've felt rather differently about the dispensation when they discovered it was for M, but this didn't explain the sudden and total reversal of Wignacourt's own stand.

What if the *very noble knight* were Wignacourt himself? Or someone in Wignacourt's inner circle? What offence could be put down to what a right thinking person like Bellori called a *disturbed* or *murky* mind – yet wasn't a crime of violence? Something ideological? An offence against religion would've brought in the inquisition straight away. M was no Bruno – there was never a hint that he had the slightest interest in doctrinal matters or that he was other than quite conformist in his religious behaviour. Everyone was. Everyone had to be. Painters might try to kill each other outside the church, but they kept up regular attendance. M's crime was strictly a matter for the knights of Saint John. There was, moreover, a strong hint in Bellori's account that M was physically maltreated in jail, and that he spent more than a little time in the *guva*. It all pointed to an offence that was deeply felt by powerful people but hard to acknowledge publicly. It might've been too compromising. They may have simply not known what to do with him.

One inference might relate all the reticence about the crime to the sudden and drastic reversal in M's relations with the Maltese leader – a sex crime. Maybe not even, technically, a crime – though this was unlikely since almost all sex was criminal when you looked into it. If it involved someone in the order and even more if it were someone close to or related to Wignacourt or one of his intimates, the response started to make sense. The institutional coyness and complicity – the crimes not named, the inconclusive inquiry into M's amazing and scandalous escape from the heart of Malta's security system, the hurry to close the matter formally – went oddly with the unspoken but lasting and implacable fury that now broke over M. Only a mixture of sexual jealousy and personal betrayal and compromised dignity, all the more intense for not being able to find open expression or normal legal redress, maybe with a further poisonous admixture of counter reformation bigotry and suppressed personal yearnings on the part of the *very noble knight*, could explain the eagerness first to get M out of Malta and then to pursue him to the ends of the earth. Which was what now happened. M knew too that from now on silent pursuers were after him.

In that closed and overwrought all male world that was part convent and part barracks, part boys' school and part criminal organization, it was hard not to think – knowing M – of the crowd of young pages the order's historian would later remember Wignacourt as having been so fond of. Particularly if the boy concerned were related to a senior knight – as the boy in his portrait looked like he was to Wignacourt. Sex with a page would've been the ultimate outrage. Even if the page weren't directly related to a senior knight. The mortal offence wouldn't be sex *qua* sex, but the boy's being had by a social nonentity. Sodomy was a mortal sin, but mortal sins were negotiable – even murder was. A little discreetly practised pederasty with one of Malta's thousands of young Islamic slaves – male slaves fetched a higher price than females – would've raised even less of an eyebrow than M's relations had in Rome with his assistants Mario Minniti and Cecco Boneri, not to mention the fleetingly mentioned *fuck boy* Giovan Battista and the *pretty* Giulietto. The pages, each with his four noble grandparents, were the male adolescent flower of the European nobility. They were not available for sex with a jumped up semiartisan, however remarkable his work. Maybe M had bedded one of Wignacourt's favourite boys.

The order of Saint John wanted M off the island. When M escaped from Malta he did three things that were impossible without the assistance of a number of people and the complicity of more. He hauled himself up out of the *guva*. He crossed tracts of open ground in a heavily garrisoned fort. He lowered himself down at least two steep walls tens of metres high. He immediately found a boat and crew big enough to take him across the open sea to Sicily and swift enough to leave the harbour unchallenged and unpursued. If his departure weren't entirely organized by an island administration appalled by the idea of a public trial – for what? – of the order's most recent and most famous new acquisition, M might've been helped by the fact that the director of prisons on Malta was a Carafa and related to M's protector in Naples, Luigi Carafa Colonna. And if he needed sea transport to Sicily, who was in a better position to provide it than the *general of the Malta galleys*, Fabrizio Sforza Colonna? Sforza was certainly moving ships between Malta and eastern Sicily around that time. When M left Malta wasn't known – when his escape was announced on October 6 some time had likely passed since the event itself. In mid September Wignacourt had written orders to Sforza about going to Messina, and Syracuse. A week later Wignacourt wrote a letter about dispatches he'd sent to Syracuse on the galleys. Syracuse was where M arrived from Malta. It was where Mario lived.

INQUISITORS PROBING HIS private life the moment he set foot in Malta, Mario Minniti in the summer of 1607 would've been on the next galley out – not waiting even for M to paint his *Jerome*. The nearest landing out of Malta was his own home town of Syracuse – Sicily's closest port and the larger island's main connexion with Malta. Mario was now no longer sharing M's umbrella of protection extended by the Colonnas, and when he got back to Syracuse he ran into the problem of the *casually committed homicide* of Ranuccio Tomassoni. He had to hole up in the Carmelite convent in Syracuse, doing a painting for its chapel while

> he tried a number of times to get a remission from the dead man's relatives, and this was always refused.

When M turned up after fleeing Malta fifteen months later, Mario had convinced the local authorities to free him, had set up house and was able to take his old friend in. He also used his persuasiveness and *the excellence of his virtue* to win a big commission for M in Syracuse. The Mario who now gave shelter and assistance to his old friend on the run was a rather different person from the wild and beautiful Sicilian boy with a turbulent past who'd shacked up with M in Rome fifteen years earlier. He was now past thirty and back home, and he was settling down with his current wife – or one of them – to what was going to be a long and successful and highly respectable career. If M had grown into an uncompromising genius, Mario had acquired the complementary attributes of staying power and business sense. Mario, now a *civilized ... gentleman*, had learnt a few lessons on how to run an art business from his old boss and M's, Giuseppe Cesari. For the next thirty years the Minniti studio was churning out art at full capacity, so that – as his loyal biographer explained a hundred years later –

> there are more than a few paintings now going under the spurious name of Minniti. The truth is they came out of his flourishing school. He had twelve young men who were all eager for the master's discipline and they all came away with good names as painters. He used them to sketch out the paintings and sometimes finish them off as well – he just added the final touches. He had so many demands for work pressing in on him, public and private commissions coming from every city in the kingdom, that he was forced to do it. As a result his work lost its glamour and a lot of weak paintings by him can be seen around, and he gets blamed for their shortcomings because they're thought to be all his own work ... if he'd been content to leave just a few works shown in public he would've been as famous as M himself. But there are so very many of his paintings that they're valued less ...

The *gentleman* Minniti and his friends in Syracuse also showed M around the archeological sights of their ancient Greek home town, and one archeologist five years later published a book on ancient Syracuse in which he recalled taking M to the remains of the prison of the tyrant Dionysius. The two paragraphs in Vincenzo Mirabella's book of 1613 gave a fleeting and unique glimpse of an M quite other than the one revealed in his paintings or in the criminal records and whose existence you'd hardly intuit. This was the M who'd been linked to a Roman circle of lawyers, poets and literary intellectuals, medical and architectural practitioners, a few semidetached church people – the kind of people who animated the academies, the informal centres of intellectual exchange that operated outside the universities and free of the church's dead hand. Its members were that nucleus of intellectuals whose counterparts elsewhere in Europe were laying the ground of modern bourgeois society and rational scientific thought.

In Italy they rarely got beyond keeping up their own informal contacts, publishing the odd heavily vetted text, indulging in dangerous clandestine atheist libertinism, doing what they could in the less ideologically charged areas of the law, medicine, architecture, the arts, working as secretaries and librarians for the aristocratic powers. Giulio Mancini's career as society physician, art collector and atheist libertine was a brilliantly opportunist version of this life. Powerful clerics like Francesco Maria Del Monte and Maffeo Barberini shared and encouraged these interests – insofar as their own hopes of being elected pope and their diplomatic work let them – and many of these friends lived entirely private lives – like Marzio Milesi, the jurist, poet and archeologist who was M's friend and passionate admirer. The personal and intellectual links were hard to trace – friendships were almost clandestine. These were the people who might've taken Italy into the modern world. This was the M who'd known Galileo and Guidubaldo Del Monte, who was the friend of Giambattista Marino – consummate libertine and willy nilly the best Italian poet of his day – the M whose interests might've been glimpsed in the titles of his twelve abandoned books, the intellectual M who was neither a painter nor a street fighter nor a lover of boys and who mostly vanished from sight.

The ruler of ancient Syracuse – the Syracuse of Pindar and Archimedes – the tyrant Dionysius, had a deep slit *cut into the living rock* in the roof of a narrow, deep and immensely high cave by the city's amphitheatre, like the narrow wedge of a chip taken out of a tree by an axe, with ripples near the top like the folds of a human ear's. A gate against the entrance made this his prison, and the great convenience of it was that the jailer had his office in a small room gouged out of the hillside at the very top of the slit, joined by a small hole but out of sight and out of mind of the prisoners on the ground hundreds of feet below. Not, however, out of earshot. The acoustics of the space below were such that the prisoners couldn't even breathe without being heard by the guard. Mirabella took M to see it and M, stirred in his *unique mental power of imitating natural phenomena*, said

You see how the tyrant, when he wanted to make a space that'd let him hear things, took his model from the way nature got the same effect. So he made his jail in the form of an ear.

The M speaking here was the otherwise unknown M the scientific intellectual – dry, essential, attentive to natural phenomena, the M whose painter's interest in the effects of light, reflected, refracted and registered by the human eye was lucid, conscious and empirical. There was no need, after reading this tiny shard of his reported thought, to think of M as intuitive and *farouche* – the man who copied nature so attentively because he was incapable of higher things. This was a tiny but unmistakeable instance of a modern empirical mind being brought to bear on a question of physics. The M speaking here related to Leonardo and Galileo, and for demonstrating this, Mirabella's fleeting anecdote had a force out of all proportion to its place in his archeological pamphlet. This was the company M kept that didn't attract the cops. Ever after M's visit, the ancient echoing prison cave in Syracuse was called *the ear of Dionysius*.

THE SENATE OF the city of Syracuse didn't need much persuading to engage M, because

> a powerful rumour was going around that he was the best painter in Italy.

M himself, after losing everything again, including the gold chain and the slaves, was badly in need of work. Syracuse was lucky – it got one of M's breakthrough paintings, at once a summation and a radical departure. M'd seen enough of the real world. He set out now into a desolate territory of the mind whose images lay inward. The painter who'd said five years earlier that a *good man ... knew how to imitate real things well* and *always* painted *with the real life model in front of him* was now working mainly from memory. The little company of favourite models he'd painted over and over in Rome, and the new group he'd formed again in Naples – the girl with the prognathous jaw, the snubnosed labourer, the bearded Spanish officer, Cecco nearly grown – were now a mental repertory of intensely recalled faces and gestures held in his mind's eye. He'd spend a year on Sicily and leave four large altarpieces, paintings that drew on the past yet were quite new in the

441

spare urgency of their doing. They'd remain M's hidden masterpieces, rarely visited, less understood, stripped and essential and steeped in an existential darkness that made, in certain moments, the shadows and the bodies of his Roman work look almost gaudy.

Now it was a matter of time and means. From memory he painted fast – the Syracuse job, a huge canvas over four metres high by three metres wide, took him less than two months, with careful preliminary study of the installation, *penitmenti* and time out to tour the archeological sites – and the daring economies speed entailed now freed him too from the rigorous formal demands he'd always made of himself – as Vincenzo Giustiniani noticed – as if in compensation for his fidelity to the real. M's painting now became almost insolent in its uncaringness for canonical form. He painted things in his mind and people still found them terribly real. The bleakness was a release from the inessential, a dumping of material ballast, a lightening earnt by years of arduous attention to the world. M's work now sang and flowed as it never had before, even as he went into the night.

Lucy was the saint of Syracuse, where she'd been denounced as a Christian by her disappointed *fiancé* after deciding to remain a virgin, then stabbed in the throat after a clash with the Roman proconsul. She was buried in the maze of palaeoChristian catacombs cut into the tufa outside Syracuse and lying under the church named after her tomb. The twelfth century church had been abandoned, but in 1608 the city had just begun a two year restoration, and M's commission was to paint the new altarpiece. He used the scope of the huge canvas to paint another great illusionistic *mise en scène* at the end of a long church, but *Lucy's burial* was a subtler and far more radical invention than the one he'd just left behind in Malta. Under a vast empty space broken only by the shadow of an archway – two thirds of the canvas was plain dark wall, or the hole and the rocks in the foreground – the little huddle of believers gathered in a confused row behind Lucy's body laid out on the ground was diminished even further in being framed and partly hidden by two giant hulking gravediggers sweating with spades in their underwear. Lucy's body was hardly noticeable at first, stretched out in the dirt beyond the labourers' tree trunk legs.

The double take the picture involved you in – the nearly instantaneous vision of the huge filthy labourers' shoulders and bums thrust in your face and the glimpse of the little upright row of mourners and the slender body lying at their feet, diminished by the enormous arch cut in the stone beyond and above them like an extension of the framing church – was unprecedented in Italian art. It was stunning less for its radical dislocations of conventional space and scale – the sense of depth and the sense of human littleness – than for the way it thrust you perving into the picture, a face in the crowd, jostling for a view of the victim's corpse and the last rites after the tragedy. To get that look you had to get down low, get up close to the filthy labourers, peer through their legs at the young girl's body. There was a certain element of jostling and perving going on among the mourners themselves, and a certain amount of confusion at the signals coming from the right, like the picture's lighting and the light in the church itself.

The officiating bishop, usefully distinguished from the other half glimpsed heads by a mitre and crozier, had his hand raised in a final benediction of Lucy's dead body, but the liturgical solemnity of the moment was obscured by the huge illuminated bum of the shaven skulled labourer on the right, and also by the bearded military figure in upper body armour who was directing the burial – his extended arm, pointing at the corpse to be transferred to the hole, exactly blocked your view of the bishop's so you saw only the hand. The worker on the left was glancing up sharply, drawing your attention not to the solemnity of the last rite but to the order on where to dump the body. You were helped, as you craned forward through the confusion, to identify the body by the downward gaze of the young deacon standing over it, and you could pick him out by his vivid red stole catching the light, the only thing in the painting that wasn't a shade of dark brown. He had the smooth repressed sexless look of a young clergyman and his fingers were laced in a demurely conventional attitude of regret – a gesture that contrasted with the more ragged and emphatic use of hands in face clasping and noseblowing of the older worn figures around him. The old woman kneeling over the corpse with her face in her hands was a reversed reprise of the appalled old woman in *John beheaded*. The labourers recalled the stooping executioner in the Malta painting, framing the corpse by bending over it.

Lucy herself was done with a few brilliant economical highlights, her outflung arms boldly foreshortened, her face and shoulder effortlessly derived from the flung back faces lit from below that'd begun with Lena's tilted face in *Mary dead* and the *Weeping Magdalen* and the *Love sleeping* he'd just done in Malta. This time it really was the hollow dead eyed face of a lifeless corpse. At first M had removed the head from the body altogether – a noncanonical variant that maybe betrayed his own renewed insecurities and maybe looked too macabre, because he attached it again and left a gash in the throat. Unable to get a look at the dead girl from the back of the crowd – one faintly glimpsed peering face just might've been his own – M had come round to the other side like an enterprizing press photographer, jumped into the grave and got his picture from there, which was why the viewpoint was so low and a huge labourer's arse took up so much of the picture. It was why the picture was so brilliantly unfocused – unlike the totally concentrated Malta *John* – with a tangle of gestures and glances over-lapping and intersecting around the painting's small, still and very dead heart. This was the catacombs of Syracuse as the streets of New York. This was a murder aftermath as seen by Weegee, the forerunner of the 1942 *Last rites*, the 1939 *Murder at the feast of san Gennaro*, the 1942 *Joy of living*.

> Weegee's work is defined by searing chiaroscuro. His pref-
> erence for working at night, the glaring lighting of the city
> streets, and the particularly inky darkness of New York
> nights all contribute to the intense tonal contrast in his
> work ... in *Car Crash Upper Fifth Ave* (1941) ... that dark-
> ness acts as a vivid framing device, calling attention to the
> victims of the crash.

You saw it first from M in 1608. *Lucy's burial* matched *Mary dead*, and took more from it than the supine figure of the dead woman. It lacked the intensity of tragic loss that weighed on the still alive seeming figure of Mary – the broken doll like corpse at people's feet made a human death something that passed almost unnoticed in the civil and religious busyness of properly disposing of the corpse, a busyness itself dwarfed and silenced in the great overhanging space above. It was as if, now, there were that much less to lose.

A PORT TOWN too close for comfort to Malta, Syracuse anyway offered few chances of work.

> M's unquiet mind ... left the comforts of his friend Min-
> niti's home

and by early December M had moved north to Messina, the big port city just across the narrow strait from Calabria at the toe of continental Italy. The odd thing about Messina as a choice of destination was that there was a large and active priory of the order of Saint John in the city. You'd think a fugitive from the order's maximum security cell on Malta, expelled by his fellow knights as *a foul and rotten limb*, and pursued by the murderous covert vendetta of a very senior knight, might've preferred a more restful destination. To move from Syracuse to Messina was high risk. That M did go there, and had a very successful and presumably rather public career that lasted six or eight months, until a quite separate piece of unpleasantness provoked his hurried departure from Messina for Palermo, raised more questions about what exactly happened between him and the knights of Malta.

In particular it raised questions about M's relations with fra' Antonio Martelli, the intimate of Wignacourt's who'd been prior of Messina for the past two years and whose portrait M had painted on Malta about eight months earlier. Martelli had been granted leave from Malta to go and run the Messina priory, and M had probably done the portrait in – say – April, maybe to mark that departure, maybe as somebody's parting gift. Martelli was a seventy four year old Tuscan and though he'd been a knight of Saint John for fifty years, he'd also until very recently been a senior military administrator in Tuscany for Ferdinando I de' Medici, Del Monte's friend and master. The political link with the Medicis and the fact of the portrait, and Martelli's personal presence in Messina during the time M was there, all implied that Martelli might've covered for M in some way. This in turn implied that M's offence in Malta had been more a personal matter than a crime against the order itself. He was, on this reading, imprisoned because he'd offended a more senior member of the order, and then expelled because he'd fled prison rather than for the crime itself – expulsion being inevitable once the escape was known publicly. Martelli might've accepted M's version of events, or been swayed by his own sympathy for him, been contacted from Florence or even have been an enemy of M's enemy within the order. M later tried to make peace with Wignacourt and sent him a painting to placate him. Maybe he didn't even know he'd been expelled – in Messina he went on calling himself a knight of Saint John of Jerusalem. Maybe he was wildly misjudging the reality, but he didn't seem to consider the damage beyond repair. If Martelli were protecting him, M might've actually been safer in Messina than he was in Syracuse. Martelli resigned his position and went home to Florence in September of 1609, just after M moved on to Palermo – it looked like Martelli's imminent departure might've prompted M's own.

Maybe Mario, already bored with domestic life, stirred once again by the prospect of the drama and the employment opportunites that came with M's company, came along with M to Messina too. Mario's long and preternaturally prolific career in Sicily was short on detail and highlights. Nothing of his was datable for sure before about 1625, but at some stage

> he left his wife with relatives and went to the city of Messina, where he spent a long time in several stays

and where in 1622 he married his second – or was it his third? – wife. And where he did a lot of paintings, many of them copies and derivations of M's own work. There were a lot more of Mario's paintings in Messina than in Syracuse – and a lot of them done for churches linked to the order of Saint John or for private clients who were knights of the order. Mario made a third, longer, less troubled and more productive return visit to Malta about fifteen years later, very different from his landfall as a runaway teenager in 1592 and the hair raising brush with the inquisition in 1607. Maybe it was while M was in Messina that Mario made his first professional contact with the knights of Saint John – it was M's style, simplified and watered down, that got him in with the order later.

Messina was where the money was, and in some ways more congenial territory for people like M and his friend. Sicily itself was dangerous ground for anyone who wasn't a well integrated conformist. It was the only part of Italy – with Sardinia – where the terrible Spanish inquisition operated, and the inquisition was not only ruthless and unspeakably cruel but so powerful that it challenged the island's secular power. Messina was different, a law unto itself – until 1675 it was a republic in its own right, a rich and pretty lawless one. The city was as big as Rome – a hundred thousand people – a strategically placed port between east and west Mediterranean, linking Italy and Sicily and Africa, another centre of privateering and the Mediterranean slave trade. Marcantonio Colonna, who was made viceroy of Sicily in 1577 as a reward for Lepanto, wrote to Felipe II that year that

> ... your majesty knows how great Messina's privileges are, and how many killers and criminals the city harbours, partly because they can get across into Calabria so easily ... it's got to the stage where the office [of governor of Messina] brings in more profit in two years than the viceroyalty of the whole island does in ten ... it's so surrounded by criminals that even inside its walls people are kidnapped for ransom.

The inquisition had gathered around it in Sicily a whole tribe of *familiars*, intermediaries and parasites from all classes around the island that made it into a proto mafia organization. *There are knights, barons, merchants, artisans, peasants and every kind of person in it*, Colonna was warned by a local lawyer when he went to take up his post.

> In Sicily the inquisition had unlimited jurisdiction even in the most atrocious crimes and maintained a network of familiars that was practically unlimited and uncontrolled.

Colonna himself estimated the inquisition mafia as numbering around thirty thousand and he reported to Felipe II in Madrid that it included *all the rich, all the nobles and all the criminals*. This flourishing mafia was just as great a drain on Spain's and the viceroy's potential income from Sicily as Messina's autonomy, and both challenged the viceroy's power. This mafia was therefore fought by Spain, whose basic plan for Sicily as for Naples was to strip the place of whatever it could move. But when Marcantonio Colonna tried to limit the inquisition's temporal powers and cut back the number of its *familiars*, he was outmanoeuvred in Madrid by the inquisitors and soundly defeated. It was always tough for someone from *the continent* who was put in authority in Sicily. *Plus ça change.*

As a flourishing international port city almost as big as Palermo, Messina was always open to the new and *very respectful of foreigners*. M soon found work – for a *foreigner*, a wealthy Genoese businessman living in the city called de' Lazzari who'd contracted on December 6 to build and decorate a chapel in a prominent Messina church at his own expense. A friend of de' Lazzari's held a high post in the order of Saint John in Messina. M got the job straight away and unsurprizingly hated the subject that'd been settled on,

> an image of the holy virgin Mary mother of god and John the baptist and other saints

and he smooth talked his way out of having to attempt some grisly reprise of the *Rosary Madonna*. Presenting himself as a *knight of Jerusalem*, using it for leverage and deploying that charm or conviction that'd always kept his relations sweet with clients, he persuaded de' Lazzari that what he really wanted over his altar was an image of Lazarus being raised from the dead. It was clearly what M wanted, and de' Lazzari was probably greatly flattered by the thought of a graceful linkage of his family name with the story of a triumph over death. The painting would be *Lazarus raised*. The theme death and life. The price a staggering thousand scudi, more than double any fee paid M in Rome or Naples.

M's notoriety for a *dark* and *disturbed* naturalistic mind led to lurid stories of how *Lazarus raised* was painted. M, they said later, got de' Lazzari to fix him up with a room in the hospital run by the order in whose church the painting would hang. They got him *the best room*.

> To paint the main figure of Lazarus in a realistic style he had a corpse exhumed that was several days old and already stinking, and he posed it in the arms of some hospital porters. They couldn't stand the stench and wanted to leave. But M in one of his rages grabbed his dagger and went for them and forced them to go on. They almost died themselves ...

Theatrically shaped to make M look perverse, violent and obsessive, this wasn't in itself preposterous – not in the light of the extraordinarily subtle handling of Lazarus's body in M's painting. And it recalled Leonardo's impassive explorations of human corpses. Even more immediately convincing was the account of what happened when the client and his friends were finally allowed to come and see the finished canvas of *Lazarus raised*, which M hadn't let them look at earlier.

> Since painting is a skill everyone's eager to have his say about, among the group there was someone who made a couple of small remarks. He didn't mean to criticize M's judgement and was only trying to impress him. M ... unsheathed the dagger he always carried on him and slashed the great painting to ribbons. When he'd taken out his rage on the poor canvas he seemed to calm down again. He reassured the stunned gentlemen that they shouldn't get upset because he'd soon do them another one. They'd like it just as well and it'd be even better done.

The spasm of rage from a man under intense pressure sounded just like earlier outbursts such as the artichoke attack in Rome, the momentary eruption into violence of unutterable frustration and the quick recovery of poise that was becoming almost habitual. It was behaviour M had earlier been able to keep from his patrons and clients, but now things were increasingly slipping from his control, as in some way they had in Malta. The incident fitted with other stories that were still doing the rounds in Messina a hundred years later, as instances of M's weirdness. Nobody knew this was a hunted man in danger of his life, and it made the testimony the more compelling.

> He was a distracted and restless man, careless about his life, and he often went to bed fully dressed with his dagger at his side and he never let go of it, out of the uneasiness of his mind which was even more agitated than the sea of Messina with its raging currents that rise and fall. He dressed badly, always went around armed and seemed more like a *sgherro* than a painter.

M was remembered in Messina as the man who threw away the huge sums he earnt in passing distractions, the quarrelsome fighter, the painter who was always badmouthing other artists and was especially contemptuous of Messina's favourite painter. Shown some of this painter's work in a city church, M singled out a canvas by a different artist not from Sicily and said loudly,

> *Now this is a picture. All the others are playing cards.*

People were particularly offended by what they saw as M's impiety, and one incident that was remembered as an instance of his baffling rudeness left a unique and harrowing glimpse of the hunted man. In Messina they didn't get the point at all. It was the only moment when M's own words on his plight would be heard. They were characteristically tersely humorous, bleak and deeply sardonic. The scene, again, showed M the distinguished visitor being taken around the city by the local gentry.

> One day he went into the church of the Madonna of Pilero with certain gentlemen, and the politest of them stepped forward to offer him some holy water. M asked him what it was for, and was told *to cancel venial sins.*
> *Then it's no use*, he said. *Because mine are all mortal.*

Homicide counted as a mortal sin. So did sodomy. What else was he thinking of?

THE STRONGEST EVIDENCE that M might've slashed his *Lazarus* canvas to shreds and redone it straight away was the state of the *Lazarus raised* he finally delivered. Even by M's recent standards it looked desperately rushed. Its extraordinary success was to make the spare essentiality of its workmanship intrinsic to the painting. A vast, empty and almost impenetrably dark black space hung over the figures, who were all on the same scale and took up no more than half the height of the canvas. Visual drama was abandoned here. There were none of the stunning leaps of proportion and depth seen in *Lucy*. All the new painting took over from that work was the frieze of tiny seeming figures lined up across the canvas under the overhanging blackness. The figure of Christ pointing across the canvas from the left was a shadowy reverse image reprise of the figure from *Matthew called*, and he and some of the shadowy heads of the crowd of hangers on behind him were so slackly and approximately done that it seemed Mario had been working in the area. Under Christ's arm a couple of labourers were holding up a stone slab, staring off beyond Christ into the source of light. Draped diagonally across the front was the exhumed Lazarus, held up by a third labourer as his two sisters on the right bent over his head. Lazarus was a marvel. All the sketchy lean urgency of the painting was concentrated on the long angular nude with the sticklike legs and long arms outstretched, one still sagging splay fingered toward a skull lying in the dirt of the crypt, the other, just galvanized with new life, becoming rigid, a little upraised, palm held out to the light.

The light was what made it marvellous. From out to the left, out where the grizzled labourers were looking in surprise, came the rush of low, golden and almost horizontal light of the setting sun, dusty, filtered and refracted and coming from a long way off. It caught and lit up, as it travelled, a bit of Christ's shoulder, the cheek, eyelid and nose of a Weegee spectator, one of the apostles most likely, standing on tiptoe behind the others, head tilted back and mouth open with the effort, trying to get a decko at the body. It glinted off the sharp edges of a couple of other heads and faces, off the nose above an unidentified gaping mouth, lit up a powerful forearm of the man holding up the slab and the arm of the man supporting Lazarus. Then it invested, fully, obliquely, centrally, the gaunt but young body of the dead man and his shred of winding sheet. The beginning of a body's inner decay was sublimely registered in the faint unevennesses below the skin that the raking light brought out – the faintly macabre baby's body of *Love sleeping* had prepared for this – but it was warmed and gilded by the light, patently tautening and revivifying in a strange reverse decomposition, gathering tension and purpose like the picture itself. The ineffably beautiful flung back young head and face was Lena's, Lucy's, the baby's – the white jaw, the tiny flecks of gold defining lips, nose, eyelid. A human face in sleep, in death, life at its most vulnerable, seen as you might look up into the face of someone sleeping beside you.

Bending over this reversed and not yet living face, locked into it with a jigsaw kiss, nose fitting nose, was the living sister's, as the *facchino* holding up the body looked on with as much wonder as was commensurate with heaving such a dead weight. The sister holding and kissing his head was as monumentally swathed as Lazarus was naked – veiled, longsleeved, only her toes showing under the dress, wrapped in a red mantle. Her expression was as full of distraught and disfiguring human intensity as his was still serenely and beautifully dead. Above her gazing down was Lazarus's other sister with her hair pinned up, a young woman who'd be seen again. These faces, these features, these folds of cloth, were picked out with breathtaking economy and sureness. The clumsy Christ, standing in the shadow, was hardly visible and strangely sidelined here. In *Matthew*, he'd drawn the rest of the painting toward him. Here, in the complex play of a dozen differently directed glances, not one of the others fell on him. The others were absorbed in Lazarus, peering over Christ's shoulder or looking past him at the source of the light that was bringing him back to life. Even Lazarus's raised right hand, tense with new life, was out of line with Christ and reaching out instead toward the light that was reanimating him.

The painting was a kind of desperately rapid summation in black and brown and gold of M's whole endeavour in painting, to make things live for you by imitating the way the play of light made them live for him. The light was bringing Lazarus back to life, as M the painter brought *natural things* to life by showing how light fell on them. The transformation of this body by light into something living was the subject of this painting. Forget *history*. Forget how everyone else had done it. If he was *drawing in paint* here, the drawing was the picking out of the essential highlights, the minimal flecks and smears and lines of white and gold that defined solid things in a darkening world. He was drawing in light. Never in his work did the light of the sun seem so precious or so gorgeous as it did now, flooding weakly into the dark of this horrendous crypt, littered with skulls and thighbones, turning a corpse into a living young man, as a good painter turned a static form into an image of pulsing life.

He aspired only to the glory of colour, and to make complexion, skin and blood and natural surface seem real.

451

Here he was after the further and impersonal glory of showing the reality of dead flesh coming to life. In mimetic sympathy, watching the paint enact the body's awakening, watching the energy tingle out to the extremity of the outflung skinny golden limbs, you were charged as you watched with the same warmth, the same enlivening energy. This was why M persuaded Giovanni Battista de' Lazzari that he wanted a painting that played on his surname and not a group picture that referred to his first.

It was as if, now, he were lightening his load, showing what he still had to show while he could. You never knew. Where were these images taking him? Into himself, into his past. He never gave up, never stopped rebuilding, but it was getting harder now. His life was speeding up. Every new stop on the road meant a new career in little, new contacts, new commissions, making himself known again. Work, work, work and then the loss of control, the outburst that undid it all. He wasn't running on empty. Turning inward had lent this new urgency to his explorations of the real. Beyond *Lazarus*, beside that foray to the uncertainty at the edge of life and death, M left in Messina a matching *summum* of something else in his work. It was contained in his first treatment of Christ's birth, his first ever *Nativity*. Probably after *Lazarus raised*, and probably because the private work so impressed, M was commissioned by the senate of Messina to paint a nativity scene as a high altarpiece for a city church. It was, coming at this moment in M's life, bound to be unusual.

The nativity was the great moment of Christian celebration, the human coming of the promised lord and saviour in the form of a child. It was the faithful's icon of earthly happiness, eclipsed in the Christian imagination only by the human Christ's later torture and death. In showing it, generation after generation after generation of Italian painters had overcome the human oddness of the religious event – the ancient father, the virgin mother, the new leader as a helpless baby – by drawing on the older Mediterranean celebrations of the mother's female fertility and the firstborn boy child's sexual power, to invest the scene of the worshipped child as a peculiarly intense event of family life. The birth in the stable was transformed into a celebration of the simple continuities of rural life and contrasted triumphantly with the exotic splendour of the wise men or kings who arrived, in a fantastic reversal of the world's real order, to adore the newborn child among the farm animals. It was all about the miraculousness of everyday life, the one Christian event that transcended ideology.

M did it as a very young and very slight girl giving birth in a refugee transit camp. He got in close in time to the actual event. The mother here wasn't seated erect on the usual implied throne, displaying the child king to admirers, but slumped still exhausted in the dirt after her birth labour, propped up with her elbow resting on a feed stall, the ox and the ass looming far over her as ordinary farm animals almost unseen in the dark at the back of the stable, staring patiently away from the little human scene and out of the picture. The mother's eyes were almost closed in her tiredness, too tired to look at her baby. The child, wrapped in a perfunctory colourless cloth, was looking up and tugging at her face, but she was staring down beyond him at the vacancy of a few glinting and shardlike yellow straws on the packed dirt floor. Looking away, too, from the four men staring at her. Her elderly husband and the three shepherds all loomed over her too, looking down on mother and baby with deep concern. They weren't so much joyful or awed as wondering whether the child would live, how it could be cared for here. One had his arms spread as if urging her to some cleaner and more comfortable place, or maybe he was trying to entertain the child. A younger one held his palms pressed together, not so much in prayer as in that southern gesture of mild reproachful despair at the futility of it all. Joseph the father looked almost blind. All were barefoot, their clothes a few rough blankets. The mother wore a shapeless red garment and a spread out black shawl – a little nearly horizontal streak of brilliant warm colour, done with a pigment derived from a plant unique to southern Italy glowing like an ember at the picture's centre and matching the vertical folds of the oldest shepherd's. Her face and the baby's were at the apex of a visual wedge of colour and form that was driven from the right into the darkness above and the darkness below, a triangle of figures defined by the descending row of heads and the line of feet. There was a lot of dark space above them and an expanse of bare dirt below them. There was a stave and a shepherd's crook and on the ground at the front was all they had beyond their clothes, the father's carpentry tools – saw, adze, set square – by an old basket with a white napkin and a loaf of coarse country bread. It was M's last still life. Lying nearby was a small stray rock. Like M, the family travelled light. These were the irreducible necessities of peasant life, and it was a place where a child's birth was a matter of deep concern. In the bleakness of this night, as the newborn child struggled with his exhausted mother, you could glimpse outside, in the gap between the shed's rough roof and its paling wall, an almost imperceptible phosphorescent glow beyond the black horizon, which showed that the darkest part of the night was over.

Bellori's city elegance was merely and quietly appalled at the whole setting of rural poverty, *the broken down shed of beams and boards falling to pieces*. Another simpler and franker local man who'd been unnerved by the rapid minimalism and the radical ambiguities of *Lazarus*, responded deeply and sincerely to the *Nativity's* simple everyday truthfulness. He described it in loving detail and praised M for moderating his style into a more modest and accessible kind of realism.

> This great work alone would've made him remembered through the centuries to come.

The Messina *Nativity* was a kind of apotheosis of all the models M had ever put into his paintings, of all those struggling girls and ancient women and worn out working men who'd served him so well with their patient playings out, and whom he'd rewarded after a fashion in the unremitting tenderness of his gaze. The monumental block of men, *as if cast in bronze*, was his last great rendering of those gaunt and sun wrinkled labourers of the *mezzogiorno* who'd defined the work he'd done since Rome. The painting itself looked a long way back, to the northern country realism of the Lombard painters whose work he'd seen as a child, the painters who'd quietly established in his own imagination the unrhetorical dignity of ordinary life – the workaday fidelity to the real that the mannerist Rome of power, intrigue, idleness and *la bella figura* had found so disconcerting when it appeared in his images. And which Rome would soon abandon for the brilliant and infinitely more congenial new rhetoric of the baroque, as M's followers, the painters of the real, dispersed to the north and to Spain to complete the invention of modern art, leaving Rome to dream its brilliant dream of power. Now, in Messina, M was completing a circle, jettisoning his own most powerful forms for the sake of an image in which the parishioners of Caravaggio would've recognized their lives. And in which the people of Messina recognized their own. M's *Nativity* earnt him another huge thousand scudi fee from the city. And as with the *Seven works* in Naples, the painting's success drew the avidity of powerful collectors – *various princes were taken with the Nativity and tried to remove it* – and the priests had to transfer ownership to the city senate to secure the canvas for the people who came to their church.

On June 10 delivery of *Lazarus raised, by the hand of the knight of Jerusalem* M was accepted and noted by the priests of the church where de' Lazzari had his new chapel, *even though* they also noted pointedly the subject wasn't the one originally stipulated. M might've finished the painting well before, if this were merely when it was installed in the just finished new chapel. He did a number of private commissions in Messina as well as the two altarpieces, none of them ever identified or located later. A Niccolò Di Giacomo left a reminder note to himself among his papers that he'd ordered four paintings in a passion cycle – the treatment left to *the painter's free choice* – from M. One of them, showing Christ carrying the cross, was already delivered and paid for, and *turned out a really beautiful work*, and the other three were promised by August. Di Giacomo must've feared he'd never get them, because he further briefly noted about M that *his mind's cracked up*. It was a rare firsthand private opinion of M, recorded at the time, but it was evidently widely shared. A hundred years later people still talked about M as *mad, round the twist, off his head*. Nobody seemed to have any idea why he was acting strangely. The completed painting for Di Giacomo also disappeared and the other three were unlikely to have been done because at some point during the summer of 1609 M abruptly left Messina and moved on to Palermo. Bellori remarked that now

> M's bad luck never left him, and fear drove him from place to place.

Apart, maybe, from the prior Martelli's imminent return to Florence and new fear of vendetta, M had another reason for leaving town. Another thing remembered long afterward was that he'd taken, in his time off work, to hanging round the boys of a grammar master called don Carlo Pepe.

> This man used to take his students down to play by the arsenal, where they used to build the galleys ... and there M used to observe the behaviour of the boys at play to stimulate his imagination. The teacher became unpleasantly suspicious of this and wanted to know why he was always hanging around. M was enraged and disgusted by the question, and got so angry that ... he wounded the very respectable man in the head. Which was why he was forced to leave Messina. Wherever he went he left the trace of his violent mind.

The *general of the Malta galleys* Fabrizio Sforza Colonna on his comings and goings from Malta would've stopped at the arsenal. Was that why M was there in the first place?

19

PALERMO & NAPLES 1609–1610

Nativity II
Salomè II
Peter's denial
John in the wild VII
John in the wild VIII
Ursula transfixed

*A*S A FUGITIVE *he went on to Palermo.* And in Palermo it turned out – or had he known already? – that the new archbishop, who'd arrived in the city a couple of months earlier on May 11, was cardinal Giovanni Doria, known to his friends as Giannettino and none other than the brother of Andrea Doria, prince of Genoa and husband of Giovanna Colonna, M's old hosts when he'd fled Rome four years earlier in the summer of 1605 – and whose cousin Marcantonio Doria was still chasing M for a painting. M had some kind of a contact in Palermo because he was immediately commissioned to do another *Nativity*, and he did it fast because in October of 1609 he was back in Naples. The contact was probably Giannettino Doria himself.

The painting M did, a *Nativity with Lawrence and Francis*, was a far less radical work than the one he'd left in Messina, both in its iconography and its formal handling. The irruption overhead of a pinched and unhappy teenage angel trailing a banderole didn't much liven it up. But it was full of ordinary life. Only the mother with the grim drawn face and her hair pinned up – a memory of the model for Lazarus's sister – and the baby, no longer even held but lying *abandoned on the ground like a thrown away cockleshell*, recalled the bleak rigour of the painting he'd just finished. Joseph was no longer a gummy eyed ancient in a brown blanket but a blond youth in a green jacket and tights, a skinny and humanly plausible working husband for this hard-bitten girl, and he was figured not statically posed like the others, but having just twisted round from his assigned place to accost an old shepherd and break the posed monotony. Only the back of his head and his projecting shoulder and his tensed legs showed. What was brilliant was his short blond hair, or blond going on grey, radiating from the crown of his head and catching the force of the strong sidelight – it belonged to one of those blond Sicilians the Normans had left behind. It also made you think of the back of the head of Wignacourt's young page. There were such marvellous things in this painting its formal inertness almost passed unnoticed. In Palermo in the summer of 1609, after the amazing innovations of Messina, M didn't have – for once – the time or the will to resist his clients' prescriptions, except in the nonconforming Joseph. He wanted to get out of Sicily and almost immediately he did. The painting he left behind was his last flash of random vigour, a last enjoyment of human presences for their own sake – never mind the unutterable sadness of the mother and her abandoned child – and it was inevitable that after the paintings of Syracuse and Messina it looked a bit retro. Describing it, Bellori wrote with exquisite terse aptness of

the lights among the shadows spreading out into the night.

Why didn't he stay longer in Palermo? Anxiety to retrace his steps, to try again for Rome? If he could swing a pardon for the Tomassoni killing, the very city he'd fled in fear of his life three years earlier might now be the only place he'd be safe. Naples was in striking distance of Rome. He had Colonna links in Naples. A convenient passage before winter set in and sailing got out of the question? Or new pursuit and fear? Baglione was unequivocal.

He was being pursued by his enemy and the best thing he could do was return to the city of Naples.

Bellori, on the Palermo *Nativity*, said the same.

After this work he didn't feel it was safe to stay any longer in Sicily and left the island and sailed to Naples, where he thought he'd stay until he got news of the pardon that would let him return to Rome.

He had to get out before the boats stopped for winter and got one of the last. It didn't help him. On October 24 – it must've been almost as soon as he got back to Naples – a terse one line *avviso* was dispatched from Rome to the court of Urbino that

> A report has arrived from Naples that the famous painter M has been murdered – other reports say disfigured.

The *other reports* turned out to be right. M was alive, but badly hurt, maybe with his face slashed. From now on his life was an enigma. Once again, when *his life was in danger* as it'd been from Tomassoni in Rome, he'd eluded his killers *in extremis* but this time it seemed they'd come closer to their mark, and after this attack there was no news of M for months. Somebody helped him recover – he was a cat with nine lives, and he did recover – but no word emerged on who or where. This was a matter of some importance, in which even the lack of news took on its own significance, because back in Naples M was wholly in the ambit – if he'd ever left it – of his patrons and protectors the Colonnas, and becoming more and more of a liability. The ante was forever being upped. They'd first visibly emerged as his helpers – if you forgot the ancient unhappy episode of *monsignor Salad*, probably their very first attempt at patronage, when M was twenty one and rebuffed them – when he'd beaten up the lawyer who was harassing him over Lena and they'd arranged his tactical withdrawal from Rome to the Dorias in Genoa. They'd given critical aid when he'd killed Tomassoni a year later, saving his skin, whisking him out of reach of the law, nursing him to recovery, putting him on the trail of Naples and Malta. After the new catastrophe of Malta, he'd got away almost certainly with Colonna help, and whether or not he'd been in touch in Syracuse and Messina, he was back in their area of influence when he got to Palermo.

But after Malta, M now presented his protectors with a completely new problem. It was one thing for the Colonna dynasty, with influence all through the church and the papal state, the Italian states, the Spanish administration and the military, to modify or pilot the outcome of legal and political processes such as M's Roman death sentence or his relations with the order of Saint John of Jerusalem. It was quite another to protect him against a wholly private – anonymous, even – determined and utterly ruthless vendetta against M's person. At the same time, the M who'd set out from Naples two years earlier, full of high hopes of a knighthood and on a charm offensive, had returned from Malta and Sicily a hunted and desperate man whose behaviour seemed to most casual observers violent and quite mad. The murderous attack by unknown assailants in October showed the Colonnas that someone really did want M dead. Maybe the Colonnas knew who M's enemy was. Maybe he was a Colonna friend. Was M – the Colonna family may plausibly have started asking each other – really worth the trouble? It wasn't as if the Colonnas were interested in art.

Other people were, of course, and this complicated the picture, because the others were friends, relatives, connexions of the Colonnas. Their relatives in Naples the Carafas had M's Lena *Weeping Magdalen*, though they'd preferred to dispose of the *Rosary Madonna*. Their relatives the Dorias in Genoa had offered M a fortune to paint for them and remained anxious to get hold of something. The Dorias were related to Ippolito Malaspina, who'd commissioned *Jerome writing* and who was also related to Ottavio Costa, who owned a clutch of canvases. Then there were the Colonnas' other relatives the Gonzagas. Vincenzo I Gonzaga, the duke of Mantua, had bought *Mary dead* two years earlier for his huge collection, and his twenty two year old son cardinal Ferdinando was about to arrive in Rome and he was shaping up as an even keener and bigger spending art collector than his father – on a par with his friend Scipione Borghese, who by fair means or foul – mostly foul – had already got hold of four paintings by M and badly wanted more. Their other relatives the Lorraines in France had the year before commissioned the *Annunciation* from M in Malta, and the Lorraines were relatives of the Medici of Tuscany, who already owned M's *Bacchus* and the *Medusa* shield. And Ferdinando I de' Medici's friend and servant Del Monte, who was also related to the Colonnas, had the second biggest collection of M's paintings in Rome, or anywhere. Federico Borromeo, who seemed to be related or closely connected to all of the above, owned the *Basket of fruit*.

The Colonnas might've been military minded philistines themselves, but they counted a lot of M's cashed up admirers in their extended family. And all these people were all mad on M's art. And if M's behaviour was getting wilder, and if he was attracting some very unpleasant attention from an unnamed person or persons, that had to be weighed against the fact that M's work had never been more eagerly sought. Everywhere he'd gone after Rome, free of the ideological fanaticism lurking at the centre of power, he'd been acclaimed. In Naples, Malta and Sicily, money and honours had been thrown at him. He'd had more work than he could handle. His reputation was at its height. He was the most famous painter in Italy, the biggest of the art superstars. And hunted like a dog.

M's fame was unchallenged now. His only rival, Annibale Carracci, had died that summer at the age of forty nine, four years into his irreversible psychic collapse. Those who now thought M *very wild*, or simply *out of his mind*, might've missed the quieter parallel tragedy of the only other great painter of the age. That other *good man* had a lot in common with M. Taciturn, generous, sometimes angry, caring only about his work, hating the role of courtier that Odoardo Farnese forced on him, careless of his appearance but jealous of his art and reputation – the description almost fitted M. Annibale Carracci too had begun as a passionate partisan of Venetian *colour* against the Tuscan and Roman tyranny of *drawing*. The difference was that M was spikier, angrier and more uncompromising in both his art and his life. Annibale Carracci's equivocal achievement had been to reconcile his Bolognese naturalism – that northern concern for real life that was so close to M's own native grounding – with what his masters asked of him in Rome. His contemptuous dismissal by Farnese was a lesson in how the aristocracy treated people who were too accommodating. If M was paying the terrible price of being his own man, Carracci had been destroyed by taking the aristocracy at its word. The only painters who really prospered in this dire time were courtier nonentities like Cesari and Baglione, and even they had their little unpleasantnesses along with the table scraps.

So the Colonnas were in a dilemma. The way to get M off their hands was to get him back into normal circulation. Back to Rome. The way to do that was to reactivate the process of seeking a pardon from Paul V, which seemed to have got nowhere in three years. Del Monte didn't in 1609 have quite the clout he'd once wielded. After his personal golden age under the Aldobrandinis, he now had to cultivate relations with the basically hostile Borghese regime. The death in February that year of Ferdinando I de' Medici had left him in tears and further unsettled his place in Rome. Del Monte was useful to M in that he never openly took his side, never became too explicitly identified – he'd probably winced every time M invoked his name to the police. Del Monte worked the informal connexions, the family network, the friendship network. Del Monte was never linked, on the record, with M after 1600 – only the most fleeting mentions – M arrested and sending a message to Del Monte's, M using his name to the cops, M seen running toward Del Monte's – and a fair slug of inference kept the connexion alive. Had they met in Naples? In late 1607 and early 1608, when M was in Naples doing the Fenaroli *Resurrection*, Del Monte had been in the city too. He was there for nearly six months. He'd left Rome in September with cardinal Montalto and other friends and relatives – all Roman politicians linked with Ferdinando I de' Medici, who was trying to improve his relations with Spain and whose fleet had lately had a spectacular military success against the infidels off the north African coast. They arrived in Naples in late October and were entertained lavishly by the viceroy Benavente, who was seen to get on particularly well with Del Monte. Getting on with people was of course Del Monte's gift – maybe they talked between courses of the *sumptuous banquet* Benavente hosted about the painting the viceroy had commissioned from M earlier that year. Three weeks later Del Monte fell suddenly and acutely ill and nearly died – doctors and medicines were rushed south from Florence and Rome and Benavente ordered four days of round the clock prayers. He recovered in the new year, and when the others returned to Rome in January, Del Monte and Montalto stayed on in Naples for another three months. It wasn't recorded whether Del Monte ever got to arrange a discreet meeting with the *bandito* M himself, let alone what might've passed between them on M's hopes of rehabilitation and what Del Monte might do for him. Del Monte in early 1608, as the hopeful reports going to Modena implied, was still doing what he could in Rome. After Malta his room for manoeuvre shrank.

The October *avviso* indicated that M was attacked so soon after his arrival in Naples that it looked as though he'd got out of Palermo by the skin of his teeth and that his pursuer had followed practically on the next galley. Both Baglione and Bellori knew about the incident, but they wrongly thought it took place just before M left Naples again – thought it was why he left. Nobody doubted it was the work of the offended *cavaliere*. Baglione wrote smugly that

> He was being pursued by his enemy and the best thing he could do was return to the city of Naples, but he was finally caught up with there and so badly wounded on the face that the slashes made him almost unrecognizable.

Bellori offered more detail.

> Trying to placate the grand master at the same time, he sent him a present of a half length *Herodias* with saint John's head in the basin. This scrupulousness did him no good at all, because one day when he stopped at the door of the Cerriglio tavern he was surrounded by several armed men who attacked him and wounded him in the face.

Bellori wasn't explicit about *vendetta* but he was referring to real things and real people. The *locanda del Cerriglio* was a famous place owned by the monastery of Santa Chiara and run by a German and not far down the hill toward the port from the Lombard church – maybe the favourite eating place and most notorious hangout in Naples, hymned in the third eclogue of his *Neapolitan muses* by Giambattista Basile, who had his finger on the pulse of Neapolitan life. *The home of good times ... makes you live to be a hundred*, said Basile, though it nearly finished M off. The painting of Herodias really existed too. It was actually of *Salomè*, a variant on the one he'd done when he was last in Naples. Bellori's most suggestive mention was of Wignacourt as the recipient of the canvas. It might've been simply an inference, that if M were in trouble with the order of Saint John the man he had to placate was the grand master. It might also have meant that Wignacourt really was himself the offended *cavaliere*, and the suggestion carried the further weight of Bellori's own apparent visit to Malta, where he'd've heard a thing or two. A gift was more likely to mollify a person than to undo a judicial process, though maybe M's experience of Scipione Borghese had made him think otherwise. In any case, M stayed in Naples for eight months after the attack outside the Cerriglio.

HIS WOUNDS HEALED, in Naples M did paintings of a strange dark splendour, an intimate glow that looked like last images from the edge. The new half length *Salomè* hardly varied formally from the one he'd done two years earlier. There was Salomè herself on the left, holding out the basin and looking wistfully away from the severed head. There was the old servant woman in the headscarf, looking into the picture from the back, almost in profile, eyes lowered and face folded over John's head. There was the workaday butcher on the right, only this time instead of holding John's head into the picture he'd turned his back on it, glancing back sadly at his work. The difference in the new painting was that the figures were now floating in dreamlike fragments in an encroaching pitchy dark. The figures were at once diminished and more vivid. The more partially they were seen, the more they flared out of the blackness. The cruel white light, that picked out Salomè's breast, the old woman's white headscarf, John's dead forehead and the worker's bare shoulder, came from the left, but on the left there was a vertical band of total blackness that took up nearly a third of the canvas. They were gliding out of sight as you gazed.

The four heads were floating around another pool of blackness at the heart of the picture, close but entirely separate, drifting away in the blackness like the memory's phantasmagoria. In a sense they were the logical conclusion of the youthfully alienated *Musicians* – trapped together for a moment in a space that wasn't really theirs. Pictorially they were exquisite, rich and austere at once – long faced intellectual Salomè, the blazing red mantle on her shoulder and arm heating the dark, doing what she had to do undaunted. The old woman, hieratic, almost beyond the human under her stiff and gleaming white head-dress, her face intricately defined as a gaunt and magnificent mask of gold lines on black, was the last of M's stony ancient Mediterranean women who'd known and foresuffered all, and here she was no longer suffering but a powerful, implacable witness. The butcher, beside these hard, gathered women was a small, gentle, vulnerable male, regret-fully fading out of the picture to the right, only his bare shoulder – a memory of the young shepherd's from Messina – caught blindingly in the pitiless white light. The brass basin was entirely defined by a single curved thread of light catching its rim.

How the painting got to Spain, as it soon did, was unknown. Maybe M never sent it to Wignacourt, even if he'd painted it for that purpose, because the copies and derivations that Neapolitan painters worked from it showed it stayed in that city for some time.

Hallucinatory forms ran through a lot of his work in early 1610 – five smallish mostly half figure paintings in all, counting this *Salomè* – like dreams of what he'd done before. But they weren't the whole story. There was a painting of *Peter's denial* that did the converse, went in Weegeelike closer than he ever had, so that the canvas was jammed with the three figures, slashing, vivid, essential – Peter on the right with glistening furrowed pate and both hands folded into his chest in the manner of someone with some heavy explaining to do, the wiry old soldier in breastplate and a fancy helmet, bearded face in deep shadow, leaning into him from the other side of the canvas, the girl's face in between, half in light and half in shade, turning to the soldier and the light behind him as she pointed at Peter, vivid, fresh, un-adorned, in a few swift lines maybe M's finest portrait of an eager young girl – as the fire in the big hearth behind them sent a shower of sparks roaring up the chimney. This was anything but the end of the road. This was a tense moment in the land of the living.

Alive and anything but tense was the first of the deeply elegiac two young *Johns in the wild* he did in early 1610. These paintings in one sense at least really were a return to origins and a completing of the circle – the boys in both paintings were barely adolescent.

M's interest in young male bodies had grown with Cecco, though it certainly wasn't limited to Cecco's body, and had become in his earlier time in Naples a pictorial fascination with the adult male nude. Now for the first time in nearly a decade he was painting barely pubescent boys again. The way they were seen, though, couldn't be more different from the vivacity of Cecco at twelve or the insolence of Giulietto. These were portraits of boys still cased in the delicate armour of childhood and filled with a deep unutterable tenderness quite alien to the sexy exultancy and the barely contained aggression of the past. They were more like the brooding older *Johns* of the early sixteen hundreds, but the models were so immature that M's earlier identification with his models' adolescent introspection was replaced by a delicate feeling for a child's vulnerability.

In the first one, the boy's body was still plump and almost undefined, with a round belly and rubbery childish legs. His face, though – the beak nosed, full lipped, black eyed face of Magna Graecia – was at once childish and full of dark knowingness. The patience in his pose showed that this boy was certainly done from life, and his eyes had a glazed stare that matched his body's slump. The look recalled Mario's more genial and sensual boredom as he'd held up his sagging basket of early fruit for the neophyte M – this John showed not so much sensual receptivity as readiness for anything. Nothing would surprise this peasant kid from the *mezzogiorno*. His human presence – the puppy fat, the slack posture, the bored look – was stirringly braced by the superb formality of the vertically hanging red drape, which wasn't entirely convincing as a desert accoutrement, but along with the warm glow of the boy's skin and the golden fuzz of the ram's fleece imparted a rather surprizing sensuous splendour to the picture. It was at once absurd and quite moving, like one of the baron Von Gloeden's less unsuccessful photo studies of Sicilian boys. It was marvellous what M could get out of a bolt of red cloth. It was a *leit motiv* in his work and never more intensely present than in these paintings of 1610, an intensifier of very different feelings, from the carnal through the tragic to the desolate, as if in itself it were a flame of human feeling, blazing or glowing against encroaching darkness.

The red drape was particularly in evidence around the spring of 1610. It became the whole organizing principle of the reclining *John in the wild*. The boy was lying on his side, resting on a rock or tree stump and propped on his elbow the way Mary had lain on the stable floor in the Messina *Nativity*. The red cloth was spread out like a picnic rug on the ledge of a rocky promontory and over the stump, and then folded up over his back, so that a flap was demurely draped over his legs and his camel hair shorts. This was a wholly unsexy and indeed quite impersonal picture. The young boy's face, wistful but openeyed and fearless, was almost entirely hidden in the shadows and his soft almost larval body seemed gripped by the enclosing shell of stiff red folds. Against the panoramic near blackness looming over him, the small nude figure and the red folds made an almost abstract image, delicate, oppressed, adrift and likely to float out of the frame. The clarified, simplified forms felt like the outcome of a struggle to render only essentials. A painting at once classically poised and full of a quite unclassical apprehension. What was the boy waiting for, staring out calmly into the gathering dark?

Now was the time that M's young patrician friend, twenty five year old Marcantonio Doria in Genoa, finally got M to do him a painting. He'd fallen greatly under M's influence five years earlier, but so far he'd had to make do with buying a lot of work by M's followers and imitators in Naples. The first hard news of it came from the Doria family's agent in Naples, Lanfranco Massa, who wrote to Genoa on May 11 to tell Marcantonio that he'd hoped to send the painting of *Ursula* north by boat that week. But there'd been an accident. The painting was just finished and

> To be sure of sending it properly dried I put it out in the sun yesterday and the heavy varnish M had put on it melted again. I want to take it back to M and get his opinion about what to do so it doesn't get ruined. Signor Damiano's seen it [a local art adviser] and he's stunned by it, like everyone else who's seen it … you should get another subject ready for M. I know he's a friend of yours and he's so far ahead of the others here that people are fighting over him and this is a good chance …

M undid the damage and the painting was sent off *in excellent condition* two weeks later. Marcantonio Doria got it on June 18. He was evidently delighted. It was put with his most valued things, with his Raphaels and Leonardos and his phial of authentic John the baptist's blood. He may have taken his agent's advice and commissioned M's painting of the reclining *John in the wild*. If he did, it never got to him. It was overtaken by the terrible and inscrutable events of that July.

Ursula was the name taken by Doria's adored stepdaughter when she went into a nunnery in Naples, and her name saint forced M to handle one of the more deliriously extravagant episodes of early

Christian martyrology. Ursula's was an unbelievably complicated story involving a British king, a Sicilian queen, a former pope and eleven thousand travelling female Christian virgins. Plus Ursula herself. The eleven thousand virgins were slaughtered by the Huns at the gates of Cologne. The chief Hun was then struck by Ursula's beauty, and expressed regret for the deaths of her travelling companions. He made her a marriage offer. When she turned him down,

> he, seeing that she despised him, transfixed her with an arrow and so consummated her martyrdom.

Painters in the past had tended to spread themselves over the panoramic possibilities of eleven thousand slaughtered virgins – it wasn't, frankly, quite M's style. The first people who saw M's version were probably more *stunned* by his radical take on the story than anything else. M'd done another Weegee, elbowed his way in to the heart of the action. Even Weegee with his police radio couldn't've arrived on the spot as soon as M. In the frame he had the two key figures, plus bits of three thrusting gawkers. On the left the enraged Hun had just let fly his arrow at point blank range, and on the right Ursula was still looking down at her breast, hands at the wound and still on her feet in total shock. It was blackest night, the figures caught in the weakest light and not another dead virgin in sight. The three quarter figures only came two thirds of the way up the canvas – the rest was blackness. Ursula was instantly recognizable as the taller sister of Lazarus and the mother of the Palermo *Nativity* – she had the same sharp features and pinned up hair. Her upper face was now a livid white mask as she bent over her wound, holding her hands with thumbs out much as Peter had. She was, as it happened, swathed below in a voluminous ruby red mantle – the rest of her was sepia monochrome. Ursula had the look that was really unknown in art until war photographers made it familiar three and a half centuries later – the mildly puzzled look of people in the instant they're killed. Leaning into her on the far left was a ridge of scaly glints that belonged to a fully armoured soldier. Free floating in the darkness in front of Ursula's death white face was an upper fragment of a man's – eyes, forehead, the bridge of his nose, with a feathered Tyrolean hunting hat pushed to the back of his Hun's head.

Over her shoulder, in the instant before she collapsed, one of M's gawkers was peering, another upper face mask almost as deathly white as Ursula's, head back, mouth open, tiptoe, supporting himself – you saw three finger joints and the tip of a thumb against black – on a stave. It came as a slightly delayed shock to recognize him as M, in a ghastly reprise of the younger guy who'd been holding up his lantern and pushing forward to get a look at the arrest in the garden eight years earlier. Maybe it was that he was caught in the cruel white light fixing Ursula. It closed his eyes to slits. He didn't seem to have aged at all. Which was odd – eight years had passed and he'd twice been near death from wounds to the head and face, the last time a few months earlier. It might've been a personal morale booster, a reassuring message for his younger friend and client, after the things he'd been hearing. It was what he was doing all the time now, reaching back over the years to remembered faces and gestures – painting a memory. Here he was reworking things a couple of months old – Ursula's hands – a year – her face – eight years – his own. It was no longer clear what was life and what was memory. Someone thought Ursula was a woman he'd brought back from Sicily. Maybe. Maybe he'd only brought her image.

The ease and rapidity with which he could deploy his actors was freeing M now to do what'd always eluded him – *action* paintings, fully realized *histories* of real human depth and complexity, dramas on canvas. Freed – when he needed to be – of *the living model in front of him*, M was able to explore spatial relations, and the human relations they reflected with oniric freedom. *Salomè*, *Peter's denial* and *Ursula transfixed* were the enthrallingly intimate outcome enabled by his great Sicilian canvases. M was now entering an extraordinary new phase of great symbolic freedom, in which real life forms were no longer the absolute, demanding exclusive fidelity, but the manifestations of a psychic drama. Never had religion seemed so irrelevant to what the canvas showed.

The total novelty in *Ursula* was the Hunnish leader – in crimson too, concertina sleeves with a gold silk band and a crimson skirt, worn under a marvellously picked out and richly ornate breastplate with a lion's head worked in metal and a great spray of metal leafwork, and armour chaps below. The breastplate seemed to match the ornate helmet in *Peter*. His hat and its plumes were implied by a smudge of lesser darkness. The glowing luminous complexity of glinting breastplate in two different metals, crumpled crimson sleeves with silk band, under the play of the Hun's hands and his bow at the instant of the arrow's release, was breathtaking. Not more so than the leader's face. The magnificently dressed barbarian leader – and M's genius had been to seize on that *she despised him* – was an unprepossessing figure, not terrible at all really. Well past his prime. Narrow shouldered, with big ears and a narrow wrinkled face, large pendulous nose, receding chin and a major five o'clock shadow problem. Neither eyes nor teeth showed a gleam. The orifices were three black pits. A small man evidently wearing lifts in his shoes. Not ridiculous, certainly not grotesque, just very sad, one of life's small losers. The ideological rejection by the Christian girl was imaged as something burningly personal. M's black hilarity managed to get away with the suggestion that this man had just slaughtered eleven thousand virgins because they laughed at him. Ursula's refusal to be his trophy wife was merely the worst moment of an already bad day. It was, when you thought about it, the magnanimity of the very greatest art to find, without diminishing Ursula's pathos or the blanching understated horror of her death, the bottomless sadness under the killer's gorgeous armour.

Salomè, Peter's denial, Ursula transfixed, the two *Johns in the wild* – they were all elements of M's renewal in 1610, a reinvention of his art as a quite new kind of painting, rapid, fluid, essential, oniric. It was as remarkable as what he'd done in Sicily and even more overlooked. The small and intimate scale of his new work, the few half figures close up, the rapidity of stroke – all these later diminished them in people's eyes and hid the newness of what M was now doing. The paintings were overshadowed by what was happening in M's life, falsified by hindsight, seen – later – as portending his death, seized on for signs of tragic desolation, terminal exhaustion, and not their signs of new life. It happened to all his work since Rome, seen as illustrating a merely personal destiny. It was quite false. Straight after M fled Rome, the work he did was inward, private, exhausted. The image of Lena in an ecstasy of despair, the infinite sadness of Cecco holding M's own severed head, Francis staring into nothingness – these were morally terminal works, bleaker than anything he was doing in Naples now – and belied by the dazzling innovation of *Seven works of mercy*, and the successive renewals of Malta, Sicily, now Naples again. The painting of Cecco Boneri as *David* seemed so final an image of his own desperation that people would ignore its style and want to believe he did it now in Naples and not in that terrible summer of 1606. But as another summer came on in 1610, M was springing back with new hope. The hope was Rome.

THE DARKEST MYSTERY was what happened now. By the time Marcantonio Doria got his painting, M was getting ready to leave Naples. He'd been in the city maybe eight months and Lanfranco

Massa's glimpse in May of Neapolitan collectors fighting for his work implied that he spent the first five or six months of 1610 solidly working. He likely did more than his five known paintings in this time – the others, once again, being lost. In Naples M was working on these paintings and living in the Carafa family's huge palazzo Cellamare in Chiaia with Luigi Carafa Colonna. By what may or may not've been a remarkable coincidence, Luigi Carafa's aunt Costanza Colonna, the marchesa of Caravaggio, was also living there at the time. She was looking over a feudal estate the Spanish were offering the family – their way of keeping people on side.

Forces were gathering around M and it wasn't clear how far M himself was aware of what was going on. The events of July made it look like he didn't know what he was buying into when he made his move on Rome. Then again, he may've understood very well, and simply had no choice. The fact – one of the very few known facts – that he went on calling himself a *knight of Jerusalem* raised at least the question that maybe he didn't even know that the order of Saint John now considered him *a foul and rotten member*. Unless he was in denial. He did know the papal authorities were still after him. He knew he was still at risk of arrest and extradition, not to mention stray headhunters. The reasons he'd gone to Malta in the first place were freshly valid now he was back in Naples and in striking distance of Rome. He knew about the vendetta from Malta – it'd provoked at least two precipitate departures in Sicily and almost overtaken him in Naples. If the order seriously wanted to eliminate M without being linked to his death, it made sense for the event to happen at some distance and after some time from the unmentioned crime. The question was of some moment, because if M had brought deep dishonour on the people like Wignacourt who'd promoted his entry to the order, then he'd also compromised Paul V, who'd so promptly made the allowance. And the pope was the order's ultimate authority in a quite direct way. Which was why M's Malta crime must've had the effect of reactivating and aggravating his Roman one. It was hard to believe the nonmention of M's name in Wignacourt's petition and the pope's concession was other than a diplomatic silence. His beatitude must've wanted to know who this killer was, and what his special merits were. And if he didn't know then he surely did in 1610.

Even more Scipione Borghese, whose precise responsibility such matters were. Indeed Borghese had gone out of his way to get jurisdiction on criminal matters assigned to him. In M's case discretion was wholly his. Borghese the art collector was also well aware of M's movements and activities. Art aside, a sense that M's unmentioned offence in Malta had also deeply offended the papacy would've been a reason for the papal administration – Scipione Borghese – to show some tacit sympathy, cooperation even, with the order's desire to eliminate M. The art, and the chance of getting more of it, complicated that consideration but didn't remove it. To these two powerful interests who were maybe feeling it was time to move against M might've been added some of his former protectors – the people, say, who'd introduced M to Wignacourt and the order in Malta. Like his beatitude they'd've been feeling ill repaid for their efforts.

In none of these three cases was a determination to remove M, or play along with such a plan, provable. It wasn't even any more likely than its opposite. The order of Saint John might've had no institutional hostility to M, and have expelled him only as a formally necessary response to his escape. His holiness might not have known or cared who it was his dispensation had helped and what'd happened later. Scipione Borghese's sole interest in M might've been to get him back at work in Rome and preferably with a personal debt to Scipione Borghese. M's protectors and promotors may have been uninfluenced by events in Malta. Nevertheless, one or more of these hostile scenarios was perfectly plausible. The determining factors, the personal elements in play, were simply unknown.

The likely forces working to aid M were intimately bound up with the hostile ones working to destroy him. This was why it was so difficult to identify either. Wignacourt, for one, was surely not indifferent to the fate of a painter he'd been so remarkably affectionate toward. Either his love for M had turned to loathing, or he went on doing what he could, which was a lot. Wignacourt's protection or Martelli's would've accounted for M's apparently trouble free time in Sicily, as far as the order was concerned. M's great painting, with the big daubed signature proclaiming his knighthood, continued to hang undisturbed in the oratory. M's portraits of the grand master went on hanging in public spaces and Martelli, dell'Antella and Malaspina all kept their paintings. The order knew – must've known – that M called himself a knight of Saint John in Messina, where they were massively present, and did nothing about it. If a perfidious and deadly waiting game were one explanation of the order's behaviour, simple benevolence was the other.

In Rome likewise, M's crime ordinarily would've weighed rather less than the enormous prestige of his work, even more glamorous and sought after in the four years of his banishment. M's art was now known at first hand and acclaimed in Milan, Genoa, Naples, Mantua, Malta and Sicily – and France and imminently Spain, while Rome had been nearly five years without a new work by Italy's and Europe's most exciting painter. The smarter cardinals surely regretted this and wanted to retrieve M for Rome's greater glory. If anyone had thought M was a burnt out case when he left Rome in 1606, ready to fade away or autodestruct, they'd been proven spectacularly wrong. It was time, the more aware people in Rome would be saying, for a rethink. Scipione Borghese, the one man who could decide M's fate, was as greedy for M's work as he'd ever been – had perhaps already been quietly commissioning or buying up work by M from Naples. One or both of two paintings that turned up undocumented and unexplained in his collection – the young *John* with the ram M'd just done, and the painting of *David* holding his own severed head – might've been bought in this way since M's return to Naples. Back from Malta and Sicily, M was already halfway back into circulation. Any movement toward a pardon would flow into whatever M's old friends and protectors like Del Monte might've still been doing to get him back. If these were doing anything, it was so low profile as not to be seen by outsiders.

It was in this connexion that the arrival of eager young cardinal Ferdinando Gonzaga in Rome in February of 1610 seemed so interesting. His father owned *Mary dead*. He was a friend or relative of a whole bunch of M's buyers and patrons, including Scipione Borghese. He was immensely rich and like Borghese he was eager to build a collection. He was already buying paintings not only from establishment figures like Roncalli and Baglione, but from M's friends and followers Antiveduto Gramatica and Carlo Saraceni, as well as the new Bolognese Guido Reni. Del Monte was advising him, as he had the duke his father, on his art purchases. Gonzaga was shaping up as a major buyer from a rehabilitated M in Rome. Who better then – from the point of view of anyone in this spectrum of M's old connexions – to front up to pope Paul V as a fresh keen twenty three year old face on the new push to pardon M? It was therefore no surprise that Baglione later reported of M that

> cardinal Gonzaga ... was negotiating his remission with pope Paul V.

Bellori repeated Gonzaga's name and added that he was successful in winning M's *liberation*. It all happened within four months of the new cardinal's arrival in Rome, and it hardly seemed to matter whether it was one of M's old friends who put Gonzaga up to it or whether it was the secretary of state Borghese. Or whether it was the Gonzaga relatives in Naples, the Carafa Colonnas and the marchesa Costanza Colonna, maybe eager to see the last of a difficult house guest, who urged the young cardinal to act. The whole network of M's powerful connexions was involved, and it was impossible to single out any one line of transmission. It was this, and the uncertainty of anyone's real motive, that made it all so sinister.

THE DORIA AGENT'S letters to Genoa in May were the last surviving evidence of M's presence in Naples. They were the last real trace of M alive. After that he effectively disappeared. There wasn't, at the end, even a body. There seemed to be a painting or two, however. The rest was all hypothetical, and it were well to remember this. Particularly as the versions of what now happened that became, in the absence of any hard evidence at all, the accepted and unchallenged accounts for the next four hundredodd years – Mancini's, Baglione's, Bellori's – were none of them longer than a sentence or two and apparently based on nothing more than hearsay. A sentence or so was enough, however, to admit discrepancies, not only among the three different versions but inside each micro account. They were all versions of the story that M died of a sudden attack of fever on an unidentified beach on the Tuscan coast. The oddest thing about this story of M's death, when you thought about it for a moment, was how it ever won credence in the first place, let alone unquestioned acceptance for nearly four centuries. The story, as it was handed down, simply didn't make sense.

Although two of the authors were on the scene in Rome at the time, and in some degree of contact with the milieux involved, the very earliest of the notes on what happened to M – Mancini's – was written down nearly a decade after the events it referred to. All three were based on hearsay. It was very hard to get the facts on a death that happened a long way away. Particularly in a deserted place a long way away. And more than ever when you weren't sure quite where the remote deserted place actually was. Or quite when the death occurred. When there was no body. No witnesses. And when the authorities were concerned you got the message about the unfortunate sudden illness. Just when, due to the graciousness of his beatitude, all the problems had been resolved. Given the shortage of hard facts, it might seem to a contemporary sensibility that M's memorializers could at least have run an attribution to their sources. Which none of them did. You could be sure, however, that the sources were highly placed – it was one of the reasons they were neither cited nor questioned. This was, after all, the Rome of Paul V. And since a very few powerfully interesting documents did come to light in the nineteen eighties, three hundred and seventy something years after they were written, it were well for once to start not with the official and literary version of M's mortal fate, but to look at the very fragmentary surviving evidence of what went on in its immediate aftermath.

The first surviving document directly concerning M, after the letter of May 11 about *Ursula*'s melted varnish, was an *avviso* dispatched from Rome to the court of Urbino on July 28. It was very short.

> A report has been received of the death of the famous painter M, a great colourist and painter from life, following his illness at port' Ercole.

This was followed up by another *avviso* to Urbino from the same source three days later, which added a couple of details.

> The celebrated painter M died at port' Ercole while he was coming to Rome from Naples for the pardon his holiness had granted him from the capital sentence he faced.

Here was the kernel of the story later taken up by Mancini and Baglione, and Bellori after them. The second dispatch gave the first explanation of what M might've been doing in the area where he was said to have died. Or rather, why he wasn't still in Naples, where informed people knew him to be working. So Gonzaga's appeal to pope Borghese had worked, M had been pardoned for the Tomassoni killing but had been mysteriously taken ill on the way back to Rome. The second report was like a hastily added postscript, as if recognizing that the first made no sense as it stood. But since port' Ercole was a long way up the western coast of Italy, as far to the north of Rome as Naples was to the south, the explanation raised as may questions as it answered. So did the reports' source, and the timing. The unsigned *avvisi* sent to Urbino from Rome since the fifteen nineties had always been particularly informative of the doings of Del Monte and his circle and particularly dense in news of the art world, of books and archeology. The Della Rovere court of Urbino was the world of Del Monte's family and his own upbringing, and it was politically allied and actively collaborating with the Medici court in Florence. The information in its Roman *avvisi* seemed to be largely sourced in palazzo Madama's information centre, and something in the tone of these two messages – the little definition of M's art – and the fact that they were sent at all, pointed to Del Monte himself as the supplier of the information. It suggested that he'd been as baffled and ignorant as anyone at the first report, and had made further inquiries.

But *when* did M die? Marzio Milesi was so moved when he heard the news that he wrote five Latin epigraphs in memory of his dead friend and three poems in Italian on M's death. It wasn't clear how long after the event Milesi composed these, but one of the epigraphs described M as a *knight of Jerusalem* and another included the information that he died at port' Ercole while returning to Rome from Naples. Not seeing his friend again after four years must've been desolating for Milesi, who in the same epigraph emotionally recorded what he thought was M's exact age in years, months and days – getting the age wrong by two years, probably because M had understated his age in Rome. M was nearing thirty nine when he died. Milesi gave the date of M's death as July 18 and this became canonical. If it were exact, the news took ten days to reach Del Monte in Rome in its briefest form, three more for the shred of context. It was a longish time, even given the transport problems, and pointed to a certain confusion about the identity of the deceased and about who to contact. It might've meant waiting until the body was buried. It might've meant settling on the version of events to report.

There certainly was confusion about this. And at the highest levels. The day after the first news of M's death left Rome for Urbino, a letter on the matter was written to the secretary of state Scipione Borghese. Its author was Deodato Gentile, who was the papal nuncio in the kingdom of Naples and bishop of Caserta. Gentile was clearly replying to an urgent demand for information from the Naples end about what'd happened to M. What Gentile had found out by July 29 greatly complicated the picture of a sudden illness en route from Naples to Rome. It also contradicted quite different news that'd already reached Scipione Borghese.

> I find poor M didn't die at Procida but at port' Ercole. The boat he was travelling on stopped at Palo and he was jailed by the captain there. In the noise and confusion, the boat pulled out to the open sea and returned to Naples. M remained in prison and freed himself by forking out a big sum of money. By land, and maybe on foot, he made it to port' Ercole where he took ill and died.
>
> When the boat got back to Naples it returned his things

to the house of the marchesa of Caravaggio, who lives in Chiaia, which was where M had set out from. I had a check made immediately to see whether the paintings are there, and I find they no longer are, except for three of them, the two Johns and the Magdalen, and they're in the marchesa's house. I sent word straight away to ask her to look after them carefully, not to let them get damaged and not let anyone see them or get hold of them, because they were bespoken and had to be kept for your most illustrious self.

In the meantime M's heirs and creditors have to be dealt with properly. I'll go and have a look and find out what can be done and I'll try in every way to see that the pictures are kept and that they end up in your most illustrious hands ...

Scipione Borghese wanted to know not what'd happened to M but what'd happened to his luggage. He'd clearly been waiting for M to arrive in Rome with a stash of fresh paintings, doubtless the *quid pro quo* for the pardon deal cardinal Gonzaga had hammered out. Three had made it back to Costanza Colonna Sforza's. Had there been more? It wasn't clear.

Even less clear was the sequence of events Gentile outlined, as a glance at a map would've shown. Procida was a small coastal island just off Naples, far too close to be a stopping place for a boat heading north. The previous month the new viceroy of Naples, the count of Lemos, had landed there on arrival from Spain, and waited before entering the city until his predecessor the count of Benavente left on July 11 – taking his canvas of *Andrew killed* by M with him back to Madrid. Lemos entered Naples on the thirteenth, presumably a few days after the departure of the painter into whose posthumous affairs he too was about to stick his oar.

This wasn't the only geographical obscurity in Gentile's account of M's last movements. What'd M been doing at Palo? A castle, a little garrison – there was almost nothing at this small coastal outpost among the malarial swamps near the mouth of the Tiber. It wasn't well connected with Rome. Travellers to Rome landed at the port of Civitavecchia a little further up the coast. But even if M or the boat had a reason for stopping there, and if M had been arrested because the *captain* knew nothing of the pardon, if M had bribed his way out and found the boat gone with his things, including the paintings that he needed to buy his freedom – if all this happened, what possible reason had he to go to port' Ercole, another nowhere settlement more than a hundred kilometres along a coast that was mainly an impassable malarial marshland, without human settlement apart from Civitavec-chia, in the blazing heat of summer, a coast infested with bandits and pirates? It seemed physically impossible to pass these swamps on foot – the idea was insane. Why was port' Ercole mentioned? Had he been heading there originally in the boat, and now trying to follow where he thought the boat had gone? The only point of port' Ercole seemed to be that it was Spanish and out of papal jurisdiction. But if he wanted or needed to land on Spanish territory, out of caution or legal require-ments for the pardon, there were other Spanish coastal stations like Gaeta much closer to Rome and Naples than port' Ercole. In Gen-tile's account, port' Ercole was both pointless and unreachable, *by land, and maybe on foot.*

For Borghese all this was secondary. What about the paintings? Two days later Gentile had to write and tell him the marchesa of Caravaggio no longer had them because the head of the order of Saint John in Naples, the prior of Capua, had sent people round to confiscate them on the grounds that M had died a knight of the order and his belongings reverted to the order. *The marchesa says this is ridiculous and the prior's wrong.* Costanza Colonna knew M had been expelled. So probably did the prior – a hardbitten and very senior military man on the Wignacourt model – but everyone wanted M's paintings. Gentile nervously assured Borghese that he'd do his very best to get them back. The count of Lemos, the newly arrived viceroy, soon heard about the paintings too and became the third distinguished party to join the scramble. The viceroy's informa-tion was wrong. He'd heard about M's death in port' Ercole, and thought that was where the confiscated paintings were. Three weeks after the marchesa lost the paintings to the prior, he wrote – with *extraordinary promptness*, given the usual slowness of Spanish official processes and the fact that he'd only taken up office a month before – a very peremptory letter to the head of the Spanish garrison at port' Ercole.

> I have been informed that the painter M died at port' Ercole and that you have confiscated all his possessions, in particular those listed in the enclosed inventory, as owing to the order of Saint John ... the prior has stated that he has no right to them as the deceased was not a knight of Malta ... I instruct you to send me the possessions listed below on the first available boat and in particular the paint-ing of John the baptist ...

Within days of the news of M's apparent death at port' Ercole, the three political powers with a stake in his fate, the papal administration, the Spanish administration and the order of Saint John of Jerusalem were at their very highest levels – the Vatican secretary of state Scipione Borghese and the Naples viceroy the conde de Lemos were two of the most powerful men in Italy – in deep conflict with each other over rights to his work. And all three were seriously uncertain or mistaken about what'd happened. Little else of their communications survived – enough to show that Borghese finally got hold of one of M's paintings of *John*, which was the boy with the ram, but over a year later and only after Lemos had kept it in Naples for an unconscionable time, first on the grounds that he was having a copy made and then with the excuse that he had to see whether M had left any heirs or any unpaid debts. The *Magdalen* and the other *John* disappeared, but since the prior of Capua was a Vincenzo Carafa and M's painting of Lena in despair turned up centuries later with the Carafa family in Naples, who were probably related, maybe the prior's brutal seizure from Costanza Colonna secured him one work. Either that or Costanza Colonna got it back. The reclining *John* came to light nearly four hundred years later in Argentina, so it looked as though Lemos might've secured this painting and taken it back to Spain. In which case each of the contending parties got one of M's paintings when he died. They'd divvied up the spoils.

20

ROME *POST MORTEM*

Peter Paul Rubens, *Herod's feast*
Cecco Boneri, *Love at the drinking fountain*

M DISAPPEARED. NO hard evidence ever came to light about what happened to him. And like his crime in Malta, like the pope's pardon, M's death somewhere between Naples and Rome in July 1610 was carefully kept out of the written records. The church funeral records from port' Ercole were preserved from these years, and the register for July 1610 contained no trace of the death and burial of anyone who might've been M. The cemetery itself yielded nothing. Somehow it was no surprise. The insistent mention of port' Ercole – so absurdly far from where M was trying to go, laden with his *things*, so evidently lacking in logistical or administrative sense – looked at best like an irrelevance and at worst like a disinformation. If the latter, it was disinformation accepted at the highest level – the viceroy fell for it, in what must've been his frantic efforts to catch up with what'd been going on in the days of his arrival in Naples. Scipione Borghese's informant the papal nuncio accepted it, and maybe though not necessarily Borghese himself, who probably had access to other and better sources.

There were signs that the death in port' Ercole took a while to establish itself as the accepted version of M's fate. There was that equally unlikely version circulating earlier of a death on Procida. And it was interesting that the very well informed Giulio Mancini, when a decade later he set down his phrasing of the by then accepted version – that M having left in the hope of recovering his situation, arrived at port' Ercole where he was overcome by a malignant fever, and at the height of his fame and around the age of thirty five or forty he died exhausted and unattended and was buried nearby –

at first wrote not *port' Ercole* but *Civitavecchia*, the logical place, which he then cancelled and corrected. If Mancini wasn't remembering something else he'd once heard, he found the official version so intrinsically implausible that he couldn't record it without error. Mancini was also struck by the parallel between M's death and that of an earlier distinguished painter from the same town, Polidoro da Caravaggio, who was *murdered in the open country alone and unaided* fiftyodd years before. In a passage eliminated from most versions of his manuscript, Mancini noted that it was *remarkable* how both painters had died *almost the same or at least a similar death*. On the matter of M's death, either suspicion or knowledge was nagging at Mancini's mind.

Of course Civitavecchia was the obvious landing point for entry to Rome. It was also a busy port where events would find witnesses and false reports be denied and disproven. If M, or anyone escorting him, like the boat crew, wanted to avoid witnesses, then inconvenient places like Palo and port' Ercole made sense. Particularly Palo, as a garrison of the papal state and quite near Civitavecchia. Before M could be granted a papal pardon he had to hand himself over to the authorities, and Gentile's report of his arrest made sense. The arrest was mentioned by Baglione, whose account tallied perfectly with Gentile's without mentioning any specific place and especially not port' Ercole.

> He embarked on a boat with a few things to come to Rome, returning on the word of cardinal Gonzaga, who was negotiating his pardon with pope Paul V. When he arrived on the beach, he was arrested in exchange and put inside the prison, where he was held for two days and then released ...

So far Baglione made the best sense of all, including the first and convincing mention of Gonzaga's role. The mention of a *beach* and a *prison* and nothing else matched Palo, which was an isolated fort on the coastline and on the way to Rome. *In exchange* referred to M's handover to papal justice, as it would in Onorio Longhi's case when he was pardoned the following year. Bellori, repeating this in his own account, mistook its vagueness to mean *in mistake for someone else* and confused things ever after. Apart from this, and a slip on *Spanish* guards – which showed he was thinking ahead to the Spanish garrison at port' Ercole, which he mentioned later – Bellori here followed Bagli-one exactly and most likely got it all from him. And up to the moment of M's arrest at somewhere unnamed very like Palo, Baglione and Bellori were entirely convincing, once you accepted that M had been prevailed on to avoid busy Civitavecchia and land instead at the isolated nearby military outpost of Palo – whose name came from the word for *swamp* and later changed to Ladispoli. This matched closely with the nuncio Gentile's letter to Scipione Borghese, which the biographers couldn't've known about.

It was when they described what allegedly happened when M was released that everyone went haywire. It was at this point that – he being distraught at the disappearance of the boat with his things – they had M staging a tantrum on the beach under the blazing sun and then running off into the malarial coastal swamps in pursuit of a boat that'd left two days earlier. Presumably a helpful guard pointed up the coast toward port' Ercole rather than southward toward Civitavecchia and Naples. *It went thataway* and M, it seemed, needed no more urging. Knowing the kind of person M was, like Baglione you got the picture.

> ... he was held for two days and then released. The boat had disappeared. He flew into a rage and headed along the beach like a madman under the blazing summer sun, to see if he could catch sight of the vessel at sea that was carrying his stuff.

Ditto Bellori. This kind of behaviour was asking for trouble. Sure enough, as Baglione put it hurriedly,

> He finally came to a place where he put himself to bed with a malignant fever. And without human aid a few days later he died, just as badly as he'd lived.

As if, someone remarked, he had a beach house at *some seaside resort.* So much for people who mocked Giovanni Baglione, *knight of Christ.* At least Baglione still scrupulously kept from claiming – as every other account now unquestioningly did – that M made it to port' Ercole. Giovan Pietro Bellori took his account over and gussied it up some decade later –

Wretchedly agitated by anxiety and suffering, running along the beach in the most intense heat of the summer sun, he gave up at port' Ercole and was seized by a malignant fever. In a few days he died ...

As you would, after running through a couple of hundred kilometres of malarial swamp in the height of summer. Bellori himself wasn't driven by Baglione's personal animus toward M, but he liked to make a nice art historical point when he could. So he falsified the year of M's death in order to say that *1609 was a sorry year for painting, having taken from us Annibale Carracci and Federico Zuccari as well* – the leading realist, the leading classicist and the leading mannerist, all in the same year.

And so M left his life and his bones on a deserted beach. While people were waiting in Rome for his return, the unexpected news of his death arrived and everyone was very sorry.

The end.

What, though, if M died at Palo? If his arrival there couldn't be concealed and the Procida story didn't make sense anyway and had to be abandoned – the boat crew knew, who'd ferried M to Palo, and the whole group of officials knew, who'd organized this from Rome and Naples, officials whose interests didn't necessarily coincide and who might therefore speak – how would you explain what happened in Palo after you took him in custody? He was famous, and you knew people would ask. How would you conceal the death? You'd tell them *he'd left*, wash your hands of his fate. You wouldn't say he'd left by boat, or by road to Rome. These might be checked. *Along the beach, along the deserted wasteland of a coast.* Why on earth would he do that? *The boat'd left him behind and gone on without his things and* – remembering M's real desperation as the boat with his vital paintings pulled out and left him trapped on the shore among his enemies – *he was very upset.* Where'd the boat gone? In reality it'd gone back to Naples, returning the paintings to where they'd come from, as per instructions. *Next place up the coast – port' Ercole.* He followed the boat as far as port' Ercole? *Sure.* Pause. A hundred kilometres? Two hundred? In this heat? *But then he died.* He died in port' Ercole? *Not in port' Ercole. Near port' Ercole. On the beach. He got a fever. The heat, the mosquitoes* ... Did anyone see this? *Oh no. Nobody saw a thing. He died alone. Of a fever.*

So the lies accumulated, each covering the one before. You could see how, under the pressure of adapting a story to the known realities, snatching at fragments of the truth to shore it up, choosing a line because it was the only safe one you could think of – *he went along the beach* – and having to take it to its logical conclusion, you might end up with a story like the one of M running up the coastline *like a madman* toward port' Ercole. The hysterical overexcitement was a nice touch – just in case anyone who knew the area as well as you did might object that only a lunatic would try such a thing. For the people back in Rome, the people who weren't sailors or garrison guards or fishermen or bandits or hired killers but quirky art world personalities and amenable clerics, it all sounded perfectly reasonable. Only a scientist and sceptic with a mind as empirically acute as Mancini's would have to struggle to suppress nagging doubts, the reflexive twitches of a relatively unconditioned intelligence.

On what'd happened to the paintings M was taking with him to Rome, it was Gentile who turned out to be right, not the viceroy. Neither M's dead body nor his last works were at port' Ercole. Or maybe his body *was* at port' Ercole, taken up the coast in a boat and dumped on the beach? It made no difference. What mattered was that the boat that took him to the fatal ambush had brought M's stuff back to Naples and returned it directly to Costanza Colonna with remarkable dispatch and efficiency. They'd known what to do. And how was it, you wondered, that while Scipione Borghese and the conde de Lemos were thrashing around and firing off threatening letters and trying to find out what the hell had happened to the paintings, the head of the order of Saint John of Jerusalem in the Spanish realm of Naples had known exactly where they were? Vincenzo Carafa had been able with a hastily mustered show of legal justification to send functionaries of the highest level around to Costanza Colonna at the palazzo Cellamare and seize M's work from the fifty five year old marchesa. The argument was that when a knight of Saint John died intestate his property devolved on the order. Costanza Colonna was unable to stop the *royal ministers* from carting off the canvases, however contemptuous she might be of the prior's justifications. The spurious reasoning was less important than the fact – the order had been able to grab the paintings before the papal nuncio's emissaries could secure them for Scipione Borghese. Who'd clearly foreseen the move. The viceroy wasn't even in the race at that point. How was Carafa so well informed so early?

It wasn't just that the head of the order of Saint John knew where the paintings were ahead of anyone else, but that he was prepared to seize them on what he knew was a wholly false pretext. When challenged by the viceroy he backed down immediately. Vincenzo Carafa, unlike Scipione Borghese or the conde de Lemos – to whom Miguel de Cervantes would dedicate his *Exemplary stories* three years later and the second part of *Don Quixote* two years after that – had no known interest in the arts, and this was his only moment in M's story. Neither would he have been likely to compromise the order out of personal greed. The whole overbearing episode had the air of a posthumous insult, as it were a public assertion that M, alive or dead, expelled or not, would be disposed of as the order of Saint John saw fit. It looked, to press the matter, like an assertion of the order's centrality to a death that everyone else seemed just then baffled about.

Which brought back all the questions about that death without a body. Nothing came out later to clear up the confusion. Even M's papal pardon, for instance, seemed quite undocumented, unlike Onorio Longhi's the next year. Had it really been conceded, as the *avviso* of July 31 stated? If it had, what was the judicial modality of M's surrender to papal *justice and mercy* – rather complicated in Longhi's case, involving a guarantor's being arrested *in exchange* for him. Why, above all, was M taken to remote Palo on his return to Rome? This was the most palpably sinister fact, given that he was never seen again and a nonsense offered to explain why. Who knew he was going there? Who was in the garrison when he got there. Gentile's phrase in his first surviving letter to Borghese had a chilling breath of verisimilitude about it –

in the noise and confusion, the boat pulled out to the open sea and returned to Naples.

It evoked M's immediate realization as the boat landed that he'd sailed into a trap, an attempt to defend himself as he'd done in the campo Marzio in Rome by the tennis courts, as he'd done by the waterfront in Naples outside the Cerriglio tavern, as he never could now, surrounded by killers on a deserted coast. It evoked the boat captain's slyly profiting from the scuffle to push off silently again with M's things, leaving M alone with his enemies. If there'd been some genuine problem – the mistaken identity theory, say, or problems over bail money, or instructions about the pardon not having reached the garrison's captain – a boat would've waited the outcome of a discussion, an order from M or the garrison captain, or it would've unloaded M's things. Unless it had prior orders to return to Naples. And it wouldn't've returned to the people at palazzo Cellamare in Naples who'd sent it, if it hadn't completed a specific mission. *Who knew?* was soon answered. Neither Scipione Borghese nor the Spanish viceroy – the two people who were supposed to know and decide everything – seemed, on the evidence of their letters, to have a clue. *But Carafa knew already* – the order of Saint John knew what'd happened before anyone else.

M's enemy from Malta found him at last.

And not without a lot of help from his friends. The knight with a personal vendetta, even if he had the support of the whole order of Saint John, had also secured the collaboration of the papal military authorities. Arranging for M to be taken to Palo and ambushed there was too big a matter to swing on a purely personal level – the whole garrison was involved. And it raised the question of how was M persuaded to go at all. Who'd promised him the pardon? What exactly had been the understanding? The pardon seemed to be inseparable from the entrapment – it was hard to see how the pardon could've been used to lure M to Palo without the collaboration of those offering the pardon – not impossible but hard. And while the pardon for a capital crime was formally the pope's gift, the mechanisms of its dispensation belonged to the papal administration. And the secretary of state was Scipione Borghese.

In the four years since M fled Rome as a *bandito* under capital sentence, Borghese, who was a creative person and not known for his initiatives on the political and administrative fronts, had been singularly active in gathering powers to himself on criminal matters. In particular, on matters concerning people in M's situation. In 1608 he'd got his uncle the pope to grant him *the power to arrest banditi*. Later that year he'd been using this new power to hassle Marcantonio Colonna IV, a great nephew of Costanza's, about handing over *banditi* found on his feudal estates. Borghese knew the Colonnas had been protecting M on their estates after the 1606 killing, and maybe he suspected that when M fled Malta in late 1608 with Fabrizio Sforza Colonna's help he'd again taken refuge on one of the Colonna territories. Borghese evidently didn't know that M was in Sicily. Then on 30 May 1609 he'd obtained a further papal

> Brief granting the power to pardon any type of *bandito* …
> for any crime,

even outside the papal state. The brief specifically gave Borghese power to pardon *those condemned to capital punishment*. And in January 1610 he'd first had himself made *Grand penitentiary* – all about granting pardons again – and then *Prefect of the signatory of justice and mercy*. Borghese was well equipped – as M was drawn ineluctably back into Rome's immediate sphere of influence in 1610 – with all the powers of arrest and all the prerogatives of mercy he needed to handle M's case on his own. He'd been getting himself ready for precisely the situation that arose in the summer of 1610. That Borghese was now ready to make a move on M was strongly implied in the information contained in a petition to the pope from Diego de Albear, *captain of the guard in the city of Naples.* In his undated appeal to his beatitude, the captain mentioned that

> cardinal Borghese has given me an order to capture a *bandito* from the papal state who is in Naples and is a most famous *bandito* …

If the *bandito famosissimo* were M, and captain de Albear carried out the arrest he was threatening to refuse – in his rather truculent petition to the holy father – that raised the question of whether M didn't go to Palo a prisoner. Instead of working out a deal at a distance, maybe Borghese just wanted M pulled in, so they could work out an arrangement in Rome later. At this point, whether M went to Palo freely or under coercion wasn't the point. That he was carrying at least one sweetener for Borghese, the *John* with the ram and maybe the other two canvases as well, made it look like a freely undertaken voyage.

There were two elements in play here. The enemy knight who wanted M dead, and the artloving cardinal nephew who wanted a live painter at his service. Since the knight's and the cardinal's interests conflicted so radically, it was hardly likely the latter would knowingly lend himself to setting the former's fatal trap for M. Neither was it imaginable that the cardinal nephew and secretary of state would act against his own interests – in a matter he cared about deeply and had been working on for years – to satisfy another individual's desire for private revenge. If the individual were immensely powerful and very close to the papacy – if he were, say, the grand master Wignacourt himself – and if the crime he was avenging were so abhorrent and shameful that it seemed private revenge were the only way of settling the score, then that would make a difference. Just conceivably – if his beatitude, for instance, were tacitly lending his weight to a private killing – enough of a difference. But it was unlikely. Scipione Borghese's greed for M's art was too strong for him to contemplate killing the goose that laid these golden eggs. The most compelling evidence that Borghese hadn't lured M to his death was the total dismay and ignorance and anxiety and anger reflected in the answers and reassurances Gentile was sending him from Naples. The papal nuncio was dealing with a man who'd been utterly thrown by the new turn of events. He was a man whose big prize had been snatched from him at the last moment and who was trying to compensate that loss by at least tracing and securing M's last surviving canvases. To lose those as well would be too much.

So there'd been no connivance. Borghese was simply exploiting M's weakened and persecuted state to lure or compel him back to Rome on Borghese's terms. He was bringing to fruition years of planning. M's inaccessibility and his ever growing fame after he left Rome must've driven Borghese mad with frustrated desire. But in July of 1610 everything was coming to fruition, the pieces were falling into place. Patiently, carefully, M was being reeled in. And then the line snapped.

For M's mortal enemy the signs of rapprochement with Rome were a most unwelcome development. He – or his agents – had tracked M through Sicily – quite closely on the evidence of M's mental state and the series of overnight bunks – and they'd nearly finished him off in Naples. They wouldn't underestimate him again. Since that attack, M had likely stopped hanging around the Cerriglio. After convalescing in the protective vastness of palazzo Cellamare he'd been hard at work there. He'd had a rough time and he was nearly forty. Even if he weren't being stalked by hired killers through the dark and narrow teeming streets of Naples, the impulse to strap on his sword and go looking for trouble came a lot less frequently now. The thought of Rome, after what he'd been through, must've made any price, any risk seem worth it. And his enemy too realized that M in Rome, the prize painter carefully guarded by a cardinal nephew with life or death in his gift, would be out of striking range forever. The utterly discreet, private and unwritten nature of negotiations among M's protectors over the terms of his surrender and pardon likely meant it was only at the very last minute that M's hunters learnt that he was about to leave for Rome and slip definitively from their grasp. They had to act fast. This time their plan – after the badly misjudged idea of a group hit against a brave and expert swordsman on the public piazza outside the busiest tavern in Naples – was brilliant. To intercept M on his way back to Rome, when he was alone and disoriented and out of sight and sound of witnesses. And, quite perfectly, it worked.

At this point events entered the murkiest area of a history clouded throughout by cunning, greed, bad faith and treachery. If Borghese weren't party to M's murder – and both interest and circumstances said he wasn't – who made it possible? Who forewarned his hunters of M's movements? Who arranged for him to head for Palo rather than Civitavecchia? The phrase in Gentile's letter to Borghese about the *noise and confusion* at Palo made it sound as though the killers' presence had been just as much a shock to the military guards on duty – that there'd been a larger fight than the killing of a single man. It was another sign that there'd been no big plan that included Borghese and the papacy. Did Borghese choose Palo, wanting to avoid publicity, or did someone at the Naples end push for Palo as more *convenient*? M's killers were waiting for him when he got off the boat. Did M even know he was going to Palo? Was he hijacked by the boat crew, acting under instructions?

And here the boat's prompt return of M's things, the dirty work done, directly to Costanza Colonna in Naples, started to look very disturbing. M's *chatelaine* and lifelong family protector from Caravaggio was also the mother of Fabrizio Sforza Colonna, convicted of unspecified major *crimes*, knight of Saint John and head of the Malta navy, the man who'd taken M to Malta and almost certainly the man who'd got him out. Fabrizio Sforza was intimate with the senior knights of the order – he was a part of its establishment. If the order's leadership tacitly endorsed the effort to kill M, or if the single enemy knight were personally close to Fabrizio Sforza, pressures would start to mount, as the last chance loomed to eliminate M, for Sforza's collaboration in the murder plan. Whatever his personal relations with M – there was no skerrick of evidence of any kind – Fabrizio Sforza, by virtue of his military position and skills, his family and his knighthood in the order of Saint John, was peculiarly well placed to help execute the vendetta. That he was still on parole for his own crimes made him vulnerable to pressures – including pressures from Scipione Borghese. The pressures to coopt Sforza might've been transmitted in turn to the general's mother. Costanza Colonna was clearly familiar with the history of M's Malta experience – she'd probably had the idea in the first place, and followed its phases closely – and was surely deeply trusted by M. She was, after all, not only his past and present protector in times of trouble but the feudal mistress who'd known him since he was born, knew him as well, probably, as anyone else alive. Did she now hand him over to his enemies? If Carafa's grabbing of M's paintings from the marchesa after M's murder looked like an ugly display of the order's power over M even in death, it also looked like an insult directed at her – she too was subordinate to the knights of Saint John. She was made subordinate, perhaps, by having lent herself to M's murder.

It was pure hypothesis. Its attraction was that if you accepted that the Colonnas were capable of betraying M – and the family wasn't exactly unpractised in the ways of *realpolitik* – you saw how the Malta killers had been able to intervene so swiftly and devastatingly during his journey to Rome, and you made sense of the oddness of the death boat's return to Costanza Colonna, the grossness of Carafa's behaviour toward the marchesa, her own distraught moment of giveaway unaristocratic shrillness in calling Carafa's claim on M's things *ridiculous*. She hadn't *wanted* M killed. You saw all the more clearly why the Vatican would've played along, once M was dead, with the coverup. The deed was done, and there was no reason to make trouble with the Colonna dynasty or the order of Saint John. They were the Vatican's people. Who, in comparison, was M?

These were impenetrable mysteries because nobody was talking. Nor would they ever. *Omertà* was universal. Still less was anything put down on paper. M was the most sensational painter of his time, in a society whose culture revolved around painting, yet the contemporary written and material record of his death consisted precisely of two terse one sentence *avvisi* originating from Del Monte's ten days and a fortnight after he was said to have died, and a couple of undated and unpublished private Latin epitaphs by his friend Milesi. From the papal archives the only thing that ever emerged was the information in Gentile's handful of letters, which presumably slipped through as business correspondence. The silence on M's death echoed the earlier silence on his offence in Malta and was determined by it. If the Vatican archives yielded nothing on his death, the archives of the order of Saint John in Malta had nothing on his crime. The only records concerned his escape and his expulsion. M was expelled for escaping and leaving Malta without the grand master's leave, not for the offence that got him imprisoned, and the records of his trial made no mention of it. His name was missing from the *List of crimes committed by the knights*. Of M's Roman contemporaries, Mancini seemed quite unaware of the offence. Baglione got to hear only the vaguest whiff of it – unless he too was being reticent about what M did – but he was quite sure that M was pursued through Sicily and attacked in Naples by *his enemy* the offended knight. Such a peculiarly personal offence had to be sexual, and in the matter of sex there was one crime – a crime the inquisition and the lay courts had been bitterly fighting over the right to judge and punish – that was by definition the crime you didn't mention. The generic *sodomy* – meaning any kind of intragender sex – was in its legal and religious dimension the *unspeakable* sin, meaning not as in modern English *mildly unpleasant* but in the full force of the Latin *nefandum*, which was to say *not to be spoken about*. It was a mortal sin and a capital crime and to engage in it, as people widely and enthusiastically but tacitly did, despite the cruellest efforts of church and state, was commonly called *nefandare*. That was, to *unspeakable-ize*.

Everyday life was one thing. In the world of the law it was an anathema to fear. You didn't speak about it, especially when people of a certain rank were involved. You didn't write about it. If M'd had sex with one of Wignacourt's noble boy pages – and in that repressed and claustrophobic life *in convento* they must've been a powerful temptation for the order of Saint John's newest recruit – maybe even surprized *in flagrante*, he would've stirred a lethal mix of religious bigotry, sexual jealousy and aristocratic snobbery in the wrong person. The wrong person might've been an older aristocratic relative – *that filthy little jumped up painter* – or it might've been the grand master himself. Wignacourt, whose particular fondness for the close and constant presence of his young pages was thought worth remarking on by the order's historian – being served by young pages was his personal innovation in the order's lifestyle – would've also felt personal treachery and burning humiliation for himself in the behaviour of the man he'd so enthusiastically sponsored in the order. Whose merits he'd so strongly urged on his beatitude Borghese. To remain silent, swiftly remove M from the island, then relentlessly pursue vendetta was a logical course of action in such a case. It was hard to think of any other offence that might've unleashed that peculiar combination of reticence and ferocity that M's *faux pas* provoked.

M grimly joked in Sicily that all his sins were mortal. His listeners thought he was just being cheap about religion, but as his painting of *John beheaded* showed, he knew how the order punished capital offences. Brother knights sewed you into a sack and threw you into the sea. Alive in some variants, already strangled in others. Maybe, after setting off in the boat with his paintings and his promises, M never even got as far as the *deserted beach*.

NOBODY IN ROME left any trace of their feelings on M's disappearance, apart from Marzio Milesi who wrote a whole string of distraught poems. Marino whipped off a facile conceit in verse, and maybe even meant what he said. Not a breath in Del Monte's correspondence about what he might've known or felt, not a word from Giustiniani. The hovering of distinguished vultures over the last paintings was the only noticeable reaction. Nobody in Rome had seen M for the last four years, and that'd've muted their feelings, and the stories of later wildnesses in Malta and Naples, if anyone knew them, must've made it seem he was already off the planet. Life went on.

Of the others who'd been involved in the fatal brawl of 1606, Ranuccio's elder brother Giovan Francesco Tomassoni had been pardoned the year before, and went on with his career as a professional soldier. He ended up as military governor of Ferrara and died in 1628. Onorio Longhi was pardoned the year after M's death and allowed back to Rome from Milan. He went back to work as an architect and was in the middle of reconstructing the church of San Carlo al Corso near Lena's old place when he died of syphilis in 1619 at the age of fifty – his son Martino jr finished off the job. Longhi owned four paintings by M when he died, including his own and his wife's portraits. All of them were later lost.

When Vincenzo Giustiniani got back from his European tour he got busy with the decoration of the palazzo he'd designed at Bassano and landscaping the gardens and writing his essays on the arts of living. The big project of his later years was preparing a great catalogue of his ancient sculpture, the *Galleria giustiniana* – it was illustrated by northern European engravers and the man in charge was Joachim von Sandrart, to whom the gouty old marchese reminisced about M and who primly urged that the nude image of Cecco at twelve be screened by a green curtain, so the boy could flaunt himself only at selected visitors. The catalogue still wasn't finished when Vincenzo Giustiniani died in 1637, leaving three hundred or so paintings. Fifteen of them were by M and the biggest group of his paintings anywhere. Many years later most of Giustiniani's paintings by M went to Germany and three of them – including the portrait of *Fillide* and the insolent first *Matthew and angel* – went up in flames with the third reich in Berlin in 1945. Cecco survived though, and is still in Berlin, grinning away sexily as *Love the winner* alongside Giovanni Baglione's unfortunate armour cased *Divine love*.

That painting's owner, Benedetto Giustiniani, died in 1621 without ever becoming pope. Neither did his neighbour Del Monte who died five years after him. They both tried. After his nearly fatal illness in Naples, Del Monte in 1608 had already started feeling elegiac, reminding an old friend in a letter about their good times passed long ago with the various *Artemisias* and *Cleopatras* who might've been boys but maybe not, *and when we played football ... and yet everything passes.* But he survived, and got over the death of Ferdinando de' Medici too and went swanning along in the arts. He was protector of the artists' academy until the end of his life. Soon after M's death he found another promising young unknown artist to take up, this time the barely twelve year old Andrea Sacchi. If twelve. He was so young in fact when he won first prize at the academy for his nude drawing of Adam and Eve *in the disobedience of the apple*, that Bellori wrote he was called by the childish diminutive of Andreuccio, or *little Andy* from then on for the rest of his life, *although he was tall and well complexioned.*

> One day, while he stood apart drawing a room in a garden, he was overtaken unawares by the cardinal Del Monte, who was out walking and quietly came up behind him to look at the drawing. When Andrea suddenly recognized the cardinal, he blushed in honest shame and made to withdraw, but the cardinal didn't want him to leave but rather to go on drawing, praising the boy's modesty, intentness and industry. The cardinal was the patron who had reestablished the academy of San Luca, a very liberal promotor of all good arts. Wherefore, turning benignly on Andrea and seeing that he was needy and not well provided with the necessities of life, the cardinal first of all clothed him anew and very handsomely, then assigned him a room and board in his own house, so that no worry might disturb his talent. Encouraged and excited by the gentleman's kindness, Andrea felt spurred to keep on going ...

Unlike some of Bellori's other emblematic moments, this one, with its discreetly powerful prelate padding up unseen to catch the boy artist at work, felt real enough to have actually taken place, and even prompted the thought that the bashful but ambitious boy might've been less ingenuous than he seemed, and have second guessed Del Monte, known his movements and his interests, and planted himself all ready to be caught blushing and unawares, intent on his art.

In the spring of 1610, a couple of months before M died, Galileo sent Del Monte one of his first telescopes, and in April Del Monte wrote to Galileo telling him he was already trying it out and discussing ways of upgrading the technology. Del Monte was also receiving and reading Galileo's books – he got the newly published *Starry Messenger* from Venice at the same time as the telescope. A year later Galileo came to Rome for two months to present his findings and suss out the climate and Del Monte was the first person he called on. In 1616, when Galileo was first warned off by the inquisition from talking about the movement of the earth, Del Monte defended him against Bellarmino. But later, when the inquisition tried and condemned old Galileo in 1633, Del Monte was no longer around to help him. The two were still writing to each other in the sixteen twenties. 1621 was the year Paul V died. Scipione Borghese was out in the cold and after fifteen years exile in Ravenna Pietro Aldobrandini came back to Rome. It was the year of Del Monte's big push for the papacy.

> Under the surface of idleness and joking they say there's a certain latent vigour of spirit ready to break out in great things if the occasion presents itself,

wrote a friendly observer hopefully before the conclave. Another *avviso* said the elderly Del Monte, *sweet natured and good humoured, must be ruled out ... the Spanish are hostile ... .* And he was. Two years later the papacy was vacant again. It was absolutely Del Monte's last throw – he was seventy four – and when Maffeo Barberini became Urban VIII there was no more chance for Del Monte. The next year the Venetian ambassador described him as

> a breathing corpse ... given over entirely to the spirit, maybe to make up for the licence of his fresher years, and he's right to be, not having anything left to think about now save how to die well.

Giustiniani's friend Ameyden had a completely different take on Del Monte now, and said that when he realized the papacy had eluded him forever, the consummate old diplomat let it all hang out. Ameyden claimed the problem hadn't been his proFrench stance but his *original sin*, and that Del Monte,

> was attracted to intimacy with boys ... not sinfully I believe, but out of natural sociability ... before the election of Urban he astutely concealed this to avoid attack, but after that he relaxed all restraint ... and openly indulged his tastes. Even when he was old and practically blind, more like a stump than a man and as little able to respond to charms, he gave money and presents to a young boy.

Life had been so much simpler before the council of Trent laid down the rules. It was within Del Monte's own lifetime that pope Julius III had made his personal monkey groomer, a fifteen year old boy he'd picked up in the street, first a cardinal and then secretary of state – it lowered the tone of the college of cardinals, but the outrage passed. The cardinal ended up in jail later, and died there. Three years after Maffeo Barberini's rise Del Monte was dead. He left five hundred and ninety nine paintings and fifty six marble statues – eight canvases by M. Giulio Mancini, who after the election of Maffeo Barberini was now personal physician to his beatitude, hovered around the death bed.

The real girls had mixed luck in life. Lena died even before M. The year after M fled Rome she went back to live with her mother and sister in via dei Greci and died there in 1610, a few months before M's failed journey back to Rome. She was only twenty eight. Anna Bianchini was dead as early as 1604, after twenty five years of wretched life at the bottom of the heap. Fillide in 1612 was forced to leave Rome for a while by the family of her current lover Giulio Strozzi, an apostolic lawyer on whom she was felt to be a bad influence. But two years later she was back in town and in October 1614 she made her will, leaving the portrait of her by M to Strozzi – was it a different one from Giustiniani's? In 1618 she died aged thirty seven and not being in order with the church was denied a fully Christian burial. Menica Calvi lasted longer – her house in via dei Greci was sumptuous, and when she died in 1633 at fifty, she left her sister a fat parcel of real estate and company shares.

YOUNG PAINTERS KEPT hearing about M in other parts of Italy and Europe and seeking him out in Rome – they kept on coming after his death. Most of the foreign painters who arrived after 1606 had no idea that M was no longer in Rome and most of the ones who came after 1610 were unaware he was already dead. There were always his Roman paintings to look at and there were Orazio Gentileschi, Carlo Saraceni, Bartolomeo Manfredi and Orazio Borgianni leading the movement – M's first, strongest and most devoted followers. The ones who'd gone on trial with him, worked for him, tried the coup at the academy to save him. The apostles turned out to be as short lived as the master. In 1616 Borgianni was dead at thirty eight. Carlo Saraceni went home to Venice and died there of the plague in 1620 at forty. Two years later Manfredi was dead at thirty five. Orazio Gentileschi, who was far older than the lot of them, stayed around until the start of the twenties and then headed north. His daughter Artemisia had become a superb painter who was even closer to M's art than her father – after her rape by Orazio's colleague, the painter Agostino Tassi, and a protracted trial in 1612 she'd gone to work in Florence – and when Orazio himself left, Saraceni, Borgianni and Manfredi were all dead. Orazio ended up in England as a court painter to Charles I – hating it – and died in London at seventy six in 1639. Twenty years after the libel trial there was nobody left in Rome who'd been a part of the struggle in the tough and heady *realistic* days of 1603. Twenty years later all had changed utterly and the terrible beauty was dead, suffocated by the rhetoric of baroque. M himself was almost forgotten.

Not in Naples, where M had a deeper influence in less time – young painters who'd known him there like Battistello Caracciolo and Carlo Sellito started a wave that broke when the plague of 1656 wiped out half the city. Naples led to Spain and directly to Diego Velázquez who was M's great heir in European art. In sheer numbers it was the young painters from the north – France and the low countries – who made M's art peculiarly their own and took it home and made it last. M's first and greatest northern admirer was Peter Paul Rubens, a very different painter whose startling homage of 1640 – when he placed M's severed head as John's on a golden platter at the centre of a vast *Herod's feast* – both acknowledged a real and deeply felt debt and expressed Rubens's own sense of M's fate thirty years earlier. Rubens the great cosmopolitan led north to Vermeer and Rembrandt, painters who mightn't've known it but owed their painterly being to M. The sense of real life, driven from Rome by brilliant unrealities, took hold in Spain and the north. Rubens, Velázquez, Vermeer, Rembrandt – they were the painters of their age in Europe and the founders of modern art and they were M's creations.

Mario Minniti hardly belonged in that company. He was a pretty terrible painter but he probably didn't mind, because his high output art studio did great business and he became a solid and respected member of the Sicilian business community and died in his sixties in 1640. Every now and then something darker and more threateningly real glimmered out of the endlessly recycled motifs of his bland religious canvases, to remind you of the years he'd spent with M. Cecco Boneri's work was altogether more formidable and his destiny more enigmatic. He seemed to part from M in Naples in 1608. Five years later he was working as a painter on a project for cardinal Montalto with Agostino Tassi, Orazio Gentileschi's former partner and Artem-isia's rapist, the year after the rape trial. Vincenzo Giustiniani knew Cecco as painter and not only a model, since he bought Cecco's painting of the merchants in the temple. Cecco later did some tough and almost satirical studies of youths with musical instruments – humorously disabused reworkings of the younger M's entranced studies of Mario – and some formidable large scale altar paintings. The most daring painting he did was a strange and brilliant piece of self mockery in which he looked back as a man and a painter on his days as a boy and an urchin model – the moment he caught M's eye. It looked right back through their relations and left you in no doubt, once you realized this was *Love the winner* in later life, what that relation was. It looked to've been done in the early sixteen twenties, when Cecco's personal traces were already lost to history.

The painting showed Cecco returning to his old role as model in a weird nude self portrait, complete with giant predator's wings, as an adult *Love at the drinking fountain*, kneeling to drink with his weaponry beside him on the ground. The resemblance of the longhaired thirty something once pretty Love, with wrinkles on his neck and already knotty joints, to M's boy Love of twenty years earlier was cruel and remarkable and quite unmistakeable. It didn't so much compare an older to a younger self as one image of himself to another. *Love at the drinking fountain* was a *trompe l'oeil* painting of another painting – whose just visible unframed top and right hand edges reached almost to the edges of the real canvas and were draped by a heavy brocade curtain that'd just been pulled back to the top right corner to reveal the canvas – as it were – freshly painted in the studio. The way of insisting that this was the image and not the reality so strongly recalled the marchese Giustiniani's green silk curtain covering M's *Love the winner* as to make you suspect the real silk curtain was already in place – over the picture of Cecco at twelve that so excited visitors as the *clou* of Giustiniani's vast collection. Draw the curtain now, Cecco's painting said, and this is what you get. In real life.

It was a painting of the painting M might've done now, if he'd still been around and still wanted to – Cecco's wry homage to his dead lover and master. The tribute was more than a reminder of how remorseless time was and what it was like to lose your looks. If M's *Love* was a laughing incitement to sex, Cecco's own *Love* was an unequivocal reminder of what he'd been doing since. The kneeling man's projecting bum and the illusionistic likeness of the drinking fountain's concave spout near his mouth to the convexity of an erect phallus hardly let you not be reminded. It was toughly funny and quite unblinking. M – who'd painted his own ruined face on the head being held up by Cecco at sixteen – would've laughed.

M'S PAINTINGS

THREE PAINTINGS BY M were destroyed in the Berlin events of 1945 and another was stolen and maybe destroyed in Palermo in 1969 – they're all well recorded in photographs and are listed here. Paintings known only through copies are excluded. So are paintings I think uncertain or wrongly deemed M's. In tracing M's life, dates matter nearly as much as attribution – I've noted the dates included in the four most significant catalogues of M's work made over the last ten years. Earlier lists are simply out of date. My dating and attributions are of course debatable – I can't swallow Gregori's insistent proposal of the *Toothpuller* as M's and I think M used help on the second versions of early paintings like *Lute Player II*. In 1996 John Spike identified the likely original of M's first known work, the *Boy peeling fruit*, in a painting auctioned that year in London. I'm persuaded too from photographs by Spike's discovery of the thrilling *Fruit & veg* – otherwise I think what follows is a conservative and fairly reliable statement of the canon as known. Park's brilliant 1985 study of *Mary dead* has persuaded me of his earlier than usual dating of that work. The date of *David II* is discussed in the text. The final *John* in Munich is a late rediscovery and missing from most catalogues.

Numbers below each entry refer to the pages on which the painting is mentioned. The major references are in bold type.

BOY PEELING FRUIT Rome 1593
Fanciullo che monda un pomo
Oil on canvas 75.5cm x 64.4cm
Rome, private collection

Marini 1989	1593
Calvesi 1990	1593–94
Cinotti 1991	1593–94
Gregori 1994	1593c

36, 44, 57, 389, 424

SICK SELF PORTRAIT 1593
Bacchino malato
Oil on canvas 67cm x 53cm
Rome, Galleria Borghese

Marini 1989	1593
Calvesi 1990	1593–5
Cinotti 1991	1593–4
Gregori 1994	1593–4

22, **39f,** 42, 44, 89, 112, 153, 273, 389

BOY WITH FRUIT 1593
Fanciullo con canestro di frutta
Oil on canvas 70cm x 67cm
Rome, Galleria Borghese

Marini 1989	1593
Calvesi 1990	1593–5
Cinotti 1991	1593–4
Gregori 1994	1593–4

44f, 49, 60, 191, 389

FORTUNE TELLER I Rome 1594
Buona ventura
Oil on canvas 115cm x 150cm
Rome, Musei Capitolini, Pinacoteca

Marini 1989	1594
Calvesi 1990	1594–95
Cinotti 1991	1594–95c
Gregori 1994	1593–94

49ff, 59f, 63, 96, 106, 109, 173

CHEATS 1594
Bari
Oil on canvas 91.5cm x 128.2cm
Fort Worth, Texas, Kimbell Art Museum

Marini 1989	1594
Calvesi 1990	1594–95
Cinotti 1991	1594–95c
Gregori 1994	1594c

51f, 55, 57, 59, 78f, 89, 93, 106, 109, 125, 172, 321

FORTUNE TELLER II Paris 1595
Buona ventura
Oil on canvas 93cm x 131cm
Paris, Musée du Louvre

Marini 1989	1595
Calvesi 1990	1595c
Cinotti 1991	1596–97c
Gregori 1994	1596–97

49ff, **59f,** 96, 106, 125, 173

MUSICIANS 1595
Concerto di giovani
Oil on canvas 92cm x 118.5cm
New York, Metropolitan Museum of Art

Marini 1989	1594
Calvesi 1990	1595–97
Cinotti 1991	1595–96c
Gregori 1994	1595c

57f, 77f, 89, 106, 109, 416, 464

FRANCIS & ANGEL 1595
San Francesco in estasi
Oil on canvas 92.5cm x 127.8cm
Hartford, Connecticut, Wadsworth Atheneum

Marini 1989	1594
Calvesi 1990	1594–96
Cinotti 1991	1595c
Gregori 1994	1594–95

77ff, 89, 106, 353

BOY BITTEN BY LIZARD I Florence 1596
Fanciullo morso da un ramarro
Oil on canvas 65.8cm x 52.3cm
Florence, Fondazione Roberto Longhi

Marini 1989	1594
Calvesi 1990	1595–97
Cinotti 1991	1595c
Gregori 1994	1595–96

74ff, 103, 174, 202

BOY BITTEN BY LIZARD II London 1596
Fanciullo morso da un ramarro
Oil on canvas 66cm x 49.5cm
London, National Gallery

Marini 1989	1594
Calvesi 1990	1595–97
Cinotti 1991	1595–96c
Gregori 1994	1595c

v. *Boy bitten by lizard I*

LUTE PLAYER I St Petersburg 1596
Suonatore di liuto
Oil on canvas 94cm x 119cm
St Petersburg, Hermitage Museum

Marini 1989	1595
Calvesi 1990	1596–98
Cinotti 1991	1595–96
Gregori 1994	1595–96

60, 62f, 75, 90, 103, 183, 191

LUTE PLAYER II New York 1596
Suonatore di liuto
Oil on canvas 100cm x 126.5cm
New York, Metropolitan Museum of Art [on loan]

Marini 1989	1594
Calvesi 1990	1596–98
Cinotti 1991	1596–97
Gregori 1994	1596–97c

60, 62, **63f,** 109

BACCHUS 1596
Bacco
Oil on canvas 95cm x 85cm
Florence, Galleria degli Uffizi

Marini 1989	1595
Calvesi 1990	1596c
Cinotti 1991	1596 or 1596–97
Gregori 1994	1596–97

58ff, 68, 74f, 103, 109, 191, 273, 460

PENITENT MAGDALEN 1597
Maddalena penitente
Oil on canvas 122.5cm x 98.5cm
Rome, Galleria Doria Pamphilj

Marini 1989	1595c
Calvesi 1990	1596–97
Cinotti 1991	1596–97
Gregori 1994	1594–95

79f, 84, 93, 109, 172, 273, 310f

REST ON THE FLIGHT INTO EGYPT 1597
Riposo nella fuga in Egitto
Oil on canvas 135.5cm x 166.5cm
Rome, Galleria Doria Pamphilj

Marini 1989	1595
Calvesi 1990	1597–98
Cinotti 1991	1596–97c
Gregori 1994	1595–96

78f, **80ff,** 89, 106, 182, 311

MEDUSA 1597
Testa di Medusa
Oil on canvas over convex poplar wood shield
    60cm x 55cm
Florence, Galleria degli Uffizi

Marini 1989	1596c
Calvesi 1990	1596–97
Cinotti 1991	1598–99
Gregori 1994	1596–97

76f, 105, 111f, 172ff, 216, 277f, 460

FILLIDE 1597
Cortigiana Fillide
Oil on canvas 66cm x 53cm destroyed 1945
ex Berlin, Kaiser Friedrich Museum, Gemäldegalerie

Marini 1989	1596
Calvesi 1990	1596c
Cinotti 1991	1598c
Gregori 1994	1596–97

88f, 91, 171, 491

JOVE, NEPTUNE, PLUTO 1597
Giove, Nettuno e Plutone
Oil on plaster ceiling 300cm x 180cm circa
Rome, Casino della Villa Ludovisi

Marini 1989	1597
Calvesi 1990	1597–98
Cinotti 1991	1597–98c
Gregori 1994	1597c

67f, 169

CATHERINE 1598
Santa Caterina d'Alessandria
Oil on canvas 173cm x 133cm
Madrid, Museo Thyssen Bornemisza

Marini 1989	1597
Calvesi 1990	1599c
Cinotti 1991	1598c
Gregori 1994	1598–99c

89f, 109, 171, 277

ISAAC & ABRAHAM I Princeton 1598
Sacrificio d'Isacco
Oil on canvas 116cm x 173cm
Princeton, New Jersey, Barbara Piasecka
   Johnson Collection

Marini 1989	1597
Calvesi 1990	1600c
Cinotti 1991	1597–98
Gregori 1994	1597–98c

113ff, 241, 245, 281, 316

JOHN IN THE WILD I Toledo 1598
San Giovanni Battista
Oil on canvas 169cm x 112cm
Toledo, Museo de la Catedral

Marini 1989	–
Calvesi 1990	–
Cinotti 1991	–
Gregori 1994	1597–98c

115, 202, 204, **281**

MARTHA & MARY 1598
Marta e Maddalena
Oil on canvas 100cm x 134.5cm
Detroit, Michigan, Detroit Institute of Art

Marini 1989	1597
Calvesi 1990	1599c
Cinotti 1991	1598c
Gregori 1994	1597–98c

93f, 106, 171, 277f

MAFFEO BARBERINI 1598
Ritratto di Maffeo Barberini
Oil on canvas 124cm x 90cm
Florence, private collection

Marini 1989	1598–99
Calvesi 1990	1599c
Cinotti 1991	1599
Gregori 1994	1598–99

173

BASKET OF FRUIT 1599
Canestra di frutta
Oil on canvas 31cm x 47cm
Milan, Pinacoteca Ambrosiana

Marini 1989	1594
Calvesi 1990	1599c
Cinotti 1991	1598–99c
Gregori 1994	1597–98c

38, **103ff,** 114, 126, 216, 277, 281, 316, 320f, 460

JUDITH & HOLOFERNES 1599
Giuditta e Oloferne
Oil on canvas 145cm x 195cm
Rome, Galleria Nazionale d'Arte Antica a
    Palazzo Barberini

Marini 1989	1599
Calvesi 1990	1599–1600
Cinotti 1991	1599 first months
Gregori 1994	1599c

95, **96,** 106, 110f, 113, 155, 171, 176, 243,
    310f, 357, 376, 421

DAVID I Madrid 1599
David e Golia
Oil on canvas 110cm x 91cm
Madrid, Museo del Prado

Marini 1989	1599
Calvesi 1990	1599–1600
Cinotti 1991	1600c
Gregori 1994	1597–98c

113, 114f

NARCISSUS 1599
Narciso
Oil on canvas 122cm x 92cm
Rome, Galleria Nazionale d'Arte Antica a
    Palazzo Corsini

Marini 1989	1600
Calvesi 1990	1599–1600
Cinotti 1991	1598–early1599
Gregori 1994	–

112f, 115, **277,** 378

MATTHEW CALLED 1599–1600
Vocazione di San Matteo
Oil on canvas 322cm x 340cm
Rome, Chiesa di San Luigi dei Francesi,
    Cappella Contarelli

Marini 1989	1599–1600
Calvesi 1990	1599–1600
Cinotti 1991	1599–1600
Gregori 1994	1599–1600

122ff, 131, 136ff, 144, 175f, 179, 181, 184, 196, 218,
    223, 239, 258, 370f, 374f, 422, 450f

MATTHEW KILLED 1599–1600
Martirio di San Matteo
Oil on canvas 323cm x 343cm
Rome, Chiesa di San Luigi dei Francesi,
    Cappella Contarelli

Marini 1989	1599–1600
Calvesi 1990	1599–1600
Cinotti 1991	1599–1600
Gregori 1994	1599–1600

130, **131ff,** 144, 160f, 175f, 179, 184, 209,
    210, 218, 222, 276f, 370f, 374f

SAUL I Odescalchi 1601
Conversione di Saulo Odescalchi
Oil on cypress wood panel 237cm x 189cm
Rome, Collezione Odescalchi

Marini 1989	1600
Calvesi 1990	1600–01
Cinotti 1991	1600–01
Gregori 1994	1600–01

78f, 144f, **160ff,** 194f, 198, 200, 210, 244, 259

PETER KILLED 1601
Crocifissione di San Pietro
Oil on canvas 230cm x 175cm
Rome, Chiesa di Santa Maria del Popolo,
    Cappella Cerasi

Marini 1989	1600–01
Calvesi 1990	1601
Cinotti 1991	1601
Gregori 1994	1600–01

144f, **164f,** 200, 223, 259, 271, 316, 376

SAUL II Cerasi 1601
Conversione di Saulo
Oil on canvas 230cm x 175cm
Rome, Chiesa di Santa Maria del Popolo,
    Cappella Cerasi

Marini 1989	1600–01
Calvesi 1990	1601
Cinotti 1991	1601
Gregori 1994	1600–01

144f, **162ff,** 200, 223, 259

MEAL AT EMMAUS I London 1601
Cena in Emmaus
Oil on canvas 141cm x 196.2cm
London, National Gallery

Marini 1989	1598–99
Calvesi 1990	1601
Cinotti 1991	1601
Gregori 1994	1601

200, 204, **206f,** 208ff, 216, 242f, 273, 311, 320, 353

LOVE THE WINNER 1602
Amor vincitore
Oil on canvas 156cm x 113cm
Berlin, Gemäldegalerie

Marini 1989	1602
Calvesi 1990	1601–02
Cinotti 1991	1601–02 or 1602
Gregori 1994	1601–02

71f, 188f, **191ff,** 196ff, 200, 202f, 209, 219f, 233f,
244, 311, 352, 356, 394, 491, 496

MATTHEW & ANGEL I ex Berlin 1602
San Matteo & angelo
Oil on canvas 223cm x 183cm destroyed 1945
ex Berlin, Kaiser Friedrich Museum, Gemäldegalerie

Marini 1989	1602
Calvesi 1990	1600–01
Cinotti 1991	1602
Gregori 1994	1602

179ff, 184f, 187, 200, 208f, 212f, 218, 290,
332, 405, 491

MATTHEW & ANGEL II Rome 1602
San Matteo & angelo
Oil on canvas 295cm x 195cm
Rome, Chiesa di San Luigi dei Francesi,
    Cappella Contarelli

Marini 1989	1602
Calvesi 1990	1602
Cinotti 1991	1602
Gregori 1994	1602

183ff, 198, 200, 242, 290, 316, 373

JOHN IN THE WILD II Rome Capitoline 1602
San Giovannino Battista
Oil on canvas 129cm x 94cm
Rome, Musei Capitolini, Pinacoteca

Marini 1989	1600
Calvesi 1990	1601c
Cinotti 1991	1599–1600
Gregori 1994	1602

195, **199f,** 202ff, 208f, 212, 244, 281f

JOHN IN THE WILD III Rome Doria Pamphili 1602
San Giovanni Battista
Oil on canvas 129cm x 94cm
Rome, Galleria Doria Pamphilj

Marini 1989	1600
Calvesi 1990	–
Cinotti 1991	–
Gregori 1994	–

202, and v. *John in the Wild II*

DOUBTING THOMAS 1602
Incredulità di San Tommaso
Oil on canvas 107cm x 146cm
Potsdam, Sanssouci, Bildergalerie

Marini 1989	1599
Calvesi 1990	1602–03
Cinotti 1991	1601–02c
Gregori 1994	1600–01

200, 204, **207f,** 209, 242f

CHRIST TAKEN 1602
Cattura di Cristo nell'orto
Oil on canvas 133.5cm x 169.5cm
Dublin, National Gallery of Ireland

Marini 1989	1598
Calvesi 1990	1602
Cinotti 1991	1602
Gregori 1994	1602

43, 200, 204, 20ff, 242f, 273, 301, 372, 394, 468

CHRIST'S BURIAL 1603
Deposizione
Oil on canvas 300cm x 203cm
Rome, Pinacoteca Vaticana

Marini 1989	1602–03
Calvesi 1990	1600
Cinotti 1991	1602–03
Gregori 1994	1602–04

202, 21f, 213, **215ff,** 271, 290, 292, 320, 385, 426

ISAAC & ABRAHAM II Florence 1603
Sacrificio d'Isacco
Oil on canvas 104cm x 135cm
Florence, Galleria degli Uffizi

Marini 1989	1603c
Calvesi 1990	1602–03
Cinotti 1991	1603
Gregori 1994	1603c

198, 200, 23f, **241ff,** 255, 316, 328

PILGRIMS' MADONNA 1604
Madonna dei pellegrini
Oil on canvas 260cm x 150cm
Rome, Chiesa di Sant' Agostino

Marini 1989	1604–05
Calvesi 1990	1605
Cinotti 1991	1604–05 first half
Gregori 1994	1604–06c

261, 263, **265ff,** 295, 300, 311, 320, 374, 381, 414

JOHN IN THE WILD IV Kansas City 1604
San Giovanni Battista
Oil on canvas 173cm x 133cm
Kansas City, Atkins Museum, Nelson Gallery

Marini 1989	1603–04
Calvesi 1990	1604–06
Cinotti 1991	1604–05c
Gregori 1994	1603–04

281f, **282f,** 292, 300, 305, 358, 371, 465

JOHN IN THE WILD V Rome Corsini 1604
San Giovanni Battista
Oil on canvas 94cm x 131cm
Rome, Galleria Nazionale d'Arte Antica a
    Palazzo Corsini

Marini 1989	1606
Calvesi 1990	1605c
Cinotti 1991	1605–05c
Gregori 1994	1603–04c

281ff, **283,** 300, 311, 316f, 465

CROWN OF THORNS I Prato 1604
Incoronazione di spine
Oil on canvas 178cm x 125cm
Prato, Cassa di Risparmi e Depositi

Marini 1989	1600–02
Calvesi 1990	1604c
Cinotti 1991	1604
Gregori 1994	1600–02

300f, 302, 305

MARY DEAD 1604
Morte della vergine
Oil on canvas 369cm x 245cm
Paris, Musée du Louvre

Marini 1989	1601 – 1605–06
Calvesi 1990	1606
Cinotti 1991	1606c
Gregori 1994	1605–06

259f, **289ff,** 299f, 306, 311, 316, 320, 332, 334,
    350f, 357, 365, 370, 372, 374f, 379f, 385ff,
    390, 411, 425, 443f, 460, 472

MOUNTOLIVE 1605
Cristo nell'orto
Oil on canvas 154cm x 222cm destroyed 1945
ex Berlin, Kaiser Friedrich Museum, Gemäldegalerie

Marini 1989	1605
Calvesi 1990	1605–06
Cinotti 1991	1603c
Gregori 1994	1605c

ECCE HOMO 1605

Ecce homo

Oil on canvas 128cm x 103cm

Genoa, Galleria Communale di Palazzo Rosso

Marini 1989	1605
Calvesi 1990	1605
Cinotti 1991	1605
Gregori 1994	1605

301ff, 305, 308, 316, 323

JEROME I Montserrat 1605

San Girolamo in meditazione

Oil on canvas 118cm x 81cm

Montserrat, Museo del Monasterio de Santa Maria

Marini 1989	1605
Calvesi 1990	1605–06
Cinotti 1991	1605–06c
Gregori 1994	1605c

316f, 404

JEROME II Rome 1605

San Girolamo scrivente

Oil on canvas 112cm x 157cm

Rome, Galleria Borghese

Marini 1989	1606
Calvesi 1990	1605c
Cinotti 1991	1606c
Gregori 1994	1605–06

315ff, 387f, 404

PAUL V BORGHESE 1605

Ritratto di Paolo V

Oil on canvas 203cm x 119cm

Rome, Palazzo Borghese

Marini 1989	1605
Calvesi 1990	–
Cinotti 1991	1605–06c
Gregori 1994	–

319

FRUIT & VEG 1605
Natura morta con frutta su un piano di pietra
Oil on canvas 87.2cm x 135.4cm
ex Madrid, Edmund Peel & Associados

Marini 1989	–
Calvesi 1990	–
Cinotti 1991	–
Gregori 1994	1601c
Spike 1996	1605c

38, 320f

GROOMS' MADONNA 1606
Madonna dei palafrenieri
Oil on canvas 292cm x 211cm
Rome, Galleria Borghese

Marini 1989	1605–06
Calvesi 1990	1605–06
Cinotti 1991	1605–06
Gregori 1994	1605–06

322, 331ff, 387

WEEPING MAGDALEN 1606
Maddalena in estasi
Oil on canvas 106.5cm x 91cm
Rome, private collection

Marini 1989	1606
Calvesi 1990	1606
Cinotti 1991	1606
Gregori 1994	1606

350ff, 358, 381f, 424, 443, 450f, 460, 476, 478

DAVID II Rome 1606
Davide con testa di Golia
Oil on canvas 125cm x 101cm
Rome, Galleria Borghese

Marini 1989	1609–10
Calvesi 1990	1609–10
Cinotti 1991	1610 or 1609–10
Gregori 1994	1605–06 or 1610

11, 355ff, 469, 472

FRANCIS I Cremona 1606
San Francesco in preghiera
Oil on canvas 130cm x 90cm
Cremona, Pinacoteca Civica

Marini 1989	1603
Calvesi 1990	1606c
Cinotti 1991	1606c
Gregori 1994	1605–06

352f

MEAL AT EMMAUS II Milan 1606
Cena in Emmaus
Oil on canvas 141cm x 175cm
Milan, Pinacoteca di Brera

Marini 1989	1606
Calvesi 1990	1606
Cinotti 1991	1606
Gregori 1994	1606c

353f, 377, 387, 401, 403

FRANCIS II Carpineto Romano 1606
San Francesco in meditazione
Oil on canvas 125cm x 93cm
Rome, Museo di Palazzo Venezia, ex
    Carpineto Romano

Marini 1989	1609
Calvesi 1990	1606–08
Cinotti 1991	1606
Gregori 1994	1605c

353

SEVEN WORKS OF MERCY 1606
Sette opere di misericordia
Oil on canvas 390cm x 260cm
Naples, Chiesa del Pio Monte della Misericordia

Marini 1989	1606–07
Calvesi 1990	1606
Cinotti 1991	1606
Gregori 1994	1606–07

369ff, 377, 380f, 393, 397f, 412ff, 421, 423,
    426, 454, 469

ANDREW KILLED 1607
Crocifissione di Sant' Andrea
Oil on canvas 202.5cm x 152.7cm
Cleveland, Ohio, Cleveland Museum of Art

Marini 1989	1607
Calvesi 1990	1609–10
Cinotti 1991	1607c
Gregori 1994	1607c

376f, 382, 393f, 398, 404, 462, 476

DAVID III Vienna 1607
David con testa di Golia
Oil on poplar wood panel 90.5cm x 116.5cm
Vienna, Kunsthistorisches Museum, Gemäldegalerie

Marini 1989	1607
Calvesi 1990	1607
Cinotti 1991	1607c
Gregori 1994	1607

377f, **378,** 379, 398

ROSARY MADONNA 1607
Madonna del Rosario
Oil on canvas 364.5cm x 249.5cm
Vienna, Kunsthistorisches Museum, Gemäldegalerie

Marini 1989	1606–07
Calvesi 1990	1606–07
Cinotti 1991	1607
Gregori 1994	1606–07

364f, **379ff,** 393, 397f, 406, 447, 460

CROWN OF THORNS II Vienna 1607
Cristo coronato di spine
Oil on canvas 127cm x 165.5cm
Vienna, Kunsthistorisches Museum, Gemäldegalerie

Marini 1989	1599
Calvesi 1990	1601–04
Cinotti 1991	1607c
Gregori 1994	1603c

394f, 397f

WHIPPING I Naples 1607
Flagellazione
Oil on canvas 286cm x 213cm
Naples, Museo e Gallerie Nazionali di Capodimonte

Marini 1989	1607
Calvesi 1990	1607
Cinotti 1991	1607
Gregori 1994	1607

393f, **395ff,** 398, 405, 414

WHIPPING II Rouen 1607
Flagellazione
Oil on canvas 134.5cm x 175.4cm
Rouen, Musée des Beaux Arts

Marini 1989	1607
Calvesi 1990	1606–07
Cinotti 1991	1607c
Gregori 1994	1607

394, **396f,** 398

SALOMÈ I London 1607
Salomè con testa del Battista
Oil on canvas 91.5cm x 106.7cm
London, National Gallery

Marini 1989	1609
Calvesi 1990	1608–10
Cinotti 1991	1607c
Gregori 1994	1607

397f, 463

JEROME III Malta 1607
San Girolamo scrivente
Oil on canvas 117cm x 157cm
Valletta, Museum of the Co-cathedral of St John

Marini 1989	1608
Calvesi 1990	1607–08
Cinotti 1991	1607
Gregori 1994	1608

404ff, 415, 417f, 438, 460

WIGNACOURT & PAGE 1608
Ritratto di Wignacourt con paggio
Oil on canvas 195cm x 134cm
Paris, Musée du Louvre

Marini 1989	1608c
Calvesi 1990	1607–08
Cinotti 1991	1608c
Gregori 1994	1608c

415f, 417, 423f, 437, 458

ANTONIO MARTELLI 1608
Ritratto di un cavaliere di Malta
Oil on canvas 118.5cm x 95.5cm
Florence, Palazzo Pitti, Galleria Palatina

Marini 1989	1608
Calvesi 1990	1608–10
Cinotti 1991	1608
Gregori 1994	1608–09

416f, 445

JOHN BEHEADED 1608
Decollazione del Battista
Oil on canvas 361cm x 520cm
Valletta, Co-cathedral of St John, Oratory

Marini 1989	1608
Calvesi 1990	1607–08
Cinotti 1991	1608
Gregori 1994	1608

418ff, **421ff,** 427, 434f, 443f, 490

LOVE SLEEPING 1608
Amorino dormiente
Oil on canvas 72cm x 105cm
Florence, Palazzo Pitti, Galleria Palatina

Marini 1989	1608
Calvesi 1990	1608
Cinotti 1991	1608
Gregori 1994	1608–09

424, 443, 450f

JOHN IN THE WILD VI Malta 1608

San Giovannino alla fonte
Oil on canvas 100cm x 73cm
Valletta, private collection

Marini 1989	1608
Calvesi 1990	1607–08
Cinotti 1991	1608c
Gregori 1994	1608–09

424, 426f, 460

ANNUNCIATION 1608

Annunciazione
Oil on canvas 285cm x 205cm
Nancy, Musée des Beaux Arts

Marini 1989	1609
Calvesi 1990	1608–09
Cinotti 1991	1609–10c
Gregori 1994	1609c

424f, **426f,** 460

LUCY'S BURIAL 1608

Seppellimento di Santa Lucia
Oil on canvas 408cm x 300cm
Syracuse, Museo di Palazzo Bellomo

Marini 1989	1608
Calvesi 1990	1608
Cinotti 1991	1608c
Gregori 1994	1608–09c

442ff, 450f, 458

LAZARUS RAISED 1609

Resurrezione di Lazzaro
Oil on canvas 380cm x 275cm
Messina, Museo Regionale

Marini 1989	1608–09
Calvesi 1990	1608–09
Cinotti 1991	1609
Gregori 1994	1608–09

447f, **450ff,** 454, 457f, 467

NATIVITY I Messina 1609
Adorazione dei pastori
Oil on canvas 314cm x 211cm
Messina, Museo Regionale

Marini 1989	1609
Calvesi 1990	1608–09
Cinotti 1991	1609c
Gregori 1994	1609

452ff, 458, 465

NATIVITY II ex Palermo 1609
Natività con i santi Lorenzo e Francesco
Oil on canvas 268cm x 197cm stolen 1969
ex Palermo, Oratorio della Compagnia di San Lorenzo

Marini 1989	1609
Calvesi 1990	1609
Cinotti 1991	1609
Gregori 1994	1609

457f, 467

SALOMÈ II Madrid 1609
Salomè con testa del Battista
Oil on canvas 116cm x 140cm
Madrid, Palacio Real

Marini 1989	1609
Calvesi 1990	1609–10
Cinotti 1991	1609–10c
Gregori 1994	1609c

462f, **463f,** 468f

PETER'S DENIAL 1610
Negazione di San Pietro
Oil on canvas 94cm x 125.5cm
New York, private collection

Marini 1989	1607
Calvesi 1990	1609–10
Cinotti 1991	1609–10c
Gregori 1994	1609–10

464, 467ff

JOHN IN THE WILD VII Rome Borghese 1610
San Giovanni Battista
Oil on canvas 159cm x 124cm
Rome, Galleria Borghese

Marini 1989	1610
Calvesi 1990	1609–10
Cinotti 1991	1609–10c
Gregori 1994	1609–10

464f, **465,** 469, 472, 476ff

JOHN IN THE WILD VIII Munich 1610
San Giovanni Battista disteso
Oil on canvas 106cm x 179.5cm
Munich, private collection

Marini 1989	1610
Calvesi 1990	–
Cinotti 1991	–
Gregori 1994	–

464f, **465f,** 469, 476, 478

URSULA TRANSFIXED 1610
Martirio di Sant' Orsola
Oil on canvas 154cm x 178cm
Naples, Banca Commerciale Italiana

Marini 1989	1610
Calvesi 1990	1610
Cinotti 1991	1610
Gregori 1994	1610

466ff, 474

NOTES

page 6
a good man   Dell' Acqua & Cinotti 1971 Doc F52 p155
natural things   Dell' Acqua & Cinotti 1971 Doc F52 p155
page 7
false gods   Paleotti 1961 Ch XIIII
page 8
There's a man   Van Mander 1604: Hibbard 1983 pp343ff
– when he's worked   Van Mander 1604: Hibbard 1983 pp343ff
M was overly   Baglione 1935 p138
he and his   Sandrart 1675: Hibbard 1983 p379
page 9
from his sweet   Bellori 1976 p232
First he had   Bellori 1976 p232
A wicked man   Stendhal 1973 p727
page 10
the obvious and   Hibbard 1983 p261
his criminality   Hibbard 1983 p261
flawed and peculiar   Hibbard 1983 p267
was probably   Waldemar Januszczak, *The Sunday Times* 22 December 1996
He lost   Mancini 1956 Vol I p226
If M hadn't   Baglione 1935 p139
deserted beach   Bellori 1976 p229
page 12
great understanding   Mancini 1956 Vol I p225
he seemed to   Mancini 1956 Vol I p246
page 13
He died badly   Baglione 1935 p139
Monsieur Poussin   Félibien 1679: *cit* Bellori pxvi n4
page 14
the great M   Bellori 1642: in Baglione 1935
too natural   Bellori 1976 p16
was extremely negligent   Bellori 1976 p232
good for nothing   Bellori: ms note in Baglione 1935 p1

the most excellent   Bellori 1976 p214
the only answer   Bellori 1976 p214
murky and combative   Bellori 1976 p232
page 15
He was dark   Bellori 1976 p232
He wasn't well built   Bellori: ms note in Baglione 1935 p137
M used   Bellori 1976 p232
his life   Bellori 1976 p229

Chapter 1

page 18
And there was war   *The Holy Bible* 1963 Vol III *Revelation* 12 p429
page 20
armed family   *cit* Canosa 1996b p78
corrupt and licentious   *cit* Canosa 1996b p92
how great human   *cit* Canosa 1996b p130
There is no moment   *cit* Canosa 1996b p129
the evident danger   *cit* Canosa 1996b p96
page 21
He goes   *cit* Canosa 1996b p109 n40
page 22
titiani alumnus   *cit* Cinotti 1983 p208
that all human   Bologna 1992 p21
page 23
to correct himself   Bologna 1992 p21
except when   Garzoni 1996 Vol II p1076
page 24
... twisted and transformed   Braudel 1995 Vol II pp755f
intolerable misery   *cit* Canosa 1996b p170
whether locals   *cit* Canosa 1996b p170
page 25
a great many   *cit* Canosa 1996b p171
With their gauntlets   Garzoni 1996 Vol II p1266
page 26
... they enjoy   Garzoni 1996 Vol II p1267
I set myself   Armenini 1988 pp247f
appeared around town   Bellori 1976 p224
page 27
studied with diligence   Mancini 1956 Vol I p223
murky and combative   Bellori 1976 p232
he ground colours   Bellori: ms note in Baglione 1935 p136
whore disfigured   Mancini 1956 Vol I pp226f n22
page 28
sound of mind   *cit* Cinotti 1983 p254
divine ability   Ziglioli 1996 p65 & n
Michel Angelo Gio.   Cinotti 1983 p247
page 30
loved nature   Vasari 1986 p558
... used to set himself   Vasari 1996 Vol 2 p781
page 31
The area   Delumeau 1975 p60
page 32
not only divine   Delumeau 1975 p66
page 34
this year we've   Delumeau 1975 p135

largely sterile   Montaigne 1962 p1226
the countryside   Delumeau 1975 p136
the scourge   Delumeau 1975 p137
page 35
forty thousand   Delumeau 1975 p147
some new death   Delumeau 1975 p149
because they live   Delumeau 1975 p152
the moaning   Delumeau 1975 p152
Without Ceres   Delumeau 1975 p152
If the mob   Delumeau 1975 p152
worse than   Delumeau 1975 p152
aged about twenty   Mancini 1956 Vol I p224
naked and extremely needy   Bellori: ms note in Baglione 1935 p136
He lived there   Bellori 1976 p213
short of money   Baglione 1935 p136
page 36
services that were   Mancini 1956 Vol I p224 & n
which served   Mancini 1956 Vol I p224
monsignor Salad   Mancini 1956 Vol I p224
called Lorenzo   Bellori: ms note in Baglione 1935 p136
who ran a shop   Baglione 1935 p136
being extremely needy   Bellori: ms note in Baglione 1935 p136
The big headman   Baglione 1935 p293
page 37
strenuous arriviste   Longhi 1982 p10
the most important   Röttgen 1980 p163
overwhelmed with commissions   Röttgen 1974 pp11f: & Röttgen 1980b p163
loved by princes   Baglione 1935 p374
was smart   Bellori: ms note in Baglione 1935 p374
page 38
forced by necessity   Bellori 1976 p213
was put   Bellori 1976 p213
said that   Giustiniani 1981 p42
He painted   Bellori 1976 p213
page 40
he did some   Baglione 1935 p136
He found   Bellori 1976 p213

Chapter 2

page 41
he was working   Bellori 1976 p213
He would have   Baglione 1935 p148
page 42
loved conversing   Baglione 1935 p148
was attacked by illness   Mancini 1956 Vol I p224
he did a lot   Mancini 1956 Vol I p224
Sicily   Mancini 1956 Vol I p224 n16
poorly dressed   Mancini 1956 Vol I pp226f n22
Giuseppe sees   Mancini 1956 Vol I pp226f n22
page 43
Giuseppe and Bernardino   Mancini 1956 Vol I pp226f n22
He left the house   Bellori 1976 p216
Then he tried   Baglione 1935 p136
He wanted   Mancini 1956 Vol I pp226f n22
gentleman amateur   *cit* Bassani & Bellini 1994 p36 n2

Tarquinio   Mancini 1956 Vol I pp226f n22
and soon   Baglione 1935 p136
his spokesman   Baglione 1935 p137 & p300
page 44
Prosperino of   Baglione 1935 p299
but after   Baglione 1935 p300
is the kind   Mancini 1956 Vol I p252
angrily called Prospero   Mancini 1956 Vol I pp226f n22
page 45
involved in some trouble   Susinno 1960 p117
a safe place   Susinno 1960 p117
with a Sicilian   Susinno 1960 p117
the spur   Susinno 1960 p117
decided to leave   Susinno 1960 p117
the use   Mancini 1956 Vol I p224
did a lot   Mancini 1956 Vol I p224
page 46
I'm a gentleman   Longhi 1595: *cit* Bassani & Bellini 1994 p47
page 47
He always   Baglione 1935 p156
I don't carry   Longhi 1595: *cit* Bassani & Bellini 1994 p11
Sometimes I   *cit* Bassani & Bellini 1994 p13
He's got   *cit* Bassani & Bellini 1994 p13
a bit   *cit* Bassani & Bellini 1994 p13
page 48
I usually   Longhi 1595: *cit* Bassani & Bellini 1994 pp13f
wants to know   *cit* Borromeo 1982 p263
on pain   Zapperi 1994 p46
page 50
a poor man   Mancini 1956 Vol I p140
the only answer   Bellori 1976 pp214f
page 51
… another deserving   Bellori 1976 p216
page 52
went around   Bellori 1976 p216
… was bought   Bellori 1976 p216
maestro Valentino   Baglione 1935 p136
Costantino, who buys   *cit* Corradini & Marini 1998 p27
page 53
cardinal Del Monte's   *cit* Corradini & Marini 1998 p27
page 54
Cardinal Del Monte   Baglione 1935 p136
page 55
Del Monte's a gentleman   *cit* Wazbinski 1994 Vol II p377
affable and gracious   *cit* Wazbinski 1994 Vol II p378
page 56
always eats alone   *cit* Wazbinski 1994 Vol I p77
you can't write   Del Monte: *cit* Wazbinski 1994 Vol I p79
seized and accepted   Van Mander 1604: Hibbard 1983 pp343ff
page 57
his cardinal   Baglione 1935 p136
painted from life   Baglione 1935 p136
page 58
There was no   Baglione 1935 p53
extremely beautiful   Baglione 1935 p54
… they were painted   Baglione 1935 p54
so beautiful   Baglione 1935 p54

page 60
the most beautiful   Baglione 1935 p136
Voi sapete   *cit* Trinchieri Camiz 1989 p206
page 61
No other banker   *Avviso* 1594: *cit* Delumeau 1975 p215
impetuous   Danesi Squarzina 1997 p767
mon cousin   Henri IV 1599: *cit* Danesi Squarzina 1996 pp94f
page 62
he could talk   Ameyden: *cit* Giustiniani 1981 p5
He'd brought   Ameyden: *cit* Bassani & Bellini 1994 p121
page 63
a woman in a shirt   Bellori 1976 p216
In the holy   Giutiniani 1981 pp21f
eunuchs   *cit* Trinchieri Camiz 1989 p220 n48
page 64
good catholics   *cit* Trinchieri Camiz 1989 p220 n48
revived the practice   Giustiniani 1981 p24
you should know   Del Monte 1579: *cit* Spezzaferro 1971 p68
like nothing   Vincenzo Galilei 1581: *cit* Spezzaferro 1971 p74
simple and natural   Vincenzo Galilei 1581: *cit* Wazbinski 1994 Vol I p82 n28
aimed only   Vincenzo Galilei 1581: *cit* Wazbinski 1994 Vol I p82 n28
what the senses   Galileo: *cit* Bologna 1992 p169

Chapter 3

page 68
People still say   Bellori 1976 p233
page 69
this painter is   *cit* Corradini & Marini 1998 p27
wears his thick   *cit* Corradini & Marini 1998 p27
page 70
… one was M   *cit* Corradini & Marini 1998 p27
M cardinal Del   Orsi: *cit* Corradini & Marini 1998 p27
half an hour   *cit* Corradini & Marini 1998 p27
shouting near   *cit* Corradini & Marini 1998 p27
it'd be   *cit* Corradini & Marini 1998 p27
although the said   *cit* Corradini & Marini 1998 p28
The said M   *cit* Corradini & Marini 1998 p28
page 71
wearing a sword   *cit* Bellini 1992 p70
I was taken   M: *cit* Bellini 1992 p70
stiff twin compasses   Donne 1978 p84
page 72
geometric military compass   Viviani 1992 p88
transparent waters   Leonardo 1995 Vol I p144
page 73
It's through   Leonardo 1995 Vol I p141
a carafe   Vasari 1986 p549
wanting people   Galileo: *cit* Bologna 1992 p35
page 74
It seems   Leonardo 1995 Vol II p264
page 75
and similarly   Leonardo 1995 Vol II p285
some weep   Leonardo 1995 Vol II pp293f
They have to   Leonardo 1995 Vol II p273

will be neither   Leonardo 1995 Vol II p273

That head   Baglione 1935 p136

page 76

very frightening   Baglione 1935 p136

clothed in   Moir 1982 p98

page 77

or perhaps   *cit* Cinotti 1983 p428

the strangest and weirdest   Vasari 1996 Vol I p630

page 78

a young pupil   Del Monte 1599: *cit* Wazbinski 1994 Vol I p95

page 79

the home   Longhi 1982 p5

… in the sixteenth   Longhi 1982 p5

He painted   Bellori 1976 p215

page 80

the truest poetrie   Shakespeare 1997: *As You Like It* p1633 l15

her face   Bellori 1976 p215

He painted   Bellori 1976 p215

page 82

donna Anna   *cit* Bassani & Bellini 1994 p74

page 83

Here's Anna   *cit* Bassani & Bellini 1994 p51

on the small   *cit* Bassani & Bellini 1994 p53

scandalous people   *cit* Bassani & Bellini 1994 p50

the two men   *cit* Bassani & Bellini 1994 p50

they wanted   *cit* Bassani & Bellini 1994 p53 n6

whipped whore   *cit* Bassani & Bellini 1994 p53

page 84

his holiness   Wazbinski 1994 Vol I p147 n13

vulgar and violent   Cajani 1970 p513

page 85

extremely beautiful   *Avviso* 1599: *cit* Bassani & Bellini 1994 p81

to extract cash   *Avviso* 1599: *cit* Bassani & Bellini 1994 p81

their estate   *cit* Bassani & Bellini 1994 p82

page 86

most ready   *cit* Bassani & Bellini 1994 p83

act in their   Medici 1599: *cit* Bassani & Bellini 1994 p83

tall and handsome   *cit* Bassani & Bellini 1994 p84

She showed   *cit* Bassani & Bellini 1994 pp86f

wept when   *cit* Bassani & Bellini 1994 p87

Better watch   *Avviso* 1599: *cit* Bassani & Bellini 1994 p87

page 87

amazed there were   *Avviso* 1599: *cit* Bassani & Bellini 1994 p88

People stood   *cit* Bassani & Bellini 1994 p89

brave … unyielding   *Avvisi* 1599: *cit* Cajani 1970 p514

She very bravely   *cit* Bassani & Bellini 1994 p89

died in   Vialardi 1599: *cit* Bassani & Bellini 1994 p89

page 88

whether in large   Clement VIII 1600: *cit* Bassani & Bellini 1994 pp94f

used their vile   *cit* Bassani & Bellini 1994 p95

page 90

to strengthen   Bellori 1976 p217

three men,   *cit* Bassani & Bellini 1994 p67

this morning   *Avviso* 1598: *cit* Bassani & Bellini 1994 p63

Chapter 4

page 93
a painting   cit Frommel 1971 p37
page 94
immense grace   Leonardo 1995 Vol I p188
page 95
melons at   Delumeau 1975 p135
page 96
particularly loved   Lomazzo 1598: *cit* Klein & Zerner 1989 p115
page 97
and the said   Zacchia 1600: *cit* Corradini 1993 Doc 17 p23
I got you   cit Corradini 1993 Doc 17 p24
So here   cit Corradini 1993 Doc 17 p25
and torn   cit Corradini 1993 Doc 17 p25
signor Ranuccio   cit Corradini 1993 Doc 17 p20
page 98
a certain signor   cit Corradini 1993 Doc 17 p21
because he ducked   cit Corradini 1993 Doc 17 p21
a certain Ranuccio   cit Corradini 1993 Doc 17 p21
I'm amazed   cit Corradini 1993 Doc 17 p22
That's all   cit Corradini 1993 Doc 17 p22
Look at   cit Corradini 1993 Doc 17 p22
thrown a small   cit Corradini 1993 Doc 17 p22
page 99
If you only   cit Corradini 1993 Doc 16 p19
I recognized   cit Corradini 1993 Doc 16 p19
I've heard you   cit Corradini 1993 Doc 16 p19
page 100
Ranuccio Tomassoni   cit Corradini 1993 Doc 18 p26
had a single   Mancini 1956 Vol II pp225f
page 101
an honoured place   Baglione 1935 p216
page 102
our age   Mancini 1956 Vol I p223
tender, impressionable   Carlo Borromeo: *cit* Prodi 1960 p33
people here understand   Calvesi 1990 p259 n22
in the darkest   Prodi 1960 p24
page 103
the purity   Bologna 1992 p127
as long   Paleotti 1961 p355
it was better   Federico Borromeo: *cit* Bologna 1992 p130
Looking at   Bryson 1995
page 104
knowing how   Giustiniani 1981 p42
M said once   Giustiniani 1981 p42
… the effects   Viviani 1992 p84
used to tell   Viviani 1992 p82
page 106
glorious is   Borromeo 1625: *cit* Cinotti 1983 p464
page 107
is closely observant   Mancini 1956 Vol I pp108f
is born   Vasari 1986 p70
is the work   Armenini 1988 pp120f
page 108
he didn't work   Baglione 1935 p137
He seemed   Baglione 1935 p374

page 109
the turning point   Clark 1993 p198
When you   Leonardo 1995 Vol I pp216f
page 110
wanted every   Leonardo 1995 Vol I p221
think about   Leonardo 1995 Vol I p222
page 111
a sign   Zuccari: *cit* Pevsner 1940 p60
called the young   Alberti: *cit* Bassani & Bellini 1994 p33
page 112
a lot of   Mancini 1956 Vol I p303
various paintings   Baglione 1935 p138
ungrateful youth   Marino 1988 Vol I p269
a new torment   Marino 1988 Vol I p271

Chapter 5

page 118
in a chair   *cit* Röttgen 1974 p20
… Matthew inside   *cit* Röttgen 1974 pp20f
… a long, wide   *cit* Röttgen 1974 p21
page 119
still boarded   *cit* Dell' Acqua & Cinotti 1971 Doc F11 p149
who's never finished   *cit* Dell' Acqua & Cinotti 1971 Doc F11 p149
a national shame   *cit* Dell' Acqua & Cinotti 1971 Doc F11 p149
and his brothers   *cit* Dell' Acqua & Cinotti 1971 Doc F11 p149
more than   *cit* Dell' Acqua & Cinotti 1971 Doc F13 p149
page 120
it was a great   Del Monte 1597: *cit* Zapperi 1994 p87
for an after   Del Monte 1597: *cit* Zapperi 1994 p87
page 122
He got   Baglione 1935 p136
page 124
seated with   Sandrart 1675: in Hibbard 1983 p378
productive … even   Paleotti 1582: *cit* Bologna 1992 p40
which trouble   Paleotti 1582: *cit* Bologna 1992 p40
page 125
without hope   Sandrart 1675: in Friedlaender 1955 pp261ff: & Hibbard 1983 p379
page 127
truly one of   Scannelli 1657: *cit* Dell' Acqua & Cinotti 1971 Doc F121 p167
it is in   Scannelli 1657: *cit* Dell' Acqua & Cinotti 1971 Doc F121 p167
page 128
darkness of   Baglione 1935 pp220f
page 129
a small   Ciotti 1592: *cit* Bruno 1994 p29
infinite individual   Bruno 1994 p58
we who look   Bruno 1995a p64
page 130
nature doesn't   Bruno 1996 p46
tied naked   *cit* Bassani & Bellini 1994 p94
to hear   *cit* Firpo 1993 p45
maintaining the   Scioppio 1600: *cit* Firpo 1993 p103
you may be   Bruno 1600: *cit* Scioppio 1600: *cit* Firpo 1993 p104
with his tongue   Scioppio 1600: *cit* Firpo 1993 p104

page 135

rent a figures   Carracci: *cit* Cinotti 1983 p532

a few hateful   Longhi 1982 p38

page 136

Christ, our redeemer,   Sandrart 1675: in Hibbard 1983 pp377f

the structure   Bellori 1976 p220

although he reworked   Bellori 1976 p220

composing a history   Mancini 1956 Vol I p108

You can't   Mancini 1956 Vol I pp108f

page 137

a contemporary   Longhi 1982 p38

page 138

he got the   Baglione 1935 p136

On the right   Baglione 1935 pp136f

page 139

helped make M   Baglione 1935 p137

while I was   Baglione 1935 p137

He said,   Baglione 1935 p137

page 140

There's a man   Van Mander 1604: in Hibbard 1983 p344

This M's   Van Mander 1604: in Hibbard 1983 p344

page 141

This surely   Van Mander 1604: in Hibbard 1983 p344

of course   Van Mander 1604: in Hibbard 1983 p344

… he doesn't   Van Mander 1604: in Hibbard 1983 p344

Yet as for   Van Mander 1604: in Hibbard 1983 p344

it's very pleasing   Van Mander 1604: in Hibbard 1983 p344

Chapter 6

page 144

egregius in urbe   Dell' Acqua & Cinotti 1971 Doc F29 p151

page 145

twelfth and most   Giustiniani 1981 p44

The cardinal   Avviso 1595: *cit* Zapperi 1994 p114

page 146

that marble statues   Avviso 1595: *cit* Zapperi 1994 p114

robust and   *cit* Zapperi 1994 p69

page 147

voraciously ate   *cit* Zapperi 1994 pp69f

hearty wines   *cit* Zapperi p70

to fill   *cit* Zapperi p70

page 148

half crazy   Spini 1982 p488

degenerated into vacancy   Freedberg 1971 p462

I was at   Longhi 1600: *cit* Corradini 1993 Doc 15 p15

page 149

unless I'm given   Longhi 1600: *cit* Corradini 1993 Doc 15 p14

any episode   *cit* Corradini 1993 Doc 15 pp14f

Not that   *cit* Corradini 1993 Doc 15 p15

Toward the statue   *cit* Corradini 1993 Doc 15 p15

A penny each   *cit* Corradini 1993 Doc 15 p15

I was walking   Longhi 1600: *cit* Corradini Doc 15 p15

page 150

I saw nobody   Longhi 1600: *cit* Corradini 1993 Doc 15 p16
With him –   Longhi 1600: *cit* Corradini 1993 Doc 15 p16
Was M carrying   *cit* Corradini 1993 Doc 15 p16
At that time   Longhi 1600: *cit* Corradini 1993 Doc 15 p16
about a month   *cit* Bertolotti 1985 Vol II p17

page 151

honours   Baglione 1935 p92
has left   Baglione 1935 p93
the person   *cit* Corradini 1993 Doc 15 p16

page 152

according to   Longhi 1600: *cit* Corradini 1993 Doc 15 p16
I went alone   Longhi 1600: *cit* Corradini 1993 Doc 15 p16
any disagreement   *cit* Corradini 1993 Doc 15 p17
No sir.   Longhi 1600: *cit* Corradini 1993 Doc 15 p17
Had he ever   *cit* Corradini 1993 Doc 15 p17
My dear sir,   Longhi 1600: *cit* Corradini 1993 Doc 15 p17

page 153

recovering from   Longhi 1600: *cit* Corradini 1993 Doc 15 p16
on the hand   Longhi 1600: *cit* Corradini 1993 Doc 15 p16
once he'd put   Bellori 1976 p232
not too tidily   *cit* Corradini & Marini p27

page 154

the defendant   Spampa 1597: *cit* Dell' Acqua & Cinotti 1971 Doc F31 p151

page 155

You fucking thief   Longhi 1600: *cit* Corradini 1993 Doc 15 p13
Open up   Longhi 1599: *cit* Corradini 1993 Doc 11 p8
with signor Ranuccio   *cit* Corradini 1993 Doc 16 p19
I don't know   Carracci: *cit* Malvasia 1967 Vol I p344

page 157

secretly far more   Del Monte 1599: *cit* Zapperi 1994 p31
everyone knows   Niccolini 1599: *cit* Zapperi 1994 p31
to his holiness's   Del Monte 1599: *cit* Zapperi 1994 p33

page 158

Christ our lord   Paleotti 1961 p290

page 159

no less   Avviso 1600: *cit* Zapperi 1994 p117 n16
Now we await   Avviso 1600: *cit* Zapperi 1994 p117 n16
very beautiful   Avviso 1601: in Dell' Acqua & Cinotti 1971 Doc F35 p151
hard shelled   Freedberg 1983 p65

page 160

he did these   Baglione 1935 p137
two large paintings   *cit* Cinotti 1983 p536

page 162

fell to   The Holy Bible 1963 Vol III *Acts* 9 p219
it is hard   The Holy Bible 1963 Vol III *Acts* 9 p219

page 163

The rear parts   Lomazzo: *cit* Longhi 1929 p114
an accident   Longhi 1982 p57
The history   Bellori 1976 p222

page 165

Pray you,   Shakespeare 1997 *King Lear* p974 l285
resident in   *cit* Parks 1985 p441
on cardinal   *cit* Corradini 1993 Doc 23 p27
so he could   Susinno 1980 p117

Chapter 7

page 167
the finest   *cit* Zapperi 1994 p15
a soft youth   Picchi: *cit* Bassani & Bellini 1994 p131
page 168
splendidly   *Avviso* 1601: *cit* Bassani & Bellini 1994 p127
had ordered   *Avviso* 1601: *cit* Bassani & Bellini 1994 p127
opposite the gateway   *cit* Bassani & Bellini 1994 p128
if you want   Calvi 1601: *cit* Bassani & Bellini 1994 p128
When I saw   Calvi 1601: *cit* Bassani & Bellini 1994 pp128f
page 169
Lieutenant I kept   *cit* Bassani & Bellini 1994 p129
signor Ottavio   Calvi 1601: *cit* Bassani & Bellini 1994 p132
who lives   M 1604: *cit* Dell'Acqua & Cinotti 1971 Doc F61 p158
a very lovely   *cit* Bassani & Bellini 1994 p131
That's the pope's   Del Monte 1597: *cit* Bassani & Bellini 1994 p132
page 170
domed canopy   *cit* Bassani & Bellini 1994 p130
to recuperate   *Avviso* 1601: *cit* Bassani & Bellini 1994 p130
taking the airs   *cit* Bassani & Bellini 1994 p131
I can't play   Calvi 1601: *cit* Bassani & Bellini 1994 p131 n21
page 171
a portrait   Salerno 1960c No 12 p136
half figure portrait   Salerno 1960c No 11 p136
famous courtesan   Cinotti 1983 p576
a very fine   Mancini 1956 Vol I p252
page 173
was acclaiming   Bellori 1976 p216
I saw   Marino 1620: *cit* Dell'Acqua & Cinotti 1971 Doc F114 p164
page 174
good, but prolix   *cit* Fulco 1980 p71
still young   Milesi: in Fulco 1980 p87 [2]
If you look   Milesi: in Fulco 1980 p87 [2]
page 175
Let the ancients   Milesi: in Fulco 1980 pp87f [3]
Admire the highest   Milesi: in Fulco 1980 p88 [4]
He stupefies   Milesi: in Fulco 1980 p88 [4]
O happy century   Milesi: in Fulco 1980 p88 [4]
my great M   Milesi: in Fulco 1980 p88 [8]
O you   Milesi: in Fulco 1980 p88 [8]
marvels   Milesi: in Fulco 1980 [10]
page 176
strengthening his darks   Bellori 1976 p217
Caravaggio, as he   Bellori 1976 pp217f
page 178
pleasures of   Dell' Acqua & Cinotti 1971 Doc F4 p147
excellent in   Baglione 1935 p100
He spent   Baglione 1935 p100
he had no   Baglione 1935 pp100f
page 179
The Contarellis   Baglione 1935 p100
because said   Dell' Acqua & Cinotti 1971 Doc F39 p152
to place above   Dell' Acqua & Cinotti 1971 Doc F39 p152
the one   Dell' Acqua & Cinotti 1971 Doc F40 p152
at the foot   Spezzaferro 1980a p52
an insolent kid   Longhi 1982 pp25f

page 181

M must have   Dell' Acqua & Cinotti 1971 Doc F40 p152

despairing ... desperate   Bellori 1976 p219

page 182

Nobody liked it   Baglione 1935 p137

When he finished   Bellori 1976 p219

greatly upset   Bellori 1976 p219

dreary   Baglione 1935 p100

statue in white   Dell' Acqua & Cinotti 1971 Doc F40 p152

page 183

Intervening with   Bellori 1976 p219

page 184

M made every   Bellori 1976 p220

page 185

Nobody liked   Baglione 1935 p137

simply because   Baglione 1935 p137

persuaded by   Baglione 1935 p137

promoter   Baglione 1935 p137

In fact   Baglione 1935 p137

page 187

as winter   Bellarmino: *cit* Zapperi 1994 p120

done in fresco   Farnese: *cit* Zapperi 1994 p120

page 188

This piece   Sandrart 1675: in Hibbard 1983 p378

a prominent   Sandrart 1675: in Hibbard 1983 pp378f

Chapter 8

page 193

going overboard   Baglione 1935 p137

we ourselves   Borromeo 1624: *cit* Bologna 1992 p123

page 194

A sitting Cupid   Baglione 1935 p137

A life size   Sandrart 1675: in Hibbard 1983 p378

Cupido di Caravaggio   Symonds 1650: in Papi 1992 p13

page 195

Francesco ... garzone   Cinotti 1983 p243

page 196

Francesco, known as   Mancini 1956 Vol I p108

page 197

Don't look,   Murtola 1603: in Dell' Acqua & Cinotti 1971 Doc F110[a] p164

If, wise painter   Murtola 1603: in Dell' Acqua & Cinotti 1971 Doc F110[d] p164

page 199

the paintings   Paleotti 1961 p289

arguments used   Paleotti 1961 p505

bodies must never   Paleotti 1961 p505

which saints   Paleotti 1961 p505

youths' lascivious   Paleotti 1961 p505

horny old ram   Moir 1983 p114

had his raiment   The Holy Bible 1963 Vol III *Matthew* 3 p5

O generation   The Holy Bible 1963 Vol III *Matthew* 3 p5

page 201

no images   *cit* Benedetti 1993 p17

page 202

nude John ... couldn't   Scannelli 1657: in Dell' Acqua & Cinotti 1971 Doc F121 p167

page 203
bathhouse art   Aretino 1545: in Klein & Zerner 1989 p123
page 204
pastor friso   Correale 1990 p35
my only lord   Cinotti 1983 p521
page 205
common bodies   Bellori 1976 p230
People started imitating   Bellori 1976 p230
workmanship   Giustiniani 1981 p42
page 207
terrifying naturalness   Scannelli 1657: in Dell' Acqua & Cinotti 1971 Doc F121 p167
In the   Bellori 1976 p23
page 209
despairing   Bellori 1976 p219
page 211
employed in   Cozzi 1961 p38
a little hunchback   Cozzi 1961 p41
page 212
excellent painter   Paravicino 1603: in Cozzi 1961 p44
midway between   Paravicino 1603: in Cozzi 1961 p44
wouldn't've even wanted   Paravicino 1603: in Cozzi 1961 p44
copious   Paravicino 1603: in Cozzi 1961 p68
in villeggiatura   Paravicino 1603: in Cozzi 1961 p45
page 213
they say   Baglione 1935 p137
the whole nude   Bellori 1976 p221

Chapter 9

page 217
two big   Baglione 1935 p401
page 219
earliest works   Nicolson 1990 Vol I p58
went off following   Mancini 1956 Vol I p246
He behaves   Mancini 1956 Vol I p246
impossible to   Van Mander 1606: in Hibbard 1983 p344
page 220
It was a   Gentileschi 1603: in Dell' Acqua & Cinotti 1971 Doc F54 p156
page 221
People didn't   Gentileschi 1603: in Dell' Acqua & Cinotti 1971 Doc F54 p156
even though,   Gentileschi 1603: in Dell' Acqua & Cinotti 1971 Doc F54 p156
The painting   Gentileschi 1603: in Dell' Acqua & Cinotti 1971 Doc F54 p156
page 222
done with love   Baglione 1935 p402
page 223
... the said M   Salini 1601: cit Bassani & Bellini 1994 p117
continually committing   Salini 1601: cit Bassani & Bellini 1994 p117
guardian angel   M 1603: in Dell' Acqua & Cinotti 1971 Doc F52 p155
an excessively free   Baglione 1935 p188
page 224
Johnny Prick   Dell' Acqua & Cinotti 1971 Doc F46 p153
page 225
to look at   Salini 1603: in Dell' Acqua & Cinotti 1971 Doc F47 pp153f
Johnny Baggage   Dell' Acqua & Cinotti 1971 Doc F46 p153

page 226

that which begins Baglione 1603: in Dell' Acqua & Cinotti 1971 Doc F46 p153

in particular Salini 1603: in Dell' Acqua & Cinotti 1971 Doc F47 p153

from a fuck Salini 1603: in Dell' Acqua & Cinotti 1971 Doc F47 p153

page 227

pretended I liked Trisegni 1603: in Dell' Acqua & Cinotti 1971 Doc F49 p154

[Mao] badly wanted Trisegni 1603: in Dell' Acqua & Cinotti 1971 Doc F49 p154

page 228

a human Trisegni 1603: in Dell' Acqua & Cinotti 1971 Doc F49 p154

and so I Trisegni 1603: in Dell' Acqua & Cinotti 1971 Doc F49 p154

a young guy Trisegni 1603: in Dell' Acqua & Cinotti 1971 Doc F49 p154

mentioned, told Trisegni 1603: in Dell' Acqua & Cinotti 1971 Doc F51 p155

and in particular Salini 1603: Dell' Acqua & Cinotti 1971 Doc F51 p155

page 229

I know how Gentileschi 1603: in Dell' Acqua & Cinotti 1971 Doc F50 pp154f

I painted Baglione 1603: in Dell' Acqua & Cinotti 1971 Doc F46 p153

page 230

I was taken M 1603: in Dell' Acqua & Cinotti 1971 Doc F52 p155

I think M 1603: in Dell' Acqua & Cinotti 1971 Doc F52 p155

To me M 1603: in Dell' Acqua & Cinotti 1971 Doc F52 p155

page 231

Of the ones M 1603: in Dell' Acqua & Cinotti 1971 Doc F52 p155

Of the painters M 1603: in Dell' Acqua & Cinotti 1971 Doc F52 p155

I don't think M 1603: in Dell' Acqua & Cinotti 1971 Doc F52 p155

– Unless it was M 1603: in Dell' Acqua & Cinotti 1971 Doc F52 p155

page 232

I don't know M 1603: in Dell' Acqua & Cinotti 1971 Doc F52 p155

maybe he does M 1603: in Dell' Acqua & Cinotti 1971 Doc F52 p155

and was young M 1603: in Dell' Acqua & Cinotti 1971 Doc F52 p155

I have never M 1603: in Dell' Acqua & Cinotti 1971 Doc F52 p155

egregius in urbe Dell' Acqua & Cinotti 1971 Doc F29 p151

page 233

well mannered gentleman Gentileschi 1603: in Dell' Acqua & Cinotti 1971 Doc F53 p155

devotion and not Gentileschi 1603: in Dell' Acqua & Cinotti 1971 Doc F54 p156

hang a little Gentileschi 1603: in Dell' Acqua & Cinotti 1971 Doc F53 p155

in the sonnets Baglione 1603: in Dell' Acqua & Cinotti 1971 Doc F53 p155

but there's also Gentileschi 1603: in Dell' Acqua & Cinotti 1971 Doc F54 p156

page 234

And I haven't Gentileschi 1603: in Dell' Acqua & Cinotti 1971 Doc F54 p156

it does Gentileschi 1603: in Dell' Acqua & Cinotti 1971 Doc F54 p156

because I write Gentileschi 1603: in Dell' Acqua & Cinotti 1971 Doc F54 p156

moderating the other Dell' Acqua & Cinotti 1971 Doc F55 p156

page 235

other decree Dell' Acqua & Cinotti 1971 Doc F55 p156

page 236

my Abraham done Barberini 1610: in Corradini 1993 Doc 142 p106

I was in Salini 1603: in Dell' Acqua & Cinotti 1971 Doc F56 p156

page 237

We came here Salini 1603: in Dell' Acqua & Cinotti 1971 Doc F56 p156

I found him Salini 1603: in Dell' Acqua & Cinotti 1971 Doc F56 p157

page 238

M's and Onorio's Salini 1603: in Dell' Acqua & Cinotti 1971 Doc F47 p153

he didn't want Della Porta 1603: in Dell' Acqua & Cinotti 1971 Doc F56 p157

a redbearded man Dell' Acqua & Cinotti 1971 Doc F56 p157

who said he Dell' Acqua & Cinotti 1971 Doc F56 p157

red in the face Dell' Acqua & Cinotti 1971 Doc F56 p157

washing out Dell' Acqua & Cinotti 1971 Doc F46 p153

Chapter 10

page 241
They never Bellori 1976 p218
in the dark Bellori 1976 p217
page 242
Leonardesque Christiansen 1986 p430
page 243
small chin Christiansen 1986 p430
The most fascinating Christiansen 1986 p430
the tightly compressed Christiansen 1986 p430
page 246
By now Mereu 1995 p90
page 247
As soon as Prosperi 1996 p219
In the late Prosperi 1996 p465
Truth is elaborated Prosperi 1996 pp467f
page 248
a priest Paravacino 1603: in Cozzi 1961 p44
It's said Vialardi 1603: *cit* Bassani & Bellini 1994 p155
page 249
Suspicio Mereu 1995 p122
praesumptio culpae Mereu 1995 p116
slanderers and defamers Delumeau 1975 p12
page 250
banally devotional Guglielmi Faldi 1963 p188
Clement ... liked them Baglione 1935 p402
For Giustiniani Baglione 1935 p403
page 251
still nailed Dell' Acqua & Cinotti 1971 Doc F46 p153
page 252
It wasn't Spanish Villari 1991 p113
imitating natural things M 1603: in Dell' Acqua & Cinotti 1971 Doc F52 p155
Pride, murky ambition Villari 1991 p126
overpower or make Villari 1991 p126
page 253
... the painters Bellori 1976 pp217f
physically dangerous Longhi 1943 p20
he got it Baglione 1935 pp146f
He was a Baglione 1935 p147
page 254
when necessary, Mancini 1956 Vol I p254
But then he Baglione 1935 p159
He painted no Baglione 1935 p159
page 255
distinguished appearance Mancini 1956 Vol I p251
At such times Mancini 1956 Vol I p251
maybe the best Mancini 1956 Vol I p251
page 256
Orazio Borgianni Baglione 1935 p142
adherents Baglione 1606: *cit* Spezzaferro 1975 pp53f
If Orazio Baglione 1935 p360
always had Baglione 1935 p156
page 257
unreliable Baglione 1935 p300
This man Baglione 1935 p300
great hatred Baglione 1935 p293

ape   Van Tuyll Van Serooskerken 1996 p251
he was given   Malvasia 1967 Vol II pp75f
page 258
attack or cause   Corradini 1993 Doc 26 p29
page 259
poor foot soldier   *cit* Bassani & Bellini 1994 p179 n12
the death   *cit* Parks 1985 p441
page 260
a very old   Montaigne 1962 p1247
The Madonna   Calvesi 1990 p330
page 261
most excellent   Mauruzi 1604: in Dell' Acqua & Cinotti 1971 Doc F57 p157
quite nonchalant   Montaigne 1960 p1250
[Roncalli] … got   Baglione 1935 p291
page 262
The experts   Mancini 1956 Vol I p109
didn't use   Bellori 1976 p229
He always had   Mancini 1956 Vol I p236
given to him   Baglione 1935 p291
perplexed   Passeri 1976 p373
page 263
moderate companion   Passeri 1976 p373
I brought them   Dell' Acqua & Cinotti 1971 Doc F59 p157
I don't know   Dell' Acqua & Cinotti 1971 Doc F59 p157
M took it   Dell' Acqua & Cinotti 1971 Doc F59 p157

Chapter 11

page 266
a mixture   Bruno 1995a pp45f
on the steps   Bruno 1995a p46
page 267
Since Rome   Guevarre 1693: *cit* Geremek 1995 p222
an edict   Avviso 1604: *cit* Bassani & Bellini 1994 p213
… he did   Baglione 1935 p137
page 268
their filthy   Bellori 1976 p231
the mass   Paleotti 1961 p500
these things   Borromeo 1624: *cit* Bologna 1992 p123
experts like   Mancini 1956 Vol I p109
page 269
saint Philip   Paleotti 1961 pp404f
soft youth   *cit* Bassani & Bellini 1994 p204
page 270
all sexually   *cit* Zeri 1997 p19
we cannot   Borromeo 1624: *cit* Bologna 1992 p124
living persons   Mancini 1956 Vol I p120
page 272
Item   Inventory 1605: in Marini & Corradini 1993 p162
page 273
some little   Baglione 1935 p136
page 274
in the end   Garzoni 1996 Vol II p1423
flat mirror   Leonardo 1995 Vol II p302
the painters'   Leonardo 1995 Vol II p302

When you   Leonardo 1995 Vol II p302

dipingere bene   M 1603: in Dell' Acqua & Cinotti 1971 Doc F52 p155

the painter's mind   Leonardo 1995 Vol I pp171f

page 275

The painter   Leonardo 1995 Vol I p173

In a small   Della Porta 1589: *cit* Alpers 1989 p41

page 276

vision is   Kepler 1604: *cit* Alpers 1989 p34

the origin   Kepler 1604: *cit* Alpers 1989 p34

Ut pictura,   Kepler 1604: *cit* Alpers 1989 p34

page 277

one large mirror   *cit* Marini & Corradini 1993 p162

mirror shield   *cit* Marini & Corradini 1993 p162

page 278

with a single   Mancini 1956 Vol I p108

… to bring out   Sandrart 1675: in Hibbard 1983 p376

He took this   Bellori 1976 p217

page 279

broken ceiling   Bruni 1605: in Dell' Acqua & Cinotti 1971 Doc F68 p159

know how to   M 1603: in Dell' Acqua & Cinotti 1971 Doc F52 p155

knowing how   M 1603: in Dell' Acqua & Cinotti 1971 Doc F52 p155

page 281

the voice of   The Holy Bible 1963 Vol III *Matthew* 3 p5

page 284

playing the lute   Tomassoni 1604: *cit* Corradini 1993 Doc 33 p42

so I put   Tomassoni 1604: *cit* Corradini 1993 Doc 33 p42

What insolence   Tomassoni 1604: *cit* Corradini 1993 Doc 33 p43

Item   Inventory 1605: in Corradini 1993 Doc 57 p63

page 285

Fright   M 1604: *cit* Dell' Acqua & Cinotti 1971 Doc F61 p158

a youth   Gabrielli 1604: *cit* Dell' Acqua & Cinotti 1971 Doc F61 p158

would've turned   Gabrielli 1604: *cit* Dell' Acqua & Cinotti 1971 Doc F61 p158

who lives   M 1604: *cit* Dell' Acqua & Cinotti 1971 Doc F61 p158

page 286

sucked cocks   M 1604: *cit* Dell' Acqua & Cinotti 1971 Doc F61 p158

a gentleman   Gabrielli 1604: *cit* Dell' Acqua & Cinotti 1971 Doc F61 p158

In any case   Tonti 1604: *cit* Dell' Acqua & Cinotti 1971 Doc F61 p158

Good night,   *cit* Dell' Acqua & Cinotti 1971 Doc F62 p158

my men   *cit* Dell' Acqua & Cinotti 1971 Doc F62 p158

Chapter 12

page 289

the death   *cit* Parks 1985 p441

page 290

the death   Longhi 1982 p63

page 291

spreading itself   Eliot 1991 p203

page 293

in the figure   Mancini 1956 Vol I p224

Some moderns   Mancini 1956 Vol I p120

It was taken   Baglione 1935 p138

had too realistically   Bellori 1976 p231

page 294

wearing a cape   Corradini 1993 Doc 38 p54

page 295

painter and poet   title page Passeri [1772] 1976

When M painted   Passeri c1670: *cit* Hess 1967 pp77f

Chapter 13

the painter   Dell' Acqua & Cinotti 1971 Doc F68 p159
He came   Bruni 1605: in Dell' Acqua & Cinotti 1971 Doc F68 p159
He smashed   Bruni 1605: in Dell' Acqua & Cinotti 1971 Doc F68 p159
the wife   Bruni 1605: in Dell' Acqua & Cinotti 1971 Doc F68 p159
page 314
They can   Bruni 1605: in Dell' Acqua & Cinotti 1971 Doc F68 p159
most illustrious   Dell' Acqua & Cinotti 1971 Doc F67 p159
scared   *cit* Bassani & Bellini 1994 p221
immensely rigorous   *cit* Bassani & Bellini 1994 p221
page 315
For the same   Bellori 1976 p223
page 316
half figure   Salerno 1960c p135
page 318
... some descriptions   Castiglioni 1957: *cit* Calvesi 1990 p351
the mediocrity   Renato Zenier: *cit* Haskell 1980 p27
page 319
The cardinal   Bellori 1976 p224
and presented   Bellori 1976 p224
page 320
offend   Corradini 1993 Doc 43 p58
page 321
vegetable love   Marvell 1996 p51
a picture   *cit* Spike 1996 p216 n6
that greater   Bellori 1976 p213
page 322
first of the   Michel 1996 p1319
didn't fit   *cit* Spezzaferro 1974 p126
to deal with   *cit* Spezzaferro 1974 p127 n4
I hurt   M 1605: *cit* Corradini 1993 Doc 67 p67
page 323
M came around   Masetti 1605: in Corradini 1993 Doc 65 p66
M's been round   Masetti 1605: in Corradini 1993 Doc 68 p67
M came round   Masetti 1605: in Corradini 1993 Doc 71 p68
page 325
a very lively   Ginzburg 1986 p173
outlined Mancini's   Ginzburg 1986 p173
page 326
Swordplay in   Longhi 1926: *cit* Calì 1980 p17
page 327
th'indifferent Italian   Donne 1978 p119
a pleasant pastime   Lithgow 1632: *cit* Posner 1971 p301
page 328
bathhouse art   Aretino 1545: in Klein & Zerner 1989 p123
stunningly beautiful   Vasari 1986 p551
thief, liar,   Leonardo: *cit* Bramly 1994 p224
the angel   Letze & Buchsteiner 1997 p178
We see   Carlo Pedretti: in Letze & Buchsteiner 1997 p178
page 329
Once the gallery   Mancini 1956 Vol I p218
From the prince's   Baglione 1935 p108
page 330
He wants   Masetti 1605: in Corradini 1993 Doc 63 p66
amorous disorders   Bellori 1976 p87
wicked life   Sandrart 1675: *cit* Wittkower 1969 p115
page 331
today or tomorrow   Masetti 1605: in Corradini 1993 Doc 74 p69

if the past's   Masetti 1605: in Corradini 1993 Doc 74 p69
he blushes   Masetti 1605: in Corradini 1993 Doc 74 p69
page 332
feathery   Parks 1985 p445
page 333
happy and satisfied   M 1606: *cit* Dell' Acqua & Cinotti 1971 Doc F75 p160
was removed   Baglione 1935 p137
the virgin   Bellori 1976 p231
page 335
prudence   Giustiniani 1981 p104
experience of holding   Giustiniani 1981 p104
Without leaving   Giustiniani 1981 p104
being able   Giustiniani 1981 p104
page 336
very lavish   Bizoni 1606: *cit* Bologna 1992 p217
There were toasts   Bizoni 1606: *cit* Bologna 1992 p217
prepared to drown   Giustinani 1981 p114

Chapter 14

page 338
28 May 1606.   *Avviso* 1606: in Corradini 1993 Doc 78 pp69f
page 339
likely to die   Corradini 1993 Doc 80 p70
Two evenings   Bertacchi 1606: in Corradini 1993 Doc 84 p71
The same day   *Avviso* 1606: in Corradini 1993 Doc 81 pp70f
page 340
had quarrelled   *Avviso* 1606: *cit* Fuda 1992 p74
a young   Bellori 1976 p224
The painter   Masetti 1606: in Corradini 1993 Doc 83 p71
… a very   *Avviso* 1606: in Corradini 1993 Doc 85 pp71f
page 341
to recount   *Avviso* 1606: in Hibbard 1983 p206 n23
maybe twelve   *Avviso* 1606: in Hibbard 1983 p206 n3
to avenge   *Avviso* 1606: in Hibbard 1983 p206 n3
page 342
finally, as   Mancini 1956 Vol I p225
he reddens   Masetti 1605: in Corradini 1993 Doc 74 p69
First they fought   Bellori 1976 p224
a young friend   Bellori 1976 p224
In his   Baglione 1935 p138
page 344
a sack   Donne 1978 p100
They all fled   Baglione 1935 p138
He fled   Bellori 1976 p225
he was forced   Mancini 1956 Vol I p225
page 345
my relative   Del Monte 1625: *cit* Fuda 1992 p76
secretly   Mancini 1956 Vol I p225
page 346
expects to be   Masetti 1606: in Corradini 1993 Doc 106 p84
bando capitale   *Avviso* 1610: in Dell' Acqua & Cinotti 1971 Doc F94 p162
the public intimation   Calvesi 1990 p141
in Rome   De Luca 1673: *cit* Calvesi 1990 p142
of severing   De Luca 1673: *cit* Calvesi 1990 p142
some zealous   De Luca 1673: *cit* Calvesi 1990 p142

page 347

by axe,   De Luca 1673: *cit* Calvesi 1990 p143

he was keeping   Longhi 1611: *cit* Calvesi 1990 p139

he has obtained   Longhi 1611: *cit* Marini 1989 p96 n301

page 348

after ten years'   Susinno 1960 p117

wasn't able   Susinno 1960 p117

He tried   Susinno 1960 p117

page 350

They all fled   Baglione 1935 p138

page 351

swollen in light   Longhi 1943 p17

one of M's   Longhi 1943 p17

page 352

savagery   Bellori 1976 p226

page 355

l'esempio avanti   Giustiniani 1981 p44

page 356

a half figure   Bellori 1976 pp223f

in that head   Manilli 1650: *cit* Cinotti 1983 p503

ye body   Symonds 1650: in Papi 1992 p13

more serious   De Luca 1673: *cit* Calvesi 1990 p142

The image of   De Luca 1673: *cit* Calvesi 1990 pp142f

Nec spe nec   Sandrart 1675: in Hibbard 1983 p379

page 359

collateral commission   Fuda 1992 p77

knight of the golden fleece   Fuda 1992 p77

Chapter 15

page 361

the richest   Cervantes Saaveda 1995 p336

Naples had   Braudel 1995 Vol I p345

page 362

The whole   Braudel 1995 Vol I pp345f

Naples was   Braudel 1995 Vol I p347

page 363

Even considering   De Maio 1983 pp23f

one of   Ghirelli 1992 p40

page 364

a particularly   Galasso 1994 p345

collateral commission   Fuda 1992 p77

the famine   Barnaba 1607: *cit* Galasso p345

He immediately   Bellori 1976 p225

page 365

Madonna and child   Pacelli 1993 p8

Political paralysis   Ghirelli 1992 p35

page 366

in favour   *cit* Macioce 1985 p293

hiding behind   Baglione 1606: *cit* Corradini 1993 Doc 110 pp87f

page 367

beardless   *cit* Corradini 1993 Doc 110 p89

and he told   *cit* Corradini 1993 Doc 110 p87

a chief of   Baglione 1606: *cit* Corradini 1993 Doc 110 p88

... they did   Baglione 1606: *cit* Corradini 1993 Doc 110 p88

page 368

You didn't Borgianni 1606: *cit* Corradini 1993 Doc 110 p89

I stayed there *cit* Corradini 1993 Doc 110 p89

I was an The Holy Bible 1963 *Matthew* 25 p50

page 370

that transforms Ghirelli 1992 p35

page 371

I was a stranger The Holy Bible 1963 *Matthew* 25 p50

I was thirsty The Holy Bible 1963 *Matthew* 25 p50

I was naked The Holy Bible 1963 *Matthew* 25 p50

I was sick The Holy Bible 1963 *Matthew* 25 p50

I was an hungred The Holy Bible 1963 *Matthew* 25 p50

page 372

just as happens Pacelli 1994 p29

The noncanonical act Moir 1982 p110

it lights Bellori 1976 pp225f

page 373

they say *cit* Villari 1994 p52

page 374

it can never *cit* Pacelli 1993 p69

page 375

singularly blackened Sade 1996 p237

The greatest Argan 1956: *cit* Marini 1989 p495

no more hallucinatory Moir 1982 p136

page 377

M original *cit* Cinotti 1983 p421

the half figure Bellori 1976 p233

page 378

a moral clearing Longhi 1982 p161

the murkiness Longhi 1982 p161

page 382

I've also *cit* Dell' Acqua & Cinotti 1971 Doc F82 p161

two stunning Pourbus 1607: *cit* Dell' Acqua & Cinotti 1971 Doc F83 p161

great friend Castro 1673: *cit* Cinotti 1983 p551

Chapter 16

page 385

and liked Magni 1607: in Corradini 1993 Doc 113 p93

page 386

I've been Magni 1607: in Corradini 1993 Doc 113 p93

It slipped Magni 1607: in Corradini 1993 Doc 114 p94

who's gone Magni 1607: in Corradini 1993 Doc 114 p94

I was afraid Magni 1607: in Corradini 1993 Doc 115 p94

All this week Magni 1607: Corradini 1993 Doc 117 p95

page 388

even when Paul V 1607: *cit* Calvesi 1995 p22

page 390

It hasn't been Masetti 1607: in Dell' Acqua & Cinotti 1971 Doc F81[a] p161

… I doubt Masetti 1607: in Dell' Acqua & Cinotti 1971 Doc F81[b] p161

page 391

The greater Masetti 1607: in Dell' Acqua & Cinotti 1971 Doc F81[c] p161

page 392

… risen out of Van Mander 1604: in Hibbard 1983 p344

page 394

one of his Bellori 1976 p232

page 399
Italy's maritime Braudel 1995 Vol II p850
apart from Jews Prosperi 1996 p109
brilliant, privileged Mallia-Milanes 1993 p15
far from austere Caylus 1710: cit Mallia-Milanes 1993 p15
might've been called Caylus 1710: cit Mallia-Milanes 1993 p15
page 400
his holiness's galleys Niccolini 1602: cit Fuda 1992 p73
general of cit Calvesi 1990 p132
page 401
loaded with Wignacourt 1607: in Macioce 1994 p215
page 402
a painter's cit Azzopardi 1989 pp29f
page 403
accidentally committed homicide Susinno 1960 p117
page 405
There was Giustiniani 1981 p42
Ever since Gerini 1829: cit Macioce 1987 p178
page 407
who push themselves Van Mander 1604: in Hibbard 1983 p344

Chapter 17

page 409
the opportunity Wignacourt 1607: in Macioce 1994 p207
page 410
once only Wignacourt 1607: in Macioce 1994 p207
that having Wignacourt 1607: in Macioce 1994 p207
would straight away Wignacourt 1607: in Macioce 1994 p207
… as it is Wignacourt 1607: in Macioce 1994 pp207f
who have desire Wignacourt 1608: in Corradini 1993 Doc 126 p97
And notwithstanding Wignacourt 1608: in Corradini 1993 Doc 126 pp97f
page 411
beloved son Paul V 1608: in Corradini 1993 Doc 127 p98
even though Paul V 1608: in Corradini 1993 Doc 127 p98
M wanted Baglione 1603: in Dell' Acqua & Cinotti 1971 Doc F46 p153
page 412
bellissimo Mancini 1956 Vol I p340
totally bizarre Scaramuccia 1674: in Dell' Acqua & Cinotti 1971 Doc F125 p169
genius of Raphael Scaramuccia 1674: in Dell' Acqua & Cinotti 1971 Doc F125 p169
They observed Scaramuccia 1674: in Dell' Acqua & Cinotti 1971 Doc F125 p169
page 413
there are three Celano 1694: cit Pacelli 1994 p218 n42
coming out De Dominici 1742: cit Pacelli 1994 p216 n35
I couldn't Cochin 1763: in Longhi 1951b p49
very fine … Cochin 1763: in Longhi 1951b p49
It's a very Cochin 1762: in Longhi 1951b p49
page 416
He painted Bellori 1976 p226
sign of merit Baglione 1935 p138
page 417
in convento cit Calvesi 1990 p160 n122
without having Wignacourt 1607: cit Macioce 1994 p209
doing the convoys Macioce 1994 p209
generously outfitted Sandrart 1675: in Hibbard 1983 p379

page 418
to decorate   *cit* Azzopardi 1989a p24
page 419
general of   *cit* Calvesi 1990 p132
We want   Wignacourt 1607: *cit* Macioce 1994 p209
page 420
In order not   Wignacourt 1607: *cit*   Macioce 1994 p209
page 421
in Turkish clothes   Bellori 1976 p226
raiment of camel's   *The Holy Bible* 1963 Vol III *Matthew* 3 p5
page 423
the beheading   Bellori 1976 p226
In this work   Bellori 1976 p226
page 424
pretty Giulietto   Murtola 1603: in Dell' Acqua & Cinotti 1971 Doc F110[d] p164
sweet languid   Murtola 1603: in Dell' Acqua & Cinotti 1971 Doc F110[d] p164
like a dead   Hibbard 1983 p262
horrid   Longhi 1951c p34
page 425
He gave   Dal Pozzo 1611: *cit* Calvesi 1990 p368
page 427
beyond the honour   Bellori 1976 p226
knight of obedience   *cit* Azzopardi 1989a Doc 2 p33
burning with zeal   *cit* Azzopardi 1989a Doc 2 p33
by a papal   *cit* Azzopardi 1989a Doc 2 p33
page 428
We took all   Contreras 1996 p43
page 429
They were all   Contreras 1996 p70
the most beautiful   Contreras 1996 p72
He was convinced   Contreras 1996 p72
My girlfriend   Contreras 1996 p77
there was   Williams 1993 p291
Young men   Williams 1993 p291
page 430
surrounded himself   Dal Pozzo 1703: *cit* Gregori 1974 p597 n16
little Gomorrah   Caylusc 1710: *cit* Mallia-Milanes 1993 p15
page 431
list of crimes   *cit* Marini 1989 p67
removed and thrown out   Azzopardi 1989a Doc 5 p39

Chapter 18

page 434
criminal commission   Azzopardi 1989a Doc 3 p34
gather information   Azzopardi 1989a Doc 3 p34
how fra' M,   Azzopardi 1989a Doc 4 p36
to strip him   Azzopardi 1989a Doc 4 p36
the said   Azzopardi 1989a Doc 4 p36
foul and   Azzopardi 1989a Doc 5 p39
page 435
prohibitions and penalties   *cit* Stone 1997 p165
After I don't   Baglione 1935 p138
M felt immensely   Bellori 1976 p227

page 436
disturbed mind   Bellori 1976 p212
knight of justice   Baglione 1935 p138
very noble knight   Bellori 1976 p227
page 438
general of   *cit* Calvesi 1990 p132
casually committed homicide   Susinno 1960 p117
he tried   Susinno 1960 p117
page 439
the excellence of   Susinno 1960 p117
civilized … gentleman   Susinno 1960 p110
there are more   Susinno 1960 p119
page 440
cut into the   Mirabella 1613: in Dell' Acqua & Cinotti 1971 Doc F112 p164
unique mental power   Mirabella 1613: in Dell' Acqua & Cinotti 1971 Doc F112 p164
page 441
You see how   Mirabella 1613: in Dell' Acqua & Cinotti 1971 Doc F112 p164
a powerful rumour   Susinno 1960 p110
good man   M 1603: in Dell' Acqua & Cinotti 1971 Doc F52 p155
with the real   Giustiniani 1981 p44
page 444
Weegee's work   Ellen Handy: in Barth 1997 p149
M's unquiet mind   Susinno 1960 p110
page 446
he left   Susinno 1960 p117
… your majesty   Colonna 1577: *cit* Braudel 1995 Vol II p692
page 447
There are knights   Castro 1577: *cit* Prosperi 1996 p180
In Sicily   Renda 1997 p112
all the rich   Colonna 1577: *cit* Prosperi 1996 p180
the continent   Robb 1996 p16
very respectful   Susinno 1960 p110
an image   Corradini 1993 Doc 133 p102
knight of Jerusalem   Dell' Acqua & Cinotti 1971 Doc F89 p161
page 448
the best room   Susinno 1960 p112
To paint   Susinno 1960 p112
Since painting   Susinno 1960 p111
page 449
He was distracted   Susinno 1960 p114
Now this   Susinno 1960 p112
One day   Susinno 1960 p114
page 451
drawing in paint   Hibbard 1983 p245
He aspired   Bellori 1976 p215
page 454
the broken down   Bellori 1976 p227
This great work   Susinno 1960 p113
as if cast   Longhi 1982 p71
various princes   Susinno 1960 p113
by the hand   Dell' Acqua & Cinotti 1971 Doc F89 p161
even though   Dell' Acqua & Cinotti 1971 Doc F89 p161
page 455
the painter's free   Di Giacomo 1609: in Dell' Acqua & Cinotti 1971 Doc F90 p162
turned out   Di Giacomo 1609: in Dell' Acqua & Cinotti 1971 Doc F90 p162
his mind's cracked   Di Giacomo: in Dell' Acqua & Cinotti 1971 Doc F90 p162
mad, round   Susinno 1960 pp106ff *passim*

M's bad luck   Bellori 1976 pp227f
This man   Susinno pp114f
general of   *cit* Calvesi 1990 p134

Chapter 19

page 457
As a fugitive   Susinno 1960 p115
abandoned   Longhi 1982 p71
page 458
the lights   Bellori 1976 p228
He was   Baglione 1935 p138
After this work   Bellori 1976 p228
page 459
A report   Avviso 1609: in Corradini 1993 Doc 136 p104
his life   Mancini 1956 Vol I p225
page 461
very wild   Del Monte 1605: *cit* Masetti: in Corradini 1993 Doc 56 p62
out of his   Di Giacomo: in Dell' Acqua & Cinotti 1971 Doc F90 p162
good man   M 1603: in Dell' Acqua & Cinotti 1971 Doc F52 p155
page 462
sumptuous banquet   Avviso 1607: *cit* Wazbinski 1996 p47 n10
He was being   Baglione 1935 p138
Trying to placate   Bellori 1976 p228
page 463
vendetta   Baglione 1935 p138
The home   Basile 1635: *cit* Samek Ludovici 1956 p135
page 466
To be sure   Massa 1610: in Pacelli 1994 pp105f
in excellent condition   Massa 1610: in Pacelli 1994 p106
page 467
he, seeing   Jacobus De Voragine 1995 Vol II p259
page 468
the living model   Giustiniani 1981 p44
page 472
cardinal Gonzaga   Baglione 1935 p138
liberation   Bellori 1976 p228
page 474
A report   Avviso 1610: in Dell' Acqua & Cinotti 1971 Doc F94 p162
The celebrated   Avviso 1610: in Dell' Acqua & Cinotti 1971 Doc F94 p162
page 475
I find poor   Gentile 1610: in Pacelli 1994 p121
page 477
by land,   Gentile 1610: in Pacelli 1994 p121
The marchesa   Gentile 1610: in Pacelli 1994 pp126f
extraordinary promptness   Green & Mahon 1951 p203
I have been   Lemos 1610: in Green & Mahon 1951 pp202f

Chapter 20

page 479
things   Gentile 1610: in Pacelli 1994 p121: & Baglione 1935 p139
page 480
having left   Mancini 1956 Vol I p225
Civitavecchia   Mancini 1956 Vol I p225 n13

murdered in   Mancini 1956 Vol I p225 n15-16
remarkable   Mancini 1956 Vol I p225 n15-16
He embarked   Baglione 1935 p138
page 481
in mistake   Bellori 1976 p228
Spanish   Bellori 1976 p228
… he was held   Baglione 1935 pp138f
He finally   Baglione 1935 p139
some seaside resort   Pacelli 1996 p186
page 482
Wretchedly agitated   Bellori 1976 p228
1609 was   Bellori 1976 pp228f
And so M   Bellori 1976 p229
page 483
he went along   Baglione 1935 p138
like a madman   Baglione 1935 p138
page 484
justice and mercy   Calvesi 1995 p23
in exchange   Baglione 1935 p138
in the noise   Gentile 1610: in Pacelli 1994 p121
page 485
the power   *cit* Calvesi 1995 p23
Brief granting   *cit* Calvesi 1995 p23
those condemned   *cit* Calvesi 1995 p23
Grand penitentiary   Calvesi 1995 p23
Prefect of   Calvesi 1995 p23
page 486
captain of   Albear 1610?: in Corradini 1993 Doc 165 p133
cardinal Borghese   Albear 1610?: in Corradini 1993 Doc 165 p133
page 488
noise and confusion   Gentile 1610: in Pacelli 1994 p121
page 489
ridiculous   Gentile 1610: in Pacelli 1994 p126
List of crimes   *cit* Marini 1989 p99 n395
page 490
nefandare   *cit* Renda 1997 pp386f
in convento   *cit* Calvesi 1990 p160 n122
deserted beach   Bellori 1976 p229
page 491
and when we   Del Monte 1608: *cit* Spezzaferro 1971 p68
page 492
in the disobedience   Bellori 1976 p537
although he was   Bellori 1976 p537
One day,   Bellori 1976 pp537f
page 493
Under the surface   *cit* Spezzaferro 1971 p59
sweet natured   *cit* Spezzaferro 1971 p59
a breathing corpse   Zenier 1624: *cit* Spezzaferro 1971 p58
was attracted   Ameyden *post*1627: *cit* Spezzaferro 1971 p60

SOURCES

M STARTED BRANCHING out in all directions. Branches were hacked off to prevent the larger story collapsing under its own weight, just as the full apparatus of notes had to be abandoned. Some of the books and articles listed below refer to elements no longer part of the text. They were too tangled to weed out, and may suggest further reading.

The Age of Caravaggio [exhibition catalogue: tr. *Caravaggio* Napoli 1985], New York 1985

Ajello, Raffaele, Haskell, Francis & Gasparri, Carlo, *Classicismo d'Età Romana. La Collezione Farnese. Fotografie di Mimmo Jodice*, Napoli 1988

'Aldobrandini', in Vol. 1, Turner 1996

Alighieri, Dante [ed. Pasquini, Emilio & Quaglio, Antonio], *Commedia* [c.1320], Milano 1987

Alpers, Svetlana, *The Art of Describing. Dutch Art in the Seventeenth Century* [1983], London 1989

Anderson, Jaynie, *Giorgione. The Painter of 'Poetic Brevity'. Including Catalogue Raisonné*, Paris-New York 1997

Argan, Giulio Carlo, *The Europe of the Capitals 1600–1700*, Geneva 1964

Armenini, Giovan Battista [ed. Gorreri, Marina], *De' veri precetti della pittura* [1586], Torino 1988

'Arpino, Cavaliere d' ', in Vol. 2, Turner 1996

Ashford, Faith, 'Caravaggio's Stay in Malta', in *The Burlington Magazine* LXVII, 1935

Atlante storico Garzanti. Cronologia della storia universale, Milano 1994

Avery, Charles, *Bernini. Genius of the Baroque*, London 1997

Aymard, Maurice [ed.], *Storia d'Europa. Volume quarto. L'età moderna. Secoli XVI–XVIII*, Torino 1995

Azzopardi, Fr. John, 'Caravaggio in Malta: An unpublished document', in Azzopardi 1978

Azzopardi, Fr. John [ed.], *The Church of St. John in Valletta 1578–1978*, Malta 1978

Azzopardi, Can. John, 'Documentary Sources on Caravaggio's Stay in Malta', in Randon 1989 a

Azzopardi, Can. John, 'Caravaggio's Admission into the Order', in Randon 1989 b

Azzopardi, John, 'Un "S. Francesco" di Caravaggio a Malta nel secolo XVIII: commenti sul periodo maltese del Merisi', in Macioce 1996

Baglione, Giovanni [ed. Mariano, Valerio], *Le vite de'pittori scultori et architetti. Dal Pontificato de Gregorio XIII del 1572. In fino a tempi di Papa Urbano Ottavo nel 1642* [1642, facsimile of copy with manuscript notes by Bellori, Giovan Pietro], Roma 1935

Baglione, Giovanni, *Le vite de'pittori scultori et architetti dal Pontificato di Gregorio XIII fino a tutto quello d'Urbano VIII* [1649, 1924] facs. Bologna 1975

Banti, Anna, 'Europa 1606', in *Opinioni*, Milano 1961

Barbiche, Bernard, 'Clemente VIII' in Vol. I, Levillain 1996 a

Barbiche, Bernard, 'Leone XI' in Vol. II, Levillain 1996 b

Barbiellini Amidei, Rosanna, 'Io Michelangelo Merisi da Caravaggio …'. in *Art e dossier* 18, 1987

Barbiellini Amidei, Rosanna, 'Della committenza Massimo', in Bernini 1989

Bardon, Françoise, *Caravage ou l'expérience de la matière*, Paris 1978

Barocchi, Paola [ed.], *Trattati d'arte del Cinquecento. Fra manierismo e controriforma*. Vol. II, Bari 1961

Barocchi, Paola [ed.], *Scritti d'arte del Cinquecento. Tomo I*, Milano-Napoli 1971

Barocchi, Paola [ed.], *Scritti d'arte del Cinquecento. Tomo II*, Milano-Napoli 1973

Barocchi, Paola [ed.], *Scritti d'arte del Cinquecento. Tomo III*, Milano-Napoli 1977

Barth, Miles [ed.], *Weegee's World. Essays by Miles Barth, Alain Bergala, Ellen Handy*, Boston &c 1997

Bartoscheck, Gerd, *Bildergalerie Sanssouci. Die Gemälde*, Berlin 1996

Basile, Giambattista [ed. Rak, Michele], *Lo Cunto de le cunti* [1634–1636], Milano 1986

Bassani, Riccardo & Bellini, Fiora, 'La casa, le "robbe", lo studio del Caravaggio a Roma. Due documenti inediti del 1603 e del 1605', in *Prospettiva* 71, 1993

Bassani, Riccardo & Bellini, Fiora, *Caravaggio assassino. La carriera di un «valentuomo» fazioso nella Roma della Controriforma*, Roma 1994

Battistini, Andrea, *Introduzione a Galilei*, Roma-Bari 1989

Bellini, Fiora, 'Tre documenti per Michelangelo da Caravaggio', in *Prospettiva* 65, 1992

Bellori, Giovan Pietro [ed. Borea, Evelina & introd. Previtali, Giovanni], *Le vite de' pittori scultori e architetti moderni* [1672], Torino 1976

Bellori, Giovan Pietro, *Le vite de' pittori scultori e architetti moderni* [1672], facs. Bologna 1977

Beltramme, Marcello, 'Le teoriche del Paleotti e il riformismo dell' Accademia di San Luca nella politica artistica di Clemente VIII (1592–1605)', in *Storia dell' Arte* 69, 1990

Benedetti, Sergio, 'Caravaggio's "Taking of Christ", a masterpiece rediscovered', in *The Burlington Magazine* CXXV, 1993a

Benedetti, Sergio, *Caravaggio. The Master Revealed*, [Dublin] 1993b

Benjamin, Walter, 'The Work of Art in the Age of Mechanical Reproduction' [1936] tr. in *Illuminations*, London 1973

Benjamin, Walter, *Angelus Novus. Saggi e frammenti* [*Schriften* 1955, tr. 1962], Torino 1995

Benjamin, Walter, 'A Small History of Photography' [1931] tr. in *One-Way Street and Other Writings* [1979], London 1997

Berenson, Bernard, *Caravaggio. His Incongruity and his Fame*, London 1953

Berne-Joffroy, André, *Le dossier Caravage*, Paris 1959

Bernini, Dante [ed.], *Caravaggio. Nuove riflessioni* [Quaderni di Palazzo Venezia 6], Roma 1989

Bertolotti, Antonino, *Artisti lombardi a Roma nei secoli XV, XVI e XVII. Studi e ricerche negli archivi romani* [1881], 2 vols, facs. Bologna 1970

Bissell, R. Ward, *Orazio Gentileschi and the Poetic Tradition in Caravaggesque Painting*, University Park & London 1981

Blunt, Anthony, *Artistic Theory in Italy 1450–1600* [1940], Oxford 1978

Boccardo, Piero, 'Doria II. (1) Gian Carlo Doria', in Vol. 9, Turner 1996

Bodart, Didier, 'Intorno al Caravaggio: la Maddalena del 1606', in *Palatino*, 1966

548

Bologna, Ferdinando, 'Il Caravaggio nella cultura e nella società del suo tempo', in *Colloquio* 1974

Bologna, Ferdinando [ed.], *Battistello Caracciolo e il primo naturalismo a Napoli* [exhibition catalogue], Napoli 1991

Bologna, Ferdinando, *L'incredulità del Caravaggio e l'esperienza delle «cose naturali»*, Torino 1992

Bon, Catarina, 'Precisazioni sulla biografia di Giovanni Baglione', in *Paragone* 347, 1979

Bon, Catarina, 'Una proposta per la cronologia delle opere giovanili di Giovanni Baglione', in *Paragone* 373, 1981

Bonnefoy, Yves, *Rimbaud* [1961], Paris 1970

Bonnefoy, Yves, *L'improbable et autres essais* [1959], Paris 1983

Bonsanti, Giorgio, *Caravaggio* [new ed.], Firenze 1991

Bonsanti, Giorgio & Gregori, Mina [eds], *Caravaggio da Malta a Firenze* [exhibition catalogue], Milano 1996

Borromeo, A., 'Clemente VIII', in *Dizionario Biografico degli Italiani*, Vol. XXVI, Roma 1982

'Borromeo: (1) Carlo II Borromeo', in Vol. 4, Turner 1996

Bossy, John, *Christianity in the West, 1400–1700*, Oxford 1985

Bossy, John, *Giordano Bruno and the Embassy Affair* [1991], London 1992

Boutry, Philippe, 'Paolo V', in Vol. II, Levillain 1996

Bramly, Serge, *Leonardo. The Artist and the Man* [1988], tr. London 1994

Brandi, Cesare, 'L'«epistème» caravaggesca', in *Colloquio* 1974

Braudel, Fernand, 'L'Italia fuori d'Italia. Due secoli e tre Italie', in Romano & Vivanti 1974

Braudel, Fernand, *The Structures of Everyday Life. The Limits of the Possible [Civilization and Capitalism 15th–18th Century. Volume I]* [1979], tr. Berkeley 1992a

Braudel, Fernand, *The Wheels of Commerce [Civilization and Capitalism 15th–18th Century. Volume II]* [1979], tr. Berkeley 1992b

Braudel, Fernand, *The Perspective of the World [Civilization and Capitalism 15th–18th Century. Volume III]* [1979], tr. Berkeley 1992c

Braudel, Fernand, *The Mediterranean and the Mediterranean World in the Age of Philip II* [1949, 1966, tr. 1972], 2 vols, Berkeley & Los Angeles 1995

Bruno, Giordano & Campanella, Tommaso [ed. Guzzo, Augusto & Amerio, Romano], *Opere*, Milano-Napoli 1956

Bruno, Giordano [ed. Angrisani, Isa Guerrini], *Il Candelaio* [1581], Milano 1976

Bruno, Giordano [ed. Ciliberto, Michele], *Un'autobiografia*, Napoli 1994

Bruno, Giordano [ed. Guzzo, Augusto], *La Cena de le ceneri* [1584], Milano 1995a

Bruno, Giordano [ed. Ubaldo, Nicola], *Il sigillo dei sigilli. I diagrammi ermetici* [1583], Milano 1995b

Bruno, Giordano [ed. Bassi, Simonetta], *Eroici furori* [1585], Roma-Bari 1995c

Bruno, Giordano [ed. Maddalemma, Manuela], *L'arte della memoria. Le ombre delle idee* [1582 & 1581], Milano 1996

Bryson, Norman, *Looking at the Overlooked. Four essays on Still Life Painting* [1990], London 1995

Buhagiar, Mario, *The Iconography of the Maltese Islands 1400–1900. Painting*, Valletta 1988

Bull, George, *Michelangelo. A Biography* [1995], London 1996

Burke, Peter, *Varieties of Cultural History*, Cambridge & Oxford 1997

Burkhardt, Jacob, *The Civilization of the Renaissance in Italy* [1860, tr. 1945], London 1995

Cajani, L., 'Cenci Beatrice', in *Dizionario Biografico degli Italiani*, Vol. XXIII, Roma 1970

Calì, Maria, *Da Michelangelo all' Escorial. Momenti del dibattito religioso nell' arte del Cinquecento*, Torino 1980

Calvesi, Maurizio, *Caravaggio* [Dossier art n. 1], Firenze 1986

Calvesi, Maurizio, 'Nascita e morte del Caravaggio', in Calvesi 1987

Calvesi, Maurizio [ed.], *L'ultimo Caravaggio e la cultura artistica a Napoli in Sicilia e a Malta*, Siracusa 1987

Calvesi, Maurizio, *Le realtà del Caravaggio*, Torino 1990

Calvesi, Maurizio, 'Novità e conferme', *Art e dossier* 66, 1992

Calvesi, Maurizio, 'Tra vastità di orizzonti e puntuali prospettive. Il collezionismo di Scipione Borghese dal Caravaggio al Reni e al Bernini', in Coliva 1994

Calvesi, Maurizio, 'Michelangelo da Caravaggio: il suo rapporto con i Mattei e con altri collezionisti a Roma', in *Caravaggio* 1995

Calvino, Italo, *Saggi 1945–1985. Tomo secondo*, Milano 1995

Campagna Cicala, Francesca, 'Intorno all' attività di Caravaggio in Sicilia. Due momenti del caravaggism siciliano: Mario Minniti e Alonzo Rodriguez', in *Caravaggio in Sicilia* 1984

Campanella, Tommaso [ed. Mollia, Franco], *La città del sole e altri scritti* [1623], Milano 1991

Campanella, Tommaso [ed. Ditadi, Gino], *Apologia di Galileo. Tutte le lettere a Galileo Galilei e altri documenti* [1622], Este 1992

Campanella, Tommaso [ed. Ernst, Germana], *La città del sole e Questione quarta sull' ottima repubblica con testi latini a fronte* [1623], Milano 1996

Canavaggio, Jean, *Cervantes* [1986], tr. Roma 1988

Canosa, Romano, *La restaurazione sessuale. Per una storia della sessualità tra Cinquecento e Settecento*, Milano 1993

Canosa, Romano, *La vita quotidiana a Milano in età spagnola*, Milano 1996a

Canosa, Romano, *Storia di Milano nell' età di Filippo II*, Roma 1996b

Cantimori, Delio [ed. Prosperi, Adriano], *Eretici italiani del cinquecento e altri scritti* [1939 &c], Torino 1992

Capialbi, Vito [ed.], *Documenti inediti circa la voluta ribellione di F. Tommaso Campanella* [1845], Cosenza 1987

Cappelletti, Francesca, 'The documentary evidence of the early history of Caravaggio's "Taking of Christ"', in *The Burlington Magazine* CXXV, 1993

Cappelletti, Francesca, 'Gli affanni e l'orgoglio del collezionista. La storia della raccolta Mattei e l'ambiente artistico romano dal Seicento all' Ottocento', in *Caravaggio e la collezione Mattei*, 1995

Cappelletti, Francesca & Testa, Laura, 'E per me pagate a Michelangelo da Caravaggio', *Art e dossier* 42, 1990a

Cappelletti, Francesca & Testa, Laura, 'I quadri di Caravaggio nella collezione Mattei. I nuovi documenti e i riscontri con le fonti', in *Storia dell' Arte* 69, 1990b

Caravaggio. Con un saggio di Mina Gregori, Milano 1994

'Caravaggio, Cecco del', in Vol. 5, Turner 1996

Caravaggio e il suo tempo [exhibition catalogue: tr. The Age New York 1985], Napoli 1985

Caravaggio e la collezione Mattei [exhibition catalogue], Milano 1995

Caravaggio in Sicilia. Il suo tempo, il suo influsso [exhibition catalogue], Palermo 1984

Caravaggio nei musei romani [exhibition catalogue], Roma 1986

Caravaggisti [*Dossier art* n. 109], Firenze 1996

Carey, John, *John Donne. Life, Mind and Art* [1981], London 1983

Castiglione, Baldassare, *Il libro del Cortegiano* [c.1518, 1528], in Cordié 1960

Castro, Américo [ed. Cipollino, Marco], *Il pensiero di Cervantes* [1925 &1972], tr. Napoli 1991

Castronovo, V., 'Borghese Cafarelli, Scipione', in Vol. XII, *Dizionario Biografico degli Italiani*, Roma 1960–1997

Cellini, Benvenuto, *La Vita* [c.1566, 1728], in Cordié 1960

Cennino d'Andrea Cennini [ed. Thompson, Daniel V. Jr], *The Craftsman's Handbook. The Italian 'Il libro dell' arte'* [c.1400, tr. 1933], New York 1954

Cervantes, Miguel de [ed. Arroyo, Florencio Sevilla & Hazas, Antonio Rey], *Novelas ejemplares I* [1613], Madrid 1993

Cervantes, Miguel de [ed. Allen, John Jay], *Don Quijote de la Mancha II* [1615], Madrid 1995a

Cervantes Saavedra, Miguel de, *The History of that Ingenious Gentleman don Quijote de la Mancha. Translated from the Spanish by Burton Raffel. Introduction by Diana De Armas Wilson*, New York & London 1995b

Chambers, D.S., 'Gonzaga: (16) Ferdinando Gonzaga', in Vol 12, Turner 1996

Cheney, Liana De Girolami, 'Zuccaro: (2) Federico Zuccaro' in Vol. 33, Turner 1996

Chiappini di Sorio, Ileana, 'Roncalli, Cristoforo', in Vol. 27, Turner 1996

Christiansen, Keith, 'Caravaggio and "L'esempio davanti del naturale" ' in *The Art Bulletin* LXVIII, 1986

Christiansen, Keith, 'Technical report on "The Cardsharps" ', in *The Burlington Magazine* CXXX, 1988

Christiansen, Keith, 'Some observations on the relationship between Caravaggio's two treatments of the "Lute-player" ', in *The Burlington Magazine* CXXXII, 1990a

Christiansen, Keith, *A Caravaggio Rediscovered: The Lute Player*, New York 1990b

Christiansen, Keith & Mahon, Denis, 'Caravaggio's second versions' [letters], in *The Burlington Magazine* CXXXIV, 1992

Christiansen, Keith, 'Thoughts on the Lombard training of Caravaggio', in Gregori 1996

Ciliberto, Michele, *Introduzione a Bruno*, Roma-Bari 1996

Cimeli Marucelliani. XII settimana per i beni culturali e ambientali [exhibition catalogue], Firenze 1997

Los Cinco Sentidos y el Arte [exhibition catalogue], Madrid 1997

Cinotti, Mia, 'Appendice documentaria', in Dell' Acqua, Gian Alberto & Cinotti, Mia 1971

Cinotti, Mia, 'La giovinezza del Caravaggio. Ricerche e scoperte', in Cinotti 1975

Cinotti, Mia [ed.], *Novità sul Caravaggio. Saggi e contributi*, Milano 1975

Cinotti, Mia, *Michelangelo Merisi detto il Caravaggio. Tutte le opere. Saggio critico di Gian Alberto Dell' Acqua. Estratto da «I pittori bergamaschi» raccolta di studi a cura della Banca Popolare di Bergamo*, Bergamo 1983

Cinotti, Mia, 'Caravaggio, gli enigmi: l'Ecce Homo «Massimi»', in Calvesi 1987

Cinotti, Mia, 'Vita di Caravaggio: novità 1983–1988', in Bernini 1989

Cinotti, Mia, *Caravaggio. La vita e l'opera*, Bergamo 1991

Cinotti, Mia & Dell' Acqua, Gian Alberto [eds], *Immagine del Caravaggio. Mostra didattica itinerante* [exhibition catalogue], Milano 1973

Clark, Kenneth, *Leonardo Da Vinci. Introduction by Professor Martin Kemp* [1939, 1988], London 1993

Cochrane, Eric [ed.], *The Late Italian Renaissance 1525–1630*, London 1970

Coliva, Anna [ed.], *Galleria Borghese*, Roma 1994

Colloquio sul tema Caravaggio e i caravaggeschi. Accademia nazionale dei lincei. Anno CCCLXXI–1974. Quaderno N. 205, Roma 1974

Contreras, Alonso de [ed. Collo, Paolo] *Storia della mia vita* [Madrid 1633, 1900], tr. Genova 1996

Cordaro, Michele, 'La tecnica pittorica del Caravaggio. Alcuni problemi di metodo', in Calvesi 1987

Cordié, Carlo [ed.], *Opere di Baldassare Castiglione, Giovanni Della Casa, Benvenuto Cellini*, Milano-Napoli 1960

Corradini, Sandro, *Caravaggio. Materiali per un processo. Con presentazione di Maurizio Marini*, Roma 1993

Corradini, Sandro, 'Nuove e false notizie sulla presenza del Caravaggio in Roma', in Macioce 1996

Corradini, Sandro & Marini, Maurizio, 'The earliest account of Caravaggio in Rome', in *The Burlington Magazine* CXL, 1998

Correale, Giampaolo [ed.], *Identificazione di un Caravaggio. Nuove tecnologie per una rilettura del San Giovanni Battista*, Venezia 1990

Cortelazzo, Manlio & Zolli, Paolo, *Dizionario etimologico della lingua italiana,* 5 vols, Bologna 1979–1988

Cozzi, Gaetano, 'Intorno al cardinale Ottavio Paravicino, a monsignor Paolo Gualdo e a Michelangelo da Caravaggio', in *Rivista Storica Italiana* LXXIII, fascicolo I, 1961

Croce, Giulio Cesare & Banchieri, Adriano [ed. Orengo, Nico], *Le sottilissime astuzie di Bertoldo. Le piacevoli e ridicolose simplicità di Bertoldino. Cacasenno* [1609, 1620], Milano 1995

Cronologia universale. Le grandi date della storia delle arti della scienza della tecnica dalla preistoria a oggi [II ed.], Milano 1994

Cummings, Frederick, 'The meaning of Caravaggio's "Conversion of the Magdalen" ', in *The Burlington Magazine* CXVI, 1974

Cutajar, Dominic, 'Caravaggio in Malta. His works and his influence', in *Malta* 1986

Danesi Squarzina, Silvia, 'Caravaggio e i Giustiniani', in Macioce 1996

Danesi Squarzina, Silvia, 'The collections of Cardinal Benedetto Giustiniani. Part I', in *The Burlington Magazine* CXXXIX, 1997

Danesi Squarzina, Silvia, 'The collections of Cardinal Benedetto Giustiniani. Part II', in *The Burlington Magazine* CXL, 1998

De Giovanni, Biagio, 'Lo spazio della vita fra G. Bruno e T. Campanella', in *Il Centauro* 11–12, 1984

Dell' Acqua, Gian Alberto & Cinotti, Mia, *Il Caravaggio e le sue grandi opere da San Luigi dei Francesi*, Milano 1971

Della Pergola, Paola, 'Una testimonianza per Caravaggio', in *Paragone* 105, 1958

Delumeau, Jean, *Rome au XVIe siècle*, Paris 1975

Delumeau, Jean, 'Roma (Epoca moderna)', in Vol. II, Levillain 1996

De Maio, Romeo, *Pittura e Controriforma a Napoli*, Roma-Bari 1983

De Maio, Romeo, *Michelangelo e la Controriforma* [1978], Firenze 1990

De Zayas y Sotomayor, Maria [ed. Piloto di Castri, Sonia], *Novelle amorose ed esemplari* [1637], tr. Torino 1995

Dizionario Biografico degli Italiani [Vols V, XII, XIII, XXI, XXIII, XXIV, XXVI], Roma 1960–1997

Donne, John [ed. Smith, A.J.], *The Complete English Poems* [1633 &c, 1971], Harmondsworth 1978

Eliot, George, *Middlemarch. A Study of Provincial Life* [1871], London 1991

Elliott, J.H., *Imperial Spain 1469–1716* [1963], London 1990

Elliott, J.H., 'The Enigma of Philip II', in *The New York Review of Books* XLIV, 14, 1997

Faccioli, Emilio [ed.], *L'arte della cucina in Italia*, Torino 1987

Fagiolo, Marcello [ed.], *La Roma dei Longhi. Papi e architetti tra manierismo e barocco* [exhibition catalogue], Roma 1982

Ferro, Filippo Maria, 'Un crime, vite, que je tombe au néant', in Cinotti 1975

Ferruzza, Maria Lucia, 'Furti d'arte in Sicilia' [interview], in *Kalós* VIII, 5, 1997

Field, J.V., *The Invention of Infinity. Mathematics and Art in the Renaissance*, Oxford 1997

Fink, Daniel A,. 'Vermeer's Use of the Camera Obscura–A Comparative Study', in *The Art Bulletin* LIII, 1971

Firpo, Luigi [ed. Quaglioni, Diego], *Il processo di Giordano Bruno* [1948–1949], Roma 1993

Firpo, Massimo, *Riforma protestante ed eresie nell' Italia del Cinquecento*, Roma-Bari 1993

Frèches José, *Caravaggio pittore e «assassino»*, Milano 1995

Freedberg, S.J., *Painting in Italy. 1500 to 1600*, Harmondsworth 1971

Freedberg, S.J., *Circa 1600. A Revolution of Style in Italian Painting*, Cambridge, Mass. 1983

Friedlaender, Walter, *Caravaggio Studies*, Princeton 1955

Frommel, Christoph Luitpold, 'Caravaggios Frühwerk und der Kardinal Francesco Maria Del Monte', in *Storia dell' Arte* 9–10, 1971

Frommel, Christoph Luitpold, 'Caravaggio, Minniti e il Cardinal Francesco Maria Del Monte', in Macioce 1996

Fuda, Roberto, 'Note caravaggesche', in *Paragone* 509–511, 1992

Fulco, Giorgio, ' "Ammirate l'altissimo pittore": Caravaggio nelle rime inedite di Marzio Milesi', in *Ricerche di Storia dell' arte* 10, 1980

Fumagalli, Elena, 'Precoci citazioni di opere del Caravaggio in alcuni documenti inediti', in Gregori 1996 a

Fumagalli, Elena, 'Crescenzi: (2) Giovanni Battista Crescenzi' in Vol. 8, Turner 1996 b

Fumagalli, Elena, 'Gramatica, Antiveduto', in Vol. 13, Turner 1996 c

Galasso, Giuseppe, 'Society in Naples in the Seicento', in Whitfield & Martineau 1982

Galasso, Giuseppe, *Alla periferia dell' impero. Il Regno di Napoli nel periodo spagnolo (secoli XVI–XVII)*, Torino 1994

Galilei, Galileo [ed. Flora, Ferdinando], *Opere*, Milano-Napoli 1953

Galilei, Galileo [ed. Flora, Ferdinando], *Dialogo dei massimi sistemi* [1632], Milano 1996

Garard, Mary D., *Artemisia Gentileschi. The Image of the Female Hero in Italian Baroque Art*, Princeton 1989

Garin, Eugenio, *Scienza e vita civile nel rinascimento italiano* [1965], Roma-Bari 1993

Garin, Eugenio [ed.], *Renaissance Characters* [1988, tr. 1991], Chicago 1997

Garzoni, Tomaso [ed. Cherchi, Paolo & Collina, Beatrice], *La piazza universale di tutte le professioni del mondo* [1585], 2 vols, Torino 1996

Gash, John, 'Painting and Sculpture in Early Modern Malta', in Mallia-Milanes 1993

Gash, John, *Caravaggio*, New York 1994

Gash, John, 'Caravaggio, Michelangelo Merisi da,' in Vol. 5, Turner 1996

Gash, John, 'The identity of Caravaggio's "Knight of Malta" ', in *The Burlington Magazine* CXXXIX, 1997

Gash, John, untitled review of Gregori 1996, in *The Burlington Magazine* CXL, 1998

Genet, Jean, *Rembrandt* [1968 & 1979], Paris 1995

Geremek, Bronislaw, *Uomini senza padrone. Poveri e marginali tra medioevo e età moderna*, Torino 1992

Geremek, Bronislaw, *La pietà e la forca. Storia della miseria e della carità in Europa* [1986], Roma-Bari 1995

Geymonat, Ludovico, *Galileo Galilei* [1957], Torino 1994

Ginzburg, Carlo, *Miti, Emblemi, Spie. Morfologia e storia*, Torino 1986

Ghirelli, Antonio, *Storia di Napoli*, II ed., Torino 1992

Gilbert, Creighton E., *Caravaggio and His Two Cardinals*, University Park, Pennsylvania 1995

Giustiniani, Vincenzo [ed. Banti, Anna], *Discorsi sulle arti e sui mestieri* [c. 1610], Firenze 1981

'Giustiniani (i)', in Vol. 12, Turner 1996

'Giustiniani (i): (1) Benedetto Giustiniani', in Vol. 12, Turner 1996

Goldscheider, Ludwig, *Michelangelo. Paintings. Sculpture. Architecture. Complete Edition* [1953], 6th ed. London 1996

Gowing, Lawrence, 'Incongruities of the actual', in *The Times Literary Supplement*, 23 March 1984

Graffiti e disegni dei prigionieri dell' Inquisizione con una nota di Leonardo Sciascia, Palermo 1977

Grassi, Luigi & Pepe, Mario, *Dizionario dei termini artistici*, Milano 1994

Greaves, James L. & Johnson, Meryl, 'New Findings on Caravaggio's Technique in the Detroit "Magdalen" ', in *The Burlington Magazine* CXVI, 1974

Green, Otis H. & Mahon, Denis, 'Caravaggio's Death: A New Document', in *The Burlington Magazine* XCIII, 1951

Greer, Germaine, *The Obstacle Race. The Fortunes of Women Painters and Their Work*, New York 1979

Gregori, Mina, 'A New Painting and some observations on Caravaggio's Journey to Malta', in *The Burlington Magazine* CXVI, 1974

Gregori, Mina, 'Addendum to Caravaggio: the Cecconi "Crowning with Thorns" reconsidered', in *The Burlington Magazine* CXVIII, 1976

Gregori, Mina [ed.], *Michelangelo Merisi da Caravaggio. Come nascono i capolavori* [exhibition catalogue], Milano 1991

Gregori, Mina [ed.], *Come dipingeva il Caravaggio. Atti della giornata di studio*, Milano 1996

Gregori, Mina et al., *Paintings in the Uffizi & Pitti Galleries*, Boston 1994

Gregory, Sharon & Bershad, David L., 'Borghese' in Vol. 4, Turner 1996

Guglielmi Faldi, C., 'Baglione, Giovanni', in Vol. V, *Dizionario Biografico degli Italiani*, Roma 1963

Guido Reni 1575–1642 [exhibition catalogue], Los Angeles & Bologna 1988

Guttuso, Renato & Ottino Della Chiesa, Angela, *L'opera completa del Caravaggio*, Milano 1967

Hale, John, *The Civilization of Europe in the Renaissance*, London 1993

Harris, Ann Sutherland, 'Gentileschi', in Vol. 12, Turner 1996

Harvey, Jacqueline Colliss, 'Camera obscura', in Vol. 5, Turner 1996

Haskell, Francis, *Patrons and Painters. A Study in Relations Between Italian Art and Society in the Age of the Baroque* [1963], *Revised & Enlarged Edition*, New Haven & London 1980

Haskell, Francis & Penny, Nicholas, *Taste and the Antique. The Lure of Classical Sculpture 1500–1900*, New Haven & London 1981

Hess, Jacob, 'The Chronology of the Contarelli Chapel', in *The Burlington Magazine* XCIII, 1951

Hess, Jacob, 'Contributo alla vita del Caravaggio' [1932–3], in Hess 1967

Hess, Jacob, 'Modelle e Modelli del Caravaggio' [1954], in Hess 1967

Hess, Jacob, 'Caravaggio's Paintings in Malta. Some Notes' [1958], in Hess 1967

Hess, Jacob, *Kunstgeschichtliche Studien zu Renaissance und Barock*, 2 vols, Roma 1967

Hibbard, Howard, *Caravaggio*, London 1983

Higginson, Peter, 'Costa, Ottavio', in Vol. 8, Turner 1996

Hinks, Roger, *Michelangelo Merisi da Caravaggio. His Life, His Legend, His Works*, London 1953

Hollingsworth, Mary, *Patronage in Sixteenth Century Italy*, London 1996

The Holy Bible. The Authorized or King James version of 1611 now reprinted with the Apocrypha, 3 vols, London 1963

Hughes, Robert, *Nothing if not Critical*, London 1990

Hyerace, Luigi, 'Minniti, Mario' in Vol. 21, Turner 1996

Ingegno, A., 'Bourbon Del Monte, Guidobaldo', in *Dizionario Biografico degli Italiani*, Vol. XIII, Roma 1971

Jacobus de Voragine [tr. Ryan, William Granger], *The Golden Legend. Readings on the Saints*, 2 vols, Princeton 1993

Johannes Vermeer [exhibition catalogue], New Haven & London 1995

Jones, Pamela M., 'Borromeo: (2) Federico Borromeo', in Vol. 4, Turner 1996

Kirwin, W. Chandler, 'Addendum to Cardinal Francesco Maria Del Monte's Inventory: the Date of the Sale of Various Notable Paintings', in *Storia dell' Arte* 9–10, 1971

Kitson, Michael, *The Complete Paintings of Caravaggio*, London-New York 1969

Klein, Robert & Zerner, Henri, *Italian Art 1500–1600. Sources and Documents* [1966], Evanston, Illinois 1989

Klemm, Christian, 'Sandrart, Joachim von', in Vol. 27, Turner 1996

König, Eberhard, *Michelangelo Merisi da Caravaggio 1571–1610*, Köln 1997

Lapucci, Roberta, 'La tecnica del Caravaggio: materiali e metodi', in Gregori 1991 a

Lapucci, Roberta, 'San Giovannino disteso'. *Germania Dederale. Raccolta privata. Analisi delle radiografie e delle riflettografie ad inrarossi* [unpublished], Firenze 1991 b

Lavin, Marilyn Aronberg, 'Caravaggio Documents from the Barberini Archive', in *The Burlington Magazine* CIX, 1967

Lemaître, Nicole, 'Pio V', in Vol. II, Levillain 1996

Leonardo da Vinci [ed. Pedretti, Carlo], *Libro di Pittura. Codice urbinate lat. 1270 nella biblioteca Apostolica Vaticana* [c.1518], 2 vols, Roma 1995

Letze, Otto & Buchsteiner, Thomas [eds], *Leonardo da Vinci. Scientist Inventor Artist* [exhibition catalogue], Tübingen 1997

Levi, Giovanni & Schmitt, Jean-Claude [eds], *Storia dei giovani. II. L'età contemporanea*, Roma-Bari 1994

Levillain, Philippe [ed.], *Dizionario storico del papato* [1994], tr. 2 vols, Milano 1996

Lewis, Charlton D. & Short, Charles, *A Latin Dictionary Founded on Andrews' Edition of Freund's Latin Dictionary* [1879], Oxford 1962

Lionnet, Jean, 'Castrati della Capella pontificia', in Vol. I, Levillain 1996

Longhi, Roberto, 'Ultimi studi sul Caravaggio e la sua cerchia', in *Proporzioni* I, 1943

Longhi, Roberto, 'Introduzione alla mostra', in *Mostra del Caravaggio* 1951a

Longhi, Roberto, 'Alcuni pezzi rari nell' antologia della critica caravaggesca', in *Paragone* 17ff, 1951b

Longhi, Roberto, 'Sui margini caravaggeschi', in *Paragone* 21, 1951c

Longhi, Roberto, 'Volti della Roma caravaggesca', in *Paragone* 21, 1951d

Longhi, Roberto, 'Un anticipo a "20 postille caraveggesche" ', in *Paragone* 105, 1958

Longhi, Roberto, 'Giovanni Baglione e il quadro del processo', in *Paragone* 163, 1963a

Longhi, Roberto, 'Le visite romane del Sandrart a Galileo nel 1633', in *Paragone* 165, 1963b

Longhi, Roberto, 'Registro dei tempi [1928]', in Longhi 1968

Longhi, Roberto, 'I precedenti [1929]', in Longhi 1968

Longhi, Roberto, 'Giovanni Baglione [1930]', in Longhi 1968

Longhi, Roberto, *'Me Pinxit' e Quesiti caravaggeschi. 1928–1934*, Firenze 1968

Longhi, Roberto, *Da Cimabue a Morandi*, Milano 1973

Longhi, Roberto, *Breve ma veridica storia della pittura italiana* [1914], Firenze 1980

Longhi, Roberto [ed. Previtali, Giovanni], *Caravaggio* [1952 & 1968], Roma 1982

Longhi, Roberto, 'I preparatori del naturalismo 1910–1911', in Longhi 1995

Longhi, Roberto [ed. Frangi, Francesco & Monagnani, Cristina], *Il palazzo non finito. Saggi inediti 1910–1926*, Milano 1995

Machiavelli, Niccolò, *Il Principe* [1532], Torino 1995

Macioce, Stefania, 'Attorno a Caravaggio. Notizie d'archivio', in *Storia dell' Arte* 55, 1985

Macioce, Stefania, 'Caravaggio a Malta: il S. Girolamo e lo stemma Malaspina', in Calvesi 1987

Macioce, Stefania, 'Caravaggio a Malta e i suoi referenti ...', in *Storia dell' Arte* 81, 1994

Macioce, Stefania [ed.], *Michelangelo Merisi da Caravaggio. La vita e le opere attraverso i documenti. Atti del Convegno Internazionale di Studi*, Roma 1996

Macrae, Desmond, 'Observations on the Sword in Caravaggio', in *The Burlington Magazine* CXI, 1964

Maczak, Antoni, *Viaggi e viaggiatori nell' Europa moderna* [1979], tr. Roma-Bari 1992

Mahon, Denis, 'Egregius in Urbe Pictor: Caravaggio Revised', in *The Burlington Magazine* XCIII, 1951a

Mahon, Denis, 'Caravaggio's Chronology Again', in *The Burlington Magazine* XCIII, 1951b

Mahon, Denis, 'Addenda to Caravaggio', in *The Burlington Magazine* XCIV, 1952

Mahon, Denis, 'Contrasts in Art-historical Method: Two Recent Approaches to Caravaggio', in *The Burlington Magazine* XCV, 1953a

Mahon, Denis, 'On some Aspects of Caravaggio and his Times', in *The Metropolitan Museum Bulletin* XII, 1953b

Mahon, Denis, 'A Late Caravaggio Rediscovered', in *The Burlington Magazine* XCVIII, 1956

Mahon, Denis, *Studies in Seicento Art and Theory* [1947], Westport, Conn. 1971

Mahon, Denis, 'Fresh light on Caravaggio's earliest period: his "Cardsharps" recovered', in *The Burlington Magazine* CXXX, 1988

Mahon, Denis, 'The singing "Lute-player" by Caravaggio from the Barberini collection, painted for Cardinal Del Monte', in *The Burlington Magazine* CXXXII, 1990

Mahon, Sir Denis, *Guercino. Master Painter of the Baroque* [exhibition catalogue], Washington 1991

Mallia-Milanes, Victor [ed.], *Hospitaller Malta 1530–1798. Studies on Early Modern Malta and the Order of St John of Jerusalem*, Malta 1993

Malta and Caravaggio. Mid-Med Bank Limited. Report and Accounts 1986, Valletta 1986

Malvasia, Carlo Cesare, *Felsina Pittrice. Vite de' pittori bolognesi* [1678, 1841], facs. 2 vols, Bologna 1967

Mancini, Giulio [ed. Marucchi, Adriana], *Considerazioni sulla pittura. Pubblicate per la prima volta da Adriana Marucchi con il commento di Luigi Salerno*, 2 vols, Roma 1956

Marin, Louis, *To Destroy Painting* [1977], tr. Chicago 1995

Marin, Louis, *Détruire la peinture* [1977], Paris 1997

Marini, Maurizio, 'Caravaggio e il naturalismo internazionale', in Zeri 1981

Marini, Maurizio, *'Ut natura pictura'. Natura come pittura. Antologia di nature morte dal XVI al XVIII secolo*, Roma 1986

Marini, Maurizio, *Caravaggio. Michelangelo Merisi da Caravaggio «pictor praestantissimus»*. *La tragica esistenza, la raffinata cultura, il mondo sanguigno del primo Seicento, nell' iter pittorico completo di uno dei massimi rivoluzionari dell' arte di tutti i tempi* [1987], rev. ed. Roma 1989

Marini, Maurizio, 'L'ospite inquieto. Le residenze romane di Caravaggio', *Art e dossier* 42, 1990

Marini, Maurizio, 'L'ultima spiaggia', *Art e dossier* 66, 1992

Marini, Maurizio, *Velázquez* [*Dossier art* n. 94], Firenze 1994

Marini, Maurizio, 'Un contributo all' iconografia del «David e Golia» del Prado', in Macioce 1996

Marini, Maurizio & Corradini, Sandro, '*Inventarium omnium et singulorum bonorum mobilium* di Michelangelo da Caravaggio "pittore" ', in *artibus et historiae* 28 (XIV), 1993

Marino, Giovan Battista et al. [ed. Ferrero, Giuseppe Guido], *Marino e i marinisti*, Milano-Napoli 1954

Marino, Giovan Battista [ed. Pozzi, Giovanni], *L'Adone* [1622], 2 vols, Milano 1988

Marino, Giovan Battista [ed. Martini, Alessandro], *Amori* [1614], Milano 1995

'Marino, Giambattista', in Vol. 20, Turner 1996

Marlowe, Christopher [ed. Steane, J.B.], *The Complete Plays. Dido, Queen of Carthage. Tamburlaine the Great. Doctor Faustus. The Jew of Malta. Edward the Second. The Massacre at Paris* [1969], London 1986

Martineau, Jane, 'Gonzaga: (15) Vincenzo I Gonzaga', in Vol. 12, Turner 1996

Martinelli, Valentino, 'L'amor divino "tutto ignudo" di Giovanni Baglione e la cronologia dell' intermezzo caravaggesco', in *Arte Antica e Moderna* 5, 1959

Marvell, Andrew [ed. Donno, Elizabeth Story], *The Complete Poems* [c.1650, 1681, 1972], London 1996

Marziale, Marco Valerio, *Epigrammi. Saggio e versione di Guido Ceronetti* [1964], Torino 1979

'Mattei', in Vol. 20, Turner 1996

Matthiessen, Patrick & Pepper, Stephen, 'Guido Reni: an early masterpiece discovered in Liguria', in *Apollo* XCI, 1970

Matvejevic, Pedrag, *Mediterraneo. Un nuovo breviario* [1987], tr. Milano 1993

Mereu, Italo, *Storia dell' intolleranza in Europa* [1979], Milano 1993

Miccoli, Giovanni, 'La storia religiosa', in Vol. I, Romano & Vivanti 1974

Michel, Christian, 'San Pietro (epoca moderna e contemporanea)', in Vol. II, Levillain 1996

Moir, Alfred, *The Italian Followers of Caravaggio*, 2 vols, Cambridge, Mass. 1967

Moir, Alfred, 'Did Caravaggio Draw?', in *Art Quarterly* XXXII, 1969

Moir, Alfred, *Caravaggio and His Copyists*, New York 1976

Moir, Alfred, *Caravaggio*, New York 1982

Moir, Alfred, 'Le sviste di Caravaggio', in Calvesi 1987

Montaigne, Michel de, *Journal de voyage en Italie par la Suisse et l'Allemagne en 1580 et 1581*, in Montaigne 1962

Montaigne, Michel de [ed. Rat, Maurice], *Œuvres complètes*, Paris 1962

Moryson, Fynes, *Shakespeare's Europe: A Survey of the Conditions of Europe at the end of the 16th century. Being unpublished chapters of Fynes Moryson's Itinerary (1617)* [1903], New York 1967

Mostra del Caravaggio e dei caravaggeschi. Catalogo con 131 illustrazioni. Seconda edizione aggiornata e riveduta [exhibition catalogue], Milano 1951

La natura morta al tempo di Caravaggio [exhibition catalogue], Napoli 1995

Nicholl, Charles, *The Reckoning. The Murder of Christopher Marlowe*, London 1992

Nicolson, Benedict, *The International Caravaggesque Movement. Lists of Pictures by Caravaggio and his Followers throughout Europe from 1590 to 1650*, Oxford 1979

Nicolson, Benedict [ed. Vertova, Lina], *Caravaggism in Europe*, 3 vols, Torino 1990

Olmi, Giuseppe, 'Paleotti, Gabriele', in Vol. 23, Turner 1996

O'Neil, Maryvelma, 'Baglione, Giovanni', in Vol. 3, Turner 1996

Ottonelli, G. Domenico & Berrettini, Pietro (Pietro da Cortona) [ed Casale, Vittorio], *Trattato della pittura, e scultura, uso, et abuso loro. Composto da un theologo, e da un pittore* [Firenze 1652], Treviso 1973

Pacelli, Vincenzo, 'New Documents concerning Caravaggio in Naples', in *The Burlington Magazine* CXIX, 1977

Pacelli, Vincenzo, 'Strumenti in posa: novità sull' *Amore vincitore del Caravaggio*', in *Prospettiva* 57–60, 'Scritti in ricordo di Giovanni Previtali', Vol. II, 1989–1990

Pacelli, Vincenzo, 'La morte del Caravaggio e alcuni suoi didpinti da documenti inediti', in *Studi di Storia dell' Arte* 2, 1991

Pacelli, Vincenzo, *Caravaggio. Le sette opere di misericordia* [1984], Salerno 1993

Pacelli, Vincenzo, *L'ultimo Caravaggio dalla Maddalena a mezza figura ai due san Giovanni (1606–1610)*, Todi 1994

Pacelli, Vincenzo, *La pittura napoletana da Caravaggio a Luca Giordano*, Napoli 1996a

Pacelli, Vincenzo, 'Una nuova ipotesi sulla morte di Michelangelo Merisi da Caravaggio', in Macioce 1996 b

Pacheco, Francisco [ed. Bassegoda i Hugas, Bonaventura], *Arte de la Pintura* [1649], Madrid 1990

Paleotti, Gabriele, *Discorso intorno alle imagini sacre e profane, diviso in cinque libri. Dove si scuoprono varii abusi loro e si dichiara il vero modo che cristianamente si doveria osservare nel porle nelle chiese, nelle case et in ogni altro luogo. Raccolto e posto insieme ad utile delle anime per commissione di Monsignor Illustriss. e Reverendiss. Card. Paleotti Vescovo di Bologna. Al popolo della città e Docese sua, Bologna 1582* [1582], in Barocchi 1961

Panazza, Gaetano, 'I precedenti bresciani del Caravaggio', in Cinotti 1975

Panofsky, Erwin, *Galileo as a Critic of the Arts*, The Hague 1954

Panofsky, Erwin 'What is Baroque?' [1934], in Panofsky 1995

Panofsky, Erwin [ed. Lavin, Irving], *Three Essays on Style*, Cambridge, Mass. & London 1995

Panofsky, Erwin, *Perspective as Symbolic Form* [1927, tr. 1991], New York 1997

Panzera, Anna Maria, *Caravaggio e Giordano Bruno fra nuova arte e nuova scienza. La bellezza dell' artefice*, Roma 1994

Papi, Giovanni, 'Cenni biografici', in Gregori 1991

Papi, Giovanni, *Cecco del Caravaggio*, Firenze 1992

Papi, Giovanni, 'Caravaggio e Cecco', in Gregori 1996

Parks, N. Randolph, 'On Caravaggio's "Dormition of the Virgin" and its setting', in *The Burlington Magazine* CXXVIII, 1985

Passeri, Giambattista, *Vite de'pittori, scultori ed architetti che anno lavorato in Roma. Morti dal 1641 fino al 1673* [1772], Bologna 1976

Pepper, D. Stephen, 'Caravaggio and Guido Reni: Contrasts in Attitudes', in *Art Quarterly* XXXIV, 1971

Pevsner, Nikolaus, *Academies of Art Past and Present,* Cambridge 1940

Pontani, Filippo Maria [ed.], *Antologia Palatina. Volume quarto. Libri XII–XVI*, Torino 1981

Posner, Donald, *Annibale Carracci. A study in the reform of Italian painting around 1590*, 2 vols, London 1971a

Posner, Donald, 'Caravaggio's Homo-erotic Early Works', in *Art Quarterly* XXXIV, 1971b

Praz, Mario, *Il Giardino dei sensi. Studi sul manierismo e il barocco*, Milano 1975

Prodi, Paolo, *Il sovrano pontefice. Un corpo e due anime: la monarchia papale nella prima età moderna*, Bologna 1982

Prodi, Paolo, 'Borromeo Federico' in Vol. XIII, *Dizionario Biografico degli Italiani*, Roma 1960–1997

Prosperi, Adriano, 'Penitenza e riforma', in Aymard 1995

Prosperi, Adriano, *Tribunali della coscienza. Inquisitori, confessori, missionari*, Torino 1996

Pupillo, Marco, 'I Crescenzi, Francesco Contarelli e Michelangelo da Caravaggio: contesti e documenti per la commissione in S. Luigi dei Francesi', in Macioce 1996

Quiviger, François, 'Armenini, Giovanni Battista', in Vol. 2, Turner 1996

Randon, Philip Farrugia [ed.], *Caravaggio in Malta*, Malta 1989

Rangoni, Fiorenza, 'Salini, Tommaso', in Vol. 27, Turner 1996

Renda, Francesco, *L'inquisizione in Sicilia. I fatti. Le persone*, Palermo 1997

Renoux, Christian, 'Urbano VIII', in Vol. II, Levillain 1996

Renucci, Paul, 'La cultura', in Romano & Vivanti 1974

Reznicek, E.K.J., 'Mander, van: (1) Karel van Mander I', in Vol. 20, Turner 1996

Ripa, Cesare [ed. Maser, Edward A.], *Baroque and Rococo Pictorial Imagery. The 1758–60 Hertel edition of Ripa's 'Iconologia' with 200 engraved illustrations* [1593, 1758–60], tr. New York 1971

Robb, Peter, *Midnight in Sicily*, Sydney 1996

Roccasecca, Pietro, 'Bourbon del Monte, Francesco Maria', in Vol. 4, Turner 1996

Romano, Giovanni, 'Immagini di gioventù nell' età moderna', in Levi & Schmitt 1994

Romano, Ruggiero, 'La storia economica. Dal secolo XIV al Settecento', in Romano & Vivanti 1974a

Romano, Ruggiero & Vivanti, Corrado [eds], *Storia d'Italia. Volume secondo. Dalla caduta dell' impero romano al secolo XVIII*, 2 vols, Torino 1974b

Romeo, Giovanni, *Aspettando il boia. Condannati a morte, confortatori e inquisitori nella Napoli della Controriforma*, Firenze 1993

Rosa, Mario, 'Sisto V', in Vol. II, Levillain 1996

Rossi, Lorenza, 'Doria I. (2) Giovanni Andrea I Doria & (3) Andrea II Doria', in Vol. 9, Turner 1996

Röttgen, Herwarth, *Il Caravaggio. Ricerche e interpretazioni*, Roma 1974

Röttgen, Herwarth, 'La "Resurrezione di Lazzaro" del Caravaggio', in Cinotti 1975

Röttgen, Herwarth, 'Cesari, Bernardino', in Vol. XXIV, *Dizionario Biografico degli Italiani*, Roma 1980a

Röttgen, Herwarth, 'Cesari, Giuseppe, detto il Cavalier d'Arpino', in Vol. XXIV, *Dizionario Biografico degli Italiani*, Roma 1980b

Rossi, Rosa, *Sulle tracce di Cervantes. Profilo inedito dell' autore del "Chisciotte"*, Roma 1997

Rossi, Sergio, 'Un doppio autoritratto del Caravaggio', in Bernini 1989

Sade, Donatien-Alphonse-François, marquis de [ed. Lever, Maurice], *Viaggio in Italia. Ovvero Dissertazioni critiche, storiche e filosofiche sulle città di Firenze, Roma, Napoli e Loreto, e sulle strade adiacenti a queste quattro città. Opera in cui ci si è impegnati a sviluppare gli usi, i costumi, la forma di legislazione ecc., riguardo tanto all' epoca antica quanto alla moderna, in una maniera più particolareggiata e più ampia di quanto non paia essersi fatto finora* [1995], tr. Torino 1996

Salerno, Luigi, 'The Picture Gallery of Vincenzo Giustiniani–I: Introduction' in *The Burlington Magazine* CII, 1960a

Salerno, Luigi, 'The Picture Gallery of Vincenzo Giustiniani–II: The Inventory, Part I', in *The Burlington Magazine* CII, 1960b

Salerno, Luigi, 'The Picture Gallery of Vincenzo Giustiniani–III: The Inventory, Part II', in *The Burlington Magazine* CII, 1960c

Salerno, Luigi, 'The Art-Historical Implications of the Detroit "Magdalen" ', in *The Burlington Magazine* CXVI, 1974

Salerno, Luigi, 'Caravaggio e la cultura nel suo tempo', in Cinotti 1975

Salerno, Luigi, 'Immobilismo politico e accademia', in Zeri 1981

Salerno, Luigi, *La natura morta italiana 1560–1805*, Roma 1984

Salerno, Luigi, 'Caravaggio nel contesto culturale italiano: gli estimatori e i committenti', in *Caravaggio* 1985 a

Salerno, Luigi [English tr. of Salerno 1985a], in *The Age* 1985 b

Sallmann, Jean-Michel, *Santi barocchi. Modelli di santità. pratiche devozionali e comportamenti religiosi nel regno di Napoli dal 1540 al 1750* [1994], tr. Lecce 1996

Samek Ludovici, Sergio, *Vita del Caravaggio dalle testimonianze del suo tempo*, Milano 1956

Sammut, Edward, 'The Trial of Caravaggio', in *Mid-Med Bank Report & Accounts*, Valletta 1986

Sandrart, Joachim von, *L'Academia Todesca della Architettura Scultura e Pittura, Oder Teutsche Academie der Edlen Bau–, Bild– und Mahlerey-Künste*, Nürnberg 1675 [extracts in Friedlaender 1955 & Hibbard 1983]

Sani, Bernardina, 'Leoni, Ottavio', in Vol. 19, Turner 1996

Santillana, Giorgio de, *The Crime of Galileo* [1955], Chicago 1966

Savage, Roger, 'Nature and Second Nature', in *Words, Wai-te-ata Studies in Literature* I, 1965

Scannelli, Francesco, *Il microcosmo della pittura*, Cesena 1657 [extracts in Dell' Acqua & Cinotti 1971 & Hibbard 1983]

Scappi, Bartolomeo, *Opera* [1570], in Faccioli 1987

Schneider, Thomas M., 'La «maniera» e il processo pittorico del Caravaggio', in Calvesi 1987

Seznec, Jean, *The Survival of the Pagan Gods. The Mythological Tradition and Its Place in Renaissance Humanism and Art* [1940, tr. 1953], Princeton 1995

Sgarbi, Vittorio, 'Il Caravaggio', in *FMR* 33, 1985

Shakespeare, William [ed. Booth, Stephen], *Shakespeare's Sonnets*, New Haven & London 1977

Shakespeare, William [eds Wells, Stanley & Taylor, Gary *et al.*], *The Complete Works. Compact Edition* [1988], Oxford 1997

Sica, Maria, 'Doria II. (2) Marcantonio Doria', in Vol. 9, Turner 1996

Simon, Bruno, 'Lepanto', in Vol. I, Levillain 1996

Smith, Marc, 'Giulio III', in Vol. I, Levillain 1996

Sohm, Philip, 'Mancini, Giulio', in Vol. 20, Turner 1996

Southorn, Janet, 'Crescenzi: (1) Pietro Paolo Crescenzi' & '(3) Francesco Crescenzi' in Vol. 8, Turner 1996a

Southorn, Janet, 'Giustiniani (i): (2) Vincenzo Giustiniani', in Vol. 12, Turner 1996b

Spadaro, Alvise, 'Note sulla permanenza di Caravaggio in Sicilia', in Calvesi 1987

Spear, Richard E., *Caravaggio and His Followers* [exhibition catalogue], Cleveland 1972

Spezzaferro, Luigi, 'La cultura del cardinal Del Monte e il primo tempo del Caravaggio', in *Storia dell' Arte* 9–10, 1971

Spezzaferro, Luigi, 'The Documentary Findings: Ottavio Costa as a Patron of Caravaggio', in *The Burlington Magazine* CXVI, 1974a

Spezzaferro, Luigi, 'La pala dei Palafrenieri', in *Colloquio* 1974b

Spezzaferro, Luigi, 'Una testimonianza per gli inizi del caravaggismo', in *Storia dell' Arte* 23, 1975a

Spezzaferro, Luigi, 'Ottavio Costa e Caravaggio: certezze e problemi', in Cinotti 1975b

Spezzaferro, Luigi, 'Caravaggio rifiutato? 1. Il problema della prima versione del *San Matteo*', in *Ricerche di Storia dell' arte* 10, 1980a

Spezzaferro, Luigi, 'Il testamento di Marzio Milesi: tracce per un perduto Caravaggio', in *Ricerche di Storia dell' arte* 10, 1980b

Spezzaferro, Luigi, 'Il recupero del Rinascimento', in Zeri 1981

Spezzaferro, Luigi, 'Il Caravaggio, i collezionisti romani, le nature morte', in *La natura morta* 1995

Spike, John T. 'The Church of St John in Valletta 1578–1978 and the Earliest Record of Caravaggio in Malta: an Exhibition and its Catalogue', in *The Burlington Magazine* CXX, 1978

Spike, John T., [untitled review of exhibition *Caravaggio: come nascono i capolavori* (v. Gregori 1991)], in *The Burlington Magazine* CXXXIV, 1992

Spike, John T., 'Un documento "di prima" per Caravaggio', in Macioce 1996

Spini, Giorgio, *Storia dell' età moderna* [1965], 3 vols, Torino 1982

Spini, Giorgio, *Galileo, Campanella e il "divinus poeta"*, Bologna 1996

Staatliche Museen zu Berlin–Preussicher Kulturbesitz, *Dokumentation der Verluste. Band 1. Gemäldgalerie*, Berlin 1995

Steinberg, Leo, *The Sexuality of Christ in Renaissance Art and Modern Oblivion. Second Edition, Revised and Expanded*, Chicago 1996

Stella, Frank, *Working Space*, Cambridge, Mass. & London 1986

Stendhal [ed. Del Litto, V.], *Voyages en Italie* [1827 & 1829], Paris 1973

Stone, Donald M., 'The context of Caravaggio's "Beheading of St John" in Malta', in *The Burlington Magazine* CXXXIX, 1997

Strinati, Claudio, 'Roma nell' anno 1600. Studio di pittura', in *Ricerche di Storia dell' arte* 10, 1980

Strinati, Claudio, 'Umano troppo umano', in *Art e dossier* 16, 1987

Strinati, Claudio, 'Caravaggio nel 1601', in Bernini 1989

Strinati, Claudio, 'Frutta e verdura per un'élite', in *Art e dossier* 109, 1996

Susinno, Francesco [ed. Martinelli, Valentino], *Le vite de'pittori messinesi e di altri che fiorirono in Messina* [1724], Firenze 1960

Sutton, Denys, 'Seventeenth-Century Art in Rome', in *The Burlington Magazine* XCIX, 1957

Touring Club Italiano, *Guida d'Italia. Napoli e Dintorni* [V ed.], Milano 1976

Touring Club Italiano, *Guida d'Italia. Roma* [VII ed.], Milano 1977

Touring Club Italiano, *Guida d'Italia. Lombardia (escluso Milano)* [IX ed.], Milano 1987

Touring Club Italiano, *Guida d'Italia. Sicilia* [VI ed.], Milano 1989

Touring Club Italiano, *Guida d'Italia. Roma* [VIII ed.], Milano 1993

Trinchieri Camiz, Franca, 'La «Musica» nei quadri del Caravaggio', in Bernini 1989

Trinchieri Camiz, Franca, 'The Roman "studio" of Francesco Villamena', in *The Burlington Magazine* CXXXVI, 1994

Turner, Jane [ed.], *The Dictionary of Art*, 34 vols, London & New York 1996

Uginet, François-Charles, 'Fabbrica di San Pietro', in Vol. I, Levillain 1996 a

Uginet, François-Charles, 'Nobiltà romana (dopo il medioevo)', in Vol. II, Levillain 1996 b

Van Mander, Karel, *Het Schilder-Boeck*, Haaerlem 1604 [extracts in Friedlaender 1955 & Hibbard 1983]

Van Tuyll Van Serooskerken, C., 'Carracci: (3) Annibale Carracci', in Vol. 5, Turner 1996 a

Van Tuyll Van Serooskerken, C., 'Spada, Leonello', in Vol. 29, Turner 1996 b

Varriano, John, 'Longhi (ii)', in Vol. 19, Turner 1996

Vasari, Giorgio [ed. Bellosi, Luciano & Rossi, Aldo], *Le Vite de' più eccelenti architetti, pittori, et scultori italiani, da Cimabue insino a' tempi nostri. Nell' edizione per i tipi di Lorenzo Torrentino, Firenze 1550,* Torino 1986

Vasari, Giorgio [tr. de Vere, Gaston du C., ed. Ekserdjian, David], *Lives of the Painters, Sculptors and Architects* [1568, tr. 1912], 2 vols, London 1996

Vattimo, Gianni et al., *Enciclopedia Garzanti di folosofia* [1981], Milano 1993

Vélez de Guevara, Luis [ed. D'Arcangelo, Lucio], *Il diavolo zoppo* [1641], tr. Milano 1997

Vendler, Helen, *The Art of Shakespeare's Sonnets*, Cambridge, Mass. & London 1997

Vida de Lazarillo de Tormes y de sus fortunas y aversidades [1554], tr. Milano 1994

Villari, Rosario, 'Il ribelle', in Villari 1991

Villari, Rosario [ed.] *L'uomo barocco*, Roma-Bari 1991

Villari, Rosario, *La rivolta antispagnola a Napoli. Le origini (1585–1647)* [1967], Roma-Bari 1994

Vivanti, Corrado, 'La storia politica e sociale. Dall' evento delle signorie all' Italia spagnola', in Romano & Vivanti 1974

Viviani, Vincenzio [ed. Borsetto, Luciana], *Vita di Galileo (con appendice di testi e documenti)* [1654], Bergamo 1992

Vodret, Rossella, 'Brevi note al *Narciso*', in Bernini 1989

Vodret, Rossella, 'Il restauro del "Narciso" ', in Macioce 1996 a

Vodret, Rossella, 'Ritratto di artista allo specchio', in *Art e dossier* 109, 1996 b

Wazbinski, Zygmunt, *Il Cardinale Francesco Maria Del Monte 1549–1626, I. Mecenate di artisti, consigliere di politici e di sovrani & II. Il «dossier» di lavoro di un prelato*, 2 vols, Firenze 1994

Wazbinski, 'Il Viaggio del Cardinale Francesco Maria Del Monte a Napoli negli anni 1607–1608', in Macioce 1996

Weegee's New York. 335 Photographs 1935–1960. Introduction by John Coplan, München 1996

Wheelock, Arthur K. Jr, 'Vermeer of Delft: His Life and His Artistry', in *Johannes Vermeer* 1995

White, Edmund, *Genet*, London & New York 1993

Whitfield, Clovis & Martineau, Jane, *Painting in Naples 1606–1705. From Caravaggio to Giordano* [exhibition catalogue], London 1982

Williams, Ann, 'The Constitutional Development of the Order of St John in Malta, 1530–1798', in Mallia-Milanes 1993

Wittgenstein, Ludwig von [tr. Miles, A.C. & Rhees, Rush], 'Remarks on Frazer's "Golden Bough" ', in *The Human World* 1970

Wittkower, Rudolph & Margot, *Born Under Saturn. The Character and Conduct of Artists: A Documented History from Antiquity to the French Revolution* [1963], New York-London 1969

Wittkower, Rudolph, *Art and Architecture in Italy 1600 to 1750* [1958], New Haven & London 1982

Wittkower, Rudolph, *Bernini. The Sculptor of the Roman Baroque* [1955], rev. fourth ed. London 1997

Wraight, A.D., *In Search of Christopher Marlowe. A Pictorial Biography*, London 1965

Yates, Frances A., *Giordano Bruno and the Hermetic Tradition* [1964], Chicago & London 1991

Yates, Frances A., *The Art of Memory* [1966, 1992], London 1997

Young, Peter Boutourline, 'Galilei, Galileo', in Vol. 12, Turner 1996

Zapperi, Roberto, 'The Summons of the Carracci to Rome: some new documentary evidence', in *The Burlington Magazine* CXXVIII, 1986

Zapperi, Roberto, *Annibale Carracci. Ritratto di artista da giovane*, Torino 1989

Zapperi, Roberto, *Eros e controriforma. Preistoria della galleria Farnese*, Torino 1994

Zeri, Federico [ed.], *Storia dell' arte italiana. Parte seconda. Dal Medioevo al Novecento. Volume secondo. Dal Cinquecento all' Ottocento. I. Cinquecento e Seicento*, Torino 1981

Zeri, Federico, *Pittura e Controriforma. L'«arte senza tempo» di Scipione de Gaeta* [1957], Vicenza 1997

Zeri, Federico & Dolcetta, Marco, *Caravaggio. Vocazione di San Matteo*, Milano 1998

Ziglioli, Roberto, 'Il Caravaggio ... a Caravaggio, in Roma', in Macioce 1996

Zingarelli, Nicola [ed. Dogliotti, Miro & Rosiello, Luigi], *Lo Zingarelli 1996. Vocabolario della lingua italiana. Dodicesima edizione*, Bologna 1996

Zuffi, Stefano, *Caravaggio*, Milano 1994

PEOPLE

Bernini, Gianlorenzo, sculptor 9, 14, 315, 319, 352

Bertolotti, Antonino, archivist 11

Béthune, Philippe de, ambassador 181, 234ff, 244f, 248f, 283, 335f

Bianchini, Anna, courtesan 82ff, 88, 93f, 109, 151, 172, 269, 273, 494

Bizoni, Bernardo, secretary 336

Bodello, Carlo, painter 367f

Boneri, Francesco [Cecco del Caravaggio], painter 10, 165, 173, 195ff, 203ff, 209, 227, 235, 242ff, 281f, 310ff, 352, 356ff, 364, 378, 394, 398, 424, 437, 441, 465, 469, 491, 495f

Borghese, Camillo: v. Paul V

Borghese, Scipione, nephew 300, 314ff, 321, 323, 334f, 337, 387ff, 400, 425, 436, 460f, 463, 470ff, 475ff, 481, 483ff, 493

Borgianni, Orazio, painter 255ff, 367f, 494f

Borromeo, Carlo, cardinal 20ff, 26, 102, 131, 326, 334

Borromeo, Federico, cardinal 102f, 105f, 193, 268, 270, 320f, 419, 425, 460

Bosch, Hieronymus, painter 377

Botticelli [Sandro Filipepi], painter 96

Bramante [Donato di Pascuccio di Antonio], architect 322

Brill, Paul, painter 102

Brueghel, Jan, painter 102ff

Bruni, Prudenzia, landlady 245, 271, 279, 310, 312ff

Bruno, Giordano, thinker 7, 121, 129f, 157, 246, 248f, 266, 284, 325, 363, 436

Brunori, Caterina, courtesan 97

Brunori, Prudenza [Tella], courtesan 97ff, 155, 269

Buonarroti, Michelangelo, artist 7, 22, 32, 79, 107, 109, 117, 126f, 135, 148, 156, 158, 174, 203

Calvetti, Olimpio, lover 85f

Calvi, Domenica [Menicuccia], courtesan 168ff, 269, 285, 494

Campanella, Tommaso, thinker 325, 363

Campani, Caterina, wife 171, 491

Canonico, Flavio, sergeant 100, 149, 151, 154f

Caracciolo, Battistello, painter 412, 495

Carafa, Antonio, duke 381

Carafa Colonna, Luigi, patron 381f, 393, 438, 458f, 470, 473

Carafa, penitentiary 438

Carafa, Vincenzo, prior 478, 483ff, 488

Caravaggio, Michelangelo Merisi da: v. Merisi

Carracci, Agostino, painter 12, 186

Carracci, Annibale, painter 12, 37, 117, 135, 144f, 155ff, 158ff, 167, 180, 182f, 186, 192, 203, 220, 230f, 251, 279, 305f, 308, 327, 329f, 334, 391, 461, 482

Castellari, banker 419

Castellini, Giovanni, archeologist 331

Castro, Pedro Fernandez de: v. Lemos

Cavaletti, Ermete, patron 261, 263, 265, 270

Cecco del Caravaggio: v. Boneri, Francesco

Cecilia, martyr 146, 250

Celio, Gaspare, painter 204

Cenci, Beatrice, feminist 84ff, 95, 130, 298

Cenci, Bernardo, brother 84ff

Cenci, Cesare, uncle 85f

Cenci, Francesco, baron 84f, 88

Cenci, Giacomo, brother 84ff, 130

Cenci, Lucrezia, stepmother 85ff, 130

Cerasi, Tiberio, cleric 144f, 159f, 165, 182, 186, 192, 200, 208, 223, 259, 355, 394

Cervantes Saavedra, Miguel de, writer 7, 210, 304, 361, 484

Cesari, Bernardino, painter 41ff, 53, 147, 171, 272

Cesari, Giuseppe [cavalier d'Arpino], painter 36ff, 41ff, 47, 49, 53, 84, 108, 117ff, 135f, 138f, 147f, 159, 171f, 178, 180, 182, 185, 218f, 222, 230f, 250f, 257, 262, 272, 348, 388ff, 398, 409, 435, 439, 461

Cézanne, Paul, painter 5, 105

Charles I of England, king 378, 495

Charles V, emperor 31

Chekhov, Anton, writer 5

Cherubini, Laerzio, jurist 259, 290, 385

Christine, grand duchess 336, 425, 460

Christo, artist 290

Clement VIII [Ippolito Aldobrandini],

PHOTOGRAPHY CREDITS

We would like to thank the following institutions for their kind permission to reproduce the paintings and prints in this book:

Banca Commerciale Italiana, Naples: *Ursula transfixed*

Gemäldegalerie Staatliche Museen, Berlin: *Love the winner*

Detroit Institute of Arts (Gift of the Kresge Foundation and Mrs. Edsel B. Ford): *Martha & Mary*

Barbara Piasecka Johnson Collection, Princeton, New Jersey: *Isaac & Abraham I (The sacrifice of Isaac)*

Kimbell Art Museum, Fort Worth, Texas: *Cheats (The Cardsharps)*

Metropolitan Museum of Art, New York, New York: *Musicians*

Nelson-Atkins Museum of Art, Kansas City, Missouri: *John in the wild IV (Saint John the Baptist in the wilderness)*

Réunion des Musées Nationaux, Paris: *Mary dead*

The John and Mabel Ringling Museum of Art, the State Art Museum of Florida, Sarasota, Florida: *Del Monte* by Leoni

Scala, Florence: *Judith & Holofernes, Matthew called, Peter killed, David II,* M by Ottavio Leoni, *Sick self portrait, Fortune teller II, Boy with fruit, Lute player I, Saul I, John in the wild II, Catherine, Pilgrim's Madonna, Grooms' Madonna, Maffeo Barberini, Scipione Borghese* by Gianlorenzo Bernini

Wadsworth Atheneum, Hartford, Connecticut: *Francis & angel (The Ecstasy of St. Francis)*